INTERNATIONAL TAXATION

SIXTH EDITION

BRET WELLS
John Mixon Chair and Professor of Law,
University of Houston Law Center

CONCEPTS AND INSIGHTS SERIES®

FOUNDATION PRESS

Cover photo courtesy of Wikipedia/'Unwicked': Singapore Skyline with Merlion in the foreground.
https://commons.wikimedia.org/wiki/File:Singapore_Skyline_2019-10.jpg

860 Blue Gentian Road, Suite 350
Eagan, MN 55121
1-877-888-1330

Published in the United States of America

ISBN: 979-8-31770-283-0

PREFACE

This book provides an overview of U.S. international taxation as of December 2025. As of the writing of this sixth edition, multiple factors have impacted the U.S. international tax regime. At the outset, it is helpful to identify these contributing factors that are shaping the U.S. international tax regime as these factors are likely to continue to contribute to its further evolution.

To begin with the obvious, Congress made significant changes to the nation's international tax laws in 2025. A full appreciation of all the implications of the 2025 tax law changes are not likely to be fully understood until future regulations and judicial decisions further illuminate its full import. Even so, important insights can already be gleaned from this 2025 legislative enactment, and so this new edition seeks to offer timely insights now even though a complete outworking of this legislation may not be fully appreciated for several more years.

In addition, the U.S. international tax regime, more than ever, is being impacted by the evolving nature of the international tax regimes of other nations. In this regard, the OECD has remained vigilant in issuing model rules and commentary for how countries should reform their domestic tax laws to better address base erosion and profit shifting activities. This OECD guidance has placed particular attention on the taxation of multinational enterprises in the digitalized global economy. The OECD refers to its model rules as its Global Anti-Base Erosion Model Rules (Pillar Two) or "GloBE" rules. The GloBE rules seek to coordinate the international tax regimes of adopting nations to ensure that a minimum tax is imposed on multinational enterprises in a harmonized manner. A specific hierarchy of taxing rights is assigned among nations under the GloBE rules. Notwithstanding the aspirational goal of a global minimum tax, the GloBE rules allow for significant exceptions and carve-outs to the actual imposition of a global minimum tax, so countries if they so choose can still engage in global tax competition through refundable tax subsidies or substance-based exclusions. As a result, tax minimization strategies of multinational enterprises appear to remain a continuing specter that haunts the tax base even for jurisdictions that purportedly adopt the GloBE rules. Numerous countries have agreed to implement these GloBE rules, but a final verdict on their efficacy remains to be determined.

At present, the United States tax regime diverges in important respects from the design parameters of the GloBE rules. Nevertheless, the OECD and the G-7 have reached an agreement that allows the nonconforming U.S. international tax system to operate as a "side-by-side system" alongside the OECD Pillar Two

GloBE rules without the need for the United States to further conform its own domestic tax laws to the OECD's envisioned GloBE framework. This concession effectively exempts U.S. multinationals from the charging provisions of the GloBE minimum tax provisions. As of the writing of this sixth edition, the details of how the nonconforming U.S. international tax regime will coexist as a "side-by-side system" alongside the GloBE rules remains to be worked out. As areas of disharmony are identified between the two approaches, one might expect further impetus for reform measures both here and abroad.

Finally, significant components of current law were enacted in the United States in 2017, 2022, and 2025 on a strictly party-line basis. The highly partisan nature of these tax enactments is in stark contrast to prior eras when major tax legislation historically had been adopted on a more bipartisan basis. An unfortunate consequence of this highly partisan backdrop to tax legislation in recent years is that it is more difficult than ever to determine which aspects of current law have sustainable bipartisan support and which aspects do not.

These realities have combined to make it much harder to write this sixth edition of International Taxation. Nevertheless, with that disclaimer in mind, this sixth edition remains committed to providing a cogent explanation of how the United States has designed its international tax regime. It continues to seek to balance the need to address the complexity of current law with the need to ensure that law students understand the policy objectives that underpin its framework.

Even though this is a challenging time to study international taxation, a law student should take solace in at least two thoughts. First, the importance of the international tax provisions unpacked in this book has never been more salient to lawyers than at the present time. Technological improvements in communication, including the explosive growth of the internet and social media platforms driven by the advancing artificial intelligence algorithms, have created a closer global community and reshaped modern discourse and commerce. In prior decades, only those lawyers who represented the largest companies or the wealthiest individuals dealt with international taxation issues, but in today's global business environment lawyers can expect that their legal practice will be impacted by international taxation rules on a recurring basis. Second, even though significant continued evolution in the international taxation laws of the United States is in some sense inevitable, future changes are likely to build upon the existing framework that you are now embarking to study. Thus, your understanding of the design goals of the existing framework provides you a firm foundation from which you can then synthesize ongoing future developments. My hope is that this book will make a significant contribution towards your mastery of these topics.

Before embarking on the topics discussed in this book, there are a few housekeeping matters that are important to address at the outset. In this preface, I want to set forth an overview of the principal sources of U.S. law and provide a brief explanation of them. Next, in the section that follows, I set forth an explanation of the diagramming conventions that are used in this book. Finally, I have a concluding acknowledgement.

Internal Revenue Code

The basic scripture of U.S. taxation is the Internal Revenue Code (the "Code"), a codification of the currently applicable provisions of income tax statutes extending back to 1913. The Code is a law of the United States; its provisions accordingly have full force to the extent consistent with the U.S. Constitution. The Code has been recodified twice since its introduction as the Internal Revenue Code of 1939. The Code currently in force is styled the "Internal Revenue Code of 1986." Provisions of the Code are cited in this book by section number only. E.g., "section 78" or "§ 78."

Income Tax Treaties

Income tax treaties between the United States and other countries also have the force of law. There is no overarching priority or precedence between treaties and statutes. They simply coexist, and inconsistencies are resolved largely ad hoc, with the help of some partly codified rules. This book follows no special form of citation to income tax treaties, which are identified simply by the country with which they are in force.

Treasury Regulations

Expounding and expanding the Code (and many income tax treaties) are extensive regulations issued by the U.S. Treasury Department. The Treasury regulations arise under a general grant of authority in the Code (section 7805) as well as under specific grants of authority under specific sections. Many regulations are interpretations of Code provisions and contain mostly interstitial and illustrative matter. Some entire segments of U.S. tax law, however, exist principally as regulations issued under broad-framed (and sometimes skeletal) statutory mandates.

Treasury regulations, to the extent consistent with the Code, have the force of law. They can, however, be attacked by taxpayers and set aside as inconsistent with statutes or treaties. Courts show some deference to Treasury regulations on close or doubtful questions, but taxpayers do succeed from time to time in persuading courts that specific regulations are inconsistent with the Code, overreaching, or otherwise invalid. Treasury regulations are cited in this book as "Reg. § _____". Regulations are usually numbered by "1." followed by the number of the Code section under which they arise. For example, "Reg. § 1.901–1(a)" is a regulation arising under section 901.

IRS Rulings

Below the regulations in the hierarchy of official pronouncements on taxation stand IRS rulings. These contain positions taken by the Internal Revenue Service or "IRS" in response to specific transactions and situations. Typically, they represent more narrowly focused applications of the tax laws than the regulations. Rulings are issued in great numbers, with far fewer formalities than regulations. Rulings are valid only if consistent with the Code *and* the regulations. They are frequently attacked by taxpayers as invalid, sometimes with success.

Rulings come in two types: published and unpublished.

Revenue Rulings. Published rulings (known as "Revenue Rulings") are collected in the Cumulative Bulletin of the Internal Revenue Service (cited here as "Cum. Bull."). A Revenue Ruling bears the number of the year and the order of its issuance. Similarly, the volumes of the Cumulative Bulletin are numbered according to the year in which their contents were issued. Thus "Rev. Rul. 78–113, 1978–2 Cum. Bull. ___" is a citation to the 113th Revenue Ruling issued in 1978, contained in the 1978 volume (Part 2) of the Cumulative Bulletin. Revenue Rulings issued in 2000 and later are numbered with the full year of issuance, as for example in "Rev. Rul. 2001–42." The IRS acknowledges published Revenue Rulings as binding precedents.

Private Rulings. Unpublished or "private" rulings are issued directly by the IRS to taxpayers who seek advance knowledge of the IRS's position on transactions they are planning. These are known as "Private Letter Rulings" and have binding force only between the Revenue Service and the taxpayer to whom they are addressed. Similar to Private Letter Rulings are Field Service Advice letters and Technical Advice Memoranda. These generally concern transactions already carried out by a taxpayer involved in administrative proceedings with the Internal Revenue Service.

Court Cases

Tax disputes can be heard before three different courts: the Tax Court, the Court of Federal Claims, and the District Courts of the United States. The District Courts are constitutional courts of the United States under Article III of the Constitution; the other two are administrative law courts. Appeals can be taken from the decisions of all three, however, to the federal courts of appeals and ultimately the United States Supreme Court. Decisions of the Tax Court are cited here to the Tax Court Reports (abbreviated "T.C."); decisions of its predecessor, the Board of Tax Appeals (which sat until 1942), are cited to volumes of the "B.T.A." Reports.

Diagramming Conventions

To an increasing extent, the substantive U.S. tax result may depend on how a foreign tax jurisdiction treats the income or the entity under non-U.S. tax law. Causing the U.S. tax result to depend in part on a contingent view of how another jurisdiction will treat the transaction under that jurisdiction's laws does promote the goals of international symmetry and seeks to ensure that "homeless income" (i.e., income that escapes taxation in any jurisdiction) is minimized, but such provisions also add considerable complexity to the U.S. tax regime.

In order to avoid confusion, the materials herein attempt to utilize diagrams that will signal when these topics are relevant and when various forms of entities are addressed. Here is a list of the diagramming conventions that are used in this book:

This diagram denotes an entity that will be treated as a "U.S. corporation" for both U.S. federal income tax purposes and for tax purposes in the relevant foreign tax jurisdiction.

This diagram denotes an entity that will be treated as a "Non-U.S. corporation" for both U.S. tax purposes and consistently as a corporation by the relevant foreign tax jurisdiction.

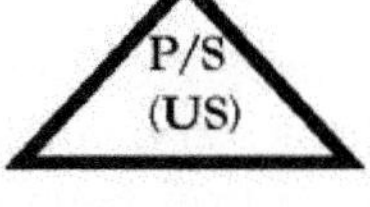

This diagram denotes an entity that will be treated as a U.S. partnership for U.S. tax purposes and is consistently treated as a U.S. partnership by the relevant foreign tax jurisdiction.

This diagram denotes an entity that will be treated as a foreign partnership for U.S. tax purposes and is consistently treated as a non-U.S. partnership by the relevant foreign tax jurisdiction.

This diagram denotes an entity that will be treated as a U.S. branch for U.S. tax purposes and is consistently treated as a U.S. branch by the relevant foreign tax jurisdiction.

This diagram denotes an entity that will be treated as a foreign branch for U.S. tax purposes and is consistently treated as a non-U.S. branch by the relevant foreign tax jurisdiction.

This diagram denotes an entity that will be treated as a foreign branch for U.S. tax purposes but is treated as a corporation by the relevant foreign jurisdiction. This entity is called a "hybrid entity."

This diagram denotes an entity that will be treated as a foreign corporation for U.S. tax purposes but is treated as a partnership or disregarded entity by the relevant foreign tax jurisdiction. This entity is called a "reverse hybrid entity."

Of course, others may use other diagramming conventions, but the hope is that using diagrams in a consistent manner throughout this book will reduce areas of potential confusion.

Acknowledgement

The first three editions of this book were written by Professor Joseph Isenbergh, Professor of Law Emeritus of the University of Chicago. His first edition was originally published in 2000 at the start of this millennium. I joined Professor Isenbergh on the fourth edition and revised it again in 2019. I am indebted to him for allowing me to join this book and ultimately take it over. This sixth edition expands upon the material set forth in earlier editions. At the end of the day, my hope is that the reader finds this sixth edition continues the tradition that Professor Isenbergh forged in terms of providing a clear, timely, and cogent explanation of the principles of international taxation. This goal is becoming increasingly more difficult to attain.

I am grateful to my research assistants who provided significant support and feedback during the revisions of this book. Marianne Standley worked as a research assistant on the fourth edition. Sarah Rabourn worked as a research assistant on the fifth edition. Hani Abdel Rasoul worked as a research assistant on the sixth edition. I am indebted to all of them for their review of early manuscripts. I am also grateful for the ongoing support of Christopher Dykes, research librarian at the University of Houston Law Center.

Bret Wells

December 2025

SUMMARY OF CONTENTS

TABLE OF CONTENTS

PART II. INBOUND U.S. TAXATION

INTERNATIONAL TAXATION

SIXTH EDITION

Part I

COMMON ISSUES FOR BOTH INBOUND AND OUTBOUND U.S. TAXATION

Chapter 1

U.S. TAXATION IN THE INTERNATIONAL SETTING

A. The Nature of International Taxation

A reader with no background in the subject would derive an imperfect idea of this book from its title. Strictly, there is no "international taxation." Only nations and their subdivisions impose taxes. The subject known as "international taxation" involves international aspects of tax systems arising in *national* environments.[1] The subject, furthermore, is rarely approached globally. Those contemplating investment or business operations in a foreign economic environment tend to limit their focus to the tax system prevailing there. It is rare even for a practicing international tax specialist to be fully operational in more than one tax system. Those scattered around the world who use the label "international taxation" as shorthand for their work are thus rarely talking about the exact same subject. Rather, they concern themselves with specific, highly differentiated, adaptations of their own national tax system's interaction with the international economic environment.

By any name, this book is mainly about *U.S.* taxation, albeit applied to economic activity with an international element. It is not, for all that, narrowly parochial. Because so much of the world's economic activity originates in the United States, and even more has the United States as its destination, a substantial part of the world's business transactions and investments are affected in some measure by U.S. taxation. Perhaps because it reaches so large a family of transactions, the U.S. system of international taxation is, I believe, the most fully elaborated of all. Its complexity and detail mirror those of U.S. taxation generally. Viewed at close range U.S. international taxation is a profusion of rules, mostly narrow and often impervious to apprehension through reading, bound together by no evident first principles or overarching themes. The subject cannot be derived in Euclidean fashion from basic postulates such as, "Income should be taxed once, but only once, by the government with sovereign power over the place it is earned or the person earning it." Rather, the U.S. international tax system is made up of specific, piecemeal responses to the way investment or business operations are carried out across national boundaries. It is a Ptolemaic system, held together with

---

1 The subject is known by other names as well, among which are "Foreign Taxation," "Taxation of Foreign-related Transactions," and "Taxation of International Transactions."

epicycles added to the structure over time as national tax authorities come to grips with changing pathways of international commerce and investment.[2]

The closest thing to a system of "international" taxation arises in income tax treaties between different countries. A treaty, by its nature, is an element of the laws of more than one nation. Although a specific country ultimately imposes the taxes affected by treatises, the treasuries of the countries joining in treaties do make concessions from their habitual taxation norms. The result is a tax regime arising under a treaty that may differ from the regime imposed by the laws of any one country. Here too the vantage point of this book is that of U.S. taxation; it is concerned almost exclusively with the income tax treaties of the United States. Dating back to the 1930s with work by the League of Nations, model treaties have been used as a framework for bilateral treaties.

Even so, it would be wrong to believe that the design of the international taxation aspects of domestic law is random or disconnected. There are noteworthy common traits among international tax regimes both in their content and their enforcement mechanisms. Someone conversant with the international elements of one tax system would likely recognize many of the features of another. Yes, each nation's laws are enacted under the legal frameworks of their own jurisdiction, but the international tax aspects of a nation's laws at the end of the day often demonstrate a family resemblance to those of other nations. What accounts for these similarities?

---

[2] One is reminded of Judge Learned Hand's observation about the complexity of the U.S. tax laws generally:

> "[T]he words of such an act as the Income Tax, for example, merely dance before my eyes in a meaningless procession: cross-reference to cross-reference, exception upon exception-couched in abstract terms that offer no handle to seize hold of-leave in my mind only a confused sense of some vitally important, but successfully concealed, purport, which it is my duty to extract, but which is within my power, if at all, only after the most inordinate expenditure of time. I know that these monsters are the result of fabulous industry and ingenuity, plugging up this hole and casting out that net, against all possible evasion; yet at times I cannot help recalling a saying of William James about certain passages of Hegel: that they were no doubt written with a passion of rationality; but that one cannot help wondering whether to the reader they have any significance save that the words are strung together with syntactical correctness. Much of the law is now as difficult to fathom, and more and more of it is likely to be so; for there is little doubt that we are entering a period of increasingly detailed regulation, and it will be the duty of judges to thread the path-for path there is-through these fantastic labyrinths."

Learned Hand, *Eulogy of Thomas Walter Swan*, 57 YALE L. J. 167, 169 (1947).

Some of the recurrent elements of international tax systems reflect specific ways international business is conducted. Because international trade must bridge different economic and commercial environments, specialized intermediaries have arisen to narrow the span. More international commerce passes through independent agents, brokers, distributors, export-import specialists, and middlemen generally than in purely domestic transactions. Joint ventures are more common, as is the use of separately chartered subsidiary corporations. Because it is typically harder and more expensive to take effective legal action outside one's native legal environment, specialized forms of financing and transfer of ownership—epitomized in the international sale financed by a letter of credit payable upon transfer of documents of title—have evolved to prevent goods and payment for them from resting simultaneously in the same hands. Concerns about the definition, scope, and protection of intellectual property in different legal environments may also induce different choices in the forms of transfers of goods or intangible property from those contained within a single country. Governments also have different degrees of leverage (usually less) over enterprises operating largely beyond their borders, and as a result have responded with separate enforcement mechanisms and collection of taxes in the international setting.

Another impetus for greater conformity is spurred by the efforts to better harmonize the tax systems of major trading partners. The European Union has attempted to harmonize the working of international taxation among EU member states for many years. But even beyond that formal league, the broader international community of nations has had an ongoing initiative to address inappropriate base erosion and profit shifting. This effort was made more formal in recent years. In this regard, starting in 2015 at the behest of the G20 nations, the OECD has set forth recommendations for how countries should reform their domestic tax laws in order to prevent inappropriate base erosion and profit shifting while mitigating instances of double international taxation of the same income by multiple jurisdictions. This work has resulted in a so-called "inclusive framework," and the OECD has issued model rules and regularly updated its commentary on how nations should reform their international taxation regimes to prevent base erosion and profit shifting. These efforts, among others, provide informal "nudges" to nations to adopt international taxation principles that broadly harmonize with those of other major trading partners. Of course, some countries are more amenable to informal nudges than others. Yet, having said that, the family resemblance that one observes in the design of international taxation laws among nations leads one to believe that these nudges have real impact on the ultimate design that countries choose to enact. And, as the United States considers its design of international taxation, a lurking issue is what impact, if any, these laws have on the competitiveness of U.S. businesses around the world, and that concern provides impetus for designing the U.S. tax regime in a manner that harmonizes with the regimes of its other major trading partners.

Thus, in a sense, it is fair to say two things that, at first blush, appear contradictory. In one sense, the study of international taxation is a country-specific study of the United States domestic laws and of U.S. tax treaties that touch on international activity. However, in another sense, your understanding of the design features of the United States system will provide you a useful means to understand the design features of other nations because there is a noticeable family resemblance that exists in the design of the international tax regime of the United States and of those of the other major trading partners of the United States.

B. "Inbound" and "Outbound" Transactions

From the perspective of the U.S. tax system, international economic activity falls into two broad classes: 1) investments or business undertakings of foreign persons in the United States and 2) investments or business undertakings of U.S. persons abroad. Informally, these are known as "inbound" and "outbound" transactions respectively. More technically, the taxation of these two classes is called "taxation of foreign persons" and "taxation of foreign income." The most fully descriptive name for this book would be "U.S. Taxation of Foreign Persons and Foreign Income."[3] A similar vocabulary is used in the international tax systems of other countries, with suitably reversed meanings, of course, for the terms "foreign," "inbound," and "outbound."

C. The Study of International Taxation

To approach the study of international taxation, a student needs little more than a reasonably well-formed notion of "income" and a basic knowledge of business and investment. Although the relevant statutes and regulations are riddled with mechanical complexities, they rest on the same essential elements as other areas of income taxation. If you know about gross income, net income, inclusion, exclusion, credits, deductions, realization, recognition, timing, and basis, you already know the underpinnings of international taxation.

---

[3] I used that nomenclature to name my treatise that is updated annually. See Joseph Isenbergh & Bret Wells, International Taxation: U.S. Taxation of Foreign Persons and Foreign Income (Wolters Kluwer 6th Ed. 2021). Much like the name given to that treatise, it is much exhaustive and detailed in its coverage in comparison to the material in this book. However, it is my belief that this book provides the essential core needed for one to master the framework for U.S. international taxation.

To gain a strong intuitive grasp of international taxation (as opposed simply to parsing its individual rules) requires further understanding of the economic activity to which it applies—business and investment in the international setting. The greatest conceptual difficulties of international taxation lie in questions of characterization. These are even more acute than in taxation generally because of the greater opportunity in the international environment to maneuver transactions into different tax regimes, some more enjoyable than others. The real question in many cases ostensibly interpreting a provision of law is "What happened?" Questions of characterization are an undercurrent running through this book, and they surface ubiquitously.

D. Matters of Terminology

Initially, there are some important points of vocabulary. In referring to various beings, the language of taxation uses common terms in uncommon ways. In tax talk, the term "person" includes human beings *and* entities. A "United States person," for example, may be an individual, a corporation, a partnership, or a trust. The term "individual" refers only to a flesh and blood human. Therefore, in these pages, the word "person" means any identifiable being or entity while the word "individual" describes the likes of you and me. I use the terms "person" and "taxpayer" more or less interchangeably in this book. In places where the context leaves no doubt, I sometimes use the word "person" to mean "individual."

Individuals and other persons whose legal status connects them closely to the United States are often described here by the term "U.S.," as in "U.S. resident," "U.S. corporation," "U.S. citizen," and, more generally, "U.S. person." A careful student, particularly one who might have taken a law school course on business organizations, will no doubt observe that most entities are actually formed under state law, not federal law. But even so, the U.S. tax system of international taxation regards them as a U.S. entity if they are formed in any particularly U.S. state. The term "American" is sometimes used instead of "U.S.," as in "American citizen." For associations and entities, the term "domestic" is used synonymously with "U.S.," as in "domestic partnership" and "domestic corporation." The term "domestic" in this context has nothing to do with families. "Nonresident alien individuals" (the technical term for foreign nationals residing outside the United States) are sometimes referred to here as "foreign individuals" or simply "foreigners." The term "foreign persons" refers to foreign individuals and foreign entities collectively.

The U.S. income tax system is administered by the U.S. Treasury Department. A division of the Treasury, the Internal

Revenue Service, is headed by the Commissioner of Internal Revenue and that agency handles the day-to-day elements of this work. In this book, I make no distinction between the Treasury and the Internal Revenue Service. I refer here to the tax authorities of the United States variously and interchangeably as the "Treasury," the "Treasury Department," the "Secretary," the "Internal Revenue Service," the "Revenue Service," the "Service," the "IRS," and the "Commissioner." No inference should be drawn from the changing vocabulary, which is meant only to relieve the tedium of uniformity.

E. The U.S. Taxing Power

The taxing power of the United States arises from Article I, Section 8, of the Constitution, granting Congress the power "to lay and collect taxes, duties, imposts and excises. . . ." This power is qualified in Article I, Section 2, requiring that "direct taxes" shall be "apportioned among the several states. . . according to their respective numbers. . .," and in Article I, Section 9, requiring that "no capitation or other direct tax shall be laid, unless in proportion to the census. . . ." Under this last clause, the Income Tax Law of 1894 was struck down by the Supreme Court as unconstitutional in *Pollock v. Farmers Loan and Trust Co.*[4] The adoption of the 16th Amendment in 1913, empowering Congress "to lay and collect taxes on incomes, from whatever source derived, without apportionment among the several states, and without regard to any census or enumeration," both eliminated all doubt on the power of the United States to tax income and left no evident limitation on that power.

The 16th Amendment has not, to be sure, prevented those who have felt aggrieved by U.S. taxation, both in and out of the United States, from raising constitutional objections. However, unlike aspirants to constitutional protection in other areas of law, they have generally fared poorly. The courts of the United States have taken the taxing power, within its stated limits, at face value and have almost invariably upheld the validity of federal taxes, whether imposed on U.S. or foreign persons.[5]

The taxing power of the United States is exercised today through the Internal Revenue Code, a codification of tax laws spanning more than 100 years, styled since the Tax Reform Act of 1986 as the "Internal Revenue Code of 1986," and known colloquially as the "Code." The Code imposes an array of taxes, of which the most important are the individual and corporate income taxes, payroll taxes on compensation from employment and self-employment,

---

[4] 157 U.S. 429, 158 U.S. 601 (1895).

[5] See, e.g., Lord Forres v. Commissioner, 27 B.T.A. 154 (1932); Ross v. Commissioner, 44 B.T.A. 1 (1941). *Lord Forres* and *Ross* are discussed further in chapter 3.

excise taxes on various goods and transactions, and estate and gift taxes. This book is concerned almost exclusively with the individual and corporate income taxes, imposed by sections 1 and 11 of the Code respectively, on "taxable income." The latter is itself derived through a plethora of specific provisions from a base of "gross income," defined in section 61.

F. The Gross Anatomy of U.S. Income Taxation

It may help, before venturing into U.S. international taxation, to consider in broad overview U.S. taxation in its own national environment. The U.S. tax system has at its core a highly elaborated form of income taxation. For tax years beginning in 2026, the U.S. income tax is imposed at moderately progressive rates on individuals and small businesses and a flat rate on corporate enterprises. For tax years beginning in 2026, the inflation adjusted marginal rate of income tax on married individuals ranges from 10 percent on joint incomes below $24,800 to 37 percent on joint incomes above $768,700.[6] However, the effective rate of tax can in practice be much lower. If the income is qualified business income, it is eligible for an extra deduction under section 199A of up to 20 percent which could reduce the marginal rate to 29.6 percent. Further, on small incomes, a rate of 10 percent or lower may apply because of exemptions, allowances, and various credits accorded to individuals in the lower income brackets. The corporate income tax is a flat 21 percent for all corporate incomes.

A core element of U.S. income taxation is the realization principle. Under the realization principle, income is not taken into account for taxation unless associated with some event, called "realization," marking a change in its owner's relation to it. Although important exceptions to the realization principle exist, pure accretion is generally not taxed until there is a realization event. The most common event of realization is the receipt of money in exchange for property or services. More broadly, realization usually (but not invariably) entails an increase in liquidity. In the vocabulary of taxation, the actual inclusion of amounts in taxable income is known as "recognition" of gain. In the vocabulary of taxation, the actual inclusion of amounts in taxable income is known as "recognition" of gain. It is therefore possible to have realization without recognition of gain, and even, in some instances, recognition without realization.[7]

---

[6] See Rev. Proc. 2025–32, Sec. 4.01, 2025–45 I.R.B. 695.

[7] See, e.g., Code Sec. 1256 (commodities futures contracts marked-to-market annually, without regard for the actual sale or exchange of such assets); Code Sec. 475 (mark-to-market election for commodity and financial traders); Code Sec. 1272 (requires accrual of income on a yield to maturity basis for debt instruments issued with original issue discount); Code Sec. 877A (requires taxation of unrealized gains on certain expatriating individuals). The Supreme Court reopened the question of

Another essential feature of the U.S. tax system is the two-level taxation of the incomes of corporations. By virtue of the treatment of corporations as separate taxable entities in the U.S. system, the earnings of a corporation from business operations or investments are generally subject to U.S. income tax (known in this case as the "corporate income tax") independently of the taxation of its shareholders. The corporation's distribution of once-taxed earnings as dividends is the occasion for further income taxation of its shareholders.

Two-level taxation of entities and their owners is something less than an absolute norm of U.S. taxation, however. Some forms of business organization, including partnerships, so-called "S" corporations, and other limited-liability entities such as LLCs are subject to a single layer of income tax. Furthermore, section 199A provides an additional deduction of up to 20 percent of qualified business income earned by individuals directly or through partnerships. This deduction that is based on the amount of qualified business income is subject to exceptions and threshold restrictions when the amount of qualified business income exceeds $315,000.

Furthermore, even when income is earned by a corporation that is subject to separate corporate taxation on its earnings, those earnings may be substantially reduced by various base erosion and profit shifting possibilities. For example, the deduction of interest by a taxable corporation removes a portion of its earnings from the reach of corporate taxation by reducing the amount of its earnings exposed to tax. The presence of debt in the capital structure of a corporation, therefore, permits part of its income to escape corporate-level tax.

It follows that the use of debt in the capital structure of corporations has important tax implications. In the international setting, the interest paid to foreign debtholders of a corporation is often exempt from tax, so that interest deducted by the corporation in one tax environment may turn into interest income received by foreign debtholders in another tax environment where it escapes tax altogether. Problems stemming from the two-level taxation of corporations and shareholders in the U.S. system, as well as the countermeasures devised by artful tax planners, are of pervasive concern in this book.

Also mitigating the force of two-level taxation of corporate incomes is the preferential rate of tax imposed on the long-term capital gains of individuals. Currently, the maximum rate of income tax on long-term capital gains for most individuals is 20 percent (for

---

whether and to what extent the realization principle is a constitutional requirement in Moore v. United States, 602 U.S. 572 (2024) but disposed of that case on narrower grounds.

lower-income individuals, the rate falls to 10 percent or even zero percent through 2025). For many foreign persons, the rate of U.S. tax on capital gains derived from passive investments in the United States is *zero* percent.

Starting in 2003, the maximum rate of income tax on dividends received from domestic corporations (and foreign corporations eligible for U.S. tax treaty benefits) was reduced to 20 percent for most individuals (and, as with capital gains, to 15 or zero percent for some).[8] This regime for dividends further blunts the force of two-level taxation for individual shareholders of corporations. Foreign persons, however, derive little or no benefit from low rates of U.S. tax on dividends under the Internal Revenue Code.

G. Worldwide U.S. Taxation

You are probably familiar with the idea that the U.S. income tax is "worldwide." The worldwide reach of U.S. income taxation flows initially, simply enough, from the absence in the Code of any limitation on the taxation of U.S. persons. Section 1 imposes a tax on the taxable income of "every individual," and section 11 does the same for "every corporation." "Gross income" (the base from which taxable income is derived) is expressly defined in section 61 to include all income "from whatever source derived." Taxation of income from all sources is precisely what is meant by "worldwide" taxation. Indeed, it is not immediately obvious on first encounter with the Code that *any* person, regardless of nationality *or* residence, escapes worldwide U.S. taxation. You could easily conclude from section 1 by itself, which imposes a tax on the income of "every individual," that the Code purported to tax every soul on earth.

1. Limits in the Code

In order to find any limitation on the taxation of *foreign* individuals, you must read to section 2(d), which scales down the tax of section 1 for "nonresident alien individuals" as provided "in sections 871 and 877." The latter provisions, in their turn, expound a tax regime reaching mainly income that is related economically to the United States. A "nonresident alien" is a non-U.S. citizen residing outside the United States. There are corollary provisions limiting U.S. taxation of foreign corporations in sections 881 and 882.[9]

This minuet of statutory cross-reference, only partly cued in the text itself, reveals the Code's true character: atomized, sprawling,

---

[8] See § 1(j).

[9] Nonresident alien individuals and foreign corporations make up a class described collectively as "foreign persons."

and opaque. For much of the Code, at least on first encounter, the only way to know what it means is to know what it means.

2. Simpler Times

It was not always so. Over a century ago, the Income Tax Law of 1894 encompassed the entire U.S. income tax, both domestic and international, in a single nearly readable sentence:

> [T]here shall be assessed. . . and paid annually upon the gains, profits, and income received. . . by every citizen of the United States, whether residing at home or abroad, and every person residing therein, whether said gains, profits, or income be derived from any kind of property, rents, interest, dividends, or salaries, or from any profession, trade, employment, or vocation carried on in the United States or elsewhere, or from any other source whatever, a tax of two per centum on the amount so derived over and above four thousand dollars, and a like tax shall be levied, collected, and paid annually upon the gains, profits, and income from all property owned and of every business, trade, or profession carried on in the United States by persons residing without the United States.[10]

Another sentence in the 1894 law contains virtually the entire system of enforcement: "[I]n computing income [a nonresident] shall include all income from every source, but unless he be a citizen of the United States he shall only pay on that part of the income which is derived from any source in the United States."

For all its endearing simplicity, the 1894 Tax Law was struck down as unconstitutional in 1895. Its basic framework, however, survives in today's law, embedded in a more than ten-thousand fold increase in girth: 1) U.S. citizens and residents are taxed on their income from all sources worldwide and 2) Nonresident foreign citizens are taxed only on income derived from the United States.

3. Dividends from Foreign Corporations

Starting in 2017, Congress provided a 100 percent foreign dividends received deduction for the foreign source portion of dividends received by a *domestic corporate* shareholder that owns a 10 percent or greater interest in the foreign corporation. This 100 percent foreign dividends received deduction in effect establishes an exemption system for foreign income earned by a *domestic corporation* from a dividend paid by a foreign corporation to which the domestic corporation is entitled to claim an offsetting deduction.

---

[10] Revenue Act of 1894, PUB. L. NO. 227, Sec. 27, 28 STAT. 509, 553 (Aug. 27, 1894).

However, the 100 percent foreign dividends received deduction is not applicable to dividends paid to individual shareholders. In addition, the 100 percent foreign dividends received deduction is not applicable to any U.S. shareholder with respect to foreign earnings of a controlled foreign corporation (sometimes referred to as "CFCs") that are deemed to be immediately taxable to the U.S. shareholders under one of the anti-deferral regimes that apply to those earnings. Any earnings that are subject to taxation under the anti-deferral regimes are subject to taxation to the U.S. shareholder, but a U.S. *domestic corporation* shareholder may then be entitled to claim foreign tax credit relief for foreign income taxes paid by the controlled foreign corporation with respect to those earnings. This juxtaposition of a potential 100 percent foreign dividends received deduction with an anti-deferral regime, which applies to those earnings and supplants the deduction, creates a hybrid regime that is neither entirely territorial in nature nor entirely worldwide in scope. The manner in which the anti-deferral regimes apply to shareholders that are U.S. corporations or to shareholders who are U.S. individuals is discussed more fully in chapter 11.

H. The Problem of Double Taxation

Worldwide taxation by the United States does not, needless to say, disarm the taxing power of other countries. Americans pursuing income outside the United States are bound to encounter tax collectors asserting their own national claims. The world is awash in possibilities of double, even triple, taxation. Countries to which Americans are themselves foreign commonly tax foreigners (as does the United States) on the basis of the "source" of their income, a term widely used by national tax systems to describe income within their reach. The short-lived 1894 Tax Law, as you may have noticed above, introduced the term "source" of income in the U.S. tax laws as a shorthand for the location of the property or business from which income is derived. This, however, is not the only plausible notion of the source of income, and other tax systems conceive the source of income quite differently. Consider the following scenario and variations.

1. A Contract in Kuwait

Suppose you are a lawyer practicing in New York City. One day, your phone rings, and a voice on the other end of the line, calling from Kuwait, asks you to do some research on a question and send your findings in the form of a memorandum. You decide that the caller, with whom you have mutual acquaintances, is creditworthy, and you go ahead with the work, consisting of some reading, some thinking, and some writing, which takes in all 20 hours of your time. Your final product is a memorandum, which you send to your Kuwaiti client, along with a bill for $10,000 reflecting your hourly rate of $500. A check for $10,000 arrives by return mail, and you give the matter little further thought beyond wishing that your local clients were as easy to deal with.

Toward the end of the year, you receive an official-looking letter from the Treasury of Kuwait, impressively adorned with a seal and crests, asking you to remit $5,000 in income tax to the Kuwaiti Treasury with respect to your $10,000 of Kuwait-source income, explaining that the rate of Kuwaiti income tax on the Kuwait-source income of foreigners from professional services is 50 percent. Although the arithmetic is sound, you are nonetheless taken by surprise. You know that your income from law practice in New York is subject to U.S. income tax, but it has not occurred to you that a foreign country might attempt to tax it as well. You ask a friend who specializes in taxation if the demand of the Kuwaiti Treasury is kosher. Your friend tells you that in the *U.S.* tax system your income has its source in the United States, not Kuwait, because under U.S. tax notions income takes its source from the place of the economic activity that gives rise to it, and you did the work in the United States. You, therefore, write back to the Kuwaiti Treasury, pointing out that all the work that produced the $10,000 fee was done in the United States and that you don't think that it should be subject to Kuwaiti tax. The Kuwaiti Treasury responds in turn that *its* tax system identifies the source of income with the source of *payment* rather than the place the underlying work was done, adding the further explanation that the $10,000 came out of *Kuwait*'s economy, reduced *Kuwait*'s claims on the world's resources by $10,000, affected *Kuwait*'s balance of payments, and that, in any event, its official determination is final.

Kuwait has won the narrow legal argument. As a matter of Kuwaiti law, you owe the tax, and while the tax does not comport with U.S. notions of the source of income, it is not self-evidently wrong. At this point, one possible course for you is to pay the tax and move on with your life. On further reflection, though, you may not care who has won the argument. Depending on your anticipated future ties to Kuwait, you can just say no—simply not pay the Kuwaiti tax claim—without further ado. Kuwait can't do anything to you unless you are planning to take your next vacation there. The United States will not enforce Kuwait's demand (or at least you don't think so). Therefore, you ignore Kuwait's tax claim.

Precisely because you can do so, and likely with impunity, the course of events just described will never occur. Kuwait's view of the source of your income in this vignette is entirely realistic (many countries take such a view), but Kuwait's relaxed approach to the collection of its tax is not. Kuwait knows full well that it has little or no leverage to collect tax from *you* and will likely not even attempt the vain act of doing so. Instead, you will receive from your Kuwaiti client a check for $5,000, along with an official form indicating that $5,000 of Kuwaiti income tax has been withheld by your client at the source and paid over to the Kuwaiti Treasury on your behalf. You can engage in the same exchange of arguments with Kuwait as above, but now *Kuwait* does not care who wins the legal point. It has the money. You cannot sue your client in Kuwait for the balance of your fee because under Kuwaiti law you have been paid in full. Kuwait's practice of withholding income tax at the source from payments of income to foreign persons has reversed the balance of power between you and the Kuwaiti Treasury on your behalf. You cannot avoid the tax.

Given the inevitability of the withheld Kuwaiti tax, your next concern is how the United States will tax your fee in light of Kuwait's action. Assume for simplicity that the United States also imposes a 50 percent income tax. The worst possibility is that the United States Treasury might take no account whatever of the Kuwaiti tax, that is, deny you any deduction or other allowance for its payment. If so, your U.S. taxable income on account of the fee is $10,000,[11] and your U.S. income tax obligation is $5,000 (at a 50 percent rate). The combined tax payments to Kuwait and the United States ($5,000 to each) add up to $10,000 and have wiped out your income from the venture. This pathetic result is absolute double taxation, to wit, the taxation of the same income by each of two countries without any allowance by either for the tax imposed by the other. If it were common, double taxation of this sort would stop international economic activity in its tracks.

Another less disastrous possibility is that the United States will allow you at least to deduct the Kuwaiti tax from your U.S. taxable income. Without digging very deeply into the U.S. tax system, a deduction of the Kuwaiti tax might be defended as an expense of carrying on the business that generated the income. With a deduction for the Kuwaiti tax, your U.S. taxable income is reduced to $5,000, on which you owe the U.S. Treasury $2,500. Taking account of the $5,000 tax paid to Kuwait, your total worldwide tax cost is $7,500. This too is double taxation, but in a milder form. While you have paid tax to two sovereigns, one of them (the United States) has made some concession for the tax paid to the other (Kuwait). The combined rate of tax is 75 percent, which is still a considerable surtax on

---

[11] Note that your U.S. income is the full $10,000 (and not the $5,000 cash you actually received) because your income includes amounts used to discharge *your* obligations, whether paid over to you or not. Readers who have taken a course in introductory income taxation may remember Old Colony Trust Co. v. Commissioner, 279 U.S. 716 (1929), in this regard.

international economic activity compared to purely domestic activities.

Better yet, you might hope (especially if you have at some point heard of the foreign tax credit) to be allowed a full dollar-for-dollar offset of the Kuwaiti tax against your U.S. income tax. If a credit for Kuwaiti tax were allowed by the United States (assuming no deduction were also allowed), your U.S. taxable income from the venture would be $10,000, entailing a pre-credit U.S. tax of $5,000, reduced to *zero* by a tax credit of $5,000 for income tax paid to Kuwait. With a U.S. tax credit, the combined amount of Kuwaiti and U.S. tax ($5,000) is the same as the 50-percent tax imposed by either country on its own. With a full foreign tax credit, there is no double taxation.

If you expected to be allowed a U.S. credit for Kuwaiti income tax in this situation, however, you would be disappointed. To be sure, the U.S. tax system normally does allow a dollar-for-dollar credit for foreign income taxes, with a view to pacifying international double taxation. This—the so-called foreign tax credit—is a concession of the U.S. Treasury to the taxing power of the country of source, but credit is accorded only for foreign taxes imposed on *foreign source* income.[12] Recall that the Kuwaiti tax here was imposed on your fee for work done in the United States, which is *U.S. source* income. True enough, Kuwait assigned a Kuwaiti source to the income you received from your Kuwaiti client, but that was a matter of *Kuwaiti* tax law. The United States applies its own principles of source, not other countries', in allowing the foreign tax credit, which defers to the taxing power of the country of source only for income on which the United States is willing to forego taxation. This forbearance does not extend to income considered within the *U.S.* tax system, to have U.S. source. Accordingly, the United States makes no particular concession for foreign taxes imposed on income from law practice in New York. Nor will the United States change its mind upon hearing from you that Kuwait takes a different view of the source of this income.

Your last resort in this situation would be to attempt to characterize the income from your Kuwaiti client as some sort of foreign source income to entitle you to utilize the U.S. credit for the tax paid to Kuwait. For example, since your work culminated in a memorandum sent to your client, you might try to cast the overall transaction as a *sale* of a written product in Kuwait, which the

---

[12] Admittedly, a de minimis rule allows individuals to claim up to $300 of a foreign tax credit ($600 for a joint return) regardless of whether foreign source income exists. See § 904(j)(2). But, even so, this de minimis allowance of foreign tax credits absent the existence of any foreign source income given that he incurred $5,000 of foreign tax.

United States might acknowledge as generating foreign source gain. This attempt would likely fail: it would be hard to convince the U.S. Treasury (and more importantly a court) that you have been compensated principally for the transfer of a physical object. That such a maneuver could even be considered to the end of a better tax result, however, reveals the special importance of the characterization of transactions in the international setting.

This vignette of an international venture illustrates a central cause of international double taxation of income: inconsistent source rules in different countries imposing overlapping taxes. Both the United States and Kuwait tax the same item of income as their own. Both have the power to tax in this instance—that is, both have a lever over the taxpayer—and so both can be "right" in the only sense that matters.[13] If all countries had perfectly consistent source rules and a system of credits, there would be no double taxation. But they don't, and there is.

I. Territorial Taxation

Many countries practice what is known as "territorial" taxation: taxation limited to income from sources within their boundaries no matter who derives it. Territorial tax systems accommodate other tax systems in the simplest possible way—by not extending their own. In a territorial tax regime, double taxation is tamed by taking no account of foreign income, whether earned by a citizen, resident, or anyone else. In fact, the nations that comprise the largest trading partners of the United States all have some form of a "territorial" tax regime for active foreign business income earned by corporations.[14] Due to a concern over a perceived reduction of international competitiveness of U.S. corporations, Congress in 2017 enacted section 245A, which in effect provides elements of a "territorial" tax regime by allowing certain domestic corporations that own a 10 percent interest in a foreign corporation to receive a deduction for the foreign source dividends from the foreign corporation. However, the United States retained worldwide taxation on U.S. individuals by restricting the scope of section 245A to domestic corporate shareholders only. The U.S. tax system is thus a hybrid of worldwide and territorial taxation.

As one should expect, whenever a tax system asserts taxing power over income from its own jurisdiction while foregoing taxation of income earned outside its taxing territory, an incentive will arise

---

13 There is, remember, no overriding international law of taxation.

14 See STAFF OF THE JOINT. COMM. ON TAXATION, BACKGROUND AND SELECTED ISSUES RELATED TO THE U.S. INTERNATIONAL TAX SYSTEM AND SYSTEMS THAT EXEMPT FOREIGN BUSINESS INCOME, JCX–33–11, 1, 7–8 (May 20, 2011) (analyzing nine major trading partners of the United States that provide for an exemption system).

to shift income to the offshore territory. Through tax planning, international economic activity originating in a territorial tax environment can sometimes elude the shoals of national taxation altogether. Returning to the vignette belabored above, suppose this time you are a Kuwaiti citizen working as a consultant in an office in *Kuwait*. Suppose further that Kuwait follows a strictly territorial method of taxation, that is, it taxes only Kuwaiti source income. A client in the United States asks you for some work, which you do for a fee of $10,000. Under the *U.S.* tax laws, you have *foreign* (i.e., non-U.S.) source income (for work done *outside* the United States). If the source rules in Kuwait turn exclusively on the origin of payment, however, you also have foreign (i.e., non-Kuwaiti) source income from the perspective of the *Kuwaiti* treasury. As a non-U.S. person, you are subject to U.S. tax only on U.S. source income (which in the U.S. Treasury's view, you do not have). Kuwait's territorial tax system, for its part, reaches only Kuwait-source income (which in the Kuwaiti treasury's view you also do not have). Economic activity involving only high-tax countries (50 percent rates in both Kuwait and the United States in this fantasy) escapes income taxation in either. This enjoyable possibility (as was taxation in the mirror-image example traversed above) flows from different and inconsistent source rules under U.S. and Kuwaiti tax laws.

Inconsistent tax principles and source rules of different countries have been known sometimes to coexist benignly—"underlap" if you will—and allow total escape from taxation by any country for those able to align their affairs artfully. The income earned in this example is known as "homeless income" that neither jurisdiction treats as its own.

The differences between territorial and worldwide tax systems are smaller than first appear. The combination of worldwide taxation and a foreign tax credit approximates in some respects the effect of territorial taxation. When foreign tax rates are roughly the same as U.S. rates, it matters little whether the U.S. Treasury simply ignores foreign income or allows an offset of its own tax by a comparable amount paid to foreign treasuries. Furthermore, few countries' taxation mechanisms are unqualifiedly territorial or absolutely worldwide. Rather, national modes of taxation fall on a spectrum from territorial to worldwide. Some countries tax the worldwide passive investment income of their own residents but not their foreign source business profits. Other countries tax the worldwide incomes of their own residents but not of their citizens residing abroad. Yet others tax the worldwide incomes only of their citizens who are also residents.

The United States, in particular, is at an important inflection point. The current U.S. international tax regime asserts worldwide taxation over U.S. individuals but defers shareholder level taxation on foreign earnings of foreign corporations owned by U.S. shareholders who are individuals. The U.S. international tax regime asserts worldwide taxation over domestic corporations on their worldwide income as well, but U.S. corporations generally enjoy a territorial tax result for foreign income earned by foreign corporations and paid to U.S. corporate shareholders. The above framework for the deferral (or as to domestic corporations the possible exemption) of income earned by foreign corporations is further garlanded by anti-deferral provisions that may cause the U.S. shareholders to be taxed immediately on the income earned by foreign corporations in which they hold interests. Finally, when earnings of a foreign corporation are immediately taxable to the U.S. shareholders under one of these anti-deferral regimes, domestic corporations are entitled to claim foreign tax credits for the foreign taxes paid on those earnings, but individuals are not absent a special election afforded under section 962 discussed in chapter 11. Thus, the U.S. tax system can at best be characterized as a hybrid regime that contains elements of both a territorial regime (particularly with respect to *domestic corporations*) and a worldwide taxation regime (particularly with respect to *individuals*), and each element has its own set of complexities.

J. U.S. International Taxation in Brief Overview

In the first four chapters, topics that are relevant conceptual building blocks to an understanding of both inbound and outbound taxation are addressed. This chapter provides a general overview of the material in this book. Chapter 2 provides an analysis of residence for tax purposes. Chapter 3 summarizes and discusses the source rules. Chapter 4 addresses the transfer pricing rules that apply to related party transactions. After addressing these questions common to both the inbound and outbound tax regimes, I then turn first to inbound taxation and thereafter to outbound taxation.

1. The Inbound Regime

The United States taxes foreign persons under two different tax regimes, imposed respectively on passive investments and active business operations. Current flows of U.S. source passive investment income—known in tax patois as "fixed or determinable income not effectively connected with a U.S. trade or business"—are taxed at a flat rate (generally 30 percent) without allowance for deductions. Business profits from the United States—known as income "effectively connected with a U.S. trade or business"—are taxed at the regular graduated rates, with allowance for the full complement of deductions and credits.

From this bare outline, it would seem that the U.S. taxation of passive investment is the more severe. To be sure, the highest marginal rate imposed on the net business incomes of foreign individuals (top marginal rate of 37 percent for individuals) is somewhat higher than the flat 30 percent rate imposed on their passive investment income, but the allowance of deductions and credits in the taxation of business income would usually be more than enough to compensate for this relatively small difference in rates. In addition, if the income earned in the United States constituted qualified business income, it would be eligible for the extra deduction under section 199A of up to 20 percent that could reduce the marginal rate to 29.6 percent. For foreign corporations, the income tax rate is 21 percent.

On closer scrutiny, however, there are gaps in the flat-rate tax imposed on investment income, large enough to make it essentially benign. Gains from the sale of U.S. investment assets (other than interests in real property) by foreign persons, including capital gains from stocks, securities, and other financial assets, are not taxed at all. Even more importantly, interest from U.S. bank deposits and from U.S. "portfolio" debt (a class including most private and public bonds and other obligations) is largely exempt from U.S. taxation in the hands of foreign persons. In chapter 5, I will explore the taxation of passive investment income of foreign persons in greater detail.

On the other side of the scale, a U.S. tax on the branch profits of foreign corporations in the United States adds a potential extra 30 percent tax on their business profits when they are removed from the U.S. economic environment. This tax, dating from the 1986 Act, extends two-level taxation of corporate profits to a larger class of foreign business operations in the United States.

Taking these additional elements into account, the taxation of active U.S. business operations emerges as the more severe. I will address the taxation of active business income in the United States in chapter 6. The taxation of active business income, however, is rarely crushing in practical effect by virtue of the combined effect of interest deductions removing earnings from the reach of U.S. taxation and the protections of various income tax treaties. The overlay of the U.S. tax treaty framework on both passive investors and for those engaged in active business activities in the United States is addressed in chapter 7. Due to a concern that the concessions accorded to foreign persons under domestic law and U.S. tax treaties may allow serious erosion of U.S. taxable income, the United States has adopted a set of backstop provisions that are designed to rein in outcomes that would otherwise be overly favorable to foreign taxpayers. These backstop provisions are discussed collectively in chapter 8.

2. The Outbound Regime

The two essential—and often conflicting—elements of U.S. taxation of foreign income are the worldwide taxation of United States citizens and residents and the status of corporations as separate taxable entities. The informing questions in the taxation of foreign income reflect one or the other of these elements, which arise respectively as the problems of double taxation and deferral. Chapter 9 sets out an overview of the general U.S. approach to outbound taxation and the general framework of U.S. taxation of direct foreign investment by U.S. persons through foreign corporations.

The Foreign Tax Credit. Since direct foreign investments and business operations of United States persons (including domestic corporations) are subject to worldwide taxation and often attract foreign income taxes along with the baseline U.S. tax, the specter of double taxation is bound to haunt the pursuit of foreign income. The principal accommodation of the U.S. tax system to the possibility of source-based taxation imposed by other countries on the business activities of U.S. persons is the foreign tax credit. From a simple idea—a dollar-for-dollar reduction of U.S. tax for income taxes paid to foreign countries—the foreign tax credit has evolved into an elaborate statutory structure. The foreign tax credit is addressed in chapter 10.

Foreign Corporations and the 100 Percent Foreign Dividends Received Deduction. The U.S. tax system generally recognizes the separate identity of corporations even when they are owned and controlled by a single person or a small group. In domestic U.S. taxation, the separate identity of corporations is the occasion for two levels of taxation of the earnings of corporations, one imposed on the income of an entity and the other on dividend distributions received by shareholders. In international transactions, however, the separateness of corporations may permit escape from current U.S. taxation of the earnings of foreign corporations beneficially owned by U.S. persons. Because a foreign corporation is a separate foreign person, it is not subject to U.S. taxation on its income derived outside the United States. The earnings of foreign corporations are subject to U.S. taxation, in the normal course of events, only when distributed to U.S. persons as dividends. Given that the distribution of a dividend is largely optional, deferral of U.S. taxation can go on indefinitely. Indeed, with the restatement to fair market value of the basis of shares at the death of an individual shareholder,[15] deferral of a dividend payment to the U.S. citizen or resident individual in that instance can become forgiveness.

---

[15] See § 1014(a).

If the foreign corporation is owned by a domestic corporation, then dividends paid to a domestic corporate shareholder that owns a 10 percent or greater interest in the foreign corporation are eligible for a 100 percent foreign dividends received deduction under section 245A. The effect of this 100 percent foreign dividends received deduction is that all U.S. residual taxation at the corporate level is eliminated with respect to foreign earnings remitted as a dividend to a U.S. domestic corporation that owns at least a 10 percent or greater interest in the foreign corporation.

Beyond that, however, if the domestic corporation in turn distributes as dividends these remitted earnings to individual U.S. shareholders, there will be further U.S. tax. Furthermore, in situations where the earnings of a foreign corporation may not reflect its actual economic income (for example, because the earnings have been shifted around among related entities to deflect them to a low-tax environment) the earnings of a controlled foreign corporation may be taxable immediately to its U.S. shareholders as ordinary income. These anti-deferral provisions are discussed in chapter 11.

The use of a foreign corporation that is not a controlled foreign corporation but is a passive foreign investment company is subject to a separate regime that is discussed in chapter 12. Final technical topics and further export incentives are discussed in chapters 13 and 14, respectively.

Complexity. This system may seem simple enough when presented in broad overview. The devil, however, is in the details, and they, trust me, are satanic indeed. Particularly in the taxation of foreign income, the proliferation of rules can be frightening. The reason for this complexity is the attempt to formalize distinctions between legitimate business operations outside the United States and maneuvers considered to be tax haven operations. The provisions governing the foreign tax credit and foreign dividends received deduction regimes forge a path that in some instances create possible international double taxation and in other instances pose excessive concessions to taxpayers or foreign treasuries. Through it all, the U.S. international taxation regime seeks to distinguish between legitimate overseas business operations, where the U.S. Treasury allows the foreign tax environment (harsh or benign) to prevail, and tax haven operations, where the U.S. Treasury steps in aggressively. The mechanics of these distinctions, real or imaginary, are often nightmarish.

3. Tax Havens and Income Shifting

Among the reasons for this complexity is the elusive nature of tax havens. A tax haven is not always immediately obvious. What makes a particular environment a tax haven is not invariably a low rate of tax but relations with other tax regimes that permit the ultimate deflection of income to a low-tax environment with which the income may have little indigenous connection. The U.S. tax system has responded with rules treating as tax havens transactional structures where there is no necessary connection between the location of economic activity and the situs of its taxation or, more concretely, where activity and taxation occur in different places.

Until fairly recently, a prime tax haven was Holland, a country sometimes perceived as having pushed its own taxation to the edge of socialism and beyond. What made Holland a tax haven was its extraordinary network of income tax treaties, allowing income from high-tax environments to flow through a Dutch-chartered entity without tax on its way to some low-tax environment bearing a more conventional resemblance to a tax haven.

You should note that a low-taxed business undertaking, domestic or foreign, is not per se a tax haven. A resort hotel and casino owned and operated by a foreign subsidiary of a U.S. corporation in the Cayman Islands (a place of pleasantly benign weather *and* taxation) is not considered a tax shelter just because Cayman Islands taxes are low. If, however, the income from a foreign owned *Miami* hotel is taxed (or more accurately, barely taxed) in the Cayman Islands and not in the United States, *that* is a tax haven operation, and if the mechanism to that end is a Dutch corporation, then the tax haven is Holland.

An essential pattern in many international tax-sheltering operations is "income shifting," which consists of arranging for income to be taxed in a country different from the one where it arose as an economic matter. The latter is typically a high-tax environment; the former is far less so. Income shifting comes in several forms, which include profit shifting and base erosion. These strategies, which often entail complex corporate structures and sophisticated business arrangements, are pursued in both inbound and outbound operations.[16]

Profit shifting and base erosion themselves fall in several different categories. Among these are the following:

1. *Interest Stripping Transactions.* A low-tax affiliate makes related-party loans to fund the capital needs of high-tax affiliates and charges interest on the related-

[16] The historical origins of the base erosion and profit shifting mistake is dealt with extensively in Bret Wells & Cym Lowell, *Tax Base Erosion and Homeless Income: Collection at Source is the Linchpin*, 65 TAX L. REV. 535 (2012); Bret Wells & Cym Lowell, *Income Tax Treaty Policy in the 21st Century: Residence vs. Source*, 5 COLUM. TAX J. 1 (2013).

party debt (interest stripping transactions).[17] In these interest stripping transactions, the high-tax affiliate is entitled to claim a tax deduction for its interest payments that are made to the low-tax affiliate while the low-tax affiliate is not subject to taxation in the high-tax country and lightly taxed in its own country.

2. *Royalty Stripping Transactions.* A low-tax affiliate acquires the intellectual property, know-how, and other intangibles of the multinational group through intangible migration strategies. After ownership of the intangibles has shifted to the low-tax affiliate, the low-tax affiliate assumes the role of "IP owner" and "internal risk taker" with respect to the intangible returns of the multinational enterprise. The low-tax affiliate then licenses the valuable intangibles to high-tax affiliates and charges those affiliates a royalty under related-party licensing agreements (royalty stripping transactions).[18] Through these royalty stripping transactions, the high-tax affiliate is entitled to claim a tax deduction on its royalty payments made to the low-tax affiliate while the low-tax affiliate is not subject to taxation in the source country and lightly taxed in its own country.

3. *Lease Stripping Transactions.* A low-tax affiliate leases tangible personal property (machinery and equipment) to foreign affiliates located in high-tax jurisdictions and charges rent for this equipment (lease stripping transactions).[19] The high-tax affiliate

---

[17] Inbound debt infused into the U.S. affiliate is widely seen as a systemic challenge. See DONALD J. MARPLES & JANE G. GRAVELLE, CONG. RESEARCH SERV., R43568, CORPORATE EXPATRIATION, INVERSIONS, AND MERGERS: TAX ISSUES 4 (2015) (noting that the inverted company "can engage in 'earnings stripping': reducing income in the U.S. firm by borrowing from the U.S. company and increasing interest deductions). For example, a foreign parent may lend to its U.S. subsidiary. This intercompany debt does not alter the overall company's debt, but does result in an interest expense in the United States (which reduces U.S. taxes paid) results in an increased portion of company income being 'booked' outside the United States in an offshore affiliate. See OFFICE OF TAX POLICY OF THE DEP'T OF TREASURY, CORPORATE INVERSION TRANSACTIONS: TAX POLICY IMPLICATIONS 22 (May 2002).

[18] See STAFF OF THE JOINT COMM. ON TAX'N, 111TH CONG., JCX–33–11, PRESENT LAW AND BACKGROUND RELATED TO POSSIBLE INCOME SHIFTING AND TRANSFER PRICING 109 (2010) at 103–04 (although diversity of techniques exist, the case studies of Charlie and Echo demonstrate IP migration with unidentified intangibles where Alpha, Bravo, and Foxtrot explicitly use licensing and cost sharing agreements to transfer the intangible value of identified intangible to a low-tax affiliate); see also DEP'T. OF THE TREASURY, REPORT TO THE CONGRESS ON EARNINGS STRIPPING, TRANSFER PRICING AND U.S. INCOME TAX TREATIES 54 (Nov. 2007).

[19] See STAFF OF THE JOINT COMM. ON TAX'N, 111TH CONG., JCX–33–11, PRESENT LAW AND BACKGROUND RELATED TO POSSIBLE INCOME SHIFTING AND

claims a tax deduction on its rental payments in the lease stripping transaction while the low-tax affiliate is not subject to taxation in the source country and lightly taxed in its own country.

4. *Supply Chain Transactions*. The low-tax affiliate buys property from one affiliate and/or resells property to another affiliate or becomes the risk-taker in the supply chain (via a contract manufacturing arrangement or commissionaire arrangement).[20] The profit margin earned by the low-tax affiliate in these supply chain transactions generally is subject only to minimal taxation.

5. *Service Stripping Transactions*. A low-tax affiliate charges high-tax affiliates for its provision of expert services including risk-taker services or technical support services (service stripping transactions).[21] The high-tax affiliate claims a tax deduction for its service fee payments that arises as part of the service stripping transaction while the low-tax affiliate is not subject to taxation in the source country and lightly taxed in its own country.

Each of the above base erosion techniques achieves the same end: profits from affiliates located in high-tax jurisdictions are shifted in a tax deductible manner to an affiliate located in a low-taxed jurisdiction.

When a U.S. subsidiary makes a cross-border tax deductible payment to a low-taxed offshore affiliate, the overall income of the multinational enterprise has not changed. The multinational enterprise has simply moved assets from one affiliate's pocket to another's. I will consider these techniques in the inbound context systematically. Each technique creates its own unique income sourcing question; the appropriate sourcing of the income earned by the offshore low-taxed affiliate for each of these techniques is

---

TRANSFER PRICING 109 (2010) at 64, n.185 (noting in the Bravo case study that the intercompany license agreement provided the low-tax affiliate with the rights that included the right to lease or otherwise commercially exploit assets acquired by the low-tax affiliate).

[20] See STAFF OF THE JOINT COMM. ON TAX'N, 111TH CONG., JCX–33–11, PRESENT LAW AND BACKGROUND RELATED TO POSSIBLE INCOME SHIFTING AND TRANSFER PRICING 109 (2010) at 11–17 (each restructuring of Alpha, Bravo, Charlie, Delta, Echo and Foxtrot provide variations of this common supply chain transaction theme).

[21] See, e.g., DONALD J. MARPLES & JANE G. GRAVELLE, CONG. RESEARCH SERV., R43568, CORPORATE EXPATRIATION, INVERSIONS, AND MERGERS: TAX ISSUES at 4 ("Royalty payments, management fees, and transfer pricing arrangements are other avenues for earnings stripping,").

addressed in chapter 3. Each of these five basic intercompany techniques creates transfer pricing issues; the regulations that address these different categories of related party transactions are addressed in chapter 4. These various techniques raise questions of the recognition and timing of income in the U.S. tax system, an analysis of which is set out in chapter 5. Each of these techniques is then addressed in terms of the application of the U.S. model treaty in chapter 7.

Finally, due to a concern that the general inbound U.S. rules do not adequately address these techniques, the United States has added to its inbound U.S. tax rules backstop regimes that bolster the basic design of the U.S. inbound taxation regime. Conceptually, an inbound base protection measure could be designed along one of the following fundamental principles: (i) impose a U.S. tax on the low-tax foreign affiliate that received the earnings stripped out of the United States tax base so that the earnings do not ultimate escape the reach of the U.S. tax system; (ii) deny a deduction for the related party earnings stripping payment so that the payor is unable to reduce its earnings that are in the United States tax base, or (iii) provide a deduction for such payments but limit the amount of such deductions. It may come as no surprise to the reader that the United States has implemented measures from all three approaches, and those backstop regimes are discussed in light of each of these earnings stripping techniques in chapter 8.

In the outbound context, U.S. multinational enterprises can utilize these same techniques to erode the tax base of a foreign jurisdiction. In chapter 11, I will explore the backstop anti-deferral regimes that attempt to prevent income shifting from the United States to an offshore tax-haven affiliate that is owned and controlled by the U.S. multinational enterprise. The U.S. multinational in the outbound context can also have its controlled foreign corporations engage in earnings stripping techniques to shift profits from foreign affiliates located in high-tax jurisdictions to foreign affiliates located in low-tax jurisdictions. I will explore how these anti-deferral provisions affect those foreign-to-foreign base erosion techniques in chapter 11 as well. As I explore the scope of the U.S. anti-deferral regimes, we will see that, with minor exceptions, the U.S. international tax regime applied to outbound operations has become increasingly agnostic about base erosion and profit shifting effects that occur solely in the foreign-to-foreign context, while remaining more vigilant and robust in protecting against stripping profits from the U.S. tax environment into an offshore controlled foreign corporation. However, excessive amounts of low-tax income that escape a minimum foreign tax are now subject to a minimum U.S. tax.

Even so, base erosion and profit shifting efforts in the foreign-to-foreign setting largely are left to be addressed, if at all, by the affected foreign jurisdiction. That said, other developed nations are considering their own measures to address base erosion and profit shifting directed at their own jurisdiction. The European Commission has launched an attack on these structures under the theory that the concessionary tax benefits obtained by the low-tax affiliate may represent illegal state aid.[22] After a multi-year study, the Organization for Economic Co-operation and Development (OECD) has issued a series of reports on base erosion and profit shifting (called its BEPS reports) that set out 15 recommendations for how countries should respond to these strategies.[23] The recommendations range from proposals on how to modify domestic laws to how the model treaties should be reformed. In 2020, the OECD issued an Inclusive Framework made up of two pillars to address international taxation with respect to virtual business activity.[24] In December 2021, the OECD issued the Global Anti-Base

---

[22] See European Commission Press Release IP/16/42, State Aid: Commission Concludes Belgian "Excess Profit" Tax Scheme Illegal; Around €700 million to Be Recovered from 35 Multinational Companies (Jan. 11, 2016); European Commission Press Release IP/15/6221, State Aid: Commission Opens Formal Investigation into Luxembourg's Treatment of McDonald's (Dec. 3, 2015); European Commission Press Release IP/15/5880, Commission Decides Selective Tax Advantages for Fiat in Luxembourg and Starbucks in the Netherlands Are Illegal Under EU State Aid Rules (Oct. 21, 2015). All European Commission press releases are accessible through the search template at http://europa.eu/rapid/search.htm (last visited Dec. 18, 2016). The U.S. government has expressed concern that these state aid cases are unfairly targeting U.S. multinational enterprises and unfairly utilize retroactive tax assessments. See Jacob J. Lew, *Lew Writes European Commission on State Aid Investigations*, 2016 WORLDWIDE TAX DAILY 29–23 (Feb. 11, 2016); see also *OECD Base Erosion and Profit Shifting Project: Hearing Before the H. Ways & Means Subcomm. On Tax Policy*, 114th Cong. (Dec. 1, 2015) (statement of Robert B. Stack, Deputy Assistant Secretary, U.S. Dep't. of the Treasury). However, the European Commission has rebuffed these U.S. criticisms. See Margrethe Vestager, *EU Official Writes U.S. Treasury Secretary on State Aid Investigations*, 2016 WORLDWIDE TAX DAILY 40–21 (Feb. 11, 2016) (asserting that the state aid investigations are complementary to the initiative to curtail base erosion and profit shifting and aim at a "proper, non-discriminative, application of tax laws in Europe."). The Netherlands and Luxembourg have recently appealed the European Commission's determination that their tax regimes represented a form of illegal state aid to the Court of Justice of the European Union. See Case T-755/15 Luxembourg v. European Comm'n (Dec. 30, 2015), 2016 WORLDWIDE TAX DAILY 31–22 (Court of Justice of the European Union reference for a state aid case); Case T-760/15, Netherlands v. European Comm'n (Dec. 23, 2015), 2016 WORLDWIDE TAX DAILY 31–23 (same).

[23] See OECD REPORT, BASE EROSION AND PROFIT SHIFTING 1–15 (Oct. 5, 2015), available at https://www.oecd.org/tax/beps/.

[24] OECD/G20 Base Erosion and Profit Shifting Project, Tax Challenges Arising from Digitalisation-Report on the Pillar One Blueprint (2021); OECD/G20 Base Erosion and Profit Shifting Project, Tax Challenges Arising from Digitalisation—Report on the Pillar Two Blueprint (2020)—The report on the Pillar Two Blueprint. More than 135 nations approved a final version of Pillar Two in 2021. See OECD/G20 Base Erosion and Profit Shifting Project, Tax Challenges Arising from the Digitilisation of the Economy-Global Anti-Base Erosion Model Rules (Pillar Two) (2021).

Erosion Model Rules (Pillar Two) and subsequently released commentary on such rules in March 2022. The Model Rules, together with the accompanying commentary, address how a jurisdiction's international taxation laws should be designed to ensure that multinational enterprises are subjected to a global minimum tax but do not suffer international double taxation in multiple jurisdictions on the same income.[25] The OECD has continued to refine and expand its guidance since then.[26] Many countries have pledged to reform their own domestic laws to adopt these recommendations. Thus, at the present time, at least one conclusion is unavoidable: the prevention of base erosion and profit shifting strategies that result in profits escaping any meaningful taxation in any jurisdiction (the creation of "homeless income") is an important policy goal that has riveted the attention of policymakers in the United States and also in other countries. Thus, in the materials that follow, common base erosion and profit shifting patterns will be set out as the basis for understanding the underlying rationale for many of the complex provisions that have been added to the U.S. international tax system.

---

[25] OECD/G20 Base Erosion and Profit Shifting Project, Tax Challenges Arising from Digitalisation of the Economy: Global Anti-Base Erosion Model Rules (Pillar Two) (2022); OECD/G20 Base Erosion and Profit Shifting Project, Tax Challenges Arising from Digitalisation: Commentary to the Global Anti-Base Erosion Model Rules (Pillar Two) (2022).

[26] See OECD, Tax Challenges Arising from the Digitalisation of the Economy—Consolidated Commentary to the Global Anti-Base Erosion Model Rules (May 2025); OECD, Tax Challenges Arising from the Digitalisation of the Economy—GloBE Information Return (January 2025).

Chapter 2

NATIONALITY AND RESIDENCE FOR TAXATION

A. Nationality

Of the essential bases of U.S. taxation, nationality raises the fewest difficulties. U.S. nationality (or citizenship—they are the same thing for present purposes) is a status defined in longstanding nationality laws. The U.S. tax system, rather than imposing a standard of its own, takes nationality as a given.[1] Tax disputes turning on nationality are not particularly common but, when they do arise, require extensive forays outside pure tax law. In the vast majority of cases, the nationality of individuals is beyond doubt. Equally clear are the tax consequences for an individual of U.S. nationality: the United States taxes the incomes of its citizens[2] from all sources worldwide, whether they reside in the United States or abroad.[3] The validity of worldwide taxation of U.S. citizens was upheld by the Supreme Court in *Cook v. Tait*.[4] Thus, along with whatever protections and benefits it confers, U.S. citizenship brings worldwide income taxation with it as its price, a quid pro quo expressly invoked in *Cook v. Tait* as justifying worldwide taxation of U.S. citizens.

---

[1] The Treasury Regulations under section 1 of the Code (in Reg. § 1.1(c)) contain a brief statement on U.S. citizenship, which does little more than refer to other laws:

> Who is a citizen. Every person born or naturalized in the United States and subject to its jurisdiction is a citizen. For other rules governing the acquisition of citizenship, see Chapters 1 and 2 of Title III of the Immigration and Nationality Act. . . . For rules governing loss of citizenship, see sections 349 to 357, inclusive, of such Act. . . .

[2] We use the terms "national" and "citizen" (as in "U.S. national" or "U.S. citizen") more or less interchangeably in this book. In some contexts, "citizenship" may not be exactly congruent with "nationality." The former term describes relations of allegiance to a range of political bodies, including cities, states, and even supranational entities. The latter term is more narrowly limited, usually, to fealty with a nation-state.

[3] A departure from worldwide U.S. taxation is the annual exclusion from income allowed in § 911 to Americans living and working overseas. See chapter 14.

[4] 265 U.S. 47 (1924). You may have noticed that early federal tax cases are often captioned as though they were disputes between two individuals. Suits for refunds of invalid or excessive taxes were originally brought against the individual Collector of each Revenue District (in this case Tait, the Collector of the District of Maryland), and challenges to assessments (nowadays Tax Court cases) were brought against the individual Commissioner of Internal Revenue (who for a long time was Guy T. Helvering). Helvering, Eisner, Bowers, Tait, and others who haunt the early reported cases, were not compulsively litigious cranks but rather officials of the United States administering the federal tax system.

If a person is a U.S. person (which term includes citizens and residents), then significant reporting obligations have been imposed on such persons as to their foreign investments and activities. U.S. persons must separately report any financial interest in foreign bank accounts (so-called FBAR reporting). In addition to FBAR reporting, the Foreign Account Tax Compliance Act (or "FATCA") requires U.S. persons who hold foreign financial assets above a certain threshold to report information about those assets. For example, U.S. persons who create a foreign trust, are a beneficiary of a foreign trust, or have transactions (including direct or indirect loans) with a foreign trust can have both U.S. income tax consequences as well as information reporting requirements. Ownership in foreign business entities also trigger significant information reporting obligations. Whereas information reporting for domestic accounts and income largely falls to financial brokers or employers, the information reporting in the foreign context often falls more heavily on the U.S. beneficial owner herself.

Further problems that arise can involve dual nationality, a loss of citizenship, or a loss of residency.

B. The Residence of Individuals

Individual residents of the United States, regardless of nationality, are exposed to U.S. tax on their worldwide incomes. By contrast, U.S. taxation of nonresident alien individuals is largely limited to income from sources in the United States. Therefore, residence is the first and most important touchstone of U.S. taxation for foreign nationals.

"Residence," as the term implies, is a measure of the extent and permanence of an individual's presence in a given place. The notion of residence, which has bearing in many legal contexts, quite early took on its own flavor in taxation. Even within taxation, the notion of residence is now made up of several separate strands. There is no across-the-board definition of a "resident" in the Code applicable to all individuals and entities for all purposes.[5] Rather, the terms "resident" and "nonresident" are attached to various persons for various purposes, with the result that there are several standards of residence germane to U.S. international taxation. The most important and pervasive is the residence of foreign nationals, which frames the boundary between worldwide U.S. taxation (imposed on foreign nationals residing in the United States, known as "resident

---

5 The word "residence" appears ubiquitously in the Code, not as a generic touchstone of tax status, but (often accompanied by the adjective "principal" or "single-family") to describe a dwelling in the physical sense. See, e.g., § 121.

aliens") and source-based taxation (imposed on foreign nationals residing outside the United States, known as "nonresident aliens").

Of lesser but significant effect is the residence of U.S. citizens. Even though they are taxed on their worldwide incomes, U.S. citizens who reside outside the United States enjoy favorable taxation of part of their income earned outside the United States.[6] A different standard of residence determines the exposure of foreign nationals to U.S. gift and estate taxes. Yet another standard of residence, in section 865, determines the source of gains from sales of personal property. There is, finally, a separate definition (in regulations) of the residence of a partnership. The precise ingredients of residence are somewhat different in each of these cases.

1. Residence Before the Enactment of Section 7701(b)

Residence is, and always has been, a question of fact at its core. For the first 70 years of the U.S. tax system, the "residence" of an individual was a factual determination shaped by cumulative administrative action and judicial decision. The notion of residence prevailing in tax questions was an amalgam of common law notions of "residence" and "domicile" drawn from outside the realm of taxation. Residence for income taxation was a physical presence in a place with the intention of remaining there indefinitely or for a substantial period of time. At the core of this idea of residence was the inner fact of intention, which can be apprehended only through difficult and uncertain inferences from external facts.

Practical determinations of residence under this common law standard came to turn on a checklist of external indicia of residence, which also served as a set of dos and don'ts for foreign nationals seeking to avoid U.S. residence. Important touchstones included the length of a stay in the United States, dwelling arrangements there and abroad, family ties in the United States, and civic and social activity there. Even lesser indicia of residence, such as the location of bank accounts and the place of issuance of driver's licenses, might come into play in close cases. The factors bearing on residence were not of equal importance, as well you can imagine. Length of stay and maintenance of a dwelling in the United States were the most important indications of U.S. residence. The fact remained, however, that determinations of residence reflected a hodgepodge of observable facts accorded weight in no perfectly settled rank or priority.

Individuals exercise significant control over many of the routine elements of daily life, often at the cost of little more than an inconvenience. Taxpayers, therefore, generally held the upper hand

---

6 See chapter 13.

under the original standard of residence. Individuals seeking to avoid the status of U.S. resident for tax purposes were advised not to marry in the United States, to leave their families behind during stays in the United States, and not to acquire U.S. drivers' licenses and checking accounts. Foreign nationals willing and able to follow these and similar constraints could spend considerable time in the United States without exposure to worldwide U.S. taxation.

C. Section 7701(b)

Case-by-case inquiry into the indicia of residence was supplanted for foreign nationals by a largely arithmetic statutory definition of a "resident alien" added to the Code in 1984 as section 7701(b). The definition of a "resident alien" in section 7701(b) on its face applies only to foreign nationals and therefore does not govern residence for U.S. citizens. Section 7701(b) does, however, apply to foreign nationals for all purposes of the Internal Revenue Code other than the estate and gift taxes (which follow a notion of residence substantially the same as "domicile" at common law). Foreign nationals are thus now subject to a single standard of residence for U.S. income taxes, social security, and unemployment taxes.

Section 7701(b) is quite fully articulated. It contains more words than the entire Income Tax Law of 1894. U.S. residence under section 7701(b) is explicitly tied to two largely objective elements: the immigration status of foreign nationals and the amount of time they spend in the United States. Section 7701(b) is not, however, in all respects a bright-line provision. At its core is a zone of indeterminacy in which the residence of foreign nationals still depends on case-by-case factual determinations.

First, a foreign national who is a "lawful permanent resident of the United States" during a calendar year is a resident of the United States in that year.[7] A lawful permanent resident, known colloquially as a "green card" holder, is an individual entitled to remain permanently in the United States in accordance with the immigration laws.[8] Immigration status and tax status are now explicitly allied, and all individuals admitted to the United States as permanent residents are subject to U.S. taxation based on residence, however little time they spend in the United States. Resident status is deemed to continue unless it is rescinded or administratively or judicially determined to have been abandoned.[9]

The second major test of residence (entirely independent of immigration status) is physical presence in the United States. A

---

7 § 7701(b)(1)(A)(i).

8 § 7701(b)(6).

9 See Reg. § 301.7701(b)–1(b)(1).

foreign national present in the United States for 183 or more days during a calendar year is a United States resident in that year.[10] The core idea of this 183-day rule is simple: 183 days is more (by a few hours) than half of a year. A foreign national who is in the United States for that length of time during a year thereby establishes a more important (or at least lengthier) connection with the United States than with any other country in that year.

The 183-day rule is known in section 7701(b) as the "substantial presence" test. Viewed at closer range, the substantial presence test has two forms, which can be thought of as "strong" and "weak" forms of the test.

1. Actual Physical Presence

Under the strong form of the test, U.S. residence results from the actual physical presence of an individual in the United States for 183 days or more during a calendar year. Actual presence establishes United States residence for the calendar year, and (unless specific exceptions apply) this determination survives any showing of intention or of a stronger or more permanent connection to another country.[11] This form of the substantial presence test is a straightjacket provision under which residence in the United States follows automatically from physical presence of 183 days. A taxpayer's intentions regarding U.S. presence do not come into play. A foreign national serving a prison term in the United States, and wishing every minute that he was somewhere else, could be a U.S. resident under this test.

2. Substantial Presence by Carryover of Days

If residence in the United States turned on nothing more than physical presence for 183 days in any given year, it would be relatively easy to work around this test. By spending 180 days in the United States for several years in a row, for example, a foreign individual could maintain a substantial permanent connection with the United States without ever becoming a U.S. resident. Similarly, a stay of 182 days at the end of one year followed by an equal stay at the beginning of the next would add up very nearly to one full year in the United States without establishing U.S. residence; a full calendar year in the United States preceded and followed by six-month stays would permit nearly two years to be spent in the United States with only one year of actual tax residence. With this much flexibility, the careful timing of gains and losses could significantly reduce the tax cost of U.S. residence.

---

10 § 7701(b)(3).

11 §§ 7701(b)(1)(A)(ii), 7701(b)(3).

A second strand of the substantial presence test extends U.S. residence in many such situations. This form of the substantial presence test takes into account not only time spent in the United States during the calendar year but also days spent in the U.S. in the two preceding calendar years, which are added to days spent in the current calendar year in measuring substantial presence. The effect is to include periods of protracted but less intense connection with the United States as periods of U.S. residence.

Days from the preceding two years are accorded less weight in arriving at the total than the days of the actual calendar year. Specifically, the tally of days spent in the United States (to be counted toward the 183) is determined as follows: 1) days from the current year are counted at their full value; 2) each day from the first preceding calendar year is counted as 1/3 of a day; and 3) each day from the second preceding calendar year is counted as 1/6 of a day.[12] The following illustration may help:

> A foreign national (who has never before been to the United States) spends 90 days in the United States in 2023, 150 days in the United States in 2024, and 120 days in the United States in 2025. In applying the substantial presence test, the individual is treated as having spent 180 days in the United States in year 2024 (the 150 days actually spent in 2024 plus 1/3 of the 90 days spent in 2023). Because this amount is less than 183, the individual is not a United States resident in 2024. In 2025 the individual is treated as having spent 185 days in the United States, consisting of the 120 days actually spent plus 1/3 of the 150 days spent in 2024 (or 50 days) and 1/6 of the 90 days spent in 2023 (or 15 days). [120 + 50 + 15 = 185.] Therefore, the threshold requirement of the extended form of the substantial presence test is crossed in 2025 but not in 2024.

Another way of looking at this test is that every day spent in the United States potentially contributes 1½ days (i.e., 1 + 1/3 + 1/6) to the count of days used in measuring substantial presence over the succeeding years.

It follows that the greatest constant-level number of days that can be spent in the United States year in and year out without triggering United States residence is 121. Repeated annual stays of 121 days eventually become measured as 181½ under this extended substantial presence test—still below 183.[13]

---

12 § 7701(b)(3)(A).

13 See Reg. § 301.7701(b)–1(e) Example (1).

United States residence cannot, however, result entirely from days carried forward from earlier years. A minimum physical presence of at least 31 days in the United States is required before substantial presence is ever triggered.[14] Without this limitation, a year following two full years of U.S. presence would be a year of U.S. residence for someone who spent only a few minutes of January 1 in the United States.

3. Closer Connection and Tax Home in a Foreign Country

The upshot of this extended formulation of substantial presence is that an individual can spend fewer than 183 days in the United States in any given year, or even fewer than 180 days consistently over a period of years, and still be treated as a U.S. resident. This possibility is rendered less likely, however, by a qualification of the substantial presence test when it is met only by carryover of days. For individuals who meet substantial presence by carryover of days during a calendar year but are actually present fewer than 183 days in the United States, the application of the 183-day test is not absolute. Under an "exception" provided in section 7701(b)(3)(B), an individual actually present in the United States on fewer than 183 days during a calendar year, despite an extended count of days exceeding 183, is not treated as a U.S. resident if it is established that, for that year, the individual 1) has a "tax home" in a foreign country and 2) has a "closer connection" to that foreign country than to the United States.

The overlay of such notions as "tax home" and "closer connection" necessarily reduces the certainty of this strand of the substantial presence test. A count of days remains a numerical threshold, but when substantial presence is met only by carryover of days (rather than actual physical presence of 183 days or more), the count of days creates, in effect, a presumption of United States residence, which can be turned back by someone whose personal epicenter is demonstrably in another country. The determination of a "tax home" raises problems that in domestic tax litigation have bordered on the Talmudic and have never been fully resolved.[15] For its part, the determination of the country to which an individual has a "closer connection" requires specific focus on that very individual,

---

[14] § 7701(b)(3)(A)(i); Reg. § 301.7701(b)–1(e) Example (2). But, any days in the prior year are counted for purposes of calculating the substantial presence in the current year if the foreign person is in the United States at least 31 days in the current year. See Reg. § 301.7701(b)–1(e) Example (3).

[15] The notion of a "tax home," incidentally, is imported into section 7701(b), with a detour through section 911, from section 162(a)(2), which allows (as you may remember from an introductory income tax course) the deduction of expenses incurred while traveling "away from home" in pursuit of a trade or business.

which in turn calls up many of the indicia of residence invoked under prior law. Sheer duration of stay is no longer an uncertain factor, to be sure, but all the others, including the place of principal residence and social, economic, and family ties, retain some force in this determination.

4. Exceptions

There are exceptions from the arithmetic of substantial presence for certain individuals, extending in favor of foreign nationals (diplomats and students, among others) whose presence in the United States, even if lengthy, does not generally imply permanence. Mechanically, these exceptions operate by excluding days spent in the United States with an exempted status from the days counted as presence in the United States.[16] Among the protected group are full-time diplomats and consular officials, teachers or trainees, and students.[17] Also excluded from the count are days spent in the United States by an individual unable to leave because of a medical condition that arose there.[18]

There is a pitfall in these exceptions. A foreign national who holds an exempt status during part of a year is not thereby inoculated against U.S. residence for the year and may still become a U.S. resident in that year by spending enough days in the United States *without* the exempt status. Consider a full-time student who graduates on June 1 from a degree program. Graduation may well bring the exempt status to an end. If the student then stays on in the United States for business or pleasure until the end of the year (another 213 days), the count of substantial presence will be more than met.[19]

D. Expatriation to Avoid Tax

1. Section 877

Until mid-2008, the Treasury's weapon against tax-motivated expatriation was section 877. The effect of section 877, roughly, was to perpetuate, for expatriates bent on tax avoidance, U.S. taxation of income originating in the United States as though they had retained their U.S. citizenship. Under section 877, a high-income U.S. citizen

---

16 § 7701(b)(3)(D). A day in the United States with an exempt status also does not enter into the count of days carried forward as fractions under the weak form of substantial presence.

17 § 7701(b)(5)(A).

18 § 7701(b)(3)(D)(ii). Note that days in the United States *do* count for a foreigner who goes there expressly for medical treatment. Only foreigners who cannot *leave* on account of sudden illness are shielded by this exception.

19 Furthermore, U.S. residence so acquired likely extends to the *entire* year, including the months with student status.

who relinquished U.S. citizenship continued, for 10 years after expatriation, to be taxed as a U.S. citizen on income from sources within the United States.

2. Section 877A

Section 877A, adopted in June 2008, replaces the 10-year chain of section 877 (in which there were a few weak links) with a far simpler "exit" tax. Under section 877A(a), a U.S. citizen who abandons U.S. citizenship, or a long-term resident alien who abandons U.S. residence, must recognize gain or loss from all property, wherever located, as though the property had been sold for its fair market value. Ironically, the economic downturn in 2020 arising from the lockdowns during the early stages of the COVID-19 pandemic probably made section 877A a more attractive escape from fealty to the U.S. Treasury, for some, than the gauntlet of the late section 877.

The exit tax applies to a U.S. citizen or long-term resident who has paid an average annual U.S. income tax greater than $124,000 for the preceding period of 5 years or whose net worth is $2 million or more.[20] The effect of section 877A thus ranges from the affluent to the colossally rich. Section 877A allows exceptions, however, for certain dual nationals who have not maintained a close connection with the United States.[21]

There are, naturally, a few additional wrinkles. Gain up to $600,000 is excluded from the amount recognized so that an expatriate can take away a significant quantity of unrealized appreciation. There also is a separate regime for certain items of tax-deferred compensation.[22]

E. Entities, Associations, and Partnerships

In the U.S. tax system, there is no characteristic of associations or entities (partnerships, corporations, and trusts) that corresponds exactly to the "nationality" or "residence" of individuals.[23] For most organizations, however, there is a place—or at least a distinct legal environment—that establishes their existence and identity. For corporations, it is the place of incorporation (or "charter"). For partnerships, similarly, it is the place under the laws of which they

---

[20] § 877(a)(2).

[21] See § 877A(g)(1)(B).

[22] See § 877A(d)–(e). This $600,000 threshold is adjusted for inflation for years after 2008.

[23] Many foreign legal systems do have a notion of corporate "residence," identified variously with a corporation's seat of management or principal place of business. Entities classified differently in different legal systems are sometimes known as "dual resident corporations."

arise. For trusts, it is the legal system in which they are acknowledged as such and which governs relations among grantors, fiduciaries, and beneficiaries. This place—sometimes called an entity's "situs"—bears importantly on its taxation.

1. Partnerships

The situs of a partnership is the place under the laws of which it is organized. Because a "general" partnership may be formed by purely private agreement, however, with no involvement of any government, the practical determination of situs is more obscure for a partnership than for a corporation. If a Frenchman and a Mexican agree to do business as partners in several states of the United States and provinces of Canada, under what law is the partnership "organized"? It is perhaps fortunate that the situs of partnerships usually matters little for tax purposes. Because partnerships are not themselves taxable entities—they are "fiscally transparent" in tax parlance—it is the nationality or residence of the individual partners that generally governs U.S. taxation of the partnership income.[24] There is also a vestigial notion in the U.S. tax system of the "residence" of a partnership apart from its status as domestic or foreign, which comes into play only in connection with the source rules for interest.[25]

2. Trusts

The situs of trusts flows from the definition of a "United States person" in section 7701(a)(30). A trust is a "United States person" (and hence subject to worldwide U.S. taxation) if 1) the trust is subject to the authority of a court within the United States *and* 2) the fiduciaries in control of the trust are United States persons. All other trusts are foreign trusts. A foreign trust escapes U.S. taxation on its non-U.S. income. U.S. beneficiaries of foreign trusts, however, are ultimately subject to full U.S. taxation on any trust income from which they benefit.

3. Corporations

In the Code, the situs of corporations and partnerships is signaled by the terms "domestic" and "foreign." A "domestic" entity (including a partnership or a corporation) is one "organized in the United States under the laws of the United States or of any State."[26]

---

[24] One situation where the situs of partnerships does matter is in withholding. Withholding of U.S. tax is required from payments of income to foreign, but not domestic, partnerships.

[25] See chapter 3; Reg. § 301.7701–5.

[26] § 7701(a)(4). Colloquially, "domestic" corporations are often called "U.S. corporations," a usage I often follow here.

All other corporations and partnerships are "foreign."[27] The situs of a corporation in U.S. taxation thus depends on the country of its incorporation.

The situs of a corporation has momentous tax consequences. A domestic corporation is subject to U.S. tax on its worldwide income; a foreign corporation only on income derived from U.S. investment or business. Because a corporation, in the end, is nothing more than a piece of paper with the official seal of a government conferring a separate legal status on a particular undertaking or body of assets, some commentators have questioned the formalism of having large tax consequences turn on which of several eligible sovereigns issues the document. However, no other basis for taxing corporations—including the nationality of their beneficial owners or the principal place of their operations or management—meshes as simply with the U.S. tax system overall. Furthermore, a number of other elements of U.S. tax law have blunted the distinction between foreign and domestic corporations in various settings.[28]

F. The Expatriating of a U.S. Corporation

1. Corporate Inversions

The U.S. tax system has competing objectives. The U.S. wants an attractive environment for foreign investment into the United States, but the U.S. also wants to preserve taxation over the active trade or business income that is earned in the United States. The current regime provides earnings stripping and base erosion techniques for foreign-owned multinational enterprises to reduce the U.S. tax liability of U.S. business activities that are unavailable to the U.S. based multinational corporation. In the succeeding chapters, I will analyze these opportunities further, but the point to be made here is that this accepted wisdom has caused many U.S. based multinational enterprises to want to become foreign-based multinational enterprises or, in other words, to enter into a corporate inversion transaction so that the post-inversion company is considered a foreign corporation for purposes of applying the U.S. inbound and outbound taxation regime. Corporate inversions are a systemic policy challenge,[29] but, at their core, corporate inversions

---

[27] It follows from these definitions that a corporation or partnership organized under both foreign and U.S. law (not a conceptual impossibility, at least for some corporations and most general partnerships) would be "domestic" but not "foreign."

[28] Among these are the special regime of taxation of U.S. shareholders of controlled foreign corporations and passive foreign investment companies, discussed in chapters 11 and 12.

[29] Corporate inversions cause significant revenue losses and ongoing policy concerns. See Congressional Budget Office, An Analysis of Corporate Inversions (September 2017), available at https://www.cbo.gov/system/files/115th-congress-2017-2018/reports/53093-inversions.pdf. In the past, Congress has attacked the corporate

are an effort by a U.S. based multinational enterprise to become foreign-based enterprises exactly because the inbound earnings stripping advantages available to foreign-based multinational enterprises are coveted by U.S. based companies. Since 2004, Congress has sought to prevent U.S. based multinationals from being able to engage in an inversion transaction or to restrict the benefits of doing so. Separately, Congress has taken steps to further backstop the inbound taxation regime and the earnings stripping opportunities that exist with respect to related party base erosion payments.

2. Section 7874

Congress, in the 2004 Act, introduced section 7874, which imposes substantial constraints on corporate inversions.

Section 7874 defines two different types of corporate inversion transactions and establishes a different consequence for each type. Certain partnership transactions also are covered. The two patterns differ in the degree of ownership change among U.S. shareholders of an expatriating U.S. corporation.

i. Eighty Percent or More of U.S. Shareholders Retain Stock Ownership

The first type of inversion is a transaction in which 1) a U.S. corporation becomes a subsidiary of a foreign-incorporated entity or otherwise transfers substantially all of its properties to such an entity, 2) the former shareholders of the U.S. corporation hold 80 percent or more (by vote or value) of the stock of the foreign-incorporated entity after the transaction, and 3) the foreign-incorporated entity, considered together with certain affiliates, does not have substantial business activities in the entity's country of incorporation, compared to the total worldwide business activities of the entire affiliated group. These rules are backed up by a set of anti-avoidance provisions.

The effect of section 7874 in this type of inversion is to treat the top-tier foreign corporation in the "inverted" corporate group as a domestic corporation for all purposes of the Code. It follows that none of the tax advantages of foreign incorporation is available. In effect, the expatriating U.S. corporation and certain of its affiliates are treated as though nothing had happened.

---

inversion phenomenon as a stand-alone problem. In my view, Congress will not eliminate the corporate inversion phenomenon until Congress eliminates the inbound earnings stripping advantages that motivate these transactions.

ii. Between Sixty and Eighty Percent of U.S. Shareholders Retain Stock Ownership

The second type of inversion is the same as the transaction described above except that the former shareholders of the U.S. corporation own less than 80 percent after the corporate inversion, so that the 80 percent ownership threshold is not met. In this case, if at least a 60 percent ownership threshold is met instead, then different rules apply to the inversion. The inversion transaction is respected (in the sense that the newly established foreign corporation is treated as truly foreign), but various specific tax penalties apply. First, there is a shareholder-level tax under section 367[30] and several other provisions. Second, and often worse, no prior tax attributes of the expatriating U.S. corporation, such as net operating loss or foreign tax credit carryovers, are available to offset the U.S. taxes triggered by the corporate inversion as described above. This second effect lasts 10 years following the inversion.

These provisions also apply to certain transactions involving partnerships that are functionally equivalent to a corporate inversion. For example, the rules extend to transactions in which a foreign-incorporated entity acquires substantially all of the business assets of a domestic partnership such that after the acquisition, at least 60 percent of the stock of the entity is held by former partners of the partnership. In this case, the various tax penalties described above apply at the partner level.

---

[30] See chapter 13.

Chapter 3

THE SOURCE OF INCOME

A. Source in General

The concept of source of income is the essential mortar—if not the keystone—in the U.S. system of international taxation. The source of income bears centrally on the taxation of both foreign and U.S. persons. Its role is more immediately evident for foreign persons. With a few narrow exceptions, foreign persons are subject to U.S. tax only on their income from sources within the United States. For U.S. persons, the source of income also plays a crucial, if less obvious, role. The source of the income received by U.S. persons determines, through the mechanism of a limitation on the foreign tax credit, the extent of allowable credits for foreign taxes as offsets to U.S. income tax.

The "source" of income is not a self-defining notion. There is no immutable, metaphysically correct notion of source of income. Within broad limits, national tax systems frame the source of income according to the desired reach of their taxing power. Nonetheless, the association of income with a place as its "source" generally does rest on some actual connection between the place and the income, and while there is no universal touchstone of that connection, there are recurrent patterns in the source of income. The developed countries, and in particular the United States, tend to associate the source of income with the economic activity giving rise to it. The source of compensation for services, for example, is the place where the services are performed. A limitation on this principle is that the relation between economic activity and resulting income may be diffused. Royalties for the use of intellectual property, for example, can reasonably be attributed both to the effort and investment of creating it and to its day-to-day use in the production of income. When matching income with economic activity is difficult—as is the case with interest income—other elements, such as the place of residence of the person paying or receiving the income, have come to serve as proxies for its economic center of gravity. Some tax systems (usually in countries that are heavy importers of capital) engage in no dissection of the economic origins of income but simply ask from whose pocket it was paid. In their view, the source of income is the source of its payment.[1] None of these notions of source is followed with unyielding consistency, and, of course, the source rules must

[1] The U.S. tax system itself follows this approach in determining the source of some scholarship and fellowship grants. See Reg. § 1.863–1(d).

also (and do in considerable degree) reflect the practical possibilities of collection of tax.

1. Big Pharma PLC's U.S. Investment

The impact of the various statutory rules on inbound activities start with the source rules, but it is helpful to frame that discussion in the context of a pattern that can be revisited and further unpacked in later chapters as well. This approach will help solidify how the various topics in the first eight chapters interact and build on the principles learned in each chapter. Thus, as a base example, suppose that Big Pharma PLC is a corporation resident in Fredonia. Its stock is publicly traded in Fredonia and has a market value of over $10 billion. Big Pharma PLC has the opportunity to acquire a U.S. pharmaceutical business that produces $200 million of operating income per year. Suppose further that this U.S. pharmaceutical business has been and can continue to be conducted such that inventory and accounts receivable could be funded with short-term working capital loans from a bank that would charge interest of $10 million per year. Finally, suppose that the business can be conducted such that the tangible and intangible property needed to operate this business generates and will continue to generate depreciation and amortization expense of $30 million per year. Thus, this U.S. business has a baseline annual net income of $160 million ($200 million less $10 million of unrelated party interest expenses less $30 million amortization and depreciation deductions). Finally, assume that Big Pharma PLC is willing to pay $1 billion worth of its stock in order to acquire this U.S. pharmaceutical business conducted by a target corporation.

To make the acquisition, Big Pharma PLC is willing to issue its stock to the target corporation's shareholders. To effectuate the acquisition, Big Pharma PLC will form a new U.S. subsidiary, called US Pharma, Inc. Immediately thereafter, the U.S. target corporation is then merged into US Pharma, Inc. in a transaction where the shareholders of the old U.S. target corporation receive Big Pharma PLC stock worth $1 billion in cancellation of their Target Corporation stock.[2] If the result of the transaction is simply that Big Pharma PLC stock is exchanged for all of the stock of U.S. target corporation as indicated in accompanying Diagram #1, then the annual income of $160 million earned at the U.S. corporate level has not been affected. Yes, the entity running the business has changed. However, after the acquisition of the U.S. pharmaceutical business of the target corporation, the U.S. business is conducted by US Pharma, Inc. in

---

[2] You may ask whether the U.S. persons who exchange their stock in a U.S. corporation for stock in a foreign corporation have any tax consequences from that exchange, and that issue is discussed further in chapter 13.

the same manner as before. As a result, the U.S. pharmaceutical business is still being conducted by a U.S. corporation (US Pharma, Inc. in the below diagram) that is subject to U.S. taxation on its worldwide income under section 61(a). US Pharma, Inc. still has an expected taxable income of $160 million going forward and, as a result, has an expected U.S. corporate tax liability of $33.6 million—the same as before the acquisition. This acquisition may well make sense for business reasons, but there has not been any noticeable tax savings from this transaction at the domestic corporate level. However, as we add additional facts and additional tax planning strategies to this basic transaction, these additional elements can be broken down separately and will provide a useful way to understand the inbound U.S. tax regime.

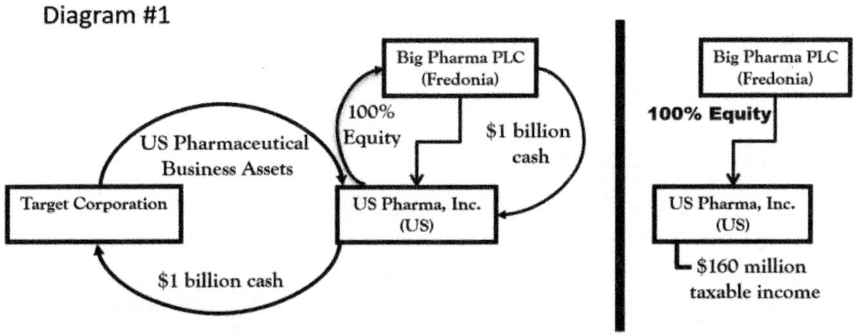

B. The Statutory Framework

The term "source" of income made its first statutory appearance in the ill-fated 1894 Act where it served as shorthand for the property or business activity from which income was derived. It soon became apparent that the source of a given item of income cannot be derived with certainty from broadly stated general principles. By 1921, the tax laws contained a detailed schedule of source rules for income of the most common types. Today extensive rules of source of income are collected in sections 861–863 and 865; many other provisions affecting specific questions of source are widely scattered in the Code.

Skim through Code sections 861–863 and 865. Even a quick perusal of the source rules reveals how extensively articulated they have become. The statutory rules cover interest, dividends, compensation for services, rents and royalties, gains from sales of property, income from insurance underwriting, and social security benefits. These items account for well over 95 percent of the income generated in the world. Some types of income are not assigned a source in the Code, however, including gain from cancellation of indebtedness, income from covenants not to compete, damage recoveries, expropriation gains, insurance recoveries, prizes and awards, scholarship grants, treasure trove or like windfalls, and unemployment compensation. Some of these are rare, even exotic; others are fairly common.

The statutory rules further separate items of income into those with a single source and those with multiple sources (such as income from compound processes of production and sale). Questions of source are further elaborated (indeed excruciatingly so) in sprawling regulations on the allocation and apportionment of deductible expense.[3]

C. Income from a Single Source

The core provisions on source in the Code, sections 861 and 862, enumerate several classes of income and assign them a source. The enumeration in these sections deals mainly with items of income that can readily be classified as belonging to a single type (such as interest, dividends, or royalties) and that have their source entirely within or without the United States.

D. Interest Income

As a general rule, interest paid by an individual, a partnership, or a trust takes its source from the payor's place of residence, while interest paid by a corporation has its source in the place of incorporation.[4] Thus, interest paid by individuals, partnerships, and trusts that are "residents" of the United States has U.S. source, as does interest paid by domestic corporations. This rule is a proxy (albeit a rough one at best) for a matching of interest with the activity that generates the income from which it is paid.

In particular, the rule placing the source of interest paid by an individual in the individual's place of residence reflects the broad expectation that borrowers are most likely to put borrowed money to work where they reside and pay the interest from funds available at that place. This is by no means the only rule one could imagine. Interest could, for example, derive its source from a tracing of the proceeds of borrowing to their actual place of use. Such a tracing rule would not necessarily be more accurate, however. Money and credit are, for the most part, fungible, and borrowers' ultimate borrowing capacity probably depends as much on the extent and location of their assets overall as on the use to be made of a specific borrowing. It is therefore entirely tenable to treat the residence of individual payors of interest as the locus of their "credit." Although reasonable, this source rule does have consequences that both borrowers and lenders

---

[3] A partial list of regulations on expense allocation includes Reg. § 1.861–8, Reg. §§ 1.861–8T through 1.861–14T, and Reg. § 1.882–5.

[4] §§ 861(a)(1), 862(a)(1).

will occasionally find somewhat startling. For example, a foreign bank lending to a U.S. resident may receive U.S. source interest even if the loan is initiated outside the United States and finances operations entirely outside the United States.

There is both difficulty and opportunity in the day-to-day operation of this source rule. A threshold problem is determining the residence of the payor of interest. Often, lenders have greater reason for concern with the physical whereabouts of their borrowers (or their assets) than with the more abstract notion of their current tax residence, which may not be readily discernible to a lender of money whose dealings with a borrower may focus narrowly on the latter's wherewithal to repay a loan. The residence of *foreign* individuals is governed by a set of explicit tests codified in section 7701(b). These tests, as you may remember from chapter 2, are tied to immigration status or length of time spent in the United States. Both elements not only may be difficult for a lender to ascertain but also may change from year to year. While there is no express statutory standard of residence for *U.S.* citizens, the Treasury also follows the tests of section 7701(b) in determining the source of interest that they pay.

1. Big Pharma PLC's U.S. Investment: Interest

Let's return to the Big Pharma PLC hypothetical where the U.S. pharmaceutical business generated $200 million of earnings before $10 million of unrelated party interest expense and $30 million of depreciation/amortization (resulting in taxable income of $160 million). But now, assume that Big Pharma PLC will transfer $1 billion of its own stock to US Pharma, Inc. in exchange for $100 million of US Pharma, Inc. stock and $900 million of US Pharma, Inc. debt that bears a 10% interest rate. The U.S. target corporation merges into US Pharma, Inc. as before, and US Pharma, Inc. transfers all of the $1 billion of Big Pharma PLC stock to the U.S. target corporation shareholders in cancellation of their Target Corporation stock. For the Target Shareholders, nothing has changed in Diagram #2 versus the result in Diagram #1. The shareholders exchange all U.S. target corporation stock for Big Pharma PLC stock as before. However, Diagram #2 has a significantly different added element: the acquisition facilitated the means to put intercompany debt of $900 million between Big Pharma PLC and its U.S. subsidiary, US Pharma, Inc. The acquisition allowed an opportunity to capitalize US Pharma Inc. with $900 million of debt in lieu of $900 million of equity. To the extent that US Pharma, Inc. is able to obtain a tax deduction for the incremental $90 million of related party interest payments ($900 million debt × 10 percent interest rate) along with its already existing unrelated party interest expense deduction, then the taxable income of US Pharma,

Inc. potentially could be reduced from $160 million to as low as $70 million.

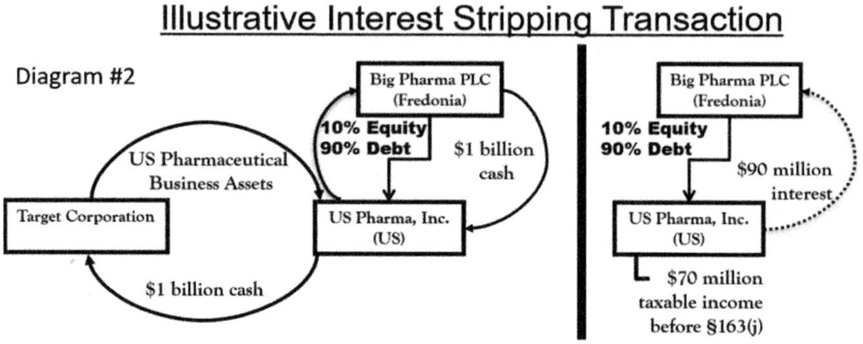

As an initial matter, section 861(a) determines the source of the interest income earned by Big Pharma PLC by the residence of the payor, and the payor in Diagram #2 is a U.S. corporation (namely, US Pharma, Inc.). Thus, as an initial matter, section 861(a) preserves for the United States its power to subject this U.S. source income to U.S. taxation even though it is earned by a non-U.S. person.

The source rules are the starting point for navigating the interest stripping technique, but those rules are not the end of the analysis by any means. In the succeeding chapters, we will learn that the United States likely will not subject Big Pharma PLC to net basis taxation and, pursuant to many U.S. tax treaties, also may disclaim taxing Big Pharma PLC on a gross basis as well. Thus, even though the interest income created in this interest stripping transaction remains U.S. source income, it nevertheless creates the potential for a "one-sided entry" from a U.S. tax perspective. The intercompany payment of $90 million of related party interest potentially provides a tax deduction to US Pharma, Inc. and shifts those profits to its parent, Big Pharma PLC. In truth, the hypothetical posited in Diagram #2 represents an aggressive form of interest stripping resulting from a high level of related party debt. In section 163(j), Congress has defined limits on the amount of interest expense that can be utilized to reduce the taxable income of US Pharma, Inc., and the rationale for envisioning such a provision can be gleaned from this example. We will explore the nuances of section 163(j) in chapter 8 so that you gain a clearer understanding of its contours and the scope of its application beyond the example set forth above, but for now it is enough to say that Congress has seen this problem and has understood that interest stripping transactions represent a potentially improper device to reduce the U.S. tax base.

A further variation that escapes any U.S. taxation due to a peculiarity of the source rules arises in a situation where the foreign person is a nonresident alien individual and not a foreign corporation or foreign partnership and borrows funds to conduct a U.S. business. Because interest paid by *nonresident* individuals has *foreign* source no matter how intense or far flung their economic activity in the United States,[5] interest deductions on what is essentially self-owed debt can shield U.S. business income from taxation. Suppose, for example, that Marcel, a citizen and resident of Fredonia, has the opportunity to acquire for $1 million a U.S. business producing $150,000 of income per year. If Marcel simply buys the U.S. business directly with his own funds, the annual income of $150,000 will attract U.S. income tax of roughly $55,500 at current rates. Instead, Marcel borrows $800,000 of the purchase price at 12 percent interest from a foreign corporation of which he owns all the stock and to which he has previously transferred the funds as a contribution to capital, securing the loan from the corporation with the U.S. business assets.

Marcel Variation on Interest Stripping Transaction

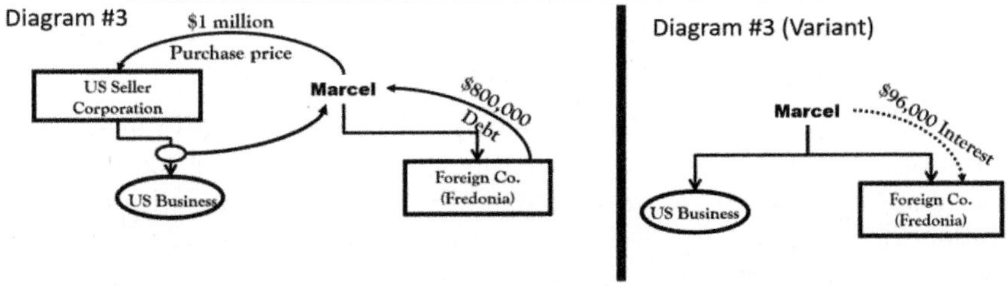

Under the source rules, the interest Marcel pays to his foreign corporation has *foreign* source. As such, it is not exposed to U.S. taxation in the hands of its recipient (Marcel's wholly-owned foreign corporation) unless it is attributable to the *recipient's* U.S. business. Marcel's foreign corporation, however (unlike Marcel), is not itself engaged in a U.S. business. Merely holding debt secured by property in the United States does not of itself constitute a U.S. business.[6] Marcel's payments of interest, on the other hand, *are* deductible from the income derived by Marcel from the U.S. business.[7] With annual interest deductions of $96,000 (12 percent of $800,000) Marcel's taxable income from the U.S. business is reduced from $150,000 to $54,000. The earnings of Foreign Co. are taxable to Marcel, in the

---

5 This assumes, of course, that their presence in the United States does not push them beyond the threshold of "substantial presence" establishing U.S. residence.

6 Even if the corporation did have a U.S. business, the *foreign source* interest it received from Marcel would still not be subject to U.S. tax unless derived from the activities of a U.S. *office*.

7 Under the regulations on interest allocation, "interest expense incurred by a nonresident alien shall be considered to be connected with income effectively connected with a United States trade or business . . . to the extent that interest expense is incurred with respect to liabilities that [are] secured by assets that generate such effectively connected income." Reg. § 1.861–9T(d)(2)(i).

normal course of events, only when distributed to Marcel as dividends. Given that the distribution of a dividend is largely optional, deferral can go on indefinitely. This is a strikingly good result for an exercise that entails little more than a day or two's paperwork.[8]

But why stop there? It may seem that Marcel could eradicate *all* U.S. taxable income by borrowing the full purchase price of $1 million at 15 percent interest from his foreign finance company. This, however, would be costly overreaching. First, the rate of interest charged on loans between related persons is subject to revision by the IRS if the interest rate exceeds an arm's length level. Second, the allowable interest deduction in such patterns is limited, under regulations, to interest on debt not exceeding 80 percent of the assets of the U.S. business paying the interest.[9] A notable consequence here of the source rule for interest (which, please remember, extends only to interest paid by individuals) is the reduction of U.S. taxable income by the deduction of interest paid by Marcel that is at the same time excluded from U.S. taxation in the hands of its immediate recipient, a person related to Marcel.

Earnings Stripping Tax Shelters. The reader should study and thoroughly understand these two fact patterns as they contain the essential elements of international tax-haven operations: the deflection of income (by deductions from income that would otherwise be heavily taxed) to an environment where it is less heavily taxed, all the while remaining under the same beneficial ownership.

If you have some experience in taxation (or have taken a tax course or two), these fact patterns may leave you faintly uneasy. In both Marcel's and Big Pharma PLC's cases, the transactions involve a self-loan between persons with congruent economic interests. There are decided cases, such as *Gregory*[10] and *Aiken*[11], with which the IRS might question the reality and the business purpose for interposing a related party transaction that channels funds out of the United States.[12] However, these interest stripping transactions are

---

8 I mean by this the time and effort of forming the foreign corporation and documenting the various loans and security interests.

9 "Interest . . . is not considered to be connected with effectively connected income to the extent that it is incurred with respect to liabilities that exceed 80 percent of the gross assets of the United States trade or business." Reg. § 1.861–9T(d)(2)(ii)(A).

10 Gregory v. Helvering, 293 U.S. 465 (1935).

11 Aiken Industries v. Commissioner, 56 T.C. 925 (1971).

12 As previously mentioned in the main text, the interest income remains U.S. source to Big Pharma PLC in the hypothetical set forth in Diagram #2. Thus, the sourcing rules under section 861(a)(1) as a preliminary matter have retained U.S. jurisdiction over the interest income earned by the non-U.S. person as a result of the related party payment by US Pharma, Inc. to Big Pharma PLC. But again, we will see

surprisingly resilient against attack. The U.S. tax system generally acknowledges the separate identity of corporations, even from their beneficial owners. Here, neither Marcel's corporation nor Big Pharma PLC's existence or participation in the debt funding are either transitory or simply function as pure conduits. The foreign corporations in each of those scenarios have their own permanent assets, and in Big Pharma PLC's case, it is a publicly traded company with substantial operations elsewhere. In the Marcel variant, that particular structure could be strengthened further against IRS attack by enlarging the range of economic activity of Marcel's foreign corporation. If it engaged in business or invested elsewhere in the world, financed other projects of Marcel's, lent to venturers other than Marcel, borrowed from other sources, and above all had other owners besides Marcel, it could not even colorably be set aside as a conduit. Even as it stands, Marcel's structure is solid,[13] and Big Pharma's structure is even more so. For Marcel, the simple rule for the source of interest by itself creates an international tax shelter. For the Big Pharma PLC variant indicated above, the interest stripping transaction creates U.S. source interest income paid to Big Pharma PLC and can only become homeless income through the use of U.S. tax treaties.

Foreign Taxes. The analysis thus far deals only with U.S. taxation. For these tax shelters to work, they must accommodate both the U.S. and Fredonian systems. Income that the United States source rules or the U.S. tax treaty network allow to escape U.S. taxation may still be subject to tax in the other jurisdiction. The Code's source rules and U.S. tax treaty provisions may have defeated the Scylla of U.S. taxation, but if Fredonia is a high-tax country, then Marcel and Big Pharma PLC still must avoid Charybdis. The plan will avail little unless the income escapes U.S. taxation and safely lands in a low-tax environment. The Fredonian system, therefore, must either be a low-tax jurisdiction in its own right or must respect the separate, untaxed status of controlled affiliates that are incorporated in low-tax jurisdictions outside of Fredonia. This raises another problem in international tax haven operations: the extent to which national income tax systems look through separately chartered entities owned by persons subject to their taxation. You will remember from the discussion of Diagram #3 that when Fredonia respects the formal separate identity of the foreign finance company as a taxpayer, the resulting tax regime creates a "deferral"

---

in succeeding chapters that the U.S. may well relinquish its taxation over this admittedly U.S. source under U.S. tax treaties.

[13] Once you appreciate that a corporation is always a pure artifact of law, it ceases to be startling that an artificial transaction such as a self-loan channeled through a corporation may have real and substantial tax effects.

of the earnings vis-à-vis the ultimate beneficial owner (namely, Marcel).[14]

The deduction arising from a related party payment allows a stream of business income that would otherwise be subject to high taxation to be earned in an offshore person's hands and is the active ingredient in virtually all international tax haven operations. In fact, it is the key feature for each of the five earnings stripping techniques that were summarized in chapter 1 and will be individually addressed in this chapter (as to sourcing) and in later chapters. The other leg of the haven is the deflection of stripped profits, free of further U.S. tax, to some benign low-tax environment. If you get to the bottom of these two inbound patterns and the patterns based on the other four inbound earnings stripping techniques and understand exactly what makes each tick, you will have the U.S. system of inbound taxation in your pocket.

2. U.S. Branch Interest Paid by Foreign Corporations

Under the general rule of section 861(a)(1), interest paid by a foreign corporation has foreign source. Under section 884(f)(1), however, "[i]n the case of a foreign corporation engaged in a trade or business in the United States. . . any interest paid by such trade or business in the United States shall be treated as if it were paid by a domestic corporation. . . ." Put more simply, interest paid by a U.S. branch business of a foreign corporation has U.S. source. Such interest is known as "branch interest." The branch interest rule treats a U.S. branch more or less as though it were a separately chartered U.S. corporation.[15]

The branch interest rule is known as a "look-through" rule because it looks through the formal place of charter of a corporation (which normally governs the source of interest that it pays) to its underlying operations. Look-through rules serve, among other ends, to counter somewhat the arbitrariness of corporate situs. The branch interest rule closes off an easy escape from U.S. taxation. However, the U.S. rules are not always a two-way street. The above look-through rule can extend U.S. source treatment to a foreign corporation that is the payor under a "look-through" mechanism, but

---

[14] Deferral would not be available to a *U.S.* person in Marcel's situation (so don't get any ideas) because the U.S. tax system looks through offshore tax haven companies and taxes their passive investment income to their U.S. shareholders. See chapters 11 through 12.

[15] This raises an intriguing possibility. Suppose a foreign corporation with a U.S. branch business would be an 80/20 company if it were U.S.-chartered (because, for example, its U.S. branch is small in relation to its worldwide business operations, which generate more than 80 percent of its income). Is the branch interest now foreign source interest paid by an 80/20 company? Literally, section 884(f)(1)(A) should have that effect. Treasury regulations under section 884(f), however, brush the possibility aside. Reg. § 1.884–4(a)(1).

note that interest paid by a U.S. domestic corporation is in all events treated as U.S. source regardless of the underlying earnings of the U.S. corporation.

E. The Source of Dividends

In its basic statement the source rule for dividends is both simple and intuitive: the source of dividends is the place of incorporation of the corporation that pays them. Thus, U.S. corporations generally pay U.S. source dividends and foreign corporations pay foreign source dividends. As with interest, the source rule for dividends is qualified with a look-through rule for dividends paid by a foreign corporation.

1. The 25 Percent Rule

If more than 25 percent of a foreign corporation's gross income is "effectively connected" with a U.S. trade or business,[16] then the dividends it pays have *U.S.* source in the same proportion that its effectively connected income bears to its total income.[17] Put more simply, if more than 25 percent of a foreign corporation's income consists of U.S. business profits, dividends paid by the corporation have U.S. source to the extent of those business profits.[18] Thus, if half of the income of a foreign corporation consists of U.S. business profits, 50 cents of every dollar it pays in dividends has U.S. source. This rule, known as the "25 percent rule," looks through the formal place of charter of a corporation to its underlying operations and income and assigns source to its dividends accordingly. In a sense, the entity becomes transparent. Were it not for the 25 percent rule (and similar look-through rules generally), the formality of the place of charter would govern the entire international tax consequences of corporate operations.

The 25 percent rule has had an important corollary. During much of the history of the U.S. income tax, the 25 percent rule, by assigning U.S. source to some part of dividends paid by foreign corporations, could trigger U.S. tax on those dividends even when paid to their *foreign* shareholders. The resulting tax was known as the "second tax on dividends." The second tax was hard to enforce given that the event triggering it was a transfer to foreign persons that might be made entirely outside the United States. It was often toned down or called off altogether by income tax treaties of the

---

[16] "Effectively connected" income and U.S. trade or business determination are discussed further in chapter 6.

[17] § 861(a)(2)(B).

[18] Below the 25 percent threshold, however, no part of the dividends paid by a foreign corporation has U.S. source.

United States with other countries. It was nonetheless a major concern of foreign investors in the United States.

After the 1986 Act, the second tax faded into insignificance. It was almost entirely supplanted by the branch profits tax of section 884, which also imposes a second layer of U.S. tax on U.S. business profits of foreign corporations.[19] The branch profits tax is imposed more uniformly, however, and is easier to enforce. The 2004 Act definitively eliminated all vestige of the second tax.

2. Constitutional Interlude

The second tax on dividends was the occasion for the courts to consider the constitutional boundaries of the U.S. taxing power when applied to foreign persons. In two cases before the Board of Tax Appeals (the predecessor of today's Tax Court), foreign taxpayers urged that the second tax on dividends could not constitutionally be imposed on them. For want of a better place, I discuss these cases briefly here. In *Lord Forres v. Commissioner*,[20] the IRS had sought to tax dividends paid by a U.K.-chartered corporation to a shareholder, Lord Forres, who was a U.K. citizen and resident. The U.K. corporation conducted its entire operations, consisting of several active businesses, in the United States. The dividends at issue were paid by the U.K. corporation to Lord Forres from its U.S. business profits. The source rules in effect at the time (and still today) assigned U.S. source to the dividends, which were accordingly (under rules that have since been changed) subject to U.S. taxation as U.S. source income. Forres put up several constitutional objections, among them that the tax reached so far beyond the territory of the United States as to deny him due process of law. It may not immediately strike you how, if at all, due process of law is implicated in this pattern. Forres was invoking a doctrine you may have encountered in a civil procedure course to the effect that a government cannot validly exercise "jurisdiction" over property and persons outside its territory. The argument went nowhere. The U.S. courts had power beyond question over assets in the United States beneficially owned by the taxpayer. The U.K. corporation's earnings were derived from a U.S. business, and the dividends were paid entirely from those earnings. Given that, it was neither unreasonable nor unfair (and hence not "undue" in the constitutional sense) to assign U.S. source to the dividends,[21] with the consequence of

[19] There is more on the branch profits tax in chapter 8.

[20] 27 B.T.A. 154 (1932).

[21] That is the effect of the 25 percent rule, remember.

extending the U.S. taxing power to a foreign citizen and resident who received them.[22]

In a later case presenting a slightly different pattern, *Ross v. Commissioner*,[23] the taxpayer was a citizen and resident of Canada who owned the shares of a Canadian holding company, which in turn owned stock investments in several U.S. corporations. Under the source rules[24] in effect at the time, the dividends Ross received from the Canadian corporation had U.S. source and were subject to U.S. income tax. The imposition of U.S. tax on dividends received by Ross from the Canadian company was upheld as constitutional even though the Canadian company had no activity in the United States, and, quite possibly, Ross had never set foot there.

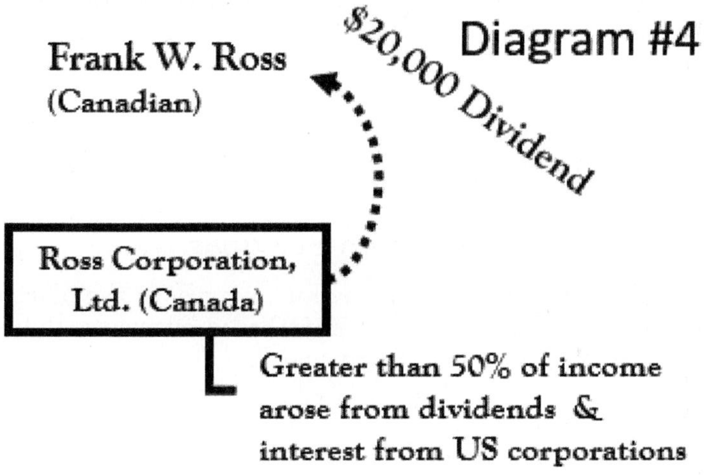

For the *Ross* case, the outcome was severe and dismal. The earnings of the U.S. corporations had undoubtedly been subject to U.S. corporate income tax. The dividends received from them by Ross's Canadian holding company had U.S. source and were

---

22 It further weakened Forres's position that a U.S. corporation doing business in the U.K. would itself have been treated at the time as a *U.K.*-resident corporation and would have paid *U.K.*-source dividends to a U.S. shareholder. If the United States had simply followed the U.K. rule of corporate residence (which is also the worldwide norm) Forres's corporation would have been a U.S.-resident corporation in the first place.

23 44 B.T.A. 1 (1941).

24 Under older source rules, dividends paid by foreign corporations had U.S. source to the extent paid from *any* U.S. source earnings. Today, under the 25 percent rule discussed above, dividends paid by foreign corporations have U.S. source only to the extent paid from U.S. business *profits*, not U.S. source income generally. Since the dividends received from U.S. corporations by Ross's Canadian holding company were not business profits, but passive investment income, the subsequent dividends paid to Ross by the Canadian company would now have entirely *foreign* source.

accordingly subject to U.S. tax in the Canadian company's hands. The U.S. tax imposed on the dividends paid by the Canadian corporation to Ross individually was therefore the *third* layer of U.S. taxation on the underlying earnings. However, *Ross* was not a case about what was sensible or humane. While acknowledging the severity of the result, the court thought the case was governed by *Lord Forres*. The dividends received by Ross were derived from assets in the United States beneficially owned by him. For this reason, the income was related to the United States in a significant way, and, equally important, the tax was ultimately collectible. That Ross could have chosen a more tax efficient form of ownership of U.S. assets did not make the tax unconstitutional.[25]

Lord Forres and *Ross* suggest that there is little constitutional constraint on the power of the United States to tax the incomes of foreign persons.[26] Note, however, that for a number of reasons—among them a concern not to create self-defeating obstacles to foreign investment—the United States does not press this power anywhere near to the limit. The tax upheld in *Ross* has long since been repealed, and today, passive foreign investors in the United States generally face a benign tax regime.[27]

F. Source of Income from Services

The source of income from personal services is the place where the services are performed.[28] Taken in broad overview, this source rule is readily fathomable. Compensation for labor or personal services performed in the United States has U.S. source; compensation for services performed elsewhere has foreign source. The rule is also reasonable. Added value from services generally arises in the vicinity of their performance. In its specific application though, there are some difficulties.

Before venturing into those difficulties, I should mention the "90-day" exception to the source rule. Compensation for services by a foreign individual present in the United States for 90 days or less during the taxable year has *foreign* source if 1) the services are

---

25 A spirited dissenting opinion in *Ross* dwells emphatically, but ultimately unpersuasively, on the unfair burden of the U.S. tax.

26 There are acknowledged constitutional limitations on the power of the individual states to tax other states and their citizens. These limitations, however, arise in the interest of harmony among the several elements making up the American nation, and are not germane to the taxation of foreigners by the United States itself. See United States v. Bennett, 232 U.S. 299, 306 (1914) (the limitation on the taxing power of the states "has no application to the Government of the United States so far as its admitted taxing power is concerned.").

27 See § 871(i)(2)(B) (exempts such dividends from gross basis taxation for nonresident individuals); § 882(d) (same for foreign corporations).

28 § 861 (a)(3).

performed for a foreign person not engaged in business in the United States and 2) if the total compensation for the services is $3,000 or less.[29] Sometimes known as the "commercial traveler exception," this exception is designed to enable foreign individuals to make short business or professional trips to the United States without suffering U.S. income tax on their salaries.[30] The $3,000 limit, while perhaps adequate to this end when first introduced in 1936, has faded into insignificance through inflation. Few engineers, accountants, executives, or even traveling salesmen, would find shelter under this provision if they spent more than a few days in the United States. As a practical matter, the statutory rule has been supplanted by more accommodating provisions in income tax treaties between the United States and the countries of origin of many business travelers.

With the 90-day exception out of the way, a specific difficulty in applying the source rule is matching compensation with services performed in different places. If services are performed only in the United States or if compensation is expressly earmarked for identifiable services performed in the United States, then source is straightforward.[31] Often, however, an individual or firm receives an aggregate of compensation for services performed in a number of places, among which is the United States. A business executive, for example, may work all over the world for a package of salary and stock options that are not explicitly allocated to services in different locations. It may seem obvious to assign source to compensation in such a case according to time spent in different places, but following through with this idea can be tricky. First, you must record or remember how much time is spent where. Second, the nature and intensity of work done may differ in different places. Should the U.S. source component of the compensation be determined by the total time spent in the United States during the year taken as a percentage of the entire year or by a comparison only of the number of actual days of work inside and outside the United States or on some other basis entirely? A three-day round-the-clock merger negotiation in New York, as an economic matter, likely accounts for more of a corporate lawyer's compensation than a three-day weekend in Bermuda cradling a brief business meeting. The 90-day rule

---

29 § 861(a)(3).

30 Note that the 90-day rule does not shield the foreign *employer* of a business traveler from U.S. taxation of income derived from the efforts of an employee or agent only briefly present in the United States

31 Fortunately, it is rarely if ever necessary to make particularized allocations of compensation for services to sources within *different foreign* countries. Compensation need only be assigned U.S. or foreign source. For most foreign persons, therefore, the important question is how much compensation has U.S. source. For a U.S. person, the proportion of foreign source income is usually all that matters.

resolves only a tiny fraction of these situations for foreign taxpayers and none for U.S. persons.

1. The NHL Player Cases

This type of source problem has recurrently afflicted professional athletes, especially players in the National Hockey League which has teams distributed widely in the United States and Canada. Athletes paid by the year have to figure out what part of their salaries have what source. Depending on how they do this, the part of any salary attributable to the offseason might have a different source from the part attributable to playing games. Add training camp, possible playoff games, and occasional postseason exhibitions into the mix, not to mention sign-on bonuses and the like for rookie players, and the question of source can turn downright messy. It may come as no surprise, therefore, that the source of the compensation of NHL players has devolved into a saga of perennial litigation. There are rulings and an Augean series of cases (over 200 docketed in U.S. courts in the 1970s, some of which were still winding their way through appeals in this Millennium) on questions of source of income concerning 1) Canadian players who want to minimize their U.S. source income exposed to U.S. tax and 2) U.S. players who want to maximize their foreign source earned income.

2. Services Performed Through Associations and Entities

Matching compensation with services is even more difficult when the services are performed through groups or associations of individuals (such as partnerships) or by firms whose employees engage in different tasks and receive widely varying compensation. Under well-established notions of agency, firms are deemed to "perform" services through their employees or agents. The source of the resulting income—the place of performance—is, therefore, the place where the corporation's employees or agents perform the services.

While an employer can reasonably be viewed (figuratively at least) as spending time in a place through the presence there of employees, the sheer length of time spent by employees performing services in a place is not self-evidently recommendable as the sole basis for assigning source.[32] Activities in some places might produce more income than in others, especially if different types of work or projects are involved. Even within a single project, more productive activity might well be reflected in higher compensation for some

---

[32] Note that the question here is not the source of employees' income received for the services—that can often be assigned a source according to time they spend in different places—but the income of the employer derived from the employees' efforts.

employees. Therefore, the source of the income of a firm with far flung service operations could plausibly be assigned according to the payroll costs incurred by the firm in different places, rather than a pure "time" basis, so that a firm engaged in performing services both in and out of the United States would have U.S. source service income in proportion to its payroll costs in the United States.

The Treasury regulations on source once determined the source of income from services, both for individuals and firms, entirely on a "time" basis, that is the number of working days spent in different places by the taxpayer or the taxpayer's employees. The Service then had the sorry experience of attacking its own regulations, unsuccessfully, in a case where allocation solely by time was favorable to the taxpayer. In *Tipton & Kalmbach v. United States*,[33] a U.S. engineering firm performed engineering, design, and construction services both in the United States and Pakistan. The taxpayer received a single overall fee for the project, but the work performed in the United States was performed by higher paid personnel than the employees working in Pakistan (in considerable part perhaps because of the large salaries drawn by Messrs. Tipton and Kalmbach themselves). The IRS, against its own regulations, sought to assign a source to the firm's compensation on the basis of payroll costs (which were higher in the United States than in Pakistan). The court, however, refused to deny the taxpayer the benefit of the regulations and upheld an allocation of source based only on the number of days of work performed by the taxpayer's employees in the United States and Pakistan, respectively. This setback induced a change in the regulations. Today, the source of income from services performed both in and outside of the United States "shall be determined on the basis that most correctly reflects the proper source of income under the facts and circumstances of the particular case," with the further provision that "in many cases" the facts will make apportionment "on the time basis. . . acceptable. . . ."[34]

The sourcing of services to the place where the services are performed provides a significant tax planning opportunity in terms of where to locate a shared service center. In this regard, a multinational enterprise can locate common support functions or expertise functions in a tax favorable jurisdiction and then can charge service fees to affiliates for providing the shared services to the related parties. In Diagram #5, in the left graphic, a foreign corporation acts as a sales agent for the distribution of a U.S. affiliate's manufactured products. That graphic is an adaption of the

---

[33] 480 F.2d 1118 (10th Cir. 1973).

[34] Reg. § 1.861–4(b)(1).

basic facts set forth in Rev. Rev. 60–55.[35] In that revenue ruling, the IRS posited that the foreign corporation receives commissions from a U.S. manufacturer for its sales efforts on behalf of the U.S. manufacturer. The foreign corporation maintained its sales and servicing personnel permanently outside the United States. The sales personnel traveled in various foreign countries to promote the sale of the U.S. affiliate's manufactured products. The U.S. domestic corporation paid a commission to the foreign corporation for its sales and marketing activities.[36] The domestic corporation would be entitled to a U.S. tax deduction for the commission expense paid to the foreign corporation. However, even though the payor can claim a U.S. tax deduction and is a U.S. person, the commission income earned by the foreign corporation is foreign source income under section 862(a)(3) because the place where the services were performed was outside the United States. Notice that this commission payment to the foreign affiliate shifts income from the multinational group out of the U.S. domestic corporation and into a foreign corporation with respect to the distribution of U.S. manufactured goods. This is a classic related party service stripping transaction.

Diagram #5 Illustrative Service Stripping Transactions

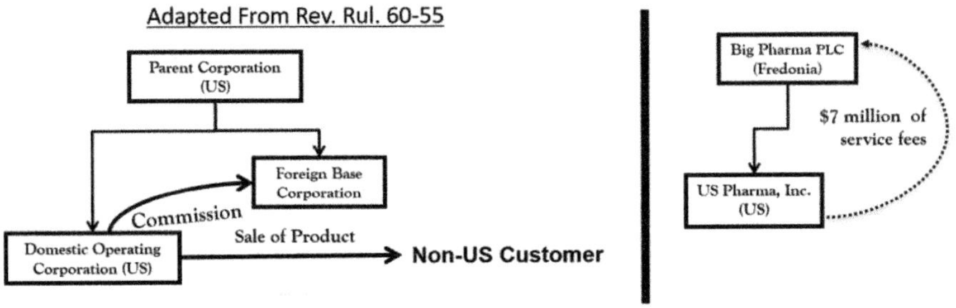

The above right graphic in Diagram #5 displays the ownership structure of Big Pharma PLC and indicates a payment to Big Pharma PLC for services fees. In this situation, Big Pharma PLC could charge its wholly-owned U.S. affiliate for management service fees, technical service fees, and administrative support services for various management, expertise, and other head office service

---

35 1960–1 Cum. Bull. 270. The diagram uses a different name for each of the corporations and adds a common U.S. parent corporation to the structure, whereas the actual ruling is silent as to the relationship and ultimate ownership of the two corporations that were the subject of the ruling. The additional corporate structure is not legally relevant in terms of the sourcing structure but does help frame the tax planning implications of the sourcing analysis in that ruling.

36 In chapter 11, we will return to this variation and will explore how the U.S. base company income rules will apply to this potential foreign base company services income under § 954(e).

functions performed for and on behalf of its U.S. affiliate from locations outside of the United States. To be sure, those fees would all be subject to the transfer pricing requirements that will be addressed in chapter 4. Subject to transfer pricing constraints, however, the sourcing of such head office fees (if arm's length in amount) would all be foreign source income to Big Pharma PLC as long as the relevant services were performed entirely outside of the United States. Additionally, the payment of those service fees, assuming they did not exceed an arm's length amount and were directly related and beneficial to US Pharma, Inc.'s U.S. business, would in turn provide US Pharma, Inc. with a deductible business expense. Diagram #5 therefore sets out the contours of two service stripping transactions that could be used to strip profits from a U.S. affiliate to an offshore affiliate.

G. Source of Rentals and Royalties

Under section 864(a)(4), "rentals and royalties from property located in the United States" have U.S. source. An immediate corollary is that rentals and royalties from property located outside the United States have foreign source. This rule applies to all classes of property—real, personal, tangible, intangible—and embraces income from the full range of transfers of the use of property, including leases, licenses, rentals, bailments, and the like. Thus, lease payments for an equipment rental in the United States have U.S. source as do film rentals from the distribution of a motion picture in the United States and royalties from the use of a patent in U.S. manufacturing operations.

The location of tangible property—real or personal—is generally straightforward. So, therefore, is the source of rentals and royalties for its use. Real property is where it is, and rents from buildings or land and royalties from mineral resources take their source unambiguously from the location of the property. Most tangible personal property is similarly easy to locate. When property is used both in and outside of the United States, an allocation of source is made according to the amount of time the property is used in different places unless different rental rates can clearly be associated with different locations.

The location of intangible property is more elusive. Unlike tangible property, it is not confined to one place at a time. Where it is located is, in fact, more a metaphysical than a physical question. Reflecting this uncertainty, section 861(a)(4) extends U.S. source to income "for the use of or for the privilege of using" intangible property in the United States. The source of income from intellectual property thus depends on where it is used. While the place of use of intangible property may be more fathomable than the abstract notion of its location, that place too is far from self-evident. This may explain the further extension of U.S. source in section 864(a)(4) to income from the "privilege" of using intangible property in the United States. Reflecting the different ways in which intangible property contributes to income, this provision may imply U.S. source for income from rights in property that are not literally "used" in the United States. For example, the writer of a play produced in the United States might license the U.S. film rights in the work to the producer of the play for the duration of its theater run to protect the play from competition in other media. Royalties from this license of film rights, even if they were measured by the use of the literary property as a play and no film were actually created or used in the United States,[37] would have U.S. source.

The above sourcing rule theoretically could create a cascading royalty problem much like the cascading dividend problem discussed earlier with *Lord Forres v. Commissioner*, but the leading case suggests otherwise. In *SDI Netherlands B.V. v. Commissioner*,[38] a Bermuda corporation licensed the worldwide rights in computer software to a Dutch corporation which in turn sub-licensed the U.S. rights to a U.S. corporation and sub-licensed the rights to use the software in other jurisdictions to other licensees. There was no dispute over the fact that any royalties paid by the U.S. licensee under the sub-licensing agreement was U.S. source income to the Dutch company, as the use of that intangible property was in the United States. However, the IRS contended that royalties paid by the Dutch corporation to the Bermuda corporation under the head license agreement also in part represented U.S. source income. In this regard, the royalties due under the head license agreement were equal to 93 percent of the royalties that were obtained by the licensee under any sub-licensing arrangement, so the calculation of royalties ultimately paid to the Bermuda corporation included in part 93 percent of the royalties received by SDI Netherlands from the U.S. sub-licensing agreement. The IRS, however, did not contend that SDI Netherlands was a conduit or agent of SDI Bermuda. The Tax Court held that the sourcing of the royalties under the head license agreement was not determined by the source of the underlying royalties paid to the Bermuda corporation because the two licenses were separate transactions. After stating the head license was a separate transaction, the court then stated that although the royalties paid by SDI Netherlands to SDI Bermuda *were derived from* the royalties received by petitioner from SDI USA, they were separate payments that "were not received from sources within the

[37] You might also think of this as a defensive "use" of the film rights to protect the income stream from the stage rights.

[38] 107 T.C. 161 (1996).

United States by SDI Bermuda under sections 881(a)." The court premised its decision in part on a desire to avoid a cascading royalty problem and cited a leading treatise that had identified this problem. The result is perhaps equitable, but it is hard to know the extent to which one can rely on the SDI precedent when a portion of a royalty payment is *derived from* the use of an underlying intangible in the United States. Section 862(a)(4), on its face, would suggest the portion of the royalty derived from the use of an intangible in the United States is in fact U.S. source income, but the *SDI Netherlands* case stipulated this fact pattern in a potential cascading royalty scenario and held otherwise.

With the above sourcing rule in mind, let's return to our Big Pharma PLC hypothetical again and assume that after its acquisition of a U.S. pharmaceutical business, US Pharma, Inc. had claimed $30 million of depreciation/amortization deductions on its tangible property. However, as that tangible personal property is replaced, US Pharma, Inc. does not purchase its own replacement equipment but instead decides to lease the replacement equipment from its parent, Big Pharma PLC. Tangible personal property, after all, needs to be substantially renovated or replaced at some point due to its ongoing wear and tear. Thus, as expenditures for replacement property are made, the acquirer of that replacement property is designated to be Big Pharma PLC. Obviously, if US Pharma, Inc. had purchased the replacement tangible personal property, then it would be entitled to depreciation deductions for that property and would incur additional interest expense on the borrowed funds used to acquire that replacement property. Consequently, in lieu of obtaining a depreciation deduction and incurring an interest funding cost, US Pharma, Inc. now will have an operating lease and will make a rental payment for the use of the leased tangible depreciable property. I will assume that the rental payment under the lease is $33 million and that Big Pharma PLC earns a reasonable profit above its economic depreciation and funding cost to acquire and rent out this replacement tangible personal property. As a final additional fact, now assume that Big Pharma PLC licenses to US Pharma, Inc. the right to manufacture and distribute pharmaceutical drugs owned and developed by Big Pharma PLC. Assume that US Pharma, Inc. sold $500 million worth of prescription drugs that relate to Big Pharma PLC's patented drugs and paid Big Pharma PLC a 10 percent royalty of $50 million for the right to have manufactured and distributed those products. Now, the $50 million royalty deduction and the $33 million of rental deduction are available to US Pharma, Inc. which is an added feature to the base case that was posited in Diagram #1. However, the effect of implementing the rental stripping strategy is that over time US Pharma, Inc. will no longer have depreciation/amortization deductions but will have gained instead a related party rental expense deduction that can be charged over the entire economic life to which the tangible property is used.

Illustrative Royalty Stripping and Rental Stripping Transactions

Diagram #6

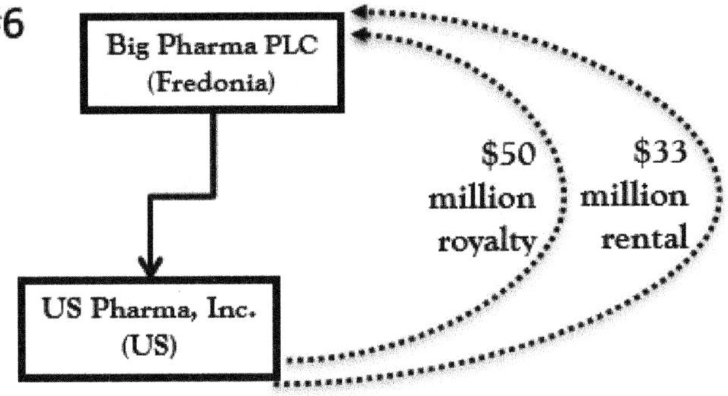

The earnings stripping benefits of the U.S. tax deduction arising from related party rental and royalty stripping payments are analogous to those that can be achieved with an interest stripping transaction but are not subject to section 163(j)'s restrictions, as section 163(j) only applies to interest payments. Thus, these rental and royalty stripping transactions provide another way of achieving earnings stripping to reduce the U.S. taxable income of US Pharma, Inc. As such, this example illustrates an important point: although transactions are separately categorized for purposes of the U.S. international laws, the reality is that inbound tax planning likely includes multiple complimentary strategies that together can create significant earnings stripping tax savings. Congress has often responded to a single earnings stripping phenomenon (like interest stripping transactions via the enactment of section 163(j)), so reducing reliance on one strategy can allow for comparable overall benefits but in a manner that avoids "overuse" of one particular technique. Only with the enactment of section 59A and section 267A has Congress begun to consider base erosion and profit shifting strategies as a common problem that must be addressed across a broad range of related party tax deductible strategies.

In this fact pattern, the $50 million of royalty income earned by Big Pharma PLC is U.S. source income because the place of use of the patents was the United States. Furthermore, the $33 million of rental income is also U.S. source income to Big Pharma PLC because the place of use for the depreciable/amortizable property is the United Sates. Thus, in the first instance, Big Pharma PLC remains potentially subject to U.S. tax jurisdiction on its U.S. source income from these transactions, but, as we will see in later chapters, the U.S. will often surrender its right to tax this royalty income and rental income under its existing tax treaties.[39] However, the critical point is that the source rules preserve U.S. jurisdiction over the foreign person that receives these base erosion payments. Under the U.S. sourcing rules, the rental income and the U.S. royalty income is U.S. source income and thus potentially subject to U.S. taxation even if earned by a non-U.S. person.

A final point is worth introducing at this point with respect to this example because it will be explored in later chapters, and that point relates to the unanswered question of how Big Pharma PLC came to own the U.S. patents of valuable pharmaceutical drugs. If Big Pharma PLC developed those patented drugs with its own personnel in its own jurisdiction and thus licensed its own entirely developed intangible property, then all would be well and good assuming the royalty rate were an arm's length rate. However, if Big Pharma PLC owns the pharmaceutical patents because US Pharma, Inc. transferred ownership of those patents to Big Pharma PLC and then licensed them back, then the outbound transfer leg of that round-tripping exercise implicates section 367(d), which will be explored further in chapter 13. Alternatively, Big Pharma PLC may have contracted and paid for the development of this intangible property under a qualified cost sharing arrangement, and that alternative is discussed further in chapter 4. The migration of valuable intangible property rights to a low-tax affiliate is thus an important predicate for a subsequent royalty stripping transaction. The issues with that migration will be addressed in chapters 4, 8, and 13.

H. Source of Notional Principal Contracts

A notional principal contract is a financial instrument that provides for the payment of amounts by one party to another at specified intervals calculated by reference to a specified index upon a notional principal amount in exchange for specified consideration or a promise to pay similar amounts. Notional principal contracts include interest rate swaps, currency swaps, interest rate caps, interest rate floors, commodity swaps, equity swaps, equity index swaps, and similar agreements.[40] Even though a notional principal contract may be referenced to dividends, interest, or some other type of referenced form of payment, the general rule is that periodic payments under a notional principal contract are sourced by the

---

[39] See Article 12 and Article 21 of 2016 U.S. Model Income Tax Treaty.

[40] Reg. § 1.446–3(a).

residence of the recipient.[41] However, notional principal contracts that arise as part of the conduct of a U.S. trade or business are sourced in the United States as part of that trade or business.[42] Significant upfront payments may be considered an embedded loan to which interest is considered to have been paid.[43] If that element exists, then the sourcing for the deemed interest portion would be by the normal rule for interest discussed above. Every notional principal contract is a derivate that references some other payment, so arguably, a notional principal contract could have received its sourcing by looking to the sourcing by which the underlying referenced amount would have been sourced, but again that is not the general rule. However, Congress changed the general rule in a limited situation by enacting section 871(m) to provide that payments under a notional principal contract would represent U.S. source income to the recipient if that instrument pays a "dividend equivalent," which is defined to be a payment that is contingent upon, or determined by reference to, the payment of a dividend from sources within the United States.

I. Gains from Sales of Property

The source of gains from sales of property is harder to wrap into a single formula than other source rules. This is so in large part because the term "sale" is a rubric covering a range of economic activity. Some sales entail only transfer of ownership, perhaps anonymously, while others imply an extended economic relationship between seller and buyer in which various types of added value may arise. For many years, the source rules themselves made no distinctions between any classes of sales and treated the sale of a gold bar where title passed on delivery in New York in the same manner as door-to-door sales in New York of imported cosmetics.[44]

1. Real Property

The simplest source rule is for gains from the sale of real property. The gains have their source where the property is located, usually a matter beyond doubt. Until 1980, this rule, as stated in section 861(a)(5), assigned U.S. source to gains "from the sale or exchange of real property located in the United States." Because the rule was framed in terms of sales of the actual property, it did not then reach many transfers of interests in real property held in a form

---

41 Reg. § 1.863–7(b)(1).

42 Reg. § 1.863–7(b)(3).

43 Reg. § 1.446–3(f)(2).

44 Both types of sale originally gave rise to U.S. source income. Where the U.S. tax system treated these undertakings differently was in their classification as a "trade or business," which brought them under correspondingly different tax regimes. See chapter 6.

other than direct ownership. For example, a sale of shares of a corporation owning real property in the United States produced gain subject to the source rule for sales of stock, a form of *personal* property. Such relatively simple devices as incorporation once permitted transfers of U.S. real estate with no resulting U.S. source income.

Today, section 861(a)(5) assigns U.S. source to all "gains, profits, and income from the disposition of a United States real property interest." A "United States real property interest" is a term of art defined (in section 897(c)) to include, along with all directly owned real property, holdings of stock in *domestic* corporations with substantial holdings of U.S. real property. Section 861(a)(5) therefore reaches gains from sales of shares in certain U.S. corporations along with gains from sales of actual real estate.[45]

2. Tangible Personal Property

For nearly 70 years, the Code contained a single short statement on the source of gains from the sale of personal property. Section 861(a)(6) assigned U.S. source to "gains, profits, and income derived from the purchase of personal property without the United States. . . and its sale or exchange within the United States."[46] This is known as the "place of sale" rule because it assigns U.S. source to property sold in the United States even if purchased outside. Section 861(a)(6) is still in the Code, although it only applies today to sales of *inventory*.

Sales of all other types of property are now governed by section 865, which was added by the 1986 Act and is as discursive as the prior rule was laconic. Section 865(a) states the general rule that:

> [I]ncome from the sale of personal property—
>
> (1) by a United States resident shall be sourced in the United States, or
>
> (2) by a nonresident shall be sourced outside the United States.

The basic principle here is that gains from sales of personal property take their source from the place of "residence" of the seller. The quotation marks around the term "residence" is not an attempt on my part to be cute. Rather, a "resident" is a specially defined notion in section 865 for purposes of this source rule. Section 865(g) defines a "United States resident" individual as 1) any U.S. citizen or resident alien with no "tax home" outside the United States[47] or 2)

---

[45] Note that section 861(a)(5) does not affect the source of gains from sales of shares of *foreign* corporations holding U.S. real estate.

[46] § 861(a)(6).

[47] § 865(g)(1)(A)(i).

any nonresident alien individual with a "tax home" *in* the United States. A "tax home" entails either a substantial residential or business presence in a given place. The "residence" of an individual for this purpose is thus akin to an economic center of gravity. Within this definition, a *resident* alien individual (as defined in section 7701(b)) can be a *nonresident* for purposes of the source rule of section 865 by maintaining a "tax home" outside the United States, while a nonresident alien individual can be a "resident" within section 865 by having a U.S. "tax home."[48]

An immediate—and notable—consequence of section 865(a) is that most sales by foreign persons of stock, securities, or commodities held as investments, even if made on U.S. securities or commodities exchanges, generate *foreign* source income. This effect is of central importance in the taxation of passive investment of foreign persons in the United States. However, as an exception to this general rule, the sale of stock in a U.S. corporation that is classified as a U.S. real property holding company is nevertheless still considered to be U.S. source income under section 861(a)(5). In chapter 8, I will explore the contours of what entities constitute a U.S. real property holding company. In transactions involving the purchase of a company, the seller is often required to provide affirmative representations and warranties about whether the company is or has been a U.S. real property holding company.

Another exception to the general "residence of the seller" source rule set forth in section 865(a) relates to the sale of depreciable personal property. In this regard, section 865(c) provides that gain from the sale of depreciable property has U.S. source regardless of the residence of the seller to the extent the property's depreciation created a reduction in the taxable income from sources in the United States. This is not a surprising rule, and the whipsaw concern to which section 865(c) is designed to address should be readily apparent. Assume that Marcel had fully depreciated equipment as part of his U.S. trade or business and then sold the equipment in a foreign country with foreign title transfer. In this scenario, to the extent that prior depreciation reduced Marcel's taxable income arising from U.S. source income, section 865(c)(1) requires the gain on the sale of the depreciable property to be classified as U.S. source income to preserve symmetry. Moreover, to the extent that the depreciable property was sold for more than its prior depreciation, then section 865(c)(2) provides that the sourcing of this excess gain

---

[48] Also, U.S. citizens and resident aliens are not treated as nonresidents with respect to any sale of personal property unless they pay to a foreign country an income tax equal to at least 10 percent of the gain derived from the sale. § 865(g)(2). Therefore U.S. persons derive U.S. source gains from sales of property in tax havens, regardless of their economic center of gravity.

would be determined as if the depreciable personal property were inventory with the consequence that the place of sale rule of section 861(a)(6) would then be applied.

3. Sale of Intangible Property

The sale of intangible property has several rules depending on the type of intangible property that is sold and the nature of the consideration that is received for the intangible property. To begin with, section 865(d)(1)(A) provides that section 865(a)'s general rule will apply to the sale of intangible property to the extent that the sale is not contingent on the productivity, use, or disposition of the intangible. In other words, a noncontingent sale of an intangible asset is generally sourced according to the residence of the seller, but this general rule is subject to several exceptions. Section 865(d)(2) defines an intangible asset as any patent, copyright, secret process or formula, goodwill, trademark, trade brand, franchise, or other like property. However, several exceptions are important to remember.

To begin with, if the sale's purchase price is contingent on the productivity, use, or disposition of the intangible asset, then the source of the gain is determined as if such payments were royalties. Note that the payment is not a royalty and section 865(d)(1)(B) does not cause the payment to be changed to a royalty. A royalty is income earned for licensing intangible property. However, even though the income is a gain arising from the sale of an intangible, that gain is nevertheless sourced in the same manner as if it were a royalty. Per section 861(a)(4) and section 862(a)(4), royalties are sourced by the location where the intangible property is able to be used by the owner. Thus, section 865(d)(1)(B) provides that one metric for an exception is whether the intangible's consideration is contingent.

Goodwill is a second important exception that exists for intangible property. In this regard, section 865(d)(3) provides that gain from the sale of goodwill is sourced according to the location where the goodwill was generated, as long as the goodwill was independent of the franchise and trademarks. The scope of this goodwill exception was addressed in *International Multifoods Corp. v. Commissioner*.[49] In that case, the taxpayer sold its Mister Donut franchises in Asia for $2.05 million and argued the goodwill was foreign source income under section 865(d)(3) because it was generated from businesses located in Asia. However, the Tax Court accepted the IRS's argument that section 865(d)(3) did not apply because any goodwill was inseverable from the Mister Donut franchises and trademarks that were sold. Because section 865(d)(3)'s exception did not extend to trademarks and franchises

---

[49] 108 T.C. 25 (1997).

and the goodwill was inextricably linked to those intangibles and the business was sold for a noncontingent amount, then section 865(d)(1)'s sourcing rule applied to source the gain entirely by the residence of the seller, resulting in U.S. source income, as the seller's residence was the United States.

4. Sale by U.S. Person Attributable to a Foreign Branch or a Foreign Affiliate

A special source rule applies to a U.S. resident who sells assets through a foreign office. However, this foreign office rule does not supplant the sourcing rules for inventory in section 865(b), the sale of intangible property for contingent consideration under section 865(d)(1)(B), the sourcing of goodwill eligible for sourcing under section 865(d)(3), or the special sourcing rule that applies to the sale of the stock in a foreign affiliate to which section 865(f) applies. However, outside of those contexts, section 865(e)(1) provides that income of a U.S. resident from the sale of property is nevertheless sourced as foreign source income if the gain arises from the sale of personal property attributable to a foreign office maintained by the U.S. resident and the gain on such sale is subject to a foreign tax equal to at least 10 percent of the income realized from the sale.

A separate sourcing exception exists under section 865(f) for the sale of stock in a foreign affiliate. In this regard, section 865(f) provides that a U.S. resident's realized gain on the sale of the stock of an 80 percent owned foreign affiliate will be considered foreign source income if the sale of the foreign affiliate occurs in a foreign country in which such affiliate is engaged in the active conduct of a trade or business and more than 50 percent of the gross income of such affiliate for the last three years was derived from the active conduct of a trade or business in such foreign country.

5. Sales of Inventory

The most important element of section 865 is what it does not do. "Inventory property"[50] is excluded from its reach by section 865(b), which defers to the source rule of section 861(a)(6). Section 861(a)(6) in turn assigns U.S. source to "gains, profits, and income derived from the purchase of inventory property... without the United States... and its sale or exchange within the United States."[51] For inventory, the old "place of sale" rule therefore survives. Until the 1986 Act, as noted above, this was the universal

[50] "Inventory property" is broadly defined to include stock in trade and any other property held for sale to customers in the ordinary course of business. §§ 861(a)(6), 865(i)(1), 1221(1).

[51] The counterpart provision of § 862(a)(6) assigns foreign source to "gains, profits, and income derived from the purchase of inventory property . . . within the United States . . . and its sale or exchange without the United States."

source rule for all gains from sales of personal property. Now, by virtue of the addition of the word "inventory," it is the source rule only for sales of inventory. Inventory sales, however, are not only by far the largest class of sales but also outweigh all others combined in economic importance.

Section 861(a)(6) governs only income from the purchase *and* sale of inventory. It deals with pure selling (retail and wholesale distribution and marketing) as opposed to selling that arises as the culmination of some other economic activity, such as manufacturing or processing. On its face, section 861(a)(6) applies only to gains from the sale *within* the United States of property purchased *outside* the United States.[52] Other combinations of purchase and sale are obviously possible. Although section 861(a)(6) does not literally say so, gains from the purchase and sale of inventory entirely inside the United States also have U.S. source, and conversely, gains from the purchase and sale of inventory entirely outside the United States have foreign source. Section 861(a)(6) must be understood, in short, to fix the source of gains in the place of sale without regard for the place of purchase.

It is one thing to put the source of gains from sales in the place of sale and quite another to say where that place is. What makes a sale "within" the United States as opposed to somewhere else? In other words, how does one determine the place of sale? Section 861(a)(6) does not say, and it is far from obvious.

Sales of goods involve a mix of physical and legal events. Generally, there is both an agreement (sometimes implicit) and an actual transfer of goods. When these events occur in the same place, there is no problem, but in international sales, they may be dispersed. Negotiations may occur in one place; the agreement may be executed in another; the goods may be delivered at yet another place; legal title may pass at another still. Any one of these could be taken as the place of sale, or a weighing of all might determine the place to which the sale relates most intensely—a "center of gravity" test in effect.

After some fits and starts, in which various tests for the place of sale were followed at different times, the U.S. tax laws have come to rest on one operative event—the passage of legal title—as the touchstone of the place of sale. Initially adopted because it was simple and easy to administer, this test of source is most notable today for the high degree of control it leaves with taxpayers over the source of income from sales. The reason for this control—which was not intended by the U.S. Treasury when it adopted the passage of

---

52 Its counterpart, section 862(a)(2), applies only to gains from the sale *outside* the United States of property purchased *within* the United States.

title test in the 1940s—is the changed role of passage of title in commercial law. The very concept of "title" has become largely irrelevant in commercial law. In the Uniform Commercial Code (which was adopted by most states only *after* the establishment of passage of title as the touchstone of source in tax matters), the transfer of rights and burdens in connection with sales no longer turns on the passage of legal title. The UCC acknowledges title only as it may bear on some other requirement outside the law of sales. The main provision in the UCC concerning the vestigial notion of "title," in fact, is that when title is germane for some purpose *other* than commercial law, it passes where the parties to a sale specify in their agreement.[53] This makes the source of gains in a range of situations a matter of the stroke of a pen, by which the parties to a sale can specify a place of passage of title that is advantageous for tax purposes. Let me add that taxpayers' control over source, while considerable, is not wholly unfettered. Under regulations, the Treasury can disregard the place of passage of title if it is artificial or has been manipulated primarily for tax avoidance,[54] but if the UCC terms did shift the risk of loss between buyer and seller (even though the risk was fully insured), then this economic result has been viewed as sufficient under the case law to withstand the government's attack on such arrangements as being artificial or made for tax avoidance reasons.[55] Even so, it follows that a Canadian seller and an American buyer cannot specify, for example, that title passes in some remote place such as Fiji. The residence of the seller or the buyer is almost always germane to a transaction of sale, however, so that passage of title in either place is very likely to hold up. Often that leaves taxpayers more than enough room to maneuver.

The advantage to taxpayers from control over source is obvious in some instances. You can readily appreciate why a foreign merchant would prefer to have foreign source income from sales of goods destined for the United States.[56] Let's suppose that our friend Marcel has become a wine merchant in his country of Fredonia. If Marcel ships wine to distributors in the United States, he should make certain that title to the goods passes in Fredonia before transport (or perhaps in some sales office Marcel maintains in a third country). Marcel's gains will then have *foreign* source from the perspective of the U.S. tax system and likely escape U.S. taxation.

---

[53] UCC § 2–401(1). Absent specific agreement between the parties, title passes as a general rule where the seller completes performance of delivery. UCC § 2–401(2).

[54] Reg. § 1.861–7(c).

[55] See A.P. Green Exports v. United States, 284 F.2d 383 (Ct. Cl. 1960).

[56] To be sure, as we shall see, even U.S. source gains from sales of goods are not subject to U.S. taxation unless "effectively connected" with a U.S. business. But U.S. source income is far more likely than foreign source income to be taxed as effectively connected.

Assume further that the Fredonian tax system follows a "center of gravity" test in determining the source of gains from sales of goods. If the agreements were negotiated and executed in the United States, the gains might then have *foreign* source in Fredonia (bearing in mind that U.S. source income is foreign source income in Fredonia). If Fredonia has a territorial tax system, it may not reach Marcel's "foreign" source gains. Artful handling of the different source rules in two countries may thus leave Marcel's gains beyond the reach of any tax.

The advantage to a *U.S.* person of being able to create foreign source income at will by steering passage of title outside the United States is also a powerful tool. Such a case was presented in *Liggett Group, Inc. v. Commissioner*,[57] where sales that involved foreign title transfer allowed the U.S. tax person to treat its income as foreign source income and to apply foreign tax credits to the extent of the foreign source income from the appropriate foreign tax credit basket.[58] U.S. persons are, after all, subject to full U.S. income tax on income of any source, domestic or foreign, but keep this pattern in mind when you come upon the foreign tax credit in chapter 10, and things will fall into place.

Consider a further scenario of a U.S. multinational enterprise that expects to have its U.S. manufacturing subsidiary produce products for export from the United States. However, suppose the supply chain were restructured so that all manufactured products were sold to a foreign affiliate who would act as a distributor for the products and would resell those goods to customers outside the United States. The revised fact pattern is set forth in the below Diagram #7.

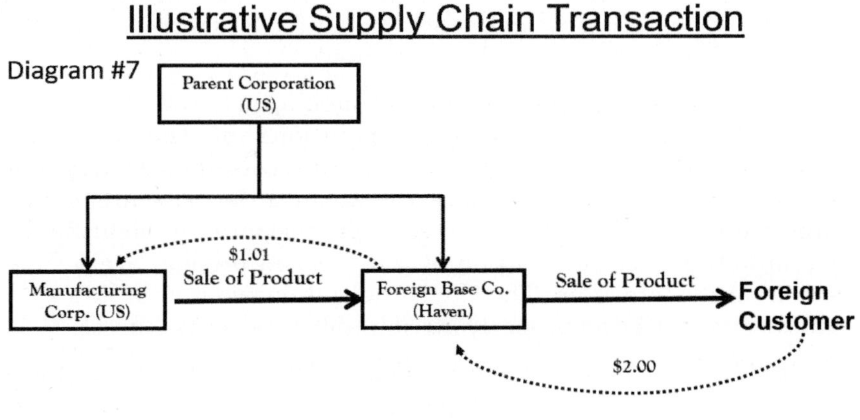

[57] 58 T.C.M. 1167 (1990).

[58] Foreign tax credit issues including the foreign tax credit basket regime is discussed in chapter 10.

By inserting a foreign base company into the structure to act as a distributor, Foreign Base Company is now able to earn a profit margin for being inserted into the trading pattern. Moreover, as long as the inventory owned and sold by Foreign Base Company is sold with title passage outside of the United States, its income would be considered foreign source income. Thus, the insertion of a related party foreign corporation into the export supply chain allows a portion of the U.S. export profits to now be earned as foreign source income by a non-U.S. entity that itself is not subject to U.S. taxation. This base company structure will be an important structure that we will return to repeatedly in connection with understanding the U.S. transfer pricing rules and also the U.S. outbound anti-deferral rules of Subpart F that seek to provide a backstop against this base erosion and profit shifting structure.

J. Income of Mixed Character

The source rules canvassed thus far deal either with income from a single source or with income with different components (such as compensation, rentals, or royalties) arising where the constituent components have a single source. Much income, however, consists of bundled gains of different components that have different sources. The activities of an integrated oil company, for example, may consist of extracting oil from the ground in one place, refining the oil into gasoline somewhere else, and selling the gasoline to a motorist at a pump in yet another place. The company may also do its own shipping of unrefined and refined products. Within the conventional U.S. income tax concepts, the first—and only—event of "realization" occurs upon the sale of gasoline at the pump. The aggregate gain from the transaction ("gross income" in tax parlance) is the difference between the proceeds of the final sale and the cost of gasoline sold (arrived at by measuring and allocating all costs incurred along the entire chain of production and distribution).

This gain is made up of several elements, each reflecting value added by significantly different operations of the taxpayer. Exploration and extraction yield crude oil of ascertainable value that is tied economically to the place the natural deposits are found; refining creates value from a process itself separately identifiable; the marketing and distribution of the finished product are a final element in the total gain. The single realization event unlocks a gain built up over time and properly attributable to several sources.

In 2017, Congress decided to adopt a decidedly pro-U.S. source posture to this complex fact pattern. In this regard, Congress modified section 863(b)(2) to provide that the source of income derived from the sale or exchange of inventory property that is produced in the United States is determined solely on the basis of where it was manufactured. For example, income derived from the sale of U.S. manufactured inventory property to a foreign jurisdiction is sourced solely to the United States even if title passage occurred elsewhere. Property that is partly manufactured within the United States and partly manufactured outside the United States must have its income allocated between the manufacturing activities.

In the 2025 Tax Act, Congress modified the manner in which the source rules section 863(b)(2) interacts with the foreign tax credit limitation and did so without modifying section 863(b)(2). In this regard, for purposes of the foreign tax credit limitation (a topic discussed in chapter 10), if a U.S. person maintains an office or other fixed place of business in a foreign country, then the portion of taxable income from the sale or exchange outside the United States of inventory property produced in the United States and which is attributable to such office or other fixed place of business is treated as foreign source taxable income but cannot exceed 50 percent of the total taxable income from the sale or exchange of the inventory property.[59] Thus, section 863(b) illustrates an unfortunate common theme in terms of the Internal Revenue Code. Section 863(b) purports to set forth a unified sourcing rule that can be used throughout the Code that is premised on a single factor: place of production. But, section 865(e)(2) changes the sourcing rule with respect to sales made from a U.S. office (discussed in the next section), and section 904(b)(6) changes the outcome of the sourcing rule for sales made through a foreign office for foreign tax credit limitation purposes. These companion provisions in effect override the singular sourcing rule of section 863(b)(2). Thus, care must be taken to properly synthesize these provisions. In that effort, one cannot simply rely on one's initial reading of the plain text of one section of the Code but must read all companion provisions that intersect with it.

K. Sales by Foreign Persons Attributable to a U.S. Office

On its face, section 863(b)(2) provides that income derived from manufactured inventory property sold in the United States but produced entirely in another country is sourced in that country even if title passage occurs in the United States. However, the sourcing rule of section 863(b)(2) is supplanted by section 865(e)(2)(A) for sales made through a U.S. office. In this regard, section 865(e)(2)(A) provides that gain of a foreign person from the sale of *any* personal property has U.S. source, "notwithstanding any other provisions [of the Code]," if the sale is attributable to a U.S. office or other fixed place of business maintained in the United States. Note, first, the

59 See Code Sec. 904(b)(6).

sweeping extent of this source rule. It applies to *all* sales (not just of inventory) and overrides *all* other source provisions. For foreign persons' sales through a U.S. office of goods produced abroad, the sourcing rule that looks to the place where manufacturing occurred under section 863(b) does *not* apply.[60] Instead, the entire gain has U.S. source. The juxtaposition of the sourcing rules for the export of U.S. manufactured property and the sourcing rule for inbound manufactured property could not provide a starker contrast.

The natural reading of the statutory provision of section 865(e)(2) is that all of the income considered attributable to *foreign* production would be considered U.S. source income as the source rule of section 865(e)(2) applies *notwithstanding any other provision.* Foreign producers selling in the United States generally avoided creating a U.S. office and deal, if at all possible, with independent distributors and brokers.[61] Those that must have their own distribution operations in the United States (such as the Japanese electronics and auto giants)[62] often create separate U.S. distribution affiliates to which they sell their produced inventory *outside* the United States. The U.S. distribution affiliate derives U.S. source gain from its resales of products in the United States, but the foreign producer derives no U.S. source gain from its production and sales outside the United States. This pattern quells the problems of source and allocation under sections 865 and 863 but raises instead transfer pricing questions under section 482.[63]

Perhaps because of these obvious planning strategies that side-step the potential pitfall of section 865(e)(2), the Treasury Department used its regulatory authority to recalibrate the scope of the sourcing impact of section 865(e)(2) so that its literal statutory language would not create a potential trap for the unwary. Under the final regulations, income that is properly allocable to the U.S. office is treated as U.S. source income, and the regulations provide a 50/50 safe harbor method and provide an alternative "books and records

---

[60] Nor does it matter where title in the goods passes to the buyer.

[61] Marcel, the Fredonian wine merchant from a few pages back, should in no circumstances establish his own sales office in the United States, at the risk of exposing his entire gains to U.S. taxation.

[62] Outfits like Sony and Toyota cannot as a practical matter channel all their U.S. sales through independent agents.

[63] See chapter 4. Section 482, furthermore, is no guaranteed antidote to excessive bureaucratic zeal. During the 1980s one part of the U.S. government (the IRS) pursued Toyota-U.S. (Toyota's U.S. distribution affiliate) under section 482, alleging that the transfer prices of cars from Toyota-Japan (the foreign producer) were so high as to shift excessive income to Japan. At the same time another part of the U.S. government (the International Trade Commission) was bringing a dumping complaint against Toyota-Japan, alleging sales of cars to the U.S. affiliate in the United States below cost.

method."[64] Under the 50/50 safe harbor method, fifty percent of the foreign manufacturer's profits are considered to be attributable to the U.S. sales office (and thus U.S. source income) whereas the other fifty percent of the profits is attributable to the place where the foreign production activities occur (and is considered foreign source income).[65] In lieu of the 50/50 safe harbor method, the nonresident seller may elect to allocate the gross income, gain, or loss under the alternative "books and records method" which requires the use of a facts and circumstances determination to allocate profits between the sales office and the place of production based on arm's length transfer pricing principles.[66]

L. Source and Characterization

Prior to the technical problem of applying the source rules outlined above is the question of classifying the income to which they apply. You can assign a source to income only if you know what it is. Ubiquitous in taxation, the problem of characterization is especially pervasive in determining the source of income. For example, a gain that could either be profit from a sale of property or a fee for brokering a sale between others will not reveal its source until its character has been resolved.[67] Many of the decided cases on the source of income ultimately turn on its classification.

Some questions of characterization are fairly tractable: interest, dividends, rents from real property, and social security benefits are in the main readily identifiable. Other types of income—such as compensation for services and gains from transfers of rights in intellectual property—melt into each other at uncertain and overlapping boundaries.

1. Services or Transfer of Property?

A free-lance writer who "sells" a story is usually treated as having transferred an identifiable property right—the copyright—while another writer (a staff reporter on a newspaper, for example) may be viewed as performing services (writing) for compensation. The boundary between these situations has been a perennial matter of dispute, both in domestic and international tax settings. To a large extent, the distinction between services and transfers of intangible property has turned on whether the creator (writer, artist, inventor, etc.) had rights in an asset separately identifiable as "property" apart

---

64 Reg. § 1.865–3(d)(2).

65 Reg. § 1.865–3(d)(2)(i).

66 Reg. § 1.865–3(d)(2)(ii).

67 A classic case of this type is United States v. Balanovski, 236 F.2d 298 (2d Cir. 1956), *cert. denied*, 352 U.S. 968 (1957).

from tax law. It follows that changes in the legal regime of intellectual property itself have affected this boundary.

2. Ingram v. Bowers

A seminal case in this area is *Ingram v. Bowers*,[68] which illustrates both the importance of characterization in international taxation and the limitations of the process. The case concerned income of Enrico Caruso. Under a 1911 agreement with the Victor Company, Caruso performed several songs at the company's recording studio in New Jersey. By the terms of the contract, Caruso was undertaking simply to sing songs which the Victor Company would record. Victor made a master recording and then made template copies from which individual records were made and sold around the world. Caruso received a royalty from the sale of each individual record by Victor.[69]

The songs were all recorded at the Victor Company's studios in the United States. The IRS accordingly took the view that Caruso's "royalty" arrangement was simply compensation for services (consisting of singing) performed in the United States. It made no difference to the IRS that the compensation for the services happened to be tied to the return derived from those services by Caruso's employer. So viewed, Caruso's entire income from the arrangement was U.S. source compensation, including the contingent amounts received from sales of records *outside* the United States.[70] Caruso's estate (he was dead by the time of the case) sought, in contrast, to characterize the transactions as licenses by Caruso to the Victor Company of rights in the recorded songs for use around the world. This characterization did not affect the source of the income from record sales in the *United States*, which would in any event have U.S. source as royalties from the "use" of property in the United States, but would have recast as foreign source income the royalties received by Caruso on account of the *foreign* (i.e., non-U.S.) sales.

Siding with the Treasury, the district court found the overall arrangement to be compensation for services. Caruso had agreed to sing and had been compensated for singing and, therefore, "the place where the work [was] done, and not the place where the later event fixing compensation occurs, is the source of the income, in cases where the income is from the exercise of a profession or vocation as

---

68 47 F.2d 925 (S.D.N.Y. 1931), *aff'd*, 57 F.2d 65 (2d Cir. 1932).

69 These terms were modified in 1919. Caruso was to record 40 songs and to receive a royalty of 10 percent of the list price of all records sold, or a guaranteed minimum of $100,000 per year. Under the 1919 agreement, Caruso also undertook to record songs for no other company.

70 The contingent element, in this view, affected only the measure, but not the nature, of Caruso's compensation.

in this case."[71] On appeal, this decision was affirmed (in an opinion by Learned Hand) on the ground that the agreements between Caruso and Victor gave Caruso no interest in the matrices and the records themselves, nor any rights in the nature of a copyright. There being no interest in intellectual property to be licensed, the characterization as a license could not stand.

As a matter of economic fundamentals, the courts could plausibly have found that Caruso's income was not, at least in substantial part, compensation for services. True, Caruso sang songs for money, but what made the singing so valuable was the unique quality of Caruso's voice. That would make Caruso's huge income akin to a rent from his exclusive control over this rare attribute. Economists view the incomes of superstar performers or athletes as rents of a sort, like the income derived by the owner of a uniquely fertile patch of land. An economist might suggest, as an example of this type of rent, Babe Ruth's $100,000 compensation from the New York Yankees in 1927, when his 60 home runs exceeded the output of any other *team* in baseball. Without his particular combination of eyesight, wrist strength, and coordination, Ruth could hardly have earned more than $2,000 as a laborer in 1927. The $98,000 difference can be thought of as a rent from Ruth's unique physical attributes. The economic return to Caruso's singing voice can be thought of in much the same way.

Rather than attempt to fathom the basic economic character of the income, however, the courts characterized Caruso's income according to the *legal* category into which his contractual arrangement with Victor fell. They focused narrowly on the terms of Caruso's contracts with Victor and, in particular, on the absence of any express transfer of rights in intangible property. The courts' approach does not betoken any intellectual failure on their part. Both the trial and appellate judges understood that Caruso's royalties fell uneasily into the class of compensation for services and reflected to a considerable extent his ownership and control of a unique productive asset. Much compensation for services, however, embodies some element of rent or return to human capital, albeit in varying degrees. A case-by-case dissection of compensation into pure returns from labor and rents is impossible. The courts could not remove Caruso from the class of recipients of compensation for services because, within the law of intellectual property as it stood, Caruso's contractual arrangement did not frame any rights in intellectual property.

---

[71] 47 F.2d 925, 927.

3. Oppenheim and Tobey

Later cases sharpen the boundaries introduced in *Ingram v. Bowers*. The Board of Tax Appeals relied on the case, although in support of the opposite result, in *Oppenheim v. Commissioner*,[72] where a foreign author was held to have transferred actual copyrights to a U.S. publisher. Oppenheim, unlike Caruso, was found to have received income from a transfer of property in the United States. Oppenheim had actually owned an item of intangible property—a copyright—whereas Caruso had simply sung for a fee.[73]

A later case brings a further wrinkle to the line between *Ingram* and *Oppenheim*. In *Tobey v. Commissioner*,[74] an American artist living in Switzerland sold his paintings through a gallery in New York. The gains thus resulted, in form at least, from the production and sale of tangible objects. The Tax Court found Tobey's gains to be "earned income" nonetheless because they were attributable to the artist's personal efforts. The source of the taxpayer's income was not the main focus in *Tobey,* however.[75]

4. Further Implications of Ingram v. Bowers as Clarified in Boulez

Ingram v. Bowers has intriguing corollaries. A practical consequence of the case (that the U.S. Treasury probably did not anticipate) is a golden (or even platinum) opportunity for foreign recording artists with a following in the United States. Where Caruso went wrong was in doing the actual singing in a New Jersey recording studio. That gave his entire compensation (the "royalties" as they were called) U.S. source no matter where records were sold to consumers. If Caruso had recorded *outside* the United States, none of his compensation would have had U.S. source. This point was not lost on star performers of later generations. Many of the iconic foreign rock stars of the 1960s recorded in places like the Bahamas (where income taxation bears as lightly as the gentle breeze). Their huge incomes from these recording arrangements, thanks to *Ingram v. Bowers,* had no U.S. source component, even though overwhelmingly, the largest market for sales of their records was the United States.[76]

---

72 31 B.T.A. 563 (1934).

73 Id. at 565.

74 60 T.C. 227 (1973).

75 The question, rather, was whether Tobey was entitled to the U.S. tax benefit accorded in section 911 to foreign "earned income." See chapter 20.

76 You may perhaps associate some of these superstar groups with such high-tax countries as Great Britain and wonder what they gained by avoiding U.S. taxation, given the fiercely high taxes in their countries of nationality. The answer lies partly in the territorial taxation of such countries—implying no tax on foreign-based business

Another implication of *Ingram v. Bowers* is that a change in the underlying intellectual property arrangement—for example, if the agreements with Victor had created for Caruso identifiable rights in the songs—might have changed the tax consequences. This possibility was both confirmed and limited in *Boulez v. Commissioner*.[77] Boulez, an orchestra conductor who had received "royalties" under an arrangement similar to Caruso's, argued that amendments of the copyright laws in the 1970s established the existence of property rights of performers in recorded works. The court agreed that under present-day copyright laws a performer may retain a property interest in recorded works. However, the court noted that this possibility arises only from express contractual agreement, which Boulez in particular had not obtained. Boulez therefore lost, but it is strongly implied in *Boulez* that the taxpayer *could* have retained intellectual property rights in the recordings by contract.

Ingram v. Bowers and *Boulez*—two taxpayer defeats—therefore contain the seeds of a favorable U.S. income tax regime for foreign performing artists. Those who have the flexibility or bargaining power to record in a place of their own choosing outside the United States can leave their agreements with record companies as silent as Caruso's on the question of the artists' property rights and thereby remove their entire incomes from the reach of U.S. taxation. Those who record in the United States are worse off from a tax standpoint, but by retaining specified property rights in their agreements, they can impart foreign source at least to their share of gains from record sales outside the United States.

5. Sergio Garcia

Whereas *Ingram v. Bowers*, *Oppenheim*, and *Tobey* involved an "all or nothing" approach to the service versus royalty characterization analysis, in other situations we find a mixed fact pattern where a single payment is separated into a payment attributable to personal services and a payment for the license of an intangible. A representative case is *Garcia v. Commissioner*.[78] In that case, Sergio Garcia entered into an endorsement contract with TaylorMade where TaylorMade was allowed to use Sergio Garcia's image, name, and voice ("image rights") in marketing campaigns for TaylorMade products, and the taxpayer agreed to perform certain

---

operations of their own citizens—and partly in the possibility of surrender of nationality of a high-tax country and the acquisition of nationality in a country with a laid-back fiscal culture. Monaco, for example, is a longstanding haven for the fiscally challenged. One of the world's best-known athletes in the 1970s was a Swede in language and culture, but a Monegasque in civil status.

[77] 83 T.C. 584 (1984).

[78] 140 T.C. 141 (2013).

services (e.g., use the sponsor's products in all golf play, act in advertisements, and make personal appearances). The sponsor compensated Sergio Garcia for his image rights and for his personal services. Importantly, under the U.S.-Switzerland income tax treaty, any U.S. source royalties paid to Sergio Garcia would have been exempt from any U.S. withholding taxes by reason of the U.S.-Swiss tax treaty whereas any U.S. sourced personal services income attributable to services performed in the United States would have been taxable to him. The taxpayer and the IRS stipulated that 69 percent of Sergio Garcia's personal services were conducted in the United States in one of the years before the Tax Court and 68 percent of the personal services were conducted within the United States for the other year that was before the court.

However, the taxpayer and the IRS disagreed on the amount of the endorsement contract that related to a payment for personal services in each of the two years. In this regard, the IRS issued a deficiency notice stating that all of the endorsement contract fees paid to Sergio Garcia were for his personal services and were not appropriately treated as royalty payments. Thus, the IRS attempted to argue that the contract must be treated in its entirety as either a license or a royalty arrangement and then asserted that Sergio Garcia's endorsement agreement should be characterized entirely as a service agreement because the payments under that agreement were "predominantly attributable" to his required athletic performances. In AM 2009–005 (June 26, 2009), the IRS addressed the consequences of endorsement contracts that require an athlete to display, wear, or use equipment, clothing, footwear, and other items (such as a patch with a sponsor's logo) during sports-related activities. In that ruling, the IRS opined that endorsement contracts should be characterized entirely as contracts for services. Citing *Boulez*, among other authorities, the IRS stated that the endorsement contract was "fundamentally a contract for services" as it required the athlete to compete in golf tournaments and to wear products to earn the fees under the endorsement contract. As a result, the IRS argued that all of the fees paid under an endorsement contract should be considered as payments for personal services and that any "star quality" aspect of the athlete who performs such services does not negate the fundamental service nature of the contract but does affect the amount of compensation that a person can command under such a contract.

The Tax Court in *Garcia v. Commissioner* disagreed with this IRS administrative position, concluding that the image rights of Sergio Garcia constituted an important and valuable intangible property right that was independent of any personal services that were separately bargained for under the endorsement contract. Even though there was only one contract between TaylorMade and Sergio Garcia, that contract encompassed two different bundled items. Relying in part on *Ferrer v. Commissioner*[79] (a favorite case found in many federal income tax casebooks), the Tax Court stated that the endorsement contract should be bifurcated between an arrangement for the licensing of Sergio Garcia's image rights and a contract for his personal services. As a result, the licensing of his image rights generated royalties that were in part U.S. source income, and as to that portion, Sergio Garcia was entitled to relief from any U.S. taxation under the U.S.-Swiss income tax treaty.

The Tax Court then sought to determine how to bifurcate the overall endorsement contract payments between the amounts paid for the intangible image rights and amounts paid for the personal services of Sergio Garcia. In the endorsement contract, Sergio Garcia and TaylorMade had agreed to a bifurcation of the contractual payments as follows: (i) 85 percent for Sergio Garcia's image rights and (ii) 15 percent for his personal services. The Tax Court found that the contract over-allocated amounts to royalties. After analyzing the facts in the specific case and considering prior bifurcation percentages used in other athletic endorsement contract cases, the Tax Court in the end allocated 65 percent of the endorsement contract payments to royalties and 35 percent of the endorsement contract payments to personal services.

M. Other Boundaries of Characterization: Products, Services, Intangible Property, and Software

Other boundaries of characterization with implications for the source of income lie between tangible products, intangible property, and services. Most consumable products and a great many services embody some intellectual property. If I transfer a product embodying protected intellectual property, such as a computer disk or a CD, have I transferred rights in intellectual property or a physical article embodying protected intellectual property? Is the transfer a sale or a license? It makes a difference in the source of my gains. If I have sold a *product* embodying intellectual property (most likely a sale of inventory), the place of passage of title would govern source. If I have sold *separate* rights in intellectual property, the source of my gains would be governed by the rule of residence in section 865.

Consumer goods, even with embedded intellectual property, are generally treated as items of inventory. A copyrighted book is simply a book, a patented vacuum cleaner an appliance, and an electronic game player complete with DVDs a toy. Computer software raises

---

[79] 304 F.2d 125 (2d Cir. 1962), *rev'g* 35 T.C. 617 (1961).

particular problems, because it is transferred 1) in consumer markets, 2) to businesses in combination with long-term service agreements, and 3) everything in between.

The Treasury Department has issued regulations on the classification of transactions involving computer programs. The transactions fall in four classes: 1) transfers of copyrights in a computer program, 2) transfers of copies of the program (copyrighted articles), 3) provision of services for the development of a program, and 4) provision of know-how relating to computer programming.[80] The first of these—the transfer of a copyright—is a transfer that brings with it full rights of modification or copying. The transfer is one of property rights and is a sale or a license depending on the extent of the rights transferred.[81] The second—the transfer of a copyrighted article—is one that brings possession and control without rights of copying or modification. It is, as transfer 1) above, a sale or a rental according to the extent and duration of rights transferred.[82] The remaining two are different types of services.[83]

1. Services—Ancillary or Integral?

A host of economic transactions involve to some degree the performance of services. The sale of goods often entails delivery or installation. Sellers of equipment or intangible property may have to demonstrate the use of the property or supervise its operation for a period of time. Ultimately, there is some element of service in *all* selling—a seller holds goods at the disposal of a buyer and assumes the physical and financial burden of ownership while doing so.

For taxation, services commonly associated with the transfer of property—delivery, when performed by the seller, is an obvious type—are assimilated to the transfer and therefore do not give rise to income with a separate source of its own. There is a point, however, where services cease to be ancillary, and are identified as separate taxable transactions. For example, if extensive training and technical assistance are provided along with a transfer of intangible property or know-how, these elements must be valued, and the service income segregated and assigned a source of its own.

2. Know-How

In this regard, the provision of "know-how" is a transaction with somewhat hazy boundaries. Sometimes it is an end in itself, but far more often, it occurs in connection with some other transfer. Know-

---

80 Reg. § 1.861–18(b)(1).

81 Reg. § 1.861–18(f)(1). See also chapter 5.

82 Reg. § 1.861–18(f)(2).

83 There are numerous examples in the regulations fleshing out these general principles. Reg. § 1.861–18(h).

how includes a variety of proprietary information directed to some practical application. Whether or not it constitutes "property," and whether the property, if any, is the object of a sale or a license depends, first, on the degree of legal protection accorded the know-how in a given legal environment and, second, on the extent of rights transferred in the transaction.

In Revenue Ruling 55–17,[84] the IRS treated the value of instruction given in connection with the transfer of know-how as having only "nominal" value and therefore as creating little income of separate source. It followed that the entire income was derived from a license of property. The IRS later retreated from any such presumptive view of the value of the services in Revenue Ruling 64–56,[85] doubtless because this view of the services proved unfavorable to the U.S. Treasury in several other contexts. The later ruling, which requires separate valuation of the services and a separate source for the associated income, remains the established position.

In Revenue Ruling 71–564,[86] the IRS determined that certain transfers of know-how, if they conveyed legally protected rights for the entire period in which the legal protection remains effective, might also qualify as sales or exchanges of property.

3. Embedded Intellectual Property

Almost all consumable products (barring perhaps such commodities as tap water and unbranded wheat flour sold by the pound) and a great many services embody some intellectual property. Even something as plain as a sponge mop may have a brand name and some proprietary mode of operation. Because most products are bundles of tangible and intangible components, the sale of a finished good also implies a license of the bundled intangible element. While the purchase of most products conveys unqualified ownership of its physical components, it generally implies only limited rights in the underlying intellectual property. The buyer of a copyrighted book can read it or burn it but cannot copy it for further sale or distribution. The buyer of a patented eggbeater can make an omelet with it but cannot replicate it for multiple sales on eBay.

A further question: if I utilized an online streaming service or online computing service, have I obtained a temporary license of that provider's intellectual property or have I simply paid for a service provided by an online provider? This question touches on a broad category of transactions colloquially known as "cloud transactions." Because a cloud transaction involves both the temporary access or

---

[84] 1955–1 Cum. Bull. 338.

[85] 1964–1 Cum. Bull. 133 (modifying Rev. Rul. 55–17).

[86] 1971–2 Cum. Bull. 179.

use another person's intellectual property, the arrangement could be analogized to an online streaming "service" and sourced akin to any other service, like paying for a movie ticket at the local movie theater or paying for a performance at the downtown concert hall. Alternatively, the arrangement might be analogized to a temporary nonexclusive license of someone else's intellectual property and analogized to a royalty payment. Depending on the analogy one employs, the relevant sourcing rule would thus be either the sourcing rule applicable to royalties or the sourcing rule applicable to services.

N. Note on Electronic Commerce

Electronic commerce has spread its tentacles widely. In much electronic commerce, the digital environment (whether you call it cyberspace, the Internet, or the Web) is simply a medium for placing orders, an alternative to mail or telephone orders. The tax questions—for example, the source and nature of income, the allocation of income and expense to different persons or factors of production, or the identity and residence of taxpayers—to this point have been viewed as much the same as in other interstate or international commerce. Conventional touchstones of taxation (such as source) have been utilized to determine the essential question of international taxation over such activities. Thus, to proceed under current rules, it is necessary to invoke analogies. If someone buys software as a download on the Internet, for example, what is the place of passage of title? One possibility is to assimilate the transaction to a transfer of a harder version of the software (such as a CD or DVD) that is transferred from a computer at the point of origin to a computer in the place of destination. Even with this elaboration, however, there are still obscure questions. If one accesses an online streaming service or social media platform, where exactly is the service performed? Is it where the hardware is located or where the customer is located who accessed the content? Exactly where is the point of origin among linked computers constituting a network? Is it the location of the customer's electronic device that places the order or accesses the streaming service or is it the place where the hardware is located that sends out a stream of electrons in response to a consumer's click or app? Furthermore, where did "title pass" or where were the "services performed" if the agreement of purchase or service were silent on the matter?

The final regulations addressing the download of computer programs is addressed in Reg. § 1.861–18. The categorization of the download of a program could represent a purchase of the program, it could represent a temporary license of a program, or it could represent a service. The final regulations under Reg. § 1.861–18 work through those distinctions.

A separate analysis is provided for cloud transactions, and those transactions are addressed under Reg. § 1.861–19. A cloud transaction includes a transaction through which a person obtains on-demand network access to computer hardware, digital content or other similar resources.[87] One example of a cloud transaction is cloud computing, which involves on-demand network access to computing resources, such as networks, servers, storage, and software.[88] In addition to cloud computing, a significant number of other cloud transactions unrelated to cloud computing are transacted through on-demand network access to technological resources. Examples of cloud transactions outside of cloud computing include streaming music and video, transactions involving mobile device applications ("apps"), and access to data through remotely hosted software.[89] A cloud transaction is defined to include all of these situations. In general, final regulations issued in 2025 ultimately determined that cloud transactions would be treated as a service.[90]

After generally categorizing a cloud transaction as a service,[91] this created a need to determine where that service was performed in a cloud transaction. Under proposed regulations issued in 2025, gross income from a cloud transaction that is sourced as services income under section 861(a)(3) or section 862(a)(3) will have its source determined under a multi-factor formula comprised of the following three factors: the intangible property factor, the personnel factor, and the tangible property factor.[92] The intangible property factor is the sum of specified research or experimental expenditures (as defined under section 174(b)) incurred during the taxable year that are associated with the cloud transaction as well as royalty and certain amortization expenses incurred during the taxable year to the extent they are for intangible property directly used to provide the cloud transaction.[93] Once the intangible property factor is determined, the portion of this factor that is attributable to sources within the United States must be identified for inclusion in the numerator. Under the proposed rules, the portion of the intangible

---

[87] Reg. § 1.861–19(b).

[88] See Reg. § 1.861–19(d) Example 1 through Example 3. The regulations also set forth three examples that address how the predominant character standard would be applied to find that an arrangement that involved cloud computing and other elements had the predominant character of a cloud transaction. See Reg. § 1.861–19(d) Examples 4 through Example 6

[89] See Reg. § 1.861–19(d) Example 7, Example 8, Example 9, Example 10, and Example 11(ii)((B) and (C). In Reg. § 1.861–19(d) Example 11(ii)(A), the transaction listed in this part was treated as a transfer of a copyrighted article.

[90] Reg. § 1.861–19(c)(1).

[91] Reg. § 1.861–19(c)(1).

[92] Prop. Reg. § 1.861–19(d)(1); Prop. Reg. § 1.861–19(d)(2), (d)(3), and (d)(4), respectively.

[93] Prop. Reg. § 1.861–19(d)(2)(i).

property factor sourced within the United States is determined based on the extent to which certain of the taxpayer's employees perform services in the United States.[94] In applying the personnel factor, the compensation paid to the taxpayer's employees whose primary function is to directly contribute to the provision of the cloud transaction is considered.[95] The tangible property factor is defined as the sum of the depreciation and rental expense for the taxable year for tangible property owned or leased by the taxpayer, to the extent the property is directly used to provide the cloud transaction.[96] Finally, the proposed regulations include an aggregation rule to aggregate substantially similar cloud transactions.[97]

As the above discussion should make clear, the digitalization of the global economy provides companies the opportunity to reach customers in other jurisdictions and compete in those jurisdictions without locating a physical business presence in that other jurisdiction. If those digital sales or services escape taxation in the economies where the customers are located, then the digital-based companies have a potential advantage versus their local brick-and-mortar competitors that sell, license, or provide onsite services from a physical presence located within the relevant jurisdiction. Remote businesses can be substantial competitors to traditional brick-and-mortar businesses without ever stepping foot into a particular jurisdiction. Does that mean that these remote businesses have no income sourced from these jurisdictions if their arrangements are services provided from outside the country or sales of products with title passage from outside the country? The European Union is considering a variation of what is called a "digital tax" that would be assessed on companies that have a significant digital presence in a country's economy even though that digital presence, under general principles, does not rise to the level of a trade or business or permanent establishment as historically understood.[98] In 2020, the OECD issued a report that was endorsed by over 135 countries that addresses the challenges posed to fiscal systems as a result of the digitization of the global economy.[99] These various initiatives seek to expand the taxation of e-commerce and streaming services due to a concern that the digitalization of the global economy is placing a significant fiscal strain on the tax base of developed nations and that new and specialized taxation regimes are needed so that the digital

---

94 Prop. Reg. § 1.861–19(d)(2)(ii).

95 Prop. Reg. § 1.861–19(d)(3)(i).

96 Prop. Reg. § 1.861–19(d)(4)(i).

97 Prop. Reg. § 1.861–19(d)(7).

98 European Commission, Proposal for a Council Directive, COM (2018) 2018/0072 (March 21, 2018).

99 OECD/G20 Base Erosion and Profit Shifting Project: Challenges Arising from Digitilisation—Report on the Pillar One Blueprint (2020).

economy is appropriately taxed in the consumer's jurisdiction and does not result in the creation of homeless income. These proposals have not yet significantly affected the U.S. international tax regime or its existing treaties (as of the beginning of 2026), but that may change. We may soon be approaching an important inflection point with respect to these questions.

Chapter 4

INTERNATIONAL TRANSFER PRICING

A thread running through the base erosion and earnings stripping questions is the problem of "transfer pricing." "Transfer pricing" is a term of art referring to the prices charged, or the process of arriving at them, for goods and services transferred between related persons not dealing at arm's length. The field has its own vocabulary. The price prevailing between related persons is called a "transfer price." Prices charged after bargaining between unrelated persons are commonly called "arm's length" prices. A price charged between related persons that approximates the result of independent bargaining is also called an "arm's length" price.

When unrelated persons deal at arm's length, the prices at which they transact reflect both prevailing competitive conditions and the specific course of bargaining between them. By contrast, among related persons—for example within a group of corporations under common control or beneficial ownership—transfer prices answer to no overriding economic principles, and the prices may reflect a largely unconstrained decision by those controlling the transactors (and ultimately the transaction) to adjust accounts within the group. If a subsidiary corporation engaged in production within a group sells its output to another affiliated subsidiary engaged in marketing, lower or higher prices between the two brother/sister companies will shift more of any overall gain to the marketing entity or leave more of the gain within the producing entity, but the prices will not affect the overall economic gain or loss of the group as a whole. Transfer prices, in short, affect the distribution, not the absolute amount, of gain or loss among related persons. The ultimate economic results achieved by a related group turn only on prices paid or charged to unrelated persons outside the group.

The U.S. tax authorities have always known about transfer pricing. From the earliest days the U.S. tax laws have had provisions designed to strengthen the Treasury's hand in dealing with transactions between related persons. The core provision in the present Code is section 482, containing three sentences. This provision is the first line of defense against inappropriate profit shifting of earnings out of the U.S. tax base, and it is the topic discussed in this chapter 4.

However, before commencing on a discussion of the transfer pricing rules, it is important to note that the U.S. transfer pricing rules are not the only defense to base erosion and profit shifting. Congress has enacted several inbound base protection regimes (discussed in chapter 8) and in the outbound context has enacted several anti-deferral regimes (discussed in chapter 11) to bolster the U.S. tax base against earnings stripping transactions. Nevertheless, to understand those other overlays, it is best to start with the U.S. transfer pricing rules.

As previously mentioned, section 482 contains only three, albeit long, sentences. The section 482 regulations further categorize the myriad of related party transactions into five broad categories: (i) related party lending, (ii) related party licensing or sale of intangible property, (iii) related party rental of tangible property, (iv) related party sale of tangible property, and (v) the provision of services between related parties. Thus, the same earnings stripping categories that we considered in analyzing the source rules in chapter 3 are helpful in terms of organizing our thinking about transfer pricing as well.

A. Transfer Pricing and Taxation

With taxation in the picture, there may be advantages to making an artful adjustment of transfer prices within corporate groups constituting integrated enterprises. If entities within a related group face different tax environments or different rates of taxation within the same tax regime, transfer pricing may bear decisively on tax consequences. For example, one affiliate may be tax-exempt, have recoverable losses, or be exposed to taxation at special rates. In the international setting, the variety of tax environments is greater and hence the possible gains from artificial transfer pricing are enhanced. Departures from arm's length prices between affiliates organized in different countries may shift taxable income to a low-tax environment and shift deductible expense to a high-tax one. Wholly discretionary transfer pricing would let firms adopt in some measure the tax environment of their own choosing. They might establish affiliates in places of benign taxation and channel transactions through them on terms making full use of beneficial features of the indigenous tax regimes. A simple example of such a device is the sale of goods at artificially low prices from one affiliate in a high-tax environment to another affiliate organized in a low-tax or no-tax jurisdiction for resale to unrelated persons at market prices. The effect is diversion of taxable profit to a low-tax environment with concomitant reduction of the profit exposed to higher tax elsewhere.

B. Examples

To make this more specific, consider Diagram #8 that sets forth all of the combined earnings stripping transactions. In this example, assume that a U.S. multinational enterprise has a Parent Corporation incorporated in the United States and is publicly traded on a U.S. stock exchange. Assume that the U.S. publicly traded parent corporation in turn owns two subsidiaries. One subsidiary is a U.S. operating subsidiary called ACME (American Company Making Everything). The U.S. parent corporation also owns a foreign corporation called Foreign Base Co. that is incorporated in a tax haven jurisdiction called "Haven." ACME produces grommets at a cost of $1 each and can sell them to non-U.S. customers for $2. If ACME sells the grommets directly, its gain is fully subject to U.S. tax. Instead, if ACME sells the grommets to its Foreign Base Co. (Haven) for $1.01 and if the Foreign Base Co. (Haven) (which is untaxed, remember) in turn sells the grommets to foreign customers for $2.00, then Foreign Base Co. will realize a profit of $0.99 on each sale. The U.S. multinational enterprise makes a $1 gross profit per grommet, of which 99 cents ($0.99) is not taxed as it conveniently resides in a foreign affiliate, namely Foreign Base Co. (Haven) located in a tax haven jurisdiction.

Diagram #8

Combined Outbound Strategy

Supply Chain Transaction, Interest Stripping Transaction, Royalty Stripping Transaction, Rental Stripping, and Service Stripping Transaction

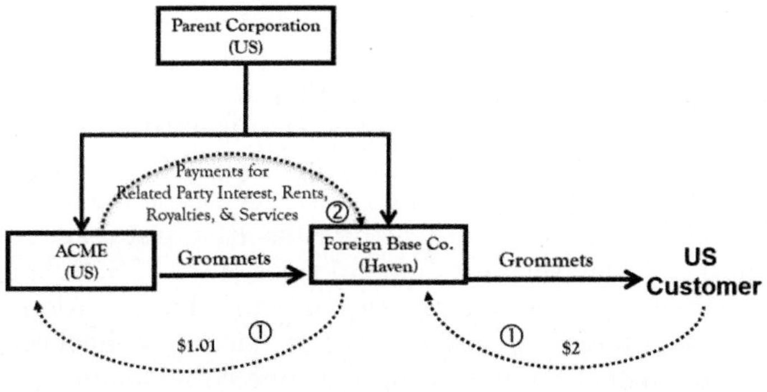

To this basic structure set forth in Diagram #8, additional related party transactions could be added to Diagram #8 albeit those additional transactions are not depicted. Thus, Foreign Base Co. could lend funds to ACME for it to fund its operations, lease equipment to ACME for use in ACME's manufacturing process, license intellectual property to ACME for use in ACME's manufacturing process, and provide technical and administrative services to support ACME's business operations. For each of these additional related party transactions, Foreign Base Co. could in turn charge interest on its loans, rent on its lease of tangible property, royalties on its licensing of intangible property, and finally service fees for the provision of its services to ACME.[1]

If the arm's length wholesale price of grommets is $1.50, ACME's low price to Foreign Base Co. has shifted an additional 49 cents ($0.49) resulting in a total of 99 cents ($0.99) of profit per grommet transferred from ACME to Foreign Base Co. (Haven)—which, significantly, is from a high-tax to a low-tax environment. If ACME had charged the arm's length price in the intra-group sale, it would have had taxable gain of 50 cents ($0.50). Similarly, if ACME makes payments to Foreign Base Co. for interest, rent, royalty, and services that exceed the arm's length standard, then the utilization of those additional related party transactions could shift additional profits from the U.S. tax base to a low-tax environment. As a pure bookkeeping matter, ACME's loss is Foreign Base Co. (Haven)'s gain, but all of the profits remain within affiliates that are entirely owned by the U.S. parent corporation, so the multinational enterprise has not alienated any profits from the group's perspective. However, as a tax matter, Foreign Base Co.'s gain is the U.S. Treasury's loss. If left unabated, Foreign Base Co. (Haven) could then remit its earnings, including the extra 49 cents from the grommet sales and any additional income derived on the related party loan, related party lease, related party license, and the related party service arrangement, back to the U.S. parent corporation as a dividend for which the U.S. parent corporation could claim a 100 percent foreign dividends received deduction under section 245A. Thus, the round-trip would allow excessive profits above the arm's length amount to be earned in Foreign Base Co. (Haven) and then returned to the U.S. parent corporation in the form of a dividend that is entitled to a 100 percent foreign dividends received deduction. This untoward result calls for a response, and this illustration provides a baseline against which to consider the U.S. transfer pricing rules (the first responder in this situation) and then the anti-deferral rules of the U.S. Subpart F regime (a further backstop against this inbound base erosion by U.S. multinational enterprises) and also the restriction of the foreign dividends received deduction to only foreign source dividends.

In inbound transactions, the U.S. Treasury is similarly vulnerable to aggressive transfer pricing. Consider the following variant of the above Diagram #8 in the following Diagram #9. In Diagram #9, Big Pharma PLC is again a Fredonian corporation that makes prescription drugs. Suppose Fredonia is a high-tax country

---

[1] Obviously, these related party transactions will also create foreign base company income issues under Subpart F, and this topic will be separately discussed in chapter 11.

that fully taxes manufacturing income in its country but provides tax incentives and concessions for "headquarters income" earned in Fredonia for income in the form of interest, rents, royalties, and management services charged to affiliates incorporated in other countries. Under these facts, if Big Pharma PLC itself sold its prescription drugs in the United States, its entire gain would attract U.S. or Fredonian tax, or both.[2] Big Pharma PLC, however, has created a distribution subsidiary (called Havenco) in Paradiso. Big Pharma PLC sells the prescription drugs to its Havenco for $1.01. Havenco resells the prescription drugs to its U.S. distribution affiliate, US Pharma, Inc., for $2x (the market price at retail). A profit of $0.99x from each sale has been shifted to Paradiso, the low-tax environment. Subsequent retail sales in the United States for $2.00 generate no further taxable gain. Nearly the entire profit from production and distribution of pharmaceutical drugs has escaped tax in Fredonia and the United States. Moreover, as depicted in the below Diagram #9, Big Pharma PLC lends funds to US Pharma, Inc., leases equipment to US Pharma, Inc. for use in its pharmaceutical business, licenses intellectual property for US Pharma, Inc. to use in its own manufacture of pharmaceutical drugs, and provides technical and administrative services to support US Pharma, Inc.'s business operations. For each of these additional related party transactions, Big Pharma PLC could charge interest on its loans, rent on its lease of tangible property, royalties on its licensing of intangible property, and finally service fees for the provision of its services to US Pharma, Inc. However, because Fredonia does not subject "headquarters income" to full taxation, the shifting of these categories of income to Big Pharma PLC also has shifted profits to a low-tax environment. If Fredonia did not have a concessionary regime for "headquarters income," then it could transfer those arrangements to Havenco to exploit.

---

2 The proportion of each tax would depend on how U.S. sales were structured.

Diagram #9

Combined Strategy

Supply Chain Transaction, Interest Stripping Transaction, Royalty Stripping Transaction, Rental Stripping, and Service Stripping Transaction

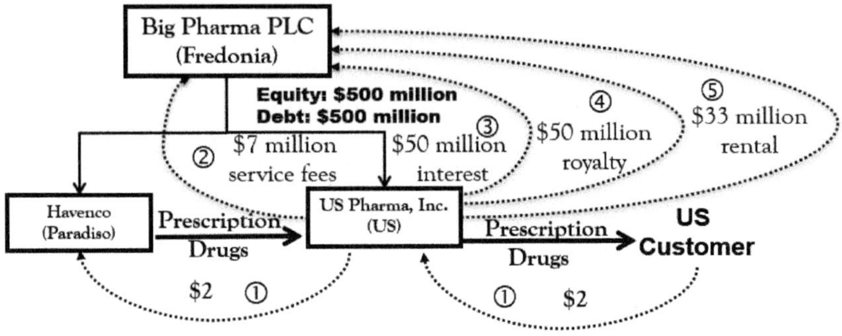

In this inbound pattern, for the U.S. Treasury the transfer price rules are the first point of leverage. For each of the five earnings stripping transactions, the Treasury can force US Pharma, Inc. to compute its taxable income on the basis of an arm's length transfer price. Thus, if the arm's length price for the prescription drugs was $1.50x, then the U.S. Treasury could treat US Pharma, Inc. *as if* US Pharma, Inc. had paid only the market wholesale price of $1.50x per prescription drug. Reining in the other half of the gain on the prescription drug trading pattern is a tax problem for Fredonia. Similarly, if the amount that Big Pharma PLC charged US Pharma, Inc. for interest, rents, royalties, and services exceeded an arm's length amount, then the U.S. Treasury could treat US Pharma, Inc. as if it had only paid an arm's length amount under those arrangements.

These base erosion examples are easy to fathom, even obvious, and so the U.S. tax laws from the very beginning had provisions designed to strengthen the Treasury's hand in dealing with artificially priced transactions between related persons. Yet, notwithstanding the longstanding authority to subject related party transactions to the arm's length standard, concern over "base erosion and profit shifting" remains a systemic concern.[3]

C. Section 482

As previously mentioned, the core provision that addresses transfer pricing among related parties is section 482, which

---

[3] See STAFF OF JOINT COMM. ON TAXATION, PRESENT LAW AND BACKGROUND RELATED TO POSSIBLE INCOME SHIFTING AND TRANSFER PRICING, 111th Cong. (Comm. Print 2010), https://www.jct.gov/publications.html?func=startdown&id=3692. See also U.S. Treas. Dept, REPORT TO THE CONGRESS ON EARNINGS STRIPPING, TRANSFER PRICING AND U.S. INCOME TAX TREATIES (2007).

empowers the IRS to reallocate income and expense in transactions among related persons so as to reflect income clearly. Section 482 reads as follows:

> In any case of two or more organizations, trades, or businesses (whether or not incorporated, whether or not organized in the United States, and whether or not affiliated) owned or controlled directly or indirectly by the same interests, the Secretary may distribute, apportion, or allocate gross income, deductions, credits, or allowances between or among such organizations, trades, or businesses, if he determines that such distribution, apportionment, or allocation is necessary in order to prevent evasion of taxes or clearly to reflect the income of any of such organizations, trades, or businesses. In the case of any transfer (or license) of intangible property (within the meaning of section 367(d)(4)), the income with respect to such transfer or license shall be commensurate with the income attributable to the intangible. For purposes of this section, the Secretary shall require the valuation of transfers of intangible property (including intangible property transferred with other property or services) on an aggregate basis or the valuation of such a transfer on the basis of the realistic alternatives to such a transfer, if the Secretary determines that such basis is the most reliable means of valuation of such transfers.

Pursuant to this three sentence mandate, the Treasury has issued extensive regulations. The regulations cover nearly the full range of transactions between related persons and are as discursively articulated as section 482 itself is laconic.

Section 482 is aimed at the unilateral advantage that related taxpayers could otherwise obtain through unchecked transfer prices. Its goal, broadly stated, is to recast transactions among affiliates on arm's length terms and adjust U.S. taxation accordingly. On its face, section 482 is not prescriptive. It does not literally obligate taxpayers to any particular course of action. Rather, section 482 empowers the Commissioner to reallocate income and expense in transactions among related persons. In practical effect, however, section 482 is a formidable weapon, among other reasons, because it is backed up by an array of penalties that can be imposed on taxpayers who have strayed from the virtuous path in transfer pricing.

Section 482 prescribes allocation of income and expense between related persons to prevent tax avoidance and "clearly to reflect" their income. Across nearly the full range of transactions, the regulations under section 482 identify clear reflection of income with arm's length pricing between unrelated persons. That is, transactions between related persons on terms that differ substantially from similar transactions at arm's length between unrelated persons are subject to immediate revision by the IRS. Conversely, when related transactors can point to identical, or comparable, arm's length transactions between unrelated persons, they are nearly immune from molestation under section 482.

D. The Regulations Under Section 482

Despite the difficulty, the regulations under section 482 embrace arm's length pricing as the test of clear reflection of income[4] and unflinchingly hold up the banner of arm's length pricing. "In determining the true taxable income of a controlled taxpayer, the standard to be applied in every case is that of a taxpayer dealing at arm's length with an uncontrolled taxpayer."[5] The regulations press hard to come up with arm's length touchstones for transactions among commonly controlled persons. To this end, they establish transfer prices based on a hierarchy of identity, similarity, or even mere analogy with arm's length transactions before retreating to arbitrary formulas and safe harbors.

E. Related Persons

Section 482 and its regulations do not assert a precise test of what makes taxpayers "related" (or, as the regulations put it, "controlled taxpayers"). A "controlled taxpayer means any one of two or more taxpayers owned or controlled directly or indirectly by the same interests and includes the taxpayer that owns or controls the other taxpayers."[6] Remaining above the arithmetic fray, the regulations further provide, "It is the reality of the control that is decisive, not its form or the mode of its exercise. A presumption of control arises if income or deductions have been arbitrarily shifted."[7] A rule of thumb is that common beneficial ownership or voting control of 50 percent or more may set the stage for an allocation under section 482. Usually, the degree of common ownership of related persons reined in by section 482 is higher because transacting persons with substantial, nonoverlapping, unrelated owners would

---

[4] Reg. § 1.482–1(a)(2) ("The purpose of section 482 is to ensure that taxpayers clearly reflect income attributable to controlled transactions, and to prevent the avoidance of taxes with respect to such transactions. Section 482 places a controlled taxpayer on a tax parity with an uncontrolled taxpayer by determining the true taxable income of the controlled taxpayer.").

[5] Reg. § 1.482–1(b)(1).

[6] Reg. § 1.482–1(i)(5).

[7] Reg. § 1.482–1(i)(4).

find it difficult to practice artificial transfer prices without protest from the outside owners.[8]

F. Arm's Length Results

The arm's length standard is initially defined in the regulations with reference to the results of the same transactions between unrelated persons. "A controlled transaction meets the arm's length standard if the results of that transaction are consistent with the results that would have been realized if uncontrolled taxpayers had engaged in the same transaction under the same circumstances."[9] Notably, the arm's length standard is cast here in terms of arm's length *results,* not merely prices (as in earlier regulations). A "result" can easily encompass the profit earned in arm's length transactions as well as the prices charged.

This basic statement in the regulations (looking to the "same transaction" and the "same circumstances") implies virtual identity between the controlled and uncontrolled transaction. On this score, however, the regulations immediately concede that "because identical transactions can rarely be located, whether a transaction produces an arm's length result generally will be determined by reference to the results of *comparable* transactions under *comparable* circumstances."[10] The magic word here is "comparable."

G. Methods: The "Best" Method

In pursuit of arm's length prices in "comparable" transactions, the regulations expound several transfer pricing "methods" applicable to different transactions such as sales of tangible and intangible property, services, loans, licensing of intangible property, and rentals of tangible property.[11] There is no fixed hierarchy among the enumerated methods, but the regulations require the use of the "best" method, or more precisely "the method that, under the facts and circumstances, provides the most reliable measure of an arm's length result."[12]

The two principal factors in determining the best method are "the degree of comparability between the controlled transaction (or

---

[8] If enterprise ***X*** shifts income to enterprise ***Y***, and only half of each enterprise is owned by the same interests, the outside owner of ***X*** (who is losing equity for someone else's tax advantage at most) is likely to speak up forcefully.

[9] Reg. § 1.482–1(b)(1).

[10] Id. (Emphasis added.)

[11] Reg. §§ 1.482–2 through 1.482–6.

[12] Reg. § 1.482–1(c)(1).

taxpayer) and any uncontrolled comparables, and the quality of the data and assumptions used in the analysis."[13]

H. Comparability

It follows that the operative standard of the regulations as a practical matter, is *comparability*. Comparability depends on "all factors that could affect prices or profits in arm's length dealings,"[14] and within comparability, there are gradations. Roughly, the regulations seek out "exact" comparable transactions before settling for "inexact" comparable transactions.

The factors underlying comparability are 1) the economic functions carried on by the taxpayers, 2) the contracts between them, 3) the risks they incur, 4) prevailing economic conditions, and 5) the nature of the property or services over which they transact.[15] Transactions need not be identical to be comparable, but the uncontrolled transaction must provide a "reliable measure" of an arm's length result.[16] Adjustments must be made to account for differences in the results of transactions that also have significant underlying comparability.[17] The greater the number of adjustments, however, the less reliable the conclusion of comparability.[18]

Transfer pricing methods, and the standard of comparability, are expounded in the regulations by setting forth a framework for analyzing specific categories of related party transactions, and so the following discussion is organized in terms of the specific transaction types identified in the regulations.

I. Interest Charged Between Related Persons

The regulations make clear that when a related party advances or lends funds to another related party, the lender must be compensated by the payment of an arm's length amount of interest. Otherwise, the IRS is authorized to make appropriate allocations to reflect an arm's length charge.[19] That said, the regulations specify that interest is not required to be charged for certain intercompany trade receivables from the sale of goods in the normal course of business. Under a safe harbor provision, a trade receivable meets this trade receivable exception if it is paid by the first day of the third month following the month of sale (generally a time period of between

---

13 Reg. § 1.482–1(c)(2).

14 Reg. § 1.482–1(d)(1).

15 Id.

16 Reg. § 1.482–1(d)(2).

17 Id.

18 Id.

19 Reg. § 1.482–2(a)(1)(i).

90 to 120 days) for sales to a related party that is located in the United States[20] and by the first day of the fourth month following the month of sale (generally a time period between 120 days and 150 days) for sales to a related party that is located outside the United States.[21] Moreover, a longer period may apply if the selling entity provides longer payment terms for unrelated customers without charging interest.[22] However, the regulations then state that in no event will an interest-free period for the sale of goods to a foreign person exceed 183 days under these exceptions.[23]

In determining an arm's length rate of interest, the regulations require that an arm's length rate be charged by looking at such factors as the principal amount of the funding, the duration of the loan, the security involved, the credit standing of the borrower, and the interest rate prevailing at the situs of the lender or creditor, in order to evaluate the comparability of the related party loan to unrelated party loans made in the same timeframe and under similar terms and conditions.[24] However, the regulations then specify a safe harbor interest rate, providing that an arm's length rate would be considered to have been charged if the interest charge is not less than 100 percent and not more than 130 percent of the interest rate published on a monthly basis by the Internal Revenue Service and known as the "applicable federal rate."[25] Thus, in the base interest stripping transaction posited in Diagram #8 and Diagram #9, the taxpayer has flexibility either to charge interest under the "applicable federal rate" safe harbor or to utilize an interest rate comparable to that of unrelated party lending arrangements made in the same period and under the same terms and conditions.

J. Services Between Related Persons

Consistent with other related party transactions, the regulations state that the provision of services for a related party must be done for an arm's length price. If it is not, the IRS is authorized to make an allocation to reflect an arm's length charge. The regulations then set forth the following methods for determining an arm's length price for related party services: (i) the cost-only services method, (ii) the comparable uncontrolled services method, (iii) the gross services margin method, (iv) the cost plus services method, (v) the comparable profits method, (v) the profit split

---

20 Reg. § 1.482–2(a)(1)(iii)(B).

21 Reg. § 1.482–2(a)(1)(iii)(C).

22 Reg. § 1.482–2(a)(1)(iii)(D).

23 Reg. § 1.482–2(a)(1)(iii)(E).

24 Reg. § 1.482–2(a)(2)(i).

25 Reg. § 1.482–2(a)(2)(iii)(B).

method, and (vii) an unspecified method.[26] The regulations then say that the taxpayer must determine the arm's length rate using the best method in the particular facts and circumstances.[27]

A detailed discussion of each of these methods is likely beyond the scope of what is needed at this point, but a further comment is in order about the cost-only method. This method acts as a safe harbor, and it allows a related party simply to recover costs with no mark-up above actual cost.[28] The cost-only method can be used only for certain internal administrative services and low-margin services that the regulations call "specified services." These so-called specified services include only those services that do not contribute significantly to the success or failure of the business and where the median comparable mark-up for such services does not exceed seven percent.[29] The regulations explicitly indicate that the following services contribute significantly and thus are ineligible for the cost-only method: (i) manufacturing-related services, (ii) production-related services, (iii) services directly related to the extraction, exploration, and processing of natural resources, (iv) construction-related services, (v) sales and distribution services, (vi) research and development services, (vii) engineering or scientific services, (viii) financial services, and (ix) insurance or reinsurance services.[30] In contrast to these excluded services, purely internal back-office and ancillary services are eligible for this cost-only method (like payroll functions, internal accounting services, etc.). Thus, this cost-only method achieves an administrative convenience goal of not requiring taxpayers to include a mark-up on low-margin administrative services that are not a core part of the business function, but taxpayers are entitled to use a cost plus method and not the cost-only method if they choose to do so. Thus, if the related party service stripping transaction posited in Diagram #8 and Diagram #9 involved a specified covered service or a low-margin service, then the taxpayer has flexibility whether or not to charge a mark-up, at least from a U.S. tax perspective. If the service stripping transaction involves services that fall outside of the "specified services" category because they do in fact contribute significantly to the success of the business, then one of the other transfer pricing methods would be the best method.

---

26 Reg. § 1.482–9(a).

27 Reg. § 1.482–9(a); Reg. § 1.482–1(e).

28 Reg. § 1.482–9(b)(1).

29 Reg. § 1.482–9(b)(2), (3) and (5).

30 Reg. § 1.482–9(b)(4).

K. Rental of Tangible Property

Again, consistent with other related party transactions, the leasing of tangible property (as posited in Diagrams #8 and #9) is required to be done on an arm's length basis, or the IRS is authorized to make appropriate allocations to reflect an arm's length charge.[31] In determining an arm's length rental rate, all the facts and circumstances are to be considered, including the period and location of the use, the owner's investment in the property or rent paid for the property, expenses of maintaining the property, the type of property involved, its condition, and all other relevant facts in order to determine the comparability of the related party transaction to independent transactions that are used as a benchmark. Thus, in the rental stripping transaction posited in Diagrams #8 and #9, the use of that transaction must comply with the arm's length standard set forth in these regulations.

L. Transfer of Tangible Property Between Related Persons

The sale of tangible property among related parties must also be done on an arm's length basis, and the regulations specify that the arm's length price must be determined based upon the "best method" from the following six methods.

1. Comparable Uncontrolled Price Method

As the regulations put it, "The comparable uncontrolled price method evaluates whether the amount charged in a controlled transaction is arm's length by reference to the amount charged in a comparable uncontrolled transaction."[32] Even though there is no formal hierarchy of methods, the regulations do take on a special glow when expounding the comparable uncontrolled price method as "the most direct and reliable measure of an arm's length price for the controlled transaction" if there are no differences or only minor differences between the controlled transaction under scrutiny and a comparable uncontrolled transaction.[33] However, in actual practice, many refer to the effort to find a comparable uncontrolled price as the search for the "elusive comparable" that is akin to a search for the Holy Grail. Except for sales of publicly traded commodity-type goods, most transactions involving goods, services, or assets likely contain some distinguishing feature that make them not exactly comparable to other goods or services. Goods may embody unique designs and other proprietary elements. Even the value of laundry

---

[31] See Reg. § 1.482–2(c)(1).

[32] Reg. § 1.482–3(b)(1).

[33] Reg. § 1.482–3(b)(2)(ii)(A).

detergent may be tied to a brand name. It is hard to compare the terms of a transfer of a Rolls-Royce and a Ferrari on the same footing. First, you would have to find transfers of generic "brand X" luxury cars, then strip away the differentiated features of Royces and Ferraris. The first step is impossible because there is no generic luxury automobile market; the second leaves open much room for argument. Thus, except for the most basic of fungible commodity sales, the comparable uncontrolled price method's applicability is uncertain.

2. The Resale Price Method

The resale price method approaches a sale between related persons from the perspective of a buyer who will resell the goods to an unrelated person. "The resale price method evaluates whether the amount charged in a controlled transaction is arm's length by reference to the gross profit margin realized in comparable uncontrolled transactions."[34] The "arm's length" transfer price under the resale price method is determined "by subtracting the appropriate gross profit from the applicable resale price for the property involved in the controlled transaction under review."[35] The "appropriate gross profit" is then computed by multiplying the applicable resale price by the gross profit margin (expressed as a percentage of total revenue derived from sales) earned in comparable uncontrolled transactions.[36]

3. Cost Plus Method

The "cost plus" method is concerned with properly compensating the *seller's* contribution to a sale of goods between related persons. "The cost plus method evaluates whether the amount charged in a controlled transaction is arm's length by reference to the gross profit markup realized in comparable uncontrolled transactions. The cost plus method is ordinarily used in cases involving the manufacture, assembly, or other production of goods that are sold to related parties."[37] Under this method, the arm's length price is the seller's cost of the property sold to a related person, increased by an appropriate markup, reflecting the value of the seller's role as producer. "The cost plus method measures an arm's length price by adding the appropriate gross profit to the controlled taxpayer's costs of producing the property involved in the controlled transaction."[38]

---

34 Reg. § 1.482–3(c)(1).

35 Reg. § 1.482–3(c)(2)(i). The "applicable resale price" is the price charged to unrelated persons after sales within a group. Reg. § 1.482–3(c)(2)(ii).

36 Reg. § 1.482–3(c)(2)(iii).

37 See Reg. § 1.482–3(d)(1).

38 See Reg. § 1.482–3(d)(2)(i).

The "appropriate gross profit" is "computed by multiplying the controlled taxpayer's cost of producing the transferred property by the gross profit markup, expressed as a percentage of cost, earned in comparable uncontrolled transactions."[39] Whenever possible, the gross profit markup should be derived from comparable uncontrolled sales made by the taxpayer involved in the controlled sale. In the absence of such sales, an appropriate gross profit markup may be derived from comparable uncontrolled sales of other producers.[40]

4. Comparable Profits Method

The comparable profits method evaluates whether the amount charged in a controlled transaction is arm's length based on objective measures of profitability (profit level indicators) derived from uncontrolled taxpayers that engage in similar business activities under similar circumstances.[41] Under the comparable profits method, the determination of an arm's length result is based on the amount of operating profit that the tested party would have earned on related party transactions.[42] The tested party's reported operating profit is compared to the comparable operating profits of uncontrolled comparables to determine whether it represents an arm's length result. Profit level indicators that may provide a reliable basis for comparing operating profits of the tested party with uncontrolled comparables include: (i) a specific rate of return on capital employed, (ii) ratio of operating profit to sales, (iii) ratio of gross profit to operating expenses, or (iv) some other method.[43]

5. Profit Split and Residual Profit Split Methods

The profit split method seeks to allocate combined operating profits among related parties by reference to the relative value of each related party's functional contribution to the combined operating profit.[44] To apply a profit split method, the relative value of each controlled taxpayer's contribution must be determined, and the regulations look to the (i) relative functions performed, (ii) risks assumed, and (iii) resources employed by each related party in the relevant business activity.[45] After this functional analysis is performed for each entity, a comparable profit split seeks to allocate the operating profits so that each related party obtains an operating profit margin that corresponds to what similarly situated

---

39 See Reg. § 1.482–3(d)(2)(ii).

40 See Reg. § 1.482–3(d)(3)(ii)(A).

41 See Reg. § 1.482–5(a).

42 See Reg. § 1.482–5(b)(1).

43 See Reg. § 1.482–5(b)(4).

44 See Reg. § 1.482–6(a).

45 See Reg. § 1.482–6(b).

uncontrolled taxpayer's would obtain for performing similar functions and activities.[46] A comparable profit split method is thus similar to the comparable profits method with one very important difference: the comparable profit method employed in Reg. § 1.482–3 tests only one party's comparable profits, whereas the profit split method employed in Reg. § 1.482–5 requires both related parties to be tested to ensure that the profit allocation for both parties does not exceed an arm's length amount.[47]

A variation to the profit split method is the residual profit split method.[48] Under the residual profit split method, the combined operating profit or loss from the relevant business activity is allocated between the controlled taxpayers following a two-step process. First, the operating income is allocated to each party to provide a market return for its routine contributions to the relevant business activity.[49] Routine contributions are contributions of the same or a similar kind to those made by uncontrolled taxpayers involved in similar business activities for which it is possible to identify market returns. "Non-routine contributions," for which it is not possible to identify market returns, are not reflected in the profit or loss attributable to the controlled taxpayer's routine contributions. Such non-routine contributions will remain after this first step and thus represent unallocated "residual profit." Therefore, in the second step, the residual profit is then divided among the related taxpayers based upon the relative value of the non-routine contributions of each related party towards the generation or creation of those residual profits.[50]

6. Other Methods

In addition to the specified methods discussed above, another method of transfer pricing may be used for sales of goods when, in the circumstances of a particular case, it provides the most reliable measure of an arm's length price under the best method principle.[51] Such an "unspecified" method should, however, "take into account the general principle that uncontrolled taxpayers evaluate the terms of a transaction by considering the realistic alternatives to that transaction, and only enter into a particular transaction if none of

---

[46] See Reg. § 1.482–6(c).

[47] Compare Reg. § 1.482–5(b)(2) (comparable profits method seeks to test only the more reliable party against a benchmark of profit level indicators) with Reg. § 1.482–6(b)(1) (profit split tests both related party's profit levels against a benchmark of profit level indicators to ensure that neither related party has an unjustified return).

[48] See Reg. § 1.482–6(c)(3).

[49] See Reg. § 1.482–6(c)(3)(i)(A).

[50] See Reg. § 1.482–6(c)(3)(i)(B).

[51] See Reg. § 1.482–3(e).

the alternatives is preferable to it."[52] Any method relying solely on "internal" data (rather than data from comparable uncontrolled transactions) is suspect under this provision although not absolutely proscribed.[53] An occasion for such an "unspecified" method is a sale of goods closely associated with "embedded" intangible property in which the buyer acquires no separate rights.[54]

M. Transfers of Intangible Property

1. The "Commensurate with Income" Clause

As by now a familiar refrain, the licensing or sale of intangible property between related parties is also required to be done on an arm's length basis, or the IRS is authorized to make appropriate allocations to reflect an arm's length charge.[55] In the context of applying the arm's length standard to the transfer of an intangible asset, the regulations set forth the following four methods: (i) the comparable uncontrolled transaction method, (ii) the comparable profits method, (iii) the profit split method, and (iv) an unspecified method. The regulations give no hierarchy but again admonish that the taxpayer must use the "best method."[56] Because intangibles are by their very nature unique, it is difficult (perhaps illusory) to establish reliably that a comparable uncontrolled transaction dealing with a different intangible is sufficiently similar to the related party intangible. The profits and market opportunities are often different with different intangibles, so even though the use of the comparable uncontrolled transaction is theoretically available as a method, it is unlikely to be the controlling method in practice. Thus, the profit split method or the comparable profits method are the more commonly used methods in situations where there is a transfer or license of intangible property.

An additional, unique element in transfer pricing of intangible property arises from the second sentence of section 482. "In the case of any transfer (or license) of intangible property. . . the income with respect to such transfer or license shall be commensurate with the income attributable to the intangible." This sparely phrased provision is shot through with difficulty. Known as the "commensurate with income" (or "superroyalty") provision, this sentence, greatly simplified, allows for continuing annual adjustments by the IRS *after* transfers of intangible property to make the results "commensurate with income." It does not command the

---

[52] See id.

[53] See id.

[54] See Reg. § 1.482–3(f).

[55] See Reg. § 1.482–4(a).

[56] See Reg. § 1.482–4(a); Reg. § 1.482–1(e).

use of an arm's length price, gauged prospectively, in transfers of intangible property. Rather, it considers the results of such transfers in retrospect and requires the pricing arrangements to reflect the demonstrated income-producing power of the intangible property. If necessary, the terms may be changed periodically in light of the subsequent economic results that actually occur.

In its operation, the "commensurate with income" provision applies after the fact, measuring income attributable to a transfer of intangible property and imputing the income back to the transferor as compensation for the transfer. The reason for this backward-looking standard is the Treasury's concern that related persons could easily undervalue transferred intangible property with an uncertain future and claim later that the transferee was just lucky. The superroyalty provision does not so much assert a strict arm's length standard but rather keeps the terms of a transfer open to revision according to subsequent results. It is as though a contingent participation were built into every transfer of intangible property between related persons, whether expressly stated or not.

The regulations provide in a broad range of situations for annual adjustment of the consideration charged for intangible property between related persons to ensure that it is commensurate with the income attributable to the property.[57] There are, however, a number of exceptions. Most important, no periodic adjustments are made if the same intangible asset was transferred to an uncontrolled taxpayer on the same terms and under substantially the same circumstances as those of the controlled transaction.[58] In other words, a taxpayer that can point to a fully comparable transfer of the same intangible property to an unrelated person at arm's length is effectively inoculated against an unhappy encounter with the superroyalty provision. However, as previously stated, because intangibles are by their very nature often unique, a comparable uncontrolled transaction that is sufficiently similar is unlikely to be found. Thus, if an actual royalty or, by reason of section 367(d)'s application, a superroyalty is deemed to apply to the fact pattern posited in the royalty stripping transaction set forth in Diagrams #8 and #9, then the taxpayer generally must use one of the other transfer pricing methods that apply to the transfer of intangibles and must also meet the commensurate with income standard.

2. Qualified Cost Sharing Arrangements

After studying the "commensurate with income" provision as set forth in Reg. § 1.482–4(f)(2) and after considering the import of the

57 Reg. § 1.482–4(f)(2)(i).

58 Reg. § 1.482–4(f)(2)(ii)(A).

IRS's power to use hindsight to its advantage in a situation where an intangible is licensed among related parties, one might have the impression that the deck is heavily stacked in favor of the government when it comes to the transfer of intangible property among related parties. However, that assessment would be premature, particularly in the case of a multinational enterprise that engages in ongoing development of its next generation of intangibles. In the context of a multinational enterprise that has ongoing development of intangibles, the IRS has allowed taxpayers the ability to assign the development rights of those intangibles to an internal funding party that bears the cost of the development under a qualified cost sharing agreement.[59]

The ability to utilize a qualified cost sharing arrangement that complies with Reg. § 1.482–7(b) to assign ownership of a developed intangible to an offshore risk-taking affiliate provides a way to shift the residual profits associated with that newly developed intangible property to an offshore affiliate and away from the U.S. affiliate that actually developed the intangible asset. Essentially, qualified cost sharing arrangements allow two or more controlled parties to share the costs and risks of a research and development project for an agreed upon scope in exchange for a specified interest in the results of that project. As the participants jointly own the developed technology, there is typically no royalty obligation for the use of the developed intangible by any participant. Consideration for use of intangibles developed in a qualified cost sharing arrangement is paid in advance during the course of development as opposed to after the development (typically as royalties) where the intangibles are developed by another person. In effect, a qualified cost sharing agreement involves multiple developers.

The IRS has struggled with its cost sharing regulations in defense of the U.S. tax base since the mid-1960s.[60] In pre-1986 cases, courts typically sided with taxpayers. While the 1986 Act did not specifically address cost sharing agreements, the legislative history indicates that the commensurate with income provisions of section 482 were not intended to prevent appropriate use of such arrangements. The regulatory experience of the succeeding decades has been that the cost sharing regulations have become more and more complicated.[61]

---

59 Reg. § 1.482–7(b).

60 Administrative guidance was initially provided in the 1966 proposed regulations. Prop. Reg. § 1.482–2(d)(4)(i), 31 FED. REG. 10,394, 10,398 (1966). When the section 482 regulations were finalized in 1968, the provisions applicable to cost sharing were considerably reduced and simplified, with the content compressed from several pages to only one paragraph. T.D. 6952, 1968–1 Cum. Bull. 218.

61 A key beginning point for this evolution was the issuance of Notice 88–123, 1988–2 Cum. Bull. 458. For an analysis of this evolution since 1988, see Bret Wells &

Where a cost sharing arrangement is put into place among parties that both contribute non-routine intangibles and where their cost shares (i.e., their expected future benefits) are equivalent to their relative contribution of the non-routine functions creating the developed intangible, then the results achieved under the cost sharing regulations should mirror the results provided by a transfer pricing method conducted within the framework of Reg. § 1.482–6. Thus, in such a fact pattern, the cost sharing arrangement formalizes an arrangement that comports with the results achieved under the profit-split approaches. On the other hand, when a cost sharing arrangement allows a multinational enterprise to choose a risk-taker entrepreneurial affiliate to fund the intangible development for an amount in excess of its functional contribution towards the creation of that developed intangible, then the cost sharing regulations allow the ownership of the intangible and its residual profits to be stripped away from the functions that created those residual profits and to be given to the offshore "risk-taker."[62]

It is helpful, perhaps, to consider some real-life examples in order to understand the import of what has just been discussed. In Congressional hearings relating to the base erosion and profit shifting phenomenon, cost sharing arrangements have played a prominent role.[63] If public statements are to be believed, in the case of Apple, Inc.,[64] its tax haven affiliate funded $5 billion of Apple's research and development expenditures and in return became the owner of Apple's developed intangibles in the European markets and was allocated $79 billion of income (or $74 billion in residual profits net of the $5 billion of research expenditures). From a normative perspective, Apple's tax haven subsidiary should not be entitled to share in the residual profits unless it met the functional standard. As a general rule, risk-taking is not a "function" that creates residual profits. Instead, the residual profits should be allocated to the

---

Cym Lowell, *Tax Base Erosion: Reformation of Section 482's Arm's Length Standard,* 15 FLORIDA TAX REV. 737 (2014).

[62] *Compare* Reg. § 1482–6(a), *with* Reg. § 1.482–7(b)(1)(i), *and* (e)(1).

[63] See *Offshore Profit Shifting Hearing (Apple, Inc.)*: Hearing Before the Permanent Subcomm. on Investigations of the S. Comm. on Homeland Sec. & Governmental Affairs, 112th Cong. 6 (2013), Staff Memorandum to the Members of the Senate Permanent Subcommittee on Investigations (May 21, 2013).

[64] The author has no personal knowledge of the Apple tax situation and, as a general rule, would not comment on a particular taxpayer's situation in my writings outside the context of decided cases. However, Apple has explicitly invited the public to consider its tax structure as part of the ongoing comprehensive tax reform debate. See *Offshore Profit Shifting Hearing (Apple, Inc.)* (statement of Tim Cook, Chief Executive Office of Apple, Inc.). Mr. Cook stated that Apple welcomes an objective evaluation of the U.S. corporate tax system, that Apple provided its information as a means to provide information "critical to any objective evaluation of its tax practices," and that Apple supports comprehensive U.S. corporate tax reform "even though it would result in Apple paying more U.S. corporate tax." Id.

affiliate whose functions actually contributed to the creation of the valuable intangible. If all functions that contributed to the creation of the developed intangible were located in Silicon Valley in the United States, then all of Apple's residual profits should be allocated to the United States. If, however, a significant non-routine European marketing intangible existed in the Apple fact pattern, and that European marketing intangible contributed towards the generation of the combined residual profits, then the residual profits should be split based on the relative contribution of the offshore marketing intangible's contribution versus the contribution of the other intangibles that contributed to Apple's combined residual profits. However, in any case, the residual profits would only be allocated to those entities whose activities contributed to the development of the intangible that generated the residual profits. Thus, under a residual profits split methodology, residual profits would not be shared with Apple's Irish risk-taking affiliate absent a substantive functional contribution (which was not readily apparent from the publicly-disclosed documents).[65] Instead, that Irish risk-taking affiliate would be provided a routine profit for its routine risk capital function. Yet, in contrast to a result that would be afforded under the commensurate with income standard, the development of intangible property under a qualified cost sharing agreement is not subject to the commensurate with income standard.[66]

A critical framing question lies at the heart of cost sharing arrangements when pre-existing platform intangibles are contributed into these arrangements: what portion of future revenue is attributable to the pre-existing platform intangible and what portion of the future revenue is attributable to the ongoing operating contributions made by the co-participants of the cost sharing arrangement? The need to make this bifurcation is plain enough: the future revenue attributable to the preexisting platform intangible should be separately valued so that the owner of the platform intangible is compensated appropriately whereas the revenue attributable to the ongoing operating contributions should be shared among the co-participants based upon their cost shares in those ongoing operating contributions.

Reg. § 1.482–7(g) provides guidance on how to segregate future revenue into different income streams so that the platform intangible developed prior to the cost sharing arrangement can be properly valued. Again, the regulations require differentiation of future

---

[65] See *Offshore Profit Shifting Hearing (Apple, Inc.)*: Hearing Before the Permanent Subcomm. on Investigations of the S. Comm. on Homeland Sec. & Governmental Affairs, 112th Cong. 6 (2013), Staff Memorandum to the Members of the Senate Permanent Subcommittee on Investigations (May 21, 2013).

[66] Reg. § 1.482–7A(a)(2) and (3).

revenue between the revenue attributable to a platform intangible and the revenue attributable to ongoing operating contributions if one is to appropriately apply the best method for valuing platform intangibles contributed into a cost-sharing arrangement.[67] In making this required differentiation, the final cost-sharing regulations envision that the following counter-factual question should be posited and analyzed: what financial benefits were available to the owner of the platform intangible in an alternative scenario where the owner of the platform intangible had chosen to license its platform intangible in lieu of entering into the cost sharing arrangement? The financial results that could have been obtained under the licensing alternative segregates the portion of the future revenue attributable to the pre-existing platform intangible.[68] Value captured by the cost sharing arrangement in excess of what could have been captured under the licensing alternative represents the portion of the revenue that should be attributed to the ongoing operating contributions made by the co-participants in accordance with their relative cost shares. Once future revenue is segregated in this fashion, the regulations require the use of an appropriate discount rate to determine the present value of the future revenue associated with the platform intangible and the present value of the revenue stream associated with the ongoing operating contributions.[69] The regulations also provide that a difference in the risk profile of the various alternatives (cost sharing alternative versus a licensing alternative) should be considered when determining the discount rates utilized to value the payment forms under the cost sharing arrangement and the licensing alternative.[70]

The manner in which different income streams are separately identified for purposes of valuing a pre-existing platform intangible was a contested issue in *Facebook v. Commissioner*.[71] In the *Facebook* case, Facebook USA and Facebook Ireland entered into a cost sharing arrangement on September 15, 2010.[72] Under the cost sharing arrangement, Facebook Ireland received the right to share in the projected future profits from all the resources, capabilities, and rights that Facebook USA contributed into the cost sharing arrangement, including profits attributable to the complementarities between Facebook's income-producing intangibles.[73] The parties

---

[67] Reg. § 1.482–7(g)(2).

[68] Reg. § 1.482–7(g)(4)(vi)(F)(1).

[69] Reg. § 1.482–7(g)(4)(vi)(F)(2).

[70] Reg. § 1.482–7(g)(4)(vi)(F)(1); Preamble, T.D. 9569, 76 FED. REG. 80,249 (Dec. 23, 2011).

[71] Facebook v. Commissioner, 164 T.C. No. 9 at 87–100 (2025).

[72] Facebook v. Commissioner, 164 T.C. No. 9 at 9 (2025).

[73] Facebook v. Commissioner, 164 T.C. No. 9 at 9 (2025).

agreed that Facebook USA had developed significant platform intangibles that pre-dated the cost sharing arrangement. Yet, in the end, the Tax Court held that significant future revenue derived from Facebook's customer user data related to ongoing operating intangibles that should be shared by the co-participants of the cost sharing arrangement and were not assignable to the pre-existing Facebook social network platform that pre-dated the cost sharing arrangement or its valuation. Thus, even when the Tax Court determined that only one party has a platform intangible, the outcome in litigation has been that significant profit shifting can be achieved to migrate profits away from the owner-developer of a already existing platform intangible through cost sharing arrangements,

Similar base erosion techniques can be achieved through the use of cost sharing arrangements utilized by non-U.S. multinational enterprises doing business in the United States in the inbound context. In this analysis, the tax planning purported to have been employed by Nestlé (a non-U.S. multinational enterprise) provides the same fundamental base erosion and profit shifting problem as the Apple and Facebook fact patterns. Thus, Nestlé's fact pattern represents an appropriate illustrative case to consider.

In *Westreco, Inc. v. Commissioner*,[74] Nestlé's U.S. affiliate (Westreco) conducted U.S.-based research that created highly valuable non-routine intangibles. The U.S. affiliate was allocated a routine service profit for its research activities, since it was designated as a "contract researcher" for Nestlé's offshore risk-taking affiliate. The offshore Nestlé "risk-taker" affiliate then turned around and charged Nestlé's U.S. manufacturing and distribution affiliates for their use of the U.S.-developed non-routine intangibles. The result of this "round-trip" tax planning was that the Swiss risk-taking affiliate kept all of the residual profits even though the intangible was created in the United States by a U.S. affiliate, was used in manufacturing activities in the United States by another U.S. affiliate, and the products produced from the intangible were distributed in the United States by a U.S. affiliate. Since all of the functions that could have contributed to the creation of the residual profits (whether research activities, manufacturing activities, or marketing activities) were conducted by U.S. affiliates within the United States, the IRS attempted to argue that the U.S. affiliates of Nestlé were entitled to the U.S.-origin residual profits arising from the creation and exploitation of this intangible and that the offshore Swiss risk-taking affiliate should not be entitled to these residual profits. However, the Tax Court disagreed, finding that the U.S.

---

[74] Westreco, Inc. v. Commissioner, T.C.M. 1992–561, 64 T.C.M. (CCH) 849 (1992).

affiliates were appropriately treated as "tested parties" and that the routine service profit left to Westreco (the research affiliate) was within the range of comparable companies. The Tax Court allowed the offshore Swiss affiliate to remain an untested risk-taker affiliate and did not address the reason that it was entitled to retain residual profits from activities that arose solely within the United States.

Nestlé in this case, like Apple in the hearings, has introduced cost sharing agreements into its inbound tax planning as well. In testimony before Congress, Nestlé's corporate officer responsible for tax matters stated as follows:

> Nestlé is a very large company, obviously. We are big boys, we can handle ourselves with the regulations and the IRS. . . I know in the transfer pricing area, for example, we have been to court now three times on our royalties [charged to U.S. manufacturing affiliates]. Our business model is, like many U.S.-headquartered companies, to maintain our intellectual property in our home country Switzerland. It is less expensive to do, because of the synergistic nature of it. So trademarks, R&D, et cetera, and we charge out globally for it, in the form of royalties for both trademarks and R&D, *although we conduct a lot of R&D [in the United States].*
>
> So dealing with the IRS on these issues, we have had battles with them, we have gone to court three times, went to trial once, summary judgment once, and then a settlement once. [At] [sic] trial, summary judgment we won 100 percent, settlement we won well over 90 percent.[75]

The Nestlé so-called "big boy planning" is interesting. Nestlé's officer admitted that the United States research function creates the intangible, yet the offshore risker-taker affiliate receives the tax ownership of the resulting non-routine intangible and then is able to charge the U.S. manufacturer/distributor affiliates a royalty to strip out the residual profits derived from activities that exploit this intangible in the U.S. marketplace. Thus, Nestlé's "round-trip planning" allows the residual profits from U.S. functions, all of which appear to be conducted within the United States by U.S. affiliates, to be stripped away from those U.S. affiliates even though the functions performed by those U.S. affiliates created the residual profits. In the end, U.S. origin profits are entirely allocated to the offshore Swiss risk-taker affiliate that funded the creation of the intangible but

---

75 See *Tax Reform and Foreign Investment in the United States: Hearing before the Subcomm. on Select Revenue Measures of the H. Comm. on Ways and Means*, 112 Cong. at 45 (2011) (testimony of Alexander Spitzer, Senior Vice President-Taxes, Nestlé Holdings, Inc.) (emphasis added).

appears to have provided no further meaningful activity towards its creation other than funding. The above discussion leads one to an unsettling conclusion: a taxpayer with advance planning and the use of qualified cost sharing agreements can obtain results that do not accord with Reg. § 1.482–6, notwithstanding the second sentence in section 482 that purports to require a broad application of the commensurate with income standard.

The failure of both the transfer pricing regulations and the litigated cases to prevent profit-shifting incomes was an important impetus for Congress to enact further backstop provisions to address these base erosion and profit shifting techniques. The enactment of the anti-deferral regime of section 951A in 2017 and its further expanded scope in 2025 (discussed in chapter 11) is an important legislative response against the practices of U.S. multinational enterprises that shift profit-making potential to foreign affiliates, and section 59A (discussed in chapter 7) is a companion regime that provides an important inbound base protection backstop against the profit-shifting strategies of foreign based multinational enterprises to shift profits from U.S. affiliates to offshore related affiliates through deductible payments. Those topics are discussed further in those succeeding chapters, but the base erosion successes identified in this chapter lays the foundation for one to understand why those further backstop regimes were viewed as necessary additions to the Internal Revenue Code.

N. Evaluation of Competing Transfer Pricing Methods

A further comment is likely needed about the various transfer pricing methods and how one should think about these alternative methodologies. The fact that the regulations specify various methods without a hierarchy and then admonish taxpayers to use whichever method is the "best method" leaves one with a checklist of methods but perhaps without a sense of the issues that are at stake. Thus, it is perhaps helpful to group the various transfer pricing methods into one of the following two fundamental categories in terms of conceptualizing the issues: "one-sided" transfer pricing methodologies and "two-sided" transfer pricing methodologies.

Under the "one-sided" transfer pricing methodologies, one party is "tested," and a routine profit is given to that tested party. The following methods should be put under the descriptive category of a "one-sided" transfer pricing methodology: (i) the uncontrolled price method, (ii) the resale price method, (iii) the cost plus method, and (iv) the comparable profits method. Each of these transfer pricing methods seek to isolate one or more (but not all) of the related party entities and identifies this sub-group of affiliates as "tested parties"[76] leaving aside one (or more than one) affiliate as an "untested party." The underlying reasoning for each of these "one-sided" transfer pricing methodologies is that if the tested party's share of the combined income meets the arm's length standard, then as a matter of logic the untested party's income by inference must also meet this standard even though it remains untested.[77] Thus, the impact of using a "one-sided" transfer pricing methodology is that the "tested party" is allocated a routine profit based on an analysis of what unrelated companies would routinely earn for their identified functions while the untested party keeps all of the residual income (i.e., the combined income less the routine profits allocated to the tested party).

A "one-sided" transfer pricing methodology may work well when there are only routine profits to be divided among affiliates. However, when residual profits exist, a "one-sided" transfer pricing methodology does not explain why residual profits should reside with any particular entity and simply assumes that the untested party should be the recipient without further explanation. This is the essential paradigm that allows the base erosion and profit shifting problem to exist. "One-sided" transfer pricing methodologies simply accept this outcome.

"One-sided" transfer pricing methodologies consequently put strong emphasis on the foundational question of which party should be the "tested party" and which party should not be tested, as it is only the "tested party" whose profits are benchmarked. The section 482 regulations answer this crucial, outcome-dispositive question by stating that the "tested party" should be the controlled party whose operating profit can be verified using the most reliable data and requires the fewest and most reliable adjustments.[78] Therefore, the "tested party" should be the least complex of the controlled taxpayers and should lend itself to comparison with uncontrolled comparable taxpayers.[79] Once agreement is reached on the risk-function responsibilities between the pertinent affiliates and which party should be the "tested party," the profit allocations are no longer controversial because the routine profits attributable to routine

---

[76] See Reg. § 1.482–5(b)(1).

[77] If a multinational enterprise's combined income ("C") is composed of the income of Affiliate A ("A") plus the income of Affiliate B ("B"), and if Affiliate A's income is tested and meets the arm's length standard, then we can assume that Affiliate B is entitled to receive the difference of "C" minus "A," which should equal "B".

[78] Reg. § 1.482–5(b)(2)(i).

[79] Id. See also Reg. § 1.482–5(e), Ex. 4. In order to determine which transfer pricing method is most reliable, the regulations articulate the best method rule that looks to the degree of comparability of the tested party with that of the uncontrolled taxpayer. Reg. § 1.482–5(c)(2)(i).

functions are common knowledge among those experienced in transfer pricing matters—both for the taxpayer and the taxing authority.

However, what is controversial, and what has made a decided impact on the outcome of the section 482 transfer pricing controversies, is the foundational question of which affiliate is framed as the complex "untested party" and which affiliate is framed as the straightforward "tested party." In a potential base erosion context where there is more than routine income on a combined basis, taxpayers will understandably desire to frame their U.S. affiliate as the straightforward "tested party" entitled to only a routine profit margin and frame their low-taxed foreign affiliate as the complex "untested party" entitled to all the residual profits without further explanation.

It is with respect to this critical dispositive framing game that "one-sided" transfer pricing methodologies make a significant difference in the ultimate outcome of a transfer pricing dispute. In this regard, a taxpayer can designate one or more affiliates of its group to be the risk-taker with respect to a particular trading pattern. The risk-taker is often located in a low-tax jurisdiction and given the "complex profit picture" through intercompany agreements executed among and with other parties. The U.S. affiliate assumes the role of non-risk taker providing only routine functions.

If the U.S. affiliate provides "straightforward" service-related functions, then it would be allocated a routine profit (typically using the comparable profits or cost plus methods). If the U.S. affiliate were to provide "straightforward" manufacturing-related activities, then it would be allocated a routine profit for those activities as well (typically using a resale profit methodology). To make such a planning structure effective, all non-routine intangibles must be owned by the offshore affiliate (via qualified cost sharing agreements, developed by the foreign affiliate itself with its own personnel, or acquired through some other form of transfer or contribution).

Again, the desired transfer pricing result is to frame the non-risk taking U.S. affiliate as the "tested party," whereas the risk taking tax haven affiliate is factually presented as "complex" and thus entitled to be framed as the "untested party" receiving all residual profits without explanation. Thus, through active advance tax planning and the use of a "one-sided" transfer pricing methodology, the groundwork is in place to create significant amounts of homeless income in tax haven jurisdictions that is blessed by the section 482 regulations and need not be explained to anyone.[80]

---

[80] The prevalence of one-sided transfer pricing methodologies is reflected in the annual statistics of the IRS Advance Pricing Agreement Program. For 2012, the

The result of this framing game lying at the heart of "one-sided" transfer pricing methodologies is an ad hoc, "all or nothing" scorecard with respect to the holdings of cases involving the IRS's efforts to tax residual profits of a multinational enterprise. The transfer pricing dispute in cases utilizing "one-sided" transfer pricing methodologies is typically over the residual profits and not the routine profit.

For example, in *U.S. Steel Corp. v. Commissioner*,[81] a location advantage for mining iron ore in Venezuela created a residual profit to the multinational group. U.S. Steel (USS) formed Orinoco Mining Company (Orinoco), a wholly-owned Delaware subsidiary, to own and exploit new Venezuelan mines. Initially, the Orinoco ore was transported to the United States in chartered vessels owned by independent companies, but in 1953, USS incorporated another wholly-owned subsidiary, Navios, Inc. (Navios), in Liberia, with its principal place of business in Nassau, Bahamas. Navios was organized for the purpose of chartering carriers transporting iron ore mined by Orinoco. Accordingly, Navios entered into shipping agreements with third parties. The prices charged by Navios to other domestic steel companies during the relevant period were the same as those charged to USS. The prices were structured in such a manner that the delivered cost of iron ore to USS would not be below the prices USS was charged for ore from unrelated U.S. mines. The consequence of this business restructuring exercise was that Navios kept all the residual profits from the Venezuelan location advantage while USS and Orinoco earned only a routine profit for their various functions.

The Tax Court agreed with the IRS that Navios should be the tested party and allocated a routine profit, and any residual profit should belong to USS. To determine the appropriate arm's length charter rate that Navios should charge in order to provide Navios with a routine shipping profit, the Tax Court extrapolated hypothetical shipping rates for 1957 through 1960 from what certain independent shippers had charged in their 1954 contracts with USS, adding adjustments to account for increased cost, risk, and profit. As a check on the accuracy of this historical approach and to determine the amount of allocation, the Tax Court also constructed hypothetical rates based on estimates of what Navios's costs had been during the taxable years in question, adjusting these estimates to allow for risk and profit, and then chose the method that, for each taxable year,

---

Program reported that the vast bulk of its cases involved routine service, distribution, or manufacturing pricing matters, with 70 percent involving distribution or related routine functions. Announcement 2013–17, 2013–16 I.R.B. 911, Part III. Only a "small percentage of the tested parties performed more complex or high value functions." Id. Similarly, the primary transfer pricing methods were one-sided methods. Id.

[81] 36 T.C.M. (CCH) 586, T.C.M. (P-H) ¶ 77,140 (1977), rev'd, 617 F.2d 942 (2d Cir. 1980).

would result in the lowest reallocation in favor of the IRS. According to the Tax Court, all excess profits above this derived profit belonged to the U.S. affiliate.

However, the decision of the Tax Court was reversed on appeal. The Second Circuit agreed with the taxpayer's assertion that the "tested party" should be USS and not Navios. The court noted that the prices charged by Navios for delivered ore to USS were the same prices as those charged by third parties. The Second Circuit recognized that allowing Navios to keep all residual profits without explanation allowed Navios to effectively become an offshore tax shelter,[82] but standing alone, this fact was insufficient to justify a reallocation of income under section 482 as Navios also "served a major business purpose unrelated to tax-shifting: allowing [USS] to reap the cost savings of using a non-United States-flag fleet."[83] The Second Circuit concluded that USS had met the standards of section 482 when it treated USS as a tested party and utilized a "one-sided" transfer pricing methodology to provide USS with a routine profit, stating as follows:

> We think it is clear that if a taxpayer can show that the price he paid or was charged for a service is "the amount which was charged or would have been charged for the same or similar services in independent transactions with or between unrelated parties," it has earned the right. . . to be free from a [section] 482 reallocation despite other evidence tending to show that its activities have resulted in a shifting of tax liability among controlled corporations. Where, as in this case, the taxpayer offers evidence that the same amount was actually charged for the same service in transactions with independent buyers, the question resolves itself into an evaluation of whether or not the circumstances of the sales to independent buyers are "similar" enough to sales to the controlling corporation under the circumstances, "considering all relevant facts." In our view, "considering all the relevant facts," the evidence was sufficient to show similar enough transactions with independent buyers to establish that the price [USS] paid Navios [for iron ore] was an arm's length price.[84]

However, the Second Circuit's opinion ignores the fundamental problem—residual profits existed within the multinational group that could not be explained by the routine functions performed by any single affiliate, including Navios. Which entity deserved those

---

[82] United States Steel Corp. v. Commissioner, 617 F.2d 942, 945 (2d Cir. 1980).

[83] Id.

[84] Id. at 947.

residual profits? By making USS the tested party, all residual profits were left inexplicably with the untested party, Navios.

The holding in *U.S. Steel* thus endorsed a significant tax planning opportunity. The *U.S. Steel* case is (in)famous because it moved the Venezuelan location advantage out of the company conducting business in Venezuela and into a tax haven subsidiary that was neither located in the country of origin or in the country where the product was shipped.

For present purposes, the critical lesson from *U.S. Steel* and its progeny is that a significant number of transfer pricing cases can be explained by the dispositive question of which party should be isolated as the "tested party" and which party should be left untested. However, few present the framing game as dramatically as *U.S. Steel* due to the fact that residual profits in that case were allocated entirely to a tax haven subsidiary that served solely a risk-taking function.[85] The risk-taker determination is, of course, a factual question upon which a taxpayer and tax authority can have dramatically different views. The cumbersome process of resolving such factual disputes is also well illustrated by *U.S. Steel*, in which the essential facts were related to the taxpayer's tax returns for 1957 through 1960, while the case was ultimately resolved in 1980.

There are other cases on this subject matter reaching similar conclusions. In *Compaq Computer Corp. v. Commissioner*,[86] a U.S. computer manufacturer, Compaq U.S., formed a subsidiary in Singapore to manufacture a component which was also purchased in substantial quantities from unrelated suppliers. The Singapore affiliate was successful in achieving worldwide material cost savings for Compaq U.S. The taxpayer designated Compaq's U.S. affiliate as the tested party and applied a "one-sided" transfer pricing methodology[87] to determine the profits allocable to that affiliate, whereas the Singapore affiliate was the "untested party" that kept all residual profits related to the location advantage. For the years at issue, the Singapore Economic Development Board had granted Compaq U.S.'s Singapore affiliate a "tax holiday," so the residual

---

85 See PPG Indus., Inc. v. Commissioner, 55 T.C. 928, 946 (1970) (sustaining the taxpayer's choice of tested party with the result that significant residual profits remain with the untested party); see also Diefenthal v. United States, 367 F. Supp. 506, 512 (E.D. La. 1973); see also Compaq Computer Corp. v. Commissioner, 78 T.C.M. (CCH) 20, T.C.M. (RIA) ¶ 99,220 (1999). In one case, the IRS asserted that an offshore subsidiary was a "consignment manufacturer." Seagate Tech., Inc. v. Commissioner 102 T.C. 149, 165–166 (1994). However, the Tax Court rejected such characterization because of the risks and responsibilities assumed by the subsidiary. Id. at 185.

86 Compaq Computer v. Commissioner, 78 T.C.M. (CCH) 20, T.C.M. (RIA) ¶ 99,220.

87 The specific method was the comparable uncontrolled price method. See Reg. § 1.482–3(b).

profits, if allocated to the Singapore affiliate, would escape any worldwide taxation. The taxpayer claimed that the Singapore affiliate was an untested party and that the U.S. affiliate was the appropriate tested party and then sought to apply a "one-sided" transfer pricing methodology in order to justify the routine profit allocated to Compaq's U.S. affiliate.

The IRS argued that the Singapore affiliate should be the tested party and that its profits should only be a routine manufacturing profit determined with a "one-sided" transfer pricing methodology.[88] The Tax Court refused to treat the Singapore affiliate as the tested party because it did not believe that the IRS presented any evidence that Compaq's U.S. affiliate was distinguishable from the comparable data set, and thus the reliability of those "comparables" was not seriously questioned. Of course, this holding simply sidestepped the critical issue because the point is that the routine functions in both Singapore and the United States could not explain the residual profits, but again the Tax Court did not address this point because the Singapore affiliate remained untested with the result that its excessive profitability did not need to be explained.

In *Diefenthal v. United States*,[89] a scrap metal dealer, Scrapco, was owned by a father and two sons, each owning a third of the total stock, respectively. Scrapco had a significant number of customers in Japan, and its business required loading scrap on ocean carriers and shipping it to Japan. In order to minimize transportation costs, Scrapco entered into alleged "voyage charters" that would fix the cost of the trip regardless of the occurrence of unforeseen delays or problems. One of the sons of the owner formed a new company, Fukaya, to conduct the shipping business with Fukaya receiving the residual profits for the geographical price difference for scrap metal sold into Japan versus its value in the U.S. marketplace. The IRS argued that the tested party should be Fukaya, not Scrapco, with the consequence that Fukaya, according to the IRS, would receive only a routine shipping profit and any excess profit attributable to the geographic differences in pricing for scrap metal belonged to Scrapco.

The court rejected the IRS's position and allowed Fukaya to be the untested party. In the course of its opinion, the court found that Scrapco had received an adequate routine profit using a "one-sided" transfer pricing methodology (in this case, using the comparable uncontrolled pricing method). The court also found no reason to believe that Scrapco was not comparable to the companies used in the transfer pricing study. Without evidence as to the unreliability of

---

88 The specific transactional method that the IRS believed was appropriate for testing the Singapore affiliate was the resale profits method.

89 Diefenthal v. United States, 367 F. Supp. 506 (E.D. La. 1973).

the comparable data set, the court accepted that Scrapco's profits should be limited solely to a routine profit comparable to the data set of companies and held that Scrapco should not share in any portion of the residual profits.

After a long line of losses where the government's theory was simply to switch the tested parties, the government finally won a significant victory in *Coca-Cola v. Commissioner*.[90] Here, the government successfully claimed that the foreign affiliates had no significant nonroutine intangible and thus could be adequately benchmarked, whereas the U.S. parent entity had intangibles and thus should not be the tested party. In *Coca-Cola v. Commissioner*, Coca-Cola had established controlled foreign manufacturing affiliates with plants located in Brazil, Chile, Costa Rica, Egypt, Ireland, Mexico, and Swaziland. The plants produced "concentrate"—syrups, flavorings, powder, and other ingredients—used in the production of Coca-Cola's branded soft drinks (including Coca-Cola, Fanta, and Sprite). These affiliates sold and distributed concentrate to hundreds of Coca-Cola bottlers in Europe, Africa, Asia, Latin America, and Australasia. The bottlers, most of which were independent of Coca-Cola, ranged from small family-owned businesses to large multinational companies. The independent bottlers used this concentrate to produce finished beverages that they marketed (directly or through distributors) to millions of retail establishments throughout the world (excluding the United States and Canada). To enable the Coca-Cola controlled foreign manufacturing affiliates to sell concentrate, Coca-Cola, the parent company, licensed Coca-Cola's intangible property, including trademarks, brand names, logos, patents, secret formulas, and proprietary manufacturing know-how.

The IRS argued that the Coca-Cola controlled foreign manufacturing affiliates should be designated as "tested parties" and then utilized the comparable profits method to benchmark their profitability with the profitability of the independent Coca-Cola bottlers as comparable parties. The taxpayer, in contrast, contended that the independent Coca-Cola bottlers were not comparable to Coca-Cola's controlled foreign manufacturing affiliates because the foreign manufacturing affiliates owned "marketing intangibles" or "IP associated with trademarks" that were allegedly created when the foreign manufacturing affiliates financed consumer advertising in foreign markets. Coca-Cola then argued that the independent bottlers by comparison were "marketing-light" businesses that operate at a different level of the market.

---

90 155 T.C. No. 10 (2020).

The Tax Court, citing Treasury regulations,[91] stated that comparability is principally judged on the basis of functions performed, contractual terms, risks assumed, economic conditions, and assets employed. Based on those criteria, the Tax Court found the independent Coca-Cola bottlers were highly comparable to the Coca-Cola controlled foreign manufacturing affiliates in all five respects. In terms of which entity owned any marketing intangibles, the Tax Court stated that the Coca-Cola controlled manufacturing affiliates played no role in arranging consumer marketing and had no voice in selecting or evaluating the services for which they were thus made financially responsible. In essence, they were passive recipients of charges that the parent company put on their books. This aspect of the Tax Court's decision represents a negative harbinger for the thesis that a funding party that provides no functional contribution towards the creation of an intangible apart from funding has any "argument in law, fact, economic theory, or common sense" as to its ownership of an internally created intangible. This aspect of the Tax Court opinion has been posited in law review articles,[92] but the above statement is the clearest articulation in a decided case of this idea to date.

Although the above survey shows some mixed results, the lessons from these cases in terms of taxpayer planning is clear. Armed with the favorable decisions utilizing "one-sided" transfer pricing methodologies and after reflecting on the taxpayer loss in *Coca-Cola*, taxpayers would understandably structure arrangements to confirm that the U.S. affiliate should be the tested party with routine profit allocable to it. For non-U.S. multinational enterprises, the residual profits may be allocated entirely to the offshore affiliate, and the IRS would be left to discover whether any non-routine profits existed and, if so, whether the U.S. affiliate owned a non-routine intangible that contributed significantly to earning those residual profits.[93] The procedural posture of the parties presents the IRS with a difficult factual contest.

In an effort to achieve better results for the federal budget, the IRS began to formulate a variety of theories upon which to argue that the tested party and the untested party should be switched. When

---

[91] See Reg. § 1.482–1(c)(2) (providing best method is determined by comparability); Reg. § 1.482–1(d) (sets forth standards for determining comparability); Reg. § 1.482–5(c)(2) (setting forth standards of comparability for the comparable profits method).

[92] See Bret Wells, *Revisiting § 367(d): How Treasury Took the Bite Out of Section 367(d) and What Should Be Done About It*, 16 FLORIDA TAX REV. 519 (2014); Bret Wells & Cym Lowell, *Tax Base Erosion: Reformation of Section 482's Arm's Length Standard*, 15 FLORIDA TAX REV. 737 (2014).

[93] See e.g., Westreco, Inc. v. Commissioner, T.C.M. 1992–561, 64 T.C.M. (CCH) 849 (1992).

the IRS argued simply that it would seek to reformulate the internal economic arrangements and risk-assignment put into place by the taxpayer, so as to place the reconstructed arrangement in a light more favorable to the government, the argument has been largely rejected with the notable exception of *Coca-Cola*.[94] However, in all cases, including *Coca-Cola*, the courts have consistently upheld the economic and contractual relationships existing among related parties when those arrangements were legitimate business transactions put into place before the risks and rewards were determined. Thus, courts have rejected the idea that section 482 permitted "substance over form" arguments. On the contrary, so long as the internal multinational enterprise's agreements allocated true economic risks and rewards, the IRS's authority under section 482 was solely to apply the arm's length standard to the economic fact pattern presented by the taxpayer.

However, where the IRS has had better success is when it could demonstrate that the "tested parties" proffered by the taxpayer were themselves "complex" and incapable of being benchmarked with routine external comparable companies.[95] For example, when the U.S. affiliate was the entity that engaged in manufacturing, the IRS would argue that non-routine manufacturing know-how created and developed by the U.S. manufacturing affiliate entitled the U.S. affiliate to more than a routine manufacturing margin. When the posture changes such that the offshore affiliate is the manufacturer and the U.S. affiliate is the distributing entity, then the IRS seeks to argue that the U.S. distributor affiliate had developed its own "marketing intangible," entitling the U.S. distributor affiliate to more than a routine distribution margin. The evolution of the concept of a "marketing intangible" is interesting and deserves a further comment. Courts have held that marketing intangibles can include customer lists, trademarks, trade names, brand names, and related customer goodwill,[96] and the IRS has asserted an even more expansive list of situations where a marketing intangible might exist in its litigating positions[97] with mixed success.

---

[94] See, e.g., Eli Lilly & Co. v. Commissioner, 84 T.C. 996, 1126–27, *aff'd in part and rev'd in part*, 856 F.2d 855 (7th Cir. 1988).

[95] It should be noted that this determination was required in *Coca-Cola* as well. See Coca-Cola v. Commissioner, 155 T.C. No. 10 (2020).

[96] See, e.g., Clarke v. Haberle Crystal Springs Brewing Co., 280 U.S. 384 (1930) (discussing goodwill in the nature of trademarks, trade names and trade brands); J.C. Cornillie Co. v. United States, 298 F. Supp. 887 (E.D. Mich. 1968) (discussing goodwill in the form of customer lists); F.W. Drybrough v. Commissioner, 45 T.C. 424 (1966), *aff'd*, 384 F.2d 715 (6th Cir. 1967) (discussing goodwill consisting of agency's file of uncollected claims). See also P.L.R. 1981–34–193 (May 29, 1981) (defining "marketing intangibles" as the right to use tradename, trademark, and related goodwill).

[97] The IRS has taken an expansive view of what constitutes an intangible in several instances. See F.S.A. 2002–30–001 (July 26, 2002) (finding project finance

As matters stand, the path is clear for the government: if residual profits exist, then it must find some non-routine intangible in the hands of the U.S. affiliate, such as manufacturing know-how or a marketing intangible, that distinguishes the tested U.S. affiliate from the comparable data set of companies proffered by the taxpayer to support its use of a "one-sided" transfer pricing methodology. If the comparable data is materially and economically distinguishable, then the U.S. affiliate can be defrocked of its "sole tested party" status due to the fact that it owns non-routine intangibles that contribute significantly to the residual profits of the combined entity.

If such a contest is waged with a U.S. multinational enterprise, then the IRS should be able to discover the offshore profits of the untested foreign affiliate so that it can learn the amount of residual profits potentially in dispute. However, if this contest is waged with a non-U.S. multinational enterprise, the IRS would likely hear that it has no right to examine the offshore books and records of foreign affiliates until and unless the IRS is able to demonstrate that a "one-sided" transfer pricing methodology is not controlling and that a "two-sided" transfer pricing methodology must be employed.[98] In either event, if the taxpayer presents a transfer pricing theory using a "one-sided" transfer pricing methodology, the IRS faces a difficult and contentious examination process because it must first contradict the characterization of the U.S. affiliate as the "tested party" by finding some unknown and undisclosed non-routine intangible. Again, from a procedural perspective, this governmental effort occurs after the taxpayer has attempted to identify all non-routine intangibles and has transferred those identified intangibles out of the U.S. affiliate and into a foreign risk-taker affiliate well before the years in issue.

---

developer's efforts to negotiate a comprehensive package of interdependent contracts to finance, construct, and operate a project constituted an intangible asset). Arguably, F.S.A. 2002–30–001 is inconsistent with the result reached in Hospital Corp. of America, Inc. v. Commissioner, where the Tax Court rejected the IRS's characterization of the negotiation of the terms of a hospital management contract as a transfer of property on the grounds that what was provided by the taxpayer did not represent a legally enforceable right and was, at best, merely a business opportunity. 81 T.C. 520 (1983), *nonacq. in part* 1987–1 Cum. Bull. 1 See also T.A.M. 2009–07–024 (Feb. 13, 2009) (concluding that network of contracts with independent foreign agents constitutes intangible asset apart from goodwill for purposes of section 367(d)); Merck & Co. v. United States, 24 Cl. Ct. 73, 91–2 U.S.T.C. ¶ 50,456 (Cl. Ct. 1991) (rejecting IRS's argument that the taxpayer's strategic planning structure and system of intercompany pricing were services that required an arm's-length payment from the subsidiary to the taxpayer).

[98] Admittedly, the IRS could attempt to discover the information from bilateral treaty partners under exchange of information agreements with that other country, but such a process is often cumbersome and not all countries have signed such agreements.

In stark contrast to a "one-sided" transfer pricing methodology, a "two-sided" transfer pricing methodology (comparable profit split and residual profit split methods in the nomenclature of the section 482 regulations) evaluates the overall income of the affiliates and determines how to allocate the combined profits between them with all parties treated as tested parties. The residual profits are divided between those affiliates that contribute to their creation in contrast to the "all or nothing" result generally prevailing in cases decided with a "one-sided" transfer pricing methodology.

Furthermore, in contrast to the transfer pricing result achieved under a "one-sided" transfer pricing methodology, the use of a "two-sided" transfer pricing methodology requires that a profit allocation to a tax haven subsidiary be affirmatively explained as a precondition for any allocation. In other words, in a "two-sided" transfer pricing methodology, no allocation of residual profits is made unless it can be affirmatively demonstrated that the affiliate's activities made a significant contribution to the creation of the residual profits.[99] The IRS, with the taxpayer, a court, or competent authorities, must determine the functions that contribute significantly to the overall residual profits and then must split the residual profits based on their relative weighting of functional importance. Although these weightings may not have been clearly understood in previous years, the current reality is that the advanced pricing agreement (the "APA" process) and the treaty mutual agreement (competent authority) processes have provided a defined pathway for resolving these disputes.

Stated differently, when a "two-sided" transfer pricing methodology is used to resolve a transfer pricing dispute, the taxpayer has the burden of showing that its allocation of residual profits follows the substantive functions that created the multinational enterprise's residual profits.[100] If the taxpayer cannot explain how a tax haven's activities functionally contributed to the creation of residual profits, it would receive a zero allocation. Nothing is left unexplained in a profit-split approach that employs a "two-sided" transfer pricing methodology because the contributions of the various affiliates must be demonstrated as a condition precedent for an allocation of income. As the income allocation tracks the functions that create the income in a "two-sided" transfer pricing methodology, an allocation of homeless income that is divorced from those substantive functions would be unachievable.

The IRS's first significant success in getting a court to utilize a "two-sided" transfer pricing methodology was the landmark case of

---

[99] Reg. § 1.482–6(b).

[100] Reg. § 1.482–6(b)(2).

Eli Lilly & Co. v. Commissioner.[101] Eli Lilly & Co. (Lilly) is a large producer of pharmaceuticals. In *Eli Lilly*, a compound was discovered in 1951 (propoxyphene and propoxyphene hydrochloride) for which Lilly received a patent in 1955 and the FDA approved the compound for the market. Several related products were marketed that used the compound as their principal active ingredient. A closely related compound (propoxyphene napsylate) was subsequently developed, for which a patent was issued in 1962, and FDA approval was obtained in 1971. Products based on this patent were then marketed. Although Lilly's Puerto Rican affiliate owned the patents, the issue remained as to the profit split between a patent owner and the U.S. affiliate that developed the market for the patented drug. The Tax Court clarified the distinction between manufacturing intangibles (owned by an offshore manufacturing affiliate) and marketing intangibles (owned and developed by the U.S. affiliate).

The Tax Court found that the marketing intangibles owned by the U.S. affiliate included the trademarks for certain pharmaceutical compounds, as well as the Lilly name and goodwill of the company. In describing the marketing intangible owned by the U.S. affiliate, the Tax Court said that the U.S. affiliate enjoyed a favorable reputation in the U.S. marketplace and had developed a marketing organization that was highly skilled. The Tax Court found that the U.S. affiliate's marketing intangible had significant value apart from the patents owned by the offshore manufacturing subsidiary. The Tax Court stated that the U.S. affiliate owned these valuable marketing intangibles because the U.S. affiliate developed this market recognition, trade name, and customer goodwill entirely from its own funds without reimbursement by the offshore Puerto Rican affiliate.[102] Concluding that both the manufacturing intangible and the marketing intangible contributed significantly to the residual profits of the multinational enterprise, the Tax Court did not believe that a "one-sided" transfer pricing methodology was appropriate as the record did not contain any transactions comparable to either affiliate on a stand-alone basis.

Accordingly, the Tax Court turned to a "two-sided" transfer pricing methodology. In this process, each identified function was provided a profit allocation. However, with respect to the residual profits remaining after the allocation of the routine profits, the court

---

[101] Eli Lilly & Co. v. Commissioner, 84 T.C. 996 (1985), *aff'd in part and rev'd in part*, 856 F.2d 855 (7th Cir. 1988).

[102] See also G.D. Searle & Co. v. Commissioner, 88 T.C. 252 (1987) (holding that the transferred manufacturing intangibles had "little value" to SCO apart from the intangibles associated with the "marketing and administrative services" provided by Searle and engaging in an effort to bifurcate the combined company goodwill between the manufacturing intangible owned by the manufacturing subsidiary and the marketing intangible owned by the distributor subsidiary).

concluded that the U.S. distributor affiliate should receive 45 percent of the residual profit for its marketing intangibles and the Puerto Rican affiliate should receive 55 percent as the owner of the manufacturing know-how and product patent based on the Tax Court's assessment of the relative contribution of each of the affiliates' functions to the generation of the residual profits.[103]

G.D. Searle & Co. v. Commissioner[104] is largely consistent and supportive of the holding in *Eli Lilly*. The Tax Court again found that there was "little hard evidence" before it and that the comparables in the record were unreliable. The Tax Court observed that the intangibles transferred to offshore affiliate SCO "were of little value to SCO without the marketing and administrative services provided by the U.S. affiliate (Searle), because SCO was unable to provide such services for itself." Additionally, Searle continued to own the new drug applications (NDAs) issued by the Food and Drug Administration with respect to the products manufactured by SCO, meaning that without Searle's services, SCO could not have sold its products. The NDAs owned by Searle "were also extremely valuable assets, without which the. . . intangibles [transferred to SCO] were of diminished value." The Tax Court found that there was no adequate evidence before it to determine how to allocate the residual profits when both the U.S. affiliate and the offshore affiliate owned significant non-routine intangibles, and therefore the Tax Court used its best judgment and determined that an allocation of profits to the U.S. affiliate equal to 25 percent of SCO's total net sales in 1974 and 1975 was appropriate in order to clearly reflect the U.S. affiliate's income. The net result of the allocation was that about 54 percent of the combined net profit of SCO and Searle from the products produced by SCO was attributed to Searle, the owner of the marketing intangible, and 46 percent was allocated to SCO, the offshore manufacturer. While the Tax Court did not articulate its conclusion as a profit split, this was the effect of its determination.

In *Bausch & Lomb v. Commissioner*,[105] a foreign manufacturing affiliate licensed valuable intellectual property from its U.S. parent, the patent owner, and the issue involved how to determine the appropriate transfer pricing result between these affiliates. After allocating a profit among the affiliates for various other routine functions, the Tax Court found that no unrelated party comparables existed for the intangible property and stated that it must construct its own arm's length royalty to allocate the residual profits from the patented product between the patent owner and the licensee of the

---

103 Eli Lilly & Co. v. Commissioner, 84 T.C. at 1130–67.

104 G.D. Searle & Co. v. Commissioner, 88 T.C. at 252.

105 Bausch & Lomb, Inc. v. Commissioner, 92 T.C. 525 (1989), *aff'd*, 933 F.2d 1084 (2d Cir. 1991).

patent. The Tax Court then used its best judgment to find that the arm's length royalty should be 20 percent, which would allow B&L Ireland, the licensee, to share in about 50 percent of the residual profits derived from the licensed technology and earn a 27 percent return on its investment over the course of the project.

The above landmark cases are representative of the larger picture. A broader cataloguing of all resolved transfer pricing disputes using a "two-sided" transfer pricing methodology demonstrates that on an aggregate basis (after eliminating a single case that is so large so as to influence adversely the overall results) courts have allocated residual profits on about a 50:50 basis between the U.S. affiliate and the foreign affiliate where both affiliates possess material, non-routine intangibles that contribute significantly to the creation of residual profits.[106] However, there is a condition precedent to this assessment—namely that significant non-routine intangibles must be found to exist in each affiliate. If that condition precedent were not met, then the use of a single tested party cannot be overcome, and the question would simply be whether the routine profit of the tested party is within the arm's length range.

O. "Blocked Income"

A further exception to the commensurate with income standard involves income that is not able to be received by the intangible owner due to a legal restriction. In this regard, commonly controlled entities do not necessarily have an unfettered ability to allocate income amongst themselves. On occasion, foreign law may prohibit the payment or receipt of income between commonly controlled entities. For example, a foreign country might prohibit the payment of royalties from a subsidiary located within its jurisdiction to an offshore affiliate. When a foreign law prohibits an entity from receiving income, that income has been referred to as blocked income. The Treasury Department has long tried to utilize section 482 as a basis to tax blocked income on the ground that the failure to do so fails to clearly reflect the intangible owner's rightful share of income. The Supreme Court, however, had ruled that income that was blocked due to a U.S. federal law restriction prevented the application of section 482 because the taxpayer failed to possess the type of complete dominion and control over the income that would cause it to be considered gross income.[107] The government at one time

---

[106] For a further analysis of section 482, see Bret Wells & Cym Lowell, *Tax Base Erosion: Reformation of Section 482's Arm's Length Standard*, 15 FLORIDA TAX REV. 737 (2014).

[107] See Commissioner v. First Security Bank of Utah, N.A., 405 U.S. 394 (1972). The Supreme Court framed its rationale based on the concept of what could be gross income and stated that only income that is subject to "unfettered command and that he is free to enjoy at his own option may be taxed to him as his income, whether he

attempted to distinguish the Supreme Court's decision in *First Security Bank* as being of precedential value only with respect to legal restrictions imposed by U.S. law,[108] but subsequent case law rejected the government's effort to so limit its holding and instead applied the blocked income exception whenever any applicable law (whether foreign or domestic) prevented taxpayers from receiving income.[109] Under this case law, the controlling question was whether or not the entities under common control affirmatively utilized their common control as a means to distort income or whether instead the distortion in income occurred by reason of a foreign law restriction outside the parties' control; when the distortion occurred due to a foreign law restriction outside the control of the parties, then section 482 was found to be inapposite.[110] At one time, former regulations allowed taxpayers to affirmatively self-elect to defer recognition of blocked income until the time when the income ceased to be blocked.[111]

The Treasury Department revisited this previously settled area of the law in 1994 in an effort to circumscribe the scope of the blocked income exception to section 482.[112] In this regard, regulations since 1994 limit a taxpayer's ability to treat an amount as blocked income to only instances when the foreign legal restriction affected

sees fit to enjoy it or not" is considered income, citing Corliss v. Bowers, 281 U.S. 376 (1930). The definition of gross income in terms of one's complete dominion and control over an amount was reinformed in later Supreme Court decisions. See Commissioner v. Glenshaw Glass, 348 U.S. 426 (1955). The Supreme Court's framing of the blocked income exception as based on a limitation on the scope of what constitutes gross income under section 61 was the subject of a vigorous dissent in that case.

[108] See Rev. Rul. 82–45, 1982–1 C.B. 89. This revenue ruling was later declared obsolete once Reg. § 1.482–1(h)(2) was promulgated in Rev. Rul. 2007–35, 2007–1 C.B. 1317.

[109] Proctor & Gamble Co. v. Commissioner, 95 T.C. 323 (1990), aff'd, 961 F.2d 1255 (6th Cir. 1992); Exxon Corp. v. Commissioner, 66 T.C.M. 1707 (1993), aff'd sub. nom. Texaco, Inc. v. Commissioner, 98 F.3d 825 (5th Cir. 1996), cert. denied, 520 U.S. 1185 (1997).

[110] Commissioner v. First Security Bank of Utah, N.A., 405 U.S. 394, 403 (1972) ("we know of no decision of this Court wherein a person has been found to have taxable income that he did not receive and that he was prohibited from receiving"); Proctor & Gamble v. Commissioner, 95 T.C. 323, *aff'd*, 961 F.2d 1255, 1259 (6th Cir. 1992) ("the Commissioner is authorized to allocate income under section 482 only where a controlling interest has complete power to shift income among its subsidiaries and has exercised that power. . . . The payment or nonpayment of royalties in no way depending on P&G's control of the various entities"); Exxon v. Commissioner, 66 T.C.M. 1707 (1993) ("the proper focus of this Court should not be upon the semantic question of whether the restriction constituted 'law', but upon whether petitioners had sufficient power or control to warrant a section 482 allocation").

[111] See former Reg. § 1.482–1(d)(6) in T.D. 6952, 1968–1 C.B. 218. The government accepted this affirmative election on the part of taxpayers if the taxpayer obtained an opinion from foreign legal counsel opining that the taxpayer's income was legally blocked. See Rev. Rul. 72–245, 1972–1 C.B. 347.

[112] Notice of Proposed Rulemaking, INTL-0401-88, 58 FED. REG. 5310 (Jan. 21, 1993); T.D. 8552, 59 FED. REG. 34,971 (July 8, 1994).

uncontrolled taxpayers under comparable circumstances for a comparable period of time.[113] If there is no evidence that the foreign legal restriction affected uncontrolled taxpayers, the taxpayer must obtain the consent of the district director as a prerequisite[114] for treating any amount as blocked income.[115]

In addition, the regulations since 1994 also attempted to more narrowly define the meaning of a foreign law restriction, providing that a foreign law restriction exists only if it (i) is publicly promulgated (in writing) and not simply imposed as part of a commercial transaction, (ii) is shown to be generally applicable to all similarly situated persons whether under common control or not,[116] and (iii) works to block payment in any and all forms[117] to the taxpayer.[118] As to this last element, if the foreign law restriction only restricts the manner of payment or its deductibility but does not restrict the taxpayer's ultimate ability to compel payment of a comparable amount in some other alternative form other than as a royalty, then the regulations conclude that the income is not truly blocked income.[119] Furthermore, the taxpayer must also demonstrate that it has exhausted all practicable legal remedies to unblock the income before it can avail itself of this exception.[120]

The validity of the Treasury Department's regulatory effort to narrow the scope of the blocked income exception was the subject of a lengthy opinion in *3M v. Commissioner*.[121] Under the stipulated facts in that case, 3M had a Brazilian affiliate that was allowed to use valuable intangible property owned by 3M's U.S. affiliate. However, during the years at issue, the authoritative Brazilian agency placed a ceiling on the amount of royalty that could be paid by the Brazilian affiliate to the U.S. affiliate. However, this practice was not publicly promulgated in writing but was simply a known practice of the Brazilian agency, so the publicly promulgated regulatory requirement was not satisfied. Furthermore, the fixed ceiling on the amount of royalty only applied to payments of royalties

---

113 Reg. § 1.482–1(h)(2)(i).

114 Reg. § 1.482–1(h)(2)(iii).

115 Notice of Proposed Rulemaking, INTL-0401-88, 58 FED. REG. 5310 (Jan. 21, 1993); T.D. 8552, 59 FED. REG. 34,971 (July 8, 1994).

116 Reg. § 1.482–1(h)(2)(v) Example 2.

117 The regulations make clear that if a payment as a dividend could be made then a payment in some form is allowed and thus no foreign law restriction exists for purposes of the regulatory definition even though foreign law prevented the payment in the form of a royalty. See Reg. § 1.482–1(h)(2)(v) Example 3.

118 Reg. § 1.482–1(h)(2)(ii).

119 Reg. § 1.482–1(h)(2)(ii).

120 Reg. §§ 1.482–1(h)(2)(ii)(B), (D).

121 160 T.C. 50 (2023). The case was fully briefed with all exhibits and stipulated facts filed as of December 2, 2016, but the Tax Court decision was not issued in the case until February 9, 2023, about seven years after the final briefing of the case.

between related parties and was not imposed on royalty arrangements involving uncontrolled taxpayers, so the Brazilian legal restriction was not generally applicable to all similarly situated taxpayers and thus failed to satisfy that element of the regulatory requirements as well. Finally, the restrictions on royalties did not prevent 3M's Brazilian affiliate from remitting dividends, and the stipulated facts indicated that 3M's Brazilian affiliate had the legal capacity to remit a sufficient amount of dividends to compensate for the fixed ceiling imposed on royalty payments. As a result, because the Brazilian legal restriction did not prevent all forms of payment, the fixed ceiling on royalties did not satisfy the regulatory definition of a foreign law restriction because it did not prevent payment in all forms. Finally, 3M did not elect to apply the deferred income method of accounting with respect to its blocked income. Thus, several of the elements added by the 1994 regulatory changes were not satisfied, and the government thus argued that 3M's U.S. affiliate was required to report additional royalty income on the ground that the blocked income exception to section 482, as refined by the 1994 regulatory changes, had not been satisfied.

The key area of contest in the litigation related to the validity of the regulations and their attempt to narrow the scope of the blocked income exception. Nine of the judges of the Tax Court held for the government over the dissent of eight judges in a closely divided court. In this regard, the Tax Court majority opinion held that the Treasury Department's adoption of Reg. § 1.482–1(h)(2) in 1994 satisfied the notice and comment requirements of the Administrative Procedure Act. The Tax Court majority opinion then addressed whether the regulations were entitled to *Chevron* deference. In this regard, the Tax Court majority opinion determined that the Congressional addition of the commensurate with income standard to section 482 in 1986 created an interpretive issue under section 482 that had not been present in the prior case law. As a result, the Tax Court majority opinion determined that the pre-1986 case law had not resolved the interpretive issues created by the addition of the commensurate with income standard to section 482 and so an interpretive gap remained to be filled by regulations with the consequence that the *Chevron* step-one test was satisfied. The Tax Court majority opinion then held that the manner in which the government applied the commensurate with income standard to the blocked income situation was a reasonable interpretation of section 482's commensurate with income requirement.

After the government's victory in *3M*, the government won again in the Tax Court in *Coca-Cola v. Commissioner.*[122] In *Coca-Cola*, the

[122] Coca-Cola v. Commissioner, T.C. Memo 2023–135 (2023).

government made section 482 adjustments that increased petitioner's aggregate taxable income by more than $9 billion, producing tax deficiencies in excess of $3.3 billion by reallocating income from foreign manufacturing affiliates, (the "supply points") to the Coca-Cola parent entity. The supply points sold concentrate to independent Coca-Cola bottlers throughout the world. The bottlers used the concentrate to produce finished beverages that they marketed to retail establishments worldwide. Coca-Cola licensed its intangible property to its various supply points for use in making the concentrate, but the Brazilian supply point paid no royalties for that intangible property and instead paid dividends of $886,823,232. In a previous decision, the Tax Court had held that the arm's-length royalty attributable to the Brazilian supply point's usage of the intangible property was $1.768 billion, so the issue before the Tax Court became whether the government was entitled to assert a transfer pricing adjustment under section 482 for the unpaid $882 million amount. Similar to the *3M* case, the Brazilian law had capped the amounts of royalties that Brazilian companies could pay to foreign parent companies, and so Coca-Cola argued that the legal import of this Brazilian law restriction was that it created blocked income of $882 million. For its part, the government argued that the Brazilian legal restriction failed to create "blocked income" if either (i) the Brazilian legal restriction had no application to royalties paid by a Brazilian company to a non-controlling (or unrelated) entity or (ii) the Brazilian law allowed the Brazilian company to pay dividends and thus did not preclude or restrict the supply point's ability to pay dividends to Coca-Cola. The Tax Court agreed with the government. Because the restrictions under Brazilian law failed to satisfy the requirements of Reg. § 1.482–1(h), the unpaid amounts were not entitled to be treated as blocked income. As an additional argument, Coca-Cola argued that the effective date for Reg. § 1.482–1(h) "grandfathered" intangible agreements entered into prior to November 17, 1985.[123] As to this grandfathering argument, the Tax Court found that the greater percentage of the intangible value related to intangible assets that were entitled to the grandfather provision and then found that Coca-Cola had failed to satisfy its burden of proof as to what portion of the aggregate transfer pricing adjustment might be attributable to exploitation of the eight grandfathered trademarks.

Several aspects of recent Supreme Court decisions arguably provide more support for the government. First, in *Moore v. United States*.[124] the Supreme Court stated that "Congress may attribute an entity's realized and undistributed income to the entity's

[123] Reg. § 1.482–1(j)(4).

[124] Moore v. United States, 602 U.S. 572 (2024).

shareholders or partners, and then tax the shareholders or partners on their portions of that income."[125] The Supreme Court based its decision by citing prior case law that afforded this attribution of income from an entity to its owner even though the income was blocked from distribution to the owner.[126] The ability to appropriately assign income so that the resulting allocation among related parties satisfies the "commensurate in income" standard would appear to be delegated authority afforded to the Secretary under section 482. Second, in *Loper Bright Enterprises v. Ramaindo*[127] the Supreme Court reiterated that agency deference is appropriate when the agency has been explicitly delegated such authority. In this regard, the statutory text of Code Sec. 482 explicitly provides that the Secretary of the Treasury Department is delegated authority to make such adjustments when the Secretary in his discretion "determines that such distribution, apportionment, or allocation is necessary in order to prevent evasion of taxes or clearly to reflect the income of any of such organizations, trades, or businesses." In Loper Bright Enterprises v. Raimondo,[128] the Supreme Court stated that "[w]hen the best reading of a statute is that it delegates discretionary authority to an agency, the role of the reviewing court under the APA is, as always, to independently interpret the statute and effectuate the will of Congress subject to constitutional limits."[129] The Supreme Court then went on to state that in that context that a court "fulfills that role by recognizing constitutional delegations, fixing the boundaries of the delegated authority, and ensuring the agency has engaged in reasoned decisionmaking within those boundaries."[130]

Yet, on appeal, the Eighth Circuit forged a different path. In a remarkable change of fortunes, the Eighth Circuit reversed the Tax Court decision in *3M*[131] and held that the Treasury Department exceeded its authority to issue a change in regulations that attempted to narrow the scope of the block incomed doctrine. Without

---

[125] Moore v. United States, 602 U.S. at 585–590.

[126] In Heiner v. Mellon, 304 U.S. 271 (1938), the Supreme Court rejected an argument that a partner must have separately applied realization requirement or constructive receipt requirement even though the partnership assets and income were unreachable by the partners. In Helvering v. Nat'l Grocery Co., 304 U.S. 282, 288 (1938), the Supreme Court also made clear that taxation of the undistributed accumulated earnings in a business could be taxed either at the corporate level or the shareholder level according to whatever Congress ultimately chose to do. The Supreme Court in its *Moore* favorably cited both of these authorities, and others, as the basis for assigning income earned at an entity to its owner for taxation. See Moore v. United States, 602 U.S. at 587–589.

[127] Loper Bright Enterprises v. Raimondo, 603 U.S. 369 (2024).

[128] Loper Bright Enterprises v. Raimondo, 603 U.S. 369 (2024).

[129] Loper Bright Enterprises v. Raimondo, 603 U.S. 369, 371 (2024).

[130] Loper Bright Enterprises v. Raimondo, 603 U.S. 369, 371 (2024).

[131] See 3M Company v. Commissioner, 154 F.4th 574 (8th Cir. 2025).

addressing or distinguishing the Supreme Court's opinion in *Moore*, the Eighth Circuit in its opinion stated that the 3M parent company entity must have complete dominion and control over the blocked income at the shareholder level before the parent company could be considered to have an income inclusion under section 482, and the Eighth Circuit held that Brazil's legal restrictions on the prevention of payments of royalties prevented this standard from being met. In its reversal of the Tax Court decision, the Eighth Circuit nowhere cited *Moore* or addressed how income that was not under the dominion or control at the U.S. shareholder level in *Moore* could still represent gross income to the U.S. shareholder in *Moore* but not so in *3M*'s context. The Eighth Circuit then stated that the Treasury Department could not simply reverse the prior Supreme Court decision in First Security Bank of Utah v. Commissioner, 405 U.S. 394 (1972), notwithstanding that Congress had made an intervening addition of the commensurate with income standard to the statute. Even if the Treasury Department had delegated authority under section 482, the Eighth Circuit opined that the agencies delegated authority still must be circumscribed by the best reading of the statute. As to the government's argument that income cannot be considered truly blocked if there were some means by which the Brazilian government might allow remittances back to the U.S. parent entity, the Eighth Circuit rejected this argument out of hand and said that the potential scope of such a legal argument was "breathtaking in its potential reach."

If other circuit courts follow the Eighth Circuit's decision, the outcome would be that foreign countries have the opportunity to design their laws to turn-off the US transfer pricing rules even if the so-called "blocked income" is ultimately repatriable back to the US parent company in some form. This aspect of the Eighth Circuit's holding is troubling as it affords a foreign jurisdiction with significant discretion to adopt formal rules that could prevent "royalties" from being paid in an amount that is commensurate with the income it generates in contravention of the expressed statutory language of the second sentence of section 482. Such an outcome is breathtaking in its potential reach. As of the publication of this edition, it remains to be seen whether the Eighth Circuit's decision will be followed by other circuit courts or even by the Tax Court in cases that are subject to an appeal to a different circuit.

P. Advance Pricing Agreements

A development at the end of the last century was the IRS's issuance of advance pricing agreements ("APAs") on intercompany transfer pricing under section 482. In the IRS's own words:

> An APA is an agreement between the Service and the taxpayer on the [transfer pricing methodology] to be applied to any apportionment or allocation of income, deductions, credits, or allowances between or among two or more organizations, trades, or businesses owned or controlled, directly or indirectly, by the same interests. The [transfer pricing methodology] thus represents the application to the taxpayer's specific facts and circumstances of the best method within the meaning of the income tax regulations under section 482 of the Internal Revenue Code. . . as agreed pursuant to negotiations between the Service and the taxpayer.[132]

The advantage of an APA for taxpayers is certainty, but certainty comes at both transactional and substantive cost. The submissions and supporting analysis required to obtain an APA are extensive. Equally if not more important, the best a taxpayer can expect in an APA is a middle-of-the road result. The IRS is unlikely to confer its blessing on transfer prices at the aggressive end of the arm's length range.

---

[132] Rev. Proc. 96–53, 1996–2 Cum. Bull. 375. This Revenue Procedure expounds general guidelines for APAs.

Part II
INBOUND U.S. TAXATION

Chapter 5

U.S. TAXATION OF FOREIGN PERSONS: FIXED AND DETERMINABLE INCOME

Thus far we have worked through several of the building blocks of U.S. international taxation—nationality, residence, the source of income, and transfer pricing, among others—but haven't yet woven them into a complete canvas of taxation of foreign persons and foreign income. This and following chapters lay out the actual U.S. tax regime applicable to inbound and outbound transactions.

A. Generalities on Inbound Taxation

The tax environment facing foreign investors and foreign-owned businesses in the United States reflects two conspicuous, and often conflicting, elements of the U.S. fiscal and economic landscape in recent decades: thirst for tax revenues and thirst for foreign capital. Impounding these dual concerns, U.S. taxation of foreign investment is a patchwork of severe and benign provisions.

There are two different tax regimes within the U.S. system of inbound taxation that apply respectively to passive investment income and active business profits from the United States. At the boundary between these regimes is the notion of a U.S. "trade or business"—a measure of the character and extent of economic activity in the United States.

In broad outline, foreign persons are taxed 1) at a flat rate of 30 percent on the *gross* amount of their U.S. source passive investment income (known as "fixed or determinable" income) and 2) at full graduated rates on *net* business profits (known in tax parlance as "income effectively connected with the conduct of a trade or business in the United States").[1]

From this bare outline, it may seem that the U.S. taxation of passive investment is the more severe. While the highest marginal rates imposed on the net business incomes of individuals (37 percent) is somewhat higher than the flat 30 percent rate imposed on passive investment income, the disallowance of deductions and the absence of lower rate brackets in the flat tax regime often make a flat 30 percent of *gross* income a substantially greater amount than the portion of *net* gain bitten off at the regular graduated rates. For corporations, the highest marginal rate is 21 percent, so the flat 30

---

1 §§ 871(b), 882(a), 884.

percent tax on *gross* income is always higher even before one considers the effect of the disallowance of deductions.

Closer scrutiny reverses this first impression. There are large holes in the flat rate tax on investment income of foreign persons. Capital gains from the sale of U.S. investment assets (other than real estate) are not taxed at all. More importantly, interest from U.S. bank deposits and from U.S. "portfolio" debt (a class including most private and public obligations) is also exempt from U.S. taxation. Because capital gains and interest represent the overwhelming bulk of income from passive investment in the United States, the tax regime on passive investment income is not fearsome after all.

On the other side of the scales, however, there is an additional tax of 30 percent on the branch profits of foreign corporations in the United States when they are removed from U.S. business investments. This tax, dating from the 1986 Act, extends two-level taxation of profits to most business operations of foreign corporations in the United States.

The overall pattern of U.S. taxation of foreign persons that emerges from these provisions is relatively benign taxation of passive investment income (represented mainly by interest and capital gains derived from financial assets) and more aggressive taxation of active business profits. This tax regime reflects, I believe, the combination of the large U.S. appetite for foreign capital that has developed in the last six decades and an accompanying wariness of relinquishing U.S. taxation over economic activity conducted from within the United States. The need for foreign capital is the aftermath of American profligacy, both at home and abroad, that has transformed the United States from the world's largest exporter of capital to its largest importer. The uneasiness over foreign control of U.S. business assets is a concomitant defensive reaction, a sort of economic nationalism that wants business activity conducted from within the United States to be subject to net basis taxation regardless of the nationality of the ultimate owner. Americans prefer the claims of foreigners to be general (in the form of bank deposits, noncontrolling corporate debt, Treasury obligations, and the like) rather than specific (such as waterfront landmarks, heartland farms, or icons of American industry). When a nonresident person participates in an active manner in the U.S. economy, then that participation represents a competitor to the other domestic participants. The United States wants that nonresident competitor to be on the same playing field as the resident person that actively conducts business from within the United States. Let me add that a similar duality of purpose in terms of the attitude directed towards the active versus passive forms of foreign investment is revealed, often more saliently, in the tax systems of many other countries.

The difference in tax cost between the two U.S. income tax regimes imposed on foreign persons can be seen as a sort of tax toll-charge on the exercise of control over economic activity in the United States, and in this context, the threshold of control is low. An ownership stake of only 10 percent by a foreign person in a U.S. enterprise, for example, either as a shareholder or as a direct owner of equity, is enough to remove the interest received by the person from the enterprise from the class of exempt portfolio interest.

Even these second-order impressions of the U.S. tax system must be further refined. The actual level of U.S. taxation of foreign-owned business operations in the United States is not crushingly high. Reasons for this include the network of income tax treaties and various artful structures of ownership cultivated by foreign owners. In broad outline, the art of planning over the years for U.S. operations by foreign persons has been the conversion of U.S. business profits into a stream of passive income enjoying some Code-favored or treaty-favored regime. More graphically, it is to shoehorn the results of active business operations into the form of passive investments. Such maneuvers, and the U.S. Treasury's countermeasures, are discussed further in later chapters.

B. The Flat Rate Tax

Sections 871(a) and 881 impose U.S. tax at a flat 30 percent rate on the U.S. source passive investment income of foreign persons if its income is not effectively connected with the foreign person's U.S. trade or business. The flat rate tax has its own separate base which departs substantially from the general pattern of U.S. income taxation. It is collected by withholding at the source.[2] Overall, the flat tax regime is not designed to be subtle but to reach a large class of U.S. source income with a simple tax that lends itself to withholding.

The flat rate tax is imposed on *gross* income which means that it permits no deductions.[3] Allocable expenses therefore produce no tax benefit. What is commonly known as "investment interest," for example, is not deductible by foreign persons to any extent.

C. "Fixed or Determinable" Income

The flat rate tax regime applies to items of income enumerated in section 871(a)(1). The core of this income consists of

---

2 §§ 1441, 1442.

3 The denial of deductions results by inference from sections 873 and 882(c), which limit the deductions of foreign taxpayers to those attributable to income "effectively connected" with a U.S. trade or business.

> interest. . . dividends, rents, salaries, wages, premiums, annuities, compensations, remunerations, emoluments, and other fixed or determinable annual or periodical gains, profits, and income

to which a few similar items are added in other provisions. The flavor of this enumeration is inclusive. The drafters clearly wanted it to reach comprehensively a certain type of income. The catchall phrase at the end ("other fixed or determinable annual or periodical gains, profits, and income") picks up similar types of income (such as royalties) not explicitly listed. This entire category of income is routinely described by tax lawyers as "fixed or determinable" income, which has become the standard shorthand.

On first reading, however, the statutory enumeration does not appear universally inclusive. Both the listed items of specific income and the broad-gauged coda could be read as limited to income occurring in flows or regular increments. One might reasonably conclude from the language of the statute that "annual or periodical" gains did not extend to purely isolated or fortuitous ones, such as found money, for example, or the proceeds of a single wager or prize fight. A number of rulings by the IRS in the early days suggested this possibility[4] but were later set aside.[5] It is now well established that "fixed or determinable" income includes virtually every type of gross income, whether arising in a lump sum or periodic flows, whether one-of-a-kind or from recurrent transactions, and whether arising in a steady, intermittent, or erratic stream. The proceeds of a single night of wagering,[6] the proceeds for a covenant not to compete in the United States,[7] the prize from entering a horse in a single race, and even found money, fall within the class.[8]

A further characteristic of most of the enumerated items of fixed or determinable income is that the tax base is readily identified. Most rents, royalties, and wages, and all interest and dividends, come in

---

[4] E.g., S.M. 975, 1 Cum. Bull. 184 (1919) (winnings of horses at a racetrack not annual or periodical income); O.D. 907, 4 Cum. Bull. 232 (1921) (commission on single transaction not annual or periodical income); G.C.M. 21575, 1939–2 Cum. Bull. 172 (prizes awarded to foreign artists for best pictures at exhibition not annual or periodical income).

[5] Rev. Rul. 58–479, 1958–2 Cum. Bull. 60 (revoking S.M. 975, O.D. 907, G.C.M. 21575, above).

[6] In Park v. Commissioner, 722 F.3d 384 (D.C. Cir. 2013), the D.C. Circuit determined that wagering "gains" subjected to the gross basis tax was to be determined on a per-session approach and not on a per-bet approach.

[7] Korfund Co. v. Commissioner, 1 T.C. 1180 (1943); Rev. Rul. 74–108, 1974–1 Cum. Bull. 248.

[8] The period that satisfies the "periodical" element is apparently *one*, which makes even once-in-a-lifetime income "periodical" income of a sort. If the amount of income can be determined by the payor, then the income in that sense is "fixed" and "determinable."

measurable amounts that have the character of gross income. Typically (but not always), these amounts arise without substantial expense by the recipient and therefore have a large component of net gain. This is at least in part the justification for taxation at flat rates without allowance for deductions. Perhaps the simplest way to understand fixed or determinable income is that it includes all gross income that can be measured by the person paying it.[9]

1. Gains from Sales of Property

From this it follows that there is one crucially important type of income that is *not* fixed or determinable income: gain from the sale of property. The amount received by a seller of property is more akin to gross receipts than gross income. From the buyer's side, there is no way to tell whether the seller has gain (which would constitute gross income) or loss. The amount of tax that a buyer should withhold from the purchase price of property is indeterminate. Congress accordingly decided to leave gains from sales of property beyond the flat rate tax when it was adopted in 1936. Capital gains of foreign investors from pure investment assets therefore are generally free of U.S. tax.

2. Fixed and Determinable Income Even When No Amount Is Actually Received

An excellent case to unpack the contours of fixed and determinable income is *Central de Gas de Chihuahua, S.A. v. Commissioner*.[10] In this case, a Mexican corporation (Chihuahua Gas) rented a fleet of tractors to a related party (Hidro) for Hidro to use as part of its U.S. business activities. The case does not definitively indicate the ownership structure of the multinational group, but it says that the parties were under common control, were related parties, and were both Mexican corporations. In the years in issue, Hidro did not actually make any payments of rent to Chihuahua Gas. The case appears to imply that Hidro had a net loss from its business operations and that it would not have received any immediate tax benefit from a rental deduction, although such a deduction would have created a larger net operating loss carryforward for Hidro with respect to its U.S. trade or business. If there had been an actual rental payment, then Chihuahua Gas would have received fixed and determinable income to which a flat 30 percent tax on *gross* income would have applied. However, Chihuahua Gas had not actually charged for the use of its tractor fleet and had not received any actual rental payment. One can

---

[9] This is crucial. When the amount of "gross income" in payments cannot be measured by the one paying them, there is no basis for withholding from gross income.

[10] 102 T.C. 515 (1994).

hypothesize why no charge among affiliates was made. Perhaps this purely internal matter was not addressed, since all companies were part of the same family of entities. Perhaps no charge was put into place because an actual rental expense would have been subjected to a 30 percent *gross* income tax on a fixed and determinable rental payment at a time when the payor affiliate could not obtain a current tax benefit on the rental expense deduction given its net operating loss position. Regardless of the actual reason, Chihuahua Gas's contention was that it did not have any fixed and determinable income under section 881 because there was no payment actually made.

Simplified Diagram of Chihuahua Gas v. Commissioner

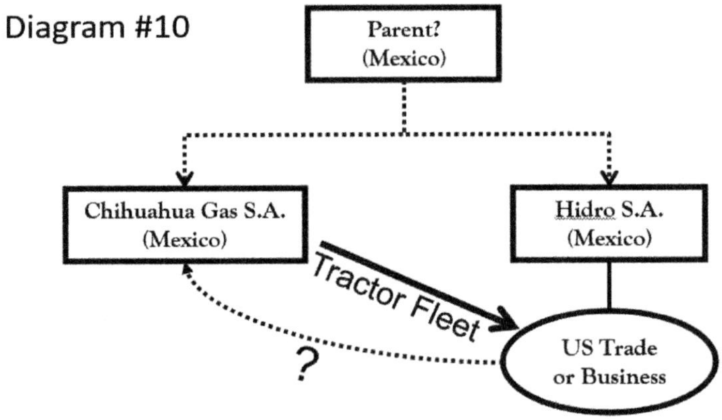

The government contended that the provision of a tractor fleet without charge failed to represent an arm's length arrangement among the related parties, and the Tax Court agreed. As discussed in chapter 4, section 482's arm's length standard underlies all related party arrangements. Thus, the government has the right under section 482 to deem a rental payment at an arm's length rate among the related parties, and once such a payment is deemed to have been made, the IRS had the right to apply section 881(a)'s flat 30 percent tax on gross *income* of the non-U.S. person that was *deemed* to have received fixed and determinable income. The Tax Court was certainly right that a foreign multinational enterprise should not be able to use non-arm's length arrangements among related affiliates to avoid the flat 30 percent tax on gross income that applies to fixed and determinable income.

However, even though the taxpayer's tax planning idea of utilizing non-arm's length arrangements to avoid the imposition of the 30 percent tax on *gross* income under section 881(a) was ultimately rejected, it is interesting to consider how this multinational enterprise could have achieved its desired tax results through other means. For example, if Chihuahua Gas had sold the tractor fleet at fair value to Hidro at a time when Chihuahua Gas did not have a U.S. trade or business, then the resulting income would have been *gain* and not fixed and determinable income. Moreover, that gain on the sale of the personal property would have all been foreign source income if title had been transferred on the tractors before arriving in the United States. Hidro then could have claimed annual depreciation deductions for the use of its purchased equipment in its U.S. trade or business. Another idea might have been to ensure that Chihuahua Gas engaged in sufficient activities within the United States to create its own U.S. trade or business presence. If that threshold had been crossed as to its own activities, then the payment of rent from Hidro to Chihuahua Gas would have constituted income effectively connected to the conduct of Chihuahua Gas's own U.S. trade or business and thus would not have been subject to a 30 percent flat tax on gross income. In that event, Chihuahua Gas could have reported its rental income as part of its U.S. trade or business and then claimed a deduction for the depreciation on its equipment used in that trade or business. In chapter 7, we will look at what would be needed to cross the threshold of having a U.S. trade or business.

The IRS has asserted a variation on this theme in Rev. Rul. 73–522, 1973–2 C.B. 226. In that ruling, a nonresident person owned rental property situated in the United States that was subject to long-term leases. The leases were referred to as "net leases." Under the net leases, the owner had transferred all maintenance and upkeep with respect to the leased property to the lessee. In this ruling, the IRS concluded that this arrangement did not represent a trade or business and that the lessor's rent income represented fixed and determinable income that was subject to the 30 percent gross basis tax under section 871. The ruling then stated that the amount of the rent subject to that 30 percent withholding included all payments made for the benefit of the lessor, including the lessee's payment of property taxes and repairs on the property. Thus, the owner's fixed and determinable income included not only the cash received but also the in-kind benefits the lessor derived from the lessee's payment of the lessor's property expenses. The law student might well remember from her federal income tax course the classic case of *Old Colony Trust v. Commissioner*, 279 U.S. 716 (1929) which, although not cited in the ruling, provides overarching support for the premise that the lessee's payment of the lessor's obligation should be treated as a constructive payment to the lessor.

D. Interest from Passive Investments

Interest is the first inclusion among the enumerated items of fixed or determinable income subject to U.S. taxation in section 871(a)(1). Little U.S. source interest paid to foreign persons, however, is actually subject to U.S. tax. Various exceptions and exemptions shield from U.S. tax virtually all interest received by foreign persons from passive investment. Interest paid to foreign persons on deposits of all kinds by U.S. banks and other financial institutions is exempt from U.S. tax pursuant to section 871(i).

E. Exempt "Portfolio Interest"

Even more importantly, since 1984, U.S. source interest from almost all types of debt obligations has been exempt from U.S. tax for foreign persons by virtue of sections 871(h) and 881(c) of the Code. These provisions exempt from flat rate tax what they term "portfolio interest" received from U.S. sources by foreign taxpayers.

Exempt "portfolio interest" includes the bulk of interest paid on passive debt obligations. Broadly, it is interest on a debt obligation held for investment by an identifiably foreign person. The design of portfolio interest in the Code aims to assure 1) that the exemption is enjoyed only by actual foreign investors and 2) that the relationship between borrower and lender is genuinely passive, i.e., that the interest truly is "portfolio" interest and not the product of some active business.

We can get a more precise picture by picking apart the Code's definition of "portfolio interest," which is interest (not derived from a U.S. business) paid on any "obligation" either 1) in registered form with a foreign owner or 2) if in bearer form, issued with restrictions on U.S. ownership.[11] Within these limitations, which are designed to prevent exempt portfolio interest from falling into the hands of U.S. beneficial owners, almost any kind of debt obligation can qualify, including bonds, notes of all kinds, and even debt on open account if it is properly recorded and not a business loan made in the ordinary course of a moneylending business.

The exemption of portfolio interest eliminates U.S. income tax on much of the return to passive foreign investment in the United States. Such an amiable tax regime would naturally induce all sorts of economic activity, including some highly entrepreneurial, to don the cloak of passive investment. Dressing ownership of U.S. business assets as ostensible debt holdings has become an obvious temptation. Section 871(h) contains a battery of provisions designed to keep the wolves from donning sheep's clothing.

---

[11] § 871(h)(2).

F. Exceptions, Limitations, and Restrictions

1. 10 Percent Shareholders

Exempt portfolio interest does not include interest received by a "10 percent shareholder" of the debtor.[12] The point of this limitation is to prevent escape from U.S. taxation for U.S. source interest paid by an enterprise to its owners and substantial equity holders. Foreign owners of U.S. businesses cannot (unless they are widely dispersed small shareholders) cast their holdings in U.S. businesses in the form of debt yielding an untaxed flow of interest. Without the 10 percent limitation for equity holders, foreign investment in U.S. businesses would routinely be structured with the highest sustainable levels of debt in order to remove the underlying business profits from the U.S. tax environment as tax-free portfolio interest.

The denial of exemption for interest paid to 10 percent shareholders means that foreign capital will not find as favorable a U.S. income tax regime when it is invested in controlling interests in U.S. businesses as when it is invested in passive financial assets. By allowing foreign investors to enjoy a tax-free regime for U.S. investment only up to the point they become substantial equity holders of U.S. businesses, the tax system attempts to favor foreign investment in economic activity that remains under American control.

A "10 percent shareholder" (despite the use of the term "shareholder") includes holders of partnership interests as well as corporate stock. For debt issued by corporations, a 10 percent shareholder means any person owning 10 percent or more of the combined voting power of all classes of stock of the corporation. The status of 10 percent shareholder of a corporation is tied to voting power rather than beneficial ownership. Foreign owners willing to leave control to others can thus expatriate U.S. source business profits in the form of exempt portfolio interest by capitalizing their ownership of U.S. business enterprises with a combination of nonvoting equity and debt.[13]

To grasp the import of the 10 percent shareholder rule, it may be helpful to revisit the interest stripping aspects of Diagram #2 that was introduced in chapter 3 and reproduced in relevant part below. The interplay between the source rule applied to interest (generally, the residence of the payor) and the 30 percent gross basis tax on fixed and determinable income (namely the related party interest paid by

---

12 § 871(h)(3).

13 In the case of a partnership, however, a 10 percent shareholder is any person who owns 10 percent or more of the capital or profits interests in the partnership. § 871(h)(3)(B).

US Pharma, Inc.) would provide an interest deduction that could reduce US Pharma Inc.'s taxable income from $160 million to $70 million.[14] If Big Pharma PLC were incorporated in a low-tax jurisdiction and if the U.S. source income were eligible for the U.S. source portfolio interest exception, the $90 million of interest would escape U.S. taxation.[15] However, because Big Pharma is a 10 percent shareholder of US Pharma, Inc., the interest is not exempt portfolio interest and is subject to the flat 30 percent gross basis tax on the $90 million interest amount. Thus, the effect of the 10 percent shareholder rule can be seen in this example: passive investors receive the benefits of the portfolio interest exemption but 10 percent shareholders (like Big Pharma PLC) are not allowed to escape the 30 percent gross basis tax on the interest earned in this inbound interest stripping transaction.

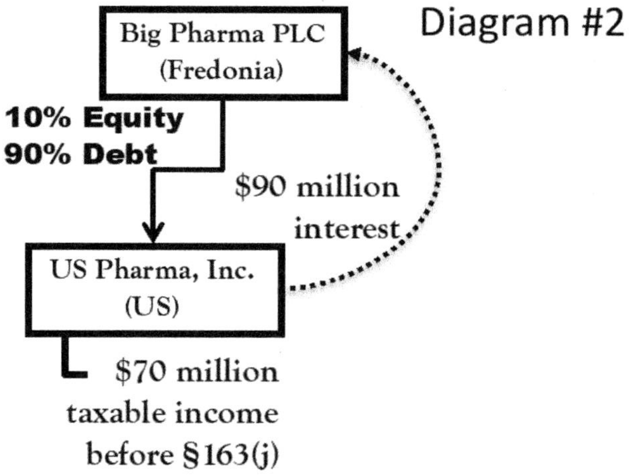

Nor would it help for Big Pharma PLC to hold the debt of US Pharma, Inc. indirectly so that no literal 10 percent shareholder would receive the interest. In this regard, consider the use of a foreign finance company. As depicted in Diagram #11, the foreign corporation (FinCo) is not directly a 10 percent shareholder (or any kind of shareholder) of US Pharma, Inc. Still, the interest paid to FinCo is not exempt portfolio interest. Attribution rules in section 871(h)(3)(C) treat FinCo for this purpose as the owner of the US

---

[14] The limitation on this interest deduction under section 163(j) modifies this result and is discussed in chapter 8.

[15] The earnings remaining in the U.S. corporation would eventually be subject to a second layer of U.S. taxation (30 percent, unless shielded by treaty) upon their distribution to Big Pharma, Inc. as dividends, but the distribution can be deferred for a long while, or Big Pharma PLC can eventually capture the value of the accumulated earnings by selling the stock, at no U.S. income tax cost.

Pharma, Inc. shares that are directly owned by Big Pharma PLC, thus making it a 10 percent shareholder by attribution. This is yet another form of look-through rule designed to forestall base erosion and profit shifting in the related party interest stripping context.

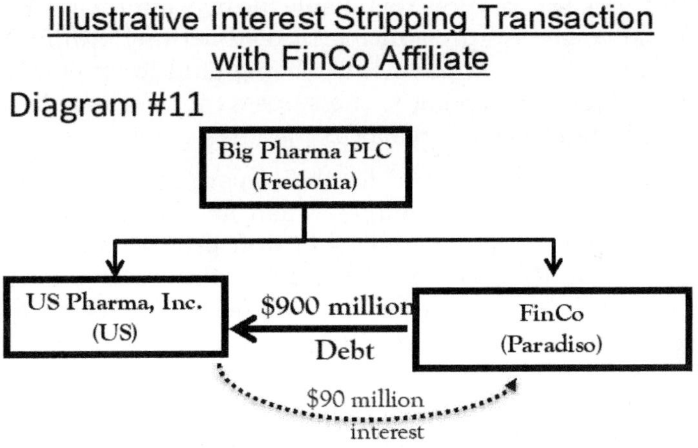

However, what Big Pharma PLC cannot do alone can be done with a second investor, as follows. Suppose that, for business reasons, another unrelated foreign investor, say a sovereign wealth fund or a private equity fund, lends funds to US Pharma, Inc. and receives interest, as depicted in Diagram #12.

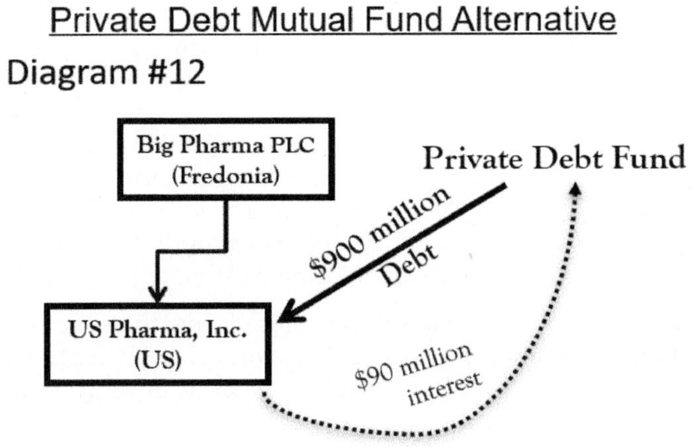

Now the interest income received by the offshore Private Debt Fund is exempt portfolio interest as no 10 percent shareholder is involved. There are constraints, though, on this possibility. If the Private Debt Fund were related to Big Pharma then by attribution under the rules sketched above the Private Debt Fund would be treated as a 10 percent shareholder and interest paid by US Pharma, Inc. would not be exempt portfolio interest and would be subject to section 881(a)'s flat 30 percent gross tax. Moreover, this alternative does not present the same base erosion and profit shifting possibility as the interest stripping transaction. Yes, the interest payment made by US Pharma, Inc. reduces its taxable income, but the multinational group is no longer simply shifting income between affiliates. Here, the $90 million interest payment is being paid to an outside party. The effect of this borrowing is the same as if US Pharma, Inc. had simply borrowed from a U.S. bank.

Thus, the policy rationale for the 10 percent shareholder can be gleaned from the above example: when an intercompany interest payment is being used as a device to shift profits among commonly owned entities, there is no relief from flat rate U.S. taxation. However, when an interest payment arises from debt issued in the public debt markets, profit shifting is not typically involved and an exception from U.S. taxation is allowed to accommodate the U.S. economy's enormous appetite for foreign capital. However, having articulated this policy rationale, we will see in later chapters that this stricture on the ability to utilize related party funding can be mitigated or supplanted by U.S. tax treaty provisions that reduce or eliminate the tax on gross income even for 10 percent shareholders.

2. Interest Paid to Foreign Banks

The unrelated debtholder in this pattern, moreover, cannot be a bank or similar full-time professional lender. In another important exception to the portfolio interest exemption, interest received by a foreign bank "on an extension of credit made pursuant to a loan agreement entered into in the ordinary course of its trade or business" is *not* exempt portfolio interest.[16] The premise of this treatment of bank loans is that a bank loan generally is more like a business transaction than a passive investment and should be taxed accordingly.[17] The rule prevents foreign banks from gaining a competitive advantage over U.S. banks in making loans to United States persons from outside the United States.

Taxpayers have attempted in various ways to maneuver around the restrictive rules for bank debt. For example, a Private Debt Fund might act as a "conduit" by borrowing from a foreign bank and re-lending to US Pharma, Inc., as in Diagram #13.

---

[16] § 881(c)(3)(A).

[17] Note, however, that 1) foreign banks *can* receive exempt portfolio interest on bona fide passive investments such as corporate bonds and U.S. Treasury debt, and 2) income tax treaties may shield some interest received by foreign banks that does not qualify as exempt portfolio interest.

Diagram #13

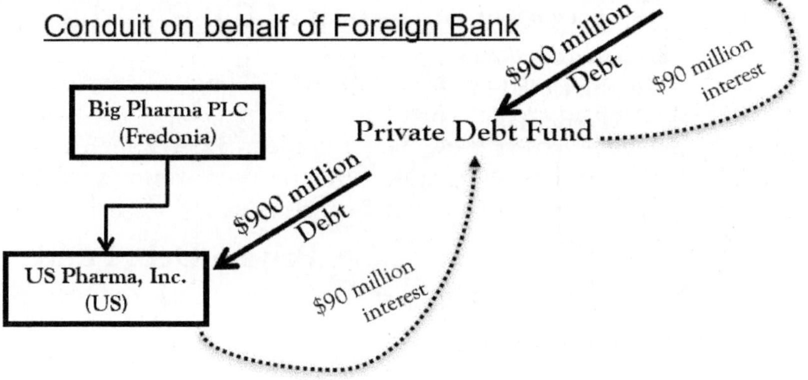

This pattern, known as back-to-back (or mirror-image) debt, is central to many international tax shelters and earnings stripping plans. We shall return to it in later chapters. In cases where the debt obligation of a fronting or conduit entity (i.e., Private Debt Fund in the diagram) is secured by US Pharma, Inc.'s obligation to the fronting entity (i.e., the Private Debt Fund in the diagram), the Internal Revenue Service might well attack the Private Debt Fund's role in the venture as a mere "conduit" and seek to deny the exempt portfolio interest exception on the grounds that the payment is in substance a payment to a foreign bank that is not entitled to that exception by reason of section 881(c)(3)(A). Under this viewpoint, the interest income received by the Private Debt Fund that must be turned over to the foreign bank is considered simply to be beneficially owned by the foreign bank from the outset. Since 1993, a set of rules on "conduits," discussed more fully in chapter 8, has strengthened the Service's hand in this type of situation.

If, however, the Private Debt Fund had borrowed on its own general credit and had no other dealings with the foreign bank, such an attack by the Service would likely fail. As a business matter, however, such a transaction is implausible. A bank would almost certainly require that the Private Debt Fund's obligation be secured by the business corporation's obligation unless the Private Debt Fund had sufficient unencumbered assets to cover the loan apart from the loan to US Pharma, Inc. In that event, the Private Debt Fund could have made the loan entirely from its own assets without having to resort to a bank loan in the first place.

A variant of this back-to-back pattern is a loan from Big Pharma PLC that is channeled through the Private Debt Fund on its way to US Pharma, Inc., as the following Diagram #14 illustrates.

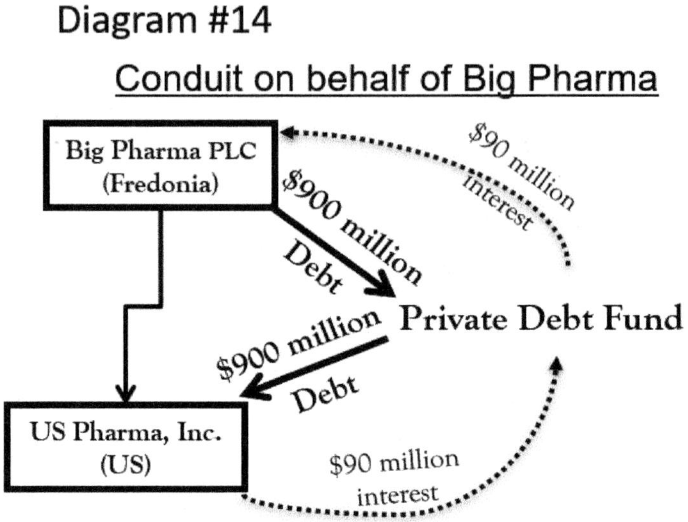

In principle, this is no different from the case involving a bank, but now, the conduit arrangement is being used as a mechanism to shift profits among affiliates, and it attempts to do so in a manner that hides the related party interest stripping activity. The pattern does raise pointed questions of enforcement. How will the IRS find out about Big Pharma PLC's back-to-back loan made through the Private Debt Fund? It is not obvious. Small private issues of debt to foreign persons that purport to generate exempt portfolio interest, to be sure, are more likely to elicit probing questions from the IRS on the relationship that exists between ultimate debtholder and the U.S. debtor on privately issued bonds. However, the IRS can make enquiries only in situations that it is able to fathom, and this type of arrangement is by no means self-identifying.

3. Contingent Interest

Another exception, dating from the 1993 Act, removes several types of "contingent" interest from the class of exempt portfolio interest. Under section 871(h)(4)(A)(i), exempt portfolio interest does not include interest determined by reference to 1) the receipts, sales, or cash flow of the debtor, 2) the income or profits of the debtor, 3) a change in the value of appreciation or depreciation of property of the debtor, or 4) dividends or similar payments made by the debtor. These rules are designed to prevent direct participations by foreign persons in the profits of U.S. business operations from escaping U.S. taxation. The import of this carve-out for contingent payments is that a foreign investor's return that is contingent upon the success of the business activity causes the nonresident person to lose the moniker of a passive investor and to don the status of an active investor.

G. Interest Derived in Different Forms

1. Interest from Mutual Funds and Other Investment Companies

Much U.S. source interest income is derived from mutual funds, including bond funds of all stripes and, more recently, exchange-traded funds (ETFs). A problem in this regard for foreign investors is that most mutual funds and all ETFs are structured as *corporations*—known for purposes of taxation as "regulated investment companies" (RICs)—in which investors own *shares*. For some purposes of taxation, RICs are taxed as conduits through which income flows unchanged; for others, they retain the character of separate corporations.[18] In general, distributions from mutual funds retain the formal aspect of *dividends,* even if attributable to *interest* income of the underlying fund. For U.S. persons, this regime has posed few problems (although the rules concerning the character of dividends from RICs were changed to reflect the maximum 15 percent rate of tax on dividends brought in by the 2003 Act). For foreign investors, however, the rate of U.S. tax on dividends is almost invariably higher than the zero-percent rate imposed on U.S. source portfolio interest. Accordingly, investment in U.S. bond funds has been unattractive for foreign persons. Instead, they have invested in offshore bond funds or directly in individual U.S. debt instruments.

2. Sections 871(k) and 881(e)

The 2004 Act introduced sections 871(k) and 881(e) which provide (simplifying somewhat) that some interest income may retain its character as interest—and hence potentially be exempt portfolio interest—when distributed by a RIC to a foreign person.

Mechanically, sections 871(k)(1)(A) and 881(e)(1)(A) exempt from flat rate tax an "interest-related dividend" received by a foreign person from a RIC. An "interest-related dividend" is a dividend designated by a RIC as an interest-related dividend in a written notice mailed to its shareholders no later than 60 days after the close of its taxable year but only to the extent of the RIC's "qualified net interest income."[19] The "qualified net interest income" of a RIC is its "qualified interest income" reduced by properly allocable deductions,[20] and its "qualified interest income," as well you expected, is interest that would be exempt from tax if received directly by a foreign person. Specifically, qualified interest income is:

---

[18] The taxation of RICs and their shareholders is governed by sections 851 through 855.

[19] § 871(k)(1)(C).

[20] § 871(k)(1)(D).

the sum of the following amounts derived by the [RIC] from sources within the United States:

(i) Any amount includible in gross income as original issue discount. . . on an obligation payable 183 days or less from the date of original issue. . . .

(ii) Any interest includible in gross income. . . on an obligation which is in registered form. . .

(iii) Any interest [from U.S. bank deposits].

(iv) Any interest-related dividend [from another RIC].[21]

There are exceptions and qualifications, corresponding to several of the limitations on exempt portfolio interest. Qualified interest income does *not* include:

(I) any interest on an obligation issued by a corporation or partnership if the [RIC receiving the interest] is a 10 percent shareholder in such corporation or partnership, and

(II) any interest which is treated as not being portfolio interest [because it is contingent interest under section 871(h)(4)].[22]

H. Dividends

U.S. source dividends, like interest, are fixed or determinable income subject to flat rate tax.[23] Unlike portfolio interest, they are entitled to no broad exemption from U.S. tax. It follows that dividends paid from earnings that have borne U.S. corporate income tax may suffer *two* layers of U.S. tax.[24] High-yield U.S. equities are not, therefore, holdings of choice for foreign investors. Low-yield equities, on the other hand, given the absence of U.S. tax on most capital gains of foreign persons, are often ideal.

I. Income from Intangible Property

The taxation of income derived from intangible property has evolved to deal with differences between the economic character of the income and the form of transaction from which it is derived. Royalties and other periodic consideration for the use of intangible

---

21 § 871(k)(1)(E).

22 § 871(k)(1)(E)(ii).

23 Dividends from *foreign* corporations, however, are exempt from flat rate tax under section 871(i)(2)(D), even if they have U.S. source through the operation of the 25 percent rule of section 861(a)(2)(B). See chapter 3.

24 Most income tax treaties reduce, but do not eliminate, the tax on dividends by the country of source.

property have always been regarded as "fixed or determinable" income even though not explicitly so listed in the Code. Royalty income, you may remember from chapter 3, takes its source from the country where the underlying royalty-producing property is used. Royalties for the use of intangible property in the United States (in a licensing arrangement, for example) are therefore taxable to foreign persons at a flat rate if not derived from a U.S. trade or business. By contrast, lump sum gains from the *sale* of intangible property have their source in the place of residence of the seller[25] and are free of U.S. tax unless related to a U.S. trade or business.[26]

1. Sale Versus License

In this regime, both taxpayers and the IRS have paid close attention to the difference between sales and licenses of intangible property. The distinction can be elusive, however. The transfer of rights in intangible or intellectual property is often less clear-cut than that of its tangible counterpart. Intangible property can often be used by several persons simultaneously. Sole possession being less critical, rights can be divided temporally, geographically, or by markets. There are certainties only at the extremes. A transfer of a copyright forever, lock, stock, and barrel, with no retained right of use, has always been a sale. The nonexclusive permission to use a secret process in exchange for a percentage of the resulting sales has always been a license.

A case filling in the middle zone is *Commissioner v. Wodehouse*.[27] Wodehouse was an English author who had ostensibly "sold" the right to serialize a novel to an American magazine publisher for a lump sum price. The IRS insisted that the single payment was nonetheless "fixed or determinable" income (a royalty in effect) subject to flat rate tax, and, despite the lump sum price, the IRS won on the ground that in the transfer of the serial rights Wodehouse retained so many other rights in the property that there had been no sale. Since *Wodehouse*, the difference between a sale and a license has turned not on the form of payment but on the extent of the rights transferred in the underlying property.

Subsequent cases and rulings have fleshed out this boundary. In general, the transfer of *all* substantial rights in intangible property is a sale and, for many purposes, the exclusive transfer of various lesser rights is also a sale. The exclusive right to use a patent in a geographical area forever is a sale, for example, as is the exclusive right to exploit a copyrighted work in a medium of expression for the

---

[25] § 865(a), (d).

[26] Remember that sales of property (other than U.S. realty) by foreign persons are generally untaxed if unrelated to a U.S. business.

[27] 337 U.S. 369 (1949).

full life of the copyright.[28] Thus, the exclusive and permanent transfer of all print rights in a work of fiction in the United States is a sale,[29] and so is a similar transfer of the stage rights or the motion picture rights. Each transfer exhausts the U.S. rights within the medium of print, stage, or screen, respectively.

There is a further question about the boundaries of a single medium of expression. For now, recognized separate media include print, stage, motion picture, and broadcast (radio and television). As cyberspace expands its power to transmit artistic and literary representations, it may come to be viewed as a separate medium of expression for this purpose.

2. Sales with Contingent Payments

The outcome of *Wodehouse* left opportunities for foreign taxpayers. As long as they transferred substantial and extensive U.S. rights in intangible property, their transactions were sales even if they received a stream of payments contingent on the buyer's subsequent use of the property. A common form of transfer of rights in intangible property is the contingent sale, where the owner of a copyright or a patent transfers all rights in it for a percentage of the proceeds derived from its use by the transferee. In legal form the transaction is a sale because the entire titular ownership in property has been transferred. In economic effect, however, it is a royalty arrangement in which the transferor retains a continuing economic interest in the intangible property.

To align taxation more closely with the economic character of contingent sales, section 871(a)(1)(D) imposes flat rate tax on U.S. source "gains from the sale or exchange. . . of patents, copyrights, secret processes and formulas, goodwill, trademarks, trade brands, franchises, and other like property, or of any interest in any such property, to the extent such gains are from payments which are contingent on the productivity, use or disposition of the property or interest sold or exchanged." As noted in chapter 3, the source of such contingent payments is determined as though the payments were royalties. Therefore, the place where intangible property is used, rather than the place of sale or the residence of the seller, governs the source of the gains. The effect of these provisions, roughly, is to tax contingent gains from the sale of intangible property as if they were royalties.

Bear in mind that gain attributable to *fixed* payments is not subject to the tax of section 871(a)(1)(D). It follows that a foreign

---

[28] See Rev. Rul. 60–226, 1960–1 Cum. Bull. 26.

[29] But not the transfer of the right of serial publication (at issue in *Wodehouse*), which does not exhaust the print medium.

seller of intangible property for use in the United States should hold out for a lump sum price rather than a contingent formula price predicated on events. It is, of course, much harder to come to an agreement on a lump sum price (because the buyer then bears the entire cost of poor results and the seller the benefit of unexpected good results), and some contingent element will often be necessary as a business matter for an exchange to go forward. In that event, the tax planner should try to confine the contingent element to the smallest possible amount in the fewest taxable years without undermining the economics of the transaction.

With section 871(a)(1)(D) in the Code, the distinction between sales and licenses is far less important for transactions in intangible property than in the days of *Wodehouse*. All contingent payments attributable to intangible property used in the United States are today subject to tax.

J. Concluding Thoughts on the Fixed and Determinable Standard and Base Erosion and Profit Shifting Phenomenon

After digesting the above rules, it is appropriate to consider whether and to what extent the fixed and determinable standard successfully protects the U.S. tax base from the base erosion and profit shifting phenomenon in the multinational enterprise context. This inquiry is not the end of the analysis because the fixed and determinable standard can be further relaxed by treaty arrangements. However, it is a helpful mile marker to consider in terms of how the U.S. source rules and the fixed and determinable standard work to protect the U.S. tax base from inbound earnings stripping techniques. In Diagram #9, which was introduced in chapter 4 and reproduced again here, Big Pharma PLC and its U.S. subsidiary, US Pharma, Inc. is depicted.

Diagram #9

Combined Strategy

Supply Chain Transaction, Interest Stripping Transaction, Royalty Stripping Transaction, Rental Stripping, and Service Stripping Transaction

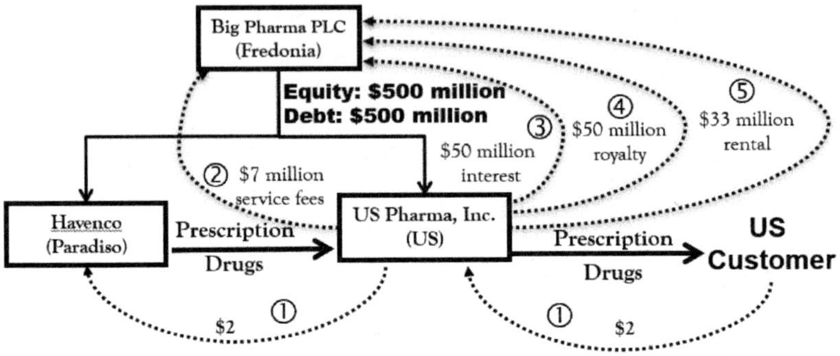

In addition, Diagram #9 sets forth each of the basic earnings stripping transactions discussed in earlier chapters in combination. There is a supply chain transaction (see the diagram at ①) that is the first depicted earnings stripping technique, a service stripping transaction (see the diagram at ②) that is the second depicted earnings stripping technique, an interest stripping transaction (see the diagram at ③) that is the third depicted earnings stripping technique, a royalty stripping transaction (see the diagram at ④) that is the fourth depicted earnings stripping technique, and a lease stripping transaction (see diagram at ⑤) that is the fifth and final depicted earnings stripping technique. As to the leased equipment, the reader should recall that the rental expense replaces US Pharma, Inc.'s ownership of its own depreciable/amortizable property for new equipment. Diagram #9 is impressive, but it simply builds on what has been discussed already. The chart depicts that at least $140 million of related party payments have been made by US Pharma, Inc. to its parent, Big Pharma PLC, apart from considering the profit shifting aspects of the supply chain transaction between HavenCo and US Pharma, Inc. A multinational enterprise with a vertically integrated business model is likely to have several means to engage in related party transactions, like the ones depicted in Diagram #9. Moreover, the use of multiple strategies allows a multinational enterprise to avoid putting all of its tax planning eggs into one tax strategy basket. In the above Diagram #9, assume that US Pharma, Inc. started with $200 million of profits before related party transactions and before any depreciation/amortization deductions. The result of the combined strategies is that at least $140 million of the $200 million of US Pharma, Inc. profits are stripped out of US Pharma, Inc. So, how do the U.S. source rules and the U.S. gross basis tax apply to these base erosion strategies?

On one side of the spectrum, the supply chain transaction and the service stripping transaction safely navigate section 881(a) without creating a category of income that would be subject to the 30 percent flat basis tax on gross income. In this regard, the supply chain transaction creates gain from the sale of inventory in Havenco, and thus it is not a category of fixed and determinable income. This inbound tax planning technique is thus unaffected by the U.S. gross income taxation of fixed and determinable income. The service stripping transaction also creates income that is not taxable under section 881(a). Service income is a potential category of fixed and determinable income in its character, but the sourcing of the service income in this fact pattern is foreign source income if Big Pharma PLC's personnel perform those related party services from facilities located outside of the United States. Thus, because the services are not U.S. source but instead are foreign source, the related party service payments are excluded from the 30 percent tax on gross income imposed under section 881(a) because the fixed and determinable income of Big Pharma PLC must be U.S. source to be subject to taxation under that regime. Thus, multinational enterprises that have trade flows or service centers can avail themselves of supply chain transactions or service stripping transactions, like those depicted above, and need not fear section 881(a).

However, the interest stripping transaction, the royalty stripping transaction, and the rental stripping transaction do create exposure under the flat 30 percent tax on gross income under section 881(a). The interest income earned by Big Pharma PLC is fixed and determinable income that is sourced by the residence of the payor and received by a 10 percent shareholder, so it is subject to the flat 30 percent tax on gross income. The royalty income earned by Big Pharma PLC that is received from US Pharma, Inc. is sourced by where the intangible property is used. So long as the intangible property licensed to US Pharma, Inc. is used in the United States, the royalty paid for the use of that intangible property is U.S. source income. As a result, the royalty income is also U.S. source fixed and determinable income subject to section 881(a)'s 30 percent tax on gross income. In like manner, the rental stripping transaction is sourced by where the underlying tangible property is used. Thus, assuming that US Pharma, Inc. utilizes the leased property in the United States, the rental income earned by Big Pharma PLC would be U.S. source fixed and determinable income subject to the 30 percent tax on gross income under section 881(a).

Therefore, the fixed and determinable standard, on the surface of these transactions, subjects three of the five earnings stripping techniques to gross basis taxation under section 881(a). That said, these three earnings stripping strategies that create an exposure to section 881(a)'s flat 30 percent tax on gross fixed and determinable income may nevertheless escape any U.S. taxation if a U.S. tax treaty modeled after the 2016 Model Income Tax Convention were to apply as Article 11 (Interest), Article 12 (Royalties), and Article 21 (Other Income provision related to income not part of a U.S. permanent establishment) would all cede U.S. taxation of these categories of fixed and determinable income when earned by a non-U.S. person that does not have a U.S. permanent establishment and is entitled to U.S. tax treaty relief. Absent such treaty relief, section 881(a)'s 30 percent gross basis tax on fixed and determinable income is an effective mechanism to protect the U.S. tax base with respect to three of the inbound earnings stripping strategies that are depicted in Diagram #9.

K. Withholding

As you may recall from the Kuwaiti contract tale discussed in chapter 1, the imposition of a gross basis tax on a nonresident person who has no connection to a jurisdiction other than the income remitted from it creates an administrative compliance conundrum. To put teeth into the system, the U.S. tax laws impose upon the payor of fixed and determinable income the requirement to withhold the 30 percent gross income tax. Section 1441 and section 1442 requires withholding by "all persons, in whatever capacity acting (including lessees or mortgagors of real or personal property, fiduciaries, employers and all officers and employees of the United States) having the control, receipt, custody, disposal, or payment of any of the items of income [subject to withholding]." The system of withholding under section 1441 and section 1442 shifts nearly the entire burden of complying with the flat rate tax from the ultimate nonresident person to those who pay out the income.

The implementing regulations define this withholding requirement in very broad terms.[30] Some exceptions are allowed, however. For example, original issue discount is fixed and determinable income, but it is specifically excluded from withholding.[31] Cancellation of indebtedness income also is fixed and determinable income, but the regulations make it clear that it is not subject to withholding if the lender does not have custody or control over the money or property of the borrower at the time of the cancellation of indebtedness.[32]

---

30 Reg. § 1.1441–2(b)(2).

31 § 1441(a).

32 Reg. § 1.1441–2(d)(2).

If the payor fails to properly withhold, then the IRS can seek collection of the gross basis tax directly from the withholding agent. The Treasury regulations require only one agent in the chain to actually withhold.[33] If no one withholds, absent a withholding agreement involving qualified intermediaries, any withholding agent in a chain of transmittal may be liable. The Treasury is free to pursue the one nearest to hand, with no apparent priority. An intermediary downstream in the chain that receives a payment from which a prior withholding agent has failed to withhold therefore cannot expect the U.S. Treasury necessarily to press its demands at the top of the chain, and might well want to withhold in self-defense, thus pulling the prior withholding agent's chestnuts from the fire.

The withholding at source from fixed or determinable income is different in basic respects from wage withholding that you may have suffered as an employee. While both instances of withholding occur on the payor side, the latter is a down payment of tax followed by a reckoning with the IRS (by filing a return) that may involve a refund or additional tax due. In the flat rate tax context, however, the tax and withholding are so thoroughly intertwined as to be nearly congruent. Withholding is set at the same rate as the tax itself and falls on the same tax base—the gross amount of fixed or determinable income from sources in the United States. From this amount there is a ready computation of gross income.

In this system, withholding and the flat rate tax have become essentially coextensive. Indeed, in the patois of international tax lawyers, the term "withholding tax" is often used to describe the flat rate tax itself.[34] A foreign taxpayer from whom the correct amount has been withheld has nothing more to pay and can expect to get nothing back. The taxpayer and the Treasury are thus quit of each other, and there is no need to file a return.[35] However, if the U.S. payor fails to withhold properly on the fixed and determinable income, then the IRS can proceed against the statutorily prescribed withholding agent for the unpaid tax.[36]

---

[33] See Reg. § 1.1441–7(a).

[34] This habit is so engrained that some international tax lawyers refer to any flat rate tax as a "withholding" tax, even if it is paid by return.

[35] The Code itself does in fact require foreign taxpayers to file returns even when the appropriate amount of tax has been withheld. § 6012(a)(1). The Treasury regulations, however, waive this requirement when tax has been withheld under § 1441 and paid over to the Treasury in an amount sufficient to satisfy tax liability in full. Reg. § 1.6012–1(b)(1)(i) and (2), 1.6012–2(g)(2)(i). However, if the correct withholding was not made, then the IRS can pursue collection against the foreign person as that person still owes U.S. tax that has not been satisfied by way of withholding and is obligated to pay the tax along with a properly filed income tax return in that scenario.

[36] See Reg. § 1.1441–10(c).

Any person or entity actually in the payment chain, subject to exceptions set forth in the regulations, is potentially liable for the withholding obligation for amounts within its control. Both payment and control are, in addition, imputed from agents to their principals. The IRS has taken the position that even "constructive" control over payment triggers the obligation to withhold, with mixed results. A favorable case for the government in this effort is *Casa de La Jolla Park, Inc. v. Commissioner*, 94 T.C. 384 (1990). In *Casa de La Jolla*, a U.S. corporation owed money to its Canadian shareholder (an individual), and the U.S. corporation directed a bank that received funds directly from customers to in turn remit those proceeds directly to a creditor of the Canadian shareholder. Even though neither the U.S. corporation nor the Canadian individual ever directly paid or received any funds, the Tax Court held that the U.S. corporation was obligated to withhold under section 1441. In light of the control exercised over the payments by the U.S. corporation vis-à-vis its arrangement with its collecting bank, the Tax Court held that the U.S. corporation was a withholding agent. This holding seems entirely sound, and the holding of the case indicates that one cannot simply shift the withholding obligation away to another person at least vis-à-vis the U.S. Treasury. However, whether one can contractually receive indemnity protection from the other party can be a matter of private contact that runs between the two parties.

A conduit arrangement presents another difficult fact pattern, as a withholding agent, absent a reason to know, would generally rely on the treaty-based intermediary as the rationale for not subjecting a payment to withholding but may be unaware that the intermediary is not the ultimate beneficial owner of the income. However, these points help to demonstrate the general rule that applies to the vast majority of situations that withholding rules are intended expansively to require a payor of fixed and determinable income to withhold on such amounts. The analysis forces the conclusion that the possible application of a tax treaty has enormous implications for interest stripping, royalty stripping, and rental stripping transactions. Thus, the gross basis income tax that applies to fixed and determinable income sets the stage for treaty shopping and the concern over how to prevent untoward use of U.S. tax treaties. That topic is addressed in chapter 7.

Chapter 6

U.S. TAXATION OF FOREIGN PERSONS: TAXATION OF A TRADE OR BUSINESS

A. The Meaning of a U.S. "Trade or Business"

The notion of a "trade or business" in the United States lies at the core of U.S. taxation of inbound transactions. As we saw in chapter 5, foreign persons' U.S. source income from passive investment is either taxed at a flat rate on a gross basis or not taxed at all. As we shall see later in this chapter, income "effectively connected" with a U.S. business is taxed on a *net* basis at graduated rates, much like the income of a U.S. person. Since a foreign person must have, or have had, a U.S. "trade or business" in order to have income "effectively connected" with it, the existence of a U.S. trade or business stands at the center of U.S. taxation of the U.S. business activities of foreign persons.

The scope of U.S. taxation over the U.S. business activities of foreign persons has changed over the years. Until 1966, a foreign person with a U.S. business—any U.S. business—was subject to full U.S. taxation on all U.S. source income. Thus, a foreign person with a huge portfolio of U.S. investment assets might become subject to U.S. taxation at graduated rates (as opposed to flat rate taxation on the gross amount of fixed and determinable income and zero taxation of capital gains) by starting a small restaurant in the United States or even giving a single lecture for money. This regime was known as the "force of attraction" rule because the U.S. trade or business appeared to "attract" all the U.S. source income of a foreign person. Today, there are separate and independent tax regimes for passive investment income and income derived from a U.S. business. Each regime applies without effect on the other.

The Code offers no comprehensive definition of a "trade or business" for either domestic or foreign taxpayers. In various places, however, the concept is expressly qualified to specific ends. For foreign taxpayers in particular, the core notion of a trade or business is left largely to administrative or judicial determination, but the notion has also been overlaid with statutory rules governing specific activities and taxpayers. This chapter surveys the general scope of a "trade or business" and one or two special enclaves. After addressing the threshold question of what constitutes a trade or business, I will then turn my attention to the question of what income is "effectively connected" to the conduct of that U.S. trade or business.

1. "Business" Versus Passive Investment

The notion of a "trade or business" is best understood in contrast to what it is not: passive investment.[1] A "trade or business" suggests something active, perhaps even entrepreneurial. Passive investment entails little more than the commitment of capital and patient expectation. Because there are near-infinite gradations of risk and involvement in the full range of economic activity, it turns out to be difficult, if not impossible, to articulate a universal test of a trade or business as opposed to passive investment. Rather, it is a fact bound determination in which several elements—including, most importantly, the nature and extent of the taxpayer's activity—weigh in the scales.

A classic case on the distinction between a trade or business and pure passive investing is *Higgins v. Commissioner*.[2] Higgins lived (in Paris) off of the income of his substantial holdings of real estate, bonds, and stock. He maintained an office in New York that generally watched over his securities. Higgins's employees did little trading but deposited checks and kept records. Because Higgins had very substantial assets, this recordkeeping and oversight entailed considerable activity. The Commissioner rejected the argument that the cost of managing the securities was an expense of carrying on a trade or business, and the Supreme Court agreed. The Court underscored the essentially factual boundary between pure passive investing and carrying on a trade or business and concluded that even though the taxpayer's activities were extensive, merely keeping records and collecting income (albeit on a large scale) is not a trade or business. Significantly though, the IRS conceded in the case—and the Court apparently agreed—that the taxpayer's ownership of rental real estate (and the attendant activity) *did* constitute a business. The difference was, one can infer, that Higgins's stocks and bonds were pure financial assets entitling him to an income stream only and giving him neither the right to participate actively in the operations of the underlying enterprises nor any liabilities beyond his commitment of capital. Higgins's ownership of buildings, by contrast, presumably gave him both the right and the obligation to

---

1 We use the terms "investing" and "investment" not in the technical economic sense of creating a new income-producing capital asset, but in the colloquial sense of acquiring ownership rights in a passive income stream.

2 312 U.S. 212, *reh'g denied,* 312 U.S. 714 (1941).

deal with the property directly as well as full liability for losses and other risks.[3]

An important inference from *Higgins* is that the existence of a trade or business depends at the outset on the nature of the interest in property from which gain is derived. Direct ownership, with the attendant responsibilities and risks, is an essential element of a trade or business, while pure financial assets that yield an income stream without involvement or liability are generally passive investments. The ownership of corporate shares therefore is not in itself a trade or business, and the trade or business of a corporation is not imputed to its shareholders or even to a single owner of all the shares.

Direct ownership is necessary but not sufficient to constitute a trade or business. The right to a stream of royalties, for example, does not put its holder in a trade or business. A landowner who turns mineral rights over to a lessee who agrees to develop the property and pay back a percentage of production as a royalty does not thereby acquire a trade or business; nor does a landowner who receives a crop share from a tenant farmer. Owners of such passive royalty interests are not involved in the underlying activity.

2. "The Taxpayer's Activity"

Higgins established the baseline that a certain type of direct ownership of assets is essential to put a taxpayer in a trade or business. That in itself is not dispositive, however. Another line of cases, with antecedents prior to *Higgins,* finds in the level of *activity* of the taxpayer an additional element of a "trade or business": if the taxpayer is active in pursuit of profit, there is a trade or business; if not, then not.

One early opinion found in the very etymology of the term "business" an entrepreneurial element:

> An occasional sale of land held as an investment is not such a business though profit results. The word ["business"], notwithstanding disguise in spelling and pronunciation, means busyness; it implies that one is kept more or less busy, that the activity is an occupation.[4]

This is a straightforwardly intuitive notion. Someone who is working up a sweat in gainful pursuits normally conveys the impression of being engaged in business, whereas someone whose

---

[3] This implication of *Higgins* is confirmed in Investor's Mortgage Security Co. v. Commissioner, 4 T.C.M. 45 (1945), where a large foreign investor in U.S. financial assets was held also to have a U.S. trade or business by virtue of its ownership of significant but lesser holdings of U.S. real property.

[4] Snell v. Commissioner, 97 F.2d 891, 892 (5th Cir. 1938).

income arises spontaneously while he lolls in a hammock does not. While the difference is plain enough in many situations, the boundary is perhaps least clear in the ownership and operation of real property which can be carried out in relatively active or passive ways. Not surprisingly, the cases in this area have largely set the level of activity amounting to a trade or business.

3. Rental Real Estate and Natural Resources

Rental real estate, in particular, is a holding that may or may not constitute a trade or business for its owner. An owner involved in the day-to-day operation of the property is clearly engaged in business. One who turns over the property entirely to independent agents, or to the tenants in net lease arrangements, may not be. The decided cases draw a somewhat shaky line between these possibilities.

"Considerable, Continuous, and Regular." In *Pinchot v. Commissioner*[5] a British citizen and resident owned several parcels of rental real estate in New York City. The properties were managed through an agent who leased them when they became idle, collected the rents, and paid the operating expenses, taxes, mortgage interest, and other necessary obligations. From time to time, properties were sold, and others were bought. The court drew the inference from the scale of the holdings themselves that the transactions of the taxpayer in managing them "must have been considerable. . . as well as continuous and regular,"[6] assuming, in effect, that income cannot arise from properties of a certain size without some active massaging:

> What was done was more than the investment and reinvestment of funds in real estate. It was the management of the real estate itself for profit. . . . It necessarily involved alterations and repairs commensurate with the value and number of buildings cared for, and such transactions as were necessary constitute a recognized form of business. The management of real estate on such a scale for income producing purposes required regular and continuous activity of the kind which is commonly concerned with the employment of labor; the purchase of materials; the making of contracts; and many other things which come within the definition of business. . . within the commonly accepted meaning of that word.[7]

---

[5] 113 F.2d 718 (2d Cir. 1940).

[6] Id. at 719.

[7] Id. Other cases have followed the standard laid down in *Pinchot* and treat ownership and operation of real estate as a trade or business. E.g., Lewenhaupt v. Commissioner, 20 T.C. 151 (1953), *aff'd,* 221 F.2d 227 (9th Cir. 1955); de Amodio v. Commissioner, 34 T.C. 894 (1960), *aff'd,* 299 F.2d 623 (3d Cir. 1962).

Left open in *Pinchot* is whether smaller holdings of real estate allow the same inference of business activity and whether an owner of real property can escape a trade or business by surrendering all control to another. The decided cases involving rental real estate are not perfectly consistent on this score but allow the inference that the ownership of even a small parcel of real estate may be a trade or business.[8] If, however, real property is subject to a long term net lease removing the owner from day-to-day involvement or control, ownership of the property by itself is not a trade or business.[9]

Net Leases and Royalty Interests. The IRS for its part has ruled[10] that a nonresident alien individual's ownership of real property subject to long-term leases shifting the burden of major costs to the lessees does not amount to a trade or business. Importantly, this ruling does not turn on the scale of the holdings. It seems therefore that a foreign person's ownership of the Empire State Building, if the property were subject to an appropriately stringent net lease, would not be a U.S. business.[11] Interests in natural resources present similar possibilities. The owner of a pure royalty interest in U.S. mineral rights is not engaged in a U.S. trade or business. Nor even, in some circumstances, is the owner of a "working" interest if the owner has turned over the day-to-day control and supervision to an independent operator.[12]

4. Other Activities

Most economic undertakings that engage taxpayers' efforts, whether directly or through agents, add up to a trade or business. Some, however, such as lending money and certain kinds of buying and selling, may fall on the passive investment side of the line.

Services. Section 864(b)(1) expressly asserts the performance of personal services in the United States to be a U.S. trade or business. This treatment extends to the broadest array of "services," including artistic and athletic performances. A single prizefight or lecture in

---

[8] Estate of Yerburgh v. Commissioner, 4 T.C.M. 1145 (1945) (a one-fifth interest in two small buildings managed by a commission agent constituted a U.S. business). Cf. Schwarcz v. Commissioner, 24 T.C. 733 (1955) (taxpayer who owned a single parcel of real property, but who was significantly engaged in operating it, *held* engaged in trade or business).

[9] Neill v. Commissioner, 46 B.T.A. 197 (1942); Herbert v. Commissioner, 30 T.C. 26 (1958).

[10] Rev. Rul. 73–522, 1973–2 Cum. Bull. 226.

[11] Foreign taxpayers preferring the graduated tax regime on net income (and they often would in such situations because their expenses are likely to amount to a significant percentage of gross rents) can *elect* to treat income from real property as though it were "effectively connected" to a trade or business. See §§ 871(d), 882(d).

[12] See Portanova v. United States, 690 F.2d 169 (Ct. Cl. 1982).

the United States, if compensated, constitutes engaging in a trade or business there.

Buying and Selling. Sales of property present a different problem. Entirely isolated sales,[13] especially of property previously put to personal use, generally do not amount to doing business, nor do sales of passive investment assets such as securities and other financial assets.

At the other end of the range, there is little doubt that sales of property representing the last step of distribution or marketing operations or the end point of production or manufacturing are a form of doing business. When the property sold is "inventory," it is by definition being turned over in the normal course of a "business." Thus, a person that regularly solicits orders for the sale of inventory has been held to be engaged in a trade or business.[14] The maintenance of a stock of inventory in the United States to which orders are regularly filled is sufficient to represent a U.S. trade or business.[15] Because selling property to customers as a habitual activity is so obviously a trade or business, the question that comes up more often, as discussed below, is *where* the business is carried out, rather than *whether* there is one in the first place.

Sales of pure investment assets, on the other hand, are not a trade or business, as the *Higgins* case and others abundantly establish. They are simply occasions for realizing gains and losses from passive commitments of capital. What makes sales of property a business, as a general matter, is some kind of added value resulting from the sale itself. A quart of milk sold by a grocer to a customer has moved a step further along its destiny of being consumed. A stock or bond, by contrast, is pretty much the same thing in the hands of successive owners, even if more or less valuable as such.[16]

There is a difficult line between inventory and investment assets. Sales of tangible property, with consumption value, are naturally more susceptible to being a business. Financial assets are most often sold anonymously on securities exchanges, not to "customers" in the colloquial sense. Such sales, unless made by a broker-dealer, rarely if ever amount to a trade or business even if frequent. A one-time sale of a painting from a private collection will also hold up easily as the disposition of an investment. Activity that

---

[13] See Continental Trading v. Commissioner, 265 F.2d 40 (9th Cir. 1959) (selling of dry milk cans was not viewed as a business activity because they were isolated activities and not done with a business objective of making a profit).

[14] Reg. § 1.864–4(b) Ex. 1; Rev. Rul. 56–165, 1956–1 Cum. Bull. 849.

[15] Handfield v. Commissioner, 23 T.C. 633 (1955).

[16] Note, however, that stocks and bonds generally do constitute inventory in the hands of a securities dealer, who, accordingly, *is* considered to be engaged in a trade or business.

is repeated is more likely to amount to a trade or business. Thus, sales of several paintings to different buyers, especially if coupled with purchases of paintings from different quarters, might well at some point become a business, but no bell rings at that point. It is undoubtedly possible, abstractly, to sell a number of tangible investment assets such as paintings in a relatively short period. As a foreign seller, however, one should go to some pains to negotiate the sales and have title pass outside the United States. That would not be possible, of course, if the paintings were sold at auction in the United States, but the more anonymous character of art auctions, being assimilable in some respects to a securities exchange, would provide considerable insulation to foreign sellers in that situation.

Stocks, Securities and Commodity Trading. As previously mentioned, *Higgins* is a leading case for how to determine the existence of a U.S. trade or business. After *Higgins*, several subsequent cases found that the taxpayer was engaged in a trade or business of stocks and securities trading and that this business was conducted in the United States.[17] Congress became concerned that applying this general trade or business standard in the context of financial trading on U.S. public stock and commodity markets could inhibit foreign investment into the United States, as some foreign investors feared creating a U.S. trade or business. As a result, Congress enacted section 864(b)(2) to remove this possible deterrent as part of the aptly named Foreign Investor Tax Act of 1966. This Act supplanted the holding of the *Higgins* case for stocks and securities trading for the trader's own account by providing that any stock and securities trading (whether by a foreign person physically present in the United States, through an employee located here, or through a resident broker commission agent, custodian, or other agent) is not treated as a trade or business, regardless of the level of activity that was conducted and regardless of whether employees located in the United States have authority to conclude contracts.[18] This exception for stocks and securities trading applies to a foreign corporation, even if the entity's principal business is stocks and securities trading.[19] A similar broad exception also applies for commodity traders that trade for their own account.[20] In all, these provisions reflect Congress's eagerness for foreign investors to invest in the U.S. public markets. At the same time, Congress did not want to extend the safe harbor of section 864(b)(2) beyond trading for one's own account. Consequently,

---

17 See Nubar v. Commissioner, 13 T.C. 566 (1949), *rev'd*, 185 F.2d 584 (4th Cir. 1950), *cert. denied*, 341 U.S. 925 (1951); Adda v. Commissioner, 10 T.C. 273 (1948), *aff'd*, 171 F.2d 457 (4th Cir. 1948), *cert. denied* 336 U.S. 952 (1949).

18 § 864(b)(2)(A)(ii); Reg. § 1.864–2(c)(2)(i).

19 Reg. § 1.864–2(c)(2)(iii).

20 § 864(b)(2)(B)(ii).

the exception in section 864(b)(2) for stock and commodity trading for one's own account does not extend to stocks and securities dealers or commodity dealers[21] that trade for the accounts of customers. Engaging in a banking business is also not eligible for this regime. Thus, although *Higgins* remains good law on the trade or business question in general, section 864(b)(2) adopts a different standard for stocks, securities, and commodity traders if they trade solely for their own account regardless of the volume of activity.

Lending Money. Holders of debt claims may be purely passive investors (as when they hold a portfolio of government bonds, for example) or may be lending money as a business (as does a bank in the course of its operations). There is, however, no self-evident line between purely passive loans, exemplified by debt securities held for investment, and loans made in the course of a lending business. Commonly, the professional moneylender is substantially involved in shaping the terms of a loan while a pure investor typically buys (or abstains to buy) bonds or other debt securities ready-made, but this is not an unequivocal boundary between a lending business and passive investment. The single buyer of a large bond issue in a private placement may negotiate aggressively over the terms of the underlying loan. Does that make the loan a business? The available authority on point suggests not.[22] An element of recurrence, and possibly even dealing with *customers* (as opposed simply to borrowers), may be necessary thresholds of an actual business.

The Tax Court addressed the contours of a money lending business in *YA Global v. Commissioner*.[23] YA Global was a Cayman Islands partnership, and it entered into an investment management agreement with Yorkville Advisors which was a general partner in YA Global. Yorkville Advisors had an office with more than 50 employees located in New Jersey. The investment management agreement provided that YA Global would render investment management services and manage YA Global's securities investment account and had authority to buy, sell or otherwise deal with their account. At the direction of Yorkville Advisory, YA Global provided funding to portfolio companies in the form of convertible debentures, standby equity distribution agreements (SEDAs) and other securities. YA Global invested primarily in microcap and low-priced public companies traded in the over-the-counter public markets.

The Tax Court first addressed whether the activities of Yorkville Advisors could be attributed to YA Global and held that such

---

[21] § 864(b)(2)(A)(ii); § 864(b)(2)(B)(ii).

[22] Consider Rev. Rul. 73–522, 1973–2 Cum. Bull. 226, discussed above, where a net lease of real property is not a trade or business even when the owner is directly involved in negotiating the lease.

[23] YA Global v. Commissioner, 161 T.C. No. 11 (2023).

attribution was appropriate because the business activities of Yorkville Advisors rose to the level of a principle-agent relationship under the commercial law standards for an agency relationship.[24] Moreover, the agency relationship was a dependent agent relationship. After finding that Yorkville Advisors was a dependent agent of YA Global, the Tax Court then found that YA Global's activities (through attribution of the activities conducted by Yorkville Advisors) rose to the level of a US trade or business because those activities were continuous and regular profit-making activities, were not limited to investment activities but represented a money lending business, and the activities did not qualify for the stock and securities exception of Section 864(b)(2) because the activities were not simply investment activities on the taxpayer's behalf but lending instead represented a money lending business to customers.

Within limits, a lender can perhaps influence the question by careful framing of the circumstances of loans. Call yourself a moneylender, and you will be taxed as one. Call yourself an investor, and that is what you may be. If you work in a storefront under a sign that boasts "Get Your Loans Here," you are in a business even if you are unsuccessful and your actual transactions are sporadic. On the other hand, if you comb the financial press for opportunities to acquire privately placed debt for investment, and often follow through, you may nonetheless retain the tax status of investor.[25] But, even in that context, if you have a hand in negotiating the terms of the privately placed debt or if you have an active role in the private placement of that debt with investors, then you may cross-over into the status of a person engaged in a money lending business. Prescriptively, this means that a foreign lender who seeks to avoid being in a U.S. business (and thereby enjoy the exemption of U.S.

---

[24] YA Global v. Commissioner, 161 T.C. No. 11 (2023). Importantly, the Tax Court explicitly rejected attribution would turn on 'whether the putative agent was acting on behalf of or for the benefit of' a foreign person by stating as follows:

> Respondent's proposed test, under which attribution would turn on "whether the putative agent was acting on behalf of or for the benefit of" a foreign person is almost certainly too broad. Courts have declined to attribute to a foreign person activities of another that benefit the foreign person. E.g. Amalgamated Dental Co., Ltd. v. Commissioner, 6 T.C. 1009 (1949). Thus, more than mere benefit to the foreign person would be required to attribute to that person the activities of another even if the tax law provides a test separate from agency law.

See YA Global v. Commissioner, 161 T.C. No. 1 at footnote 8. After making this negative statement against a broad attribution standard, the Tax Court then went on to state that it need not decide whether activities can be attributed for tax purposes even in the absence of an agency relationship due to the fact that the Tax Court found that an agency arrangement existed under commercial law standards.

[25] See Yaeger v. Commissioner, 889 F.2d 29 (2d Cir. 1989) (extensive investing during entire lifetime by individual for own account, including involvement in underlying businesses, *held* not a trade or business).

source portfolio interest) should try as much as possible to *look* like a passive investor.

As a practical matter, the volume of transactions matters much in loans made directly to borrowers and may be the single most important factor. For a lender seeking to avoid a U.S. trade or business, therefore, it is better to lend a few billion to one person than a few thousand each to millions of people.

Manufacturing. Making things (i.e., manufacturing and production) is undoubtedly a trade or business. It involves the commitment of capital and labor to the creation of added value and, in some form or other, almost invariably culminates in a sale or exchange of something. Surprisingly, no decided case expressly holds that manufacturing as such is a trade or business. There is, however, little doubt of this conclusion, notwithstanding some ancient cases and rulings that manufacturing is not by itself a trade or business.[26]

5. Business "in the United States"?

Once the existence of a trade or business is established at the threshold, there is the further question whether the taxpayer is carrying on the trade or business *in the United States* or in some other place. There are varying degrees of presence in the United States that, cumulatively, establish a trade or business there. A resort hotel in Monaco clearly is engaged in business. Equally clearly, it does not have a *U.S.* business simply by virtue of receiving American guests nor, one imagines, does a foreign mail order or online retail firm merely because some orders come to it from the United States. But what if these enterprises regularly run advertisements in the New York Times? As activities in support of foreign operations are imported into the United States, the threshold of a U.S. trade or business is eventually crossed.

In general, purely promotional activities do not rise to the level of a trade or business. Either of the foreign enterprises just described could therefore engage in advertising in the United States without crossing the line. Similarly, the mere purchase of goods in the United States for resale elsewhere does not amount to doing business.[27] On the other side of the line, any complete cycle of production in the United States or the sale of inventory from locations within the United States *is* a U.S. trade or business.[28]

---

[26] See R.J. Dorn & Co. v. Commissioner, 12 B.T.A. 1102 (1928); 32 Op. Atty. Gen. 336 (1920). Cf. United States v. E.C. Knight Co., 156 U.S. 1, 12 (1895) (manufacturing in itself not "commerce" within meaning of Sherman Antitrust Law).

[27] Cf. Consolidated Premium Iron Ores Ltd. v. United States, 28 T.C. 127 (1957) *(nonacq.)*.

[28] See United States v. Balanovski, 236 F.2d 298 (2d Cir. 1956), *cert. denied,* 352 U.S. 968 (1956).

Here again, sales of property pose the greatest difficulty. A sale of "inventory" implies the existence of a trade or business,[29] but where? Does passage of title to goods in the United States establish a trade or business there? Probably not. A foreign seller must engage in some actual economic activity in the United States, at least by imputation. But how much and of what kind? What if the foreign seller also engages in promotion in the United States to generate orders, such as advertisements in U.S. publications or other media? Does this, coupled with the passage of title here, establish a U.S. business? Again, more likely not, but it is less clear.[30] As for sales through brokers, distributors, agents, and employees, they raise questions of the imputation of a business, which are discussed next.

By the same token, the lack of any physical location at all is not dispositive either, if in fact the foreign person is engaged in regular and continuous business activity within the United States. In *Adams Challenge (UK) Limited v. Commissioner*,[31] the taxpayer was a U.K. company that owned a multi-purpose support vessel called the M.V. Adams Challenge. The M.V. Adams Challenge had a class 2 dynamic positioning system, a diving system, and a helipad. The vessel owner entered into a time charter arrangement with Epic Diving & Marine Services (EPIC) for EPIC to use it for staging its own underwater activities. EPIC had contracted to do oil and gas decommissioning work with respect to offshore oil and gas wells located in the U.S. outer continental shelf. All the actual decommissioning work would be done by EPIC and its own employees, as EPIC maintained a service crew on the vessel to engage in these diving operations. The personnel of Adams (U.K.) Challenge had no part in the decommissioning work, but they did navigate and position the vessel wherever EPIC instructed. The M.V. Adams Challenge was operated in the outer continental shelf in U.S. territorial waters 60% to 85% of the time for each year in a continuous three year period. The Tax Court held that these activities occurred "in the United States," and after so finding the Tax Court then held that Adams Challenge (U.K.) Limited had a U.S. trade or business as a result of its ongoing and continuous activities under the time charter arrangement with EPIC. This trade or business existed even though the vessel never physically rested anywhere, nor was it ever connected at any time to the ocean floor. Thus, although none of these activities was from a "fixed place" within the United States, the operation of the M.V. Adams Challenge nevertheless was held to have established a U.S.

---

29 Inventory by its nature is property sold to customers in the normal course of business.

30 There is no decisive authority on point, but Piedas Negras Broadcasting v. United States, 43 B.T.A. 297 (1941), suggests this result.

31 154 T.C. 37 (2020).

trade or business for Adams (U.K.) Challenge Limited because it represented continuous and regular business activity conducted from within the United States.

In the end, the above analysis leads one back to the central point: the legally relevant question in determining whether a trade or business exists is whether regular and continuous business activities are being conducted from within the United States. A fixed physical location can help demonstrate the continuing nature of an activity and its conduct within the United States, but the central inquiry is not predicated on the existence of a physical location as that, in the end, is not the legally dispositive issue.

6. The Imputation of a Trade or Business

It is entirely possible to be engaged in a trade or business without conducting the underlying activity with one's own hands. Someone can be in the coal business without ever donning a miner's hat, and, as many readers of this book either know or suspect, it is possible to practice law as a senior partner without ever venturing into a law library. A taxpayer's "activities" can be the measure of a trade or business only if, across a broad spectrum of situations, the activities of some are imputed to others. Beyond one or two explicit statutory rules, however, principles of imputation can be derived only at some pains from cases and rulings that, on this score, are far from perfectly consistent.

Some imputation of a trade or business is statutory and automatic. There are two specific statutory rules of imputation. Under section 875, a trade or business is imputed 1) from a partnership to each partner[32] and 2) from a trust or estate to each beneficiary.[33] In *United States v. Balanovski*, 236 F.2d 298 (2d Cir. 1956), *cert. den.*, 352 U.S. 968 (1956), one partner conducted business in the United States on behalf of a partnership, and this activity caused all of the partnership income, including the share that was allocable to the other partner who resided in Argentina, to be effectively connected with the conduct of a U.S. trade or business.

Beyond the above two statutorily prescribe cases for attribution, the imputation of a trade or business in other contexts is all case by case. A trade or business is generally imputed from agent to principal (especially from an employee to an employer) and between others who stand in relations of delegation and control. A senior partner who plays golf while a junior associate toils is nonetheless engaged in a trade or business. There is nothing talismanic about the agency relationship however. An "agent," as that term is understood at

---

32 § 875(1).

33 § 875(2).

common law, is subject to a high degree of control by the principal. Moreover, the agent's activities do not have to involve concluding contracts on behalf of the principal to constitute a U.S. trade or business. For a dependent agent (as opposed to an independent agent), regularly soliciting or securing customer orders or maintaining a stock of goods is sufficient for the dependent agent to create a U.S. trade or business for its principal.[34] It is this control, rather than the terms used to describe the relationship, that permits the activities of a dependent agent to be regarded as those of the principal. This can be inferred from a number of decided cases but is nowhere fully articulated. Relationships of lesser control—such as independent contractors or brokers—are generally not occasions for the imputation of a trade or business even if that independent agent has the authority to solicit orders or conclude contracts or maintain a stock of goods.[35] However, the sparseness of explicit authority on point makes it somewhat hazardous to bank on this conclusion.[36]

A difficult case of imputation is presented in *Handfield v. Commissioner*, 23 T.C. 633 (1955). In *Handfield*, a Canadian maker of postal cards called "Folkards" transferred Folkards to American News Company that in turn would display the Folkards in racks at its newsstand locations. If, however, Folkards did not sell, then Handfield agreed that the Folkards were fully returnable and that full credit would be refunded to American News regardless of the condition of the returned postal cards. Thus, American News was not obligated to buy any definite amount of merchandise from Handfield, and American News was obligated only to account for the merchandise which had been sold. The Tax Court also reached the conclusion that the agreement afforded Handfield control over the retail price that Folkards were sold. All these, taken together, led the Tax Court to conclude that the arrangement was an agency relationship in the form of a contract of consignment. The Tax Court then held that Handfield was engaged in business in the United States. Although the exact reasoning of the Tax Court is subject to some uncertainty, it appears that the Tax Court believed that Handfield held a stock of goods in the United States (the Folkards),

---

[34] Reg. § 1.864–7(d)(1); Rev. Rul. 70–424, 1970–2 Cum. Bull. 150.

[35] Reg. § 1.864–7(d)(2).

[36] A further difficulty in decided cases is that the specific nature of an agency relation may be ill-defined, taken for granted, or both. See, e.g., cases like Lewenhaupt v. Commissioner, 20 T.C. 151 (1953), *aff'd,* 221 F.2d 227 (9th Cir. 1955); de Amodio v. Commissioner, 34 T.C. 894 (1960), *aff'd,* 299 F.2d 623 (3d Cir. 1962), where the finer points of the relationship between a foreign taxpayer and an agent in the United States remain obscure. In a practical sense one can understand the outcome of these cases (a U.S. business was found to exist in both) as characterization, among other things, of the relation between a foreign person and a U.S. agent as one of sufficient control to involve the foreign person in a U.S. business.

and the agency activities of American News was imputed to Handfield.

The decision in *Handfield* contemplates that the consigned goods represented a stock of goods that remained beneficially owned by Handfield while located within the United States. Moreover, these consigned goods were being used to fill orders. The court in *Handfield* also contemplates that American News acted as an agent with respect to the consigned goods, but that is where the clarity appears to end. The decision in *Handfield* does not premise its finding on whether or not the American News' "agency status" was that of an independent agent or was instead a dependent agent. Rather, the existence of an agent with a stock of goods was by itself sufficient for the holding in *Handfield* that a U.S. trade or business had been created. The facts of the case would logically lead one to conclude that American News was in fact an independent agent unless the major item sold at its newsstand was the consigned Folkards, which is an unlikely assumption given that newsstands typically sell any number of items including a variety of newspapers, magazines, and other convenience items for day travelers.

The reason the above imputation is difficult is because in 1972 the Treasury issued final regulations that purport to set forth the standards for determining when an agent's activities will be imputed to a foreign principal. In relevant part, Reg. § 1.864–7(d)(2) states that "[t]he office or other fixed place of business of an independent agent . . . shall not be treated as the office or other fixed place of business of his principal who is a nonresident alien individual or a foreign corporation, irrespective of whether such agent has authority to negotiate and conclude contracts in the name of his principal, and regularly exercises that authority, or maintains a stock of goods from which he regularly fills orders on behalf of his principal." The regulation seems clear that an independent agent who maintains a stock of goods does not create a U.S. trade or business for a foreign person.

So, how is one to reconcile the holding of *Handfield* with Reg. § 1.864–7(d)(2)? Again, this Treasury regulation was issued long after the decision in *Handfield*, and yet the regulation is silent as to its intended impact on the prior *Handfield* decision. One can read the regulations as overruling prior case law to the extent an independent agent's holding of a stock of goods was found to have created a U.S. trade or business under the prior case law. The court in *Handfield* did not reach the question of whether or not American News was an independent agent or dependent agent, but the facts augur against the notion that that American News was a dependent agent. If American News was an independent agent, then the subsequently enacted regulations can be viewed as overruling Handfield *sub silencio*. But, this is certainly not the Service's view. The Service has repeatedly cited *Handfield* as good law on how to determine whether an agent's activities with consigned goods creates a U.S. trade or business without ever attempting to rationalize *Handfield*'s holding with the language set forth in the subsequently enacted regulations. So, if one were to assume *Handfield* remains good law, then an attempt to construe *Handfield* in a manner to harmonize it with the promulgated regulations presents a difficult case. Perhaps *Handfield* poses a concern any time consigned inventory is given to an agent. In any event, whether and to what extent this prior case law remains precedential or has been supplanted by the 1972 Treasury regulations is unsettled to this day.

Another difficult authority is Rev. Rul. 70–424, 1970–2 C.B. 150. In this ruling, the Service posits a situation where an agent regularly secures orders for a foreign principal, but the ruling is silent as to whether the agent "has a stock of goods located in the United States." Without positing this fact, the ruling concludes that an agent that regularly secures orders on behalf of a foreign principal creates a U.S. trade or business for the foreign principal in the United States.

Now, consider the same fact pattern as posited in Rev. Rul. 70–424 in the context of the regulations that were issued two years later. Those regulations speak about imputation from a dependent agent to a foreign principal and states that a dependent agent creates a U.S. trade or business for the foreign principal if either of the following are true:

1. The domestic subsidiary corporation regularly negotiates and concludes contracts in the name of its foreign parent corporation, or

2. Maintains a stock of merchandise from which it regularly fills orders on behalf of the foreign parent corporation.

Yet, neither of the above two situations that justify imputation of a dependent agent's activities rise to the threshold needed in the regulations based on the posited facts in Rev. Rul. 70–424. In that ruling, the agent only had the authority to secure orders and not to conclude contracts, so the dependent agent in Rev. Rul. 70–424 did not fit into the framework of the first category of dependent agents that can be imputed to a foreign principal as articulated in the regulations. And, as to a dependent agent that regularly fills orders, that category of agents must maintain a stock of merchandise with which orders are filed. The posited facts in Rev. Rul. 70–424 do not specify that the secures order agent in that ruling had or maintained any stock goods. So again, how is one to reconcile this 1970 revenue ruling with the subsequently issued 1972 regulations? The regulations were issued after the issuance of Rev. Rul. 70–424, so one might read the 1972 regulations as having amplified and clarified the earlier revenue ruling *sub silencio*. But, as an objection to that reading of the regulatory import, it is important to note that the Service has never modified, amplified, or withdrawn Rev. Rul. 70–424. Rather, Rev. Rul. 70–424 remains outstanding as the Service's administrative position even though it seems to afford a broader imputation of a dependent agent's activities than what the regulations appear to contemplate.

B. Effectively Connected Income ("ECI")

U.S. taxation of business profits of foreign persons is built on the notion of income "effectively connected" with a U.S. trade or business. The "effectively connected" income of a foreign person is subject to U.S. tax on a net basis at regular graduated rates. This regime of graduated rates is the same net income tax regime to which U.S. persons are generally subject under the Code. As with U.S. persons, tax is payable by return.

1. The Basic Statutory Scheme

Under section 871(b)(1), a nonresident alien individual is taxed "as provided in section 1. . . on his taxable income which is effectively connected with the conduct of a trade or business within the United States." The reference to section 1 and "taxable income" incorporates the essential rules of the U.S. income tax. Deductions are allowed for business expenses and specific personal itemized expenses. The same distinctions between business and personal expenses apply as well as between current expenses and capital outlays. The relevant depreciation and amortization allowances are available. Foreign corporations are subject to a similar tax regime on their effectively connected income by virtue of the specific reference in section 882(a)(1) to the tax imposed on corporations by section 11. Simplifying somewhat, foreign taxpayers are taxed on their "effectively connected" income as though they were U.S. residents with no other gains. The receipt of effectively connected income thus opens up for a foreign person the full intricacies of the Internal Revenue Code.

Effectively connected income is defined at some length in section 864(c). The main focus is on its relation to a U.S. trade or business. Only a foreign person who at some time has been engaged in a U.S. business can have effectively connected income.[37] The trade or business need not, however, exist in the same year as the one in

---

[37] § 864(c)(1)(B).

which the income arises if there is a requisite economic or commercial relationship between the income and the trade or business.

Once the existence of a U.S. trade or business is established, there are different tests of effectively connected income for income of different source and character. *U.S. source* income is effectively connected according to rules contained in sections 864(c)(2) and 864(c)(3). A small class of *foreign source* income is effectively connected under rules in section 864(c)(4). There is considerable further articulation within these categories.

2. Fixed or Determinable Income and Capital Gains

Fixed or determinable income and capital gains are effectively connected according to a two-pronged statutory test in section 864(c)(2):

> In determining whether [U.S. source fixed or determinable income and capital gains and losses] is effectively connected with the conduct of a trade or business within the United States, the factors taken into account shall include whether—
>
> (A) the income, gain, or loss is derived from assets used or held for use in the conduct of such trade or business, or
>
> (B) the activities of such trade or business were a material factor in the realization of the income, gain, or loss.

These two standards are known as the "asset use" and "activities" tests respectively. These are intuitive tests and in some degree overlapping. Regulations under section 864 fill in the broad-brush statement of section 864(c)(2).

Assets Used in the Business. The use of some assets constitutes a business in itself. Income from such use (which almost invariably is fixed or determinable) is therefore effectively connected. Rents from real estate or equipment leasing, for example, are effectively connected under the asset use test if the rental operations giving rise to them are a trade or business. Similarly, film rentals from movie distribution, if the distributor owns the films, are effectively connected (or not) according to the asset use test. If, however, the distributor has no proprietary interest in the films, the rentals might be viewed as flowing from an *activity*. The rentals might still be effectively connected but under the activities test described below.

In some cases, assets used in support of a business generate income that does not have the immediate look and feel of business profits. Some common items of fixed or determinable income (such as interest or dividends) received by the owner of a business, for example, have the same form as income derived from passive investments. These may nonetheless be effectively connected under the asset use test if they are derived from the working capital or inventory of a business. Instances of effectively connected interest and dividends include interest on bank balances held in support of the current operations of a business, interest derived from a business's accounts receivable, and interest or dividends on stock or bonds held as inventory by a securities dealer.

Activities. Income is effectively connected under the second prong of section 864(c)(2) if the "activities" of the business were a "material factor" in its realization.[38] This material factor standard looks to whether there is a causal connection and whether active participation was an element in the generation of the income.[39] Since the performance of services in the United States is usually a "trade or business," compensation for services is effectively connected under the activities test because the services are obviously a material factor in producing the income. Besides its immediate application to income from personal services, this standard also reaches royalties derived from active licensing operations and gains from assets sold by traders whose activity has crossed the threshold of a business.

Some income—that derived from a restaurant, for example—results from a combination of sales of inventory and services. Since both elements are likely to be effectively connected to an underlying business conducted in the United States, albeit under different statutory tests, the exact breakdown of the income is not of crucial importance.

3. Other U.S. Source Income

The reader may have noticed that the two tests of section 864(c)(2) do not reach the single most important class of business profits, namely, gains from the sale of inventory.[40] Gains from both manufacturing and merchandising most commonly take the form of profits from the sale of inventory to customers. Such gains are, however, neither derived from the sale of capital assets nor fixed or determinable and therefore fall outside the reach of section 864(c)(2). Consider, for example, a foreign corporation that produces and sells automobiles in the United States. It is about as fully engaged in a

---

[38] Reg. § 1.864–4(c)(2)(ii).

[39] Reg. § 1.864–6(b). For a helpful case that works through the effectively connected income standard in the context of a financial business that was not eligible for the stocks and securities trading safe harbor of section 864(b)(2), see InverWorld Inc. v. Commissioner, 71 T.C.M. (CCH) 3231, 1996 T.C.M. (RIA) ¶ 96,301.

[40] British readers should know that what is called "inventory" in American usage (materials and goods turned over in the normal course of a business) is generally called "stock" in Great Britain. In the United States (and in this book) the latter term refers to the shares of a corporation.

trade or business as you can get, but it derives no fixed or determinable income from its operations because gains from the sale of inventory are not fixed or determinable income.[41] The "asset use" and "activities" tests of section 864(c)(2) therefore have no bearing on whether this corporation's gain is effectively connected. Common sense tells us that this corporation should derive taxable business profits from its U.S. operations. Section 864(c)(3) formalizes this intuition along with some effects that are far less obvious.

Section 864(c)(3) casts as effectively connected to a U.S. trade or business all U.S. source income *not* covered by section 864(c)(2). Accordingly, *any* U.S. source income of a foreign person engaged in a U.S. business, other than fixed or determinable income or capital gain, is automatically treated as effectively connected to the U.S. business. Section 864(c)(3) is sometimes known as the "Other Income" clause.

Section 864(c)(3) is cast in the form of the old "force of attraction" principle: the entire residual class of U.S. source gains is attributed to a U.S. trade or business. Since the overwhelming bulk of such gains are from sales of inventory in the United States, which have U.S. source by virtue of passage of title in the U.S., the results of this "attraction" are generally reasonable. An item cannot by definition be "inventory" without being part of a trade or business; its sale therefore produces a business profit. A large class of U.S. source business profits, including all gains from the sale of goods and various income at the periphery (such as gains from the operation of a restaurant), are effectively connected by virtue of section 864(c)(3).

Often there is an economic connection between a U.S. business and "other" U.S. source income made effectively connected by section 864(c)(3). If a foreign corporation opens a department store in the United States, section 864(c)(3) quite naturally makes the profits from U.S. sales effectively connected. A foreign dealer of objets d'art whose U.S. sales are frequent enough to constitute a trade or business would also derive effectively connected income under section 864(c)(3) unless both the dealer had no U.S. office and title to the sold property passed legitimately outside the United States.

Section 864(c)(3), however, makes "other" U.S. source income effectively connected whether or not it has an economic connection to a U.S. business. Its effect can be startling. A European mail order business, for example, might have a number of U.S. customers and significant U.S. source income without being engaged in business in the United States. If the owner of the business were to perform personal services in the United States, even in the form of a lecture

---

[41] For more on this score, see chapter 5.

or two on a wholly unrelated subject, or if the business opened a small branch in the United States in some entirely different line, such as a restaurant, the entire U.S. source income of the business (including the mail-order profit) would become effectively connected. This would result because section 864(c)(3) operates entirely by attraction rather than by requiring any actual connection between items of income and specific business activity. Alternatively, a European business might purchase U.S. commodities at a U.S. export terminal and resell those commodities to foreign customers with risk of loss being transferred at the U.S. port of origin. As we learned in chapter 3, such an inventory sale would represent U.S. source income as the risk of loss occurred at the U.S. load port and would therefore be subject to this force of attraction rule. Thus, in the course of reaching inventory sold by U.S. businesses, section 864(c)(3) may reach much more.

For example, in *YA Global*,[42] after determining that the taxpayer was engaged in a US money lending trade or business, the Tax Court then held that all of the income from sales of personal property was effectively connected income of that U.S. trade or business. In that case, the U.S. office that created the U.S. trade or business of YA Global was "a material factor" in the production of YA Global's income, and so the income represented effectively connected income for that reason.[43] However, the government argued (and the Tax Court agreed) that even if the assets and activities of the U.S. trade or business had not been a material factor in the generation of the income, the income nevertheless would have remained effectively connected income by reason of Code Sec. 864(c)(3) because the U.S. source property gain arose from the sale of personal property that was not a capital asset but instead property that was held for sale to customers. The Tax Court came to this holding that YA Global was itself a dealer in securities and thus sold inventory because the portfolio companies to which YA Global regularly purchased securities were its customers for purposes of determining the dealer status of YA Global.[44]

---

[42] YA Global v. Commissioner, 161 T.C. No. 11 (2023).

[43] Code Sec. 864(c)(5)(B)); Code Sec.865(e)(3). The court established the connection between YA Global's U.S. office and its sales of securities. The Tax Court then noted that, for purposes of determining effectively connected taxable income within the meaning of Code Sec. 1446(c), Code Sec. 865(e)(2)(A) treats income from sales of personal property as U.S.-source income if that income is attributable to a U.S. office or other fixed place of business maintained (or attributable to) the partnership.

[44] The Tax Court relied on Code Sec. 475(c)(1)(A) for this result and also based its decision of its determination on YA Global's status as a dealer on Reg. § 1.475(c)–1(a)(2) which assigns dealer status to taxpayers who regularly offer to enter into security positions. By regularly offering to enter into private placements of the portfolio company debt, the Tax Court determined that YA Global was in fact a dealer in securities.

This makes section 864(c)(3) a potential minefield which can punish foot faults severely. A foreign artist selling paintings on consignment through an independent gallery in the United States more than likely does not have U.S. taxable income,[45] but if the artist gives a single lecture for a fee in the United States—sufficient by itself to constitute a U.S. business—section 864(c)(3) may swallow up all of this hapless taxpayer's U.S. source gains.

4. Foreign Source Income

Several narrowly specific types of *foreign* source income are attracted to a U.S. trade or business and treated as "effectively connected" under sections 864(c)(4) and 864(c)(5). These Code provisions, themselves quite elaborate, are backed up by extensive and detailed regulations, complete with numerous examples.[46]

At the outset, no such attraction can occur unless the foreign taxpayer has an office or other fixed place of business in the United States and the income is attributable to this office. The following types of foreign source income may then be effectively connected with the U.S. business:

> 1) Rents or royalties derived from the U.S. business for the use of intangible property outside the United States.
>
> 2) Financial gains (e.g., dividends, interest, gains from securities) resulting from a U.S. banking business or from the operations of an active securities investment company.
>
> 3) Gains from the sale "through" the U.S. office of inventory or like property, unless the property is sold for use outside the United States and a foreign office of the taxpayer participates materially in the sale.[47]

The 2004 Act added to effectively connected income (when the other conditions of section 864(c)(4) are met, naturally) foreign source income or gain that is "equivalent" to any of the listed items of foreign source income. The notion of "equivalent" income is far from self-explanatory. Income likely to be affected would include payments "in

---

45 The U.S. source gains from the sale of the artist's "inventory" are not fixed or determinable and therefore escape U.S. taxation in the absence of a U.S. trade or business.

46 Reg. §§ 1.864–5, 6, 7.

47 § 864(c)(4)(B). These rules pre-date the current source rules of section 865(e) for sales of property through offices or fixed places of business in different countries, discussed in chapter 3. Under today's source rules, sales of inventory by nonresidents (as defined in section 865) through a U.S. office have *U.S.* source, unless sold for use outside the United States with participation by a foreign office as well. Hence the situations in which one might encounter the third-listed strain of foreign source effectively connected income are few and far between.

lieu of" dividends or "in lieu of" interest derived from securities lending transactions (known as "repos" in financial vernacular), income "equivalent to interest" (which includes various fees linked to lending and the time value of money), income from notional principal contracts (known as "swaps" of various kinds), and other amounts that are economic equivalents of foreign source rents, royalties, interest, dividends, and other such gains.[48]

In determining the existence of a "U.S. office or other fixed place of business" (something of a term of art in this context), more than the physical space actually occupied by the taxpayer is taken into account. The office of an agent in the United States is imputed to the principal.[49] This imputation arises, however, only if the agent is a dependent agent. There is no imputation of the office of an independent agent (such as a general commission agent or broker) acting in the ordinary course of business.

To get the flavor of this type of foreign source effectively connected income, consider the following possibilities: 1) A foreign filmmaker distributes motion pictures all over North America through a sales and distribution office maintained in the United States. The rentals from film distribution in Canada (which have non-U.S. source) are effectively connected nonetheless. 2) A U.S. branch of a foreign bank makes a mortgage loan to a customer in Mexico City;[50] the loan is negotiated and cleared through the U.S. branch office. Interest on the loan (which has foreign source by virtue of the residence of the borrower/payor) or "points" (which should be considered, most likely, income "equivalent to interest") would be effectively connected to the U.S. branch business. 3) Our friend Marcel, in this incarnation a French wine merchant, opens a sales office in Detroit, Michigan, through which he sells wine to customers in Windsor, Ontario. Marcel, although a nonresident alien, has a "tax home" in the United States, which makes him a U.S. "resident" for the source rules of section 865 (with the further effect that the source rules of section 861(a)(6) for sales of inventory, rather than section 865(e), continue to apply). If title to the goods passes in Canada, Marcel's gains have foreign source but are effectively connected nonetheless.[51]

---

[48] This checklist is based, by analogy, on the regulations on "income equivalent to interest" in Reg. § 1.954–2(h)(2)(i).

[49] § 864(c)(5)(A).

[50] See Rev. Rul. 86–154, 1986–2 Cum. Bull. 103.

[51] The third example (involving Marcel) is somewhat forced, as doubtless you observed. How often will a French wine merchant have a "tax home" in the United States? This underscores the point of footnote 47 above—that you will rarely encounter this type of foreign source effectively connected income.

5. Sale of Partnership Interest

In 2017, Congress enacted section 864(c)(8) to provide that the sale by a nonresident alien individual or a foreign corporation that owns an interest in a partnership engaged in a U.S. trade or business is considered effectively connected income to the extent that the gain on the sale of the partnership interest results from gain in the assets of the underlying U.S. trade or business. Section 864(c)(8)(C) provides a coordination rule so that any gain attributable to a U.S. real property interest that is taxable under section 897 is not included again by reason of section 864(c)(8) to avoid double counting. This statutory rule had long been the IRS position,[52] but Congress enacted section 864(c)(8) to reverse the Tax Court decision in *Grecian Manesite Mining, Industrial & Shipping Co. v. Commissioner*,[53] where the Tax Court stated that the sale of a partnership interest would be entirely sourced by the residence of the seller under the law that existed prior to section 864(c)(8).

6. Deferred Gains from a Trade or Business

There are, finally, provisions in section 864(c) that treat certain deferred income or gains as effectively connected. Sections 864(c)(6) and 864(c)(7) extend the scope of effectively connected income to include several types of income attributable to a U.S. business but arising in a year when the business no longer exists.

Section 864(c)(6) treats as effectively connected, in the year it is "taken into account," deferred income attributable to the performance of services, the sale of property, or any other "transaction" occurring in another year if the income would have been effectively connected in the year of the actual sale, services, or transaction. This provision draws within the "effectively connected" class such income generated by a U.S. business that is realized in some later year when the business no longer exists. Thus, deferred compensation for the performance of services in the United States or installment payments from sales of business assets or inventory are taxed as effectively connected income at graduated rates even if received at a time when the taxpayer has no economic activity in the United States. These rules are often, but not invariably, hard on taxpayers. In the case of services, for example, the rules may well improve the tax regime of less affluent former U.S. residents who have returned to their countries of origin and who might otherwise

---

[52] See Rev. Rul. 91–32, 1991–1 Cum. Bull. 107.

[53] 149 T.C. 63 (2017).

suffer flat rate taxation of 30 percent (instead of tax at 10 or 15 percent rates) on their low-bracket U.S. source retirement income.[54]

Under section 864(c)(7), when property once "used or held for use in connection with the conduct of a trade or business within the United States" is disposed of within 10 years of that use, the determination of whether the resulting gain is taxable as "effectively connected" is made "as if" the disposition "occurred immediately before" the property ceased to be used in a U.S. trade or business. The effect of this "as if" determination is generally to treat the gains as effectively connected because that is the usual fate of gains from property used in a U.S. business. Inventory or equipment from a U.S. business may thus bear the mark of that business, as a tax matter, for a decade.

7. Effectively Connected Election

As we saw earlier in this chapter, interests in U.S. real estate or natural resources can be held without creating a trade or business. In that case, the current income of foreign persons from the property is not effectively connected and is therefore taxed at flat rates without deductions. This is highly disadvantageous in the common situation where the combined operating expenses, interest, and depreciation or depletion would, if available as deductions, significantly offset income taxable on a net basis. Rental real estate often produces tax losses when full account is taken of these deductions. A royalty interest in natural resources may also give rise to significant deductions for depletion and other costs if taxable on a net basis.

To pacify this problem, there is an election for foreign taxpayers to treat income from real property in the United States as effectively connected with a trade or business regardless of its actual character.[55] The election extends to all income from real property, including income from natural resources. However, the IRS has ruled in Rev. Rul. 91–7, 1991–1 C.B. 110 that a foreign person cannot make this election until some income is generated. This can be problematic as carrying costs such as taxes and interest are not eligible to be capitalized until there is a trade or business. The ruling is silent on how much income from real property is necessary to support an election under Code Sec. 871(d) or 882(d). It is foreordained that the Service will strain to dismiss relatively small amounts as de minimis. The most I can add is that the more income received the earlier, the

---

[54] This point applies to retirement income in the form of deferred compensation, but not to social security payments.

[55] The election is codified in § 871(d) and 882(d).

better. Once the election is made, it is binding on the taxpayer for future years and can be revoked only with the consent of the IRS.

8. Deductions Allowable Against Effectively Connected U.S. Tax Return Filing Obligation

Timely Tax Return. As a prerequisite to claiming deductions, a taxpayer is required to file a timely federal income tax return.[56] The government's requirement that a timely tax return be filed has been upheld in *Swallows Holding Ltd. v. Commissioner*.[57] The taxpayer can request a waiver for this timely filing requirement if the taxpayer can establish that its failure to timely file was reasonable and in good faith and acts cooperatively to determine its income tax liability, but this waiver is one that is at the discretion of the Commissioner to grant.[58] The outright denial of deductions as a result of a failure to file a timely tax return makes the stakes quite high in determining whether a foreign person has a U.S. trade or business. To ameliorate this risk, a foreign corporation can timely file a protective tax return, claiming that it is filing the return in order to preserve its right to claim deductions while claiming that it does not believe its activities create a U.S. trade or business.[59] Of course, one can certainly envision what audit attention such a tax filing may generate, but at least the taxpayer preserves the ability to claim a U.S. tax deduction for expenses incurred in the conduct of the foreign person's activities should those activities be found to constitute a U.S. trade or business.

Allocable and Apportionable Expenses. As a general rule, expenses that are definitely related to the foreign person's effectively connected income are allowed as a deduction. If an expense relates to both activities that generate effectively connected income and also to activities that do not, then the expense must be apportioned among those two classes of activities and only the amount apportioned to the effectively connected income is allowed as a deduction. Special apportionment rules are provided for particularly fungible expenses, such as interest expense, research and development expenses, stewardship expenses, legal and accounting costs, and non-federal taxes. These special apportionment rules seek to provide an administrable rule with respect to costs that cannot be definitively associated with any particular category of income.

---

56 See § 874(a); § 882(c)(2).

57 515 F.3d 162 (3rd Cir. 2008).

58 See Reg. § 1.882–4(a)(3)(i).

59 See Reg. § 1.882–4(a)(3)(vi).

Chapter 7

INCOME TAX TREATIES

A. Overview

The only true "international" element of international taxation arises in tax treaties. An income tax treaty is, literally, an act of law "between nations." An income tax treaty frames a tax regime for economic activity connected with the treaty countries that may differ in important respects from both the wholly domestic taxation of either country and any treaty regime between other countries.

Income tax treaties provide for adjustments between the income tax systems of different countries. So also, as we shall see, does the foreign tax credit. The difference lies in the mutual character of income tax treaties. While the foreign tax credit is available to all comers, with little regard to similar measures adopted by other countries,[1] an income tax treaty is typically composed of a set of negotiated adjustments and concessions between the tax laws and treasuries of two countries. While the foreign tax credit is both unilateral and multilateral, income tax treaties are strictly bilateral.

The central concern of income tax treaties, as with the foreign tax credit, is double taxation. Treaties generally limit the extent of taxation imposed by each of the treaty countries on transactions that touch on both. The provisions of a typical income tax treaty include an enumeration of specific abatement or exemption of taxation for residents of one country on certain types of income from the other. Items commonly shielded from full taxation in the treaty country of their source are interest, dividends, royalties, and business profits. On first encounter you might conclude that an income tax treaty was designed to confer tax advantage on certain taxpayers. Although tax treaties may have that effect, that is not what they are mainly about. Rather, they are principally concerned with the apportionment of tax revenues between the treasuries of the treaty countries.

Reduced rates or exemption for income derived from one treaty country by a resident of the other country usually imply a larger share of tax for the latter. Most countries allow their residents some form of foreign tax credit for income taxes paid on foreign income. If the foreign tax is abated or eliminated, the foreign tax credit falls

---

[1] By this we mean that the foreign tax credit does not depend on similar allowances under foreign law. It *does* depend on the nature of the foreign taxes imposed. But it is a unilateral concession by the United States in that a bona fide income tax imposed by almost any country may be credited, without regard for any specific agreement with the United States.

away as well. Therefore, when a treaty provides, for example, that a resident of one country is not taxed on interest income derived from another, the interest income is not entirely tax-exempt as a result. The country of residence will now tax the income and at a rate undiminished by any credit it might otherwise have allowed under its own tax laws for taxes imposed by the other country. In this event, the effect of the treaty provision for interest income is simply to shift tax revenues from the treasury of one treaty country to that of another. Treaties, in short, serve to allocate tax revenue between countries rather than to exempt income altogether.

Given this basic function, income tax treaties most commonly arise between relatively high-tax countries. An out-and-out tax haven has little to offer by way of concessions in an income tax treaty with an industrial or commercial country, and treaties between such disparate partners are rare.

It does not follow, however, that income tax treaties make no difference in the taxation of individuals and enterprises. If income tax rates were always exactly the same in countries entering into treaties, treaties would indeed affect only the treasuries of the two countries and not taxpayers. Because rates differ, the practical effect of treaties often is to create a more favorable tax regime than would otherwise be available. If income tax rates in the country of source are *higher* than in a taxpayer's country of residence, exemption from tax in the country of source under a treaty improves the tax regime of the taxpayer in the other country. At the extreme, if one country does not tax foreign source income at all, and the country of source also does not tax the income by virtue of an income tax treaty, income derived in one country by a resident of another escapes taxation altogether. This is rarely the intended result of an income tax treaty. It is not unknown, however, for tax treaties to create avenues of complete exemption for certain income. Once uncovered, these avenues are pursued to the hilt by tax-averse international investors.

In entering into treaties, countries generally seek to protect the interests of their own treasuries, taking into account the patterns of their habitual economic relations with specific other countries. For example, countries that import technology and capital can be expected to pursue terms in treaties that leave the taxation of royalties and license fees in the country of source. This is so because countries that import intellectual property for use within their borders are, under the standard source rules, the countries of source of royalties from the property,[2] and therefore may be able to collect tax on the royalties. Countries that export capital and technology can

---

[2] Under sections 861 and 862, remember, royalties have their source in the place of use of the underlying property.

be expected to press for exemption in the country of source and for taxation by the country of residence of the owner of the capital or technology.[3] The position of the United States in treaty negotiations, in this light, has consistently been that the country of source should defer to the country of residence in taxing royalties from intellectual property. In contrast, developing countries, which are predominantly importers of capital and technical assistance, commonly seek to leave primary taxation of royalties and license fees with the country of source.

Countries may well prefer one pattern in their treaties with some countries and a different one in others depending on the flow of investment between them. If the flow of capital and income between two countries were exactly equal, any rule would have the same effect in the end. Any concession to foreign residents made by the country of source would be offset by an equal increase in its taxation of its own residents deriving income from the other treaty country. This is not a common situation, however, even in the very long run.

1. Advancement of Trade

Besides allocating revenue, tax treaties aim at facilitating business transactions and other economic exchanges between the treaty countries that might otherwise be inhibited by intrusive national taxation. Beyond the cost of actual tax payments, the mere fact of exposure to the tax system of another country imposes significant transactional burdens on enterprises venturing beyond their national boundaries. Dealings between tax authorities and taxpayers in connection with the collection of an income tax can be protracted and difficult. This is one of the concerns underlying the provisions of income tax treaties for allocating the taxation of business profits between the treaty countries. The central element to this end in treaties is the threshold of taxation known as a "permanent establishment."[4]

There were few income tax treaties in force before the Second World War. The first income tax treaties of the United States were, not surprisingly, with Canada and Great Britain. As the post-war economies developed, the treaty network of the United States grew to include virtually all the industrial and commercial countries, to which have been added in the last 20 years a fair number of

---

[3] This will afford them larger tax collections from their own residents that receive royalties from other countries.

[4] Generally, the business profits of an enterprise of one country are not taxable in the other unless derived from business conducted through a permanent establishment.

developing countries as well.[5] The extension of income tax treaties probably received some impetus from the development of international organizations, such as the General Agreement on Tariffs and Trade (that later became the World Trade Organization, or WTO) and the Organization for Economic Co-operation and Development (OECD).

There is no single mold for income tax treaties. Each treaty is separately negotiated with a foreign country and may reflect a particular set of economic relations. As discussed above, income tax treaties between economically developed countries function principally to allocate tax revenue between national treasuries. Between developed and developing countries, tax treaties may impound subsidies and economic aid in the guise of particular tax concessions.

B. Model Treaties

1. The OECD Model Treaty

Although any given treaty may differ from all others in some respect, treaties between economically similar countries bear a family resemblance. In the interest of international commerce, the Organization for Economic Co-operation and Development (OECD) has issued (and periodically revised) a Model Income Tax Treaty which exerts a strong influence on the form and content of income tax treaties among developed countries. The OECD model treaty is consistent in many respects with the U.S. Model Treaty.

2. The U.S. Model Treaty

To set the framework of its treaty negotiations, the U.S. Treasury has drafted and issued over the years successive versions of a U.S. Model Income Tax Treaty. The U.S. Model Treaty is similar in many respects to the OECD Model Treaty but also reflects unique concerns of the United States, particularly regarding tax-haven operations. The U.S. Model Treaty establishes the official profile of U.S. treaty policy, consisting of a compendium of the baseline positions the United States puts on the table in negotiating income tax treaties. The following chapters on income tax treaties are based on the current (2016) version of the U.S. Model Treaty. You should bear in mind, though, that no U.S. income tax treaty is exactly congruent with the U.S. Model Treaty, and in fact the 2016 U.S. Model Treaty has several new provisions that have not existed in any existing U.S. tax treaty. However, many provisions that first surfaced in one or another version of the U.S. Model Treaty have

---

[5] The United States has signed income tax treaties with Indonesia, Mexico, and China, for example.

become staple elements of the recent income tax treaties between the United States and other countries.

3. United Nations Model Treaty

Developing nations have expressed concern that the OECD Model Treaty was overly accommodating to developed nations. Thus, the United Nations developed a model convention that is more accommodating to the concerns of developing nations. It is developed and updated by the U.N. Committee of Experts on International Cooperation in Tax Matters, a subsidiary body of the Economic and Social Council. The U.N. model treaty generally favors greater taxing power over income in the country of source of that income. Among other things, the U.N. model treaty provides for a lower standard for a permanent establishment and generally provides greater withholding on fixed and determinable income.

C. Residence in Income Tax Treaties

Income tax treaties involve the taxation of persons who are normally subject to the taxing power of one or both of the treaty countries. The basic pattern is forbearance by the country of source from taxing some income (that it would otherwise tax by reason of source) of a "resident" of the other treaty country. Broadly speaking, a "resident" of a country in an income tax treaty is a person within the class that can invoke the benefits of the treaty. Residence, being the status on which treaty benefits are most commonly predicated, is more important in this regard than nationality. Even a national of one country, who does not reside there, may not be able to claim benefits accorded in a tax treaty to "residents" of that country. By the same token, a resident of one country, even though not a national, can often claim the benefit of the income tax treaties between that country and others.

1. Treaty "Residence"

The notion of "residence" has its own special flavor in income tax treaties, having absorbed some aspects of citizenship. It is rarely congruent with the notion of residence established by the national tax laws of any treaty country. In the U.S. Model Treaty, a

> "resident of a Contracting State" means any person who, under the laws of that State, is liable to tax therein by reason of his domicile, residence, citizenship, place of management, place of incorporation, or any other criterion of a similar nature, and also includes that State and any political subdivision or local authority thereof.[6]

---

6 U.S. Model Treaty, art. 4(1).

Under the U.S. Model Treaty, all persons whose status exposes them to worldwide taxation by the United States are U.S. residents, as are national, state, and local governments. Thus U.S. citizens along with "residents" can invoke the benefits of the U.S. Model Treaty. A corporation is a U.S. resident within this definition by virtue of being chartered in the United States, which of itself implies worldwide U.S. taxation.[7] As so defined, the idea of "residence" is perhaps better conceived as a form of "fiscal domicile." That is, "residence" is the degree of presence or connection in a country that triggers taxation there. The concept includes citizenship to the extent that citizenship is itself a basis for taxation under the laws of a given country—which in the United States, of course, it is.

Individuals and corporations subject to worldwide taxation under U.S. tax laws are thus residents of the United States under the general terms of the U.S. Model Treaty. These include foreign nationals who are U.S. residents under section 7701(b) (that is, individuals who either have the requisite immigration status or meet the "substantial presence" test) and all corporations incorporated in the United States. This definition of a resident works best (and perhaps only) in treaties between countries that tax incomes on a worldwide basis. Countries with more territorial tax systems have no reason to grant to U.S. citizens residing in third countries tax concessions that ultimately benefit the U.S. Treasury when similar concessions made by the U.S. Treasury to their own citizens are of different effect. Thus, for example, the income tax treaty between the United States and Italy (a country with a relatively territorial income tax system) defines a resident of a State as "any person who, under the laws of that State, is liable to tax therein by reason of his domicile, residence, place of management, place of incorporation, or any other criterion of a similar nature."[8] In this treaty, individual *citizens* of either country are not, as such, treated as residents.

The definition of a "resident" in the U.S. Model Treaty is followed by the immediate qualification that a resident of a Contracting State "does not include any person who is liable to tax in that State in respect only of income from sources in that State or of profits attributable to a permanent establishment in that State."[9] As a result, foreign individuals and corporations do not become U.S.

---

[7] Other countries determine corporate residence according to an entity's principal place of business or seat of management. The U.S. Model Treaty accommodates this standard, to an extent, by providing that a corporation is a resident of a treaty country if it is liable to tax there by reason of its "place of management." Art. 4(1). By this standard, a corporation chartered in a third country would be a resident of a treaty country if it had connections with the treaty country sufficient to make it a resident corporation under that country's own tax laws.

[8] Treaty with Italy, art. 4(1).

[9] U.S. Model Treaty, art. 4(1)(a).

residents merely by receiving U.S. source income that is subject to U.S. tax. Thus, on the question of whether a person or entity is a "resident" of the other contracting state, the United States defers to how the other contracting state treats the entity or person. A few examples will help in this regard.

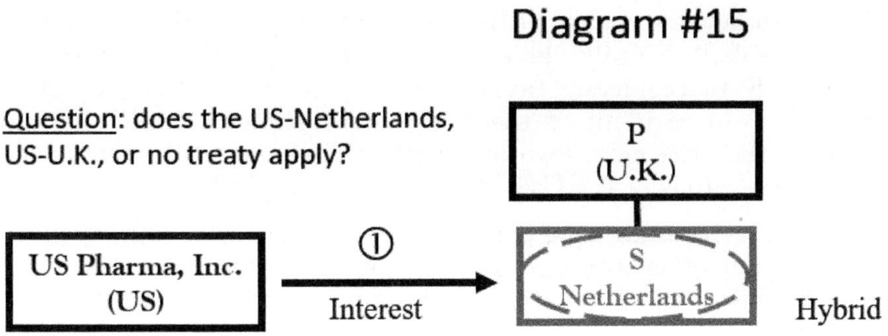

In Diagram #15, US Pharma, Inc. is shown to have made an interest payment to a Netherlands hybrid entity (i.e., an entity that is treated as a disregarded entity for U.S. tax purposes but as an actual entity for Netherlands tax purposes). If the Netherlands subjects S to taxation on its interest income as a Netherlands entity, then the U.S. will apply the U.S.-Netherlands tax treaty. At first blush, this conclusion is counterintuitive as the recipient entity for U.S. tax purposes is a disregarded entity, so how can it be that this entity is entitled to tax treaty protection under the U.S. tax treaty? The answer is that the status of an entity is determined by the other contracting state. As long as the Netherlands regards the entity as subject to its taxation as a Netherlands resident entity, then the entity is entitled to treaty benefits under the U.S.-Netherlands tax treaty. However, if the Netherlands did not treat S as a resident entity for its tax purposes, then the U.S.-Netherlands tax treaty would not apply.[10] Suppose, however, that S is not treated as a Netherlands resident for purposes of the Netherlands tax regime, but the United Kingdom subjects the income earned in the S entity to taxation of its resident, P. Would the U.S.-U.K. tax treaty apply? The answer is "yes" because the interest paid by US Pharma, Inc. is included in P's income and thus subject to taxation in the U.K. on a residency basis, so in this scenario, the income is eligible for the U.S.-U.K. tax treaty.[11] As a further variation, let's assume that the hybrid entity is incorporated in the Netherlands and that the Netherlands does treat the entity as a separate corporation but does not tax that entity on a residency basis because its place of management is located

[10] See U.S. Model Treaty, art. 1(7); Rev. Rul. 2004–76, 1974 Cum. Bull. 111 (Situation 1).

[11] Reg. § 1.894–1(d); Rev. Rul. 72–378, 1972–2 Cum. Bull. 668.

in a different jurisdiction. In this scenario, the S entity is not entitled to relief under the U.S.-Netherlands tax treaty because it is not subject to taxation as a resident in the Netherlands.[12] If, however, the country where S's place of management is located subjects S to taxation in that jurisdiction and if that other jurisdiction has a tax treaty with the United States modeled after the 2016 U.S. Model Treaty, then that other jurisdiction's tax treaty with the U.S. would be available.[13] Finally, let's assume now that the Netherlands subjects S to residency taxation and that the United Kingdom subjects P (a resident of the U.K.) to taxation on the S income directly, then the most favorable withholding rate under either the U.S.-Netherlands or the U.S.-U.K. tax treaty could be used.[14]

Again, the organizing point here is that the other country must treat the entity as subject to taxation on a residency basis, and if it does so, then the U.S. treaty with that jurisdiction can be applied. If it does not, then the U.S. treaty with that jurisdiction would not apply. If one keeps that thought in mind, then the above myriad of alternatives with hybrid entities can all be sorted out. However, even if an entity is properly viewed as a resident under Article 4, the "limitations on benefits" provisions of Article 23 may limit the availability for treaty relief with respect to a resident of the treaty jurisdiction. The outworking of the limitations of benefits provisions of the U.S. Model Treaty and how those provisions further restrict the availability of treaty relief is dealt with separately below.

2. Resolving Dual Residence

Within the Model Treaty's definition of residence, it is entirely possible for persons (individuals or corporations) to be residents of both treaty partner jurisdictions. To apply the treaty to that person, the person needs to be placed as a resident of one of the two jurisdictions. For example, another country tying residence to a specific duration of physical presence could claim as a resident a person also claimed by the United States under the extended form of its "substantial presence" test. The U.S. Model Treaty therefore contains, along with its definition of residence, a set of tie-breaking rules to establish a single country of residence under the Treaty, largely eliminating the possibility of dual residence. These are layered, in Article 4(3), in a sequence of clauses, each one of which comes into play when the previous one has failed to resolve an overlap of residence. First, "an individual. . . resident of both Contracting States . . . shall be deemed to be a resident of the State

[12] Rev. Rul. 2004–76, 2004–2 Cum. Bull. 111.

[13] Id.

[14] Rev. Rul. 73–564, 1973–2 Cum. Bull. 435.

in which he has a permanent home available to him."[15] For individuals who have only one home, there is no problem. Further, this provision offers those who have some wealth and a degree of flexibility in their lifestyles a measure of control over their "residence" under income tax treaties. Someone who owns a dwelling in one country and always stays in hotels (or similarly transient quarters) in other countries can assert exclusive residence in the country of the permanent dwelling.[16]

The constraint of staying in hotels is one that many who divide their time between two countries may not find appealing, however, which leads to the next rule. An individual who "has a permanent home available to him in both States. . . shall be deemed to be a resident of the State with which his personal and economic relations are closer," a place also known in the U.S. Model Treaty as the "center of vital interests."[17] This test has a flavor similar to the U.S. standard of residence applied to foreign individuals before 1984 that was predicated on a weighing of essential connections between an individual and a place.

If the overlap survives these tests (for example, because the taxpayer has no vital center or no permanent home anywhere), the U.S. Model Treaty continues, "[i]f the State in which [an individual] has his center of vital interests cannot be determined, or if he does not have a permanent home available to him in either State, he shall be deemed to be a resident of the State in which he has an habitual abode."[18] This leaves us to determine exactly what is an "habitual abode." An apartment, even a pied-à-terre, certainly qualifies. What about the abode of a special friend with whom the taxpayer is very, very close? What if the taxpayer always stays at the same hotel? In the same room? To be safe, individuals seeking to avoid U.S. residence might do well to spread their sojourns in the United States among different hotels and their attentions among different special friends.

Moving on, an individual who has an habitual abode in both countries (or neither) is treated as a resident of the country of his nationality.[19] Finally, the residence of an individual who has dual nationality (or none) is a matter for determination by the "competent authorities" of the treaty countries.[20] The "competent authorities" (who surface ubiquitously in income tax treaties) are the tax

---

15 U.S. Model Treaty, art. 4(3)(a).

16 Holding a dwelling under a long-term lease is probably the equivalent of ownership in this situation.

17 U.S. Model Treaty, art. 4(3)(a).

18 U.S. Model Treaty, art. 4(2)(b).

19 U.S. Model Treaty, art. 4(2)(c).

20 U.S. Model Treaty, art. 4(2)(d).

authorities of the respective treaty countries. In effect, the IRS gets together with its foreign counterpart to thrash out the taxpayer's residence when none of the tie-breaking rules resolves a case of dual residence.

If you picked up the U.S. Model Treaty and quickly read a few provisions conferring tax benefits on foreign "residents," you might conclude that the United States accords treaty benefits to its own citizens who reside in treaty countries. This is not so. The United States (and some other countries as well) reserves in its treaties its taxing power over its own citizens and residents who happen to reside in another country. All U.S. income tax treaties contain some form of a provision reserving to each of the treaty countries the right to tax its own residents and citizens as though the treaty were not in force. In such provisions—known as "saving" clauses—each treaty country "saves" its taxing power over its own constituents. A discussion of savings clauses is discussed later in this chapter under its own heading.

3. Business Profits—Permanent Establishments

The main event in most income tax treaties is a provision concerning the taxation of active business operations of an enterprise of one treaty country in the other. Generally, the business profits of an enterprise of one treaty country are not taxable in the other treaty country unless they are attributable to a "permanent establishment" in that country. There is some such provision—with different shadings—in all income tax treaties. In the U.S. Model Treaty, the provision governing business profits—and it is entirely typical—is the following:

> The business profits of an enterprise of a Contracting State shall be taxable only in that State unless the enterprise carries on business in the other Contracting State through a permanent establishment situated therein. If the enterprise carries on business as aforesaid, the business profits of the enterprise may be taxed in the other State but only so much of them as is attributable to that permanent establishment.[21]

A permanent establishment is both a threshold of taxation of business profits and a limitation. Only if a foreign enterprise has a permanent establishment may the country of source tax its business profits, and then only those "attributable" to the permanent establishment. The key questions, then, are the exact contours of a

---

[21] U.S. Model Treaty, art. 7(1). The sparse punctuation is original.

"permanent establishment" in a given treaty and the range of business profits attributable to it.

Before pursuing those questions, however, we first consider the reasons underlying the taxation of business profits in income tax treaties.

4. Marcel's Wine Business

It may be easier to understand the idea underlying the taxation of permanent establishments through an example. Consider again our friend Marcel, now a citizen and resident of France engaged in the production and sale of French regional wine. Marcel wants to expand his sales outside France. He need not look far. There are a number of contiguous or nearby countries[22] (and the United States just a boat trip away) that offer promising markets for French wine. Entering these markets will involve at some point warehousing goods, wholesale distribution, and retail sales, but Marcel, at least initially, probably will not want to do these things himself. In nearly every commercial country, a class of independent distributors, agents, wholesalers, and others has arisen to facilitate the acquisitive undertakings of those (inside or outside the country) for whom it would not be feasible to provide such support for themselves. Marcel is therefore likely to enter markets in Europe and the United States with the help of such intermediaries, who, in the normal course of their business, also serve as marketing intermediaries for other enterprises. By acting through a pre-existing network of independent distributors and agents, a producer like Marcel might easily sell wine in a score of different countries, where he would not have been able to afford to create his own exclusive commercial infrastructure.

What about the taxation of these operations? If Marcel's foreign sales conducted through independent intermediaries were exposed to unmodified taxation in the countries of destination, Marcel might find himself subject to a battery of different tax obligations. By virtue of regular sales of inventory in the normal course of business, Marcel could be considered—at least within a technical meaning often followed in national tax laws—to be "doing business" in many countries. That would be so, most likely, in the United States, with the further consequence that Marcel would have "effectively connected" income there as a matter of U.S. law. To the extent national tax systems tax something like effectively connected income of foreign persons (and most do), Marcel might find himself with taxable business profits under *many* national tax laws.

---

[22] Belgium, Luxembourg, Germany, Austria, Holland, the U.K., Switzerland, Denmark, and Sweden are affluent countries that import wine.

This would be a dreadful result for Marcel, not because of the tax cost per se—France would allow him a foreign tax credit for the non-French taxes—but because of the burden of dealing with all the national tax authorities. The mechanics of taxation of business profits are not easy. Income taxation, generally based on filed returns, entails extended dealings with national tax authorities. For each separate foreign operation, you have to measure the income of relevant source and the allocable deductions under different national tax laws. This would add up to a significant burden on Marcel's foreign operations.

Enter income tax treaties with "permanent establishment" clauses. None of Marcel's operations outside France in this situation would be subject to income tax in the country of source. All the countries in this scenario are connected by such treaties. With a permanent establishment as a threshold of taxation of business profits by the country of source, the far-flung sales of an enterprise can be carried out within the regime of a single country's national tax laws (in Marcel's case France). Merchants like Marcel can extend their operations into other countries through independent agents without multiplying the burdens of tax compliance. Marcel in particular can deal solely with the French tax authorities and pay income tax in France with respect to his worldwide operations.

The shield of business profits from taxation offered by treaties extends, however, only to foreign undertakings pursued *below* a specific level of sustained activity or investment. Suppose that Marcel found a particularly favorable reception for his products in Holland. He might also find it convenient, in order to pursue his Dutch business more efficiently, to open his own sales office there and to rent or buy warehouse space for his own exclusive use. These steps would create for Marcel a permanent establishment in Holland and expose him to Dutch income taxation on his business profits earned there, but, having a more extensive presence in Holland, Marcel would also be in a better position to deal with the accounting and administrative incidents of Dutch income taxation. By establishing a substantial and protracted presence in Holland, Marcel can be deemed to have accepted the same terms of participation in the Dutch economy as those afflicting home-grown Dutch enterprises.

"Enterprise". The threshold of a permanent establishment applies in many treaties (but not all) to an "enterprise" of the other treaty country. It should be noted first that the precise definition of terms such as "enterprise" and "business profits" varies from treaty to treaty. There is no generalized notion of an enterprise substitutable among all income tax treaties. Most treaties contain, moreover, only a partial definition of the term "enterprise." In Article

3(1) of the U.S. Model Treaty, the definition is more fully articulated than most:

> c) the terms "enterprise of a Contracting State" and "enterprise of the other Contracting State" mean respectively an enterprise carried on by a resident of a Contracting State, and an enterprise carried on by a resident of the other Contracting State. . .;
>
> d) the term "enterprise" applies to the carrying on of any business. . . .

Business Profits. "Business profits" are not expressly defined in the U.S. Model Treaty, but their character follows from the definition of a "business" in Article 3(1)(e). "[T]he term "business" includes the performance of professional services and of other activities of an independent character." This statement is a broad description, not an exhaustive enumeration. It follows that "business profits" are pretty much what they sound like: income from business operations. The treaty notion of "business profits" has no exact counterpart in the U.S. domestic tax laws. There is a family resemblance, to be sure, between business profits and income "effectively connected with a trade or business" under the Code, but there are differences as well. "Effectively connected" income is composed of several different elements bound together in a complex definition while business profits partake of a more broadly drawn, but unified, economic character.

A common provision in income tax treaties (which pacifies what would otherwise be difficult questions of characterization) is that business profits do not include items of income dealt with separately in other provisions of the treaty.[23] This does not mean, however, that the other income escapes full taxation. Items of income set apart from business profits, including interest, compensation for services, and royalties, are nonetheless taxed as though they were business profits when similarly derived from a permanent establishment.[24]

"Permanent Establishment". A "permanent establishment" is the major threshold of taxation, for business undertakings, between the tax regimes of treaty countries. There is, however, no universal notion of a "permanent establishment" good for all treaties. The

---

[23] In older treaties lacking such a provision the respective spheres of the provisions governing business profits, rentals, natural resource royalties, and other items of income can be difficult to unravel. The U.S. Model Treaty contains a variant of this provision to the effect that where business profits overlap with income dealt with in other provisions of the treaty, the other provisions are not affected by the provisions for business profits. U.S. Model Treaty, art. 7(6).

[24] This regime of full taxation is generally prescribed in the separate provisions governing the taxation of these types of income. See, e.g., U.S. Model Treaty, art. 12(5) (royalties derived through a permanent establishment taxed as business profits).

elements of permanent establishments vary from treaty to treaty, reflecting agreement between the treaty countries over their respective spheres of taxation. The threshold for the taxation of business profits in the U.S. Model Treaty is fairly high because the United States, as a matter of policy, has always leaned toward taxation by the country of residence rather than the country of source. Many other countries, among them developing countries, countries that import capital, and countries with economies built on basic industries, take a different view and seek in their treaties to set fairly low thresholds of taxation by the country of source on the business profits of foreign enterprises.

Exporters of capital or goods, in contrast, and highly commercial countries usually prefer the threshold of taxation to be high for the foreign operations of their own enterprises in treaty countries. Often a significant presence is required for a permanent establishment in treaties between developed economies while a far lesser presence will suffice under treaties among developing countries or between countries of different levels of development.[25]

The definition of a permanent establishment in the U.S. Model Treaty is typical of treaties between developed countries:

> 1. For the purposes of this Convention, the term "permanent establishment" means a fixed place of business through which the business of an enterprise is wholly or partly carried on.
>
> 2. The term "permanent establishment" includes especially:
>
>   a) a place of management;
>
>   b) a branch;
>
>   c) an office;
>
>   d) a factory;
>
>   e) a workshop; and

---

[25] The exact definition of a permanent establishment sometimes reflects narrowly parochial concerns of the treaty countries. A former treaty between the United States and Canada, for example, included the use of "substantial equipment or machinery" (such as construction equipment or harvesting combines) in a treaty country as a permanent establishment there. 1942 Treaty with Canada, Protocol 3(f). The point was to bring the seasonal operations of builders and agricultural harvesters, who frequently cross the U.S.-Canada border, within the tax reach of the country where the activity was conducted. Most likely this provision, which in any event is no longer in the current U.S. treaty with Canada, was for the benefit of the Canadian treasury because of greater U.S. ownership of construction equipment or harvesting combines used in Canada than vice versa.

f) a mine, an oil or gas well, a quarry, or any other place of extraction of natural resources.[26]

In addition, a special rule exists for building sites and installation sites. In this regard, paragraph 3 provides as follows:

> 3. A building site or construction or installation project, or an installation or drilling rig or ship used for the exploration or exploitation of the sea bed and its subsoil and their natural resources, situated in one of the Contracting States constitutes a permanent establishment only if it lasts, or the activities of the rig or ship lasts, for more than twelve months. For the sole purpose of determining whether the twelve-month period referred to in this paragraph has been exceeded:
>
> a) where an enterprise of a Contracting State carries on activities in the other Contracting State at a place that constitutes a building site or construction or installation project and these activities are carried on during periods of time that in the aggregate do not last more than twelve months; and
>
> b) connected activities are carried on at the same building site or construction or installation project during different periods of time, each exceeding thirty days, by one or more enterprises that are connected persons with respect to the first-mentioned enterprise,
>
> these different periods of time shall be added to the periods of time during which the first-mentioned enterprise has carried on activities at that building site or construction or installation project.

Note that the above rule prevents splitting of contracts between affiliates working in geographically related areas. The effort to integrate different work sites that are part of a single project is a longstanding interpretive position of the IRS,[27] and this position has

---

[26] Art. 5. The U.S. Model Treaty also includes construction projects lasting more than 12 months among permanent establishments, while expressly excluding shorter ones. Art. 5(3)

[27] PLR 8526005 (March 8, 1985); GCM 39,373 (March 1, 1985). In LMSB-4-0909-037 Directive (10/30/2009), the IRS stated that it believes that many foreign contractors working on the outer continental shelf of the United States do not comply with U.S. tax requirements.

been endorsed in prior technical explanations of the U.S. Model Treaty.[28]

An illustrative case applying this construction and building site analysis is provided in *Adams Challenge (UK) Limited v. Commissioner*,[29] which was discussed on the U.S. trade or business issues earlier in chapter 5. To restate the facts, the taxpayer *Adams Challenge* was a U.K. company that owned a multi-purpose support vessel called the M.V. Adams Challenge. The M.V. Adams Challenge had a class 2 dynamic positioning system, a diving system, and a helipad. The vessel owner entered into a time charter arrangement with Epic Diving & Marine Services (EPIC) for EPIC to use it for staging its own underwater activities. EPIC had contracted to do oil and gas decommissioning work with respect to offshore oil and gas wells located in the U.S. outer continental shelf. All the actual decommissioning work would be done by EPIC and its own employees, as EPIC maintained a service crew on the vessel to engage in these diving operations. The personnel of Adams (U.K.) Challenge had no part in the decommissioning work, but they did navigate and position the vessel wherever EPIC instructed. The M.V. Adams Challenge was operated in the outer continental shelf in U.S. territorial waters from 60% to 85% of the time for each year in a continuous three year period. After determining that the taxpayer's activities constituted a U.S. trade or business under the Code, the Tax Court then addressed whether the taxpayer's effort to avail itself of the benefits of the U.K. tax treaty allowed the taxpayer to avoid a permanent establishment. Importantly, a taxpayer entitled to treaty relief is eligible to elect the more favorable of domestic law or the benefits of an applicable treaty. In analysing the tax results under the U.K. tax treaty, the Tax Court held that these activities occurred "in the United States." But even so, the taxpayer argued that its activities did not create a permanent establishment as defined in Article 5(3) because its activities involved a ship that had nothing to do with the "exploitation of oil and gas wells" as all wells that were worked on had ceased production years earlier or had never produced oil and gas." Nevertheless, the Tax Court held that the decommissioning work related to the exploitation of oil and gas wells because decommissioning wells is part of the life cycle of the exploitation of natural resources. Thus, because the decommissioning work occurred for longer than twelve months, the activities met the threshold for a permanent establishment under a treaty provision that was similar to the one found in Article 5(3) of the 2016 U.S. Model Treaty.

---

[28] See U.S. Treasury Department Explanation to the 2006 U.S. Model Treaty, art. 5(2).

[29] 154 T.C. 37 (2020).

Like most income tax treaties, the U.S. Model Treaty also contains an enumeration of elements (even though fixed and relatively permanent) that *do not* constitute a permanent establishment in a treaty country:

> 4. [T]he term "permanent establishment" shall be deemed not to include:
>
> a) the use of facilities solely for the purpose of storage, display, or delivery of goods or merchandise belonging to the enterprise;
>
> b) the maintenance of a stock of goods or merchandise belonging to the enterprise solely for the purpose of storage, display, or delivery;
>
> c) the maintenance of a stock of goods or merchandise belonging to the enterprise solely for the purpose of processing by another enterprise;
>
> d) the maintenance of a fixed place of business solely for the purpose of purchasing goods or merchandise, or of collecting information, for the enterprise;
>
> e) the maintenance of a fixed place of business solely for the purpose of carrying on, for the enterprise, any other activity of a preparatory or auxiliary character;
>
> f) the maintenance of a fixed place of business solely for any combination of the activities mentioned in subparagraphs (a) to (e), provided that the overall activity of the fixed place of business resulting from this combination is of a preparatory or auxiliary character.[30]

These excluded elements bear a family resemblance. While they all betoken a presence in a country that is less than a complete industrial or commercial cycle (consisting of the manufacture or the combined purchase and sale of goods), they do permit a significant level of economic activity without engaging the full tax regime of the host country. Not surprisingly, an enterprise of one treaty country can be a customer for goods and services in another without tax consequences there.

Besides resulting from a substantial physical presence, a permanent establishment can arise by imputation from an agent. Under Article 5(5) of the U.S. Model Treaty, for example,

---

30 U.S. Model Treaty, art. 5(4).

"[notwithstanding the requirement of a fixed place of business] where a person. . . is acting on behalf of an enterprise and has and habitually exercises in a Contracting State an authority to conclude contracts in the name of the enterprise, that enterprise shall be deemed to have a permanent establishment in that State." An enterprise thus need not have its own presence in a country as a condition of having a permanent establishment there. The presence of an agent with the authority to enter into binding contracts may be imputed to the principal as a permanent establishment. This arises when enterprises repeatedly send executives or other officers to a country to negotiate and enter into contracts. Even if they are careful to maintain no fixed place of business (by operating, for example, from hotels), their activity, if "habitual," may create a permanent establishment for the enterprise. The possibility is especially pervasive in industries (such as entertainment) where much business takes the form of deals concluded by the owners, managers, and agents of an enterprise.

An agent whose activities are limited to those exempted from the category of permanent establishments (as enumerated in Article 7(4) of the U.S. Model Treaty quoted above) does not, however, create a permanent establishment for the principal.[31] Thus, an agent can habitually enter into binding contracts for the display of goods, the purchase of goods, advertising, or various combinations of these activities without thrusting a permanent establishment upon the principal. Concluding contracts of sale, however, or engaging in most forms of production are generally steps of no return.

There is a further, vitally important qualification of the imputation of a permanent establishment from an agent to a principal: it does not extend to most *independent* agents. Under Article 5(6) of the U.S. Model Treaty, an enterprise does not have a permanent establishment in a country if it carries on business there solely "through a broker, general commission agent, or any other agent of an independent status, providing that such persons are acting in the ordinary course of their business."

This is the provision that permits Marcel to extend distribution and sales of French wine to Europe and the United States without becoming a taxpayer all over the place. It removes from permanent establishments virtually the entire class of commission agents, brokers, and independent distributors through which one can do business in foreign markets, along with many other intermediaries of independent status. This remains so even if the independent agents have the authority to conclude contracts. The requirement of "independent" status, however, implies that an agent or intermediary

---

[31] U.S. Model Treaty, art. 5(5).

can be neither an employee nor even under the day-to-day control of the principal. It is perhaps necessary as well for the agent to have at least one other client, if not several.

Which Is Which? An immediate practical problem is to determine who are dependent and independent agents, a distinction not always visible to the naked eye. This issue was front and center in *Taisei Fire and Marine Insurance Co., Ltd. v. Commissioner.*[32] In *Taisei*, a U.S. insurance agent, Fortress Re, Inc., sold insurance contracts for nine Japanese underwriters. Under management agreements entered into with each of the underwriters, Fortress Re had discretion to execute reinsurance contracts on behalf of the Japanese underwriters that would bind them if those reinsurance contracts were within certain pre-determined coverage limits. The parties stipulated that Fortress Re, Inc. represented the underwriters in the ordinary course of business, and the only issue was whether Fortress Re, Inc. was an "agent of an independent status" for purposes of Article 5(5) of the U.S.-Japan tax treaty. The court agreed with OECD commentary and U.S. Technical Explanations to its treaties that the controlling standard to decide whether Fortress Re was an independent agent centered on the inquiry as to whether Fortress Re was both legally and economically independent. The underwriters did not have any ownership interest in Fortress Re, nor did the underwriters have any director, officer, or employee that worked for Fortress Re. The court found no evidence that the Japanese underwriters acted in concert or as a "pool" to control Fortress Re. Thus, the court found that Fortress Re was legally independent. As to economic independence, the court found that Fortress Re did not have any guaranteed revenue. Moreover, the management contracts allowed for each party to terminate the arrangement, and several had a notice period of only 6 months. Based on these findings of fact, the court found that Fortress Re was not economically dependent on any particular underwriter and that the loss of an underwriter would not inhibit its opportunity to cover its business operating costs. Consequently, the court concluded that Fortress Re was in fact an independent agent because it was both legally and economically independent of the Japanese underwriters. *Taisei* is an important case both for the issue that it considered but also for its reliance on OECD commentary and on a non-U.S. case in Germany as analogous guidance.

Profits "Attributable" to a Permanent Establishment. Another question concerning business profits is: how are they properly allocated to a permanent establishment? Or more simply, how do we determine the taxable income of a permanent establishment? In the

---

[32] 104 T.C. 535 (1995) (*acq.*).

Code, there are elaborate rules for determining the income "effectively connected" with a U.S. trade or business and even more elaborate regulations governing allocable expenses. Treaty provisions on business profits "attributable" to a permanent establishment are, by contrast, broadly drawn.

In determining the business profits attributable to a permanent establishment, most treaties require an "arm's length" standard. In Article 7(2) of the U.S. Model Treaty, "there shall in each Contracting State be attributed to [a] permanent establishment the business profits which it might be expected to make if it were a distinct and independent enterprise engaged in the same or similar activities under the same or similar conditions." This provision empowers the tax authorities of the treaty countries to allocate business profits to and among permanent establishments from related persons as though they had dealt with each other on an arm's length basis, as unrelated persons would have done.

Article 7(2) also implies that a permanent establishment is treated as a separate and distinct enterprise in its dealings with its own home office. Therefore, instead of allocating income and expense between a permanent establishment and its home office as items arising within a single entity (which in titular effect they are), Article 7(2) of the Model Treaty invites computation of the permanent establishment's income according to a notional course of dealing between the permanent establishment and its home office as though it were a separately chartered subsidiary dealing at arm's length with its parent. Suppose, for example, that the home entity produced inventory and shipped it to a U.S. permanent establishment for sale to customers. Article 7(2) implies that income from the sale would be reckoned and attributed to the permanent establishment as though the home entity had sold the inventory to the permanent establishment at an arm's length price (to be determined under transfer pricing principles such as those of section 482) and not as gain from a foreign person's U.S. sale through a U.S. office. On this basis, a considerable part of the gain would be attributed to the home office beyond the reach of U.S. taxation. The computation of income under the Code (and specifically section 865(e)(2)) potentially would be different.[33]

Most treaties require an actual connection between a permanent establishment and "attributable" business profits. The U.S. Model Treaty, for example, specifically limits the business profits to be attributed to a permanent establishment to those derived from the assets or activities of the permanent establishment.[34] This suggests

[33] See chapter 6.

[34] U.S. Model Treaty, art. 7(2).

a standard analogous to the "asset use" and "activities" tests for effectively connected income under the Code. Article 7(2) would not countenance a "force of attraction" mechanism like the one in Code section 864(c)(3), which treats all residual U.S. source income as effectively connected.[35] Enterprises therefore need not fear that economically unrelated business profits or other income will be attributed out of the blue to a permanent establishment under the Model Treaty.

Article 7(7) of the U.S. Model Treaty does, however, specifically provide for business profits generated by a permanent establishment and deferred to a later year to be "attributed" to the permanent establishment. "[A]ny income or gain attributable to a permanent establishment or fixed base during its existence is taxable in the Contracting State where such permanent establishment or fixed base is situated even if the payments are deferred until such permanent establishment or fixed base has ceased to exist." This provision deals with deferred business profits in much the same way as the Code.[36]

D. Compensation for Personal Services

In addition to business profits, most income tax treaties deal with more specific types of income similar to business profits. Of particular concern to individuals working or plying a trade in foreign lands are the provisions for personal services.

The treaty regime for compensation for personal services is similar to the one imposed on business profits. Treaties aim to make it easier for residents of one country to work in the other and, to this end, establish thresholds of taxation for income from personal services in the country of source that allow considerable services to be performed there without local taxation. The result, generally, is that business travelers and other mobile workers are taxed only in their country of residence or citizenship.

Although the exact terminology varies, many treaties divide services into two classes: 1) "dependent services," which means services performed as an employee under the close direction of an employer, and 2) "independent services," which generally means services performed as an independent contractor or in self-employment, including most professional services such as legal advice or medical treatment. In addition, treaties commonly make special provision for the compensation of performing artists and athletes as well as the incomes of students, teachers, and scholars.

The U.S. Model Treaty follows a different nomenclature, although in substance its rules for personal services fall within the

---

[35] See chapter 6.

[36] See chapter 6.

treaty mainstream. It refers to income from "dependent personal services" as "income from employment," and it lumps income from independent personal services with other types of business income.

1. Income from Employment

On "income from employment" (more widely known as "dependent personal services" in tax treaties), the U.S. Model Treaty follows a nearly universal pattern, known as the "183-day rule." At the baseline, income from employment is taxable in the country in which the services are performed,[37] but—and these are key qualifications—income from services performed in a treaty country by a resident of the other treaty country is *not* taxed in the country where they are performed if 1) the employee is present there for 183 days or less during the taxable year, 2) the compensation is paid by an employer who is not a resident of the country of performance, and 3) the compensation "is not borne by a permanent establishment or a fixed base which the employer has" in that country.[38] In short, an employee of an employer in one treaty country can spend up to 183 days annually in the other treaty country without being taxed there. Employees of enterprises in countries with a broad treaty network can therefore move quite freely within the treaty countries while remaining subject to income tax only in their country of residence.[39]

2. Independent Personal Services

In the U.S. Model Treaty, the term "business" is defined to "include. . . the performance of professional services and of other activities of an independent character."[40] The treaty regime for income from independent personal services is thus subsumed to the treatment of business profits. An individual resident of one treaty country performing services in an *independent* capacity is taxed only in the country of residence unless the services are performed in the other treaty country *and* the income is attributable to a permanent establishment.[41]

This regime for independent personal services is generally accommodating. It covers lawyers, doctors, consultants, and piano tuners who ply their trades outside their countries of residence in treaty countries where they have no office or fixed place of business. A lawyer can thus travel to another country to advise a client without

---

[37] U.S. Model Treaty, art. 14(1).

[38] U.S. Model Treaty, art. 14(2).

[39] Bear in mind that what is involved here is the taxation of the salary income of the employee, *not* the employer's business profits derived from the employee's activity, which may well be subject to tax in the country of source.

[40] U.S. Model Treaty, art. 3(1)(e).

[41] U.S. Model Treaty, art. 7(1).

being taxed there as long as the lawyer's firm maintains no office there. If it does, the treaty provisions on business profits offer less protection, if any. A question not explicitly addressed in the Model Treaty is how close a connection between services and a permanent establishment is necessary to bring the resulting income within taxation by the country of source.[42]

In many treaties, the permanent establishment rule is combined with a limitation (usually 183 days) on the period during which income from independent personal services is exempt from tax in the country of source. Under the U.S. treaty with the United Kingdom, for example, independent services performed in one treaty country by a resident of the other can be taxed in the former country *either* if the individual performing them has a "fixed base regularly available" in that country *or* if the individual spends more than 183 days in that country within a taxable year.[43] This dual threshold of taxation of independent personal services is the closest thing to a norm in income tax treaties and appears in the treaties between the United States and Australia, Belgium, China, Cyprus, Finland, France, Germany, Hungary, Iceland, Italy, Japan, New Zealand, Norway, Poland, Romania, and the United Kingdom.

Some treaties impose more restrictive rules, reducing the period of exempt presence to 90 days, in some instances with a dollar limitation as well.[44]

Readers should note that this skeletal summary does not capture a number of specific features of individual treaties. Some impose time *and* dollar limitations; others impose them in the alternative. When you are faced with an actual question of compensation, there is no substitute for recourse to the exact terms of the currently applicable treaty.

Johansson and "Loan-Out" Companies. The treaty regime for personal services is of great practical importance because it permits movement of people between countries that would otherwise be constrained by tax barriers. It often influences the patterns of business travel between treaty countries. Not surprisingly, various acquisitive undertakings have been shoehorned into forms designed to benefit from the 183-day rule. Residents of third countries, for example, are frequently tempted to set up residence and employment in a treaty country in order to invoke the 183-day rule. A widely noted

---

[42] Earlier versions of the U.S. Model Treaty addressed this question with the additional requirement that the permanent establishment be "regularly available" to the foreign resident performing independent services. Today, it would appear that more is required to support taxation of services income by the country of source.

[43] Treaty with United Kingdom, art. 14.

[44] E.g., Barbados, Denmark, Egypt, Malta, and the Philippines.

case in this regard is *Johansson v. United States.*[45] In *Johansson* a professional boxer (and citizen of Sweden) sought to claim the benefits of the income tax treaty between the United States and Switzerland. Johansson established "residence" in Switzerland and created a Swiss corporation, Scanart S.A., which ostensibly employed him to engage in championship prize fights in the United States against Floyd Patterson. Johansson was thus attempting to fight in the United States in the guise of an employee of a Swiss corporation. Literally, Scanart S.A. undertook to provide an opponent for Floyd Patterson in the person of its employee Johansson. Scanart paid Johansson its entire receipts for his services of administering and receiving beatings (he did some of both), minus amounts contributed to a pension fund for Johansson, who was Scanart's sole employee (and most likely its sole shareholder as well). Since Johansson spent fewer than 183 days in the United States in the years in which he fought Floyd Patterson, he claimed exemption from U.S. taxation on his compensation from Scanart (a Swiss entity) under the income tax treaty then in effect between the United States and Switzerland (which contained a variant of the 183-day rule).[46]

Under attack from the IRS, the arrangement failed in court. The court found that Scanart had no independent identity and accordingly that Johansson was in effect fighting on his own behalf. Scanart had come on the scene late and had done little that was visible to the naked eye. The court essentially refused to take Scanart seriously as an entity and concluded that Johansson's pugilistic endeavors were more nearly those of an independent contractor than of an employee.

The *Johansson* case has cast a long shadow. The structure attempted unsuccessfully there is known as a "loan-out" company and has been widely used by performers and athletes. The tax objectives of such arrangements include income-splitting, deferral of taxable gain, and the advantageous use of income tax treaties. Although the taxpayer lost, *Johansson* does not systematically foreclose these possibilities. Rather, it suggests a road map to success by avoiding its pitfalls. If Scanart had employed several boxers, had had real economic activity in Switzerland, and had taken on other indicia of reality, the arrangement could have succeeded.[47]

---

[45] 336 F.2d 809 (5th Cir. 1964).

[46] Scanart itself, to be sure, was probably subject to U.S. taxation because it was doubtless engaged in business in the United States and might well have had a U.S. permanent establishment to boot; but Scanart's taxable income would in any event have been fully offset by deductions for compensation paid to Johansson personally and amounts paid into his pension fund.

[47] See, e.g., P. R. Bass v. Commissioner, 50 T.C. 595 (1968) (Swiss corporation owning U.S. oil interests entitled to treaty benefits by virtue of its significant business activity).

"Artistes and Athletes" Clauses. More broadly, performers and athletes have often been able to gain advantage from the standard treaty provisions on compensation for services. They move around a lot and derive income from many countries. As residents of a country connected to others through a useful network of treaties, and not itself given to fierce taxation, performers and athletes could enjoy virtual exemption from taxation under standard treaty provisions governing the performance of services. Under a treaty that exempts "independent" personal services from taxation in the country of source (as does the U.S. Model Treaty), a performer could fairly easily arrange to work as an independent contractor and avoid creating a "fixed base" in the country of performance. Even under a treaty that has only the standard 183-day rule for "dependent" personal services, a performer can seek shelter by arranging to be employed by a "loan-out" company (ultimately under his or her control) incorporated in a well-chosen treaty jurisdiction.

For that reason, most recent treaties, and the U.S. Model Treaty, have special provisions for performers and athletes limiting the tax benefits available for their compensation and explicitly undercutting the use of loan-out companies. The typical "artistes and athletes" clause strengthens the taxing hand of the country of source.[48] In Article 16(1) of the U.S. Model Treaty, for example, "income derived by a resident of a Contracting State as an entertainer, such as a theater, motion picture, radio, or television artiste, or a musician, or as a sportsman, from his personal activities as such exercised in the other Contracting State. . . may be taxed in that other State, except where the amount of the gross receipts derived by such entertainer or sportsman, including expenses reimbursed to him or borne on his behalf from such activities does not exceed thirty thousand United States dollars ($30,000) or its equivalent in the taxable year concerned."[49] This is an explicit exception to the Model Treaty's taxation of personal services generally. With the $30,000 floor (which leaves the second stringers and members of the chorus mostly unaffected), the provision aims squarely at top athletes and headliners. Article 16(2) extends this regime to income paid to "loan-out" companies on account of the services of performers and athletes.

3. Students, Trainees, and Scholars

Another group widely favored in income tax treaties is students, with whom scholars are often (but not always) associated. In the U.S. Model Treaty:

---

48 Note that the term often used in treaties is not "artist" but "art*iste*." "Artiste" is an old-fashioned word for a performing artist (a singer, for example) and does not describe a painter or sculptor.

49 U.S. Model Treaty, art. 16(1).

> Payments received by a student or business trainee who is, or was immediately before visiting a Contracting State, a resident of the other Contracting State, and who is present in the first-mentioned State for the purpose of his full-time education at an accredited educational institution, or for his full-time training, shall not be taxed in that State, provided that such payments arise outside that State, and are for the purpose of his maintenance, education or training.[50]

Under this provision, the financial support of foreign students is not taxed by the country in which they study when it "arises" outside that country. The reasons for these terms, one imagines, is to prevent the largesse of governments and other institutions toward students of their own country from being diverted into the treasuries of the foreign countries where the students pursue their studies. Since the Internal Revenue Code unilaterally grants foreign students much the same protection as the U.S. Model Treaty,[51] the provision may serve in some instances mainly to improve the position of American students studying outside the United States.

The U.S. Model Treaty provides an additional exemption for remuneration from personal services performed in the host country to the extent of $10,000 or its equivalent in the currency of the other Contracting State annually.[52] This provision serves to prevent taxation of subsistence wages eked out by starving students in part-time jobs.

Article 20(1) of the U.S. Model Treaty also applies to "business trainees." A "business trainee" is someone who is in a treaty country temporarily for the purpose of securing training necessary to qualify to practice a profession or professional specialty. A business trainee can also be a person who is employed, or under contract with, a resident of the treaty country for the primary purpose of acquiring technical, professional, or business experience from a person other than the employer.[53] As long as the training is received from someone other than the employer, an employee can receive tax-free payments for maintenance, education, and training from an employer residing outside the host country. Thus, the exemption for business trainees depends on receiving the *training* from someone other than the employer, but the exempt payments themselves may be received directly from the employer.

---

[50] U.S. Model Treaty, art. 20. In the case of a business trainee the exemption from tax lasts only one year. Id. Some treaties, including those with France and Germany, offer students even greater protection from taxation during overseas study.

[51] See § 872(b)(3).

[52] U.S. Model Treaty, art. 20(2).

[53] U.S. Model Treaty, art. 20(3).

Somewhat less widespread than protection for students and trainees are treaty benefits for teachers and scholars. The U.S. Model Treaty, for example, does nothing for them. Some older treaties, however, accord visiting professors from one country a two-year period of tax exemption in the other.[54]

E. Interest, Dividends, Royalties, Rents, and Other Gains

Passive investment in a foreign country commonly generates interest, dividends, and royalties, in various combinations. Interest and royalties (but rarely dividends) also arise from active business operations. Recall that in the Code, U.S. source passive investment income paid to foreign persons is subject to a flat 30 percent tax on the gross amount. Since most countries welcome passive foreign investment—which adds to the capital available to an economy without bringing indigenous business activity under direct foreign control—most income tax treaties offer significant concessions by the country of source in taxing passive investment income paid to residents of the other treaty country. A widespread pattern, epitomized in the U.S. Model Treaty, is exemption for interest and royalties in the country of source and reduced rates of tax for dividends.

1. Interest

In the U.S. Model Treaty, "interest derived and beneficially owned by a resident of a Contracting State shall be taxable only in that State."[55] With this, interest is exempt in the country of its source in the hands of a resident of the other treaty country. The Model Treaty defines interest broadly as "income from debt claims of every kind."[56]

There is a separate regime for interest income "determined with reference to receipts, sales, income, profits or other cash flow of the debtor."[57] For interest of this type received by U.S. residents from other treaty countries, the basic exemption of interest income in the Model Treaty does not apply. Instead, the contingent interest is taxed similarly to a dividend and not above 15 percent. This provision, which mirrors the exclusion of contingent interest from exempt portfolio interest in the Code, aims at the use of equity-flavored debt instruments which were once great favorites of foreign investors in the United States.

---

[54] E.g., Treaty with Japan, art. 19.

[55] U.S. Model Treaty, art. 11(1).

[56] U.S. Model Treaty, art. 11(4).

[57] U.S. Model Treaty, art. 11(2)(a).

Unlike the Code's exemption of U.S. source "portfolio" interest, the broader exemption of interest income in the U.S. Model Treaty applies to interest paid to 10 percent (and greater) shareholders and other owners and is available to foreign banks for interest on loans not made through a permanent establishment in the United States.[58] Further study is needed here, as this outcome marks an important divergence from the outcome of an interest stripping transaction under domestic law. You will remember that in chapter 5 we concluded that the related party interest stripping transaction in Diagram #9 (which is depicted as a $50 million interest payment at ③ in Diagram #9) would have been subject to the 30 percent gross basis tax under section 882, as the income was fixed and determinable income to which the portfolio interest exemption would not have applied by reason of the 10 percent shareholder rule.

Diagram #9

Combined Strategy

Supply Chain Transaction, Interest Stripping Transaction, Royalty Stripping Transaction, Rental Stripping, and Service Stripping Transaction

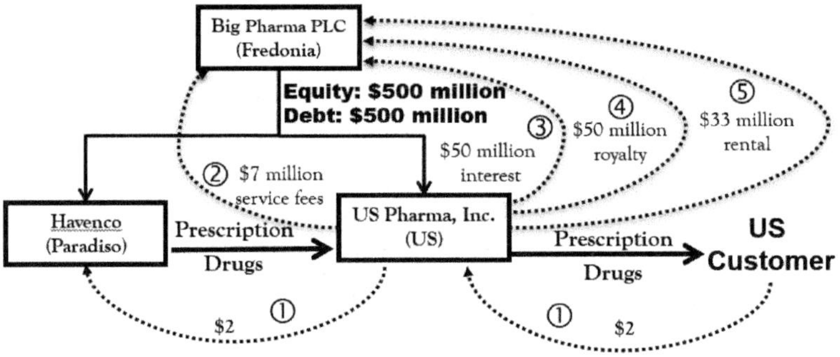

In contrast, Article 11(1) of the U.S. Model Treaty provides for exemption from U.S. taxation if the lender is entitled to claim tax treaty relief regardless of whether the lender is a 10 percent shareholder. Thus, the potential for pursuing an interest stripping strategy as depicted in Diagram #9 is restored by reason of the treaty relief, so that determining whether Big Pharma PLC is entitled to rely on the U.S. Model Treaty becomes an enormously important question. What if Fredonia does not have a tax treaty with the United States? Can Big Pharma PLC incorporate a new finance subsidiary in a jurisdiction that has a U.S. tax treaty and route the interest stripping transaction through it and gain access through that finance subsidiary to treaty benefits that Big Pharma PLC could not have obtained on its own? The idea of creating an intermediate treaty-

[58] Section 881(c)(3), in contrast, denies to most U.S. source interest paid to foreign banks the character of exempt portfolio interest. See chapter 5.

based entity to engage in transactions with another affiliate is commonly referred to as "treaty shopping," and we will unpack the limitations that have been put into place on such treaty shopping later in this chapter. The reason why that issue is so important is clearly seen here: Big Pharma PLC needs a tax treaty if it wants an inbound interest stripping transaction that is not subject to the flat 30 percent gross basis tax that applies to fixed and determinable income. The possibility of treaty shopping is an active ingredient in many treaty-based international tax shelters.

The 2016 U.S. Model Treaty introduced a restriction on the possibility of sheltering interest with a reduced withholding rate when that interest benefits from a "special tax regime" in the jurisdiction of residence.[59] For this purpose, a special tax regime includes either a concessionary rate of taxation for interest income or notional deductions that offset the gross interest income and is expected to result in the lesser of a 15 percent tax rate on the interest or a rate that is 60 percent or less than the general nontreaty rate.[60] The provision is not in any existing U.S. tax treaty, and it represents a new milestone. The provision conditions the relinquishment of source country taxation over the profits that are stripped out of the source country on the other jurisdiction's assertion of meaningful taxation over that income in the recipient's jurisdiction. In addition, the 2016 U.S. Model Treaty prevents a company that engages in a corporate inversion after the date this new provision is implemented from being able to use the reduced withholding rates on interest.[61] It was widely understood that a major impetus for a corporate inversion was to engage in inbound interest stripping transactions, and this provision is designed to address that strategy.

2. Dividends

Treaties rarely exempt dividends, unlike interest, from taxation entirely in the country of source. Dividends received from one treaty country by residents of another are generally subject to reduced rates of tax by the country of source. In the U.S. Model Treaty, the tax imposed on dividends by the country of source is reduced to 15 percent for the bulk of dividends and to 5 percent if the recipient is a corporation owning at least 10 percent of the voting stock of the corporation paying the dividend.[62] Some such two-tiered reduction of the normal national rates is the standard tax regime for dividends in treaties.

---

[59] See Article 11(2)(c).

[60] See Article 3(*l*).

[61] Article 11(2)(d).

[62] U.S. Model Treaty, art. 10(2). Recall that in the Code the baseline tax imposed on dividends received by foreign taxpayers is 30 percent.

The U.S. Model Treaty also provides that one country may not tax dividends paid by a corporation chartered in the other treaty country except in specific narrow situations.[63] This clause eliminates what is known as the "second tax" imposed under the U.S. tax laws on certain dividends paid *by* foreign corporations.[64] Most other treaties make similar provision for the second tax on dividends. On the other side of the scales, the 2016 U.S. Model Treaty removes the benefit of the reduced withholding rates on dividends from a company that engages in a corporate inversion after the date this new provision is implemented into a treaty.[65]

3. Royalties

In the U.S. Model Treaty, royalties received by a resident of a treaty country are taxable only in that country.[66] This taxation solely on the basis of the recipient's residence implies exemption from tax in the country of source. A similar treatment of royalties is found in a number of treaties between the United States and developed countries.[67] An equally common pattern is taxation at a reduced rate by the country of source on royalties.[68]

More difficult is determining the boundary of "royalties." In the U.S. Model Treaty, "royalties" are defined as income from the use of a broad range of intangible property as well as certain contingent gains from the sale of such property:

> The term "royalties" as used in this Convention means:
>
> payments of any kind received as a consideration for the use of, or the right to use, any copyright of literary, artistic, scientific or other work (including cinematographic films), any patent, trademark, design or model, plan, secret formula or process, or for information concerning industrial, commercial or scientific experience.[69]

A notable element of this definition is the specific inclusion of income from motion pictures among royalties (and hence the tax-favored group) and the absence of any mention of computer software or audio and video tapes and disks. A number of treaties differ on this score. The characterization of royalties under treaty provisions raises the

---

[63] U.S. Model Treaty, art. 10(9).

[64] This provision is largely redundant in practical effect because § 884(e) also calls off the second tax on dividends paid by foreign corporations subject to the branch profits tax, which is nearly all of them.

[65] U.S. Model Treaty, art. 10(5).

[66] U.S. Model Treaty, art. 12(1).

[67] E.g., The treaties with Belgium, Germany, the Netherlands, the United Kingdom, and several of the former Soviet Republics.

[68] E.g., Canada (10 percent), France (5 percent), and Japan (10 percent).

[69] U.S. Model Treaty, art. 12(4).

same kinds of questions that arise in nontreaty cases. In *Boulez v. Commissioner*,[70] for example, involving a recording contract of a foreign orchestra conductor, the IRS characterized the income received as compensation for services rather than royalties, as in *Ingram v. Bowers*,[71] under both the Code and U.S. treaty with Germany and prevailed on both fronts.

The 2016 U.S. Model Treaty for the first time implemented a limitation on reduced rates for royalties when the royalties benefit from a "special tax regime" in the country of residence.[72] For this purpose, a special tax regime includes either a concessionary rate of taxation for royalty income or provides for notional deductions that offset the gross royalty income and result in the lesser of a 15 percent tax rate or a rate that is 60 percent of the general statutory rate.[73] In addition, like the treatment of dividends after a corporate inversion, the 2016 U.S. Model Treaty also prevents a company that engages in a corporate inversion after the date this treaty provision is implemented from enjoying the reduced withholding rates on royalties.[74]

As was true with the analysis of a related party interest stripping transaction, it is worth pausing again here to note the marked divergence that the U.S. Model Treaty affords for royalty stripping transactions from the result obtained under section 881. Again, in chapter 5, we concluded that the related party royalty stripping transaction in Diagram #9 (which is depicted as a $50 million royalty payment at ④ in Diagram #9) would have been subject to the flat 30 percent gross basis tax under section 881, as the income is fixed and determinable income to which the gross income tax applied. Now, the licensor in a royalty stripping strategy avoids any source country taxation under the U.S. Model Treaty *if* the licensor of the intangible property is eligible for tax treaty relief. Again, Big Pharma PLC *needs* a tax treaty if it wants to engage in an inbound royalty stripping transaction and not be subject to the gross income tax at a rate of 30 percent. The importance of tax treaty relief for the inbound multinational enterprise is becoming more and more apparent.

---

70 83 T.C. 584 (1984).

71 See chapter 3.

72 U.S. Model Treaty, art. 12(2)(a).

73 U.S. Model Treaty, art. 3(1)(*l*).

74 U.S. Model Treaty, art. 12(2)(b).

Diagram #9

Combined Strategy

Supply Chain Transaction, Interest Stripping Transaction, Royalty Stripping Transaction, Rental Stripping, and Service Stripping Transaction

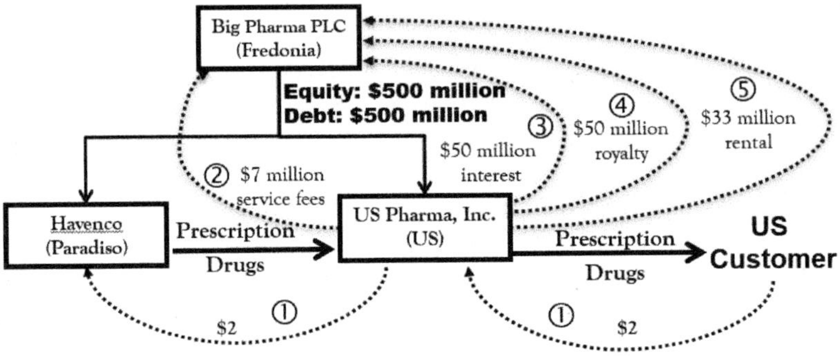

A final point should be made as to the royalty clause in the U.S. Model Treaty. The provisions governing royalties in the U.S. Model Treaty do not apply to royalties earned as part of the business profits of a permanent establishment. If the royalties are "effectively connected" with a business conducted in a treaty country through a permanent establishment, they are subject to tax in that country as business profits.[75] Roughly speaking, therefore, the property producing the royalties must be an investment asset in the hands of its owner at the time the royalties are received if they are to be exempt under the Model Treaty. That does not mean that the asset must not have originated from the operations of an active business, only that the posture of the recipient of the royalties must be, or have become, relatively passive. The writer of a book, therefore, cannot also publish and actively distribute it in a treaty country without losing, in all likelihood, the protection of the royalties under the treaty.

4. Rentals from Tangible Property

In contrast with royalties, most U.S. income tax treaties make no explicit provision for rentals derived from tangible personal property. The U.S. Model Treaty, for example, has no article directly governing rents of this type.[76] One could easily conclude that rentals from tangible property were simply subject to the baseline tax of the country of source, which in the United States would be a flat rate tax of 30 percent. As it turns out, Article 21 of the Model Treaty (an "Other Income" clause) eliminates tax by the country of source for all

---

75 U.S. Model Treaty, art. 12(5).

76 In contrast, the U.N. Model Treaty has an explicit provision that addresses movable property. See U.N. Model Treaty, art. 22(2).

rents not attributable to a permanent establishment or real property, with taxation resulting only in the country of residence of the recipient of the rents. The treaty with the United Kingdom is similar in this regard.[77]

More commonly, treaties leave the taxation of rents in the country of source. This results because the treaties make no specific provision for the taxation of rents and also contain no "Other Income" clause shielding unspecified income from taxation by the country of source.

5. Income from Real Property

Under the U.S. Model Treaty, income from real property is taxable in the country in which the property is located.[78] This is the simplest of provisions, and some near-equivalent of it is found in every income tax treaty. It follows that, even under treaties, income from foreign investment in real estate is subject to income tax in the country of source.

In the U.S. Model Treaty, the term "real property" derives its meaning from the law of the country imposing the tax, although certain types of property—such as "property accessory to real property (immovable property), livestock and equipment used in agriculture and forestry, rights to which the provisions of general law respecting landed property apply, usufruct of real property (immovable property) and rights to variable or fixed payments as consideration for the working of, or the right to work, mineral deposits, sources and other natural resources"—are treated as real property in all events.[79] Income from real property, for its part, is defined expansively to include income from agriculture and forestry. Bear in mind as well that United States tax law (for example, in section 897) contains a sweeping definition of "real property."[80]

Many income tax treaties expressly identify some of the constituents of the class of real property. Common inclusions are mines, quarries, and all other exploitations of natural resources. Occasional exclusions are ships and aircraft. These would be widespread norms, one imagines, even if the treaties were silent on those items. Less clear is the treatment of livestock and agricultural and forestry equipment when not expressly mentioned. Under U.S. law, some but not all of these items are real property.[81] With all the

---

77 There is further discussion of "Other Income" clauses below.

78 U.S. Model Treaty, art. 6(1).

79 U.S. Model Treaty, art. 6(2).

80 See chapter 8.

81 Property used to *grow* or *harvest* timber or crops is real property, but not property used to process them. See Reg. § 1.897–1(b)(4)(i)(A).

variations of national laws, there is bound to be some uncertainty which can be resolved only by consulting local counsel.

Another common provision is the exclusion of interest on mortgage debt from the class of income from real property. The U.S. Model Treaty contains no explicit rule, but the result is not in doubt. As mentioned above, the student should again note that the U.S. Model Treaty that addresses rent only applies to the rental of real property and that rental of tangible personal property is addressed in the "other income" clause of the U.S. Model Treaty.

Finally, consistent with domestic law, paragraph 5 of Article 6 allows a resident of a treaty jurisdiction to elect to compute the tax on its real property income on a net basis as if such income were business profits attributable to a permanent establishment. However, any such election is binding on the taxpayer for the taxable year of the election and all subsequent taxable years unless the competent authority of the jurisdiction where the property is situated agrees to terminate the election.

6. Gains from the Sale of Real Property

Treaties almost invariably make gains from the *sale* of real property subject to tax in the country in which the real property is located. There is sometimes a separate provision to this effect, as in the U.S. Model Treaty (Article 13(1)), but more commonly there is a single provision for income from real property and gains from the sale of real property. Regardless of the format, the essential rule is always the same: the country in which real property is located retains priority of taxing power.

The U.S. Model Treaty extends the taxation of real estate by a treaty country to sales of shares of corporations (no matter where incorporated) holding assets consisting principally of real estate in that country as well as to sales of interests in partnerships, trusts, and estates with similar assets.[82] Several recent treaties, including those with Australia, Canada, and the United Kingdom, are similar on this score. This treatment is consistent with section 897 of the Code, which imposes tax on gains of foreign taxpayers from sales of "U.S. real property interests," a class that includes shares of domestic corporations owning U.S. real estate as well as direct holdings of real estate.[83]

[82] U.S. Model Treaty, art. 13(2).

[83] Unlike the treaties, however, section 897 does not directly reach interests in foreign corporations.

7. Capital and Other Gains from Sales of Personal Property

As a rule, treaties provide that gains from the sale of personal property are taxed only in the seller's country of residence. Capital gains of residents of treaty countries are therefore not subject to U.S. taxation even when derived from assets, such as investment securities, that have some relation to the U.S. economy. Since the baseline treatment of capital gains of foreign taxpayers under the Code is similarly benign, the treaty regime adds little to what is already there. That being so, the few atypical treaties, such as the treaties with India and Thailand, that allow each treaty country to tax capital gains in accordance with its own national tax laws entail in practice a tax regime little different from that enjoyed by residents of countries with more fully developed treaty protection for capital gains.

Treaty protection (like that of the Code) generally extends only to gains from a specific and narrow class of property. Real property, as the discussion above confirms, is not covered. Nor, for the same reason, does the protection reach personal property that represents beneficial ownership of real property (such as shares of corporations owning real property). Contingent gains from dispositions of intangible property are commonly treated as "royalties" rather than as gains from the sale of property.[84] Finally, gains from the sale of personal property attributable to a permanent establishment are never shielded under treaties as "capital gains." What this means in overview is that the gains protected by treaties consist pretty much of gains from pure investment assets, principally financial assets. Some physical assets, such as art and antiques, are also shielded but only when they are sold independently of a permanent establishment.

One difference between treaties and the Code is in the treatment of gains from sales of property by a business that does not possess its own permanent establishment in a treaty country. A dealer in property can make sales that are effectively connected with a U.S. business and still avoid U.S. taxation under the treaty regime *if* the gains are not attributable to a permanent establishment. To illustrate the point, consider an artist or an art dealer selling pieces from inventory in the United States. The sales would not generate effectively connected income under the Code if there were no U.S. trade or business. The existence of *any* U.S. trade or business of the seller, however, would alter this result, even if the trade or business bore no direct relation to the sales of art. The artist could not, for example, present a seminar in the United States, or teach, or give a

---

[84] See, e.g., U.S. Model Treaty, art. 12(2).

lecture tour, or perform any personal services in the United States, without exposing the gains from sales of property to becoming effectively connected income under the Code.[85] Treaties, in contrast, normally shield sales of property in the United States by a person who has no U.S. permanent establishment. A foreign antique dealer from a treaty country can therefore mix a few sales with a lecture tour in the United States, whereas one from a nontreaty country must be far more guarded.

8. "Other Income" Clauses

A provision found in a number of treaties is a residual "other income" clause. In the U.S. Model Treaty, it is Article 21(1). "Items of income of a resident of a Contracting State, wherever arising, not dealt with in the foregoing Articles of this Convention shall be taxable only in that State." Three qualifications of this provision exist. First, in Article 21(3), the country of source is allowed to retain taxing jurisdiction over other income that is attributable to a permanent establishment or fixed base by the country of the permanent establishment's location. Second, under Article 21(2)(a), guarantee fees that are subject to special tax regime in the recipient's jurisdiction are allowed to be taxed by the country of source. Finally, under Article 21(2)(b), a guarantee fee paid by a corporation that engaged in a corporate inversion is not allowed to receive treaty relief. Because the U.S. Model Treaty blankets most items of income quite thoroughly, the effect of Article 21 is not huge. Some of its pockets are nonetheless worth noting. For example, the U.S. Model Treaty makes no specific provision for rentals derived from tangible personal property. Article 21 therefore shields them from tax by the country of source in the hands of a resident of a treaty country as noted above. Income from the cancellation of indebtedness, from court-awarded damages, from prizes and awards, and from pure windfalls might also flourish under the umbrella of Article 21.

As was true with the analysis of interest and royalties, it is worth again pausing here to reflect on the marked divergence of the U.S. Model Treaty from purely national tax law. In chapter 5, we concluded that the related party rental stripping transaction for the lease of tangible personal property illustrated in Diagram #9 (which is depicted as a $33 million of rental payments at ⑤ in Diagram #9) would have been subject to a flat rate 30 percent income tax under section 881 as fixed or determinable income to which the gross income tax applied. Thus, the potential for employing a rental-stripping strategy is restored under the U.S. Model Treaty *if* the lessor of the tangible personal property is eligible for U.S. tax treaty relief. Again, the Big Pharma PLC *needs* a tax treaty if it wants to

---

85 See § 864(c)(3) and further discussion in chapter 6.

engage in an inbound rental stripping transaction and not be subject to the gross income tax at a rate of 30 percent that applies to fixed and determinable income. The importance of tax treaty relief for the inbound multinational enterprise is now fully apparent for the inbound base erosion opportunities it affords.

Diagram #9

Combined Strategy

Supply Chain Transaction, Interest Stripping Transaction, Royalty Stripping Transaction, Rental Stripping, and Service Stripping Transaction

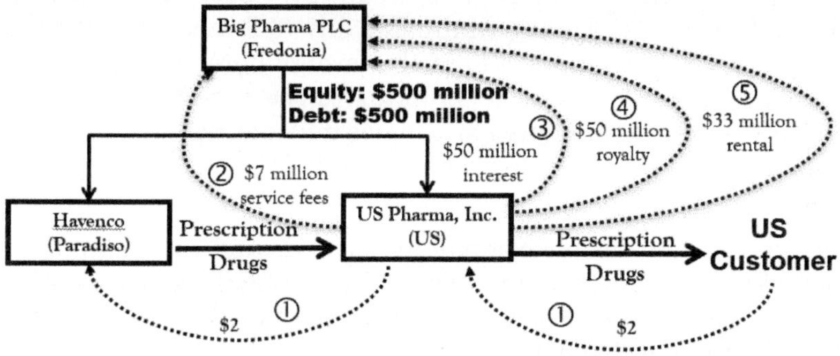

A final point should be made as to the "other income" clause in the U.S. Model Treaty. The "other income" clause of the U.S. Model Treaty also bears importantly on the taxation of dual residents. The tie-breaking rules on residence confer the benefits of residence on individuals who would otherwise be dual residents (and hence exposed to "saving" clauses in both treaty countries) but offer no protection for items of income not actually covered by the treaty. The breadth of the "other income" clause of the U.S. Model Treaty, in contrast, makes the protection of dual residents very nearly complete. Only a small handful of treaties, however, have "other income" clauses as expansive as the U.S. Model Treaty's.

9. Concluding Comments on Interest Stripping, Royalty Stripping, and Rental Stripping Transactions Under the 2016 Model Treaty

We have taken a winding path and have come to a somewhat startling place. The source rules discussed in chapter 3 and the taxation of fixed and determinable income discussed in chapter 5 worked together to allow the United States to retain the power to tax the fixed and determinable income earned in inbound related party earnings stripping transactions. Those rules did not reach the purchase and sale of inventory among related parties, and they did not apply to service stripping transactions where the foreign affiliate provided services from a location outside the United States. Thus, two of the five common earnings stripping strategies were effective in removing profits from the U.S. affiliate to an offshore affiliate and U.S. gross basis taxation. Even so, the three most powerful earnings stripping techniques (namely, interest stripping transactions, royalty stripping transactions, and rental stripping transactions) were unsuccessful in avoiding U.S. taxation on the income earned by the foreign person from a related party. The income from each of those transactions would generally have U.S. source, and would be fixed or determinable income. Thus, the flat rate of 30 percent would have applied to the gross income earned by the foreign related party (Big Pharma PLC in our Diagram #9) in all three of those cases, even though the U.S. Model Treaty eliminates any U.S. taxation on those three strategies in situations where the foreign person is entitled to claim relief under a treaty that conforms to the U.S. Model Treaty. Thus, all five earnings stripping strategies may spring back to life for an inbound multinational enterprise, but *only if* U.S. tax treaty relief is available.

The tables have been completely turned, and an unbalanced situation exists at this juncture. The student should feel somewhat uneasy about this current state of affairs and upon further reflection would expect further developments in the law. One possible course of correction would be that the U.S. Model Treaty would walk back its concessionary rates for fixed and determinable income earned among related parties, but that has not been the chosen course. Instead, two lines of attack have been mounted to address this unevenness. First, a significant effort has been exerted to restrict *inappropriate* treaty shopping, which is the next topic to be addressed in this chapter. However, where treaty relief is not denied but the resulting inbound base erosion inappropriately and excessively reduces the U.S. tax base, further backstop regimes have been enacted to circumscribe those treaty-based related party earnings stripping and base erosion strategies. That topic is addressed further in chapter 8. The reason both of these efforts have been needed follows from the U.S. Model Treaty, and this sets the stage for the treaty shopping discussion that follows later in this chapter and the need for additional inbound base erosion backstop regimes that is taken up in the next chapter.

10. Non-Discrimination Clause

Article 24 provides that a national of a treaty state shall not be subjected to taxation or any requirement connected therewith that is more burdensome than the taxation and connected requirements to which nationals of that other contracting state may be subjected. In addition, the taxation of a permanent establishment of an enterprise of a contracting state shall not be less favorably levied than with respect to enterprises of that other contracting state carrying on the same activities. The United States' view is that inbound base erosion protections, like those set forth in chapter 8, do not violate this non-discrimination clause. As discussed in chapter 8, the United States requires a foreign person to timely file a tax return in order to claim deductions,[86] and this requirement has been held to restrict the scope of Article 7's allowance of properly attributable business deductions.[87] In addition, the Tax Court has held that this precondition of filing a return is a prerequisite to claiming deductions that applies solely to foreign persons is not discriminatory within the meaning of this treaty provision.[88]

The requirement to allow a treaty-based resident to have the opportunity to rely on either the more favorable provisions of either the tax treaty or of domestic law requires a consistent application. In Rev. Rul. 84–17,[89] a company had three separate activities that created, respectively, a profitable permanent establishment, a profitable U.S. trade or business, and an unprofitable U.S. trade or business. The first activity created a permanent establishment on a stand-alone basis and was profitable. The second activity did not rise to the level of a permanent establishment but would have represented a U.S. trade or business and was profitable. Like the second activity, the third activity did not rise to the level of a permanent establishment but would have represented a U.S. trade or business, but it generated a loss. The ruling concluded that the company could either elect to apply the treaty provisions as to all three activities or elect to apply domestic law as to all three, but importantly the taxpayer could not pick and choose.[90]

11. Savings Clause

Because treaty benefits are generally couched in terms of residence, residence in one of the treaty countries is often a necessary condition to obtain them. It is rarely a sufficient condition, however. Many countries, and among them the United States, do not surrender in their treaties any of their taxing power over their own citizens and residents.

---

86 § 871(d); § 882(d).

87 Swallows Holding Ltd. v. Commissioner, 515 F.3d 162 (3rd Cir. 2008).

88 Adams Challenge (U.K.) Ltd. v. Commissioner, 156 T.C. No. 2 (2021).

89 1984–1 Cum. Bull. 308.

90 Taxpayer had no decision to make on the first activity, as it was taxable regardless of the relevant treaty versus domestic law standard. But, left to its own devices, the taxpayer would have preferred to claim treaty relief to avoid taxation on the profitable second activity that did not rise to the level of a permanent establishment but to not claim treaty relief for the third activity so that the trade or business loss arising as part of that activity would be deductible. The revenue ruling excludes this cherry-picking approach.

Income tax treaties almost invariably contain a provision—widely known as a "saving clause"—reserving to each of the treaty countries the right to tax its own residents and citizens as though the treaty did not exist. By such a provision, each treaty country "saves" its taxing power over its own constituents. In the 2016 U.S. Model Treaty the savings clause is conspicuously inserted near the beginning, in Article 1(4): "Notwithstanding any provision of the Convention . . . a Contracting State may tax its residents (as determined under Article 4 (Residence)) and its citizens." The 2016 U.S. Model Treaty then further provides in Article 1(4) that this savings clause also extends to "a former citizen or former long-term resident of a Contracting State may be taxed in accordance with the laws of that Contracting State." In other treaties, especially older ones, the saving clause is sometimes buried deep in the text, often in provisions that seem purely administrative.[91] In the income tax treaty with Austria, for example, the saving clause is in Article XV(1). In the treaty with Belgium, the saving clause is in Article 23(1), which is (inaccurately) captioned "Relief from Double Taxation." So, when giving an opinion on a treaty, always read more than the few lines in question.

The holding of *Filler v. Commissioner*, 74 T.C. 406 (1980) illustrates this rule. In *Filler*, a U.S. citizen resided in France and may well be a French resident. Even so, he still could not assert treaty benefits against the United States. In that particular case, the taxpayer had wanted to avail himself of the dependent services provision of the treaty to avoid U.S. taxation, but the taxpayer was unable to do so because the savings clause retained jurisdiction in the United States to tax its citizens irrespective of the treaty provisions. As a result, the U.S. citizen in *Filler* was subject to U.S. taxation on all worldwide income, including the U.S. source income, regardless of whether or not French taxation also applied to him as a French resident.

Saving clauses are rarely absolute. Some allowances are made by countries under treaties even to their own citizens and residents. Article 1(5) of the 2016 U.S. Model Treaty, for example, removes a number of provisions from the reach of the saving clause. Social security benefits are taxable only by the country paying them and child support payments are not taxable at all under the treaty, even if paid to a resident or citizen of the United States. And various treaty benefits are preserved for pensioners, students, exchange scholars,

---

[91] I must admit to having concluded once, as a beginning lawyer, that a U.S. citizen residing and working in a foreign country was not subject to U.S. taxation on his salary because of an apparently unequivocal provision in the relevant treaty exempting the salaries of "residents" of each country from taxation in the other. Of course I had missed the saving clause (which was included under a rather misleading heading).

teachers, trainees, government officers, and diplomats, regardless of residence. U.S. citizens and lawful permanent residents, however, cannot claim the latter benefits from the United States. In other treaties of the United States, the foreign tax credit is extended, for the benefit of U.S. persons, thus providing clarity as to whether a tax regime is an income tax regime in the U.S. sense.[92]

F. Treaty Shopping and the U.S. Treaty Based Response

The United States has largely won the battle on treaty shopping only to find that it has lost the larger war over earnings stripping through its tax treaty network. Thirty years ago this chapter would have represented a step-by-step user's guide for setting up international tax shelters based on income tax treaties. However, treaty shopping is largely no longer the path of choice, and the limitations on benefits provisions of the U.S. Model Treaty and the preceding modifications to U.S. domestic law have played a key role in addressing traditional treaty shopping strategies. Nevertheless, as the United States moved to more aggressively limit treaty shopping techniques, the reality is that its treaty partners have stepped in to provide tax haven benefits that are comparable to what tax haven locations provided in the past. Thus, earnings stripping transactions can be done from a developed nation directly, and the income shifted to that jurisdiction is afforded favorable tax treatment in the treaty jurisdiction. This is a remarkable outcome—one that the United States has only recently addressed to any extent. In response to this race to the bottom, the OECD has initiated a multi-year project to address base erosion and profit shifting (called its "BEPS" project). The OECD has issued 15 action items that it believes nations should take to address inappropriate base erosion and profit shifting. The proposals are far ranging and set forth proposals for modifying treaty provisions and domestic laws.

All of the U.S. major trading partners now have some form of territorial tax regime, and the great majority provide concessionary taxation of "headquarters income" that can and should be read as including homeless income or profits that have been stripped from another jurisdiction. As was said in chapter 1, what makes a particular environment a tax haven is not invariably a low rate of tax but relations with other tax regimes that permit the ultimate deflection of income to a low-tax environment. Thus, to a growing

---

[92] The Treasury Department asserts in its technical explanation to its model treaty that it reviews the other jurisdiction's tax regime to determine whether its tax regime is an income tax regime in the U.S. sense before agreeing to this provision. The Treasury Department's affirmative endorsement of the foreign jurisdiction's tax regime benefits the foreign treasury as well because it provides certainty to U.S. investors as to the creditability of local taxes.

extent, developed nations now represent a "friendly" jurisdiction for earning offshore profits shifted to them from other group companies. The original design was that a source country would relinquish its taxation over income in deference to the country of residence and that this merely represented a reallocation of the taxing jurisdiction between the bilateral treaty partners. However, when such reallocation results instead in a relinquishment of all taxation, this calls into question the original rationale for the source country's relinquishment of its own taxation. What was originally envisioned as a reallocation of taxation rights to avoid international double taxation instead represents a path to avoid all taxation. The original goal was to mitigate international double taxation, not to create international tax exemption.

Table #1 provides an interesting insight into this reality. All of the companies in Table #1 were incorporated in an undeniable "tax haven" jurisdiction at the beginning of 2008, but as treaty shopping restrictions grew increasingly stifling and the implementation of those strictures became more certain, the inbound tax planning into the United States that relied on treaty shopping structures was exposed to greater risk. The result was that each of the multinational enterprises redomiciled out of its tax haven jurisdiction and reincorporated into either Switzerland or Ireland to become an undeniable resident of those jurisdictions and thus eligible for U.S. tax treaty relief directly without the need to avail themselves of an intermediate treaty-based entity through which to route transactions.

Table #1: Representative List of 2008–2009 Redomiciling Transactions

Switzerland	**Ireland**
Tyco Int'l	Covidien, a Tyco spin-off
Tyco Electric, a Tyco spin-off	Ingersoll-Rand
Foster Wheeler	Cooper Industries
Transocean	Seagate Technology
Weatherford Int'l	Accenture
ACE Limited	
Noble Corporation	

In addition, since that period, companies that have migrated from the United States through a business combination have simply incorporated into a jurisdiction that would not be considered a tax haven, and Table #2 sets forth a representative list of transactions or mergers that have occurred in the post-2009 era that provide empirical evidence for this reality. Thus, it is now possible, in fact quite natural, simply to incorporate a multinational enterprise in a developed nation that has a favorable tax treaty with the United States and all the while obtain very favorable tax treatment for "headquarters" or "group company" income.

Table #2: 2009–2013 Expatriation Transactions	
ENSCO	United Kingdom
Eaton/Cooper	Ireland
Pentair/Tyco spin-off	Switzerland
Aon Corporation	United Kingdom
Jazz Pharmaceuticals/Azur Pharma	Ireland
Alkermes/Elan Corp	Ireland
Rowan Companies	United Kingdom
DutchCo, a Sara Lee spin-off	The Netherlands
Global Indemnity	Ireland
Omnicron/Publicis Groupe	Netherlands
Perrigo/Elan	Ireland
Activas/Warner Chilcott	Ireland
Applied Materials/Tokyo Electric	Netherlands

For example, Ireland and the Netherlands historically provided special tax concessions for holding companies that earn group financing income. The United Kingdom has recently adopted a "patent box" regime that provides a concessionary low tax rate for all intangible income returns, thus making it an excellent host for royalty-stripping transactions. These countries also do not provide expansive controlled foreign corporation provisions and allow for a participation exemption on foreign dividends remitted back to the international holding company. Thus, although these countries are not viewed as "tax havens" per se, the reality is that the effort to attract international headquarters of multinational enterprises has brought on a "race to the bottom" to attract these corporate centers with the consequence that meaningful residence-based taxation is not asserted. Thus, the source country's relinquishment of its own taxation over the income facilitates the creation of homeless income. Even so, it is helpful to understand the battery of measures added to the U.S. tax system that restrain or eliminate treaty shopping, as that background will lay the foundation for understanding the evolution of taxpayer planning and the development of further base protection measures that have occurred.

To that end, the following discussion sets forth the United States efforts to prevent unwanted treaty shopping by non-treaty persons that seek to avail themselves of U.S. tax treaty relief. The United States' effort to restrict treaty shopping has certainly cut off that pathway to a meaningful extent, but the reaction to such efforts is that companies that were then denied access to treaty shopping benefits simply responded by redomiciling into jurisdictions that would allow them to establish their headquarters there to become resident companies, affording them tax haven benefits for income directed there.

1. The Origins of Treaty Tax Havens

Treaty tax havens came about largely by accident. Among the elements abetting their rise were the break-up of the great colonial empires after World War II and the unquenchable thirst of the U.S. economy for foreign capital. During the 1950s, the United States entered into income tax treaties with former colonies of the United Kingdom and the Netherlands that had become separate sovereign nations. The terms of these treaties were initially the same as those of U.S. treaties with the mother countries even though the tax systems of the newly independent countries were far different. The U.S. tax treaty with the Netherlands Antilles, for example, when first adopted in 1955 was essentially the same as the existing treaty with the Netherlands. For over 30 years it was the main working part in several treaty tax shelters.

Also, part of the landscape during this period were persistent balance-of-payments deficits of the United States with the rest of the world. Beginning in the 1950s, large and increasing amounts of U.S. dollars accumulated outside the United States. Their foreign holders did not invariably return them to the U.S. banking system. Instead, vast quantities of U.S. dollars remained on deposit in foreign banks and became the wherewithal of wholly foreign financial transactions. U.S. dollars on deposit in a bank outside the United States are known as "Eurodollars."[93] The capital markets in which Eurodollar obligations and instruments arise are known as the "Eurodollar market."

---

[93] A "Eurodollar" is a dollar-denominated bank deposit anywhere in the world outside the United States. The term is somewhat misleading. In the period immediately following World War II most Eurodollars were in banking centers such as London, Geneva, and Luxembourg, hence the name "Eurodollar." In the 1970s the term "petrodollar" (reflecting its origin as payment for oil imported by the United States) was sometimes heard.

Because interest rates in the Eurodollar market were often lower than in U.S. capital markets, it became beneficial to U.S. companies to raise capital by borrowing Eurodollars. A major obstacle to such financing, initially, was the U.S. tax on U.S. source interest. Before the exemption of U.S. source "portfolio" interest from U.S. tax in 1984 (now codified in sections 871(h) and 881(c)), foreign persons were subject to 30 percent flat rate U.S. tax on U.S. source interest unless protected by a treaty in their country of residence. Also, to invoke a treaty against the U.S. Treasury might attract unwanted attention from their own national treasuries. The 30 percent flat tax thus put a serious crimp on borrowing by U.S. enterprises on the Eurodollar market (or, for that matter, from any foreign lender).[94]

2. Netherlands Antilles Finance Corporations

Sometime in the 1950s someone got the wondrous idea that the U.S. flat rate tax could be eliminated by channeling Eurodollar loans through a Netherlands Antilles corporation. The method was to use a Netherlands Antilles finance corporation as the middle party in "back-to-back" or "mirror-image" debt.

A U.S. enterprise seeking to borrow from foreign holders of dollars would first create a subsidiary corporation chartered in the Netherlands Antilles. The Antilles corporation would issue bonds, typically bearer bonds denominated in U.S. dollars, in some convenient financial center such as Luxembourg or Geneva where Eurodollars congregate. The proceeds of this first borrowing were then re-lent by the Antilles corporation to its U.S. parent (the ultimate borrower) at *nearly* identical interest rates and maturities. The obligation of the U.S. parent to the Antilles corporation in the second borrowing stood as security for the bonds issued by the Antilles corporation to the ultimate lenders. Often, the U.S. parent guaranteed the Antilles bonds as well. Coordinated borrowings channeled in this fashion through an Antilles entity are known as "back-to-back" or "mirror-image" debt. The pattern is shown schematically in the below Diagram #16, illustrating a mirror-image arrangement in which Eurodollar bonds are issued to foreign lenders, to whom interest flows from a U.S. borrower through a Netherlands Antilles finance subsidiary.

[94] Bear in mind that it was (and still is) alien to the culture of many potential foreign lenders to suffer any tax whatsoever on interest income.

Diagram #16

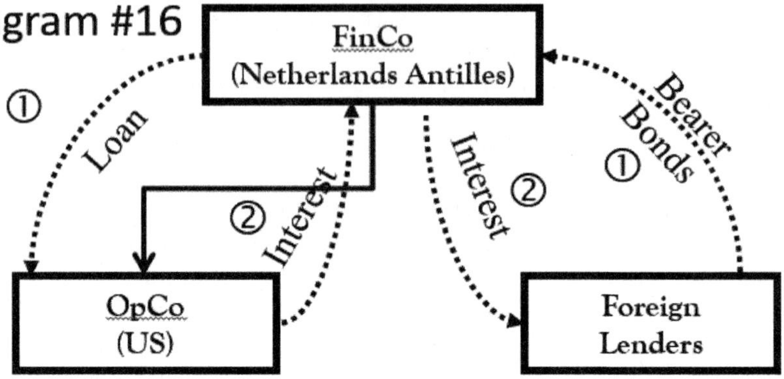

The income tax treaty between the Netherlands Antilles and the United States eliminated U.S. flat rate tax on the interest paid by the U.S. borrower to the Antilles corporation. The Netherlands Antilles, for its part, does not impose withholding tax on interest paid by Netherlands Antilles corporations to foreign persons. In this structure, therefore, no withholding tax was imposed on interest at any point in the chain.

The U.S. treaty with the Netherlands Antilles thus permitted lenders all over the world to lend to U.S. borrowers through Antilles finance companies at no U.S. tax cost. Observe that nothing much happened in the Netherlands Antilles. The only involvement of the Netherlands Antilles in this structure was the issuance of a corporate charter to the finance subsidiary. Neither the U.S. borrower nor the foreign lender has any economic or other connection to the Netherlands Antilles.[95] The parties to this financing transaction in effect appropriated the Netherlands Antilles treaty to shield interest on a loan coming into the United States from a third country which could be almost anywhere.

In light of this possibility, the Netherlands Antilles Treaty came to be known as the United States' "income tax treaty with the world," and because the borrower and lender in effect shopped around for the treaty environment that pacifies U.S. tax on interest, the underlying pattern was also known as "treaty shopping." The structure—in which a treaty-favored finance entity rests between back-to-back loans like corned beef between two slices of rye—is also called a treaty "sandwich." Treaty sandwiches—with some variations in fillings and condiments—flourished in international investing until quite recently when the U.S. Treasury began to devastate their habitat through countermeasures.

[95] The finance corporation's accounts were usually kept in a financial center bank—often Luxembourg or Geneva—which was also where the interest on the Eurodollar bonds was paid out.

3. Treaty Sandwiches

Several elements in this sandwich warrant attention. First, consider what makes a country a tax haven in a practical sense. It is not necessarily the absence of an income tax. The Netherlands Antilles was not at the time a zero tax jurisdiction. It imposed an income tax of roughly 30 percent on Antilles-based corporations. What made the Antilles a tax haven in this sandwich was the absence of any withholding tax on Antilles source interest paid to foreign persons by Netherlands Antilles corporations, coupled with the provisions of its income tax treaty with the United States. Interest received by the Antilles corporation from the U.S. borrower *was* subject to Antilles income tax, but, at the same time interest paid out by the Antilles corporation was deductible in the Netherlands Antilles. Because of the matching terms of the back-to-back loans channeled through the Antilles finance subsidiaries, interest deductions largely offset Antilles taxable income. Only the excess of interest received by an intermediate Antilles corporation over the interest it paid out—a relatively small amount—was taxed in the Netherlands Antilles.

You may wonder why the interest rates in both legs of the back-to-back loans weren't exactly the same, which would have eliminated *all* taxable income in the Netherlands Antilles. The answer lies in the need to gain the cooperation of the Netherlands Antilles government. To induce the Netherlands Antilles tax authorities to grant favorable rulings to the mirror-image loan arrangement (needed to secure deductions and forestall taxation of the full amount of interest in the Netherlands Antilles) it was necessary to build a taxable profit into the operations of the Antilles corporation by creating a spread between the interest it received and the interest it paid. Thus, if the Eurodollar bonds issued by the Antilles corporation paid interest of 10 percent, that entity's own loan to its U.S. parent might yield 10¼ percent. The resulting 1/4 percent profit would be subject to Netherlands Antilles income tax. This tax (sometimes known as the Netherlands Antilles "toll charge") was the compensation exacted by the Netherlands Antilles treasury for the beneficial use of its income tax treaty. Depending on the size of the underlying loan, the required spread ranged from 1/8 to 1 full percent. In the case of a $100,000,000 loan, for example, a 1/4 percent spread would entail an annual toll charge of roughly $75,000 (a tax of 30 percent imposed on $250,000, which is 1/4 percent of $100,000,000).

Given the palpably artificial connection of the Netherlands Antilles with the overall transaction, the parties had reason for uneasiness about the certainty of the tax benefits of a treaty sandwich. Beyond the "toll charge," no money ever went to the

Netherlands Antilles. The Antilles entity did little besides pay and receive nearly matching amounts of interest and principal. This is the type of situation in which the IRS has on occasion been successful in persuading courts to disregard an intermediate entity as a pure conduit lacking in "substance." If channeling of interest through the Netherlands Antilles were ignored, the structure would collapse into a direct loan from the United States to the holder of a Eurobond with interest subject to flat rate U.S. tax and withholding.[96]

What gave particular urgency to these concerns was the case of *Aiken Industries v. Commissioner*.[97] In *Aiken* (simplifying a bit), a Bahamas corporation ("Bahamas") owned all the shares of a U.S. corporation ("US Co.") and all the shares of an Ecuadorian corporation. Bahamas lent money to US Co. under a note ("US Co. note" depicted in ①) providing, naturally enough, for the payment of principal and interest. Less than a year later, the Ecuadorian subsidiary of Bahamas created its own wholly-owned Honduran subsidiary ("HavenCo") to which Bahamas then transferred the US Co. note in exchange (as depicted in the exchange indicated at ②) for nine demand notes, each requiring HavenCo to pay one-ninth of the principal amount owed by US Co. under the US Co. note with interest at the same rate. The course of events is illustrated in Diagram #17.

Diagram #17

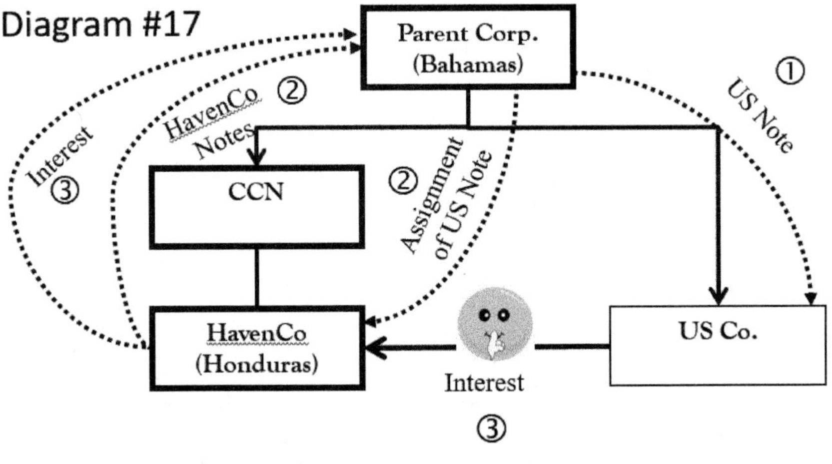

At the time HavenCo was created (but not today, so don't get any ideas), there was an income tax treaty in force between the United States and Honduras exempting interest "received" by a corporation of a treaty country from withholding tax in the country of source. The point of the exchange of notes between Bahamas and HavenCo was therefore to permit the interest paid by US Co. (as depicted in ③ in

[96] These were the days before the exemption of portfolio interest. See chapter 5.

[97] 56 T.C. 925 (1971), *acq.*, 1972–2 Cum. Bull. 1.

Diagram #17) to escape U.S. withholding tax under the treaty with Honduras. HavenCo itself would offset its interest income with interest deductions. The basic pattern is back-to-back mirror-image loans through a treaty country.

The IRS attacked HavenCo's claimed benefit under the Honduran treaty. The standard approach of the Treasury at the outset in "form and substance" cases is to yell "sham" in a crowded courtroom with the expectation (or the hope at least) that intellectual panic will ensue. *Aiken* was no exception. The first contention of the IRS in the case was that the very existence of HavenCo should be disregarded for tax purposes, with the consequence that the interest paid by US Co. would be treated as paid directly to Bahamas and subject to U.S. withholding tax. However, HavenCo was demonstrably a real Honduran corporation, and the Tax Court correctly declined to deny or ignore its existence.

Although the court acknowledged HavenCo as a real corporation, the taxpayer in *Aiken* still lost. The Tax Court concluded from the perfect identity of the terms of the notes payable *to* and *by* HavenCo that no interest was in fact "received" by HavenCo in the sense of being reduced to its dominion and control. All interest ostensibly received by HavenCo was subject to an immediate obligation to pay it out again. Nothing of value ever vested in HavenCo. The court's holding was underpinned by the "business purpose" doctrine derived from *Gregory v. Helvering*[98] to the effect that a transaction with no economic purpose other than income tax reduction may be denied its ostensible character for income tax purposes. The court inferred the absence of a business purpose from the exact symmetry of the transaction and the impossibility of a profit for HavenCo which "obtained exactly what it gave up in a dollar-for-dollar exchange [and] was committed to pay out exactly what it collected, and. . . made no profit on the acquisition of [US Co.'s] note in exchange for its own."[99] The court summed up its holding as follows:

> In effect, [HavenCo], while a valid Honduran corporation, was a collection agent with respect to the interest it received from [Bahamas]. [HavenCo] was merely a conduit for the passage of interest payments from [US Co.] to [Bahamas], and it cannot be said to have received the interest as its own. [HavenCo] had no actual beneficial interest in the interest payments it received, and in substance, [US Co.] was paying the interest to [Bahamas]

---

98 293 U.S. 465 (1935).

99 56 T.C. at 934.

> which "received" the interest within the meaning of [the treaty].[100]

There is an obvious similarity between the pattern struck down in *Aiken* and the sandwiches using Netherlands Antilles finance corporations to bring Eurodollars into U.S. capital markets. Compare the relationship of HavenCo, US Co., and Bahamas with the similar array of entities in the outline of a Eurodollar financing above. You may wonder, in this light, why the Treasury did not invoke *Aiken* in the period before 1984 (when U.S. source portfolio interest became exempt from U.S. tax for foreign persons) to attack mirror-image loans channeled through Netherlands Antilles finance corporations. There are, to be sure, differences between the latter and *Aiken*. On its facts, *Aiken* applies to interest received by a corporation that does not and cannot derive a profit from the overall transaction. The finance company in the Antilles-based financing, for its part, earned and retained a small profit by virtue of paying out interest at a lower rate than the rate of interest it received from a U.S. borrower. While this distinction proved crucial in a later case, as we shall see below, that is not why the IRS initially held back the *Aiken* card. The IRS simply didn't dare play it for fear that it would succeed.

In the 1970s and early 1980s, U.S. capital markets had become heavily dependent on hundreds of billions of dollars of foreign capital flowing into the United States through the Netherlands Antilles window. The Treasury's pursuit of tax revenue was overwhelmed in this situation by its boundless craving for foreign capital. Benign taxation of Netherlands Antilles finance companies was the avenue of foreign capital into the United States.[101] The IRS even issued favorable advance rulings in the 1970s acknowledging treaty exemption for U.S. source interest paid to Antilles-based finance intermediaries.

The volume of financings channeled through Netherlands Antilles corporations was so great in the 1960s and 1970s (reaching by some estimates a total of $500 *billion*) that the toll charges became a major underpinning of the Netherlands Antilles economy.

After the exemption from U.S. taxation of U.S. source "portfolio" interest[102] paid to foreign persons in the 1984 Act, U.S. borrowers no

---

[100] 56 T.C. at 935.

[101] Note further that *Aiken* involved a transfer between related persons of *existing* debt (subject to U.S. taxation) to a treaty-favored environment. The Treasury had no particular reason to care whether foreign investors already subject to U.S. tax had incentives to shift to a more favorable regime, but it could not risk shutting down the largest single source of *new* foreign investment in the United States.

[102] §§ 871(h), 881(c). The exemption reflects Congress's and the Treasury's acknowledgement that the United States could not afford to tax interest derived from foreigners' passive investment in U.S. capital markets.

longer needed the Netherlands Antilles window to raise capital abroad on favorable tax terms. The Treasury therefore no longer had any reason to look the other way from treaty sandwiches. Before the ink on the 1984 Act was dry, the Service, having apparently awoken to the true meaning of *Aiken*, invoked the case to deny exemption under the treaty with the Netherlands Antilles for interest paid from U.S. sources to a finance corporation chartered in the Netherlands Antilles that was itself an intermediary in a sequence of back-to-back loans.[103]

4. Active Business Sandwiches

You may wonder why the IRS (or taxpayers) cared about back-to-back debt channeled through the Netherlands Antilles after the exemption of portfolio interest. U.S. borrowers since then have been able to issue their bonds to any foreign person in the world and pay interest exempt from U.S. tax.

Obviously, the treaty window remained vital for active business operations. Not all U.S. source interest is exempt portfolio interest. In particular, interest paid to a 10-percent shareholder of a borrowing entity is not. Therefore, a foreign *equity* owner of a U.S. business cannot extract the earnings from it in the form of exempt portfolio interest simply by placing debt in its capital structure.[104] The tax exemption for interest in treaties, however, is usually broader than the exemption of portfolio interest in the Code. For this reason, treaty sandwiches remained essential in sheltering income from active business operations. Consider again Diagram #9, which for convenience is reproduced again below.

---

[103] Rev. Rul. 84–152 and 84–153, 1984–2 Cum. Bull. 381, 383. The question of the reach of the *Aiken* case surfaced in the courts at long last in Northern Indiana Public Service Co. v. Commissioner, 115 F.3d 506 (7th Cir. 1997), *affirming* 105 T.C. 341 (1995), involving a prototypical sandwich of back-to-back loans channeled through a Netherlands Antilles finance company. The IRS flung its entire arsenal at the taxpayer but lost in both the Tax Court and the court of appeals. By then, however—because recent statutory provisions had rendered back-to-back debt largely ineffective for securing treaty benefits—the outcome no longer mattered much.

[104] See chapter 5.

Diagram #9

Combined Strategy

Supply Chain Transaction, Interest Stripping Transaction, Royalty Stripping Transaction, Rental Stripping, and Service Stripping Transaction

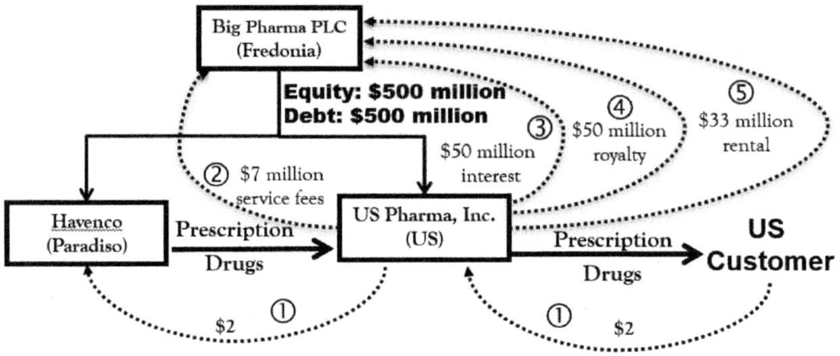

For purposes of this example, assume that Fredonia does not have an income tax treaty with the United States, so Big Pharma PLC would not be eligible for tax treaty relief on the interest paid on the interest stripping transaction depicted in ③ in the diagram. The plan of Diagram #9 by itself, however, would be of little tax benefit. Interest paid to Big Pharma PLC on the debt of a corporation beneficially owned by Big Pharma PLC is *not* exempt "portfolio interest" because portfolio interest does not include interest received by owners of substantial equity holdings in the paying corporation either directly or indirectly.[105] Therefore, if Fredonia had no income tax treaty with the United States, interest paid by the U.S. corporation to Big Pharma PLC would be subject to U.S. withholding tax of 30 percent.

Until the repeal of the U.S. treaty with the Netherlands Antilles in 1988, the solution to Big Pharma PLC's tax problem took the form of a back-to-back loan channeled through a Netherlands Antilles corporation. Big Pharma PLC could eliminate the U.S. withholding tax on the interest paid by the U.S. corporation, without exposing itself to current taxation overseas, by interposing one or more well-chosen corporations in the chain of ownership. Big Pharma PLC might, for example, borrow $500 million in Fredonia and contribute those borrowed proceeds plus $500 million of its own cash in exchange for stock of a Bermuda corporation, which would in turn contribute $500 million to the capital of a Netherlands Antilles corporation in exchange for its stock and would lend to it the balance of $500 million for a note bearing interest at, say, 11.75 percent. The Netherlands Antilles corporation would then create a U.S. corporation with the same capital structure (that is, $500,000 of stock

105 See chapter 5.

and $500 million of debt—at 12 percent—both held by the Netherlands Antilles corporation) which in turn would acquire and operate the target U.S. business. The overall pattern is in Diagram #18 which is a variation on the finance subsidiary structure that was posited in Diagram #11 discussed in chapter 5.

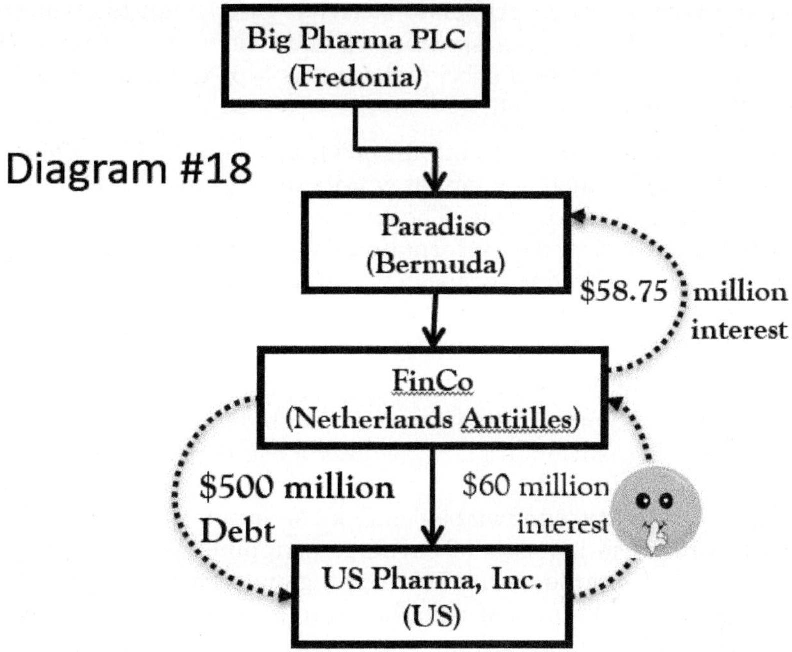

The hoped-for consequences of this structure were the following. The U.S. corporation would pay and deduct interest of $60 million to the Netherlands Antilles corporation, reducing its taxable income by $60 million and saving $12.6 million on its U.S. corporate income taxes. The $60 million of interest paid out would be free of U.S. withholding tax under the treaty with the Netherlands Antilles. The interest income of the Netherlands Antilles corporation would be largely offset by deductions for interest paid to the Bermuda corporation of $57.5 million (which would also be free of withholding tax in the Netherlands Antilles). The relatively small spread between the interest received and the interest paid by the Netherlands Antilles corporation (1/4th percent of the $500 million principal, or $1.25 million) would be the only income subject to tax there.[106] Finally, the interest income received by the Bermuda corporation would accumulate there free of income tax.

---

[106] The annual tax cost at the Netherlands Antilles rate of 30 percent on $1.25 million would be $375,000.

The upshot of the structure is that a portion of the income derived from a business in the United States is removed from the reach of the U.S. taxing power and comes to rest offshore beyond the taxing power of any country. If Fredonia is itself a high-tax jurisdiction, interest paid by Big Pharma PLC on its borrowings there might also offset Fredonia taxes. The result is a tax-free income stream (derived from economic activity in a high-tax country) sandwiched between two streams of deductions offsetting highly taxed income. A common sobriquet for this type of structure was in fact a "Bermuda Sandwich."[107]

The Bermuda entity is often known as a foreign (or "offshore") "base company" which accumulates untaxed income carved out of a stream of high-taxed income. The earnings of the base company can be used to start other international ventures (including more sandwiches). If Fredonia doesn't tax the earnings of offshore corporations until they are repatriated, taxation of the base company's income may be deferred indefinitely.[108]

This type of structure is also described as "earnings stripping" or "interest stripping." Business profits that would otherwise be subject to U.S. taxation are stripped out of the U.S. tax environment by interest deductions and come to rest in a low-tax environment instead. All treaty sandwiches and most other international tax shelters are variant forms of earnings stripping. We have already encountered a simple earnings-stripping pattern in chapter 3, in connection with the source rule for interest paid by an individual. There, Marcel deducted from U.S. business profits a stream of interest payments made to his own foreign finance company that suffered no U.S. tax on the interest because under the source rules the interest paid by Marcel has *foreign* source.

Several elements of the sandwich structure warrant further attention. First, don't try this at home. A *U.S.* shareholder cannot use a structure of this type to strip business profits earnings away from U.S. taxation. If Big Pharma PLC were a U.S. person there would be no U.S. tax benefit whatsoever. Reflect on Subpart F and

---

107 There were further elaborations of sandwich structures depending on the specific tax, financial, and currency rules in the country of the ultimate investor (here Fredonia). Another part of the filling (between Bermuda and Big Pharma PLC) might be, for example, a Swiss bank trust account or a Liechtenstein Anstalt or Stiftung. You may not know what these are (and that reflects well on you), but anyone likely to use them in a sandwich probably did.

108 Of course, Big Pharma PLC may have to put off spending those earnings as well. But if consumer interest is tax deductible in Fredonia, Big Pharma PLC can gain further tax advantage by borrowing to consume immediately and repaying the debt with delayed repatriation of earnings, having enjoyed the benefit of the interest deductions in the interim.

the PFIC rules.[109] If Big Pharma PLC were a U.S. person, the Bermuda corporation would be a controlled foreign corporation (and probably a PFIC too). As a U.S. person, Big Pharma PLC would be subject to immediate U.S. taxation on the earnings of the Bermuda corporation as though he had received them directly. Therefore, *only* a foreign person can use a treaty sandwich to shelter the earnings of a U.S. business. This limitation has not escaped the attention of U.S.-based multinational enterprises that covet the earnings stripping flexibility that can exist for a foreign-based multinational enterprise.

Second, if Fredonia is a high-tax country, Big Pharma PLC has the further problem of dealing with Fredonian taxes. Whether it can do so depends on how aggressively Fredonia taxes controlled foreign corporations and other "offshore" operations of Fredonian persons. It depends, in other words, on the extent of possible "deferral" of *Fredonian* tax on foreign income. If Fredonia has rules similar to the United States, such as Subpart F and the PFIC rules, Big Pharma PLC cannot succeed. The interest income of the Bermuda corporation (being passive investment income) would be subject to full current taxation in the hands of its controlling shareholder. If, on the other hand, Fredonia does not look through the controlled foreign corporations of its own citizens and residents, then the sandwich works for Big Pharma PLC in Fredonia.

Until about 40 years ago, the United States was the only country that systematically imposed current taxation on controlled foreign corporations owned by its citizens and residents. It has since moved in somewhat the opposite direction, while many other high-tax countries have sharply curtailed the possibility of deferral of taxation through controlled foreign corporations. France and Germany, for example, have provisions similar to Subpart F capturing the passive income of controlled foreign corporations. Other high-tax countries, such as the Netherlands and Switzerland, still allow extensive deferral.

In sum, if Big Pharma PLC is from a high-tax environment, a treaty sandwich will not avail it unless the multinational enterprise can pacify both U.S. taxes and its own national taxes.

This is the point in the story to introduce some of the countermeasures mobilized by the U.S. Treasury against treaty sandwiches and other international tax shelters. After a slow start in the 1980s, the Treasury's arsenal now has an impressive array of countermeasures.

---

[109] See chapters 11 and 12 to refresh your memory.

5. The End of the Antilles Treaty

The following bears repeating: the U.S. Model Treaty is exactly that—a model treaty. As of now, no U.S. tax treaty has the provisions in place that apply to a special tax regime. Thus, one is left with an interesting juxtaposition. The United States now has a mechanism to address the creation of low-tax or homeless income by use of its treaties either by an entity that earns that income in the other jurisdiction but will not be taxed on that income, but again those provisions in practice are not universally contained in the United States treaties currently in force. Thus, remedies outside of the U.S. income tax treaty have been implemented in the interim as a parallel effort. In the discussion that follows, we will explore the interim state that exists in the U.S. tax treaty network, and all of this lays the foundation for understanding why Congress was moved to enact further backstop regimes that will be discussed in detail in chapter 8 to address the creation of homeless income and inappropriate base erosion and profit shifting.

The treaty with the Netherlands Antilles, of course, contained no limitation on benefits. When the U.S. Treasury asked the Netherlands Antilles to renegotiate its income tax treaty to include a limitation on benefits, the Netherlands Antilles naturally refused. The Treasury countered in mid-1987 simply by terminating the treaty, effective January 1, 1988.[110]

The demise of the treaty with the Netherlands Antilles brought one of the classic tax-haven possibilities to an end. The spread of anti-treaty-shopping clauses in the treaty network of the United States also narrowed the range of alternatives, but limitations on benefits in treaties are of little effect unless they are universal. It hardly mattered how many treaties had restraints on treaty shopping as long as there was at least *one* treaty with a potential tax haven country that did not. Even as the environment for treaty shopping grew less hospitable in the late 1980s, treaty tax havens hung on in an effort to serve as a safe respite for those who combed through the U.S. treaty network with the goal of finding one.

6. The Dutch Sandwich

It remained possible until 1994 to use the treaty between the United States and the Netherlands, which offered its guests surprisingly broad protections. What made the Netherlands a tax haven was (surprise!) its own income tax treaty with its former colony, the Netherlands Antilles. A combination of entities organized in the Netherlands and the Netherlands Antilles was for a time the

---

[110] The treaty exemption for interest on *existing* debt was preserved, however, by separate tax legislation.

most promising structure for treaty-favored investment in the United States. There were several variations. A simpler ownership structure involved a U.S. business corporation owned by a Netherlands corporation, itself owned by a Netherlands Antilles corporation, and itself then in turn owned by the ultimate investor (in our case, Big Pharma PLC). As in the sandwich described above, the capital structure of the Netherlands corporation would mirror that of the U.S. corporation with back-to-back debt so that U.S. source interest flowing to the Netherlands corporation would be exempt under the U.S.-Netherlands treaty while interest paid out by the Netherlands corporation would be deductible from taxable income in the Netherlands and exempt from Dutch withholding tax under the Netherlands' own treaty with the Netherlands Antilles. The pattern can be seen in Diagram #19.

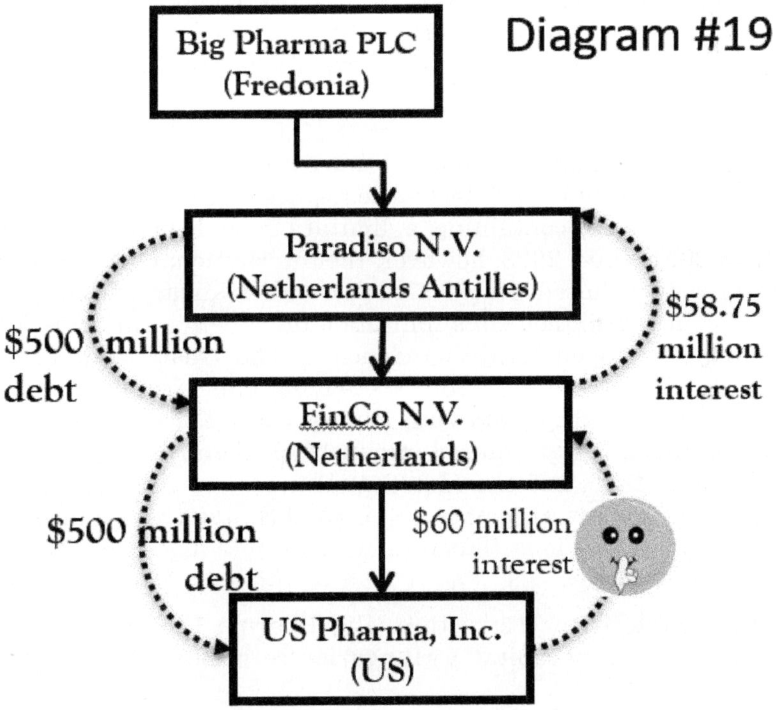

This type of structure was called a "Dutch sandwich" because it cradled a Dutch entity between two others.[111] Between the mid-1980s and 1994, the Dutch sandwich was the top treaty tax haven. Then in

[111] There was no need for a tax haven entity (Bermuda or Cayman Islands) above the Netherlands Antilles corporation in a Dutch sandwich. After the repeal of the Netherlands Antilles' treaty with the United States, the Netherlands Antilles dispensed with its own income tax, which it had previously maintained solely to avoid the appearance of being a pure tax haven.

1992, after more than 10 years of negotiations, the United States and the Netherlands agreed on a new income tax treaty, containing a limitation on benefits provision aimed at treaty shopping, which became effective in 1994.[112] This did not spell the end of treaty sandwiches, though, because the U.S. treaty with Luxembourg (which also had a treaty with the Netherlands Antilles) still had no limitation on benefits. The Dutch sandwich for a time became the Luxembourg sandwich.[113]

The U.S. Treasury set out to renegotiate the treaty with Luxembourg. A new Luxembourg treaty (with limitation on benefits, naturally) was signed in 1997 but did not go into effect until 2001. The Luxembourg sandwich therefore enjoyed a significant career. The composition of the sandwich required considerable modification at various points, however, because of several additional statutory countermeasures against international tax shelters added to the Treasury's arsenal in the 1990s. The next step in this historical traversal of treaty sandwiches is an excursion into these measures

7. The Last Few Crumbs

The treaty shopping venues at this point have been closed down. A Luxembourg topping has lost its zest since a new income tax treaty with Luxembourg, containing a limitation on benefits, went into effect in 2001. Until 2008, however, the international tax-averse had in reserve the United States' treaties with Hungary, Iceland, and Poland which remained *sans* limitation on benefits. All three found their way into open treaty sandwiches. The treaty with Iceland, however, fell in December 2008,[114] leaving only two: Hungary and Poland. Of these, the treaty with Hungary was the most interesting to tax planners. It was entered into in 1979 when Hungary was part of the Soviet Bloc, and the idea that Hungary might become a tax haven venue for investment in the United States was as far beyond imagination as the idea that billions of people might one day own computers.

In a 21st century structure, Big Pharma PLC would create, entirely with equity capital, a Hungarian corporation with a branch

---

[112] The United States could not simply terminate the treaty with the Netherlands unilaterally, as it had done with the Netherlands Antilles. Given the large trade between the Netherlands and the United States and the high level of Dutch investment in the United States (the highest of any country, per capita), the United States *must* have a tax treaty in effect with the Netherlands.

[113] To picture a Luxembourg sandwich, just substitute a Luxembourg corporation for the Dutch corporation in Diagram #19.

[114] See Tax Notes Today, December 16, 2008 (revised treaty with Iceland, with strong limitation on benefits, enters into force).

in Switzerland[115] engaged in financial operations, such as lending money. The Hungarian entity would lend through its Swiss branch to another entity, also beneficially owned by Big Pharma, that is engaged in a U.S. business (US Pharma, Inc.) as depicted in Diagram #20. Under the treaty between the United States and Hungary, the interest paid to the Hungarian corporation would be free of U.S. tax, within the constraints of section 163(j). Meanwhile, neither Hungary nor Switzerland would impose significant tax on the interest income. If the Hungarian corporation allowed its interest income to accumulate, it would be beyond the reach of the conduit regulations under section 7701(*l*), even expansively construed.

Diagram #20

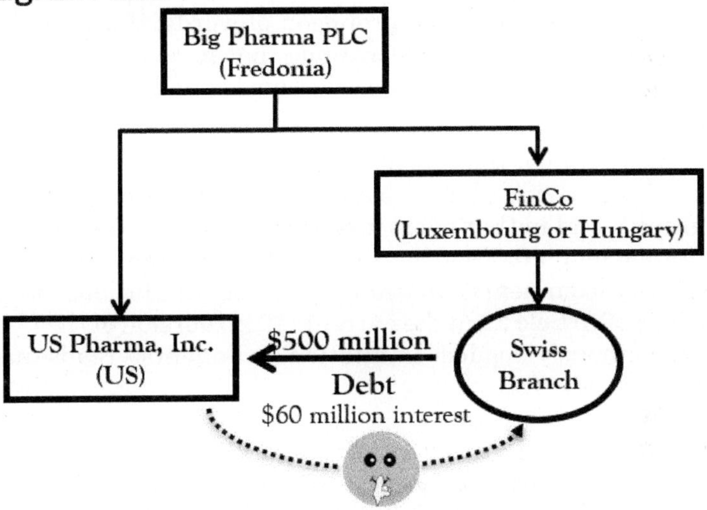

The sands of Balaton are running through the hourglass, however. In February 2010, the Treasury announced that it had concluded negotiations with Hungary over a new income tax treaty with a "comprehensive limitation on benefits."[116] In 2013, the Treasury Department announced that it had signed a new tax treaty with Poland that contains a modern "limitations on benefits" provision. However, due to the objection of one U.S. senator, both of these treaties have been stalled in their ratification process and still have not been ratified, and it is unclear when the U.S. Senate will act to ratify these treaties. However, in the interim, the United States terminated its 1979 treaty with Hungary effective January 1, 2024. Thus, the opportunity to utilize the Hungary treaty is no longer available, and the ratification of a new treaty with a limitation on

---

[115] Note that a Swiss branch appears in this example from inertia. Other countries might equally well host this branch.

[116] Tax Notes Today, June 8, 2009.

benefits provisions remains before the Senate. The ratification of these remaining two treaties may take a while longer[117] but ultimately is likely.

G. Limitations on Treaty Benefits

The Treasury's first point of attack on treaty shopping during the 1980s came in the negotiation of new treaties, but tax treaties take time to renegotiate. Therefore, as will be addressed in the next chapter, Congress and the Treasury simultaneously implemented domestic law provisions that override treaties or that would unilaterally provide an alternative response. With that said, the U.S. Model Treaty has contained a form of a limitations of benefits provision since 1977. The basic purpose of this provision remains clear even within the lavish profusion of words: it attempts to limit the benefit of a treaty to corporations that have some real economic connection with the treaty jurisdiction beyond the formality of a corporate charter.

Unfortunately, there is no easier way to unpack the limitations on benefits provision than simply to work through its relevant paragraphs, and in that effort it is best to set forth the full text of the paragraphs and, after setting them forth here, to then provide some explanatory comments. In that vein, the limitations on benefits provisions of Article 22 in the current (2016) version of the U.S. Model Treaty, ominously headed "Limitation on Benefits," reads (in part) as follows:

> 1. Except as otherwise provided in this Article and in paragraph 6 of Article 10 (Dividends), paragraph 3 of Article 11 (Interest) and paragraph 3 of Article 12 (Royalties), a resident of a Contracting State shall not be entitled to the benefits of this Convention otherwise accorded to residents of a Contracting State unless such resident is a "qualified person" as defined in paragraph 2 of this Article at the time when the benefit would be accorded
>
> 2. A resident of a Contracting State shall be a qualified person at the time when a benefit otherwise would be accorded by this Convention if, at that time and, with respect to clause (i) of subparagraph (f) of this paragraph, on at least half of the days of any twelve-month period that

[117] Hungary is said to be unenthusiastic about the new treaty. See Tax Notes Today, February 27, 2009.

includes the date when the benefit otherwise would be accorded, the resident is:

a) an individual;

. . .

c) a company, if the principal class of its shares (and any disproportionate class of shares) is regularly traded on one or more recognized stock exchanges, and either:

Public Company Rule

i) its principal class of shares is primarily traded on one or more recognized stock exchanges located in the Contracting State of which the company is a resident; or

ii) the company's primary place of management and control is in the Contracting State of which it is a resident;

d) a company, if:

Public Company Subsidiary Rule

i) at least 50 percent of the aggregate vote and value of the shares (and at least 50 percent of any disproportionate class of shares) in the company is owned directly or indirectly by five or fewer companies entitled to benefits under clause (c) of this subparagraph, provided that, in the case of indirect ownership, each intermediate owner is a resident of the Contracting State from which a benefit under this Convention is being sought or is a qualifying intermediate owner; and

ii) with respect to benefits under this Convention other than under Article 10 (Dividends), less than 50 percent of the company's gross income, and less than 50 percent of the tested group's gross income, is paid or accrued, directly or indirectly, in the form of payments that are deductible for purposes of the taxes covered by this Convention in the company's Contracting State of residence (but not including arm's length payments in the ordinary course of business for services or tangible property, and in the case of a tested group, not including intra-group transactions): (A) to persons that are not residents of either Contracting State entitled to the benefits of this Convention under subparagraph (a), (b), (c) or (e) of this paragraph; (B) to persons that are connected persons with respect to the company described in this subparagraph and that benefit from a special tax regime with respect to the deductible payment; or (C) with respect to a payment of interest, to persons that are connected persons with respect to the company described in this subparagraph and that benefit from notional deductions described in subparagraph (e) of paragraph 2 of Article 11 (Interest);

. . .

Ownership and Base Erosion Test

f) a person other than an individual, if:

i) persons that are residents of that Contracting State entitled to the benefits of this Convention under subparagraph (a), (b), (c) or (e) of this paragraph own, directly or indirectly, shares or other beneficial interests representing at least 50 percent of the aggregate vote and value (and at least 50 percent of the aggregate vote and value of any disproportionate class of shares) of the shares or other beneficial interests of such person, provided that, in the case of indirect ownership, each intermediate owner is a qualifying intermediate owner; and

ii) less than 50 percent of the person's gross income, and less than 50 percent of the tested group's gross income, is paid or accrued, directly or indirectly, in the form of payments that are deductible for purposes of the taxes covered by this Convention in the person's Contracting State of residence (but not including arm's length payments in the ordinary course of business for services or tangible property, and in the case of a tested group, not including intra-group transactions): (A) to persons that are not residents of either

Contracting State entitled to the benefits of this Convention under subparagraph (a), (b), (c) or (e) of this paragraph; (B) to persons that are connected persons with respect to the person described in this subparagraph and that benefit from a special tax regime with respect to the deductible payment; or (C) with respect to a payment of interest, to persons that are connected persons with respect to the person described in this subparagraph and that benefit from notional deductions described in subparagraph (e) of paragraph 2 of Article 11 (Interest).

Active Business Test

3. a) A resident of a Contracting State shall be entitled to benefits under this Convention with respect to an item of income derived from the other Contracting State, regardless of whether the resident is a qualified person, if the resident is engaged in the active conduct of a trade or business in the first-mentioned Contracting State, and the income derived from the other Contracting State emanates from, or is incidental to, that trade or business. For purposes of this Article, the term "active conduct of a trade or business" shall not include the following activities or any combination thereof:

i) operating as a holding company;

ii) providing overall supervision or administration of a group of companies;

iii) providing group financing (including cash pooling); or

iv) making or managing investments, unless these activities are carried on by a bank, insurance company or registered securities dealer in the ordinary course of its business as such.

b) If a resident of a Contracting State derives an item of income from a trade or business activity conducted by that resident in the other Contracting State, or derives an item of income arising in the other Contracting State from a connected person, the conditions described in subparagraph (a) of this paragraph shall be considered to be satisfied with respect to such item only if the trade or business activity conducted by the resident in the first-mentioned Contracting State to which the item is related is substantial in relation to the same or complementary trade or business activity carried on by the resident or such connected person in the other Contracting State. Whether a trade or business activity is substantial for the purposes of this paragraph shall be determined based on all the facts and circumstances.

c) For purposes of applying this paragraph, activities conducted by persons connected to a resident of a Contracting State shall be deemed to be conducted by such resident.

Derivative Benefit Test

4. A company that is a resident of a Contracting State shall be entitled to a benefit under this Convention, regardless of whether the resident is a qualified person if, at the time when the benefit would be accorded, and on at least half of the days of a twelve-month period commencing or ending on the date when the benefit otherwise would be accorded:

a) at least 95 percent of the aggregate vote and value of its shares (and at least 50 percent of any disproportionate class of shares) is owned, directly or indirectly, by seven or fewer persons that are equivalent beneficiaries, provided that, in the case of indirect ownership, each intermediate owner is a qualifying intermediate owner; and

b) less than 50 percent of the company's gross income, and less than 50 percent of the tested group's gross income, is paid or accrued, directly or indirectly, in the form of payments that are deductible for purposes of the taxes covered by this Convention in the company's Contracting State of residence (but not including arm's length payments in the ordinary course of business for services or tangible property, and in the case of a tested group, not including intra-group transactions): (i) to persons that are not equivalent beneficiaries; (ii) to persons that are equivalent beneficiaries only by reason of paragraph 5 of this Article or of a substantially similar provision in the relevant comprehensive convention for the avoidance of double taxation; (iii) to persons that are equivalent beneficiaries that are connected persons with respect to the company described in this paragraph and that benefit from a special tax regime with respect to the deductible payment, provided that if the relevant comprehensive convention for the avoidance of double taxation does not contain a definition of a special tax regime analogous to the definition in subparagraph (*l*) of paragraph 1 of Article 3 (General Definitions), the principles of the definition provided in this Convention shall apply, but without regard to the requirement in clause (v) of that definition; or (iv) with respect to a payment of interest, to persons that are equivalent beneficiaries that are connected persons with respect to the company described in this paragraph and that benefit from notional deductions of the type described in subparagraph (e) of paragraph 2 of Article 11 (Interest).

Headquarter Company Test

5. A company that is a resident of a Contracting State that functions as a headquarters company for a multinational corporate group consisting of such company and its direct and indirect subsidiaries shall be entitled to benefits under this Convention with respect to dividends and interest paid by members of its multinational corporate group. A company shall be considered a headquarters company for this purpose only if:

a) such company's primary place of management and control is in the Contracting State of which it is a resident;

b) the multinational corporate group consists of companies resident in, and engaged in the active conduct of a trade or business in, at least four countries, and the trades or businesses carried on in each of the four countries (or four groupings of countries) generate at least 10 percent of the gross income of the group;

c) the trades or businesses of the multinational corporate group that are carried on in any one state other than the Contracting State of residence of such company generate less than 50 percent of the gross income of the group;

d) no more than 25 percent of such company's gross income is derived from the other Contracting State;

e) such company is subject to the same income taxation rules in its Contracting State of residence as persons described in paragraph 3 of this Article; and

f) less than 50 percent of such company's gross income, and less than 50 percent of the tested group's gross income, is paid or accrued, directly or indirectly, in the form of payments that are deductible for purposes of the taxes covered by this Convention in the company's Contracting State of residence (but not including arm's length payments in the ordinary course of business for services or tangible property or payments in respect of financial obligations to a bank that is not a connected person with respect to such company, and in the case of a tested group, not including intra-group transactions):

(i) to persons that are not residents of either Contracting State entitled to the benefits of this Convention under subparagraph (a), (b), (c) or (e) of paragraph 2 of this Article; (ii) to persons that are connected persons with respect to such company and that benefit from a special tax regime with respect to the deductible payment; or (iii) with respect to a payment of interest, to persons that are connected persons with respect to such company and that benefit from notional deductions described in subparagraph (e) of paragraph 2 of Article 11 (Interest).

If the requirements of subparagraph (b), (c) or (d) of this paragraph are not fulfilled for the relevant taxable year, they shall be deemed to be fulfilled if the required ratios are met when averaging the gross income of the preceding four taxable years.

6. If a resident of a Contracting State is neither a qualified person pursuant to the provisions of paragraph 2 of this Article, nor entitled to benefits under paragraph 3, 4 or 5 of this Article, the competent authority of the other Contracting State may, nevertheless, grant the benefits of this Convention, or benefits with respect to a specific item of income, taking into account the object and purpose of this Convention, but only if such resident demonstrates to the satisfaction of such competent authority a substantial nontax nexus to its Contracting State of residence and that neither its establishment, acquisition or maintenance, nor the conduct of its operations had as one of its principal purposes the obtaining of benefits under this Convention. The competent authority of the Contracting State to which the request has been made shall consult with the competent authority of the other Contracting State before either granting or denying a request made under this paragraph by a resident of that other Contracting State.

The above is quite an impressive provision, isn't it? Through its numerous twists and turns this provision's main goal is to limit treaty benefits to actual individual residents and the resident entities of that jurisdiction that have a substantial economic and/or beneficial ownership connection to that treaty jurisdiction. But to articulate this "substantial connection" goal, the limitations on benefits provision sets forth a series of complex paragraphs for companies. Again, the prior section's historical explanation of how treaty shopping was accomplished is helpful in explaining why this provision exists in the manner in which it exists, as the treaty shopping phenomenon was the loadstar for how the limitations on benefits provisions were envisioned. In broad terms, the limitations on benefits provisions of Article 22 seek to prevent "treaty shopping" where an investor from a third country routes investment into the United States through a company that is a resident in a treaty partner jurisdiction unless a sufficient nexus to that treaty jurisdiction exists with respect to the treaty-benefitted income. Identifying what represents a "sufficient nexus" is where the juice is and why the provision has become so complex.

In paragraph 1, the general rule is set forth that provides that residents are only entitled to benefits accorded to residents only to the extent provided in the limitations on benefits article.

Then, in ¶ 2 through ¶ 5, the contours for when a company that is incorporated in a treaty jurisdiction will be eligible for treaty benefits is unpacked as follows:

1. **Public Company Rule.** In ¶ 2(c), publicly traded companies incorporated in the other contracting state are eligible for treaty benefits if the principal class of its shares is regularly traded on one or more recognized stock exchanges and the company satisfies at least one of the following additional requirements: (i) the company's principal class of shares is primarily traded on one or more recognized stock exchanges *located in the Contracting State* of which the company is a resident or (ii) the company's primary place of management and control is *in its State of residence.* Thus, it is not enough that a company be publicly traded. It must either have its principle class of shares traded principally in the country of residency, or its place of management must be in the country of residency.

2. **Public Company Subsidiary Rule.** In ¶ 2(d), a subsidiary of a company that is owned by a company that meets the publicly traded exception set forth in subparagraph (c) is described in this paragraph. However, in the 2016 U.S. Model Treaty, ¶ 2(d) for the first time subjects the public company's subsidiary to a base erosion test, similar to the one that has long existed in ¶ 2(f), as a precondition for the subsidiary to

be eligible for treaty relief as a Public Company Subsidiary. This change was controversial. The 2016 Model Treaty also restricts the benefits of a treaty if deductible payments are made to a connected company that is subject to a "special tax regime" with respect to the receipt of that payment.[118]

3. **Ownership and Base Erosion Test.** In ¶ 2(f), a further exception was provided that is commonly referred to as the "ownership and base erosion test." This test is commonly available for companies that are neither publicly traded nor meet the Public Company Subsidiary rule. This provision thus is logically relevant for a privately held company or a company that is a subsidiary of a public company of a third country. The "ownership and base erosion test" is a two-part test, and both prongs must be satisfied for the resident to be entitled to treaty benefits under ¶ 2(f). The ownership test of clause (i) provides that a subsidiary incorporated in the treaty jurisdiction is entitled to treaty benefits if five or fewer publicly traded companies described in ¶ 2(c) are the direct or indirect owners of at least 50 percent of the aggregate vote and value of the subsidiary's shares. If the publicly traded companies are indirect owners, however, each of the intermediate companies must be a resident of one of the Contracting States. The base erosion prong of clause (ii) of ¶ 2(f) is satisfied with respect to a person if less than 50 percent of the person's gross income for the taxable year is paid in the form of a deductible payment to a nonresident person or to related person that would have the receipt of that income subject to a "special tax regime."[119]

4. **Active Business Test.** If a company were not a "qualified person" so that treaty benefits by reason of paragraph 2 are unavailable, then a resident company may still be able to claim treaty benefits if it can satisfy paragraph 3's "active business test." In this regard, subparagraph (a) sets forth the general rule that a

---

118 U.S. Model Treaty, art. 22(2)(d)(ii). This provision is similar to the one that was proposed by the OECD's Action Item #6 in its Base Erosion and Profit Reports. See OECD/G20 Base Erosion and Profit Shifting Project, *Preventing the Granting of Treaty Benefits in Inappropriate Circumstances, Action 6—2015 Final Report* (2015).

119 U.S. Model Treaty, art. 22(2)(f)(ii). This provision is similar to the one that was proposed by the OECD's Action Item #6 in its Base Erosion and Profit Reports. See OECD/G20 Base Erosion and Profit Shifting Project, *Preventing the Granting of Treaty Benefits in Inappropriate Circumstances, Action 6—2015 Final Report* (2015).

resident of a Contracting State engaged in the active conduct of a trade or business in that State may obtain the benefits of the Convention with respect to an item of income derived in the other Contracting State. The item of income, however, must be derived in connection with or incidental to that trade or business. Paragraph 3(b) sets forth a limitation on the ability of connected companies to aggregate their activities for purposes of satisfying the trade or business test and requires a factual connection between that trade or business in the residence country and the item of income for which treaty benefits are sought. This limitation prevents a holding company from relying on the activities of connected active companies in the same country to satisfy the active-trade-or-business test. The limitation in paragraph 3(b) was motivated by a concern that the existing active-trade-or-business test can, in certain circumstances, allow third-country residents to treaty shop through an entity that has an active trade or business in a treaty partner.

5. **Derivative Benefits Test.** In the 2016 U.S. Model Treaty, the United States provided for a "derivative benefits test" that in effect expands the class of owners beyond the scope in paragraph 2(f)'s "ownership and base erosion test." Much like paragraph 2(f)'s "ownership and base erosion test," paragraph 4's "derivative benefits test" utilizes a two-prong test. Under the ownership prong of the derivative benefits test, 95 percent of the tested company's shares must be owned, directly or indirectly, by seven or fewer persons that are equivalent beneficiaries. For dividends, interest, royalties, or a branch profits tax, a person will be an equivalent beneficiary only if that person is eligible for a withholding rate at least as low as the withholding rate under its own treaty with the United States as would have applied under the convention between the United States and the company claiming treaty benefits. The base erosion prong of the derivative benefits test is substantially the same as the base erosion test that exists under ¶ 2(f). Consistent with the restriction that was put in ¶ 2(f), the 2016 Model Treaty also restricts the benefits of a treaty if deductible payments are made to a connected company

that is subject to a "special tax regime" with respect to the receipt of that payment.[120]

6. **Headquarters Company Test.** The 2016 U.S. Model Treaty includes a "headquarters company test" in ¶ 5. This provision allows companies that serve as the active headquarters company of a multinational corporate group to enjoy treaty benefits if the headquarters company exercises its *primary* management and control functions (and not just supervision and administration) in its residence country with respect to itself and its geographically diverse subsidiaries, and the multinational group of companies operates active businesses in at least four countries. The headquarters company test also includes a base erosion test. Furthermore, a headquarters company is only entitled to benefits with respect to dividends and interest paid by members of its multinational corporate group. As a recurring pattern, the 2016 Model Treaty also restricts the benefits of a treaty for an entity claiming benefits under this paragraph if deductible payments are made to a connected company that is subject to a "special tax regime" with respect to the receipt of that payment.[121]

The above discussion is helpful in both understanding the strictures that have been added to the U.S. tax treaty limitations and in understanding the evolution of inbound planning, but again, the ability to achieve a low-tax result is still available for many companies.

H. Back to Basics

After reviewing the historical evolution of treaty shopping and the creation of homeless income through the tax treaty network, one has reason to be skeptical that the above provisions will be effective in preventing the creation of homeless income. Even if the above provisions achieve their intended goals, it would take years, perhaps decades, to fully implement the full scope of these provisions into all of the U.S. tax treaties that are currently in force. What is more, many countries offer concessionary regimes for headquarter income

---

120 U.S. Model Treaty, art. 22(4)(b). This provision is similar to the one that was proposed by the OECD's Action Item #6 in its Base Erosion and Profit Reports. See OECD/G20 Base Erosion and Profit Shifting Project, *Preventing the Granting of Treaty Benefits in Inappropriate Circumstances, Action 6—2015 Final Report* (2015).

121 U.S. Model Treaty, art. 22(5)(f). This provision is similar to the one that was proposed by the OECD's Action Item #6 in its Base Erosion and Profit Reports. See OECD/G20 Base Erosion and Profit Shifting Project, *Preventing the Granting of Treaty Benefits in Inappropriate Circumstances, Action 6—2015 Final Report* (2015).

and have demonstrated a willingness to modify their laws to circumvent the full brunt of efforts to restrict the creation of homeless income.

Even so, it is interesting to note that a basic, almost primitive, earnings-stripping possibility survives even after these extraordinary efforts on the part of the Treasury Department to restrict the creation of homeless income. It rests on the use by a foreign individual of the source rule for interest to strip business profits away from the U.S. tax environment, a pattern we first encountered in Diagram #3 introduced in chapter 3. None of the recent developments canvassed here, including section 163(j), the conduit regulations, and limitations on treaty benefits, lays a glove on this maneuver. Review the pattern in chapter 3. As long as the taxpayer has less than $25 million of gross receipts, section 163(j) does not come into play. There is no multi-party financing, just a single debt between two parties that cannot be recombined, and no treaty exemption or other benefit is invoked by anyone.

Diagram #3 (Variant)

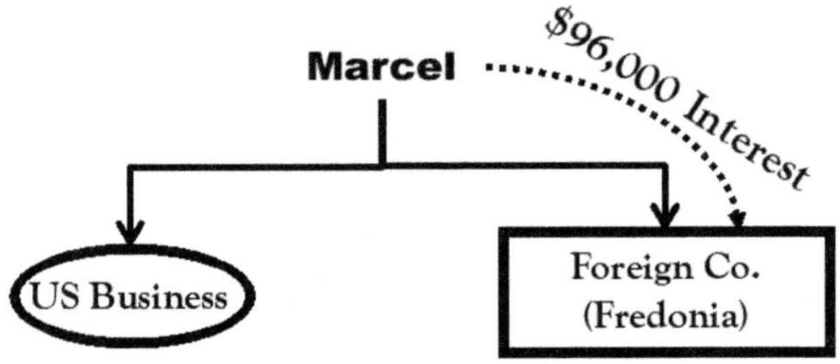

In the pattern observed in chapter 3, this maneuver suffers from constraining nontax limitations. There can be only one owner who must, from the perspective of the U.S. tax system, be a direct proprietor. Direct ownership by an individual is not a flexible form of ownership of a U.S. business. Historically, this has severely limited the type and size of businesses that could avail themselves of the tax advantage. The problems include difficulties of management and the owner's unlimited liability. It is hard to imagine an automobile assembly plant or a chain of retail stores organized as an individual's directly-owned sole proprietorship.

I. Check the Box

A development in a different area of U.S. tax law has considerably enlarged the potential range of this form of investment in U.S. business assets. The check-the-box regulations on the tax character of entities[122] allow a foreign owner of a U.S. business in Marcel's position to hold assets in a separate entity and still be taxed as an individual proprietor. Let's revisit Marcel's purchase of a U.S. business in chapter 3 in this light.

This time, instead of acquiring the U.S. business directly, Marcel forms a Limited Liability Company (LLC) to which he transfers $200,000 as equity capital. The LLC elects to be fiscally transparent under the check-the-box regulations. The LLC borrows $800,000 from a foreign corporation also owned by Marcel and purchases the U.S. business for $1 million, securing the $800,000 loan from Marcel's finance corporation with the U.S. business assets. Diagram #21 may remind you of a pattern of ownership we have already encountered in Diagram #3 in chapter 3, although in Diagram #21 it is somewhat disguised. Think back to Marcel's form of ownership of a U.S. business in chapter 3, which was coupled with a loan to Marcel from his own foreign finance corporation. When you take into account the effect of the check-the-box election, the two forms of ownership are exactly the same from the perspective of the U.S. tax system. The LLC is a single-owner entity that has checked the box (i.e., has elected to be fiscally transparent). It is therefore, for U.S. tax purposes, a form of direct ownership of assets by Marcel. The loan from the foreign finance company to the LLC is simply a loan directly to Marcel. The interest paid by the LLC has foreign source, just as though it had been paid by Marcel (which, for tax purposes, it has been).

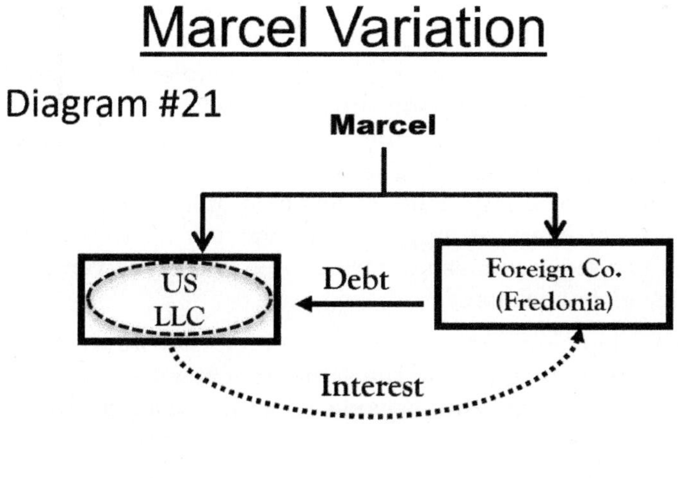

[122] See Reg. § 301.7701–2(b)(8) (setting forth foreign entities that are per se corporations for U.S. tax purposes); Reg. § 301.7701–3(a) (allowing taxpayers the ability to elect the tax classification of a foreign entity that is not a per se corporation).

If indeed we eliminate the LLC from this pattern (which is what happens in effect when Marcel checks the box of fiscal transparency), we can redraw the relations between the players and events as in Diagram #3. Look familiar? The check-the-box regulations let Marcel have his cake and eat it. Marcel can preserve the advantage of the corporate form of ownership—limited liability with more flexible capital and management structure—while retaining the earnings stripping tax advantage resulting from the source rule for interest paid by individuals. With an LLC, in fact, the range of this type of earnings stripping pattern structure is considerably extended. The electing LLC can have only one owner (or it would be a partnership for U.S. tax purposes and the interest it paid would have U.S. source). But, if the business generates in excess of $25 million in gross receipts, then section 163(j) could now restrict the benefits of this structure but would not entirely eliminate them.

Diagram #3 (Variant)

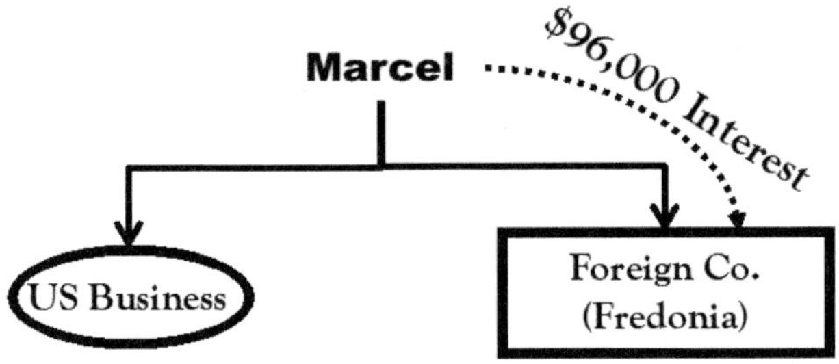

We have come full circle. The last example of an international tax shelter is the one we encountered first. It is built, somewhat prosaically, on the source rule for interest paid by individuals. Perhaps because of the very lack of moving parts—it involves no treaties or mirror-image debt—it has held up better than the others. But, the point of the example is to demonstrate that gaps in how different tax regimes mesh is foreseeable, perhaps even probable in a complex global economy.

With that said, the future career of this above variation is tenuous. This is not because the structure can easily be attacked—it is surprisingly sturdy—but because it can fall to a statutory stroke of the pen. A small change in the source rule for interest would stop it cold. Rather than spell it out, I leave to you to ponder what that might be. In a subject with so transitory a form as international taxation it is natural to end with an unanswered question.

Chapter 8

INBOUND BASE PROTECTION MEASURES THAT BACKSTOP INBOUND TAXATION

Thus far, we have worked our way through the general framework for taxing a foreign person's passive investment income in chapter 5 and for taxing a foreign person's income that is effectively connected to the conduct of a U.S. trade or business in chapter 6. These provisions, in combination with the source rules discussed in chapter 3, provide the general framework for how the U.S. tax regime applies to inbound operations. However, these inbound taxation rules, if left without further modification, provide significant inbound tax base erosion and profit shifting opportunities. In chapter 4, we saw how the arm's length standard was the first line of defense against earnings stripping transactions. Even so, significant earnings stripping opportunities remain viable within the confines of the arm's length standard. Some of the opportunities exist within exceptions to taxation of the gross amount of fixed or determinable income[1] discussed in chapter 5. However, as discussed in chapter 7, a larger and more significant source of earnings stripping opportunities arises from provisions of the U.S. Model Treaty that reduce or eliminate the imposition of U.S. taxation on potentially more important forms of related party earnings stripping that would have been subject to gross basis taxation.[2] If Congress were dissatisfied with the perceived inappropriate base erosion, one might envision that Congress would reform the deficient parts of the fixed and determinable income standard or would walk back its elimination of the 30 percent gross basis tax through treaty relief for these earnings stripping transactions. However, that has largely not been the historical response, or in any event the treaty reform efforts have been slow to come.

Instead of the above straightforward approach, Congress has chosen to pursue a parallel path of enacting backstop regimes to redress perceived excessive erosion of the U.S. tax base with the consequence that the statutory picture has been further complicated.

---

[1] For example, service stripping transactions avoid the fixed or determinable standard if the services are performed outside the United States, and supply chain transactions in which goods are sold is not fixed or determinable income.

[2] For example, interest stripping, royalty stripping, and rental stripping transactions all involve fixed and determinable income that otherwise would be subject to gross income taxation, but the U.S. Model Treaty eliminates taxation of these passive forms of income.

Each of these backstop regimes is worthy of separate study, but a common feature of all of them is that each regime represents an effort to bolster the inbound taxation regime against perceived inappropriate inbound base erosion techniques. Even so, reasonable minds can and do differ on whether these provisions effectively implement Congress's expressed policy goals and whether these base protection measures create unintended consequences beyond their core mission.

A. Gains from Sales of U.S. Real Property

Until 1980, sales by foreign persons of real property in the United States had essentially the same tax consequences as their sales of other property. If ownership of the property constituted a trade or business or if the property was used in a trade or business, gain or loss from the sale was "effectively connected." If the taxpayer had no trade or business or if the real property was not connected to one, gain or loss upon a sale entailed no tax consequences.

The interplay of these and other rules created a favorable tax regime for foreign ownership of U.S. real estate operations. A foreign person who owned and operated U.S. real estate as a trade or business could use the full range of deductions (interest, depreciation, etc.) to shelter the income from the property. The property could subsequently be sold on an installment basis with a small down payment in the year of sale. Most of the gain would ultimately be recognized in years in which the taxpayer was engaged in *no* U.S. trade or business and would therefore escape U.S. tax altogether. Even better results could flow from the ownership of U.S. real estate through a corporation. Current income from the property would be offset by deductions within the corporation, whereas the gain from appreciation in value could be derived from the sale of the stock by the shareholders, a transaction usually attracting no U.S. tax. Moreover, the non-taxation of U.S. real property gains could often be structured to avoid immediate or ultimate taxation in the foreign investor's jurisdiction. Many other countries would have expected the United States to tax income arising from real estate located within the United States, and when it did not do so an opportunity presented itself to create "homeless income" from these investments that escaped taxation in all jurisdictions. The opportunity to create "homeless income" from U.S. real property earnings was perceived as creating a competitive advantage for foreign ownership of U.S. real property. Thus, Congress believed that a further backstop regime was needed.

1. Section 897

Under section 897(a)(1), gains and losses of foreign taxpayers arising from the disposition of a "United States real property interest" are treated as "effectively connected" with a United States trade or business. Gains reached by section 897 are therefore taxed at graduated rates, as gains derived from business operations, regardless of their actual character. By virtue of being treated as effectively connected, the gains are brought essentially within the tax regime imposed on U.S. persons for gains of the same type. Section 897 makes the taxation of gains from U.S. real estate directly owned by foreign persons nearly unavoidable.[3]

"United States Real Property Interests." Numerous holdings are swept into the class of "United States real property interests," some obvious, some less so. A "United States real property interest" is defined in section 897(c)(1)(A) as

> (i) an interest in real property (including an interest in a mine, well, or other natural deposit) located in the United States or the Virgin Islands, and
>
> (ii) any interest (other than an interest solely as a creditor) in any domestic corporation unless the taxpayer establishes. . . that such corporation was at no time a United States real property holding corporation during the shorter of—
>
> > (I) the period . . . during which the taxpayer held such interest, or
> >
> > (II) the 5-year period ending on the date of the disposition of such interest.

Both direct holdings of real property located in the United States or the U.S. Virgin Islands and many types of shareholdings in domestic corporations that own U.S. real property are treated as United States real property interests within this definition. Among the numerous questions flowing from this provision are the nature of "real property" and the scope of an "interest" in real property.

Scope of "Real Property." Under section 897, as elaborated in the regulations, "real property" includes a broad range of holdings. Besides land, all mineral deposits and natural resources (including timber and agricultural crops) are treated as real property until they are actually extracted or severed from the land.[4] A royalty interest in minerals, for example, is an interest in real property. All

---

[3] Tax can, however, be deferred for a time by using a foreign corporation to hold U.S. real property, as discussed further at the end of this chapter.

[4] Reg. § 1.897–1(b)(2).

"improvements," including buildings and other inherently permanent structures, are interests in real property.[5] Virtually any structure with walls constitutes a "building." "Inherently permanent structures" include parking lots, swimming pools, paved areas, wharves, docks, fences, billboards, outdoor lighting, oil rigs, silos, and much, much more.[6] Structural components (plumbing, heating, elevators, etc.) are also real property.[7]

"Real property" also includes "furnishings" and other "personal property associated with the use of the real property."[8] This category encompasses pipelines, railroad tracks, and other traditional fixtures, as well as power lines and transmission units. The regulations extend the range of "associated" property to mining equipment, farm machinery, and even draft animals.[9] Construction equipment is also "associated" property if it is used by the landowner. All furniture and equipment used in lodgings held for rental (both permanent housing and hotels) and offices is included.

"Interests" in Real Property. The range of "interests" in real property reached by section 897 is as broad as the types of property. Fee ownership, co-ownerships, leaseholds, options, and all other possessory or beneficial interests in property are "interests" under section 897.[10]

Also included among U.S. real property interests—and this is a critical element—is an interest in any *domestic* corporation that qualified as a "United States real property holding corporation" (hereafter "U.S. RPHC") at *any* time during the previous five years while owned by a foreign person.[11] A U.S. RPHC, in overview, is a corporation (domestic *or* foreign) the principal assets of which include United States real estate.

The terminology of section 897 is a little tricky and requires close attention. Only an interest in a *domestic* corporation can be a "U.S. real property interest," but *any* corporation holding U.S. real property can be a U.S. RPHC. In other words, a U.S. RPHC that is also a domestic corporation may be a United States real property interest.

The status of U.S. RPHC is defined by the degree of concentration of the entity's holdings of U.S. real property. More specifically, a U.S. RPHC is any corporation holding U.S. real

---

5 Reg. § 1.897–1(b)(3).

6 Reg. § 1.897–1(b)(3)(iii).

7 Reg. § 1.897–1(b)(3)(ii).

8 § 897(c)(6)(B).

9 Reg. § 1.897–1(b)(4)(i)(A).

10 § 897(c)(6)(A).

11 § 897(c)(1)(A)(ii).

property with a fair market value equal to 50 percent or more of the fair market value of its combined holdings of real property worldwide and assets used in the conduct of a trade or business.[12] In applying this 50 percent test, only real property (both U.S. and foreign) and active business assets are taken into account. Otherwise, portfolio holdings, passive investments, or interests in subsidiary corporations could routinely be used to dilute real property holdings and avoid section 897 altogether. Because of the five-year period established in section 897(c)(1)(A)(ii)(II), a domestic corporation that was once a U.S. RPHC may be treated as a U.S. real property interest for five years thereafter.

The test period for the status of U.S. real property interest is the shorter of five years or the taxpayer's holding period. Thus, while a U.S. real property interest lasts five years after the dreaded RPHC ratios are established, the taint is removed by an ownership change and does not carry over to a purchaser (i.e., acquirer). An *acquired* interest is not a U.S. real property interest unless the status of U.S. RPHC exists at the time of acquisition or thereafter.

Effects of Valuation. To the end of identifying gain attributable to the ownership of U.S. real estate, the definition of a U.S. RPHC is in fairly obvious ways both overinclusive and underinclusive. Being predicated entirely on values, the definition of a U.S. RPHC identifies *gains* attributable to U.S. real estate only accidentally, if at all. Suppose that more than half the assets of an entity consist of U.S. real estate that has declined in value and remaining personal property whose value has gone up sharply. A foreign person's gain upon the sale of shares of the entity may be swept within section 897 even though 1) the gain is not attributable to U.S. real estate and 2) gain from the sale of the same properties owned directly would escape U.S. tax altogether. For example, the sale of shares of a U.S. corporation holding land that has declined in value along with a portfolio of stocks that have increased enormously could attract the tax of section 897(a) even though the entire gain was attributable to the investment securities. If the investment portfolio does not constitute a trade or business, section 897 would apply even if the investments were worth considerably more than the land because assets not used in a trade or business are not counted as part of the non-real-estate assets of a corporation in testing its status as a U.S. RPHC. Section 897 can thus make the ownership of certain U.S. corporate shares a veritable minefield for foreign persons.

As a result of changing valuations, a corporation could quite easily fall into the class of U.S. RPHCs without having been created for (or even having significantly engaged in) U.S. real estate

---

[12] § 897(c)(2).

operations. A business that owned its own land and buildings and was going through a period of poor profits and liquidity might readily become a U.S. RPHC. For example, Chrysler Corporation (now part of Fiat Chrysler), though not widely perceived as a real estate investment company, might well have been a U.S. RPHC during the recession of 1981–83 when the value of its operating assets fell perilously close to zero and its real estate probably represented nearly the entire equity in the company. More obviously, virtually any oil company would be a U.S. RPHC given the inclusion of natural resource holdings within the class of real property. This could have potentially surprising consequences to foreign portfolio investors on U.S. stock exchanges.

Publicly Traded Stock. To soften such untoward effects, and more generally to preserve the appeal of U.S. portfolio holdings for foreign investors, section 897(c)(3) provides an exception from the category of U.S. real property interest for holdings of stock regularly traded on an established securities exchange if the holding constitutes less than *five* percent of its own class of stock. This exception largely removes concerns foreign investors might otherwise have over holdings of publicly traded U.S. equities.[13]

Real Estate Investment Entities. The stock of a real estate investment trust held by a qualified shareholder also is not treated as an investment in U.S. real property. Thus, any gain on the sale of a real property interest owned by the real estate investment trust is not treated as a disposition of a real property interest by a qualified shareholder.[14] A qualified shareholder generally includes a foreign person who is eligible for treaty benefits or is a publicly traded foreign partnership or publicly traded collective investment vehicle. This very favorable exception to the U.S. real property interest designation does not apply if the qualified shareholder has an applicable investor (a foreign person) that owns more than 10 percent of the qualified shareholder.

2. Foreign Corporations

A foreign corporation, even if loaded with U.S. real property (and hence a U.S. RPHC), is not a U.S. real property interest. This may

---

[13] It does not take care of all the problems, however. Renault S.A. (a French corporation) bought a large block (well over 5 percent) of American Motors stock in the 1980s, at a time when American Motors was quite possibly a U.S. RPHC by virtue of the depressed value of its operating assets. When Renault later sold its American Motors stock (to Chrysler), I am not sure anyone gave much thought to section 897, which may well have applied. Of course, if Renault sold its American Motors stock at a *loss* (eminently possible), the effect of § 897 was salutary: the resulting effectively connected *loss* could have offset other U.S. business profits. (But did Renault have any?)

[14] § 897(k)(2).

seem to offer an easy escape to foreign persons from the tax of section 897. They need only hold U.S. real property through foreign corporations. Sales of the shares are not subject to U.S. tax. There is less here than meets the eye, however. The U.S. real estate remains a U.S. real property interest in the hands of the foreign corporation. If it has increased in value, it can't be sold (or otherwise disposed of) without triggering the tax of section 897 on the *corporation*. What guarantees this result is section 897(d), by which *any* disposition of U.S. real property by a foreign corporation is subject to tax. The use of a foreign corporation to hold U.S. real estate therefore offers at most deferral of U.S. taxation on appreciation in the property. While that may sometimes be worthwhile, the tax benefit may also be limited because the real estate cannot regain a fair market value basis for depreciation without suffering the tax. Furthermore, if the property is a principal residence, the $250,000 exclusion of gain from income upon sale (granted by section 121) is available only if the property is owned directly by a foreign individual.

3. Closing Note on Section 897

An ironic sidelight on section 897 is that, initially, the Treasury did not want it. When it was adopted in late 1980, at the tail end of a period of oil crisis and inflation, foreign money was flowing into U.S. real estate at unprecedented levels. Section 897 was—and this is unusual for a tax measure—a grassroots provision from Congress reflecting concern that America's best assets were being sold to tax-beating "foreigners" who had caused the very inflation that put Heartland America beyond Americans' economic reach. From the Treasury's perspective, however, foreign investment in U.S. real estate was a way of righting the balance of payments by bringing Petrodollars back into the U.S. economy.

Only a few years later the situation had reversed. Oil price declines and recession kept foreign investors away from Heartland America in droves. Early proponents of section 897 then urged its repeal. But by then the Treasury had grown fond of it.

B. Section 163(j)

The ability of a U.S. taxpayer (or a foreign taxpayer with a U.S. trade or business) to make tax deductible interest stripping payments to an offshore affiliate enables a powerful earnings stripping technique. This reality is made even more real due to the fact that taxpayers have considerable flexibility to determine the capital structure of a wholly-owned U.S. affiliate. The intercompany payment represents no net reduction in the overall combined income of the multinational enterprise, but the U.S. tax base is eroded in the process because the interest payment represents a potential deductible payment that reduces the effectively connected income of the U.S. trade or business. When income is shifted from the United States to another jurisdiction but that other jurisdiction asserts taxing jurisdiction over the income at a rate comparable to the United States rate, then the earnings stripping transaction affects the coffers of the United States government, but it does not create an overall tax savings for the multinational enterprise. However, the multinational enterprise, with planning, is often able to redirect the earnings stripped via related party interest payments from the U.S. tax base to an affiliate that is located in a low-tax jurisdiction that will not impose a comparable rate of tax to that of United States. Thus, the ability to erode the U.S. tax base via the use of an interest stripping transaction provides the avenue to shift profits to a low-tax jurisdiction that can potentially create a significant tax advantage and competitive advantage for inbound foreign-based multinational enterprises. A U.S.-based multinational enterprise can also utilize strategies that shift profits to a low-tax jurisdiction, but the United States has outbound tax measures that apply to prevent the inbound interest stripping technique with respect to U.S. source interest payments. However, those extra-territorial backstop provisions generally do not apply to a foreign-based multinational enterprise. Thus, a further inbound base protection measure is needed in that context.

Congress responded to this interest stripping concern starting in 1989 with the enactment of section 163(j). The explanation of section 163(j) given by a congressional committee underscores the element of self-loan in the earnings stripping pattern:

> [I]t is appropriate to limit the deduction for interest that a taxable person pays or accrues to a tax-exempt entity whose economic interests coincide with those of the payor. To allow an unlimited deduction for such interest permits significant erosion of the tax base. Allowance of unlimited deductions permits an economic unit that consists of more than one legal entity to contract with itself at the expense of the government. . . [A] limitation on the ability to 'strip' earnings out of this country through interest payments in lieu of dividend distributions are appropriate. The uncertainty of present law (particularly the debt-equity distinction) may allow taxpayers to take aggressive positions that inappropriately erode the U.S. tax base.[15]

Section 163(j) does not deny treaty benefits directly. Instead, it disallows certain earnings stripping deductions for purposes of

---

[15] H. Rep. No. 247, 101st Cong., 1st Sess. 1241–1242 (1989) (1989 House Report).

computing the taxable income of the payor entity. Thus, the U.S. tax base is preserved not by taxing the foreign recipient on the income but by reducing or curtailing the benefits of the tax deduction that is afforded to the payor of the interest payments. In 2017, Congress rewrote section 163(j) to refocus the provision. Section 163(j) is a complex provision of which I shall summarize only the broad elements here. It is also a somewhat blunt, all-purpose weapon. Its effect is by no means limited to tax haven operations. It disallows excess interest deductions whether they are paid to related parties or whether interest is paid to an entirely unrelated party or even when the interest income is exposed to high foreign taxes. Section 163(j), therefore, preserves a certain amount of business profits for U.S. taxation in all events. Section 163(j) thus both constrains treaty tax havens *and* apportions the taxation of business profits between the United States and other high-tax jurisdictions with which it has income tax treaties.[16]

Under section 163(j), an interest expense deduction is disallowed with respect to "excessive" business interest expense whether or not the business interest expense is paid to a related party and whether or not it is U.S. source interest expense or not. There is no safe harbor based on a debt-to-equity ratio as existed under section 163(j) prior to 2017, but the provision is generally applicable only to taxpayers with gross receipts that exceed $25 million, and, even as to those taxpayers, "business interest" does not include interest paid by an employee, interest paid by certain electing real property businesses, interest paid by certain electing farming businesses, and interest paid by certain utility businesses (electrical, water, sewage, or gas distribution or steam distribution).

For taxable years after 2017, section 163(j) disallows an interest deduction to the extent that a taxpayer's interest expense exceeds the sum of (1) the taxpayer's business interest income, (2) 30 percent of the adjusted taxable income of the taxpayer for the taxable year, and (3) the floor plan financing interest of the taxpayer for the taxable year. Floor plan financing interest is interest on indebtedness used to finance the acquisition of motor vehicles held for sale to retail customers and secured by the inventory so acquired. Because that carve-out appears to have limited application outside the auto dealership context, it is not considered further here. Thus, the provisions that have broad applicability are the taxpayer's business interest income and the definition of "adjusted taxable income."

For this purpose, "adjusted taxable income" is defined as the taxpayer's taxable income attributable to its trade or business but

---

16 For this reason, several high-tax treaty partners of the United States have taken a jaundiced view of section 163(j).

excluding all of the following: (i) business interest income, (ii) business interest expenses, (iii) net operating loss deductions, (iv) the 20 percent qualified business income deduction under section 199A, (v) deductions for depreciation, amortization, or depletion, and the amounts included in gross income under section 951(a), section 951A, and section 78 (topics discussed in chapter 10). If the taxpayer's interest expense (whether related party or not) exceeds 30 percent of adjustable taxable income plus business interest income plus floor financing interest, then it is limited. The amount of any business interest not allowed as a deduction for any taxable year may be carried forward indefinitely.

A comparison of the outcomes under Diagram #2 and Diagram #9 is helpful for understanding the nuances of section 163(j). Therefore, let's return to the Big Pharma PLC hypothetical depicted in Diagram #2. The essential facts again were as follows. U.S. target corporation had $200 million of earnings and had $10 million of unrelated party interest expense. As part of the acquisition, Big Pharma PLC transferred $1 billion of its own stock to US Pharma, Inc. in exchange for $100 million of US Pharma, Inc. stock and $900 million of US Pharma, Inc. debt bearing a 10 percent interest rate. Finally, please assume that US Pharma, Inc. has no business interest income, no net operating loss, and is ineligible to claim any benefits under section 199A. In this scenario, apart from section 163(j), US Pharma, Inc. is posited to have had taxable income of $70 million (i.e., $200 million profits less $30 million depreciation less $10 million unrelated interest and $90 million related party interest).

Diagram #2

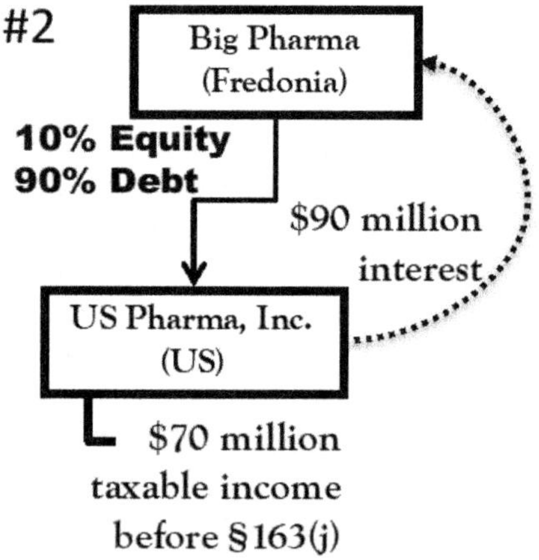

On these facts, section 163(j) starts with taxable income of $70 million and then adds back all interest expense ($100 million) and depreciation ($30 million) to arrive at adjusted taxable income of

$200 million. Section 163(j)'s 30 percent cap means that US Pharma, Inc. can only claim an interest expense deduction of up to 30 percent of its adjusted taxable income or $60 million (i.e., $200 million adjusted taxable income multiplied by 30 percent). As there was no business interest income or floor financing interest expense or net operating loss to consider, no further adjustment is needed; the section 163(j) limit is simply $60 million. Thus, US Pharma Inc. is entitled to only claim a deduction for $60 million of its total $100 million of interest expense payments. The deduction related to the excess $40 million is disallowed in this example. The disallowed interest expense can be carried forward to a year where interest expense is less than the section 163(j) limit in the carryforward year. Consequently, in the above example, US Pharma, Inc. would have $110 million of taxable income after application of section 163(j)'s limitation (i.e., $70 of taxable income before considering section 163(j)'s limitation plus $40 million of disallowed interest expense deductions) resulting in a corporate tax liability of $23.10 million. Thus, US Pharma, Inc. still obtained a partial benefit from its interest stripping transaction, but its interest deduction was limited to only 30 percent of adjusted taxable income in this example.

Table #3: § 163(j) Limitation (as applied to Diagram #2)		
1	Taxable income (*before* § 163(j) limitation)	$70.00
2	*Less* Business interest income	$0.00
3	*Plus* Business interest expense ($90 related party; $10 unrelated)	$100.00
4	*Plus* Net Operating Loss deduction	$0.00
5	*Plus* section 199A deduction	$0.00
6	*Plus* Depreciation, Amortization, & Depletion	$30.00
7	*Less* Inclusions by Reason of § 951 or § 951A	$0.00
8	*Less* Other adjustments allowed by IRS	$0.00
9	Adjusted taxable income (ATI) (L1 − L2 + L3 + L4 + L5 + L6 − L7 − L8)	$200.00
10	Limitation (30% of ATI per L9)	$60.00
11	*Plus* Business interest income	$0.00
12	*Plus* Floor financing interest	$0.00
13	§ 163(j) Limit (L10 + L11 + L12)	$60.00
14	Excess interest expense (Excess of L3 over L13)	$40.00
15	Taxable income (*after* § 163(j) limitation) (L1 + L13)	$110.00
16	Corporate Tax Liability (at 21%) (L15 × 21%)	$23.10

Now, let's apply the section 163(j) framework to the facts considered in the combined Diagram #9 which is reproduced again below. By way of reminder, Diagram #9 sets forth each of the basic earnings stripping transactions discussed in earlier chapters in a collective or combined fashion. In this regard, there is a supply chain transaction (see the diagram at ①) that is the first depicted earnings stripping technique, a service stripping transaction (see the diagram at ②) that is the second depicted earnings stripping technique, an interest stripping transaction (see the diagram at ③) that is the third depicted earnings stripping technique, a royalty stripping transaction (see the diagram at ④) that is the fourth depicted earnings stripping technique, and a lease stripping transaction (see diagram at ⑤) that is the fifth and final depicted earnings stripping technique and replaces the strategy of US Pharma, Inc. owning its own depreciable/amortizable property.

Diagram #9

Combined Strategy

Supply Chain Transaction, Interest Stripping Transaction, Royalty Stripping Transaction, Rental Stripping, and Service Stripping Transaction

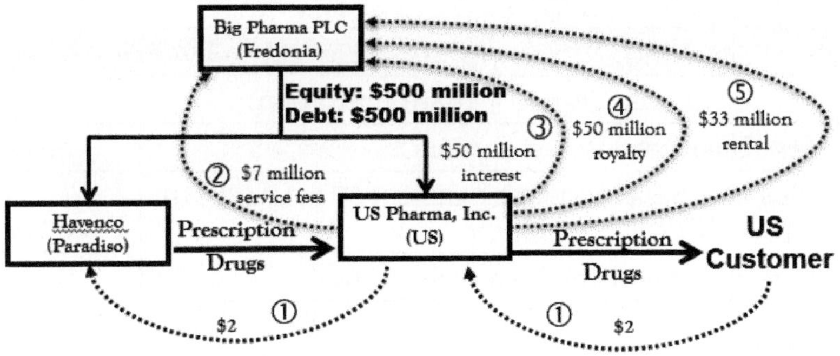

The above facts indicate that at least $140 million of related party tax deductible payments are made by US Pharma, Inc. to its parent, Big Pharma PLC, before considering the profit shifting aspects of the supply chain transaction that exists between HavenCo and US Pharma, Inc. In addition, as in the earlier example, please assume that there is an additional $10 million of unrelated party interest expense. However, because the rental stripping transaction depicted in Diagram #9 replaced the competing option of having US Pharma, Inc. acquire and depreciate its own equipment, please now assume there is no depreciation deduction.

On these facts, section 163(j) starts with taxable income of $50 million ($200 million of profits before related party payments and interest less $140 million combined related party payments less $10 million unrelated party interest). From this taxable income, section 163(j) adds back all interest expense ($60 million in total in this alternative example). Thus, adjusted taxable income is now $110 million. US Pharma, Inc. is limited in its ability to claim an interest expense deduction up to $33 million (i.e., 30 percent of its adjusted taxable income of $110 million). As there was no business interest income, floor financing interest expense, net operating loss, or section 199A deduction to consider, no further adjustment is needed, and the section 163(j) limit is simply $33 million. Thus, US Pharma Inc. is entitled to only claim a deduction for $33 million of its total $60 million of interest expense payments. The deduction related to the $27 million of interest expense that exceeds the 30 percent of adjusted taxable income threshold (now $33 million) is disallowed in this example. The disallowed interest expense can be carried forward to a year where interest expense is less than the section 163(j) limit. Thus, in the above example, US Pharma, Inc. would have $77 million of taxable income after application of section 163(j)'s limitation (i.e., $50 of taxable income before considering section 163(j)'s limitation plus $27 million of disallowed interest expense deductions) resulting in a corporate tax liability of $16.17 million ($77 million of modified taxable income multiplied by 21 percent).

Table #4: § 163(j) Limitation (as applied to Diagram #9)		
1	Taxable income (*before* § 163(j) limitation)	$50.00
2	*Less* Business interest income	$0.00
3	*Plus* Business interest expense ($50 related; $10 unrelated)	$60.00
4	*Plus* Net Operating Loss deduction	$0.00
5	*Plus* Section 199A deduction	$0.00
6	*Plus* Depreciation, Amortization & Depletion	$0.00
7	*Less:* Inclusions by Reason of § 951 or § 951A	$0.00
8	*Less* Other adjustments allowed by IRS	$0.00
9	Adjusted taxable income (ATI) (L1 – L2 + L3 + L4 + L5 + L6 – L7 – L8)	$110.00
10	Limitation (30% of ATI per L9)	$33.00
11	*Plus* Business interest income	$0.00
12	*Plus* Floor financing interest	$0.00
13	§ 163(j) Limit (L10 + L11 + L12)	$33.00
14	Excess interest expense (Excess of L3 over L13)	$27.00
15	Taxable income (*after* § 163(j) limitation) (L1 + L14)	$77.00
16	Corporate Tax Liability (L15 at 21%)	$16.17

Several comparisons are in order. Note that the final taxable income after section 163(j) in the Diagram #9 scenario is $77 million. Note also that the taxable income before application of section 163(j) was $70 million in the Diagram #2 scenario but $110 million after section 163(j)'s application. The point of comparison is to show that because section 163(j) applies only to interest stripping transactions; it is not applicable to the other base erosion and profit shifting techniques. Thus, reliance on those other earnings stripping strategies served to side-step in part section 163(j) and provide alternative strategies that provided earnings stripping benefits without reliance only on aggressive interest stripping transactions. Section 163(j)'s targeted focus on interest payments ignores the other complementary forms of earnings stripping that can be achieved with other tax-favored payments to related persons, such as rents, royalties, and service fees. Thus, section 163(j) is not entirely able to fulfill its core mission of addressing inbound earnings stripping—at least as broadly understood. Another point is in order: note that the use of the rental stripping transaction provides a potential inbound earnings stripping benefit that can extend beyond the depreciable life of a leased asset and provide rental stripping benefits for the entire economic life of the asset, but this strategy does have a negative consequence under section 163(j) because depreciation expense is a favorable add-back to the calculation of adjusted taxable income for purposes of computing the section 163(j) limit.

C. Conduit Regulations Under Section 7701(*l*)

In chapter 7, we spent considerable time looking at the limitations on benefits provisions of the U.S. Model Treaty, but please remember that this is simply a *model* treaty. Once the United States decides to advance such a model, it must then renegotiate existing treaties to amend them to conform to the new model or enter into new treaties that replace the earlier versions. That process takes time, sometimes a lot of time. Thus, while the process for addressing base erosion and profit shifting was being worked out through treaty negotiations, the reality is that the United States Congress and the Treasury Department were eager to have inappropriate treaty shopping addressed more quickly in advance of the addition of a limitation of benefits provision in each and every U.S. bilateral tax treaty. Thus, in parallel with the Treasury Department's effort to deal with treaty shopping in the bilateral context by adding limitations on benefits provisions into existing and new treaties, the 1993 Act brought the Treasury another (unilateral) weapon in its campaign against sandwiches and other international tax havens: section 7701(*l*). Understated in form, section 7701(*l*) is potent in reach. Under the somewhat cryptic heading "Regulations Relating to Conduit Arrangements," section 7701(*l*) reads, "The Secretary may prescribe regulations recharacterizing any multi-party financing transaction as a transaction directly among any 2 or more of such parties where the Secretary determines that such recharacterization is appropriate to prevent avoidance of any tax imposed by this title." Someone who did not have in mind the history of sandwiches and other tax-favored structures using finance intermediaries would be hard pressed to divine what section 7701(*l*) is about. In fact, this single sentence changes the balance of power between taxpayers and the Treasury in the matter of conduits, earnings stripping, and back-to-back debt.

Reread section 7701(*l*). It gives the Treasury the power to recharacterize certain "multi-party financing" transactions. To understand what that means consider the outcome of the *Aiken* case, discussed in chapter 7, where a court in effect excised a treaty-favored Honduran corporation from a chain of back-to-back loans on the ground that it was a "conduit." In consequence the structure was recast as a loan directly from a Bahamas corporation to a U.S. corporation, with interest (subject to flat rate tax, naturally) flowing the other way. With section 7701(*l*) in place, the IRS can reshuffle back-to-back loans systematically and cut treaty-favored entities out of sandwich structures altogether.

The regulations under section 7701(*l*) are known as the "Conduit Regulations." These regulations are a decidedly fierce read. What you should glean from them at a minimum is that they treat most chains of debt and many combinations of debt and leases or licenses as multi-party financing transactions. If there is a significant possibility of tax avoidance, the IRS can disregard the participation of any intermediate entity as a "conduit." Here also, an example may make things easier to understand. Let's return to the Dutch sandwich in Diagram #18. The back-to-back debt binds together a multi-party financing transaction involving three entities. The Treasury can therefore recharacterize the transaction as a debt running directly between the U.S. corporation and the Netherlands Antilles corporation. Because there is no longer a U.S. treaty with the Netherlands Antilles, interest on the loan as recharacterized (which is not exempt portfolio interest, because of Marcel's stock ownership) is subject to flat rate U.S. tax.

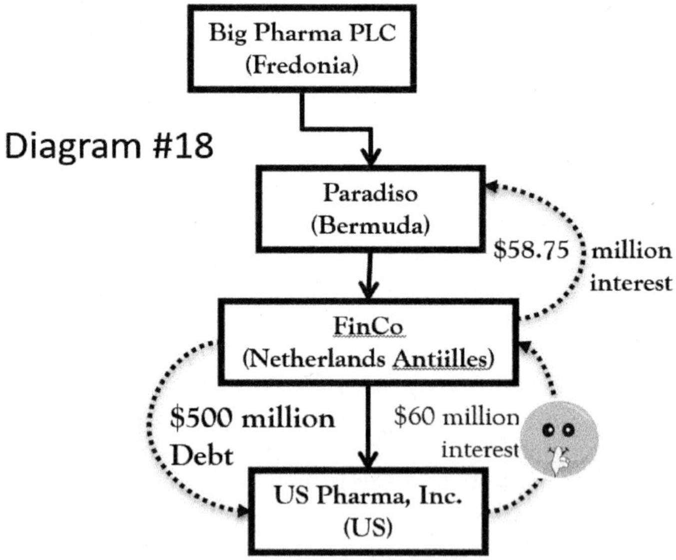

Therefore, even without a limitation on benefits provision in the applicable U.S. income tax treaty, the Conduit Regulations under section 7701(*l*) would have defeated treaty sandwiches built on back-to-back debt. After the United States and the Netherlands included a limitation on benefits provision into the U.S.-Netherlands treaty, taxpayers might then attempt to substitute a Luxembourg corporation for the Netherlands corporation in the classic Dutch sandwich but doing so would avail nothing given the broad reach of the Conduit Regulations. Under the Conduit Regulations, the Luxembourg variant would be cast as payment of interest from the United States straight to the Netherlands Antilles.

1. The Luxembourg Option (1993–2001)

You might think, in this light, that section 7701(*l*) finished off treaty sandwiches once and for all, but it didn't. The Conduit Regulations, to be sure, drove the final stake in the heart of treaty sandwiches built on back-to-back debt.[17] Treaty tax havens were not entirely finished off, however. Even with the Conduit Regulations in place, there remained a way to set up a treaty-based tax shelter, if the underlying treaty had no limitation on benefits.

The design of this structure eliminates the back-to-back debt so that no "multi-party financing" is involved. In an earlier form, the structure made use of the U.S. treaty with Luxembourg combined with helpful elements of the national tax systems of Luxembourg and Switzerland. Luxembourg does not tax income derived from financing operations by foreign branches of Luxembourg corporations. Switzerland, for its part, also does not tax the income from financing operations of Swiss branches of Luxembourg corporations.

To work around section 7701(*l*), Big Pharma PLC would therefore set up the following structure of ownership of business assets in the United States. Big Pharma PLC would create, entirely with *equity* capital, a Luxembourg corporation with a branch in Switzerland engaged in lending money. The Luxembourg entity would lend through its Swiss branch to another entity, also beneficially owned by Big Pharma PLC, engaged in the U.S. pharmaceutical business. Under the treaty between the United States and Luxembourg, the interest paid to the Luxembourg corporation would be free of U.S. tax within the limits imposed by the earnings stripping backstop of section 163(j). Meanwhile, neither Luxembourg nor Switzerland would impose significant tax on the interest income. In Diagram #20 you will find a simplified version of

---

[17] Earlier provisions such as section 163(j) were more like steaks than a bullet to the heart. They killed through a build-up of cholesterol rather than a single sharp blow.

the structure in which Big Pharma PLC owns the stock of a Luxembourg corporation with a financing branch in Switzerland.

Diagram #20

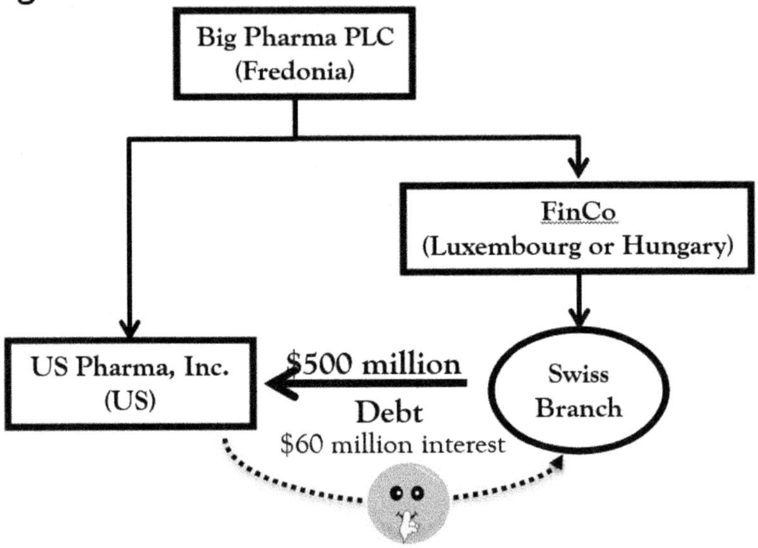

While it may look vulnerable, this structure is not readily assimilable to a "multi-party financing transaction" subject to the conduit rules. The key element is Big Pharma PLC's all-equity interest in the Luxembourg corporation (the Swiss branch). There is no back-to-back debt. Because the interest income accumulates in the Luxembourg entity rather than flowing through it along a chain of debt, there is no evident "multi-party financing transaction" that the Treasury could seek to recombine under the Conduit Regulations. A multi-party financing transaction must have at least three parties and *two* legs of debt. Here, there is only a single layer of debt. In other words, the final incarnation of the treaty sandwich has only one slice of bread. However, to work, the branches in the structure must have a certain substance, including an actual staff. The structure is cost-effective only for much larger enterprises, like Big Pharma PLC. However, if Big Pharma PLC used this structure for interest stripping into the United States and lent from the Swiss branch to its affiliates throughout continental Europe and beyond, then the structure could have sufficient substance to provide an effective avenue of foreign investment in U.S. business operations.

D. Hybrid Entities and Payments

Much like the dual path that was taken to deal with treaty shopping (limitation on benefits provisions and a simultaneous effort under the conduit regulations), the problem of homeless income has been addressed through tax treaty provisions and simultaneously through domestic backstop provisions that were enacted more quickly. Again, in chapter 7, we saw that the U.S. Model Treaty contains a provision that would restrict treaty relief for interest and royalties that are part of a "special tax regime" of the other contracting state. This treaty provision is designed to prevent low-taxed income from escaping U.S. withholding taxes when such income is untaxed in the other country. However, that provision is at present in none of the actual U.S. tax treaties currently in force, and it will take time to amend those treaties to include such a provision, perhaps decades. Instead of waiting for that remedy, Congress has reacted again using domestic law as a means to backstop a perceived inappropriate treaty outcome in situations involving hybrid entities and hybrid payments first by enacting section 894(c) and then later by enacting section 267A. Section 894(c) attacks the hybrid problem by overriding the reduced withholding rates otherwise allowable under an income tax treaty (a treaty override), while section 267A allows the concessionary rate of taxation on the recipient of the hybrid payment but denies a deduction to the payor of such a payment. Thus, these two provisions attempt to attack a common problem but use different means to do so.

1. Section 894

The principle of relinquishing tax jurisdiction over fixed and determinable income for interest, rents, and royalties under a tax treaty presupposes that the income would be taxed in the other jurisdiction. The tax treaty simply modifies the international comity afforded among the countries to give greater weight to residency jurisdiction taxation over source country taxation. However, the premise behind this rebalancing between residency versus source taxation is that the country of residence would in fact assert jurisdiction over that income. What happens if they do not do so because it does not believe it is their income? In that situation, the relinquishing of gross income taxation on fixed and determinable income has become a means to create homeless income—income taxed in no country. The opportunities for creating this homeless income are uniquely presented through the use of hybrid entities, which as you will remember is the term used to describe an entity that is treated as a separate taxable entity for one jurisdiction's purpose but not as a separate taxable entity for the other jurisdiction. With the advent of the U.S. regime that allows elective treatment of many foreign entities,[18] instead of waiting for treaties to be individually renegotiated and amended, Congress enacted section 894(c) as a holistic remedy in the form of a treaty override provision.

---

[18] See Reg. § 301.7701–3(b)(2).

Section 894(c)(1) provides that a foreign person shall not be entitled under any income tax treaty of the United States to any reduced rate of any withholding tax imposed if (i) such item is not treated for purposes of the taxation laws of such foreign country as an item of income of such person, (ii) the treaty does not contain a provision addressing the applicability of the treaty in the case of an item of income derived through a partnership, and (iii) the foreign country does not impose tax on a distribution of such item of income from such entity to such person. Also, section 894(c)(2) provides authority for the Treasury Department to issue regulations to determine other instances where treaty benefits should not be available with respect to any payment received by, or income attributable to any activities of, an entity organized in any jurisdiction (including the United States) that is treated as a partnership or is otherwise treated as fiscally transparent under the U.S. tax laws but as not transparent for purposes of the tax laws of the other jurisdiction. Thus, section 894(c)(2) allows the Treasury Department to address both the use of hybrid entities and reverse hybrid entities. The Treasury Department has issued extensive regulations. The regulations treat an item of income as earned by a resident of a treaty jurisdiction only if the resident jurisdiction asserts taxing jurisdiction over that payment.[19] Thus, if an entity is fiscally transparent in the jurisdiction to which it was formed for foreign law purposes, it is not treated as a treaty resident of that country. If an interest holder in a fiscally transparent entity is subject to taxation in its own resident jurisdiction over the income earned through a fiscally transparent entity, then treaty relief can be available only if the interest holder in the hybrid entity derives income that is taxable in its own resident jurisdiction. This determination is made on an item of income basis. The regulations then seek to unpack what is meant by fiscally transparent in terms of the underlying hybrid entity[20] and the interest holder.[21]

The regulations also discuss the situation where the U.S. tax rules respect an entity as a separate entity whereas the foreign jurisdiction treats an entity as a fiscally transparent entity (a domestic reverse hybrid entity). The regulations deny treaty benefits for payments *to* a domestic reverse hybrid entity.[22] In addition, payments by a domestic reverse hybrid entity are treated as derived by the interest holder only if the interest holder is treated as deriving income from the payment.[23] If, however, a payment is received by a

---

[19] Reg. § 1.894–1(d)(1).

[20] Id.

[21] Reg. § 1.894–1(d)(3).

[22] Reg. § 1.894–1(d)(2)(i).

[23] Reg. § 1.894–1(d)(2)(ii).

domestic reverse hybrid entity and treated as a dividend for any tax purposes (U.S. or foreign) and the payment by the domestic reverse hybrid entity would generally have been treated as an interest payment, then the payment is recast as a dividend and no deduction is allowed to the domestic reverse hybrid entity for making the payment, and the withholding rate for dividends would apply to the domestic reverse hybrid entity's payment.[24]

2. Section 267A

The payment of a related party interest or royalty payment, as a prima facie matter, reduces the tax base of the jurisdiction where the payment is deducted. The underlying assumption is that the other jurisdiction more appropriately has a right to tax that income, but should this deference change if the other jurisdiction does not believe that the receipt of this type of payment is taxable under the laws of the other jurisdiction? If both jurisdictions disclaim taxation over the cross-border payment, then the income represented by that payment is in fact "homeless income" taxed nowhere. Multinational enterprises are quite skilled in creating discontinuities of these sorts between jurisdictions. When such "homeless income" escapes taxation everywhere, the result goes beyond simply the avoidance of international double taxation or simply an allocation of taxing authority to another jurisdiction. What is created is a tax arbitrage between the jurisdictions that affords a windfall due to the discontinuities among jurisdictions. Of course, it is impossible to expect a sovereign nation to have its laws completely align with those of another sovereign nation. Thus, discontinuities in some sense are inevitable, and so international tax arbitrage has plagued developed nations for many years.

The United States, following the lead of the OECD,[25] responded to this concern by enacting section 267A. In broad terms, section 267A denies a deduction for any disqualified related party interest stripping or royalty stripping payment made pursuant to a hybrid transaction or by, or to, a hybrid entity. This is a somewhat elegant idea. Instead of repudiating the treaty provision that allows a lower withholding rate on the payment of interest or royalties, section 267A allows that income to remain low-taxed but eliminates the deduction

---

[24] Reg. § 1.894–1(d)(ii)(B).

[25] The Organisation for Economic Co-operation and Development (OECD) Action 2 of its Base Erosion and Profit BEPS project provide recommendations for hybrid and branch mismatch arrangements. See *OECD/G20, Neutralising the Effects of Hybrid Mismatch Arrangements, Action 2: 2015 Final Report* (2015) and *OECD/G20, Neutralising the Effects of Branch Mismatch Arrangements, Action 2: Inclusive Framework on BEPS* (2017). The European Union Council has directed that all EU members must have laws to address hybrid transactions. See EU Council Directive at (13), FISC110:ECOFIN648, 2016/0011 (July 5, 2016).

for the payment of that income if it is not treated consistently as income in the other jurisdiction. Thus, the recipient of the income retains its treaty concessionary rate, but the payor (which is a U.S. person) is not allowed a deduction for a "hybrid payment." Thus, this provision side-steps the unilateral treaty override that section 894(c) creates but achieves the same economic equivalent outcome without a treaty override. Note that a disqualified related party payment is only defined as an interest or royalty payment, so evidently a rental stripping payment or service stripping payment is not addressed by section 267A. Moreover, a related party interest or royalty payment is a hybrid payment as defined under section 267A only to the extent that: (1) there is no corresponding income inclusion to the related party upon receipt of such payment under the tax law of the country of which such related party is a resident or (2) such related party is allowed a deduction with respect to such amount at the time of its inclusion under the tax law of the other country. If the income is taxable under the U.S. Subpart F rules (a topic discussed in chapter 11), then it has not become "homeless income," as it will be subject to taxation eventually back in the United States and is not considered a hybrid payment that is subject to section 267A. However, if the income is not subject to taxation either under the U.S. anti-deferral rules or in the other jurisdiction, then it is a hybrid payment that is subject to disallowance of its interest or royalty payment deduction. A hybrid entity is any entity which is either: (1) treated as fiscally transparent for U.S. tax purposes but not so treated for purposes of the tax law of the foreign country or (2) treated as fiscally transparent for purposes of the tax law of the foreign country of which the entity is resident for tax purposes but not so treated for U.S. tax purposes (reverse hybrid entity).

This provision thus attacks base erosion and profit shifting by disallowing a deduction for such payments. Thus, section 267A follows the remedy forged by section 163(j) (namely deduction disallowance). However, the comparison to section 163(j) likely ends there, as section 267A utilizes a markedly different framework than does section 163(j). Section 163(j) does not ask the question of whether or to what extent a deductible interest payment is taxable in the other jurisdiction. Section 163(j) doesn't even restrict its disallowance to related party interest payments. Instead, section 163(j) simply sets a bright-line standard for the extent by which profits can be reduced by an interest deduction. Thus, the amount of an interest stripping payment is subject to limitations but is not per se disallowed except when it exceeds the applicable limitation. In contrast, section 267A does not ask any of those questions. Instead, section 267A would allow a related party interest payment or royalty payment to be deductible but only if the payment is taxable in the other jurisdiction where the payment is received. Thus, section 267A makes the availability of a U.S. tax deduction for a related party interest payment or royalty payment contingent on how the foreign jurisdiction treats the payment.

E. Base Erosion Alternative Tax

The above approaches represent targeted responses, but, as we have seen with Diagram #9, the issue of base erosion and profit shifting spans a broader category of transactions than are addressed by section 163(j), section 267A, or section 897. What amount of U.S. profits should one be able to reduce through earnings stripping transactions? None? All? Congress answered this question by stating that very large companies can achieve the benefits of earnings stripping transactions but only for one-half of its pre-base erosion profits but did so in a counter-intuitive way.

In a now common response, instead of amending its inbound provisions that enabled earnings stripping to flourish, Congress chose instead to enact yet another base protection measure in the form of a new minimum tax under section 59A that would seek to restrict the benefits of excessive amounts of inbound earnings stripping strategies more broadly defined.

1. Section 59A

Section 59A imposes a base erosion alternative tax ("BEAT") equal to the excess of a minimum tax rate of 10.5 percent (which is 10.5/21st or one-half of the regular 21 percent rate specified in section 11) but applies this one-half concessionary rate of tax on *modified taxable income*. An added minimum tax is then applied to the extent the section 59A computation exceeds the regular tax liability computed under section 11. The scope of the BEAT does not seek to draw a distinction between foreign-based multinational enterprises and U.S.-based multinational enterprises. However, the BEAT applies only to the very largest multinational enterprises (whether ultimately owned by a U.S.-based or a foreign-based parent corporation)—namely those that over the preceding three-year period have average annual gross receipts of $500 million or more.

The key concept for unpacking the BEAT is "modified taxable income" which is defined as the corporation's regular taxable income but adding back specific payments. The category of payments that are added back to arrive at "modified taxable income" are payments that meet two definitions: (i) they are within the category of payments that constitute "base erosion payments" and (ii) the base erosion payments result in a "base erosion tax benefit" to the taxpayer. These two criteria are discussed immediately below and then demonstrated through the use of the facts posited in Diagram #9.

Base Erosion Payments. A base erosion payment means any amount paid or accrued by a taxpayer to a foreign person that is a *related* party (defined as a 25 percent or more common ownership)[26] and with respect to which a deduction is *allowable*. Thus, a related party payment of interest, rents, royalties, services, or other amounts that provide an immediate deduction is a base erosion payment. In addition, a payment for the purchase of depreciable or amortizable property is also included in this definition. However, a base erosion payment does not include any amount paid for property that will result in an amount that is included in costs of goods sold unless the particular party engaged in a corporate inversion after November 9, 2017. Thus, the purchase or sale of inventory property with a related party is not a base erosion payment, so the earnings stripping opportunities afforded by related party supply chain transactions is not covered by the BEAT. This failure to cover all forms of earnings stripping transactions limits the effectiveness of the BEAT in achieving its goals, as taxpayers are likely to attempt to use supply chain transactions to replace other strategies to side-step the BEAT. A base erosion payment also does not include payments for related party service reimbursements with respect to services that are eligible to use the cost-only service method described in Reg. § 1.482–9 which was discussed in chapter 4. If related party services are eligible for the cost-only method but were in fact subject to a mark-up, then only the extra mark-up amount is considered a base erosion payment.[27] Thus, synthesizing the above observations leads to the following conclusion: a base erosion payment encompasses related party payments for interest stripping transactions, lease stripping transactions, royalty stripping transactions and service stripping transactions (but special exceptions exist for services eligible for the cost-only safe harbor). Finally supply chain transactions that involve the purchase and resale of inventory are not subject to these rules unless the taxpayer had engaged in a corporate inversion after November 9, 2017.

The BEAT also excludes from the definition of a base erosion payment any qualified derivative payments. A qualified derivative

---

[26] Related party means: (i) any 25-percent owner of the taxpayer, (ii) any person who is related to the taxpayer or any 25-percent owner of the taxpayer, within the meaning of sections 267(b) or 707(b)(1), and (iii) any other person related to the taxpayer within the meaning of section 482. For these purposes, section 318 regarding constructive ownership of stock applies to these related party rules except that 10-percent is substituted for 50-percent in section 318(a)(2)(C), and for these purposes section 318(a)(3)(A), (B) and (C) do not cause a United States person to own stock owned by a non-U.S. person.

[27] Reg. § 1.59A–3(b)(3)(i).

payment means any payment made by a taxpayer pursuant to a derivative with respect to which the taxpayer: (i) recognizes gain or loss as if such derivative were sold for its fair market value on the last business day of the taxable year (and such additional times as are required by this title or the taxpayer's method of accounting), (ii) treats any gain or loss so recognized as ordinary, and (iii) treats the character of all items of income, deduction, gain or loss with respect to a payment pursuant to the derivative as ordinary.

The U.S. Treasury also utilized its regulatory authority to exclude from base erosion payments any related party interest stripping transaction that relates to TLAC securities[28] that apply to regulated banks and payments that will be treated as effectively connected income for the recipient.[29] In addition, through its regulatory authority, the Treasury Department provided a further exception to a base erosion payment for any payments that represent effectively connected income of the foreign payee.[30] Finally, the Treasury Department exercised its regulatory authority to provide that a transfer of property as part of a nonrecognition transaction is also not considered a base erosion payment.[31]

Base Erosion Tax Benefit. Once a base erosion payment is identified, it must then be determined whether it created a "base erosion tax benefit." A base erosion tax benefit means: (i) any deduction allowed for the taxable year with respect to a base erosion payment, (ii) in the case of a base erosion payment with respect to the purchase of property of a character subject to the allowance for depreciation (or amortization in lieu of depreciation), any deduction allowed for depreciation or amortization in lieu of depreciation with respect to the property acquired with such payment, or (iii) any reduction in gross receipts with respect to a payment described above to a surrogate foreign corporation (as defined there) in computing gross income of the taxpayer for the taxable year. The Treasury Department provided in its regulations that taxpayers can elect to waive the benefits of a deduction and if so then the portion of the payment to which a deduction is waived is not treated as a base erosion payment that gives rise to a base erosion tax benefit.[32]

---

[28] See Reg. § 1.59A–3(b)(3)(v). A so-called "TLAC security" is a security that ensures "total loss absorption capacity" for a regulated bank. Total loss-absorbing capacity is an international standard, finalized by the Financial Stability Board that is intended to ensure that global systemically important banks have enough equity and bail-in debt to pass losses to investors and minimize the risk of a government bailout.

[29] Reg. § 1.59A–3(b)(3)(iii).

[30] Reg. § 1.59A–3(b)(3)(iii).

[31] Reg. § 1.59A–3(b)(3)(viii)(A).

[32] Reg. § 1.59A–3(c)(6)(i).

Any base erosion tax benefit where the tax imposed by sections 871 or 881 has been deducted and withheld under sections 1441 or 1442 is not taken into account in computing modified taxable income as defined above.[33]

Combined Example. Now, let's apply the section 59A framework to the facts considered in the combined Diagram #9 which is reproduced again here. By way of reminder, the diagram sets forth each of the basic earnings stripping transactions discussed in earlier chapters in a collective or combined fashion. In this regard, there is a supply chain transaction (see the diagram at ①), a service stripping transaction (see the diagram at ②), an interest stripping transaction (see the diagram at ③), a royalty stripping transaction (see the royalty stripping transaction (see the diagram at ④), and a lease stripping transaction (see diagram at ⑤). For purposes of this problem, it is assumed that all of the related party payments made to Big Pharma PLC were not subject to U.S. withholding tax due to an applicable U.S. tax treaty.

Diagram #9

Combined Strategy

Supply Chain Transaction, Interest Stripping Transaction, Royalty Stripping Transaction, Rental Stripping, and Service Stripping Transaction

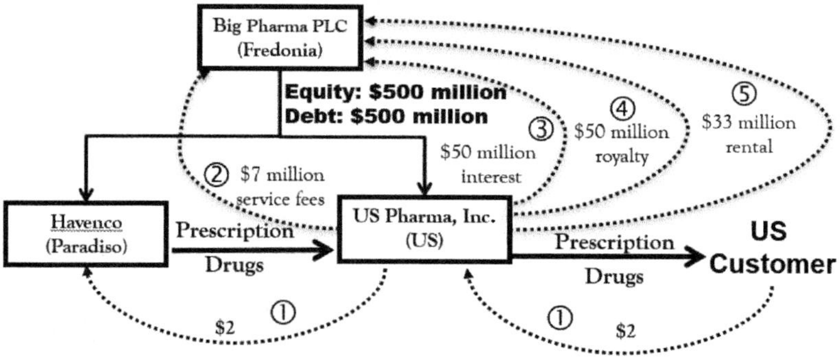

As indicated in the discussion accompanying Table #4 that addressed section 163(j)'s limitation, the facts in Diagram #9 result in a regular corporate taxable income of $77 million, since regular taxable income was increased from $50 million to $77 million after application of section 163(j)'s limitation that disallowed $27 million of interest expense. Thus, after applying section 163(j)'s disallowance of $27 million of interest expense, regular taxable income was $77 million, and this resulted in a regular corporate tax liability of $16.17 million. But now, this same set of facts must be analyzed under section 59A. Section 59A starts with regular taxable income, which

---

33 See § 59A(c)(2)(B).

means *after the application of section 163(j)*. Thus, the starting point for applying section 59A is $77 million. From this amount, base erosion payments that create a base erosion benefit are added back to arrive at modified taxable income. The base erosion payments in Diagram #9 are the related party tax deductible payments paid by US Pharma, Inc. to Big Pharma PLC, with certain exceptions. Most notably, the supply chain transaction is not a base erosion payment as long as the goods that are sold are inventory so that US Pharma, Inc.'s payment would be treated as part of cost of goods sold.[34] In addition, the service stripping transaction would not be considered a base erosion payment if the services were eligible for the cost-only method and charged without a mark-up.[35] For the remainder of this analysis, let's assume that the service stripping transaction involve services that are ineligible for the cost-only method. Thus, the full $7 million service fee would be considered a base erosion payment in its entirety. The rental stripping transaction ($33 million) and the royalty stripping transaction ($50 million) are both base erosion payments. These payments also provided a base erosion tax benefit and so all of them are added back into the calculation to arrive at modified taxable income.

The determination of the amount of the interest stripping transaction that represents a base erosion payment that afforded a base erosion tax benefit is more complex. On these facts, US Pharma, Inc. paid $50 million of related party interest expense and paid $10 million of unrelated party interest expense, but $27 million of its interest expense had been disallowed under section 163(j). So, what amount of the $50 million of related party interest expense created a base erosion tax benefit? Again, only the related party interest expense that was allowed as a deduction is considered as a base erosion payment that provided a base erosion tax benefit.[36] Section 59A(c)(3) makes clear that any disallowed interest is first allocated to unrelated party interest so that the related party interest is treated as providing an allowable deduction to the extent possible.[37] Thus, on these facts, because $10 million of unrelated party interest expense existed, the first $10 million of the $27 million disallowed interest is deemed to have been attributable to the unrelated party interest so that only the remaining excess amount of $17 million of disallowed interest expense is attributed to the $50 million related party interest payment. So, the amount of the related party interest

---

34 See § 59A(c)(2)(B).

35 A base erosion benefit, as defined in section 59A(c)(2), includes a related party payment that provides a deduction or relates to the purchase of depreciable property. Purchase of inventory property where recovery of basis is through cost of goods sold to arrive at gross income under Reg. § 1.61–3(a) is excluded from this definition.

36 See § 59A(d)(1).

37 See § 59A(c)(3).

payment that created a base erosion tax benefit was $33 million of the $50 million, as $17 million did not provide a tax benefit. Therefore, $33 million of the related party interest stripping transaction is treated as a base erosion payment that provided a base erosion tax benefit. Thus, total base erosion payments of $140 million (L2 + L3 + L4 + L5 in Table #5) are added back to the regular taxable income of $77 million to arrive at modified taxable income of $217 million. The minimum tax liability is equal to 10.5 percent of modified taxable income for $22.785 million (10.5 percent minimum tax rate × $217 million of modified taxable income). Because the tax amount computed under section 59A (i.e., $22.785 million) exceeds the regular tax amount of $16.17 million, US Pharma, Inc. is required to pay an additional minimum tax under section 59A of approximately $6.615 million. The above analysis is set forth in the following Table #5.

Table #5: Example of Base Erosion Anti-Abuse Tax (BEAT)		
1	Regular Taxable Income after § 163(j) (See Line 13 of Table #4)	$77.00
2	Base Erosion Payment: Related Service Stripping	$7.00
3	Base Erosion Payment: Related Interest Stripping*	$33.00
4	Base Erosion Payment: Royalty Stripping	$50.00
5	Base Erosion Payment: Rental Stripping	$50.00
6	Modified taxable income (L1 + L2 + L3 + L4 + L5)	$217.00
7	10.5% of modified taxable income (10.5% × L6)	$22.785
8	Regular U.S. tax (See Line 15 of Table #4)	$16.170
9	BEAT (excess of L7 over L8)	$6.615

* Base erosion payments are payments to related foreign persons that result in a U.S. tax deduction. Because $27 million of interest expense is disallowed and the first $10 million is allocated to unrelated party interest, $17 million of related party interest is nondeductible and thus provided no base erosion benefit.

As a further variation, assume that the interest stripping transaction was subject to a 10 percent withholding tax pursuant to a U.S. tax treaty but that the remaining related party service stripping payments, royalty stripping payments, and rental stripping payments were not subject to any U.S. withholding under a U.S. tax treaty. In this variation, because a withholding rate of one-third of the statutory 30 percent rate (i.e., 10% treaty rate divided by normal 30% gross basis rate) was imposed, one-third of the $33 million of allowable related party interest payments are now no longer treated as a base erosion payment per section 59A(c)(2)(B). Consequently, under this further variation, only $22 million (two-thirds of L3 in Table #5) of the interest stripping transaction is now treated as a base erosion payment that provided a base erosion tax benefit. Thus, under these modified facts, modified taxable income would now be $206 million. Because 10.5 percent of $206 million (or $21.63 million) exceeds the regular corporate tax liability of $16.17 million by $5.46 million, the base erosion minimum tax is now $5.46 million.

Several final observations are perhaps helpful here. First, if the U.S. gross income tax on fixed or determinable income had not been reduced by treaty concession on the royalty stripping payments, rental stripping payments, and interest stripping payments, then none of those amounts would have been a base erosion payment under section 59A. Thus, in a sense, section 59A represents a "back to the future" experience. When the effect of concessionary treaty relief provides "excessive" earnings stripping opportunities, a limitation is placed on the benefit by denying the deduction benefit to the payor while the concessionary taxation of the recipient is not directly changed. Second, section 59A is the broadest attempt to address earnings stripping to date, but even so it still excludes supply chain transactions from its reach unless the entity involved had engaged in a corporate inversion after November 9, 2017. Thus, one would expect multinational enterprises to restructure their related party arrangements to maximize their supply chain transactions. Finally, unlike section 163(j) that applies to taxpayers with gross receipts above $25 million, section 59A only applies to taxpayers with gross receipts that equal or exceed $500 million. If protecting the U.S. tax base is an important policy concern, then why is section 59A's application limited to only the very largest companies? More comments are likely relevant in terms of thinking about the asymmetries that exist between section 59A, section 163(j), section 267A, and section 897, but these comments hopefully illuminate the common policy goal of regulating the amount of earnings stripping and base erosion that can be achieved. Even so, the resulting statutory enactments have diverged in their scope and application and thus have created considerable additional complexity.

F. The Branch Profits Tax

Until the adoption of the 1986 Act, the repatriation of U.S. earnings by a foreign corporation had no tax consequences in itself. Section 884 now imposes an additional 30 percent "branch profits tax" on earnings removed from the United States. The branch profits tax adds a second layer of U.S. income tax on earnings received by foreign corporations from U.S. business operations. The tax has, roughly, the effect of treating U.S. business operations of foreign corporations (commonly called "U.S. branch businesses") as though they were separately incorporated entities that make taxable dividend distributions to their foreign shareholders. The branch profits tax makes two-level taxation of foreign corporations' U.S. business operations more uniform than the regime that preceded it.

1. Why?

Before venturing into the mechanics of the branch profits tax (which are somewhat frightening), it may be helpful to review the problem that gave rise to it. Foreign corporations doing business in the United States can choose between three forms of organization of their venture. The simplest is a direct branch operation in the United States. A foreign corporation that does business in the United States directly, with assets that it owns as a proprietor, is said to have a U.S. "branch" which in turn is to say that the foreign corporation has a U.S. trade or business or a U.S. permanent establishment. A branch business is a direct presence of a foreign person in the United States. The other two possibilities entail the use of separately chartered subsidiary corporations to own and operate a U.S. business. The separate subsidiary can be domestic (that is, U.S.-chartered) or foreign (that is, chartered in a foreign country).

A problem, before the 1986 Act, was that a foreign corporation's direct branch business in the United States might be taxed differently from a separate subsidiary. The reason for the difference lies in source rules for dividends and in the range of application of the "second tax" on dividends that followed from the source rules. Consider, for example, Big Pharma PLC (a Fredonian corporation) with widely dispersed foreign shareholders carrying out a U.S. business through a wholly-owned U.S. corporate subsidiary, US Pharma, Inc., as illustrated in the right-side of Diagram #22.

Diagram #22

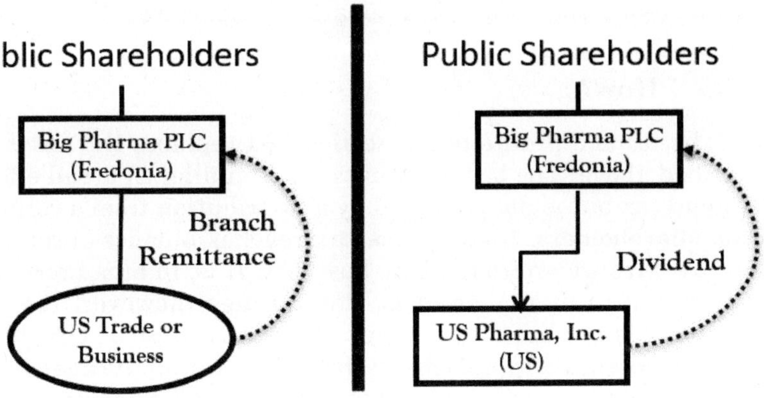

The business profits of the U.S. subsidiary are subject to U.S. corporate taxation. Dividends paid by the subsidiary to its foreign parent, being paid by a U.S. corporation, also have U.S. source and are subject to U.S. flat rate tax. This form of organization therefore entails two layers of U.S. tax on fully repatriated business profits of the Fredonian corporation,[38] which is the norm of U.S. corporate taxation. If the subsidiary conducting a U.S. business in this pattern was foreign-chartered, it made no difference before the 1986 Act.[39] Dividends paid by the foreign subsidiary to its parent, coming entirely from U.S. business profits, would also have U.S. source under the source rules (specifically the 25 percent rule[40] for dividends from a foreign corporation, which you may recall from chapter 3) and would be subject to the "second" U.S. tax on dividends.

Conducting the U.S. business as a direct branch, however, would eliminate the second tax if the U.S. business operations were small in relation to the worldwide operations of the foreign corporation. Suppose Big Pharma PLC derived 10 percent of its gross income from a U.S. branch business, as in the accompanying Diagram #22. The U.S. business profits, then and now, would be taxed as effectively connected income, but before the introduction of the branch profits tax, that would have been the full extent of U.S. taxation. The repatriation of the profits to the Fredonian home office had no U.S. tax consequences. No part of any dividend distribution by the Fredonian corporation to its individual shareholders has U.S. source,

[38] Dividends from the Fredonian corporation to its individual shareholders (A, B, C, etc.) are free of U.S. tax, but two layers of U.S. tax have already been paid.

[39] It still doesn't, although the mechanics of taxation are somewhat different with the branch profits tax.

[40] Dividends from a foreign corporation with more than 25-percent "effectively connected" income have a proportional component of U.S. source income. § 861(a)(2).

and therefore no part suffered U.S. tax.[41] In this regime, the taxation of a U.S. branch of a foreign corporation was often more advantageous than that of a separately chartered U.S. or foreign subsidiary.[42]

2. How?

The branch profits tax of section 884 replaces the "second tax" described above. The branch profits tax is similar in broad effect to a dividend tax but is not triggered by a distribution from a corporation to its shareholders. Instead, the tax reaches business profits when they are withdrawn from a U.S. business. It is, in broad terms, a tax on remitted profits. Viewed at closer range, however, the branch profits tax is not literally a tax on the repatriation of U.S. business profits by foreign corporations; rather, it is a tax on the disinvestment of those profits from U.S. business assets even if they remain within the U.S. economic environment. The tax brings all U.S. business operations of foreign corporations within the same tax regime, generally subjecting them to two layers of U.S. tax.

Mechanically, the branch profits tax is distinctly complicated. It is triggered by a reduction in a foreign corporation's U.S. business assets to the extent of any prior business profits. In effect, the tax falls on profits disinvested from a U.S. business. Think of it as a tax on a notional dividend from an imaginary separate subsidiary holding a U.S. branch business.

3. The "Dividend Equivalent Amount"

Section 884(a) imposes a tax of 30 percent of the "dividend equivalent amount" of a foreign corporation in each taxable year. The "dividend equivalent amount" is defined in section 884(b) as the corporation's "effectively connected earnings and profits" ("ECEP") "for the taxable year," adjusted up or down by decreases or increases respectively in the foreign corporation's "U.S. net equity."[43] Specifically, a foreign corporation's ECEP for the taxable year are 1) *reduced* by the excess of the foreign corporation's "U.S. net equity" at the end of the taxable year over its "U.S. net equity" at the beginning of the taxable year and 2) *increased* by the excess of the foreign corporation's U.S. net equity at the beginning of the taxable year over its U.S. net equity at the close of the year.[44] Mnemonically, think of

---

[41] The Fredonian corporation, remember, is below the 25 percent threshold of U.S. source in § 861(a)(2).

[42] Technically, of course, a foreign subsidiary would have its own U.S. branch business—but one accounting for 100 percent of its gross income, which would impart U.S. source to its entire dividends under the 25 percent rule.

[43] § 884(b); Reg. § 1.884–1 (a)(2), (3). "U.S. net equity" is U.S. business assets.

[44] § 884(b)(2)(A).

ECEP as reduced by an increase in U.S. net equity and increased by a reduction.

4. The Taxable Event

If you ponder these provisions for a while, it may hit you that if a foreign corporation leaves its effectively connected earnings invested in a U.S. branch business the amount of its taxable ECEP will be just offset by the resulting *increase* in its U.S. business assets. Therefore, there is no branch profits tax. However, if the foreign corporation pulls its profits out of the U.S. business (sending them to a bank account in its home country, for example), the corresponding decrease in its U.S. business assets will expose its taxable ECEP to the branch profits tax.

Note, further, that the branch profits tax can be triggered by any reduction of a foreign corporation's U.S. *business* assets even if the amounts disinvested are not actually repatriated but remain in the United States. A simple shift of the accumulated business profits of a U.S. branch business into passive investments or even a U.S. bank account is sufficient. If a foreign corporation takes its U.S. business profits and parks them in U.S. Treasury notes, for example, it will suffer the branch profits tax. The bonds, to be sure, may yield exempt portfolio interest, but the branch profits tax inflicts a heavy tax toll charge on a foreign corporation's purchase of the bonds with profits withdrawn from a U.S. business.

Suppose that Big Pharma PLC did not appreciate that it had a U.S. trade or business (a U.S. branch) and thus did not file a U.S. tax return and upon audit it is determined that it had a U.S. trade or business. As discussed in chapter 6, Big Pharma PLC is entitled to claim U.S. tax deductions for its definitely related expenses *only if* it timely files a federal income tax return.[45]

Alternatively, suppose that Big Pharma PLC's branch had interest that was subject to disallowance by reason of section 163(j)'s limitations on deductible interest. Can these nondeductible payments be deducted for purposes of computing the effectively connected earnings and profits? Certainly, the payments transferred assets out of the branch, and if the transfer did not reduce effectively connected earnings and profits, then the mismatch creates a branch profits tax exposure immediately. How should one determine U.S. effectively connected earnings and profits when there are significant disallowed expenses?

One plausible answer is that these disallowed expenses are similarly not allowable as a deduction for determining effectively

---

[45] See § 874(a); § 882(c)(2).

connected earnings and profits. Under this view, the effectively connected earnings and profits are determined simply by looking to the effectively connected income less the U.S. tax obligation. This is a harsh result because the effectively connected earnings and profits would then be higher than the remaining assets of the branch even if the branch did not remit any assets back to its head office. However, after positing this nightmare scenario, the better view seems to be that the disallowed amounts are deductible for purposes of computing the effectively connected earnings and profits. In this regard, Treasury regulations seem to suggest that expenses that are allocable or apportionable under Reg. § 1.861–8 are allowed as a reduction to effectively connected earnings and profits with no stipulation that the expenses must have been allowed as a deductible item.[46]

5. Relation to the Former Second Tax

Even before the repeal of the "second tax" in 2004, foreign corporations exposed to the branch profits tax did not suffer the second tax in normal circumstances. Section 884(e)(3)(A) calls off the flat rate tax of sections 871 and 881 on dividends paid by a foreign corporation from its earnings for any taxable year in which it is subject to the branch profits tax.

A corollary of this effect is that the branch profits tax largely ended the differences in taxation of U.S. branches and separate subsidiaries of foreign corporations. Consider the Fredonian corporation in the diagrams above. Dividends from a foreign-chartered subsidiary with U.S. business operations are no longer subject to the second tax. However, because distributions do reduce the earnings of the subsidiary's earnings invested in U.S. business assets, they are subject to the branch profits tax. The tax cost is the same (30 percent of the distributed amount).

The effect of the branch profits tax, in some instances, is somewhat different from that of the former second tax. When it applied, the second tax reached a portion of *all* dividends paid by a foreign corporation regardless of their economic origin. The branch profits tax, in contrast, only reaches earnings withdrawn from U.S. business assets. Suppose, for example, that profits from the Fredonian corporation's U.S. branch business (as depicted in

---

[46] Reg. § 1.884–3(f)(3). The nuances of the earnings and profits adjustments under section 312 likely allows the consideration of nondeductible expense but the answer is not entirely certain. See Divine v. Commissioner, 500 F.2d 1041, 1053 [34 AFTR 2d 74–5331] (2d Cir. 1974), *rev'g and remanding* 59 T.C. 152 (1972); BITTKER & EUSTICE, FEDERAL INCOME TAXATION OF CORPORATIONS AND SHAREHOLDERS AT ¶ 8.04[5] SEVENTH EDITION, WARREN, GORHAM & LAMONT (2000), with supplements.; Rudick, " *'Dividends' and 'Earnings or Profits' Under the Income Tax Law: Corporate Non-Liquidating Distributions*," 89 U. PA. L. REV. 865, 887 (1941).

Diagram #22) account for 50 percent of its gross income. With the second tax, half of any dividends of the corporation to its shareholders would have been subject to U.S. tax,[47] regardless of the location of the assets used to pay the dividends. With the branch profits tax, *all* amounts distributed to shareholders originating from U.S. business assets would be subject to additional U.S. tax, but none of the amounts distributed from assets already outside the U.S. economic environment would be subject to it. The Fredonian corporation can therefore distribute as dividends to its shareholders earnings attributable entirely to business activity outside the United States at no U.S. tax cost. Such a distribution does not trigger the branch profits tax because it entails no reduction of U.S. assets.

6. The Branch Interest Tax

Closely related to the branch profits tax is the tax of section 884(f) on interest paid by U.S. branch businesses of foreign corporations. It is considerably more complex than the branch profits tax (itself no slouch in that department), and we will attempt here to give only a fleeting glimpse of this tax.

To fathom the branch interest tax, it is necessary to think back to the "branch interest" rule of section 884(f)(1)(A), discussed in chapter 3, by which interest "paid by" a branch business of a foreign corporation in the United States is treated "as if. . . paid by a domestic corporation." It follows that U.S. branch interest paid by foreign corporations may have U.S. source. If paid to a related person, the branch interest would not be exempt portfolio interest (because of the 10 percent shareholder rule) and hence might be subject to flat rate U.S. tax. On the positive side of the ledger, such interest would normally be deductible in determining the effectively connected U.S. income of the branch business. More precisely, the interest would be "allocable" as a deduction to effectively connected income.

Under regulations on expense allocation, interest paid by a foreign corporation *outside* the United States (and hence not literally "branch interest" subject to section 884(f)(1)(A)) may nonetheless be allocable as a *deduction* to the effectively connected income of a U.S. branch business of the foreign corporation. A foreign corporation may therefore in some instances deduct more interest from the income of a U.S. branch than was actually paid by the branch. Without further statutory provision, the "excess" interest would have foreign source (being outside the branch interest rule of section 884(f)(1)(A) because it is not "paid by" the branch) and would not be subject to U.S. tax in the hands of its recipient even if the latter were a related person.

---

[47] Under the source rules, the dividends have a 50-percent component of U.S. source income.

The branch-level interest tax undoes this potential tax advantage and then some. Under section 884(f)(1)(B), if the amount of interest allocated as a deduction to the effectively connected income of a foreign corporation exceeds the amount of interest that its U.S. branch business actually pays, the excess is subject to the branch interest tax. Mechanically, the foreign corporation is subject to flat rate tax "as if" the excess interest had been paid *to it* by a wholly-owned U.S. subsidiary. Note that the foreign corporation is taxed as though it had *received* an amount of "excess" interest that it actually paid out. This amount of interest would have U.S. source, would not be exempt portfolio interest, and would hence be subject to flat-rate U.S. tax unless shielded by an income tax treaty.

The branch-level interest tax is thus imposed on a notional base to which no actual receipts may correspond. It is, furthermore, determined with reference to a class of *deductions* that are established only in regulations. From the face of the Code itself, both the object of the tax and its amount are difficult to apprehend.

Beyond these generalities, little of the branch interest tax is readily fathomable without recourse to the extensive regulations on branch interest issued under sections 882 and 884. Unless your future self is deeply, perhaps pathologically, involved with international taxation, you will get through life without any further concern for the branch interest tax.

7. Treaties and the Branch Profits Tax

The branch profits tax is a second-level U.S. tax on business profits of foreign corporations similar in effect, but not form, to a tax on dividends. The branch profits tax is not literally imposed on a dividend payment but is imposed directly on the earnings of a foreign corporation that are repatriated from the United States. Treaty provisions concerning dividends paid by foreign corporations therefore provide no literal protection from the branch profits tax, whether they apply to the baseline U.S. tax on dividends received from U.S. sources by foreign taxpayers or to the "second" tax on dividends.

The U.S. Model Treaty expressly allows the imposition of a branch profits (or similar) tax on the business profits of a foreign corporation attributable to a permanent establishment, along with other gains treated as effectively connected income in U.S. taxation.[48] The branch profits tax is limited, however, to the 5-percent rate imposed on dividends paid by domestic corporations to 10-percent corporate shareholders.[49] The branch profits tax, far more than the

[48] Art. 10(8)(a).

[49] Art. 10(8)(b).

second tax on dividends, is now where the question of corporate double taxation is played out.

The treaties the United States entered into since 1986 (when the branch profits tax was adopted) allow the imposition of a branch profits tax on the profits of a corporation chartered in one treaty country derived from business operations in the other, but with limitations that make the branch profits tax essentially equivalent to the taxation of dividends under the treaty. The typical provision limits the branch tax to after-tax profits attributable to a permanent establishment and to the rate of tax imposed on dividends from related corporations, often 5 percent.[50]

8. Section 884(e)

Older treaties rarely make explicit provision for the branch profits tax. Section 884 and the associated regulations, however, coordinate the branch profits tax and the taxation of dividends under treaties that are silent on the matter. Specifically, section 884(e)(2) limits the rate of the branch profits tax (normally 30 percent) imposed on a corporation of a treaty country to the maximum rate of U.S. withholding tax provided under the relevant treaty for dividends from a wholly-owned U.S. subsidiary of a foreign corporation.

There is more fine print in section 884(e). A reduced rate of branch profits tax in a treaty applies only to "qualified" foreign corporations, which are corporations of treaty countries, of which at least 50 percent of the stock is owned by individual residents of the treaty country or by individual citizens or residents of the United States.[51]

9. Possible Conflicts with Treaties—Questions of Precedence

You may have noticed (and several foreign governments have forcefully pointed out) that the Code's section 884(e) is inconsistent with (and may well limit in practice) some of the treaty provisions mentioned above. That is true, and that's life. In the U.S. legal system there is no absolute precedence between statutes and treaties. Each may contradict or displace the other.

This element of U.S. law is formalized in section 7852(d)(1): "[f]or purposes of determining the relationship between a provision of a treaty and any law of the United States affecting revenue, neither the treaty nor the law shall have preferential status by

---

[50] See, e.g., the Treaty with the Netherlands, art. 11.

[51] § 884(e)(4)(A). Also "qualified" are publicly traded corporations primarily traded on securities markets of their country of incorporation, as well as their wholly-owned subsidiaries. § 884(e)(4)(B).

reason of its being a treaty or a law." The baseline rule of precedence in resolving conflicts is that the later enacted prevails over the earlier. Absent more specific provision or inference, therefore, statutes displace prior inconsistent treaties, and treaties displace prior inconsistent statutes.[52] That means in practice that a provision buried in section 884(e) of the Code can and does modify rights ostensibly established by valid treaties.

To mitigate the severity of conflicts (and the pain of surprise), Code section 894(a) provides a general balm: "[t]he provisions of [the Code] shall be applied to any taxpayer with due regard to any treaty obligation of the United States which applies to such taxpayer." The broad terms of this language, however, are not entirely reassuring. The relation between statutes and treaties in taxation is difficult, and it is hard to be specific. Let me try to tide you over with the following. To the extent that treaty benefits are accorded with reference to baseline U.S. taxation, they prevail. For example, a treaty exemption for royalties is effective notwithstanding the U.S. tax that would otherwise be imposed. Were it not so, what would be the point of treaties? However, provisions in the Code, such as section 884(e), that expressly purport to *limit* treaty benefits also prevail, even over equally explicit treaty provisions.

---

52 See Whitney v. Robertson, 124 U.S. 190, 194 (1888).

Part III
OUTBOUND U.S. TAXATION

Chapter 9

OUTBOUND TAXATION IN OVERVIEW

As discussed in earlier chapters, the main concern of the U.S. tax system regarding *inbound* transactions is to define the thresholds of U.S. taxation for foreign persons investing or doing business in the United States. The key to tax planning for inbound transactions is hence to keep the economic presence of foreign persons in the United States below the relevant thresholds, where possible, or to minimize the effectively connected taxable income in order to reduce or eliminate U.S. tax exposure.

The essential structure of outbound U.S. taxation—the taxation of income derived by U.S. persons outside the United States—follows from two premises that are in basic respects at odds: the worldwide taxation by the United States of its citizens and residents and the status of foreign corporations as separate taxable entities.

A. Double Taxation

One immediate corollary of worldwide U.S. taxation is possible double taxation. A U.S. person is at the outset fully subject to U.S. taxation on foreign income. Any tax imposed abroad therefore threatens to be a second layer. A pressing concern of a U.S. person pursuing foreign income is that any foreign taxes be imposed instead (rather than on top) of U.S. tax. Foreign tax advisers (viewing the question from their perspective as an inbound one) can help in creating a structure with the least exposure to foreign taxation. There are limits to what they can accomplish, especially when an outbound U.S. venture plays out in a high-tax environment, just as there are limits to the reduction of U.S. taxes that can be gained for foreign persons here. Nor can American enterprises afford simply to steer clear of high-tax foreign venues because there, often, is where the money is. Countries with rich markets and developed commercial infrastructures that may reward investment by U.S. persons also tend to impose significant taxes.

B. Less than Single Taxation

On the other end of the spectrum from the concern over international double taxation is the opposite concern of "no taxation" or the creation of "homeless income." Again, as indicated in earlier chapters, homeless income refers to profits that are diverted to a low-tax jurisdiction but arose from activities conducted elsewhere. Homeless income can be created as a result of asymmetries that exist in the application of the tax laws of different countries to a transaction that interacts with those countries. Homeless income can also be created through earnings stripping transactions where a low-tax subsidiary is allowed to engage in related party transactions with high-tax affiliates, with the consequence that profits and profit-making opportunities are contractually shifted to the low-tax subsidiary. I organized these earnings stripping transactions into related party interest stripping transactions, royalty stripping transactions, lease stripping transactions, service stripping transactions, and supply chain transactions. Not every tool in this tax minimization toolbox will work in every country. Some countries impose significant withholding taxes on service fees. Other countries deny the ability to remit foreign exchange for cross-border royalties or subject those payments to a rigorous governmental approval process in an effort to force multinational enterprises to contribute their know-how to their in-country subsidiary. Other countries may impose substantial withholding taxes on interest, rents, and royalties. Still other countries may restrict the amount of related-party interest expense that can be deducted through the adoption of various thin capitalization regimes akin to section 163(j). Other countries may impose significant customs duties or value added taxes on the import and sale of inventory in its jurisdiction. However, few (if any) jurisdictions comprehensively eliminate all means to engage in earnings stripping transactions. Thus, sophisticated taxpayers that have an integrated business model are able to customize their trading patterns and investment into a foreign jurisdiction to utilize the tax planning techniques that are not addressed in the local environment. Regardless of whether homeless income arises due to a tax arbitrage transaction that captures an asymmetry between different jurisdictions or involves an earnings stripping technique, each of these various strategies achieves a common base erosion and profit shifting goal: profits ultimately settle in an affiliate located in a low-taxed jurisdiction.

C. Competing Norms of International Neutrality

Moreover, in thinking about outbound taxation it is also helpful to recognize that a fundamental design weakness confronts any and all outbound international tax regimes: whenever effective tax rates in different countries differ among the impacted countries, it is difficult for any country, acting unilaterally, to design an international tax regime that achieves neutrality among all economic participants.[1] From this premise, there are two primary ways that

---

[1] STAFF OF JOINT COMM. ON TAXATION, 112TH CONG., DESCRIPTION AND ANALYSIS OF PRESENT-LAW RULES RELATING TO INTERNATIONAL TAXATION SCHEDULED FOR A HEARING BEFORE THE HOUSE COMM. ON WAYS & MEANS 74 (JCX–40–99) (June 28, 1999) [hereinafter DESCRIPTION AND ANALYSIS OF PRESENT-LAW RULES RELATING TO INTERNATIONAL TAXATION]. The coexistence of both types of neutrality in a single national tax system is not impossible, however. For example, a

one can approach neutrality: capital import neutrality and capital export neutrality.[2]

Capital export neutrality generally seeks to tax resident taxpayers on their worldwide income and then provide a foreign tax credit for taxes that the resident taxpayer pays in the host country. As a result, capital export neutrality promotes the goal of having a taxpayer make foreign investment decisions independent of tax reasons, as the income is ultimately subject to worldwide taxation with an appropriate foreign tax credit that avoids double taxation. However, to the extent that the host country imposes a tax rate below that of the taxpayer's country of residence, then the resident jurisdiction subjects the foreign earnings to residual residency-based taxation. Thus, although international double taxation is avoided through the foreign tax credit mechanism, the taxpayer's worldwide income is subject to the same worldwide tax rate as the resident jurisdiction regardless of where earned.

In contrast to capital export neutrality, capital import neutrality is gauged from the perspective of the country where the investment is made (the host country). Under this approach, all firms operating in the host country bear tax at the same host country rate. The country of residence would then provide an "exemption" on income earned in the other jurisdiction. By not asserting taxation over extra-territorial income, the country of residence is assuring that its own citizens and residents do not bear a tax burden greater than any other competitor that conducts business operations in the same host country. Thus, when a resident jurisdiction has a territorial tax system or an exemption system, capital import neutrality is attempted to be achieved (that is, neutrality among all participants located in that same host country regardless of where their ultimate country of residency may be). Capital import neutrality is often called

---

national tax consisting of a tax on the worldwide *consumed* income of citizens and residents of the taxing country, coupled with a foreign tax credit, can achieve both capital import and capital export neutrality across a broad range of situations. For domestically based taxpayers, investment decisions both at home and abroad have the same tax costs (unless foreign taxes are much higher than domestic). For foreign investment in the taxing country, a shadow tax could be imposed mirroring the tax on wholly domestic investment of the foreign taxpayers. These two boundaries of neutrality can be advanced together or separately within a single system of taxation imposed on consumed income. Taxation of consumed income can also achieve a considerable degree of progressivity where that is viewed as an indispensable policy objective. For more on the taxation of consumed income see Joseph Isenbergh, The Future of Taxation (September 2010). U of Chicago Law & Economics, Olin Working Paper No. 509. Available at SSRN: https://ssrn.com/abstract=1536725 or http://dx.doi.org/10.2139/ssrn.1536725.

2 A third neutrality standard is called "national neutrality" which would allow a deduction for the foreign taxes that are paid in another country. To the extent that non-income foreign taxes are only deductible and not afforded a U.S. foreign tax credit, national neutrality is furthered.

"competitive neutrality" by those who endorse this type of regime because all competing firms in the same market are subject to the same tax burden, and so this form of neutrality encourages the most efficient capital ownership of resources within a given capital importing country. Under a territorial regime, if the host country's tax rate were lower than the tax rate of the country of residence, then the resident taxpayer would have an incentive to reduce their tax burden by moving business operations and investment out of the country of residence and into the host country.

In a purely territorial tax regime, parity can be achieved between U.S. multinational corporations (U.S. MNCs) and foreign multinational corporations (Foreign MNCs) in the foreign jurisdictions in which those firms compete, but such parity comes at the cost of creating a tax preference for overseas profits of U.S. multinational enterprises earned in regimes where the tax rate is below the U.S. tax rate as compared to the domestic profits of U.S. corporations. If, instead, a worldwide tax regime were adopted, then parity can be achieved between U.S. multinational enterprises and purely domestic business entities, but such parity comes at the cost of creating a competitive disadvantage for U.S. multinational corporations versus foreign multinational corporations in low-tax jurisdictions. These two regimes can be summarized as follows:

Territorial Tax Regime

Advantage:	Disadvantage:
U.S. MNC and Foreign MNC Neutrality	**Domestic Business Entity Non-Neutrality**
The overseas profits of the U.S. multinational enterprise bear the same tax cost as the overseas profits of Foreign MNC competitors thus preserving competitiveness of U.S. MNCs vis-à-vis Foreign MNCs.	If the overseas profits of the U.S. multinational enterprise were lower-taxed versus the profits of a purely domestic enterprise, a tax advantage would exist for generating overseas profits. This preference arguably places domestic enterprises at a competitive disadvantage and may create an incentive to migrate activities overseas.

Worldwide Tax Regime

Advantage:	Disadvantage:
Neutrality with Domestic Business Entities	**Non-Neutrality with Foreign MNCs**
If overseas profits of the U.S. multinational corporation are subjected to United States taxation on a current basis, then the U.S. multinational corporations bears the same worldwide tax cost on all of its global income, thus preserving horizontal equity between U.S. multinational corporations and purely U.S. domestic enterprises.	If the extra-territorial business profits of U.S. multinational corporation are subjected to significant additional U.S. taxation (either on a current or deferred basis), then U.S. multinational corporations would have a competitive disadvantage versus foreign multinational corporations (either on a current or deferred basis).

D. The Tax System's Dual Response

The complexity of U.S. taxation of foreign income (which will become apparent in short order) reflects its attempts to balance the competing goals of capital export neutrality and capital import neutrality. In 2017, a schism appeared in the U.S. international tax system as the U.S. international tax system now has significant elements of both a worldwide tax regime and a territorial tax regime. In 2025, a significant expansion in immediate U.S. taxation to the U.S. shareholder of income earned through controlled foreign corporations was adopted, but that income is taxed at a concessionary rate. The coordination of these competing elements into one outbound international tax regime entails significant complexity.

1. Direct Conduct of Foreign Activities of U.S. Persons

For direct investment of U.S. persons outside the United States, the United States follows a worldwide taxation regime. To prevent international double taxation in that regime, the U.S. tax system allows a foreign tax credit. Said differently, for U.S. persons with direct investment in a foreign country, all worldwide income is taxable immediately but may also give rise to a tax credit for foreign income taxes paid, within the framework of section 901. The contours of what taxes are eligible for the foreign tax credit and the limitations on allowable credits are discussed in chapter 10.

2. Foreign Corporations

For a number of reasons, the most common form of organization of foreign business ventures conducted by U.S. persons is a separate foreign corporate entity rather than a direct branch of a domestic corporation or an individual proprietorship. Both U.S.-chartered and foreign-chartered entities are used but the latter predominate. In part, this is for business reasons. A locally chartered entity can make it easier to deal with foreign tax and regulatory authorities. Often though, taxation is the main concern. In form, a foreign corporation is a foreign person. If owned by U.S. shareholders, however, it embodies the economic interests of United States persons. Despite this manifest economic reality, foreign corporations are treated by the U.S. tax system across a broad range of situations as foreign taxpayers and as such may receive foreign income beyond the reach of immediate U.S. taxation. When the foreign corporation is a controlled foreign corporation (more than 50 percent owned by U.S. shareholders), the income earned by the foreign corporation is immediately includible in the U.S. shareholder under one or another of the U.S. anti-deferral tax regimes. The anti-deferral exceptions that apply to controlled foreign corporations are addressed in chapter 11. When the foreign corporation is not a controlled foreign corporation but is a ten percent owned foreign corporation, a more narrowly tailored anti-deferral regime applies in that context and any income not made subject to that narrowly tailored anti-deferral regime is generally not taxable to the U.S. shareholder. The tax consequence of receiving a dividend from a ten-percent owned foreign corporation diverges, however, depending upon whether the U.S. shareholder is an individual (fully taxable) or a domestic corporation (nontaxable due to a 100 percent corporate foreign dividends received deduction). Finally, if a foreign corporation is less than ten percent owned, then the more narrowly tailored anti-deferral regime applies and any income not subjected to taxation under that anti-deferral regime remains fully taxable when distributed as a dividend to a U.S. person regardless of whether the U.S. person is a corporation or an individual.

Individual. As a general rule, dividends from a foreign corporation are taxable to the U.S. individual under section 61(a)(7). However, qualified dividends are eligible for a preferential tax rate for individuals.[3] A "qualified dividend" includes a dividend received from a qualified foreign corporation as long as the U.S. individual shareholder meets the holding period requirements with respect to its ownership of the stock in the foreign corporation.[4] A qualified foreign corporation includes any corporation incorporated outside the United States that either (i) is eligible to claim the benefits of a U.S. tax treaty or (ii) is traded on a U.S. stock exchange but only if the foreign corporation is not a passive foreign investment company or an entity that engaged in a corporate inversion.[5] If the dividend paid by a foreign corporation fails to satisfy the requirements for a qualified dividend, then the dividend is taxable at ordinary income rates for the individual shareholder. The favorable deferral of immediate U.S. taxation on the foreign earnings of a foreign corporation owned by U.S. shareholders provides a significant potential tax advantage for the individual U.S. shareholder as the income earned by a foreign corporation generally avoids any U.S. taxation until the shareholder actually receives an actual dividend. This "deferral benefit" can result in a permanent benefit if the earnings are indefinitely reinvested overseas. As might be expected, this deferral benefit is subject to limitations in the form of several anti-deferral regimes. The anti-deferral regimes that apply to controlled foreign corporations are addressed in chapter 11. The alternative regime that applies to passive foreign investment companies is addressed in chapter 12. If the earnings of the foreign corporation were immediately taxable to an individual U.S. shareholder under one of the anti-deferral regimes, then the above tax results are altered and will be explored extensively in those chapters. Even so, it is helpful to understand the general rule so that the exceptions and alterations discussed in chapters 11 and 12 are understood in their correct context.

Domestic Corporation as Shareholder of Foreign Corporation. The combination of the 2017 Act and 2025 Act significantly redirected the U.S. outbound taxation regime in terms of how it applies to a domestic corporate shareholder. In this regard, as a general rule, if a domestic corporation owns 10 percent or more of a

---

3 § 1(h)(11)(A).

4 § 1(h)(11)(B)(i)(II) and (iii).

5 § 1(h)(11)(C)(i), (ii) and (iii).

foreign corporation[6] and receives a dividend from that foreign corporation, then section 245A provides a domestic corporate shareholder with a 100 percent foreign dividends received deduction with respect to the foreign source portion of the dividend[7] as long as the applicable holding period requirements[8] are met and the foreign corporation is not a passive foreign investment company.[9] The effect of claiming a 100 percent foreign dividends received deduction for the foreign source portion of a foreign dividend is that the U.S. taxation over that foreign dividend is effectively eliminated. Because the 100 percent foreign dividends received deduction effectively eliminates any residual U.S. taxation with respect to repatriation of the foreign earnings back to the domestic corporate shareholder, international double taxation is avoided with respect to the repatriation of the foreign corporation's earnings eligible for this foreign dividends received deduction. To obviate the possibility of a double tax benefit, section 245A(d)(1) disallows the foreign tax credit with respect to foreign earnings that are eligible for the 100 percent foreign dividends received deduction. Again, as might be expected, favorable nontaxation of foreign dividends to a domestic corporate shareholder is subject to restrictions that will be addressed in chapters 11 and chapter 12. Moreover, if a foreign corporation is more than 50 percent owned by U.S. shareholders, it is a foreign controlled corporation and its earnings will be subjected to immediate U.S. taxation on all its net earnings from all CFCs. If the foreign corporation is not a controlled foreign corporation, then the anti-deferral regimes are more targeted in their application. If the earnings of the foreign corporation are immediately taxable to a domestic corporate shareholder under one of the anti-deferral regimes (addressed in more detail in chapters 11 and 12), then the ability to claim a dividends received deduction is lost. Nevertheless, as with individuals, it is helpful to understand the above general framework before one approaches the nuances of the anti-deferral regimes and the foreign tax credit regimes in greater detail.

3. Controlled Foreign Corporations

The general rules set forth above provide specialized treatment with respect to income earned in a foreign corporation regardless of whether that U.S. shareholder is a domestic corporate shareholder or a U.S. individual. In its treatment of foreign corporations, the U.S. tax system makes a central distinction between foreign corporations

---

[6] The detailed rules for determining the 10-percent ownership threshold and the attribution rules of section 245(A)(b)(1) incorporate the standards for determining ownership under section 951(b).

[7] § 245A(a).

[8] § 246(c)(5).

[9] § 245A(b)(2).

dominantly owned or controlled by United States persons versus foreign corporations in which United States persons hold lesser interests. Foreign corporations actually controlled by U.S. shareholders are known as "controlled foreign corporations" (or "CFCs") and fall under a tax regime quite different from domestic corporations or wholly foreign corporations. The foreign operations of CFCs are often subjected to immediate taxation to the U.S. shareholders, but the actual amount of such taxation can mitigated by foreign tax credit relief or may otherwise be subjected to a preferential tax rate. A narrowly defined type of passive income of foreign corporations that are *not* CFCs is also subject to current U.S. taxation.

When the earnings of a controlled foreign corporation create an immediate income inclusion to the U.S. shareholder under one of the anti-deferral regimes, then the provisions of those anti-deferral regimes work to limit the extent of international double taxation. Thus, the critical first issue is to determine the application of these anti-deferral regimes, as that analysis sets out the framework for when the general rules mentioned above are supplanted and when they are not.

4. The Entity Question: Check-the-Box Election, Per Se Entities, and Default Rules

Because foreign operations conducted by a U.S. person through a separately chartered corporation may be taxed much differently from direct branch operations or partnership operations, an important threshold question is the characterization of entities, foreign and domestic, for tax purposes. Many readers have no doubt already encountered this question—known as entity classification—in other tax and business courses.

To compress a half-century of prior law into a paragraph, an organization, even if it was not possessed of an official corporate charter, would be taxed as a corporation if it displayed a preponderance of corporate characteristics (the essential characteristics being limited liability, unlimited life, centralization of management, and free transferability of interests). Conversely, an organization or association (even if ostensibly a corporate entity) was treated as a "fiscally transparent" form of ownership[10] if it lacked a preponderance of corporate characteristics. By this standard, virtually all regularly chartered corporations were taxed as such,

---

[10] By a "fiscally transparent" entity I mean a form of ownership where the income and losses of the organization flow through to the owners, who may be direct proprietors or partners. Fiscal transparency is sometimes called "flow-through" or "pass-through" taxation.

while many limited partnerships, even though registered under state law, were acknowledged as flow-through entities.

This standard, while never easy, was especially hard to apply to foreign entities with features that do not line up perfectly with those of entities organized in the United States. In addition to the standard, full-bore corporation, there exist in many countries a variety of limited-liability organizations, including SARLs, GmBHs, and Limitadas, which have some but not all of the classical corporate characteristics. In the old regime, taxpayers and the Treasury doggedly scoured these forms of organization, one by one, to determine the balance of their corporate characteristics. The emergence of limited liability companies (LLCs) in the United States during the past two decades brought the problem home.

In 1996, the Treasury swept away the tangle in one stroke when it issued regulations permitting a "check-the-box" election for the tax characterization of a broad class of entities by their owners.[11] The "check-the-box" regulations have fundamentally changed the landmarks of entity classification.[12] Shortly afterwards, it was quipped that the elective U.S. entity classification and the opportunities for hybrid mismatches that it created served as the greatest tax-planning development since the invention of numbers.[13]

The determination of an entity's tax status entails slightly more than just checking a box. There is no unqualified election for all entities. In order to elect (or more colloquially "check the box"), an entity must first establish its character as a separate entity,[14] and then it must fall within a group that is eligible to choose its own tax status. At several stages, the rules differ somewhat for domestic and foreign-chartered entities.

Once identified as separate, a business entity with two or more owners is classified for tax purposes as either a "corporation" or a "partnership."[15] A separate entity with a single owner is either a corporation or is "disregarded" for tax purposes.[16] To be "disregarded" means to be "treated in the same manner as a sole proprietorship, branch, or division of the owner."[17] For several types of single-owner

---

[11] These regulations are codified in Reg. § 301.7701.

[12] It is important to bear in mind, however, that *publicly traded* partnerships are taxed across the board as corporations, without election, by virtue of section 7704.

[13] The complexities that these mismatches create increasing policy challenges for the Treasury Department and augur against the wisdom of such a regime. See Bret Wells, *U.S. International Taxation; A Matter of Taxpayer Election?*, 24 HOUS. BUS. & TAX L.J. 195 (2022).

[14] Reg. § 301.7701–1(a)(1).

[15] Reg. § 301.7701–2(a).

[16] Id.

[17] Id.

and multiple-owner entities, the classification at this stage is elective (which is what I mean by "checking the box").[18]

Several types of separate entities, however, are automatically classified as corporations regardless of the number of owners. These include entities specifically denoted as "corporations," "joint-stock companies," "insurance companies," and "banks" chartered by the states or the United States.[19] Also included is a long list of foreign-chartered entities analogous to business corporations under U.S. law. These include the classic Inc.s (Corporation), S.A.s (Sociedad Anonima or Sociêté Anonyme), A.G.s (Aktiengesellschaft), SRSFs (San Ren Sei Fuseki), KKs (Kabushiki Kaisha), NVs (Naamloze Vennootschap), PLCs (Public Limited Company), and others that are the basic forms of state-chartered business corporations around the world.[20]

An entity that escapes classification as a corporation under this per se rule "can elect its classification for federal tax purposes."[21] Eligible entities include partnerships, limited partnerships, joint ventures, LLCs, GmbHs, SARLs, Limitadas, and many more. An entity with at least two members can elect to be classified as either a corporation or a partnership. An entity with a single owner can elect to be classified as a corporation or to be disregarded as an entity altogether.[22] This is the election that known and loved as "check-the-box."

If an eligible entity fails to make an election, there are default rules. When a *domestic* business entity fails to elect its tax status, it is classified by default as a partnership if it has two or more members and disregarded as an entity if it has a single owner.[23] An eligible *foreign* entity that fails to elect is treated 1) as a partnership if it has two or more members and any member has unlimited liability, 2) as a corporation if no member has unlimited liability, or 3) disregarded as an entity if it has a single owner with unlimited liability.[24]

5. The Resulting Hybrid Entity Implications

The electivity afforded by the check-the-box election regime provides significant deference to taxpayers in choosing whether to treat an entity as a corporation, a partnership, or a disregarded entity. This flexibility, in turn, provides the opportunity for taxpayers

---

18 Reg. § 301.7701–3(a).

19 Reg. § 301.7701–2(b)(1)–(7).

20 Reg. § 301.7701–2(b)(8)(i).

21 Reg. § 301.7701–3(a).

22 Id.

23 Reg. § 301.7701–3(b)(1).

24 Reg. § 301.7701–3(b)(2)(i).

to create entities that are regarded as one form of entity in the foreign jurisdiction and as a different form of entity in the United States. Again, in the following materials, I will refer to hybrid entities as along the following two fundamental lines:

This diagram denotes an entity that will be treated as a foreign branch (or disregarded entity) for U.S. tax purposes but is treated as a corporation (a separate entity) by the relevant foreign jurisdiction. This entity is also called a "hybrid entity."

This diagram denotes an entity that will be treated as a foreign corporation for U.S. tax purposes but is treated as a partnership or disregarded entity by the relevant foreign jurisdiction. This entity is called a "reverse hybrid entity."

Affording taxpayers with the flexibility to create hybrid entities and reverse hybrid entities (that is, entities treated differently in two different jurisdictions) provides opportunities for taxpayers to create mismatches between taxing jurisdictions that can allow income to escape taxation. Congress has become concerned about the use of hybrid entities and reverse hybrid entities and thus to an increasing extent has made the U.S. domestic law and U.S. tax treaty provisions contingent on whether an entity is a hybrid entity or a reverse hybrid entity and/or on whether the transaction with the entity is treated in an inconsistent manner between the two jurisdictions. On one level, this effort to condition a favorable U.S. tax concession on the consistent treatment of that income in the other jurisdiction makes sense. If the U.S. is deferring taxation over income under the assumption that the other jurisdiction has a stronger or more compelling right to tax that income, then that underlying assumption presupposes in some sense that the other jurisdiction will in fact seek to tax that income. If the other jurisdiction does not act to tax the income, either in law or in fact, then this scenario calls into question the wisdom of the original premise behind the initial favorable U.S. tax concession. Thus, in order to attack the perceived evils of tax arbitrage transactions, Congress increasingly has made a U.S. domestic law and/or tax treaty concession contingent on how the other jurisdiction will treat the transaction. However, conditioning a U.S. tax concession on how another jurisdiction will treat a transaction creates complexity in analyzing the U.S. tax results, particularly if the U.S. tax advisor is not conversant with the tax laws of the other relevant jurisdiction.

Chapter 10

DIRECT FOREIGN INVESTMENT: THE FOREIGN TAX CREDIT REGIME

A. Background and Overview

The foreign tax credit (or "FTC") regime is a unilateral measure adopted by the U.S. tax system. On the surface at least, the U.S. tax system asks nothing from foreign treasuries in return for the credit. In fact, the foreign tax credit is virtually a necessary concomitant of the U.S. system of taxing the worldwide incomes of citizens and residents. Countries that impose tax only territorially (that is, solely on income from sources within their boundaries) make a similar concession to the taxing power of other nations simply by not extending their own.

The foreign tax credit rests on a simple idea: income taxes paid to the U.S. Treasury are reduced (credited, in tax argot) by the amount of foreign income taxes paid by U.S. persons to foreign governments. The result is that in combination a single level of income taxation is achieved (and double taxation is avoided) through the mechanism of a credit for income taxes paid in the host jurisdiction.

If you have not yet mastered the difference between a tax credit and a deduction, now is the time to do so. A credit is a dollar-for-dollar reduction of U.S. income tax by the amount credited. The tax saving from a credit is therefore the exact amount of the credit itself. If, for example, the U.S. and foreign income tax rates were both 50 percent, there would be a foreign tax of 50 cents on a dollar of foreign source income. The U.S. tax on the foreign income—pre-credit—would also be 50 cents (U.S. tax is worldwide, remember) but would be fully offset by a 50-cent credit for the foreign income tax. The tax ultimately paid to the U.S. Treasury on foreign source income would therefore be zero, and the taxpayer's overall effective tax rate on this income would be 50 percent, the same rate paid on income derived by a U.S. person entirely within the U.S. environment. International double taxation of income is thus avoided by the allowance of a foreign tax credit.

In contrast, a deduction is a reduction of taxable income by the amount of a given outlay and reduces tax at the marginal rate of taxation otherwise applicable to the amount deducted. The tax saving from a deduction is the amount of tax that would otherwise have been imposed on the deducted amount. Deduction of the foreign tax in the example above would reduce taxable income by 50 cents, leaving 50 cents subject to U.S. taxation. After U.S. tax of 25 cents (at the 50 percent rate) the taxpayer would have 25 cents left over after payment of all taxes. When deducted (rather than credited) the payment of foreign income tax of 50 cents would reduce U.S. income tax by only 25 cents.[1] The taxpayer would end up paying tax (to two different countries) at an overall effective rate of 75 percent. This result violates the single taxation of income principle for income earned in these jurisdictions. For this reason, it is almost invariably preferable to credit an amount against taxes than to deduct it from taxable income.

1. Early History

Surprisingly, the earliest U.S. income tax laws provided no credit for foreign taxes. The only allowance for foreign income taxes in the 1913 Act was a deduction for taxes paid to foreign governments as a cost of doing business. One reason for the oversight could have been that income tax rates were quite low in the 1913 Act—the income tax then was hardly more than a nuisance—and income taxes were not widespread outside the United States. If a U.S. enterprise subject to a 1 percent income tax under the 1913 law was also subject to a 1 percent income tax on its foreign income, the total income tax burden (after deduction of the foreign income tax from U.S. taxable income) was 1.99 percent. While this is a large *relative* increase in the tax cost of foreign international operations—it nearly doubles because at low rates a deduction from foreign taxes produces only a small U.S. tax saving—in absolute terms the total tax is not painfully high.

With the sharp increases in income tax rates (both in the United States and abroad) and rapid growth of U.S. foreign trade during World War I, the problem of foreign income taxes became more pressing. By 1918, the top marginal rate of U.S. tax on income was 60 percent, and rates were similarly high in Europe. A U.S. firm doing business in the U.K. might be exposed there to income taxation of 50 percent. If the U.S. rate was the same, all that remained from, say, 100 of pre-tax U.K. source income (after deduction of the U.K. tax from U.S. taxable income) was 25.[2] The total combined income tax on foreign income was thus 75 percent, much higher than the tax imposed on the wholly domestic operations of a U.S. or U.K. firm.[3]

---

[1] At a 50-percent rate, a deduction of one dollar reduces income tax by fifty cents. At a 30-percent rate, by 30 cents, etc. Here, at a 50-percent rate, a deduction of 50 cents reduces income tax by 25 cents.

[2] Deduction of 50 of U.K. tax paid leaves 50 of taxable income subject to U.S. tax of 25 (at 50 percent), for a final after-tax income of 25.

[3] Note that in *relative* terms the double taxation is milder than in the example above with lower rates.

While there is some U.S. tax benefit from the deduction of U.K. tax, there remains a far heavier tax burden on foreign income compared to domestic.

This over-taxation of foreign income was an obvious deterrent to foreign commerce, and was remedied in the Revenue Act of 1918, which allowed a "credit" against U.S. income taxes for "income. . . taxes paid. . . to any foreign country."[4] From this modest kernel, a truly stultifying set of rules has arisen framing the foreign tax credit.

In the simple formulation of the 1918 Act the amount of the credit was unlimited up to the amount of U.S. tax. Every dollar of foreign income tax paid could displace a dollar otherwise paid to the U.S. Treasury. When foreign income taxes were higher than U.S. taxes, the credit could therefore do more than offset U.S. tax on foreign income; the credit could reduce the U.S. Treasury's tax on *U.S.* source income.

Suppose, for example, that in Year 1 the Fredonian income tax rate is 70 percent and the U.S. rate 50 percent. Suppose further that a U.S. person has 100 of Fredonian income and 100 of U.S. source income. Income tax paid to Fredonia is 70. Year 1 is summarized in Table #6 below. If credit is allowed against U.S. income tax for the full amount (70) paid to the Fredonian government (as was the case in the 1918 Act), the U.S. tax of 100 (pre-credit) is reduced to 30 by the foreign tax credit. The U.S. Treasury collects no tax on foreign source income and only 30 percent of the pre-credit tax on *U.S. source* income despite the basic 50 percent U.S. rate. Part of the U.S. tax otherwise payable on *U.S.* source income has been displaced by the credit. In this situation, the U.S. taxpayer is better off than under a regime of pure territorial taxation in which foreign source income and taxes are simply not taken into account.[5] In this regime, the effective overall rate of taxation of worldwide income paid to all governments is the U.S. effective rate, regardless of the foreign tax rate.

---

4 Revenue Act of 1918, ch. 18, § 222(a), 40 STAT. 1057 (Feb. 24, 1919).

5 If U.S. taxation were purely territorial, foreign income or loss would not enter into taxable income, and foreign income taxes would similarly be ignored. *U.S. source* income would be taxed at the regular U.S. rates, no matter what the results of foreign operations or foreign income taxes.

Table #6: No Section 904(a) Overall Limitation				
		(a)	(b)	c = a + b
		Fredonia	U.S.	Worldwide Total
1	Income	100	100	200
2	Foreign Taxes	70	0	
3	U.S. Income Tax (before FTC) (Assume 50% U.S. Tax Rate)			100
4	Foreign Taxes			70
5	U.S. Income Tax (after FTC)			30

2. Introducing the Credit Limitation: Defining Appropriate and Inappropriate Cross-Crediting

While this system has some merit as a matter of global efficiency,[6] it was unsatisfactory to the U.S. Treasury. Congress responded in 1921 with a limitation on the foreign tax credit. In the 1921 Act, the credit for foreign income taxes was limited to "the same proportion of the [U.S.] tax. . . which the taxpayer's. . . income. . . from sources without the United States. . . bears to his entire. . . income."[7] This exact language survives in today's Code[8] but embedded in a vastly more complex statutory architecture. The provision limits the credit to the amount of U.S. tax attributable to foreign source income.

Mechanically, the limitation turns on a fraction—the ratio of foreign source income to total income—multiplied by the U.S. tax (determined initially without regard for the credit). The limitation on the foreign tax credit can therefore be expressed as a three-factor formula consisting of the U.S. income tax (before credit) times the ratio of foreign source income to total worldwide income:

$$\text{Credit Limitation} = \text{U.S. Income Tax (Pre-Credit)} \times \frac{\text{Foreign Source Income}}{\text{Total Income}}$$

Another way of expressing the limitation is that the foreign tax credit cannot exceed the U.S. effective rate of tax on foreign source income. This is more readily apparent if the factors in the formula are rearranged. The credit limitation can be stated as foreign source

---

[6] The uniform tax cost of worldwide operations of U.S. persons under such a system is allocatively neutral—a good thing—but foreign governments have opportunities to tax U.S. persons strategically, at the expense of the U.S. Treasury.

[7] Revenue Act of 1921, ch. 136, § 222(a)(5), 42 STAT. 227 (Nov. 23, 1921).

[8] § 904(a).

income multiplied by the ratio of U.S. tax to total taxable income, as you can observe below:

$$\text{Credit Limitation} = \text{Foreign Source Income} \times \frac{\text{U.S. Income Tax}}{\text{Total Income}}$$

In this formulation, the fraction is U.S. income tax (pre-credit) expressed as a percentage of total income or, simply, the effective rate of U.S. income tax. The limitation thus states the amount of tax resulting from the imposition of the effective U.S. tax rate on foreign source income.

On seeing the limitation formula for the first time (and realizing, or being told, that it limits the foreign tax credit to the U.S. effective rate of income tax on foreign source income), some wonder why the Code itself does not adopt this formulation. In other words, why doesn't section 904 simply limit the credit to the U.S. effective rate of tax on foreign source income? In fact, the statutory formula sets out a necessary order of steps in determining the limitation. The difficulty with any other order results from the graduated U.S. tax rates. With a graduated rate schedule, there is no self-revealing effective U.S. rate. Since different rates apply to different segments of income, you don't know the effective rate of U.S. income tax until you have calculated the tax and stated it as a percentage of taxable income.

The first determination must therefore be the pre-credit U.S. income tax. The limitation formula then gives you the amount of U.S. tax imposed on foreign source income. This implies a necessary order of steps to follow in determining the credit limitation. First, compute the U.S. income tax on worldwide income without regard for the credit. Second, determine the ratio of foreign source income to worldwide income (the "limitation fraction"). Third, multiply the U.S. tax (pre-credit, remember) by the limitation fraction. The result is the limitation on the foreign tax credit. These steps are equivalent to determining the U.S. tax attributable to foreign source income (or applying the effective rate of U.S. tax to foreign source income). Any other order, however, leaves greater room for error. When we get to the separate FTC limitation baskets, things will get far more complicated, but these steps will remain the basic drill that you should follow in determining the credit limitation.[9]

3. Effect of the Limitation

The limitation is just that. It does not determine how much credit will be allowed, which depends initially on how much foreign

---

[9] You will follow these steps within separate categories of income, however.

tax is paid, but sets a ceiling that the credit cannot exceed. When the foreign income tax rate is lower than the U.S. rate, foreign income taxes can be credited in full, within the limitation, and the U.S. Treasury will collect a balance that is the excess of the U.S. rate over the foreign rate. The upshot of the credit coupled with the limitation is that the effective rate of tax on the foreign source income of a United States person is the higher of the U.S. or the foreign rate.

With the limitation in place, the situation in Table #7, where foreign income taxes are higher than U.S. taxes, comes out differently. The limitation prevents any reduction of U.S. taxation of U.S. source income, as shown in Table #7. Under the 1921 formula, the limitation on the foreign tax credit is 50, determined as follows. U.S. tax pre-credit is 100 (50 percent of worldwide income of 200). The limitation fraction (the ratio of foreign source income to worldwide income) is 100/200, or 1/2. The credit limitation is therefore: 100 × 1/2 = 50. Of the tax of 70 paid to Fredonia only 50 can be credited. The U.S. Treasury therefore collects 50. Now the burden of the higher foreign income taxes falls on the taxpayer rather the U.S. Treasury, which collects a tax equal to the full effective rate applied to U.S. source income.

Table #7: No Section 904(a) Overall Limitation				
		(a)	(b)	c = a + b
		Fredonia	U.S.	Worldwide Total
1	Income	100	100	200
2	Foreign Taxes	70	0	70
3	U.S. Income Tax (Before FTC) (Assume 50% U.S. Tax Rate)			100
4	Limitation on FTC (100 × 50%)			50
5	U.S. Income Tax (after FTC)			50
6	Excess FTC (L2 – L5)			20

You may remember from chapter 1 (in the vignette of the contract in Kuwait) the assertion that the foreign tax credit is allowed only for foreign taxes imposed on foreign source income. This, in fact, is not perfectly accurate. The Code no longer restricts the foreign tax credit (as it did in the 1918 Act) to foreign taxes imposed on foreign source income. The limitation on the foreign tax credit, however, has roughly the same effect, albeit as an indirect result of the limitation mechanism. The credit is limited by the ratio of foreign source income to total worldwide income. For a taxpayer who has suffered foreign tax on *U.S. source* income (and has no foreign source income), the numerator of this ratio is zero—so that the limitation on the credit is zero as well. A foreign tax imposed on U.S. source income therefore runs into a limitation of zero on the credit before the first penny has been credited. In practical effect, then, only foreign taxes on foreign source income can be credited.[10]

4. Excess Credits and Carryovers

The amount (i.e., 20 in L6 of the above Table #7) by which the Fredonian income tax of 70 exceeds the credit limitation of 50 (per L5 of the above Table #7) cannot be credited in the year paid but is not permanently lost as a foreign tax credit. As a general rule, the amount of foreign income tax above the credit limitation paid in any given year (sometimes known as an "excess credit") can, under section 904(c), be carried back to the previous taxable year and forward to the ten following taxable years. An excess credit carried back or forward to a given year is treated as though it were a creditable tax paid or accrued in that year and can therefore offset U.S. tax imposed on foreign source income in that year. As an exception to this general carryover rule, the last sentence in section 904(c) prevents any carryover with respect to any foreign taxes associated with net CFC tested income inclusions under section 951A. An analysis of the income inclusions under section 951A will be more fully addressed in chapter 11.

The limitation on the foreign tax credit also applies in the carryover year, of course. If there is no room for any more credit within the limitation in that year, the excess credit will carry over to the following year and so on until it is either credited or expires uselessly beyond the carryover period. There is in effect a 12-year window (the carryback year, the year of payment, and the 10 carryforward years) within which a foreign income tax can be credited. If foreign income tax rates fluctuate but are on average equal to or lower than U.S. rates over time, foreign income taxes may be credited in full within the limitation. Even with credit carryovers, however, if foreign income tax rates are persistently higher than U.S.

---

10 Note, however, that in the limitation there is no specific tracing of foreign taxes to income of any particular source. Rather, the limitation works as an aggregate. If a foreign country taxes a U.S. person's U.S. source income but does not tax the person's foreign source income, credit may be allowed for the foreign tax ostensibly imposed on U.S. source income. But that is so only because a foreign government has failed to tax foreign source income, and the untaxed foreign source income allows a sufficient limitation on the credit to build up to accommodate the foreign tax on U.S. source income. It would be more accurate to say that foreign taxes are creditable without regard for the source of the income on which they are imposed, but that in the absence of foreign source income, they are not creditable at all.

rates, excess credits will pile up and eventually expire unused, having provided no U.S. tax benefit.

Returning to our Fredonian situation, suppose that in Year 2 the Fredonian income tax rate falls to 30 percent while the taxpayer's income from all sources remains the same. The credit limitation in Year 2, as in Year 1, is 50 (100 of U.S. tax pre-credit multiplied by the limitation fraction of 1/2). The Fredonian income tax of 30 is well within the limitation and can be credited in full. If Year 2 were taxed in isolation, the U.S. Treasury would collect 70 (the pre-credit U.S. tax minus 30 of Fredonian income tax). The excess credit of 20 from Year 1 is carried forward, however, and treated as a foreign income tax paid in Year 2.[11] The 30 of Fredonian tax actually paid and the carryover of 20 from Year 1 add up to a foreign tax of 50 treated as paid in Year 2. This amount is just within the credit limitation and creditable in full. The U.S. Treasury collects 50, as demonstrated in the below Table #8.

Table #8: No Section 904(a) Overall Limitation with Carryover

		(a)	(b)	c = a + b
		Fredonia	U.S.	Worldwide Total
1	Income	100	100	200
2	Foreign Taxes	30	0	30
3	U.S. Income Tax (before FTC) (Assume 50% U.S. Tax Rate)			100
4	Limitation on FTC (100 × 50%)			50
5	U.S. Income Tax (after FTC)			50
6	Current Year FTC (see L2)			30
7	Carryforward FTCs (see L6 of Table #7)			20

If we combine the two years as a single tax period, the average rate of Fredonian tax is 50 percent and all Fredonian income tax paid in the period is credited.[12] The limitation-with-carryover system is

[11] I have made the simplifying assumption that Year 1 is also the first year of operations, so that no credit carryback is available.

[12] If the Fredonian income tax rate fell only to 50 percent in Year 2, the credit carryover could not be credited in that year because the credit limitation would then just accommodate the Fredonian income tax of 50. The Year 1 excess credit would then carry over undiminished to Year 3. If the Fredonian income tax rate and the U.S. rate remain at 50 percent thereafter, the Year 1 excess credit will carry forward from year to year uncredited until it expires after Year 11.

roughly similar to combining a block of 12 years as a single period for allowing the foreign tax credit.

5. "Overall" and "Per-Country" Limitations

The limitation is the central technical rule of the foreign tax credit. The basic mechanism of the 1921 limitation survives in the Code today (in section 904(a)) and is still discernible through effusive statutory overlays. Its present form is a compromise of currents that have run through the foreign tax credit for more than a century. In the 1921 Act, the limitation was based on the taxpayer's overall foreign income, and that form of the limitation is hence known as the "overall" limitation. At other times, the limitation has been computed separately on the basis of the income and the taxes arising in each foreign country. In that form, it was called the "per-country" limitation and limited the credit for income taxes paid in *each* foreign country to the same proportion of U.S. tax (pre-credit) that the income from that country bore to total income. The fraction underlying the per-country limitation for each country is income from sources *within that country* over total income. In other words, the per-country limitation limited the credit for taxes paid to each country to the effective rate of U.S. tax on income from sources within that country. With the per-country limitation, there were as many separately computed limitations as there were separate countries from which a U.S. taxpayer derived income.

Although the per-country limitation has been repealed and the original overall limitation modified extensively, these methods warrant attention here in their basic form. It is difficult to understand the mechanics of the present limitation (which, it turns out, is an elaboration of the overall limitation) without some sense of the different effects of the overall and per-country limitations. In the overall limitation, the rest of the world is treated as a single taxing sovereign. All foreign results—gains, losses, and income taxes—are homogenized to arrive at a single limitation, by which credit for the aggregate of foreign income taxes is bounded. The per-country limitation, by contrast, requires a discrete reckoning for each foreign country. To illustrate the different forms of limitation, assume the existence of the following operations in three foreign countries of a United States person that also has U.S. operations. Assume further (for arithmetic simplicity) that all three foreign countries impose a 50 percent income tax and that the U.S. effective income tax rate is also 50 percent. Here, the taxpayer has worldwide income of 200[13] and has paid foreign income tax totaling 100 (50 each to France and the U.K.). The limitation determined under the "overall" formula of

[13] This is the sum of gains of 100 each from the U.K., the U.S., and France (or 300) minus a loss of 100 from Denmark.

the 1921 Act is 50.[14] Therefore, only 50 of the foreign tax of 100 paid can be credited against U.S. tax.[15]

Table #9: Per Country Limitation					
		France	U.K.	Denmark	U.S.
1	Income	100	100	(100)	100
2	Foreign Taxes	50	50	0	0

Under the per-country limitation, there are separate limitations of 50 each for the United Kingdom and France[16] while the limitation for Denmark is zero.[17] Foreign income taxes paid are thus creditable in full,[18] and the U.S. Treasury collects nothing.[19]

You might conclude from this example that the per-country limitation, which preserves full credit for foreign income taxes, was more favorable to taxpayers. The particular combination of foreign income, losses, and taxes in this case seems plausible if not realistic. Consider, however, a different U.S. taxpayer with different foreign operations. Here, a U.S. person pays a 90 percent income tax to Kuwait and a 10 percent income tax in the Bahamas. Under the overall limitation, the amount of foreign income tax paid (100 in total, consisting of 90 paid to Kuwait and 10 paid to the Bahamas) is credited in full. As depicted in the below Table #10.[20]

---

[14] The U.S. tax pre-credit is 100. Overall *foreign* source income adds up to 100 (gains of 100 each from the U.K. and France, minus a loss of 100 from Denmark). The limitation fraction is therefore 100/200 or 1/2.

[15] The additional 50 of foreign tax can be carried back or forward to other years, and possibly credited then.

[16] The separate limitation fraction for the U.K. is 1/2 (U.K. income of 100 over worldwide income of 200). The U.S. tax pre-credit (100) multiplied by this fraction gives a limitation of 50. The computation for France is the same.

[17] For Denmark the limitation is zero because Danish source income in the numerator of the limitation fraction is zero.

[18] Income taxes paid both to France (50) and the U.K. (50) are fully offset by a credit within the respective country limitation (50 in each case).

[19] The differences in the two forms of credit limitation reflect, among other things, the different effect of losses. Under the overall limitation, the loss in Denmark reduces total foreign source income and, therefore, the limitation and credit. Under the per-country limitation, U.K.-source and French source incomes are not reduced by Danish losses, which reduce total taxable income but not the credit for taxes paid to other countries.

[20] U.S. tax pre-credit is 150 (50 percent of worldwide income of 300). The limitation fraction is 2/3 (200 of foreign source income over 300 of total income). The limitation is therefore 100 (150 × 2/3), which accommodates the entire foreign income tax paid.

Table #10: No Section 904(a) Overall Limitation (Cross-crediting)				
		Kuwait	Bahamas	US
1	Income	100	100	100
2	Foreign Taxes	90	10	0

Under the per-country limitation, only 60 of the foreign income tax paid can be credited. The separate limitations for Kuwait and the Bahamas would each be 50.[21] That allows full credit for the Bahamas tax with room to spare. Credit for Kuwait's tax of 90, however, would be limited to 50. The taxpayer will therefore pay income tax of 90 to the U.S. Treasury.[22] The uncredited 40 of Kuwaiti tax could be carried back and forward as an excess Kuwaiti tax but will almost surely run into the separate limitation for Kuwait in other years unless there is a drastic change in Kuwait's tax system. Meanwhile, the overabundant separate limitation for the Bahamas is useless as long as Bahamian income tax remains very low.

It is important to understand the difference between these two forms of the limitation. In the overall limitation, all foreign income and foreign income taxes are lumped together. As a result, the taxpayer can credit the very high taxes paid to Kuwait against U.S. income tax attributable to low-taxed Bahamian income. This is known as "cross-crediting." Here, foreign tax imposed at higher-than-U.S. rates is credited against U.S. income tax that would otherwise be imposed on low-taxed foreign source income. The possibility of cross-crediting mitigates the effect of the limitation, which was adopted, at least in part, to prevent full credits for higher-than-U.S. taxes. With the per-country limitation, there is no cross-crediting between income taxes of different foreign countries. Low-taxed foreign income cannot soak up high income taxes paid to another foreign country by enlarging the available credit limitation.

6. Stakes Involved in the Foreign Tax Credit Limitation Regimes

The example with Kuwait and the Bahamas may strike you as thoroughly contrived upon first encounter. What kind of U.S. taxpayer would have such far flung and disparate foreign operations? But it is in fact entirely realistic. This explains the perennial incentive of U.S. taxpayers with high-taxed foreign income to create

---

21 U.S. tax pre-credit is still 150. The ratio of Kuwait-source (and Bahamas-source) income to total income is 1/3 (100/300) each. The limitation for each country is therefore 150 × 1/3 = 50.

22 There is a credit of 10 for Bahamas tax and 50 for Kuwaiti tax against the precredit U.S. tax of 150.

or "find" enough low-taxed foreign source income to preserve credits for the foreign taxes through an enlarged limitation. The restructuring of the credit limitation in the 1986 Act brought severe, but not invariably fatal, restrictions on this possibility. The 2017 Act revived a considerable part of the possibilities of cross-crediting, and the 2025 Act allows significant cross-crediting particularly within the section 951A basket. Before contending with the nuts and bolts of the foreign tax credit and its limitation in its present form, we will first make a side trip through the question of creditable foreign income taxes.

B. The Foreign Tax Credit: Creditable Foreign Taxes[23]

The foreign tax credit is allowed for foreign "income. . . taxes."[24] While the mechanics of the credit are piled high with statutory detail, on the question of creditable taxes, the Code says little beyond those two words. We must look elsewhere to determine what is a "tax" and when it is imposed on "income." Although the former question is conceptually prior—something has to be a tax before it can be an income tax—it barely surfaced in case law and rulings until the 1970s. In the early years, the dominant question on creditable taxes was whether a foreign tax was imposed on "income." To frame your thoughts on these questions, read the following story.

1. Your Vacation in Canada

Suppose you are taking a vacation by automobile in Canada. You come upon a sign that says, "Maple Leaf Berry Farm. Pick Your Own Blueberries. $2 a Pound." You spend a few hours picking blueberries. As you leave the farm, your berries are weighed, and you pay the specified amount. A day or two later, you come upon a government-owned national park with a sign saying "Royal Canadian Berry Park. Pick Your Own Blueberries. Free." You drive in and pick up a storm. As you are leaving the park with your haul, a Canadian Mountie directs you to a sign that says "Income Tax Station. Weigh Your Berries Here." You say, "But the berries are free, why should I have to weigh them?" The Mountie answers, "Free they are, but we have to weigh them in order to value them and compute your Canadian income tax." The Mountie explains that the value of the berries is taxable income to you. The Canadian government seeks not to be paid

---

[23] For a more detailed discussion of one author's view of the evolution of the foreign tax credit eligibility standards, see Bret Wells, *The Foreign Tax Credit War*, 2016 BYU L. REV. 1895 (2016). For more detail on the other co-author's views, see Joseph Isenbergh, *The Foreign Tax Credit: Royalties, Subsidies, and Creditable Taxes*, 39 TAX L. REV. 227 (1984).

[24] § 901(b)(1).

for the blueberries you gathered from its land[25] but to collect an income tax on your economic gain. You have expended your labor to create a tangible consumable product. Because you have no recoverable basis in your labor, the full return is taxable gain. On reflection you realize that, although the U.S. income tax does not typically reach self-gathered fruit, the Canadian government's claim is sound from first principles. You have derived from your labor an accretion to wealth which is taxable compensation within an idealized income tax. The Canadian tax system is truer to the notion of income on this point than the U.S. system, so you pay the Canadian income tax and move on.

Embedded in this homely vignette are the essential questions concerning creditable foreign income taxes. These are 1) whether a payment made to a foreign government is indeed a "tax" and 2) if so, whether it is imposed on "income." The former, somewhat amplified, is the threshold question whether the relationship between the taxpayer and the foreign government is one that gives rise to a tax at all. When there is an extensive course of economic dealing between a taxpayer and a foreign government, ostensible taxes are hard to disentangle from an overall contractual relationship in which consideration changes hands, in the form of rents or royalties for benefits received by the taxpayer. In order for your payment to be regarded as fully a "tax," the Canadian government must be deemed to have foregone any return from its ownership of berry bearing lands. Conversely, if your payment is recast as some sort of proprietor's "rent" to the Canadian government, then Canada has abstained to exercise its taxing power. Judging by Canada's express assertion (the berries are "free," but it is imposing "tax") the former has occurred, but the situation ultimately is indeterminate.[26] If the return is satisfactory in amount to the Canadian government, to call it a proprietary crop share or a tax is a matter of indifference.

Essentially the same questions—with amounts at stake multiplied by a hundred billion or so—have arisen in connection with the operations of the U.S. international oil industry. In most oil-exporting countries (including all the OPEC countries), mineral resources are owned exclusively by the state. U.S. oil companies engaged in oil exploration and development in these countries extract oil that in the first instance is owned by the state. They are compensated, often, with a share of the oil that they recover from the

---

25 The Mountie adds: "They are indeed beautiful berries, but I come to seize your berry, not to praise it."

26 Suppose the sign outside the national park read: "Pick Your Own Blueberries. Tax Free. Pay Only the Posted Price." Suppose further that the posted price was a percentage of the value of the berries equal to the Canadian federal income tax on that amount of income.

ground while the state keeps the balance. The companies are also subject to "income tax" in most oil-exporting countries. Determining which parts of the huge amounts that pass from U.S. oil companies to foreign governments are, respectively, owners' "royalties" and true income taxes has been *the* epicenter for determining what portion of a payment to a foreign government is in fact a tax payment.

2. Is a Foreign Tax an "Income" Tax?

As noted above, this was the dominant question on creditable taxes until the 1970s. The early case law, which involved small-scale transactions, was accommodating to taxpayers. In a pair of cases in the 1920s, the Board of Tax Appeals (the predecessor of the Tax Court) took an expansive view of creditable foreign "income" taxes. In *Keen v. Commissioner,*[27] the Board allowed credit for a French tax imposed on a tax base equal to a multiple of the estimated rental value of a residence maintained in France by a U.S. citizen. In *Burk Brothers v. Commissioner,*[28] the Board found creditable a tax imposed by India on the export of animal hides based on the value of the hides and reduced by the relevant costs. In these cases, the Board of Tax Appeals required neither a tax base corresponding precisely to U.S. notions of net income nor an event of realization of the sort extolled in *Eisner v. Macomber.*[29]

Biddle and *Bank of America.* The Supreme Court gave the IRS a potent counter-weapon in two sentences of dictum in *Biddle v. Commissioner.*[30] In *Biddle,* in the course of deciding whether a U.S. shareholder of a British corporation subject to an integrated British corporate tax could be treated as having "paid" the taxes imposed on the corporation, the Court threw in the following thought as to what constitutes an income tax:

> 'Income taxes paid,' as used in our own revenue laws, has for most practical purposes a well understood meaning to be derived from an examination of the statutes which provide for the laying and collection of income taxes. It is that meaning which must be attributed to it.[31]

The Treasury embraced this dictum language in *Biddle* as scriptural.[32] Since *Biddle,* the standard for a creditable tax has been

---

27 15 B.T.A. 1243 (1929), *nonacq.*

28 20 B.T.A. 657 (1930), *nonacq.*

29 252 U.S. 189 (1920).

30 302 U.S. 573 (1938).

31 Id. at 579.

32 For those of you who remember your law school course in the legal process, let me point out that the Court's statement is mere *dictum* on the question of the nature of *income* taxes. The Court was deciding whether the British tax had been *paid*

an income tax within U.S. tax notions as epitomized by the Internal Revenue Code.

The *Biddle* dictum states rather than resolves the problem. The Code being as it is, both vast and byzantine, the contours of an "income tax" don't exactly jump off the page. With only a few exceptions,[33] however, the U.S. income tax is imposed on realized net gain. Accordingly, two questions run through the decided cases. Does the foreign tax at issue fall on "net" income (rather than gross), and is it triggered by an event of "realization"?

In working out these U.S. principles,[34] early cases and IRS rulings had held that taxes levied on "imputed income" could be eligible for U.S. foreign tax credit relief if net income is what was attempted to be taxed and was so taxed.[35] In general, these cases and early IRS rulings took an expansive view of credit eligibility, allowing considerable latitude to the foreign country to define the manner in which a formulary tax arrived at the net income it intended to tax.[36] Thus, although the diversity of foreign taxes made the pre-1983 case law inconsistent at the outer edges, the substantive law was one that was based on a principle-based approach: if the foreign tax was designed to tax net income and did in fact tax net income in practice, then U.S. foreign tax credit relief was appropriate in order to prevent international double income taxation.

(the focus of its actual *holding)* within the meaning of U.S. tax laws, not whether the tax was imposed on "income."

[33] Consider, for example, the U.S. flat rate tax on the *gross* amount of U.S. source fixed or determinable income.

[34] Some have called for a broader allowance of creditability of taxes beyond foreign income taxes. See Joseph Isenbergh, *The Foreign Tax Credit: Royalties, Subsidies, and Creditable Taxes,* 39 TAX L. REV. 227, 230–31 (1984).

[35] See Keen v. Commissioner, 15 B.T.A. 1243 (1929) (a tax on presumed income was calculated on nondomiciled persons who maintained a residence in France; income was presumed to be a minimum of seven times the rental value of their residence; held, French tax was an income tax eligible for U.S. foreign tax credit relief); Hatmaker v. Commissioner, 15 B.T.A. 1044 (1929) (same); Burk Brothers v. Commissioner, 20 B.T.A. 657 (1930) (Indian tax on goat skins was calculated based on the difference between the average sales price of goat skins in their destination from the average sales price in Calcutta and reduced by certain transportation expenses; held, the presumptive tax was an income tax entitled to U.S. foreign tax credit relief); Rev. Rul. 53–272, 193–2 Cum. Bull. 56 (a Haitian tax was imposed on business income computed by multiplying the rental value of the land and buildings by five and assessing an income tax on this imputed income; IRS held this was an attempt to tax presumed income and was eligible for U.S. foreign tax credit relief); Rev. Rul. 56–658, 1956–2 Cum. Bull. 501 (Cuban tax on sugar mill operators assessed based on the amount of sugar produced times the average price for sugar and reduced by 60 percent for "deemed expenses;" held that this presumptive tax was creditable as an attempt to tax income).

[36] See ELISABETH OWENS, THE FOREIGN TAX CREDIT: A STUDY OF THE CREDIT FOR FOREIGN TAXES UNDER UNITED STATES INCOME TAX LAW 43–46 (1961).

An important articulation for how to harmonize these decisions came in *Bank of America v. United States*.[37] In the *Bank of America* case, the Court of Claims offered a formulation of the *Biddle* standard for creditable income taxes. At issue in *Bank of America* was credit for foreign taxes imposed on the gross income of a U.S. bank. The Court of Claims declared that the standard for determining foreign tax credit eligibility was as follows: "a direct income tax is creditable, even though imposed on gross income, if it is very highly likely, or was reasonably intended, always to reach some net gain in the normal circumstances in which it applies." This standard, known as the "*Bank of America* standard," operates within the constraints of *Biddle*, but it also countenances departures from strict conformity with U.S. norms and thus gives taxpayers a little breathing space. A tax can reach "some net gain" in the normal circumstances in which it applies without being strictly based on net "taxable" income as defined in the Internal Revenue Code.[38] Most commentators, in this light, understand the *Bank of America* standard to allow credit for some foreign taxes similar to the Code's flat rate tax on the gross amount of tax that applies on passive investment income subject to the fixed or determinable standard, and Treasury regulations now confirm this understanding.[39]

The first case on creditable taxes after *Bank of America* was *Inland Steel Co. v. United States*,[40] and it largely reasserts the same standard. *Inland Steel* concerns the creditability of an Ontario mining tax imposed on a tax base from which only operating expenses were allowed as deductions but not interest, depletion, royalty payments to private owners, or depreciation. The tax was imposed whether or not the ore produced by the taxpayer was sold. The Claims Court denied the allowance of a foreign tax credit on the following grounds:

> When the mass of the omitted items in the [Ontario tax] are considered together and in combination as applied to plaintiff's mining business, it is clear to us that tax does not seek to reach, or necessarily reach, any concept of net gain from the mining business which would be recognized as such in this country . . . . The exclusions are far too

---

37 459 F.2d 513, 519–520 (Ct. Cl. 1972).

38 Note, however, that all the taxes actually under review in *Bank of America* were held *not* to be creditable. These taxes were imposed on the gross income of enterprises engaged in active business. Because no deductions were allowed for the cost of producing the income, while the underlying business activity necessarily entailed expenses, the court concluded that the taxes would not predictably reach only net gain.

39 See Reg. § 1.901–2(b)(4)(C)(ii).

40 677 F.2d 72 (Ct. Cl. 1982).

> widespread and important to permit the conclusion that some net gain is sure to be reached.[41]

The *Bank of America* standard, as expressed in *Bank of America* and *Inland Steel*, thus looked at whether the foreign levy was likely to reach some amount of net gain. When that standard could not be met using U.S. principles, then the foreign tax was not considered to be an income tax in the U.S. sense.[42]

3. The Regulations on Creditable Taxes

The regulations on creditable foreign taxes under section 901 purport to be—and probably are—a comprehensive statement of doctrine. Their length certainly testifies to the tenacity of their drafters. It was understood at the time of their 1983 amendment that the Treasury Department's goal in making amendments at that time was to restrict the scope of eligible taxes that the prior case law had blessed. Much of the complexity since then is attributable to the Service's efforts to further restrict the scope of the foreign tax credit eligibility rules to outright disallow foreign tax credit relief for foreign taxes generated in "inappropriate transactions."[43] This later reformulation was and is a fundamentally different objective than the original goal of simply defining when a regime imposed an income tax. Of course, "inappropriate" is in the eye of the beholder, and so this further effort to reinvent the eligibility rules adds complexity and invites considerable dispute. It is in the midst of this reformulation of the Treasury Department's regulations in 1983 when *Bank of America* and *Inland Steel* would be afforded a remarkable profile. Even though the decisions in *Bank of America* and *Inland Steel* were themselves trial level decisions that were not reviewed by any circuit court, these cases obtained prominence in the preamble to the prior 1983 final regulations which lauded them as enlightened articulations of how U.S. principles should be applied.[44] The prior 1983 final regulations adopted the "predominant character standard" that was articulated in the *Bank of America* case, which in

---

[41] Id. at 85.

[42] The Tax Court endorsed and explained the *Bank of America* standard in Bank of Am. Nat'l Tr. and Sav. Ass'n v. Comm'r, 61 T.C. 752 (1974). In that case, the Tax Court explained the controlling standard in the following terms: "Perhaps the test which we and the Court of Claims have articulated will not provide that magic touchstone whereby every situation in this area can be precisely located in the spectrum of foreign taxes ranging from pure net income taxes on one end to pure excise, sales, or privilege taxes on the other. But we are convinced that the test is not 'manufactured out of whole cloth,' as petitioner would have us believe, and that it provides a rational and manageable basis for interpretation of section 901(b)(1)." See Bank of Am. Nat'l Tr. and Sav. Ass'n v. Comm'r, 61 T.C. 752, 762–63 (1974).

[43] The prior 1983 final regulations effort to impose more formality that goes beyond the *Bank of America* standard is addressed in further detail in Bret Wells, *The Foreign Tax Credit War*, 2016 BYU L. REV. 1895, 1960–1962 (2016).

[44] T.D. 7918, 48 FED. REG. 46,272, 42,273 (Oct. 12, 1983).

turn focused on whether or not a foreign levy reached some amount of net gain in the normal circumstances in which it applied, but then the prior 1983 final regulations grafted onto this *Bank of America* standard the requirement that a foreign levy must meet some familiar design hallmarks of the U.S. tax system (realization, gross receipts, and net income) in order to be eligible for foreign tax credit relief.[45]

In contrast, the 2022 final regulations repudiated the *Bank of America* standard. In its place, the 2022 final regulations require the foreign tax regime to utilize a foreign tax base that closely conforms to the tax base used in the United States determine the amount of net gain under U.S. law.[46] The preamble to the 2022 final regulations only cites *Bank of America* for the proposition that a foreign levy must provide cost recovery and not for its predominant character standard. And, the preamble to the 2022 final regulations only cites *Inland Steel* for the proposition that the foreign tax is determined to be an income tax or not based on principles of U.S. law. However, from this point onward, the 2022 final regulations eschew the reasoning of *Bank of America* and *Inland Steel* in favor of a more restrictive close conformity standard not found in the case law. The 2022 final regulations remove all reference to the "predominant character standard" applied in "normal circumstances." The case law that had articulated the use of U.S. principles had done so as part of its effort to determine whether or not a foreign levy attempted to reach some amount of net gain. Whether the amount of net gain corresponds to the same amount of net gain that the U.S. tax laws would have calculated was not the critical determinate historically, but now it is under the 2022 final regulations.

The impetus for the Treasury Department to amend its final regulations in 2022 was a desire to deny foreign tax credit relief for novel extraterritorial taxes such as digital services taxes, diverted profits taxes, or equalization levies. However, once that regulatory project was undertaken, the Treasury Department used it as the occasion to then add heightened close conformity requirements into its foreign tax credit eligibility standards. This aspect of the 2022 amendments to the final regulations have implications far beyond the articulated and announced core policy concern surrounding novel extraterritorial taxes that were the stated impetus for the 2022 regulatory reform effort.

The regulations start from the longstanding position of the Service that "a tax either is or is not an income tax, in its entirety,

---

[45] See Former Reg. § 1.901–2(b)(1) in T.D. 7918, 48 FED. REG. 46,272, 46,296 (Oct. 12, 1983).

[46] See Reg. § 1.901–2(b).

for all persons subject to the tax."[47] This means that it is insufficient for a taxpayer to demonstrate that a foreign tax in fact took a portion of the taxpayer's own net income. Taxpayers must show that a foreign tax functions as an income tax across the entire range of situations where it applies.

Once past the thresholds that what was levied was a "tax" and that this levied tax was "paid," the regulations proceed to define the contours of an "income" tax. A tax meets this standard if it is "a net income tax,"[48] and the regulations assert that the foreign levy is an income tax "only if the foreign tax meets the regulatory net gain requirement."[49] This standard is further resolved into requirements of realization, gross receipts, cost recovery, and attribution.[50] The regulations then state that a tax will meet the net gain requirement "if and only if" each of four formal requirements are met.[51]

First, the foreign levy must satisfy the realization requirement. "Realization" in these regulations includes all realization events under U.S. tax principles, as well as earlier and subsequent events used as occasions for reckoning gain or loss.[52] Realization for this purpose also includes a number of events prior to realization events in the U.S. sense, specifically: 1) the recovery or recapture of a previously allowed tax deduction or credit,[53] 2) increases or decreases in the value of property, and 3) the "physical transfer, processing, or export of readily marketable property" at any time, and 4) a pre-realization event related to a deemed distribution or deemed income inclusion.[54] The third rule accommodates foreign taxes triggered by the export of goods from the country of production.[55]

Second, there is the further requirement that the foreign tax base be predicated on actual "gross receipts."[56] If not imposed on actual "gross receipts," a foreign tax still passes muster under an alternative gross receipts test if and only if the deemed gross receipts results from a deemed realization event that meets the requirements

---

47 Reg. § 1.901–2(a)(1)(i).

48 Reg. § 1.901–2(a)(1)(ii).

49 Reg. § 1.901–2(a)(3). The contours of the net gain requirement is set forth in Reg. § 1.901–2(b).

50 Reg. § 1.901–2(b)(1) through (5).

51 Reg. § 1.901–2(b)(1).

52 Reg. § 1.901–2(b)(2)(i)(A).

53 Reg. § 1.901–2(b)(2)(i)(B).

54 Reg. § 1.901–2(b)(2)(i)(C).

55 Some countries tax gains from basic products (such as crude oil) when they physically leave the country. The alternative of waiting for a realization event in the U.S. sense (which in the case of a fully integrated oil company would be the sale of gasoline at the pump) is impractical.

56 Reg. § 1.901–2(b)(3)(i)(A). This aims principally at the compulsory use of artificial "posted prices" as an income tax base in some oil-exporting countries.

of Reg. § 1.901–2(b)(2) and the deemed gross receipts are reasonably calculated to produce an amount that is not greater than fair market value.[57] The existing regulations then sanction usage of "deemed gross receipts" only when they arise in an insignificant realization event or as part of a pre-realization timing or recapture event.[58] The existing regulations assert that a foreign tax imposed as a mark-up on costs (such as a tax imposed on a cost plus 5% basis)[59] fails to satisfy the formal gross receipts requirement. Juxtaposed against this portion of the regulations is a statement in the final regulations that a foreign law that purports to impose a tax on gross receipts but determines those gross receipts through a "simplified transfer pricing method" based on a mark-up on costs does satisfy the gross receipts test.[60] How this latter regulatory clarification is to be reconciled with the earlier restriction is left to the reader to discern. To this author, the import seems to be that foreign law must make some affirmative statement indicating that its use of a cost-plus methodology is a transfer pricing methodology applied to deemed gross receipts and not an attempt to adopt an alternative means of taxation other than gross receipts. If a taxpayer must determine the policy goals of the local law and not just its economic effect, then such an inquiry would appear to create subjective uncertainty in the application of these regulations.

Third, the regulations require the foreign levy to satisfy a cost recovery requirement. The "cost recovery" test is close to the core of the notion of a creditable income tax.[61] In *Inland Steel*[62] and *Bank of America*,[63] the foreign tax credit stood or fell on the possibility of cost recovery. However, the Treasury Department through its regulatory authority has attempted to restrict the scope of creditable taxes through the formulation of a cost recovery requirement that is more stringent than what the case law had required. In this regard, Reg. § 1.901–2(b)(4) provides that the regulatory formulation of the cost recovery requirement is satisfied only if the tax allows 1) the recovery of *all* significant costs and expenses (including capital outlays)

---

57 Reg. § 1.901–2(b)(3)(i)(B).

58 Reg. § 1.901–2(b)(3)(i)(B), (C) and (D).

59 Reg. § 1.901–2(b)(3)(ii)(A). The regulations make plain that a tax based on a posted price that exceeds the fair market value of the posted property is another instance where the gross receipts test is failed. See Reg. § 1.901–2(b)(3)(ii)(C). But, this aspect of the existing regulations is consistent with the outcome of the prior 1983 regulations. See former Reg. § 1.901–2(b)(3)(ii) Example 3 in T.D. 7918, 48 FED. REG. 46,272, 46,278 (Oct. 12, 1983). Thus, the area of significant change resides with respect to how a tax applied on incurred costs is treated under the gross receipts test.

60 Reg. § 1.901–2(b)(3)(ii)(B).

61 Cost recovery and the computation of "net gain" are of course definitionally correlated.

62 Inland Steel Co. v. United States, 677 F.2d 72 (Ct. Cl. 1982).

63 Bank of Americas v. United States, 459 F.2d 513, 519–520 (Ct. Cl. 1972).

attributable under reasonable principles to gross receipts, or 2) the recovery of costs and expenses computed under a method that approximates or exceeds the amount of actual costs and expenses. These tests are alternatives. A tax that meets either one is therefore treated as satisfying the cost recovery requirement. Furthermore, although foreign law can allow for a different period for cost recovery than is allowed under U.S. law, the cost recovery requirement is not met if the deferral of cost recovery effectively represents a denial of such recovery. Taken as a whole, the final regulations posit that an income tax in the U.S. sense must allow for a recovery of *all* significant business expenditures (or their economic equivalent) in some reasonable period unless there is a similar analogue to the disallowance provision under U.S. law. In addition, in the computation of the tax base, the foreign jurisdiction must utilize transfer pricing principles that comply with the arm's length standard without taking destination-based criterion (like customer location) into account.[64]

Given that a disallowance of any significant cost causes the foreign levy to fail as an income tax in the U.S. sense in its entirety, the determination of what costs are "significant" has profound importance. The regulations provide a general rule that the significance of a particular cost or expenditure is determined based on whether it constitutes a significant portion of the total costs and expenses of all taxpayers subject to the tax.[65] The existing regulations, however, then provide a list of "per se" significant costs and expenses. Included within that group of expenditures are the following: capital expenditures, interest, rents, royalties, wages or other payments for services, and research and experimentation expenditures.[66] Again, a disallowance of any significant expense would cause the entire foreign levy to be ineligible for foreign tax credit relief in its entirety.[67]

However, after articulating this seemingly absolute standard that *all* significant costs must be recovered, the regulations then provide that disallowance provisions that bear a family resemblance to disallowance provisions that exist in the U.S. tax laws do not cause the cost recovery requirement to be failed.[68] The final regulations state that a disallowance intended to limit base erosion or profit shifting represents an acceptable variation, but then the regulations take pains to provide only examples of base protection measures that

---

[64] Reg. § 1.901–2(b)(5)(ii).

[65] Reg. § 1.901–2(b)(4)(i)(C)(1).

[66] Reg. § 1.901–2(b)(4)(i)(C)(1).

[67] Each separate levy is separately tested as an all or nothing proposition. See Reg. § 1.901–2(d)(1).

[68] Reg. § 1.901–2(b)(4)(i)(C).

are found in existing U.S. tax law.[69] In this regard, a foreign tax is considered to permit recovery of significant costs and expenses if the foreign tax law limits interest deductions (an otherwise designated "per se" significant cost) so as not to exceed 30 percent of a reasonable measure of taxable income (determined either before or after depreciation and amortization) as such a regime is similar to section 163(j).[70] Moreover, a disallowance regime that disallows interest and royalty deductions in connection with hybrid transactions based on principles similar to those underlying section 267A is also an acceptable variation.[71] Finally, the disallowance of expenses based on public policy considerations similar to those disallowances contained in section 162 also represents an acceptable departure that does not run afoul of the net income requirement.[72] These examples set forth in the regulations represent a nonexhaustive list.[73]

This close conformity requirement raises as many questions as it answers. The U.S. tax laws are not static. This close conformity standard applies to the U.S. tax law as it exists year-by-year. Thus, a foreign tax that limits interest deductions in a manner similar to section 163(j) or that disallows royalty deductions in a manner similar to section 267A can deviate along those lines without running afoul of the "all significant costs" requirement because those deviations conform to how existing U.S. tax law deviates from the Plutonic ideal income tax.[74] However, even if a foreign jurisdiction did have a regime that closely conformed to the United States tax laws at some point in time, Congress or the foreign jurisdiction may amend their tax laws at any time thereafter. If one just focused on the United States, one could imagine very different tax laws depending on the political party that is in power. Thus, even if foreign tax law closely correlated to U.S. tax law at some point in time, it is an open question whether it would remain so over time or at least would remain so over all periods of time. The regulations, if literally applied, would require an annual exhaustive review of the current design of each country's tax laws on an annual basis because the question is not simply did the foreign jurisdiction assert taxation over some amount of net gain but rather did the foreign jurisdiction design its tax base in a manner that closely conforms to the U.S. tax laws in that particular year of comparison.

---

69 Reg. § 1.901–2(b)(4)(i)(C)(1).

70 Reg. § 1.901–2(b)(4)(i)(C)(1).

71 Reg. § 1.901–2(b)(4)(i)(C)(1).

72 Reg. § 1.901–2(b)(4)(i)(C)(1).

73 Reg. § 1.901–2(b)(4)(i)(C)(1) (note the use of the term "for example" as illustrating the rule and not limiting the rule).

74 Reg. § 1.901–2(b)(4)(i)(C)(1); Reg. § 1.901–2(b)(4)(iv)(C) Example 3 (sets forth an example of a thin capitalization regime that is based on section 163(j) as it existed prior to 2022).

This analysis requires a taxpayer to holistically determine how foreign law applies to everyone before the taxpayer can determine if anyone might fail the regulatory disallowance threshold. If somewhere or somehow a significant expense were disallowed to someone in an amount that did not fit safely within a disallowance exception or disallowance safe harbor, then the foreign levy would be denied eligibility for everyone subjected to that levy. This "all or nothing approach" approach creates a daunting due diligence challenge for determining whether a foreign levy is eligible for foreign tax credit relief for anyone at all. It is a hard enough task to determine how a foreign levy applies to a particular taxpayer. It is a still harder challenge to determine how a foreign levy applies "under the normal circumstances in which it applies," which is the standard envisioned by the 1983 final regulations. But, it is an exponentially more daunting challenge to determine how a foreign levy applies to everyone subjected to the levy, which is the standard required by the 2022 final regulations. The level of effort needed to satisfy this heightened threshold is daunting.

The fourth and last eligibility requirement set forth in the 2022 regulations for foreign tax credit relief is the so-called "attribution requirement." The attribution requirement purports to limit foreign tax credit relief to only those foreign taxes that are levied in a manner that satisfies a jurisdictional nexus standard that conforms with the jurisdictional nexus standards found in U.S. tax law.[75] This attribution requirement thus seeks to deny credit relief for a variety of novel extraterritorial taxes (such as digital services taxes, diverted profits taxes, or equalization levies) that assert taxing jurisdictional rights beyond traditional norms of international taxation or at least beyond the norms of what are found in U.S. tax law.

If a foreign country imposes taxation based on the activities conducted by a nonresident taxpayer, then the foreign tax law must determine the amount of income subject to tax based on the nonresident's activities located in the foreign country (including its functions, assets, and risks located in the foreign country) in order to satisfy the attribution requirement.[76] Thus, nexus rules applied to nonresident persons that are consistent with the rules found in section 864(c) of the U.S. tax laws for taxing income effectively connected with a U.S. trade or business or with the nexus rules articulated in Articles 5 and 7 of the U.S. Model Income Tax Convention for taxing profits attributable to a permanent establishment satisfy the attribution requirement.

---

[75] Reg. § 1.901–2(b)(5).

[76] Reg. § 1.901–2(b)(5)(i)(A).

In order for a foreign tax to meet the attribution requirement as applied to a resident taxpayer, the foreign tax must be designed to determine income and expense utilizing arm's length principles that do not take destination-based criteria (like customer location) into account.[77] Importantly, the foreign tax must be applied in a manner that closely conforms to the manner in which the U.S. tax regime determines net income and must also utilize sourcing and jurisdictional nexus norms that conform to existing U.S. tax laws.

The sourcing conformity requirement that undergirds the attribution requirement, whether applied to resident or nonresident persons, creates the real possibility that a foreign jurisdiction's taxes may fail the requirements of section 901 even though the United States already has a bilateral tax treaty with that jurisdiction. So, the next logical question is does this newfound attribution requirement override existing U.S. treaties? The final regulations answer this question by stating that a foreign levy treated as an income tax under an applicable U.S. income tax treaty qualifies as a "foreign income tax" if paid by a U.S. citizen or resident that elects the benefits under the treaty.[78] The final regulations then provide that because a controlled foreign corporations is not treated as U.S. resident under U.S. income tax treaties, that entity (as a resident of a third country) does not qualify for this treaty-based foreign tax credit exception.[79] Thus, the final regulations clarify that taxes paid from an entity located in a U.S. treaty partner jurisdiction to a controlled foreign corporation located in a third-country jurisdiction are separate levies that must independently satisfy the attribution requirement of section 901 or section 903. However, if the foreign country has agreed under its treaties with other jurisdictions to apply a source rule consistent with the U.S. source rule, then that treaty provision's sourcing rule would be relevant in the determination of whether or not the foreign jurisdiction applied a sourcing rule that conforms to the U.S. rule.[80]

The Treasury Department's effort to graft an attribution requirement onto the foreign tax credit eligibility standards is controversial, and the addition of this new attribution requirement opens the door to a larger debate over whether the Treasury Department's regulatory amendments made in 2022 represent the best reading of the statutory intent of section 901. In *Loper Bright*

---

[77] Reg. § 1.901–2(b)(5)(ii).

[78] Reg. § 1.901–2(a)(1)(ii).

[79] This is made clear in the preamble to the final regulations. See T.D. 9959, 87 FED. REG. 276, 292 (Jan. 4, 2022). However, the regulations provide that if the source rule is changed under a treaty to which the CFC is entitled to rely then the modified source rule would potentially be tested to determine if the jurisdictional sourcing requirement is met. See Reg. § 1.901–1(a)(1)(ii).

[80] Reg. § 1.901–2(a)(1)(ii).

Enterprises,[81] the Supreme Court overruled its prior *Chevron* regulatory deference standard and instead stated that a court's charge is to review an agency decisions to determine the best reading of a statute using the full scope of its statutory interpretive toolkit.[82] In contrast, under its prior *Chevron* deference standard, the Supreme Court generally deferred to agency determinations if the relevant statute was ambiguous and the agency's regulatory interpretation was a reasonable interpretation of an ambiguous statute.[83] The Supreme Court in *Loper Bright Enterprises* did say that due respect should be afforded to the views of the Executive Branch, but the Supreme Court also said that an agency's interpretation of the law is afforded deference only to the extent that the agency's interpretation has the power to persuade the court. Thus, after its decision in *Loper Bright Enterprises,* the Supreme Court appears to have returned to a deference standard that it had previously employed in *Skidmore v. Swift & Co.*[84] Now that the *Chevron* deference standard has been overruled in *Loper Bright Enterprises,*[85] an unresolved question is whether the Treasury Department's effort to graft an attribution requirement into section 901 represents the best reading of section 901 or is an ultra vires expansion beyond its statutory text.

The historical record that underlies section 901 poses a substantial risk that the Treasury Department's newfound

---

[81] Loper Bright Enters. v. Raimondo, 603 U.S. 369 (2024).

[82] Loper Bright Enters. v. Raimondo, 603 U.S. 369 (2024). Instead of applying its prior Chevron deference standard, the Supreme Court in *Loper Bright Enterprises* stated instead that "it makes no sense to speak of a "permissible" [agency] interpretation that is not the one the court, after applying all relevant interpretive tools, concludes is best." In overruling its prior Chevron deference standard, the Supreme Court then went on to state that "[i]n the business of statutory interpretation, if [the agency's interpretation] is not the best, it is not permissible."

[83] The prior deference standard in vogue prior to the standard articulated in Loper Bright Enterprises originated in Chevron U.S.A., Inc. v. Nat. Res. Def. Council, Inc., 467 U.S. 837 (1984) (stating that "if the intent of Congress is clear, that is the end of the matter, for the court, as well as the agency, must give effect to the unambiguous expressed intent of Congress" [so-called *Chevron* Step 1]; but, if Congress has left a gap to fill then the Court looks to whether the regulation is a permissible construction of the statute [so-called *Chevron* Step Two]).

[84] Skidmore v. Swift & Co., 323 U.S. 134, 140 (1944). The Court cabined its judicial deference afforded under Skidmore in the following manner:

> "[I]nterpretations and opinions" of the relevant agency, "made in pursuance of official duty" and "based upon. . .specialized experience," "constitute[d] a body of experience and informed judgment to which courts and litigants [could] properly resort for guidance," even on legal questions. *Id.* at 139–140. "The weight of such a judgment in a particular case," the Court observed, would "depend upon the thoroughness evident in its consideration, the validity of its reasoning, its consistency with earlier and later pronouncements, and all those factors which give it power to persuade, if lacking power to control." *Id.* at 140.

See Loper Bright Enters. v. Raimondo, 603 U.S. 369 (2024).

[85] Loper Bright Enters. v. Raimondo, 603 U.S. 369 (2024).

attribution requirement may not withstand scrutiny. In this regard, when section 901 was enacted in 1918 (effective starting in 1919), it read as follows: "The amount of any income, war-profits and excess-profits taxes paid during the taxable year to any foreign country, *upon income derived from sources therein*, or to any possession of the United States."[86] Prior to 1921, the United States had not articulated a comprehensive concept of source, but the above italicized language suggests that a jurisdictional nexus and sourcing conformity requirement akin to the attribution requirement initially was part of the foreign tax credit eligibility requirements, but not for long.

In 1921, Congress enacted the foreign tax credit limitation regime as the means to address the over-crediting of foreign tax credits so that the foreign tax credit could not be used against U.S. source income.[87] Simultaneously with the enactment of section 904's predecessor, Congress removed any jurisdictional nexus or sourcing conformity requirement from section 901's predecessor so that it would then read as follows: "The amount of any income, war-profits, and excess-profits taxes paid during the same taxable year to any foreign country, or to any possession of the United States."[88] In relevant part, this aspect of section 901 remains unchanged to this day.

Congress's decision to affirmatively remove any reference to any sourcing or jurisdictional nexus requirement from section 901(b)(1)'s predecessor occurred at the very same time that Congress elsewhere in the 1921 Act affirmatively addressed the scope and nature of sourcing rules that should exist in the United States.[89] In 1932, Congress made it explicitly clear that the rules for allocating and apportioning U.S expenses between U.S. source income and foreign source income must be utilized in order to determine the foreign tax credit limitation so that foreign tax credit relief is limited to situations where the taxpayer had ***net*** foreign source income,[90] but again Congress did not alter the scope of credit eligibility standard under section 901 based on sourcing or jurisdictional nexus conformity. Thus, Congress thought a lot about the interaction of the

---

[86] See Revenue Act of 1918, PUB. L. NO. 65–254, § 222(a), 40 STAT. 1057, 1073 (Feb. 24, 1919).

[87] See Revenue Act of 1921, § 222(a)(5), § 238(a), 42 STAT. 227, 249, 258 (Nov. 23, 1921).

[88] See PUB. L. NO. 67–98, § 222(a)(5), § 238(a), 42 STAT. 227, 249, 258 (Nov. 23, 1921).

[89] See PUB. L. NO. 67–98, § 217(d) and (e), 42 STAT. 227, 244 (Nov. 23, 1921).

[90] See PUB. L. NO. 72–154, § 131(e), 47 STAT. 169, 212 (June 6, 1932) (added an explicit cross-reference to the sourcing rules of former Code Sec. 119, which was the predecessor to Code Sec. 861). The courts have held that the sourcing rules are utilized in order to determine the foreign tax credit limitation. See International Standard Electric Corp. v. Commissioner, 1 T.C. 1153 (1943), aff'd, 144 F.2d 487 (2d Cir. 1944).

sourcing rules, the foreign tax credit limitation regime, and the scope of the foreign tax credit eligibility rules in this era, and at that time Congress withdrew any jurisdictional nexus or sourcing conformity requirement from its statutorily prescribed foreign tax credit eligibility standards with its 1921 amendment to section 901. Congress has never revisited that decision to remove sourcing or impose a jurisdictional nexus conformity into the eligibility requirements found in section 901. Instead of continuing to impose a jurisdictional nexus or a sourcing conformity rule into section 901 as had existed at its first formulation, Congress instead confined its use of its sourcing rules to the foreign tax credit limitation computation.

The removal of any jurisdictional nexus and sourcing conformity rule along with the concurrent adoption of the predecessor to section 904 demonstrates that Congress recognized that sourcing was an important consideration in that era but in the end chose to make sourcing relevant only for the foreign tax credit limitation computation and not relevant in the foreign tax credit eligibility context. The current version of section 901 contains the added words "or accrued" but otherwise Code Sec. 901 has remained unchanged in relevant part since 1921[91] as can be seen in the following redline version that shows the statutory changes made from the 1921 Act onward to section 901:

> The amount of any income, war profits, and excess profits taxes paid <u>*or accrued*</u> during the same taxable year to any foreign country, ~~*upon income derived from sources therein,*~~ or to any possession of the United States.[92]

Thus, the text and the amendments made to section 901 demonstrate that Congress thought about sourcing in the context of section 901, and when it did so it removed sourcing from the eligibility requirements of section 901 since 1921 onward. The statutory provision of section 901 had to be amended to reach this result, which adds further impetus to the argument that sourcing conformity is not a prerequisite for a foreign levy to be eligible for foreign tax credit relief given how section 901 was amended to remove such a requirement.

What is more, the Treasury Department's prior regulations explicitly recognized that section 901 had no sourcing or jurisdictional nexus conformity requirement through the end of 2021. Prior to 2021, the Treasury Department's longstanding acceptance

---

[91] See Code Sec. 901(b).

[92] A hat tip is owed to Robert Culbertson who first provided this redline version of Code Sec. 901 to demonstrate how it has amended in relevant part since its inception. See Robert E. Culbertson, *Sense and Sensibility and Creditability: Redefining an Income Tax "in the U.S. Sense,"* 104 TAX NOTES 147, 196–198 (Oct. 11, 2021).

that no sourcing conformity requirement existed under section 901 can be seen in the fact that prior 1983 final regulations explicitly granted foreign tax credit relief to a foreign levy that would have failed a sourcing conformity requirement.[93] Given the statutory text in section 901, the historic amendments to section 901 that removed any sourcing conformity requirement, and given the longstanding regulatory interpretation that had allowed foreign tax credit relief for foreign levies that had utilized a divergent sourcing rule from that found in the United States, a significant argument can be made that the imposition of an attribution requirement fails to represent the best reading of section 901 and its currently enumerated statutory provisions.

Perhaps due to the reality that the treaty partner would not have envisioned the restrictive nature of these 2022 final regulations, the final regulations provide a safe harbor by stating that a foreign levy treated as an income tax under an applicable U.S. income tax treaty qualifies as a "foreign income tax" if paid by a U.S. citizen or resident that elects the benefits under the treaty.[94] Furthermore, perhaps in tacit recognition to the impractical nature of complying with these heightened standards, the Treasury Department through two notices has also indicated that taxpayers can continue to rely on the "predominant character standard" of its prior 1983 final regulations that had envisioned a more lenient standard in lieu of applying the more onerous and stricter close conformity standards of the 2022 final regulations while the government continues to study this issue further.[95] This is truly a remarkable state of affairs. The 1983 regulations were withdrawn, and final regulations were published in the federal register to replace those 1983 regulations in 2022, but subsequent notices now inform taxpayers that they may rely in part on prior withdrawn regulations except with respect to the attribution requirement which taxpayers must affirmatively satisfy.

PPL v. Commissioner[96] *Redux.* The Supreme Court decided the *PPL* case in the midst of the Treasury Department's evolving regulatory standards for applying section 901. In addition, the implications and continuing precedential value of *PPL* also remain matters of controversy where reasonable minds can and do differ. The

---

93 See former Reg. § 1.903–1(b)(3) Example 3, 48 FED. REG. 46,272, 46,296 (Oct. 12, 1983). In the regulatory example, a withholding tax was applied on technical services performed outside the jurisdiction that applied the withholding tax. Nevertheless, the 1983 regulations concluded that the withholding taxes were creditable. For a further discussion of this example, see Gary B. Wilcox and Lucas Giardelli, *Will Jurisdictional Nexus Survive Chevron Step 1*, 105 TAX NOTES 2153 (Mar. 7, 2022).

94 Reg. § 1.901–2(a)(1)(iii).

95 Notice 2023–55, 2022–32 I.R.B. 427; Notice 2023–80, 2023–52 I.R.B. 1583.

96 See PPL Corporation v. Commissioner, 569 U.S. 329 (2013).

PPL decision was rendered before the 2022 amendments to the Treasury Department's regulations, so it was decided prior to the Treasury Department's rejection of the *Bank of America* standard in favor of its close conformity standard. Yet, the Supreme Court decision in *PPL* occurred after the Treasury Department had endorsed the *Bank of America* standard in its prior 1983 final regulations but then had added formalistic design hallmarks of the U.S. income tax that must also be satisfied as a separate prerequisite for foreign tax credit relief. Thus, consideration of the continued relevance of the *PPL* case is important for at least three reasons: (i) the decision was a unanimous decision of the Supreme Court where the Supreme Court was asked to require, in addition to the *Bank of America* standard, further regulatory formalistic design hallmarks that loosely mirrored U.S. tax laws, (ii) the Supreme Court rejected the government's effort to apply the prior 1983 final regulations to disallow a foreign tax credit for a foreign tax that did assess taxation on some amount of net gain even though that foreign tax levy did not meet the formal design hallmarks found in a U.S. income tax law at that time, and (iii) the government has attempted through its 2022 final regulations to add even greater formal close conformity requirements in contravention of the *PPL* holding.

In *PPL*, the Supreme Court considered whether a U.K. windfall profits tax imposed as a one-time 23 percent formulary assessment on all privatized utility companies was eligible for U.S. foreign tax credit relief. The 23 percent U.K. windfall profits tax was applied to the difference between a company's "profit-making value"[97] and the price for which it was privatized.[98] Under the case law that pre-dated the 1983 regulatory changes, the above-described U.K. windfall profits tax would likely have been eligible for foreign tax credit relief under the *Bank of America* standard. Earlier iterations of U.K. excess profits tax regimes were found to be creditable,[99] and IRS administrative practice had also stated that a wide range of excess profits regimes met the eligibility standards set forth in the pre-1983

[97] For this purpose, "profit-making value was defined as its average annual profit per day over an initial period that was generally a four year period and then this amount was multiplied by 9. The number 9 was chosen as a baseline "price-to-earnings ratio." Although described as a tax on excess value, the tax had the economic effect of a tax on excess profits because the calculation of "value in profits terms" was based on average net income over the four-year period, rather than on an actual measure of value (which could have easily been established from market data). Thus, from an economic point of view, the U.K. windfall profits tax was a tax on excess profits. See Brief For Amici Curiae Rosanne Altshuler, Richard M. Bird, Malcom Gillis, Arnold C. Harberger, Gary C. Hufbauer, Charles E. McLure, Jr., Jack Mintz, & George R. Zodrow in PPL v. Commissioner at 8–9, 569 U.S. 329 (2013).

[98] See Entergy v. Commissioner, 683 F.3d 233, 234 (5th Cir. 2012).

[99] See Robertson v. Commissioner, 176 F.2d 704 (3d Cir. 1949); Ethyl Corp. v. United States, 75 F. Supp. 461 (Ct. Cl. 1948); Colombian Carbon Co. v. Commissioner, 25 B.T.A. 456 (1932), acq., 1932–1 Cum. Bull. 2.

case law.[100] The IRS had even ruled that a tax levy imposed on average profits that spanned multiple years, much like the U.K. windfall profits tax that was the subject of the *PPL* litigation, was entitled to foreign tax credit relief.[101] However, these cases and administrative pronouncements preceded the 1983 regulatory amendments to Reg. § 1.901–2(b), and as the Tax Court recognized in its *Texasgulf* decision, " "[r]egulations [under Reg. § 1.901–2] can supersede prior case law to the extent that they provide requirements and definitions not found in prior case law."[102] Thus, the *PPL* case is interesting exactly because the taxpayer substantively satisfied the *Bank of America* standard (a conclusion that the IRS National Office appears to have accepted before the litigation, or at least did not reject),[103] but even so the U.K. windfall profits tax failed to comply with the formal design hallmarks that the prior 1983 final regulations added.

To add further intrigue, the government did not contest the Tax Court's factual finding that the U.K. tax was a tax that did apply to some amount of net income for all taxpayers. In this regard, the Tax Court found that the U.K. windfall profits tax was designed to reach net income and did in fact tax net income in all cases.[104] The

---

100 See Rev. Rul. 68–318, 1968–1 Cum. Bull. 342 (Italian tax on profits in excess of a six percent of capital); Rev. Rul. 56–51, 1956–1 Cum. Bull. 320 (Cuban tax on profits in excess of 1/10th of estimated real worth of capital). Another ruling concluded that a tax imposed at variable rates was creditable. Rev. Rul. 74–435, 1974–2 Cum. Bull. 204 (Swiss Cantonal tax imposed at variable rates on multi-year profits was creditable).

101 See Columbian Carbon Co. v. Commissioner, 25 B.T.A. 456, 463 (1932), acq., 1932–1 Cum. Bull. 2 (Service contested timing of accrual, but not creditability, of U.K. tax based on average profits of three-year period preceding assessment year); see also Rev. Rul. 69–446, 1969–2 Cum. Bull. 150 (Swiss National Defense Tax, imposed on average profits for the two years preceding the assessment year, is an income tax).

102 See Texasgulf, Inc. v. Commissioner, 107 T.C. 51, 69 (1999) *aff'd* 172 F.3d 209 (2d Cir. 1999). Also, the government was categorical to the Tax Court, stating that the pre-1983 case law was of "little consequence" and that the 1983 final regulations superseded prior case law. See Reply Brief of Respondent in PPL v. Commissioner at 93–99, 135 T.C. 304 (2010).

103 It is interesting to note at this point that the IRS National Office appeared to have agreed that the pre-1983 case law was supportive of the taxpayer's position even before the PPL litigation, but after analyzing that favorable case law the IRS National Office then argued that the government had authority to change the standards for creditability in its final 1983 Treasury regulations and then stated as follows: "analysis of pre-regulation case law does not assist in the resolution of this case, since Taxpayer does not dispute that the U.K. Windfall Tax must satisfy the net gain test of the regulations to qualify as a creditable tax." See PLR 200719011 (May 11, 2007).

104 The Tax Court stated as follows:

> Parliament did, in fact, enact a tax that operated as an excess profits tax for the vast majority of the windfall tax companies. The design of the windfall tax formula made certain that the tax would, in fact, operate as an excess profits tax for the vast majority of the companies subject to it.
>
> Because both the design and effect of the windfall tax was to tax an amount that, under U.S. tax principles, may be considered excess profits realized by the vast majority of the windfall tax companies, we find that it

government's disagreement was not that the U.K. windfall profits tax was applied on some basis other than net income. Its complaint was that the design of the U.K. windfall profits tax did not contain the formal design hallmarks of a U.S. income tax system that the prior 1983 final regulations required.

Thus, the facts set forth in the *PPL* case squarely put in issue whether the prior 1983 final regulations could require formalistic design hallmarks of a U.S. income tax to be met as a precondition for foreign tax credit relief for a foreign tax that was designed to reach some amount of net gain (thus satisfying the *Bank of America* standard). The Supreme Court *unanimously* held that the U.K. windfall profits tax was entitled to U.S. foreign tax credit relief, but the Court's opinion omitted any detailed discussion of the formal design tests set forth in the prior 1983 final regulations.

Instead of discussing how the 1983 final regulations had attempted to impose additional formalistic design hallmarks on top of the *Bank of America* standard, the Court attempted to harmonize the regulatory formal design hallmarks in the prior 1983 final regulations with the pre-1983 case law, stating that Reg. § 1.901–2(b) "codified longstanding doctrine dating back to *Biddle*."[105] The Court omitted any serious discussion of the government's assertion that its formal regulatory requirements sought to bring "structure and clarity" not found in the earlier case law.[106] The Supreme Court

---

> did, in fact, "reach net gain in the normal circumstances in which it [applied]", and, therefore, that its "predominant character" was "that of an income tax in the U.S. sense."

See PPL v. Commissioner, 135 T.C. at 340–341 (2010).

[105] See PPL v. Commissioner, 569 U.S. at 324.

[106] Compare PPL v. Commissioner, 569 U.S. at 341–343 (where Court discusses portions of the government brief dealing with pre-1983 case law), with Brief of the Respondent in PPL v. Commissioner at 33–43, 569 U.S. 329 (2013) (No. 12–43) (where the government asserts that the formalistic three-pronged test set forth in the 1983 Treasury regulations is entitled to deference under Mayo Foundation for Med. Educ. & Research v. U.S., 562 U.S. 44 (2011)). The government's argument was more robust in its brief before the Third Circuit and the Fifth Circuit as the following excerpt from its briefs in those proceedings so indicates:

> [T]he Tax Court was required to accord the regulation Chevron deference. See Mayo Found. for Med. Educ. & Research v. United States, 131 S. Ct. 704 (2011). Moreover, "[b]ecause § 901's exemption from taxation is 'a privilege extended by legislative grace,'" the regulation had to be "strictly construed." Texasgulf, Inc. v. Commissioner, 172 F.3d 209, 214 (2d Cir. 1999) (quoting Inland Steel Co. v. United States, 677 F.2d 72, 79 (Ct. Cl. 1982)).
>
> Instead, the Tax Court paid only lip service to the regulation. Although it discussed the regulation in summarizing the relevant legal principles (PPL Op. 24–26), the court went on to apply its own test for determining the predominant character of the windfall tax. Thus, the court considered at length the historical background and purpose of the windfall tax and its effect on the companies subject to the tax. It made no effort whatsoever to explain whether the windfall tax met any of the three regulatory subtests, all of which had to be met for the tax to be creditable.

applied *Biddle* for the purpose of determining whether the U.K. windfall profits tax was assessed on net income and found that its formal design, which did not comply with the formal design hallmarks set forth in the prior 1983 final regulations, was not fatal. As to the argument that the prior 1983 final regulations established formalistic requirements that must be met in form,[107] the Supreme Court stated that this notion cannot be squared with the black-letter principle that "tax laws deal in economic realities, not legal abstractions."[108] The Supreme Court eschewed any effort to apply the formal requirements of the prior 1983 final regulations and instead used a holistic analysis that harkens back to the pre-1983 case law, opining that substance over form principles compel a conclusion "that the windfall profits tax is best viewed as nothing more than a tax on actual profits above a threshold."[109] By not resolving the *PPL* case within the formal guidelines of the regulatory tests, the decision can be read as a full-throated endorsement of the *Bank of America* standard notwithstanding that the Treasury Department, through its prior interpretive regulations, had attempted to circumscribe that standard by adding formal design hallmarks of a U.S. income tax that must separately be met. Instead of giving dispositive significance to the added regulatory formalistic design requirements, the Supreme Court placed a heavy judicial gloss over the prior 1983 final regulations to "harmonize them" with "longstanding doctrine dating back to *Biddle*" when in fact the Treasury Department's prior regulations had attempted to impose formal requirements not found in the prior case law.

After its defeat in *PPL*, the government doubled-down on its regulatory efforts. In the preamble to its 2022 final regulations, the government asserted that the Supreme Court decision in *PPL* involved prior regulations and so that decision has no significant ongoing precedential value now that the Treasury Department has updated its final regulations. Therefore, instead of conforming its regulations to a substance-over-form approach in a manner consistent with the unanimous Supreme Court decision in *PPL*, the Treasury Department in 2022 set forth stricter formal conformity requirements that require a foreign jurisdiction's tax law to be designed so as to reach an amount of net gain that closely conforms

---

Compare Appellants Opening Brief in Entergy v. Commissioner at 24–25, 683 F.3d 233, 238 (5th Cir. 2012) with Appellants Opening Brief in PPL v. Commissioner at 21–22, 665 F.3d 60 (3rd Cir. 2011).

[107] See PPL v. Commissioner, 135 T.C. at 330 ("Respondent argues that the 1983 regulations alone control the creditability of the windfall tax because those regulations subsume or supersede prior caselaw and "neither require nor permit inquiry into the purpose underlying the enactment of a foreign tax or the history of a foreign taxing statute.").

[108] PPL v. Commissioner, 569 U.S. at 340.

[109] PPL v. Commissioner, 569 U.S. at 341.

to the amount of net gain that the United States tax laws would determine before the foreign levy is afforded foreign tax credit relief under section 901.

In contrast, in *PPL*, the Supreme Court appears to have repudiated any regulatory effort to require a close conformity standard for determining credit eligibility under section 901, and in the process of doing so the Supreme Court reformulated its own *Biddle* doctrine as follows:

> Instead of the foreign government's characterization of the tax, the crucial inquiry is the tax's economic effect. See Biddle, supra, at 579, 58 S. Ct. 379 (inquiry is "whether [a tax] is the substantial equivalent of payment of the tax as those terms are used in our own statute"). In other words, foreign tax creditability depends on whether the tax, if enacted in the U.S., would be an income, war profits, or excess profits tax.[110]

The above Supreme Court reframing of its own *Biddle* doctrine in *PPL* represents a more lenient standard than what the Treasury Department has articulated as its understanding of the strictures of *Biddle* doctrine. The Supreme Court's framing of its *Biddle* doctrine in *PPL* posits that the *Biddle* doctrine only requires that a foreign levy be one that hypothetically could have been enacted in the United States within the delegated constitutional authority afforded to Congress under the Sixteenth Amendment. That articulation of the *Biddle* doctrine is a vastly different formulation than what the Treasury Department's view that the *Biddle* doctrine requires a foreign tax levy to closely conform to an actual tax provision already found under the existing United States tax laws.

Viewed through this prism, in 2022, the level of disagreement between the judiciary and the Treasury Department over the appropriate standards that are to be applied to determine eligibility for foreign tax credit relief has never been greater. However, perhaps there are signs that the Treasury Department is de-escalating the current tension, at least in part. In this regard, as previously indicated, the Treasury Department in 2023 issued two notices that allow taxpayers to continue to apply its prior withdrawn 1983 final regulations in lieu of being subjected to the stricter conformity standards of the 2022 final regulations, except that the added attribution requirement of the 2022 final regulations remains applicable.[111] Thus, except for the added attribution requirement, these two notices allow taxpayers to continue to rely on the withdrawn 1983 final regulation which in turn makes the Supreme

---

110 PPL Corp. v. Commissioner, 569 U.S. 329, 335 (2013).

111 Notice 2023–55, 2022–32 I.R.B. 427; Notice 2023–80, 2023–52 I.R.B. 1583.

Court's *PPL* decision applicable to taxpayers who elect to apply those prior 1983 final regulations. This guidance thus reduces the potential for a controversy between the Treasury Department and the courts over the continued validity of the Supreme Court's interpretation of the *Biddle* doctrine in *PPL* as the Treasury Department appears to be conceding that the Supreme Court's reading of section 901 as set forth in its *PPL* decision remains the best interpretation of section 901 for analogous cases or controversies.

As to the Treasury Department's effort to graft an attribution requirement into section 901 in 2022, the Treasury Department remains steadfast in its resolve that this aspect of its 2022 final regulations is an appropriate restriction on the potential scope of section 901. The Treasury Department remains committed to not allowing foreign tax credit relief for novel extraterritorial taxes. The Treasury Department maintains that its addition of the attribution requirement is appropriate because it views these novel extraterritorial tax measures as not similar to tax measures to which section 901 has been historically applied. Whether or not the Treasury Department's outright disallowance of foreign tax credit relief for these novel extraterritorial tax regimes represents the best reading of section 901 remains a debatable matter and likely will remain so until a future judicial decision squarely addresses this controversial position.

4. Is the Foreign Payment a "Tax"?

A basic tension exists within the foreign tax credit regime, and this basic tension has created increasing complexity and increasing risks of international double income taxation. The basic tension relates to the question of how the U.S. government should address the problem of cross-crediting of excess foreign tax credits generated in objectionable transactions. Congress has believed that section 904 is not a sufficient response in and of itself against perceived manipulation in the amount of allowable U.S. foreign tax credits generated in a particular class of transactions. Thus, although section 904 expresses an overall or aggregate approach to the cross-crediting phenomenon, Congress has simultaneously pursued a parallel effort to disallow foreign tax credits for foreign payments generated in objectionable transactions.

This question came into sudden sharp focus in the mid-1970s, after the October 1973 Middle East conflict and ensuing oil embargo, in connection with payments by U.S. oil companies to governments of oil-exporting countries.

The Problem of Oil Payments. The problem had been simmering for a long while. U.S. oil companies have been engaged in exploration and production outside the United States since the 1920s. In that connection, they have made huge payments to foreign governments. Everywhere in the world (except a few common law countries) the state owns all mineral resources. As such, it is in a position to act as an owner (and receive an economic rent from its property) as well as a tax collector (and demand a portion of an enterprise's profit). Being ultimately indifferent to the rubric covering the money it receives, a government that owns minerals can cast as a "tax" amounts received from mineral developers that would look much like a proprietor's royalties in dealings between purely private parties. If the characterization as a "tax" holds up, a U.S. taxpayer engaged in the extraction of minerals might derive, through the foreign tax credit, a full reduction of U.S. taxes for amounts that, if paid in purely private dealings, would only be deductible from income as royalties.[112]

Agreements between U.S. oil companies and foreign governments were structured in this light. By the mid-1970s, income taxes on gains from oil exploration and development in some oil-exporting countries (that also owned the oil in the ground) were as high as 80 percent. In some instances, furthermore, there was no general income tax at all. If the formally designated royalty component of the arrangement was small (or nonexistent) in relation to a tax, it was easy to infer that the ostensible "tax" contained an element of royalty, i.e. a consideration for a specific interest in the oil rather than a generalized payment in consideration of public goods. The foreign government could be understood to be acting more as an owner of minerals than as a tax-collecting sovereign. Part of the payment termed a "tax" could readily be considered the price of an interest in minerals resources purchased from the government, and you cannot reasonably expect a tax credit for goods or services purchased from a government any more than from a private person.

The question surfaced dramatically in a 1976 IRS ruling denying credits for ostensible payments of income taxes under production-sharing agreements between a U.S. oil company and the Indonesian

---

112 H.R. 91–413, 91ST CONG. 89, 107, 110 (1969) ("Your committee recognizes the substantial difficulties of ascertaining in these situations whether a payment which is labeled as a tax payment is, in fact, a tax or a royalty. It does not believe, however, that it is appropriate to allow these "tax payments" to offset U.S. tax which would otherwise be imposed on other foreign income (either from the same country or from another country.")); see also the following statement of Senator Long, which is illustrative of the concern expressed at that time: "The [Saudi Arabian] king collected a royalty and he levied a tax on the companies. The companies concluded that they could only deduct their royalty but they were entitled to a tax credit if they were paying a tax. Therefore, some tax expert—and anybody with any brains as a tax expert would figure this one out—simply said 'If Saudi Arabia were charging you the same amount as a tax, you would get a credit for it, which would be worth twice what a deduction would be worth. So why do you not tell the King over there that if he would assess that payment as a tax, you could afford to pay him a lot more, and you both would be better off, because you would owe the U.S. Government less?" 121 CONG. REC. 7490 (1975) (statement by Sen. Long).

government.[113] The IRS's position in the ruling was that no "tax" was paid under the agreements and that the total amount received by the Indonesian government was merely a royalty. The crucial vice of the arrangement, in the IRS's view, was the combination of 1) a guaranteed return for Indonesia, consisting of a single combined amount of ostensible "royalties" and "taxes," predicated on the quantity of oil extracted by the U.S. company and 2) the failure of the contract to allow for full cost recovery. It followed that payments designated "taxes" might be paid without regard for the company's economic gain or loss. "Thus, the effect of the [agreement] and the other prohibitions is to assure that the government will retain a fixed percentage of oil produced in any year regardless of whether [the taxpayer] has any net gain from such production. Such an assured share of production retained by the mineral owner is characteristic of a royalty and not of a tax within the United States concept of the terms."[114]

The problem was easier to state than to fix. The Treasury tried and ultimately rejected several different approaches. The first response of the Treasury was to require that the foreign government receive a reasonable and independent royalty before any payment from an oil developer could be treated as a tax. That approach proved unworkable, however, because there is no immediate touchstone of a "reasonable" royalty. Each area of exploration and development is unique. The royalty widely used in Texas, for example, would be far too small for most of Saudi Arabia, where the oil is generally cheaper to extract.[115]

The next idea was more promising and became the standard of creditable income taxes in connection with natural resource payments. It occurred to the Treasury that while it may be hard, even impossible, to find an objective touchstone of a "reasonable" royalty, there is often a readily available test of a "reasonable" tax. At first this may seem surprising or even sophistry. The tax and the royalty are complementary components of a single amount received by a foreign government. When one is established, the other is the residual amount by default. Why should it be easier to establish a reasonable amount of income tax within the fixed combined amount than a reasonable royalty? The answer lies in the available comparison with the amount of income tax paid by persons who have *no* course of dealing with the government. The "reasonable" income tax is the income tax borne by persons who have no specific transactions with the government. In countries with income taxes,

---

113 Rev. Rul. 76–215, 1976–1 Cum. Bull. 194.

114 Id. at 197.

115 If the oil is easily accessible, the landowner's royalty should be greater, because the explorer/developer incurs lower cost and risk.

this is readily observable. The creditable amount, put anthropomorphically, is the amount that the government "wants" to collect as a tax in its sole capacity as taxing sovereign. Therefore, in proposed regulations on creditable taxes issued in 1980, the Treasury required, as a condition of the foreign tax credit, that the amount termed an "income tax" be comparable in amount with the amount of tax paid by persons who did not deal with the government. This is known as the "comparability" requirement and has itself gone through a mutation or two.

In an early version of the regulations, the comparability requirement was imposed in draconian fashion. Unless the amount termed a "tax" paid by an oil developer was very nearly the exact same amount as a general income tax paid by others, the oil tax was not "comparable," and *no* tax credit was allowed for *any* part of the payment to the foreign government. A near miss on comparability meant *no* foreign tax credit at all under these early regulations. U.S. taxpayers (mostly oil companies) objected that foreign governments could not be presumed to have foresworn their taxing power altogether simply because they also exacted royalties, and that the amounts paid to governments therefore necessarily had *some* component of tax for which credit should be allowed. Initially, the Treasury countered that it was neither feasible nor even within its statutory power to break down ostensibly single foreign levies into separate components of creditable taxes and deductible royalties.

The difficulty, from the Treasury's perspective, is as follows. Suppose that a foreign government owns all of the country's mineral resources and imposes a general income tax of 50 percent and a special oil tax of 75 percent on the profits of oil producers from oil concessions. There is a strong inference that part of this supernormal tax payment of 75 percent is a royalty, compensating the government for its ownership of the oil in the ground. But what part? If the producer derives 125 of gross income from oil extraction at a production cost of 25, that leaves 100 of net extractive income on which the tax at the special oil rate would be 75. Since the general income tax is 50 percent (which would entail a tax of 50 applied to this taxpayer's net income), it may seem that the combined total payment of 75 should break down into 50 of tax and 25 of royalty.

If this amount of tax (50) strikes you as right, though, you're wrong. The problem with subtracting the difference in percentage points is that it doesn't take into account the *deductibility* of a royalty under a general income tax.[116] Let's assume that the royalty is 25 and the tax is 50. Then deduct the royalty of 25 from 100 of net income. That leaves 75 of net taxable income and 37.5 of tax, which is clearly

[116] Income tax, by contrast, is not itself deductible from taxable income.

wrong. You must consider that with a 50 percent income tax rate every dollar of royalty reduces taxable income by one dollar and *tax* by 50 cents. The correct approach is to work backward from the taxpayer's after-tax net income, in this case 25. To be left with 25 after paying a 50 percent income tax, the taxpayer must have started with 50 of pretax income.[117] Therefore, the tax component of the total payment of 75 is only 25, and the royalty must be 50. In short, you must allow for the deductibility of a royalty in dissecting the combined payment into its royalty and tax components.[118]

Splitting Payments Made by Dual Capacity Taxpayers. In a later version of the regulations (which remains in force today), the Treasury did allow single combined payments to foreign governments to be divided into separate components of deductible royalty and creditable income tax. The current regulations on creditable taxes sport a "splitting" formula for breaking down payments to foreign governments made by "dual capacity taxpayers." When a "dual capacity taxpayer"[119] is subject to a different type or level of taxation from other taxpayers, the element of pure income tax is broken out separately. The regulations are complicated, but their core is a "safe harbor formula" for separating tax and nontax components. This is only a safe harbor, however, and taxpayers can seek to identify the royalty and tax components under a facts and circumstances standard if they do not want to follow the safe harbor method.

The splitting formula under the safe harbor reconstructs the amount that would have been paid under the foreign country's general income tax and treats that amount as a creditable tax. The safe harbor formula takes into account the deductibility of the amount of any payment properly characterized as a royalty under a general income tax.

Mechanically, the qualifying amount of tax under the safe harbor formula is the following:[120]

$$(A - B - C) \times \frac{D}{1 - D}$$

A is the amount of "gross receipts,"

B is the amount of "costs and expenses,"

---

[117] If the tax rate is 50 percent, the amount of tax that you must pay to be left with 25 after tax is 25.

[118] If you fail to make that allowance, furthermore, then the foreign tax system, by disallowing a deduction for royalty payments, is inconsistent with U.S. income tax notions, as prescribed in *Biddle*.

[119] These are the taxpayers that also transact business with the government.

[120] Reg. § 1.901–2A(e)(1).

C is the amount actually paid by the dual capacity taxpayer to the foreign government, and

D is the applicable tax rate under the general income tax.

If we insert the numbers from the example above into the formula, we have gross receipts ("A") of 125, costs and expenses ("B") of 25, and the amount paid to the foreign government ("C") of 75. The term (A – B – C) is therefore (125 – 25 – 75), or 25. With the general income tax rate 50 percent (0.5), the factor D/(1 – D) is .5/(1 – .5), or 1. The amount of tax paid is therefore 25 (25 × 1/1). It may seem like magic, but the formula is a more general form of the computation done above to work backward from after-tax to pretax income and from there to the tax paid. (A – B – C) is simply after-tax net income, the amount the taxpayer is free to take home after payment of all costs, royalties, and taxes. From that amount, it is relatively easy to figure out the tax that was paid.[121]

The safe harbor approach is logical and after some practice is fairly straightforward in the results that it produces, but a substantial number of taxpayers have chosen to try their hand under the facts and circumstances standard. As a result, a fascinating jurisprudence has developed that has allowed extraction taxes to remain creditable income taxes in an amount in excess of the generally applicable income tax under the more generous facts and circumstances test set out in Reg. § 1.901–2A(c).[122]

No Tax Payment Due to Subsidy. Another important question is whether a foreign tax is offset by some other element of value. The question arises in a situation where the taxpayer makes an income tax payment to a foreign government but the foreign government gives a refund to the taxpayer of that amount in some form. The IRS has long taken the position that an indirect refund of the taxes means that a foreign income tax was not "paid" to the extent of the refund.[123]

---

[121] It is easy when there is a single tax rate (here 50 percent). When foreign income tax rates are graduated, it is far more difficult. The effective rate of tax paid is not self-revealing from net after-tax income. You, therefore, have to plug different rates into the formula by trial and error until you find one that works.

[122] See, e.g., Exxon Corp. v. Commissioner, 113 T.C. 338 (1999) (UK petroleum tax held to be creditable); Texasgulf, Inc. v. Commissioner, 107 T.C. 51 (1996), *aff'd* 172 F.3d 209 (2d Cir. 1999) (holding that Ontario mining tax was creditable); Phillips Petroleum Co. v. Commissioner, 104 T.C. 256 (1995) (Norway's surtax on petroleum activities was held to be creditable under 1980 temporary regulations); Rev. Rul. 76–215, 1976–1 Cum. Bull. 194 (the Indonesian petroleum tax was modified after Rev. Rul. 76–215 had denied its eligibility for foreign tax credit relief and the modified version was found to be eligible for U.S. foreign tax credit relief).

[123] A more extensive analysis of this evolution is set forth in Joseph Isenbergh, *The Foreign Tax Credit: Royalties, Subsidies, and Creditable Taxes*, 39 TAX L. REV. 227 (1984).

Congress eventually codified this into law in the 1986 Act by enacting section 901(i) which provides that a foreign income tax:

> Shall not be treated as a tax. . . to the extent. . . the amount of such tax is used (directly or indirectly) by the country imposing such tax to provide a subsidy by any means to the taxpayer. . . or any person to the transaction. . . and. . . such subsidy is determined. . . by reference to the amount of such tax.

The issue of when another party receives a "subsidy" of some sort is a difficult question, and the Treasury regulations have not made this analysis much easier. However, if the other party is a state-owned entity, then the courts have refused to treat the benefit to the state-owned entity as a "subsidy to another person." This issue was directly litigated in *Amoco v. Commissioner*,[124] where the Seventh Circuit treated any benefit received by the national owned petroleum company of Egypt as simply an internal government accounting issue and not a true benefit to an independent party outside of the government itself. However, when the effect of a tax is refunded to a private party that is not owned by the government in some manner, then a prohibited indirect subsidy could be found to exist.[125]

Compaq-Style Financial Arbitrage Transactions. In the 1990s, the government's war on questionable foreign tax credit transactions resurfaced over the cross-crediting of excess foreign tax credits generated by abusive financial arbitrage transactions. In Notice 98–5,[126] the government expressed strong hostility against taxpayer attempts to cross-credit taxes generated in abusive financial arbitrage transactions and identified five transactions of interest to discuss the contours of its policy concerns. The Treasury Department argued that each of the five transactions of interest set forth in Notice 98–5 lacked economic substance because these transactions made no sense apart from their generation of U.S. foreign tax credit benefits. When a transaction has an economic justification only in consideration of the U.S. tax savings from the generation of excess U.S. foreign tax credits, then the transaction does not have a sufficient non-tax business purpose, at least according to Notice 98–5. Again, the fundamental point is that the government signaled a willingness to restrict foreign tax credit eligibility standards to attack the cross-crediting of excess credits generated from

---

[124] 138 F.3d 1139 (7th Cir. 1998), *aff'g* 71 T.C.M. 2613 (1996).

[125] See Riggs National Bank v. Commissioner, 81 T.C.M. 1023 (2001) (Taxpayer paid Brazilian withholding taxes on interest paid on cross-border loans but borrower was given a refund of a portion of the withheld tax; held no foreign tax credit to the extent of the indirect subsidy).

[126] 1998–1 Cum. Bull. 334, withdrawn by Notice 2004–19, 2004–1 Cum. Bull. 606.

"objectionable transactions" in situations where the IRS deems section 904 as ill-suited to address the abusive transaction of concern.

The formulation of the economic substance doctrine set forth in Notice 98–5 was challenged in *Compaq Computer v. Commissioner*.[127] Compaq had recognized a long-term capital gain of approximately $232 million. Upon learning of this capital gain, an investment banker structured a series of financial transactions that allowed Compaq to purchase ten million Royal Dutch ADRs for approximately $887.6 million cum-dividend and to sell these shares ex-dividend for approximately $868.4 million. Compaq, using the "next-day" settlement rules, settled the purchase-trades on September 17, 1992. However, for the sale-trades, Compaq used regular settlement rules and settled the sales-portion of the transaction on September 21, 1992. As a result of the difference in settlement dates, Compaq was the owner of ten million Royal Dutch ADRs on the dividend record date of September 18 and thus was entitled to receive a dividend of approximately $22.5 million. The Dutch withholding taxes on this dividend was approximately $3.4 million, so Compaq actually received a net dividend of $19.1 million. Compaq also incurred a capital loss of $20.7 million. Thus, the transaction (which was completed in approximately one hour) created a net cash loss of approximately $1.6 million to Compaq (see Line 4(a) netted against Line 5(a) in Table #11).

Table #11: Compaq Excess FTC Arbitrage				
			(a)	(b)
			IRS Position	Compaq Position
1	ADR Sale Price	868.4		
2	Investment Banker Fee	(1.5)		
3	ADR Purchase Price	(887.6)		
4	Capital Loss (L1−L2−L3)		(20.7)	(20.7)
5	Dividend (Gross $22.5 less $3.4)		19.1	22.5
6	Foreign Withholding Taxes (Foreign Tax Credits)			3.4

On the above facts, the Tax Court denied foreign tax credit relief because the financial arbitrage transaction lacked an adequate nontax business purpose due to the fact that Compaq's trades were pre-wired, created a negative cash flow of $1.6 million, and were done

[127] See Compaq Computer Corp. v. Commissioner, 277 F.3d 778 (5th Cir. 2001), *rev'g* 113 T.C. 214 (1999); IES Indus. v. U.S., 253 F.3d 350 (8th Cir. 2001) (same).

solely to generate $3.4 million of U.S. foreign tax credits.[128] The Fifth Circuit reversed the Tax Court decision, agreeing with Compaq that the gross dividend is used to determine whether there was a pre-tax profit motive and concluding that a pre-tax profit was the only prerequisite for the transaction to have an adequate business purpose and to possess economic substance.[129] Thus, according to the Fifth Circuit, as long as Compaq possessed a pre-tax profit ($1.8 million calculated as the difference between Line 4(b) and Line 5 (b) in the above Table #11), it was irrelevant that this pre-tax profit suffered a pre-planned effective foreign tax rate of 189 percent (or $3.4 million in the above table).

As cases such as the *Compaq* case were making their way to the courthouse, Congress in 1997 enacted section 901(k) to provide for a minimum holding period as a precondition to claiming U.S. foreign tax credit relief for dividend withholding taxes,[130] but Congress excepted certain foreign-licensed securities dealers from these holding period requirements.[131] The legislative history to section 901(k) makes it clear that Congress' concern was that tax motivated transactions were being done to transfer foreign tax credits in the marketplace in short-term trades.[132] In 2004, Congress added section

---

[128] The Tax Court used the economic substance doctrine to deny U.S. foreign tax credit benefits in this transaction, claiming that Compaq failed to possess a sufficient non-tax business purpose and was motivated solely by the desire to obtain U.S. foreign tax credit benefits. In the course of its opinion, the Tax Court reasoned as follows:

> The foreign tax credit serves to prevent double taxation and to facilitate international business transactions. No bona fide business is implicated here, and we are not persuaded that Congress intended to encourage or permit a transaction such as the ADR transaction, which is merely a manipulation of the foreign tax credit to achieve U.S. tax savings.

See Compaq Computer v. Commissioner, 113 T.C. at 226.

[129] The Fifth Circuit reversed the Tax Court's application of the economic substance doctrine, reasoning that Compaq's economic profit is to be judged by looking at its pre-tax gross dividend and stating that foreign income taxes should not be considered as an expense, thus rejecting Notice 98–5's interpretation of the economic substance doctrine. Compaq Computer v. Commissioner, 277 F.3d 778, 785 (5th Cir. 2001); see also IES Indus. v. U.S., 253 F.3d 350 (8th Cir. 2001) (same).

[130] PUB. L. NO. 105–34, 1053(a), 111 STAT. 788 (1997). When Congress originally enacted section 901(k) in 1997, it required the taxpayer to hold the stock at least 16 days within a thirty day period that included the dividend record date. Congress amended section 901(k) to change the thirty day period to a thirty-one day period. PUB. L. NO. 108–311, 406(g)(1), 118 STAT. 1166 (2004).

[131] See § 901(k)(4). Commentators indicated that this exception represented a compromise that allowed securities dealers to continue to benefit from these foreign tax credit generator transactions but excluded the retail user of these techniques. See Lee A. Sheppard, *"What Did Wall Street Give Up for Deferral?,"* 76 TAX NOTES 1665 (Sept. 29, 1997). However, section 901(k)(4) does not exclude a securities dealer unless it is held in the active conduct in a foreign country of a business as a securities dealer, a requirement that may prevent US-based securities dealers from being eligible for this exception. See Lehman Brothers Holdings, Inc. v. U.S., (1:10-cv-06200), 2015 WL 2359256 (S.D.N.Y. May 8, 2015).

[132] See H.R. REP. NO. 105–148, 105th CONG. 1st SESS. at 545 (June 24, 1997) ("[S]ome U.S. persons have engaged in tax-motivated transactions designed to transfer

901(*l*) to impose a similar holding period requirement for instruments that incur interest withholding taxes, but again Congress excepted securities dealers from these new holding period requirements.[133] Thus, even though Congress failed to address the fundamental tax arbitrage aspects of the Compaq transaction, and its new minimum holding period requirements had selective application, these provisions demonstrate an attempt to deny foreign tax credit relief for objectionable short-term financial arbitrage transactions that were executed by retail customers of securities dealers.

In the end, Congress' codification of the economic substance doctrine reversed the holdings of cases like *Compaq* in section 7701(*o*)(2)(B), which explicitly directed the Treasury Department to issue regulations requiring foreign taxes to be treated as expenses for purposes of calculating the reasonably expected pre-tax profit potential of a transaction.[134] Thus, the remedy for the foreign tax credit generator transactions set forth in Notice 98–5 was

---

foreign tax credits from persons that are unable to benefit from such credits . . . to persons that can use such credits. These transactions sometimes involve a short-term transfer of ownership of dividend-paying shares. Other transactions involve the use of derivatives to allow a person that cannot benefit from the foreign tax credits with respect to a dividend to retain the economic benefit of the dividend while another person receives the foreign tax credit benefits."); S. REP. NO. 105–33, 105th CONG. 1st SESS. at 175–6 (June 20, 1997) (same).

[133] AMERICAN JOBS CREATION ACT OF 2004, § 832 (effective October 22, 2004) (adding new § 901(*l*)); see also H.R. CONF. REP. NO. 108–755, 108th CONG. 2nd SESS. at 621 (October 7, 2004) (adopting version of the house bill); H.R. REP. NO. 108–548, 108th CONG. 2nd SESS. at 201 (June 16, 2004) ("The Committee believes that the present-law holding period requirement for claiming foreign tax credits with respect to dividends is too narrow in scope and, in general, should be extended to apply to items of income or gain other than dividends, such as interest."). The determination of what risk mitigation strategies create a tolling of the holding period creates considerable complexity in the application of this law. See Nicholas Bogos, *A Risk-Based Analysis of Credit Derivation Under SSRP Standard (Part 1)*, 112 TAX NOTES 587 (Aug. 14, 2006); (Part 2), 112 TAX NOTES 655 (Aug. 21, 2006); and (Part 3), 112 TAX NOTES 259 (Aug. 28, 2006).

[134] Sections 7701(*o*)(2)(A) and (B) set forth the following criteria for analyzing whether a pre-tax profit potential is substantial enough to satisfy economic substance concerns:

> (2) SPECIAL RULE WHERE TAXPAYER RELIES ON PROFIT POTENTIAL—
>
> (A) IN GENERAL—The potential for profit of a transaction shall be taken into account in determining whether the requirements of subparagraphs (A) and (B) of paragraph (1) are met with respect to the transaction only if the present value of the reasonably expected pre-tax profit from the transaction is substantial in relation to the present value of the expected net tax benefits that would be allowed if the transaction were respected.
>
> (B) TREATMENT OF FEES AND FOREIGN TAXES—Fees and other transaction expenses shall be taken into account as expenses in determining pre-tax profit under subparagraph (A). The Secretary shall issue regulations requiring foreign taxes to be treated as expenses in determining pre-tax profit in appropriate cases.

legislatively codified in the enactment of section 7701(*o*)(2)(B), and specific authority was given to the U.S. Treasury Department to handle these objectionable transactions in a targeted manner under the codified economic substance doctrine. By directing the U.S. Treasury Department to issue regulations that would treat a foreign tax payment as a transactional expense, section 7701(*o*)(2)(B) sets forth a pre-tax profit test that coherently addresses the cross-crediting concerns of these financial arbitrage transactions.

STARS War: The Government Strikes Back (Again). The foreign tax credit war shifted to a more sophisticated variation in what the government came to call a "structured passive investment arrangement." As indicated in the preceding section, the financial arbitrage transactions in *Compaq* were uneconomic except for the tax credit benefits generated in those overall transactions. Thus, in a sense, those cases are easy cases from an economic substance and business purpose perspective even though the courts failed to arrive at the right answer and caused Congress to enact section 7701(*o*)(2)(B) in response.

However, the next generation of financial arbitrage transaction would be substantially more complex yet present the same fundamental cross-crediting phenomenon. Unlike *Compaq*, the highly structured financial arbitrage transactions that utilize a "structured passive investment arrangement" often generate a pre-tax profit on an overall basis even if the foreign tax cost is treated as an expense in the transaction. Thus, from the vantage point of the justification for the overall investment decision, the entire transaction has an overall business purpose and makes overall economic sense. However, the problem in these structured passive investment arrangements is that the transaction step that creates the highly structured bolt-on passive investment vehicle is extraneous to the underlying investment assets. It does provide some incremental pre-tax borrowing savings to the U.S. taxpayer, but the U.S. taxpayer incurs a substantially larger incremental foreign tax cost that far exceeds the incremental borrowing savings generated by the bolting-on of this otherwise extraneous passive investment vehicle.[135] Thus, if the "bolt-on feature" of the transaction were

[135] The structures vary, but the essential facts are that a foreign lender invests in a foreign subsidiary ("FSub"). For foreign tax purposes, the foreign lender is treated as a stockholder and is entitled to be exempt on the income from its stock investment in its resident jurisdiction. The foreign lender is willing to accept a lower return than would be required if the foreign lender made a straight taxable interest-bearing loan. Because foreign law treats the payments to the foreign lender as a dividend, the structured passive investment arrangement does not allow FSub to deduct its payments to the foreign lender. The incremental additional tax cost due to the foregone interest expense deduction is about twice as much as the reduced borrowing cost. Thus, if one were to view the addition of this bolt-on structure passive investment arrangement in isolation, the pre-tax benefits are significantly less than the foreign

isolated and separately tested as an independent business decision whose addition must be justified on a stand-alone basis, then the bolting-on of the otherwise extraneous passive investment vehicle fails to have a justifiable business purpose because the addition of this otherwise extraneous transaction step creates incremental financial benefits smaller than the incremental foreign tax cost incurred as a result of its addition. Importantly, in these structured passive investment arrangements, the taxpayer knows upfront that the incremental savings in borrowing cost arising from the inclusion of the otherwise extraneous transaction step will be less (often only half) of the amount of the incremental additional foreign tax cost incurred by reason of the inclusion of the otherwise extraneous transaction step.[136]

Prior to the enactment of section 7701(*o*), the Treasury Department was unsure of its prospects for victory against such structures, so yet again it decided to amend its section 901 regulations expressly to attack this new generation of foreign tax credit generator transactions,[137] thus adding more complexity and clutter to the already complex regulatory framework for section 901. In this regard, the Treasury Department created a rifle-shot provision in Reg. § 1.901–2(e)(5) that treats any tax payment made as part of a structured passive investment arrangement as a "voluntary" (non-compulsory) foreign tax payment. By classifying taxes generated in a structured passive investment arrangement as "voluntary," these taxes fail to meet the basic requirement of a "foreign tax," as a foreign tax must be a compulsory payment (not a voluntary payment) in order to be eligible under section 901 for U.S. foreign tax credit relief.[138] In its attack on these structures, the Treasury Department provided a highly particularized set of factors that must be satisfied before an investment structure would be classified as a "structured passive investment arrangement."[139]

---

tax cost of engaging in this structure. But, the ability to cross-credit the foreign taxes against other low tax income makes the transaction economical.

136 See Salem Fin., Inc. v. United States, 112 Fed. Cl. 543, 561 (2013), *aff'd in part and rev'd in part and remanded*, Salem Financial, Inc. v. United States, 786 F.3d 932 (Fed. Cir. 2015) (Bx payment, or interest rebate, was equal to 51% of the foreign tax cost); see also Expert Report of Michael I. Cragg at ¶ 76, Salem Financial, Inc. v. United States, 112 Fed. Cl. 543 (2013).

137 See Notice of Proposed Rulemaking, 72 FED. REG. 15,081 (March 30, 2007) (announced special rules for structured passive investment arrangements in proposed regulations); T.D. 9416, 73 FED. REG. 40,727 (July 16, 2008) (made amendments to regulations in unrelated areas); T.D. 9535, 76 FED. REG. 42,038 (July 18, 2011) (finalized in final regulations the regulatory rules for structured passive investment arrangements).

138 See Reg. § 1.901–2(e)(5)(i).

139 See Reg. § 1.901–2(e)(5)(iv)(B) sets forth six detailed criteria that must be met which in general are as follows: (i) a special purpose vehicle, (ii) a U.S. party exists who is eligible for foreign tax credit relief, (iii) direct investment is made, (iv) foreign

Although the STARS transactions have created a spirited debate about their effectiveness under the law prior to section 7701(*o*)'s enactment, the enactment of section 7701(*o*) effectively ends that controversy prospectively because section 7701(*o*) gives the government all the tools that it needs to deny foreign tax credit relief for foreign taxes generated in these so-called STARS transactions.[140] Section 7701(*o*)(5)(D) provides that the economic substance doctrine can be applied to an individual transaction step to determine the independent business purpose and economic substance of the particular transaction step that generates U.S. tax benefits, and section 7701(*o*)(2)(B) explicitly directs the Treasury Department to issue regulations that treat foreign taxes as an expense for purposes of assessing the profit motive for the individual transaction step that is tested.

U.S. Tax Versus Foreign Tax Permanent Basis Differences and Section 901(m). An early method of generating excessive amounts of foreign tax credits arose in instances where foreign law attempted to define taxable income on a basis that was different from (and broader than) the U.S. definition of taxable income thus creating a permanent tax basis difference between the two jurisdictions. In this situation, foreign taxes for the full amount were claimed by the U.S. taxpayer even though a significant portion of the foreign taxes related to items of income that were excluded from any U.S. taxation. In G.C.M. 26062, 1949–2 Cum. Bull. 110, the IRS argued that foreign taxes assessed on amounts that were excluded from U.S. taxation should not be eligible for U.S. foreign tax credit relief because the allowance of those credits inflated the amount of foreign tax credits beyond what was required to avoid international double income taxation and generated inappropriate cross-crediting. The government asserted that international double income taxation was already avoided if the United States did not assert taxing jurisdiction over the item that foreign law sought to tax, so providing a cross-crediting opportunity for taxes assessed on excluded income was arguably too generous. This argument represented an early effort to prevent inflated amounts of U.S. foreign tax credit relief, but this early effort to deny foreign tax credit relief for taxes paid on items that would never be part of the U.S. tax base was largely rejected by the courts.[141]

---

tax credit benefit exists to a counterparty, (v) a foreign counterparty exists, and (vi) the U.S. party and foreign counterparty have inconsistent tax treatment.

[140] Evidently, the acronym STARS was the acronym used by the promoter of these passive investment trust structures and stands for Structured Trust Advantaged Repackaged Securities transaction. See Bank of New York Mellon v. Commissioner, 140 T.C. 15, 1617 (2013) (where Tax Court indicates the acronym and its origin).

[141] See Helvering v. Nell, 139 F.2d 865, 870–71 (4th Cir. 1944); I.B. Dexter v. Commissioner, 47 B.T.A. 285, 290–91 (1942), *acq.*, 1948–2 Cum. Bull. 1; Brace v. Commissioner, 11 T.C.M. (CCH) 906, 907, T.C.M. (P-H) ¶ 52,265, at 800–801 (1952); United States v. Rexach, 200 F. Supp. 494, 496 (D.P.R. 1961) (considering the

Consequently, after largely failing to convince the courts to engage in a facts and circumstances inquiry to determine whether foreign tax credit relief was appropriate as a precondition to the grant of such relief under section 901, the IRS in 1954 abandoned its arguments that foreign tax credit relief should be available only when true international double income taxation were possible with respect to the underlying item that was assessed foreign tax.[142] Here things remained until 2010.

Congress eventually addressed the cross-crediting opportunities afforded by tax basis differences with the enactment of section 901(m).[143] In general, section 901(m)(1) denies U.S. foreign tax credit relief for any foreign taxes attributable to the disqualified portion of foreign income arising in a covered asset acquisition. Section 901(m)(2) provides that a covered asset acquisition includes any transaction that is treated as an asset acquisition for U.S. tax purposes but is treated as a stock purchase for foreign income tax purposes. Thus, section 901(m) can apply in instances where (i) stock in a foreign entity is sold and a section 338 election is made, (ii) stock in a foreign entity is sold and the foreign entity is considered a disregarded entity for U.S. tax purposes, or (iii) an interest in an foreign entity is sold and the foreign entity is treated as a partnership for U.S. tax purposes.[144] Section 901(m)(3)(a) provides that the disqualified portion of foreign taxes is the incremental foreign income tax paid as a result of a permanent tax basis difference.[145] The purpose of section 901(m) is to deny foreign tax credit relief for foreign taxes imposed on foreign income that is not taxable in the United States under the theory that international double income

argument raised by the Service that the foreign tax credit is allowed only for items subject to U.S. tax an "extinct question"); but see Hubbard v. United States, 17 F. Supp. 93 (Ct. Cl. 1936) (ruling in favor of the IRS that foreign tax credits should not be allowed to the extent assessed on amounts that were not taxable in the United States).

142 The Service formally abandoned this position in Rev. Rul. 54–15, 1954–1 Cum. Bull. 129; see also Reg. § 1.904–6(a)(1)(iv) (places foreign tax credit for items not subject to U.S. tax in the general basket, thus accepting their creditability and placing them in the basket that provides the most protection against the cross-crediting phenomenon).

143 See PUB. L. 111–226, § 212 (August 11, 2010).

144 See Joint Comm. on Taxation, "Technical Explanation of the Revenue Provisions of the Senate Amendment to the House Amendment to the Senate Amendment to H.R. 1586, Scheduled for Consideration by the House of Representatives on August 10, 2010" (JCX–46–10) (Aug. 10, 2010) at 10.

145 § 901(m)(3)(A) achieves this by stating that the disqualified portion means the ratio of the aggregate percentage basis differences allocable to such taxable year divided by the income which the foreign tax is applied. § 901(m)(3)(C)(i) provides that the basis difference means the excess of the adjusted basis of such asset immediately after a covered asset acquisition over the adjusted basis of such asset immediately before the covered asset acquisition. § 901(m)(3)(B)(i) provides the general rule that the basis difference will be allocated to taxable years using the applicable recovery method for U.S. income tax purposes.

taxation is already avoided due to the nontaxability of that particular item that was subjected to foreign taxation. The below illustration sets forth the analysis:

> USP purchases the stock of a foreign target (FT) for $100. FT made substantial use of its assets in its trade or business. The inside basis (i.e. FT's basis in its assets, as opposed to the outside basis of the FT stock) is $40. FT is treated as a disregarded entity for U.S. tax purposes so that the acquisition is viewed as an asset acquisition for U.S. tax purposes but as a stock acquisition for foreign law purposes. Thus, the basis of the assets is stepped up for U.S. tax purposes, but no basis step-up exists for local tax purposes as the transaction is treated as a stock purchase for local tax purposes.[146] Assume that the additional $60 of basis step-up is amortized over a 15-year period ($4 of additional amortization annually). Assume that FT has $24 of income (before the additional amortization) and pays a foreign tax at a 25 percent tax rate, so on these facts FT pays a total of $6 of local income tax. Consequently, in this situation, $4 of the $24 of FT's income will never be subject to U.S. taxation due to the $4 of additional amortization deductions, so the corresponding $1 of foreign tax assessed on this excluded $4 of income need not be given foreign tax credit relief because double taxation is already avoided on the $4 of foreign income to which this $1 of tax relates. Consequently, section 901(m) disallows the $1 of foreign tax that is attributable to the income that is sheltered by reason of the amortization of the tax basis difference that was created by reason of the covered asset acquisition.[147]

The justification for section 901(m) harkens back to the policy arguments first expressed in G.C.M. 26062. For U.S. tax purposes, the assets in the above illustration have experienced a basis step-up in a transaction where no foreign taxable event occurred. The amortization of this additional stepped-up basis creates a permanent reduction in the portion of the foreign income that will be taxed in the United States versus what will be subject to tax in the foreign jurisdiction where no basis step-up was provided. Thus, in this situation, for U.S. tax purposes, the buyer can obtain a basis step-up in the underlying FT assets in a transaction where the seller was not

---

[146] The same result could have been achieved if FT was acquired and a section 338 election were made and then immediately after the acquisition of FT a check-the-box election were made to treat FT as a disregarded entity.

[147] For a further analysis of the interplay between section 901(m) and section 338(g), see Lowell Yoder, *Section 338(g) Election for a Foreign Tax Continues to Provide Benefits to Buyer After New Section 901(m)*, 40 TAX MGM'T INT'L J. 347 (June 10, 2011).

subject to a taxable event in a foreign jurisdiction, thus creating a permanent basis difference between the United States and the relevant foreign jurisdiction. Therefore, the foreign taxes associated with the income that is excluded (excluded by reason of the additional U.S. amortization deduction) is disallowed under section 901(m) because international double income taxation is already pacified with respect to the particular item of income to which those taxes relate.

Foreign Tax Credit Splitter Transactions. Section 909 provides a matching rule to prevent the splitting of income away from the underlying income. The genesis of section 909 lies in *Guardian Industries Corp. v. United States.*[148] In that case, a U.S. domestic corporation owned a Luxembourg entity (the acronym of which was "GIE") that was treated as a corporation for U.S. tax purposes but treated as a flow-through entity for Luxembourg tax purposes. Thus, it was a reverse hybrid entity. GIE earned income and paid an associated Luxembourg income tax of approximately $3.4 million. Because the entity was regarded as a separate foreign corporation for U.S. tax purposes, Guardian Industries took the position that the Luxembourg income was earned by GIE and thus was not the income of Guardian Industries for U.S. tax purposes. However, because Luxembourg law treated Guardian Industries as the technical taxpayer that was liable for the Luxembourg taxes, Guardian Industries, citing the technical taxpayer rule of Reg. § 1.901–2(f), claimed that it was the technical taxpayer of the Luxembourg income taxes and as such was entitled to claim direct foreign tax credits. The Federal Circuit agreed, holding that Guardian Industries was entitled to claim U.S. foreign tax credits for the Luxembourg taxes and was not taxable on the income earned by GIE until those earnings were remitted as a dividend. Thus, the foreign tax credits were "split away" from the income to which it related.

Diagram #23

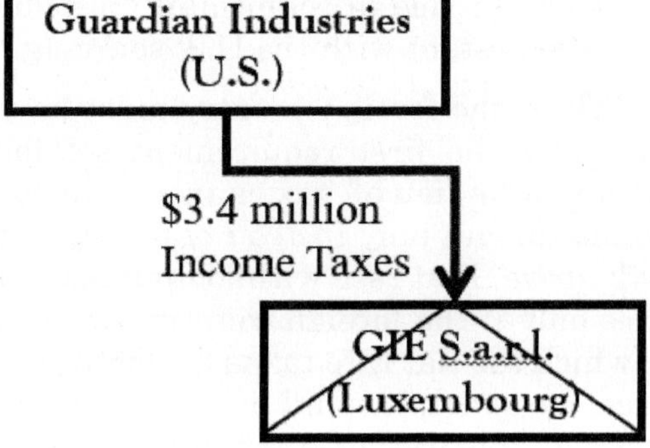

148 477 F.3d 1368 (Fed. Cir. 2007).

In response to this case and similar techniques, section 909 provides that any foreign tax that is part of a "foreign tax credit splitter event" may not be taken into account if the associated income is earned by a "covered person" until such time as that income is included in the taxpayer's own income. For this purpose, a covered person is any person that is under 10 percent or more direct or indirect common control. A splitter event is now worked out in painstaking detail in regulations. Moreover, the Treasury Department is given authority under section 909(c)(2) to disallow such credits permanently if the income is not taxable. Presumably if the income is included in a later year but entitled to receive a 100 percent foreign dividends received deduction under section 245A, the foreign tax credits would be forever lost in order to avoid a double benefit.

5. Credit for "in Lieu of" Taxes

There is one more component of creditable taxes. Section 903 of the Code adds to the range of creditable taxes any foreign tax paid "in lieu of a tax on income. . . otherwise generally imposed by any foreign country." These are known as "in lieu of" taxes. An "in lieu of" tax is a substitute for an income tax that is otherwise generally imposed. To satisfy this "substitution" requirement, a four-part inquiry is required in Reg. § 1.903–1(c) as follows:

1. Is there a generally-imposed net income tax?
2. Is the foreign levy imposed completely "in lieu of" and not in duplication of the generally imposed income tax?
3. Does the imposition of the "in lieu of" tax have a close connection to the exclusion of the income from taxation under the generally applicable income tax?
4. Does the generally imposed income tax apply a sourcing rule (a conforming "jurisdiction to tax" rule) that is consistent with the U.S. sourcing rules?

Thus, the foreign country must have in force a general income tax under the first requirement set forth above. Furthermore, a creditable "in lieu of" tax cannot be imposed *in addition to* a general income tax but only *instead of* to satisfy the second requirement set forth above. Flat rate withholding taxes are creditable as "in lieu of" taxes only if the foreign country also imposes a general income tax for which the flat rate tax is a substitute. Sales taxes or value-added taxes, for example, paid by taxpayers that also pay income tax are not creditable. Because of these constraints, the "in lieu of" credit is not widely available for foreign taxes that fail to qualify as full-bore "income" taxes.

The final regulations require that the "in lieu of" tax must have a close connection to its substitution for a general income tax to satisfy the third requirement set forth above. This close connection standards sets forth a required finding that the foreign country made a deliberate and cognizant choice to impose the "in lieu of" tax instead of its generally imposed net income tax.[149] This "but for" requirement is met under the final regulations only if the imposition of the "in lieu of tax" bears a "close connection" to the failure to impose a generally-imposed net income tax on the excluded income. A close connection exists if the generally-imposed net income tax would apply by its terms to the income but for the fact that the excluded income is expressly excluded.[150] If the statutory language does not provide such formal documented linkage between the two levies, then the taxpayer must provide proof based on foreign tax law, or the legislative history of either the tested foreign tax or the generally-imposed net income tax, that the foreign country made a cognizant and deliberate choice to impose its substitute foreign levy instead of imposing a generally-imposed net income tax.[151] The context of the enactment of the two levies can reduce the taxpayer's burden of proof to show the close connection in the two levies.[152] In this regard, the close connection standard can be satisfied without resort to the legislative history of a foreign jurisdiction if a generally-imposed net income tax does not apply to the excluded income and the otherwise eligible "in lieu of" tax were enacted contemporaneously with the generally-imposed net income tax.[153] However, if the levies were enacted at different times, then the taxpayer's burden of proof is heightened to demonstrate the country's desire to have a close connection between the two levies.[154] Not all income derived by persons subject to the tested foreign tax need be excluded income, as long as the tested foreign tax applies only to amounts that relate to the excluded income.[155]

The existing regulations require that the generally-imposed net income tax, if it were to be applied on excluded income, must in turn have met the attribution requirement imposed by Reg. § 1.901–2(b)(5) to satisfy the fourth requirement listed above.[156] Thus, the existing regulations require all in lieu of taxes—that otherwise satisfy the requirements of section 903—to also satisfy the same attribution requirement that the government has announced applies

---

149 Reg. § 1.903–1(b)(1), 1.903–1(c)(1)(iii).

150 Reg. § 1.903–1(c)(1)(iii).

151 Reg. § 1.903–1(c)(1)(iii).

152 Reg. § 1.903–1(d)(5) Example 5.

153 Reg. § 1.903–1(c)(1)(iii).

154 Compare Reg. § 1.903–1(d) Example 5 with Reg. § 1.903–1(d) Example 6.

155 Reg. § 1.903–1(b)(1), 1.903–1(c)(1)(ii).

156 Reg. § 1.901–2(b)(3); Reg. § 1.901–2(b)(5); Reg. § 1.903–1(b)(2)(ii); Reg. § 1.903–1(c)(1)(iv).

to any section 901 creditable tax, thus conforming the regulatory requirements for purposes of section with the new attribution requirement set forth in section 901.[157]

However, the final regulations provide a special rule for applying the substitution requirement to gross basis withholding taxes.[158] To qualify as a "covered withholding tax" that is entitled to this special rule, the withholding tax must satisfy three rules. First, the withholding tax must be imposed on gross income of persons who are nonresidents of the foreign country.[159] Second, the withholding tax must meet the non-duplication standard, meaning that it cannot be in addition to a net income tax that is imposed by the foreign country on any portion of the income subject to the withholding tax.[160] The Treasury Department made clear that if a withholding tax applies to certain gross income of nonresidents who are also subjected to the generally-imposed net income tax in the event the nonresident had a taxable presence in the foreign country, the withholding tax cannot meet the substitution requirement even with respect to nonresidents that do not have a taxable presence in that country.[161] Third, the withholding tax must meet the source-based attribution requirement.[162] The effect of this special rule is that a sourced-based withholding tax that is applied to nonresident taxpayers in lieu of a generally applicable foreign income tax does not need to satisfy the close connection standard.[163]

C. The Credit Limitation of Section 904

1. The "Overall" Limitation of 1921

The limitation on the foreign tax credit, as we saw earlier, is designed to prevent high taxes on foreign income from offsetting U.S. tax on U.S. source income. When we last looked in on the credit limitation, it was the 1921 version. This is an "overall" limitation that established a single limitation on the credit for all foreign income taxes on the basis of the ratio of foreign source income to worldwide income. While the credit overall could not exceed the U.S. effective rate of tax on foreign source income, some very high foreign income taxes could be credited in full if the taxpayer also had sufficient low-taxed foreign source income to build up the amount of the limitation.

---

157 Prop. Reg. § 1.903–1(c)(1)(iv).

158 Reg. § 1.903–1(c)(2).

159 Reg. § 1.903–1(c)(2)(i).

160 Reg. § 1.903–1(c)(2)(ii).

161 T.D. 9959, 87 FED. REG. 276, 358 (Jan. 4, 2022).

162 Reg. § 1.903–1(c)(2)(iii).

163 Reg. § 1.903–1(c)(2).

With the original overall limitation, U.S. taxpayers subject to foreign income taxes higher than the U.S. rate had ready opportunities for "cross-crediting" by seeking out low-taxed foreign source income, which would enlarge the limitation on the credit and thereby permit the high foreign taxes to be credited in full. Low-taxed foreign income in this situation is a shelter of sorts for U.S. taxes, not because it is beyond the reach of U.S. taxation, but because it enlarges the credit for *other* foreign taxes that would otherwise exceed the credit limitation. In this regime, U.S. taxpayers had non-economic incentives to shift income-producing operations offshore to low-tax environments.[164] An integrated oil company, for example, might move an oil refinery from the continental United States to the Bahamas.

For years, the U.S. tax system took a benign view of such devices through its allowance of the unmodified overall limitation. Under this regime, all sorts of operations of U.S. taxpayers—from marketing offices to oil refineries—have sprung up in tax-haven jurisdictions. One of the simplest ways to create low-taxed foreign source income is to make deposits in foreign banks which yield interest often untaxed by the country of source. However, since 1986, Congress has become much more concerned about the cross-crediting problem. Earlier in this chapter, we looked at how the foreign tax credit eligibility rules have been used to prevent transactions that generate excessive amounts of foreign tax credits from being eligible for the foreign tax credit at all. Now, we will examine how Congress has determined to police the cross-crediting phenomenon through a series of separate foreign tax credit limitations applied to separate categories (or "baskets") of foreign income as a means to limit perceived inappropriate cross-crediting of high-tax foreign income against a different category of low-tax foreign income. In 2017, Congress once again reformulated the separate limitation categories or "baskets" so that a separate foreign tax credit limitation would be applied separately to each separate limitation basket.[165] The current limitation on the credit remains an "overall" limitation under section 904(a) that is then applied separately under section 904(d) to four separate categories (or baskets) of foreign income.

2. The Current System

The basic statement of the limitation is in section 904(a): "The total amount of the credit. . . shall not exceed the same proportion of

---

164 Note that a wholly unlimited foreign tax credit (as in the 1918 Act) would eliminate this particular economic distortion. Such a suggestion, however, meets with a sullen reception from the U.S. Treasury.

165 From this point onward, I use the terms "separate limitation category" and "separate limitation basket" (or simply "basket") interchangeably.

the tax against which such credit is taken which the taxpayer's taxable income from sources without the United States. . . bears to his entire taxable income for the same taxable year." This statement of the limitation is unchanged from the one originally adopted in 1921.

Section 904(a), however, states only the broad framework of the limitation. The mechanics of the limitation are further articulated in section 904(d)(1), which provides that the limitation established in section 904(a)

> shall be applied separately with respect to—
>
> (A) any amount included in gross income under section 951A (other than passive category income),
>
> (B) foreign branch income,
>
> (C) passive category income, and
>
> (D) general category income.

For reasons that will become clear later, the basket characterization follows a hierarchy that underlies the statutory regime. Passive income is the first stop given the ordering rules. Passive basket characterization displaces the opportunity for that income to be considered foreign branch basket income whenever income is passive and low-taxed income regardless of whether it is earned in a foreign branch or in a foreign corporation.[166] Also, the passive basket characterization displaces the possibility of characterizing income in the separate basket established for income that is taxed as "net CFC tested income" as defined under section 951A by virtue of the ordering rules that exist between taxation under the Subpart F regime of section 951(a) and taxation under the section 951A regime of section 951A.[167] Foreign branch basket income is foreign income earned through a qualified business unit outside the United States. The general basket is a residual category if the income is not placed somewhere else. Thus, except for financial services businesses, the general basket does not trump the passive basket where income overlaps both baskets. Next, income that is not passive income but is earned in a foreign branch of a U.S. person is placed in the foreign branch basket. Income earned in a controlled foreign corporation may be passive income, general basket income, or the section 951A basket income but could never be foreign branch basket income.

---

[166] See § 904(d)(2)(J).

[167] See § 904(d)(1)(A); § 951A(c)(2)(A)(i)(II) (excludes any Subpart F income from the definition of net CFC tested income).

"Passive Category Income". The principal ingredient of "passive category income" is "passive income" as defined in section 904(d)(2) via an obligatory cross-reference to section 954(c). "Passive income" includes dividends, interest, royalties, rents, and annuities, along with a miscellany of gains from financial assets.[168] However, "passive income" does not include any item of high-taxed income that otherwise would have been considered passive income.[169] This "high tax kick-out" rule from the passive basket provides a clear insight into the purpose of the passive basket: highly mobile investment type income is presumed to be low-tax, and this income is placed in its own separate basket that prevents the cross-crediting of excessive foreign tax credits against this category of income. If income is described as passive income and is not subject to the high tax kick-out, then that income is placed in the passive basket because the passive basket takes priority over all other baskets. The effect of this separate limitation basket for passive income is to minimize the opportunity of taxpayers to reduce the residual U.S. taxation of low-tax passive income by cross-crediting foreign taxes paid on other types of income. With that said, if an item of investment income were in fact subject to high foreign tax, then that particular item of high tax investment income would be exposed to the "high tax kick-out" and removed from the passive basket so that its excess credits cannot be cross-credited or used to reduce the residual U.S. taxation over other passive income. Where does it land? It is provisionally placed in the foreign branch basket if it was earned in a foreign branch but otherwise is placed in the general basket.

As a further exception to the passive basket, and as a concession to banks and other financial businesses, the receipt of "financial services income" by a person predominately engaged in the conduct of a banking, insurance, or financing or similar business is not considered "passive income" but instead falls in the "general category" basket.[170] The effect of removing financial services income earned by banks from the passive basket and putting that income in the general basket is to allow cross-crediting of taxes among all financial services businesses income and other general basket income. Congress became convinced that an active financial services business should not be subject to the same cross-crediting strictures as those taxpayers that earn passive investment income. However, as discussed earlier in this chapter, Congress has refined the eligibility for claiming any U.S. foreign tax credit relief for transactions that inappropriately generated excess foreign tax

---

168 See § 954(c)(1).

169 See § 904(d)(2)(B)(iii) and (2)(F).

170 See § 904(d)(2)(C)(i).

credits in objectionable transactions or were themselves not viewed as tax payments at all.

Finally, a special rule exists with respect to dividends, interest, rents, and royalties paid by one controlled foreign corporation to another controlled foreign corporation.[171] In chapter 11, we will explore the contours of what is meant by a controlled foreign corporation, but the idea is that if a payment is made between controlled foreign corporations, then the foreign tax credit basket in which the payment is placed in the hands of the recipient controlled foreign corporation is determined by looking to the foreign tax credit basket from which this payment came out of in terms of the payor controlled foreign corporation. Said differently, the recipient controlled foreign corporation "looks through" the dividends, interest, rents, and royalties paid by another controlled foreign corporation and sees the underlying basket characterization of the item of income that was paid out of the payor controlled foreign corporation. The foreign tax credit basket is determined by looking through the payment to the underlying basket characterization of the payor. Moreover, if the payment of interest, rents or royalties reduced the passive income of the payor, then to that extent the recipient must treat that payment as passive income.[172]

Foreign Branch Category Income. "Foreign branch income" means business profits earned by a U.S. person attributable to one or more qualified business units located in foreign jurisdictions.[173] Since this provision applies only to direct branches of a U.S. person, it cannot interact with the section 951A basket and supplants the application of the general basket as the general basket is the basket to which any undesignated items are placed. The separate existence of a basket for foreign branches creates a dichotomy for how the active business income of a company is categorized depending on whether it is earned in a foreign branch or in a controlled foreign corporation. If the income is earned in a foreign branch and it is not passive income, then it will be foreign branch basket income. If the income is earned in a controlled foreign corporation and is not passive income, then it will either be global intangible low-taxed income or general basket income but cannot be foreign branch basket income, as it is not earned directly by a U.S. person through a foreign branch.

Net CFC Tested Income. Income that is subject to taxation under section 951A is stripped out of the general basket and placed in a separate section 951A basket. Thus, this foreign tax credit basket relies on a determination of the nature of the income under section

171 See § 904(d)(3)(A).

172 See § 904(d)(3)(C).

173 See § 904(d)(2)(J).

951A. Once income is tainted by that characterization, it falls in the section 951A basket. To understand the scope of this basket, one needs to unpack section 951A, which is discussed in chapter 11. Importantly, unlike any other foreign tax credit basket, section 904(c) does not allow foreign tax credits in the section 951A basket to be carried forward or backward to any year, creating a current year "use it or lose it" scenario.

"General Category Income". "General category income," as you expected, is everything else. It includes all active business income and in particular the bulk of financial services income.[174] *Within* the general category basket, the full cross-crediting of foreign income taxes is still possible. Most large U.S. enterprises with foreign operations, whether in commercial, financial, or manufacturing, are unaffected by the basket system and operate under a single overall limitation for their worldwide operations, even if these are far-flung, varied, and subject to highly different tax regimes. Most of the icons among U.S. multinational corporations (Microsoft, Procter & Gamble, and Ford Motors, among others) fall within this class at least as a preliminary matter. If the foreign income earned in controlled foreign corporations meets the threshold to be considered net CFC tested income, then the income is removed from the general basket and placed in the section 951A basket.

3. Relevance of Source Rules in the Limitation

With the limitation in mind, you may more readily understand the importance of the source rules that we explored earlier.[175] The only income that can fall in a foreign tax credit basket in the first place is income that has foreign source. If the income does not have foreign source, then it is not placed in a separate limitation basket under 904(d) and is not included in the overall limitation of section 904(a).

However, even though the source rules are the beginning point, Congress has chosen to alter the foreign tax credit limitation to exclude items of foreign source income and foreign source deduction. For example, section 904(b)(4)(A) provides that for purposes of computing the section 904(a) foreign tax credit limitation, a domestic corporation that is a U.S. shareholder of a specified 10-percent owned foreign corporation must compute its foreign-source taxable income (and entire taxable income) by disregarding the foreign-source portion of any dividend received from that foreign corporation for which the 100 percent foreign dividends received deduction is taken. Section 904(b)(4)(B) extends this exclusion from the entire taxable

---

[174] See § 904(d)(1)(D); § 904(d)(2)(A)(ii)).

[175] See chapter 3.

income of the taxpayer any deductions properly allocable or apportioned to any stock that is attributable to income described in section 245A. The effect of this provision is to exclude from the foreign tax credit limitation calculation any amounts that are entitled to a 100 percent foreign dividends received deduction under section 245A.

In addition, section 904(b)(5) provides that any indirect expense deduction (including for expenses related to interest expense or research and development expenses or stewardship expenses) that would have been allocated or apportioned to income in the section 951A category will only be allocated or apportioned to U.S. source income. The effect of this provision is to ensure that any indirect expenses that would have otherwise been apportioned to the Code Sec. 951A category of income would not decrease the ability to utilize foreign tax credits in the section 951A foreign tax credit limitation basket. And, by treating that allocation as resourced to U.S. source income, the effect is that no other foreign category basket is not negatively impacted by those expenses either, but this provision only relates to indirect expenses related to the section 951A basket.

4. Implications of the Basket System

The basket system currently in place does constrain cross-crediting in the foreign operations of U.S. persons that have foreign income placed in the passive basket or excess foreign earnings that become subject to taxation under section 951A. However, the full range of financial services income derived from an active business (including insurance, banking, and financial operations) is included within the general category basket. Therefore, U.S. multinational enterprises that have, for example, a mix of manufacturing, marketing, and banking operations abroad may nonetheless compute a single overall limitation.[176]

Taxpayers whose foreign income consists of a combination of passive income, section 951A, foreign branch income, and various types of active business income will have foreign income in four separate baskets and will compute separate limitations on the foreign tax credit for each basket. There will be no more than four baskets, however, even if foreign business operations are varied and complex.

The following Table #12 summarizes two years of operations of an imaginary U.S. corporation. Assume the U.S. income tax rate is 21 percent. The foreign income tax rate, on both business income and passive income, fluctuates from year to year:

---

[176] Income from all three operations is general category income.

Table #12: Separate § 904(d) Basket Hypothetical									
	Foreign Source General Basket			Passive Basket					
	General Basket Income	General Basket FTC Limitation	General Basket FTCs	Passive Basket Income	Passive Basket FTC Limitation	Passive Basket FTCs	U.S. Source Income	Worldwide Income
		(a)	(b)		(a)	(b)		
Year 1	100	21	40	100	21	10	250	450
Year 2	100	21	10	100		25	250	450

In Years 1 and 2, the separate limitation in both the general category basket and the passive category basket is 21. The foreign income tax on passive basket income in Year 1 (10) is creditable in full. There is, however, an excess credit of 19 above the limitation in the general basket which carries forward to Year 2. The lower foreign tax on passive basket income in Year 1 has provided no cross-crediting benefit with respect to the high taxes that are in the general basket. In Year 2, the actual tax of 15 on general category income can be used in Year 2, and 6 of the carryover of 19 from Year 1 of excess general basket credits are able to be utilized in Year 2. There is also in Year 2 an excess limitation of 11 in the passive basket, but again the excess general basket credits are not able to be utilized against the separate basket of the passive basket.[177] At the end of Year 2, foreign income taxes in the passive basket has been fully utilized but 13 of the Year 1 general basket tax credit remain unused and can be carried forward to a future year.

5. The Special Case of Oil and Gas

From the bare-bones summary of the basket system just expounded, it would seem that the cross-crediting of high taxes on oil extraction income and low taxes on oil refining income would still be viable. Income from oil extraction and from oil refining both fall in the general category income basket, so the low-taxed Bahamas refining income should build up a limitation in the general category basket for the ultra-high Kuwait taxes on extraction income, right? Actually, no. There is a set of special rules codified in section 907 governing oil and gas income, above and beyond the basket system of section 904(d)(1).

Section 907 is highly complex. Its effect is roughly equivalent to creating an additional separate limitation basket for oil and gas income. Under section 907(a), amounts claimed as taxes paid on "combined foreign oil and gas income" are creditable in a given taxable year (if they otherwise qualify as creditable taxes) only to the

177 § 904(c).

extent they do not exceed the applicable U.S. tax on that income. In 2008, Congress combined foreign oil and gas extraction income and foreign oil-related income into a new combined category called "foreign oil and gas income" and applied the section 907 limitations on this new combined category.[178] The applicable U.S. tax is determined for a corporation as the product of the amount of combined foreign oil and gas income for the taxable year and the highest marginal tax rate for corporations.[179] Excess foreign taxes may be carried back one year and carried forward 10 years but only credited against U.S. taxes on combined foreign oil and gas income. Importantly, section 907 applies before (and in addition to) the rules on creditable foreign taxes paid by dual-capacity taxpayers.

D. Overall Losses

The U.S. tax system is an annual accounting system, and the annual nature of its accounting system can create inequities in the application of the foreign tax credit limitation. These inequities can go in two directions.

First, suppose that a U.S. person has a foreign source loss of $1 million and U.S. source domestic income of $1 million so that the overall taxable income in that year is zero. The effect of the foreign loss was that the U.S. tax on U.S. source income was reduced. If in a later year the taxpayer has foreign income of $1 million, an asymmetry would arise if the taxpayer were able to fully utilize foreign tax credits. On a multi-year basis, the foreign income is nil, but the mismatch between years (foreign losses in the first year and foreign income in the later year) allowed a reduction of U.S. taxation of U.S. source income and overstated the foreign tax credit limitation. In effect, U.S. taxation over U.S. source income has been reduced due to the double benefit of the mismatch in different years of a deductible foreign loss against U.S. source income in one year and the utilization of foreign tax credits in another year. Given the rationale for the overall foreign tax credit limitation of section 904(a), one would expect that this outcome is inconsistent with the goals of the overall limitation that has been in place since 1921.

In response, Congress enacted section 904(f) in 1976. Under the overall foreign loss provisions of section 904(f), a portion of the foreign source taxable income earned after an overall foreign loss

---

[178] See PUB. L. NO. 110–343, DIV. B, § 402 (2008). Thus, although high extraction taxes no longer are limited to solely foreign oil and gas extraction income, they still cannot be cross-credited against non-oil and gas income such as income arising from the chemical processing businesses of integrated companies.

[179] § 907(a). For an individual, the limitation is the product of the amount of combined foreign oil and gas income for the taxable year and a fraction, the numerator of which is the tax against which the credit is taken and the denominator of which is the taxpayer's entire taxable income.

year is recharacterized as U.S. source taxable income for foreign tax credit purposes. Unless a taxpayer elects a higher percentage, generally no more than 50 percent of the foreign source taxable income earned in any particular taxable year is recharacterized as U.S. source taxable income. Recapturing the overall foreign loss reduces the foreign tax credit limitation in one or more years following an overall foreign loss. Even so, Congress recognized that a taxpayer might dispose of its foreign assets used in its foreign operations before an overall foreign loss can be fully recaptured. In that situation, the disposition of foreign branch assets might leave the mechanism reflected in Code Sec. 904(f)(1) ineffectual as the taxpayer would no longer have any future foreign-source income to be recharacterized as U.S.-source. To remedy that potential situation, Congress as a second step added Code Sec. 904(f)(3) to increase the recapture percentage from 50 percent to 100 percent with respect to the realized gain upon a disposition of foreign trade or business assets including the realized gain on the disposition of stock in certain majority-owned controlled foreign corporations.

The sourcing asymmetry, however, could cut in the opposite direction too. Suppose that a U.S. person has a U.S. source loss of $1 million and has an overall foreign income of $1 million and that the net result is U.S. taxable income of zero. The effect of the overall domestic loss is that it reduces the taxable income for the year below the amount of net foreign source income for the year with the consequence that the taxpayer's ability to utilize foreign tax credits in that particular year is diminished. This in turn may create excess foreign tax credits that are unused in that year. Any such excess foreign taxes may be credited, if at all, in a subsequent taxable year but only if there is sufficient foreign tax credit limitation in that later year. If in the later year, the U.S. person has U.S. source taxable income of $1 million but does not have any foreign source income, an asymmetry has occurred. The mismatch of U.S. source losses of $1 million in the first year and U.S. source income of $1 million in the later year reduced the foreign tax credit limitation in the earlier year, and there may follow the double taxation of foreign source income over time. Although the inequity here is just the other side of the same problem, fixing this inequity on behalf of taxpayers did not happen for almost thirty years after section 904(f). To ameliorate this asymmetry that harmed taxpayers, Congress in the 2004 Act added section 904(g) to address an overall domestic loss recapture scenario. Under 904(g)(1), a portion of a taxpayer's U.S. source income is recharacterized as foreign source income in an amount equal to the lesser of (1) the amount of the overall domestic loss for years prior to such taxable year or (2) fifty percent of the taxpayer's U.S. source income for such taxable year.

The application of the overall foreign loss recapture provisions of section 904(f) and the overall domestic loss recapture rules of section 904(g) becomes even more complicated in their application when those provisions are applied to the separate foreign tax credit limitation baskets.

E. Dual Consolidated Losses of Dual Resident Entities

A corporation can be dual incorporated by having its charter registered in two different jurisdictions. If an entity were incorporated in the United States or had its registration filed in the United States, then it would be treated as a U.S. corporation for U.S. tax purposes. A dual registered corporation could also arise because another jurisdiction treats an entity as a resident corporation if it has its place of management and control in that jurisdiction regardless of where it is legally incorporated. Thus, it is possible for a company to be treated as a domestic corporation simultaneously in two different jurisdictions at the same time and at the very same moment on the same day or hour. In the United States, this entity would be entitled to join the U.S. consolidated group as part of its consolidated tax return, a topic that you would likely explore further in a corporate taxation course. In the United Kingdom, Australia, and other similar jurisdictions, the entity would be entitled to obtain group relief. Thus, losses incurred in this entity would be eligible to be used in both jurisdictions to offset the income of both groups of companies. Congress believed that the use of a single loss to create a duplicate benefit in two different consolidated groups in two different jurisdictions was excessive, so it enacted section 1503(d) to disallow the use of any dual consolidated loss in the United States unless the taxpayer demonstrates that the loss was not used and will not be used to provide a tax benefit in a different jurisdiction on a group basis. As with many areas of U.S. international taxation, extensive regulations have been issued that work out these requirements in significant detail that is beyond the scope of what is likely helpful here, but an example may be helpful.

In Rev. Rul. 87–27,[180] in somewhat simplified facts set forth in Diagram #24, a U.S. corporation ("W") formed another U.S. corporation that had its place of management in the United Kingdom, so it was a dual resident corporation. The dual resident corporation's sole asset was the stock of a U.K. company that conducted operations only in the United Kingdom. The dual resident corporation borrowed funds to purchase its U.K. subsidiary and generated a loss. This loss was deducted on a group basis in the U.K. tax return as the dual resident corporation was able to obtain group relief for its loss

[180] 1987–1 Cum. Bull. 134.

through its U.K. subsidiary for U.K. tax purposes. The IRS held that the loss in the dual resident company was a dual consolidated loss as it was potentially usable on a group basis in the United Kingdom to offset another entity's income and was potentially included in the U.S. consolidated return with W. Thus, Rev. Rul. 87–27 held that section 1503(d) disallowed this dual consolidated loss from being used in the United States on those facts.

Against this backdrop of the statutory text and purpose of section 1503(d), the Treasury Department has issued extensive regulations to address a variety of situations where a payment (whether a regarded payment or disregarded payment for U.S. tax purposes) between separate units of an entity may also run afoul of the prohibited double deduction benefit that section 1503(d) was enacted to disallow.[181] The inner-workings of these regulations are complex and require many hours of careful study. They are beyond the scope of an introductory course on international taxation and are not addressed further here.[182]

---

[181] See Reg. § 1.1503(d)–1 through Reg. § 1.1503(d)–8.

[182] If further study were desired, one could consult the latest update to JOSEPH ISENBERGH & BRET WELLS, INTERNATIONAL TAXATION: U.S. TAXATION OF FOREIGN PERSONS AND FOREIGN INCOME at Chapter 7 (Wolters Kluwer 6th ed.).

Diagram #24:

Simplified Rev. Rul. 87-27

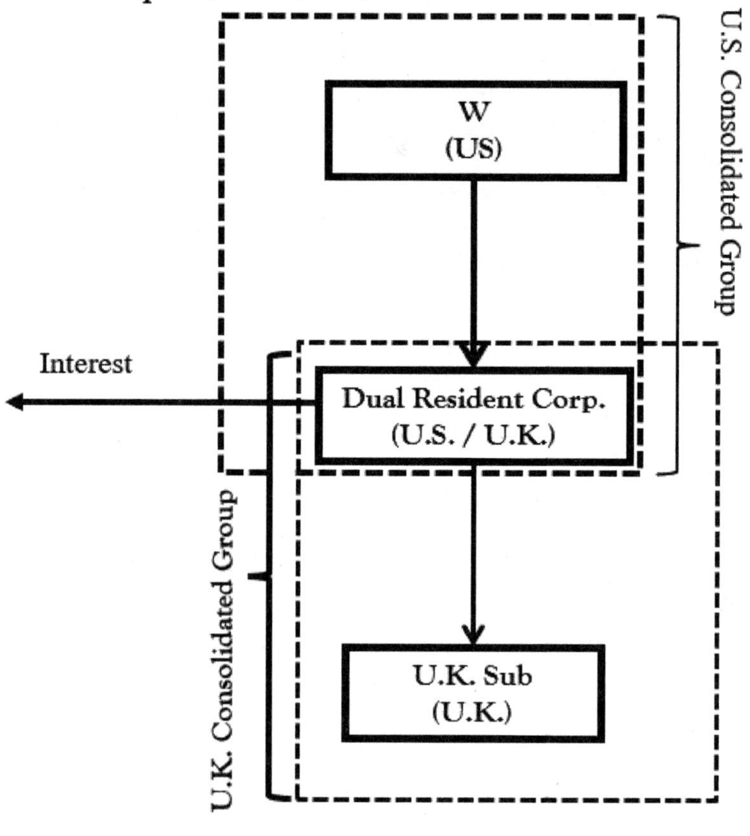

Chapter 11

CONTROLLED FOREIGN CORPORATIONS

A. General Overview

For nearly 70 years, there have been different tax regimes imposed on U.S. shareholders owning shares of foreign corporations. The broad lines of today's regime for foreign corporations with U.S. shareholders appeared in the early 1960s. The 2017 Act added substantial new anti-deferral elements to an already elaborate and complex array of provisions. The 2025 Tax Act expanded further upon those anti-deferral elements.

At dawn, the Revenue Act of 1962 substantially curtailed the use of foreign base companies, and deferral in general. Congress augmented its original Subpart F regime in the 2017 Act with a second anti-deferral regime. A cluster of Code sections extending from 951 through 965 set forth the contours of these two anti-deferral regimes: the "Subpart F" regime and a second anti-deferral regime imposed on net CFC tested income found in section 951A. These two regimes impose current U.S. taxation on many of the tax-haven operations of foreign corporations controlled by U.S. persons (known unsurprisingly as "controlled foreign corporations"). The original 1962 version of Subpart F left most active business operations unmolested. The 2017 Act added the section 951A regime to impose a minimum U.S. tax on global intangible low-taxed income earned in the controlled foreign environment, and the 2025 Act greatly expanded its scope.

Before venturing further into the Subpart F regime of section 951 and the net CFC tested income regime of section 951A, let me mention that these anti-deferral regimes represent a pinnacle of statutory complexity. Their inner plumbing is thoroughly monstrous. The core of Subpart F is a single tightly coiled sentence in section 951(a)(1) imposing current U.S. tax on the "pro rata share" of a "United States shareholder" in various types of income of a "controlled foreign corporation" (hereafter, a "CFC"). In like manner, the income inclusion rules for net CFC tested income found in section 951A are modeled in the same tight fashion and impose current U.S. tax on a "United States shareholder" of a "controlled foreign corporation" with respect to that shareholder's "pro rata share" of net CFC tested income. The main building blocks for the Subpart F regime and for the net CFC tested income regime are the definition of "control" that makes a foreign entity a "controlled foreign corporation" and the definition of a "U.S. shareholder" which identifies the person who is subjected to the income inclusion from the controlled foreign corporation. At those junctures, the Subpart F regime and the net CFC tested income regime are in harmony. However, where they diverge is with respect to the income of the controlled foreign corporation that is subject to an immediate income inclusion to its U.S. shareholder. The Subpart F regime applies first if there is an overlap, so this chapter begins with an analysis of the common definitional problem of "controlled foreign corporations" and "United States shareholders" and then explores the triggering events that create income inclusions under the Subpart F regime. After addressing those areas, this chapter explores the contours for income inclusions required under the net CFC tested income regime. The chapter then concludes with some refinements of these regimes related to natural persons who are U.S. shareholders.

As a threshold matter, the statutory changes made to section 951A in the 2025 Act had the effect of generally ending deferral for the annual net earnings arising in controlled foreign corporations, albeit the income inclusion that is required to the U.S. shareholder under section 951A may afford a domestic corporate U.S. shareholder with a concessionary tax rate by reason of the extra deduction allowed by reason of section 250. These mechanics will be discussed at the end of this chapter. But for now, the significant expansion in the scope of section 951A calls into question whether the nuanced interaction between the subpart F regime and the net CFC tested income regime is overly complex. For the law student and for the tax lawyer who specializes in this area of the law, the scope and reach of the subpart F regime must be understood if for no other reason than because the subpart F regime contained in section 951 applies first, before the broader net of section 951A can be applied. When the subpart F regime is triggered, the tax consequences of an income inclusion that arise under section 951 presents different outcomes than what would occur if there were an income inclusion by reason of section 951A. So, for the law student and for the tax lawyer who specializes in this area of the law, the scope and reach of the subpart F regime must be appropriately positioned first before one can determine the extent to which a controlled foreign corporation's earnings are subjected to immediate income inclusion under section 951A. One is left with the impression, however, that significant simplification could be achieved if the subpart F regime were curtailed now that the income inclusion regime of section 951A has been greatly expanded. But for now, careful calibration between these two anti-deferral regimes is essential.

In any event, the first two legally relevant issues before unpacking these two anti-deferral regimes is to determine when a foreign corporation is a controlled foreign corporation and then which shareholders are U.S. shareholders responsible for income inclusions under one or the other of the subpart F regime of section 951 or the net CFC tested income regime of section 951A. That is the topic that this book turns to next. After those two elements are affixed, then the next question in the three-part analysis is to determine whether the income of the CFC is includible to the U.S. shareholder under the subpart F regime of section 951 or under the net CFC tested income regime of section 951A. The scope and contours of the income that is subjected to those two anti-deferral regimes are addressed in the order of their priority: first as subpart F income to the extent described therein and then thereafter secondarily as net CFC tested income.

1. Controlled Foreign Corporation Defined

A "controlled foreign corporation" (a.k.a. "CFC") is defined in section 957(a) as "any foreign corporation if more than 50 percent of (1) the total voting power of all classes of stock. . . entitled to vote or (2) the total value of the stock, is owned. . . by United States shareholders on any day during the taxable year of such foreign corporation." Note that control is established *either* by voting power *or* by the value of stock.[1] Because *more* than 50 percent ownership or control is required, however, a foreign corporation owned exactly equally by foreign persons and United States shareholders (or even by United States shareholders and U.S. persons not qualifying as United States shareholders) is *not* a CFC.

2. "United States Shareholder"

"United States shareholder" is a term of art defined in section 951(b) as "a United States person. . . who owns. . . 10 percent or more of the total combined voting power of all classes of stock entitled to vote of such foreign corporation."[2] A United States shareholder (hereafter sometimes referred to as a "U.S. shareholder") is thus not simply any U.S. person that owns shares of a foreign corporation but one holding 10 percent or more of its voting power. Thus, if twenty U.S. persons each own 5 percent of the stock of a foreign corporation, the foreign corporation has no U.S. shareholder as defined in section 951(b) even though its only shareholders are U.S. persons. If non-U.S. shareholders (and this includes U.S. persons who hold less than 10 percent of the voting power) own at least 50 percent of the value and voting power of a foreign corporation, then the foreign

---

1 Before the 1986 Act, only voting power mattered in determining control.

2 The elided portions of these two definitions refer to the different types of ownership—direct, indirect, and constructive under section 958—that satisfy the control requirement. This is discussed below.

corporation is not a CFC.[3] Because the term "U.S. shareholder" is a specific term of art that can diverge from its expected plain meaning, this book will use the term "U.S. shareholder" and will not separate those words. When what is meant is a domestic corporation that is a U.S. shareholder, I will refer to that person as a domestic corporate U.S. shareholder. When what is meant is an individual who is a U.S. shareholder, I will use the term individual U.S. shareholder. That usage perhaps does not lend itself to the most natural reading, but it does have the advantage of ensuring clarity.

3. Indirect and Constructive Ownership of CFCs and Attribution

A further element of the definition of control of a controlled foreign corporation is a set of rules of indirect ownership and attribution of stock ownership, under which a person is treated as owning shares of stock held indirectly through entities or owned by related persons so that the status of "United States shareholder" cannot be avoided by creating long chains of lower-tier subsidiaries or by spreading shares among family members or beneficially owned entities.[4]

Under section 958(a)(2), stock owned by any foreign entity is treated as owned proportionately by its shareholders, partners, or beneficiaries. Suppose, for example, that a U.S. person owns 40 percent of the stock of a foreign corporation that owns 40 percent of the stock of a second foreign corporation. The U.S. person owns indirectly 16 percent of the stock of the lower tier foreign corporation. Indirect ownership through foreign entities is the equivalent of actual ownership for nearly all purposes of Subpart F, including current taxation. Indirect ownership implies beneficial ownership.

Constructive ownership determined under section 958(b) arises for more limited purposes, which include, most importantly, the determination of "United States shareholders," the status of "related" persons, and certain thresholds of ownership for investments in U.S. property. Section 958(b) incorporates the attribution rules of section 318 (which govern the attribution of stock ownership for most domestic tax purposes), with important modifications. Section 318 contains rules both of family and entity attribution.

---

[3] Although nonvoting ownership may be taken into account in determining control, only a U.S. shareholder of a CFC is subject to current taxation under Subpart F. Small portfolio shareholders and even large owners of nonvoting stock escape current taxation. This is in contrast with the taxation of U.S. shareholders of PFICs, discussed in chapter 12.

[4] § 958.

The constructive ownership rules of section 958(b) are as follows:

(1) *Family Attribution.* Ownership of stock is imputed to an individual from a spouse, children, grandchildren, and parents.[5] Family attribution does not, however, extend to imputing stock owned by a foreign individual to an individual U.S. citizen or resident, except for the purpose of taxation of investments in U.S. property under section 956.[6]

(2) *Attribution from Entities.* Stock held by partnerships, trusts, and estates is imputed to the partners or beneficiaries in proportion to their interests.[7] Stock owned by a corporation is imputed to its 10-percent (or greater) shareholders in proportion to their stock holdings.[8] In applying these rules, an entity owning more than 50 percent of the total voting power of a corporation is treated as owning *all* the stock entitled to vote, which is then attributed under the rules of section 318(a)(2) to partners, beneficiaries, and shareholders.[9]

(3) *Downward Attribution to Entities.* Stock owned by partners and beneficiaries is imputed to the relevant partnership, estate, or trust. Stock is imputed from a 50-percent or greater shareholder of a corporation to the corporation.[10] However, after generally incorporating the constructive attribution rules of section 318(a), section 958(b)(4) turns off the downward constructive attribution rules to entities. However, section 951B restores downward attribution in limited situations.

(4) *Options.* The owner of an option to acquire stock (or of an option to acquire an option) is treated as the owner of the stock.[11]

(5) *Operating Rules.* Both direct ownership and indirect ownership under section 958(a) are treated as actual ownership in applying the rules of constructive ownership under section 958(b). Also, constructive ownership is generally treated as actual ownership for the purpose of applying the attribution rules repeatedly. Attribution can thus occur through a chain of corporations, trusts, or partnerships; and ownership resulting from entity attribution will itself trigger family attribution.

Family attribution, however, is applied only once. Similarly, attribution *to* entities is not applied in combination with attribution

---

5 § 318(a)(1).

6 § 958(b)(1).

7 § 318(a)(2).

8 § 318(a)(2); § 958(b)(3).

9 § 958(b)(2).

10 § 318(a)(3).

11 § 318(a)(4).

from entities if the effect is to treat partners, beneficiaries, shareholders, and the like, as owning each other's stock.[12]

An important aspect of these rules is that attribution *from* entities under section 958(b)(2) applies more broadly than the stand-alone application of section 318. If a partnership, estate, or corporation owns more than 50 percent of the voting stock of a corporation, it is considered constructively to own *all* the voting stock of the corporation,[13] which again is a broader attribution principle than set out in section 318(a)(2). This means that a foreign corporation can be a CFC even when beneficial ownership by U.S. persons is very small. Suppose, for example, that a U.S. corporation owns 60 percent of the voting stock of a foreign corporation that owns 60 percent of a second-tier foreign corporation that owns 60 percent of a third-tier foreign corporation, and so on down the line to the sixth tier. The sixth-tier foreign corporation is a CFC, even though less than 5 percent of its stock is beneficially owned by a U.S. person. A seventh-tier 60 percent subsidiary would also be a CFC, with U.S. beneficial ownership below 3 percent.

As mentioned above, section 318(a)(3) applies downward attribution principles to attribute stock from the entity's owners to the entity. In this regard, any stock owned by a partner is automatically considered to be owned in its entirety by a partnership regardless of the ownership interest of the partner in the partnership.[14] The downward attribution to corporations at least contains a threshold requisite ownership level before downward attribution, but the effect is still pronounced even in that context. In this regard, if 50 percent or more in value of the stock in a corporation is owned, directly or indirectly, by or for any person, such corporation shall be considered as owning the stock owned, directly or indirectly, by or for such person.

Although stating the rule may be clear to some, an illustrative case is provided as a means to unpack the application of these attribution rules. Many more variations are possible, but this illustration helps frame the type of analysis that one must utilize.

FACTS: Agricola S.A. is a foreign corporation owned by the following persons: (i) Jose, a resident alien, owns 9% of the stock of Agricola S.A. and 10% of the stock in Cargyll, Inc., a US corporation, (ii) Cargyll, Inc. owns 20% of the stock of Agricola S.A., (iii) Maria is Jose's sister. Maria is a US citizen but resident of Fredonia. Maria owns 6% of the stock of Agricola S.A. and 5% of the stock of Chiquita.

---

12 § 318(a)(5). These qualifications of the attribution rules are necessary to prevent interlocking ownership of all stock by everyone.

13 § 958(b)(2).

14 § 318(a)(3)(A).

(iv) George is a US citizen and US resident and owns 25% of the stock of Chiquita and no direct ownership in Agricola S.A., (v) Chiquita, a Swiss corporation, owns 40% of the stock of Agricola S.A., (vi) Partnership P is a Fredonian partnership that owns 25% of the stock in Agricola S.A. The partners in Partnership P are Jorge (70 percent partner) and Sarah (30 percent partner). Jorge is a citizen and resident of Fredonia and is Maria's husband. Sarah is a US citizen and related to no other person. These facts are depicted in the below combined diagram:

Diagram #25

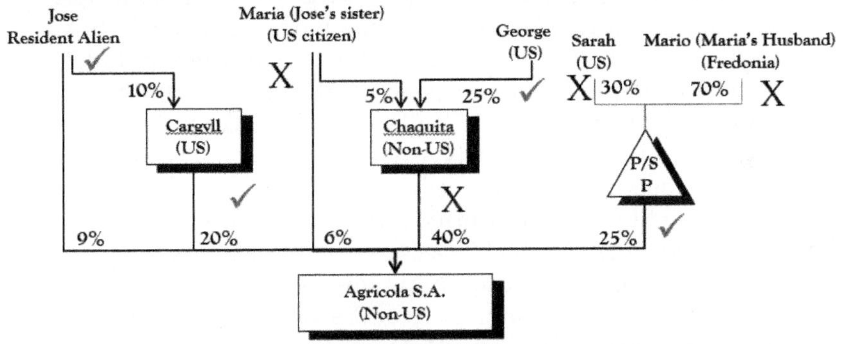

ANSWER: Section 957(a) provides that Agricola S.A. is a controlled foreign corporation if more than 50 percent of its vote or value in its stock is owned by US shareholders. Section 951(b) defines a US shareholder as a US person who owns 10 percent or more of the combined voting power of stock in a foreign corporation. For the definition of a US person, Section 951(b) cross-refences section 957(c), and section 957(c) in turn incorporates the definition of section 7701(a)(30) but then modifies that definition further in section 957(c). Furthermore, section 951(b) cross-references section 958 which in turn sets forth the ownership criteria that is applied to determine how much a US person (as determined in section 957(c)) owns directly or constructively by the US person for purposes of the US shareholder determination under section 951(b). Ownership, as determined in Section 958, utilizes a two-part approach. Section 958(a) adopts a definition of direct stock ownership in Section 958(a)(1) that is then expanded by a unique set of rules in Section 958(a)(2) to address stock held through foreign entities. Section 958(b) then further expands the "direct ownership" of Section 958(a) to include "constructive ownership." In its definition of constructive ownership, Section 958(b) starts with the constructive ownership rules of section 318(a) but then Section 958(b) provides its own further set of tweaks to those section 318 rules with the consequence that a unique standard for determining constructive stock ownership is forged. The purpose of this problem is to work through how to identify a US person and then to demonstrate how one is to determine that US person's direct and constructive ownership of stock under these rules.

(A) Jose, as a resident alien, is defined as a US person under section 7701(a)(30)(A). Thus, section 957(c) includes him within the scope of a US person who could be a US shareholder if his stock ownership meets the requisite 10% ownership threshold of section 951(b) after application of the stock attribution rules of section 958. Section 958(a)(1) starts with the stock that Jose directly owns of 9% of the stock in Agricola S.A. Once his direct ownership is identified, section 958(b) then adds to that amount the stock that Jose constructively owns. Section 958(b) incorporates the attribution from entity rules of section 318(a)(2) but then section 958(b)(3) reduces the ownership threshold needed for upward entity attribution to owners of 10% of the entity's stock. Because Jose owns 10% of the stock of Cargyll, Inc., he is deemed to constructively own a proportionate share of the stock in Agricola S.A. that is owned by Cargyll, Inc. under this threshold set forth in section 958(b)(3). Thus, Jose is deemed to constructive own 2 additional shares (10% x 20). The actual shares (9 shares) and the constructive shares (2 shares) owned by Jose thus total 11 shares which gets him above the 10% threshold for being classified as a US shareholder under section 951(b).

(B) Cargyll, Inc., as a domestic corporation, is defined to be a US person under section 7701(a)(30)(C). Thus, section 957(c) includes Cargyll, Inc. within the scope of a US person who could be a US shareholder if the requisite 10% ownership threshold of section 951(b) is satisfied after application of the stock attribution rules of section 958. Section 958(a)(1) starts with the stock that Cargyll, Inc. directly owns. Cargyll, Inc. owns 15 shares directly and thus exceeds the 10% threshold in section 951(b) to be classified as a US shareholder.

(C) Maria, as a US citizen, is defined to be a US person under section 7701(a)(30)(A). Thus, section 957(c) includes her within the scope of a US person who could be a US shareholder if the requisite 10% ownership threshold of section 951(b) is satisfied after application of the stock attribution rules of section 958. Section 958(a)(1) starts with the stock that Maria directly owns of 6% in Agricola S.A. However, section 958(a)(2) further expands her stock ownership to include a proportionate share of the stock owned indirectly through foreign entities regardless of her ownership interest in the foreign entity. Thus, she is considered to own 2 shares (5% ownership in Chiquita x 40 shares of Agricola S.A. owned by Chiquita). Note the divergence with how foreign entities are treated versus domestic entities under these attribution rules. In the discussion of Jose, it was indicated that section 958(b)(2) only applies the entity attribution of section 318(a)(2) to domestic entities when a 10% ownership threshold is exceeded. In contrast, Maria is deemed to own a proportionate interest of stock owned through a foreign entity regardless of her ownership threshold in that foreign entity. So, Maria has 8 shares owned directly under section 958(a)(1). The constructive ownership rules of section 958(b) now must be applied to Maria to determine whether she owns more stock through constructive ownership. The beginning point for applying Section 958(b)'s constructive ownership rules is section 318(a). Family attribution under section 318(a)(1) does not include attribution between siblings, so Maria is not deemed to constructively own the stock that is owned by Jose, her brother. If Jose had been Maria's father, son, or grandchild, then she would be attributed his stock under family attribution and would then exceeded the threshold. But, section 318(a)(1) does not apply family attribution among siblings, so she is not deemed to constructively own the stock of her brother. Under section 318(a)(1), Maria normally would be attributed the stock owned by her spouse per Section 318(a)(1)(A)(i), but section 958(b)(1) modifies that rule so as not to apply spousal attribution if the spouse is a nonresident alien individual. Because Maria's spouse (Mario) is a nonresident alien individual, section 958(b)(1) cuts-off spousal attribution of his stock to her. If Mario and Maria were to move to the United States so that Mario became a resident alien, then Maria will be attributed his stock under spousal attribution as the restriction in section 958(b)(1) would no longer apply. This nuance highlights the need for Agricola S.A. to keep dibs on where Maria and Mario reside as part of its determination of whether it is a controlled foreign corporation. But, returning to the posited facts, Maria owns a total of 8 shares directly (6 actually plus 2 through her ownership in Chiquita) which is below the 10 percent threshold. Thus, even though she is a US person, she is not a US shareholder within the meaning of section 951(b) as she does not have stock ownership that exceeds the 10% threshold after application of the attribution rules of section 958.

(D) George, as a US citizen, is defined to be a US person under section 7701(a)(30)(A). Thus, section 957(c) includes him within the scope of a US person who could be a US shareholder if the requisite 10% ownership threshold of section 951(b) is satisfied after application of the stock attribution rules of section 958. Section 958(a)(1) starts with the stock that George owns directly, which is zero. However, section 958(a)(2) further expands his stock ownership to include a proportionate share of the stock owned indirectly through foreign entities regardless of his ownership interest without a minimum ownership threshold for applying this rule. Thus, he is considered to own 10 shares (25% ownership in Chiquita x 40 shares of Agricola S.A. owned by Chiquita). As a result, he is a US shareholder within the meaning of section 951(b) because he is a US person whose ownership is 10 percent or more in Agricola S.A.

(E) A domestic partnership is treated as a US person under section 7701(a)(30), and section 957(c) incorporates this inclusion without modification. Because Partnership P owns 25% of the stock of Agricola S.A., the partnership entity is a US shareholder within the meaning of section 951(b) as its actual stock ownership exceeds the 10 percent threshold.

(F) Sarah, as a US citizen, is defined to be a US person under section 7701(a)(30)(A). Thus, section 957(c) includes her within the scope of a US person who could be a US shareholder if the requisite 10% ownership threshold of section 951(b) is satisfied after application of the stock attribution rules of section 958. Section 958(a)(1) starts with the stock that Sarah directly owns in Agricola S.A., which is zero. However, section 958(a)(2) further expands her stock ownership to include a proportionate share of the stock owned indirectly through foreign entities regardless of her ownership interest without a minimum ownership threshold for applying this rule. Thus, she is considered to own 8 shares (40% ownership in Partnership P x 20 shares of Agricola S.A. owned by Partnership P). Because she falls below the 10% threshold, she is not a US shareholder.

CONCLUSION: Agricola S.A. is a controlled foreign corporation. The U.S. shareholders Agricola S.A. own more than 50% (i.e., 64%) of the stock of Agricola S.A. as follows: Jose-9, Cargyll-20, George-10, and Partnership P-25. However, even though Agricola S.A. is a CFC, Prop. Reg. § 1.958–1(d) provides that the determination as to whether the partners of Partnership P are US shareholders is made as if Partnership P was a foreign partnership. Because Sarah (a US person) only owns 8% of the Agricola S.A. stock indirectly, Sarah is not a US shareholder. See Prop. Reg. § 1.958–1(d)(3) Ex. 1. The other partner, Mario, is not a US person. Thus, the partnership is counted as a US shareholder for purposes of determining the CFC status of Agricola S.A., but it is not treated as a US shareholder for purposes of the subpart F inclusion. Only its partners are responsible for the subpart F inclusion and only when those ultimate partners satisfy the US shareholder determination as applied at their level.

The above example hopefully provides some refinement for how to apply the attribution rules to determine a U.S. shareholder under section 958. In practice, the determination of a U.S. shareholder will often be found to be straightforward, but even so careful reading and attention is needed as the analysis can get involved where multiple shareholders exist in the ownership structure of a foreign corporation.

4. Foreign Controlled United States Shareholders

In the previous section, this material indicated that downward attribution to an entity is generally prohibited due to section 958(b)(4). However, the prohibition against downward entity attribution prescribed in section 958(b)(4) is partially superseded through the companion provision of section 951B. Section 951B was added in the 2025 Act to provide for downward attribution in a limited situation within the context of a foreign corporation that is majority owned by a foreign parent entity. In that context, section 951B allows for downward entity attribution so as to create a foreign controlled foreign corporation.

However, unlike the broad array of situations that would implicate downward attribution of stock by reason of an outright repeal of section 958(b)(4), section 951B provides for downward attribution only of foreign controlled foreign corporations and only to a foreign controlled U.S. shareholder. The narrowly targeted application of downward entity attribution thus occurs in situations where two elements exist: (i) a foreign controlled U.S. shareholder is found to exist and (ii) a foreign controlled foreign corporation also exists and owns directly or indirectly stock in a U.S. entity. As a result, to appreciate the intended application of section 951B, one must unpack those two concepts.

A foreign controlled U.S. shareholder is a U.S. person that is more than 50 percent owned by a foreign corporation. A foreign controlled foreign corporation is a foreign corporation, other than a CFC, where more than 50 percent of its ownership interest is constructively owned by a foreign controlled U.S. shareholder as a result of downward attribution of its stock to the foreign controlled U.S. shareholder by reason of section 318(a)(3). However, even if a foreign controlled U.S. shareholder exists by reason of section 951B and there are foreign controlled foreign corporations constructively owned by such shareholder, the foreign controlled U.S. shareholder must have direct or indirect ownership under section 958(a) before that shareholder is subjected to an income inclusion. Said differently, the U.S. shareholder must have actual direct or indirect ownership as defined in section 958(a) rather than simply constructive ownership by reason of section 958(b) before that entity is subjected to an income inclusion even though constructive ownership of the foreign controlled foreign corporation exists.

The reader may agree that the immediately preceding paragraph was written in plain English and yet still fail to apprehend the intended application of section 951B. Thankfully, a single picture is worth a thousand words, and in that regard the below Diagram #26 serves to illuminate the intended application of section 951B.

Diagram #26

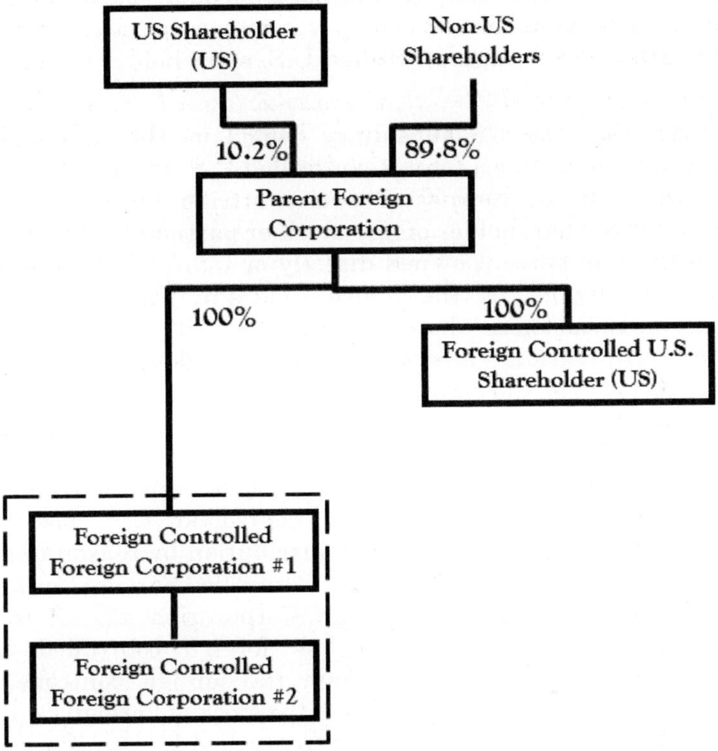

In the above Diagram #26, the Parent Foreign Corporation is a foreign corporation but it is not a controlled foreign corporation because it is not more than 50 percent owned by U.S. shareholders. Due to the prohibition on downward attribution of section 958(b)(4), the foreign corporations owned directly or indirectly by the Foreign Parent corporation are not controlled foreign corporations under the standard application of Code Sec. 957. Thus, the US shareholder who owns 10.2 percent of the foreign parent corporation is not required to have any inclusions. Moreover, that top-level U.S. shareholder is not a foreign controlled U.S. shareholder as that top-level U.S. shareholder is not more than fifty percent owned by the Parent Foreign Corporation, so section 951B has no impact on that top-level U.S. shareholder.

The US entity owned by the foreign parent corporation is a U.S. person that is more than 50 percent owned by the foreign-owned parent corporation, so that US entity constitutes a foreign controlled U.S. shareholder within the meaning of Code Sec. 951B. The above diagram indicates that the foreign controlled U.S. shareholder is a domestic corporation, but even if it were a US partnership it would still be considered a foreign controlled U.S. shareholder as any U.S. juridical person[15] (whether a US corporation or US partnership) that is more than fifty percent owned by a foreign corporation can satisfy the definition of a foreign controlled U.S. shareholder under section 951B.

Given that the US subsidiary owned by the parent foreign corporation constitutes a foreign controlled U.S. shareholder, section 951B now requires downward entity attribution to the foreign controlled U.S. shareholder of any stock or partnership interest that is more than 50 percent owned directly or indirectly by the foreign parent corporation. In the above diagram, the foreign parent corporation owns more than 50 percent of the stock (directly or indirectly) in various foreign corporations depicted as Foreign Controlled Foreign Corporation #1 and Foreign Controlled Foreign Corporation #2. So, due to the downward attribution required by section 951B, the stock in these entities is constructively owned by reason of downward attribution to the foreign controlled U.S. shareholder. Because the foreign controlled U.S. shareholder constructively owns (via downward attribution by reason of section 951B) more than 50% of both Foreign Controlled Foreign Corporation #1 and Foreign Controlled Foreign Corporation #2, all of those foreign affiliates are designated as foreign controlled foreign corporations. However, even though the foreign controlled U.S. shareholder constructively owns all of the stock of Foreign Controlled Foreign Corporation #1 and Foreign Controlled Foreign Corporation #2, the constructive ownership rules do not apply for purposes of determining the amount of the income inclusions as those inclusions are required only for the pro rata interest that is directly or indirectly held (not constructively held) by the U.S. shareholder.[16] As a result, even though the foreign subsidiaries owned by the foreign parent corporation are foreign controlled foreign corporations, because the foreign controlled U.S. shareholder has no direct or indirect ownership in those foreign controlled foreign corporations, no income inclusions under Subpart F or the net CFC tested income regime are required.

Suppose, however, that the Foreign Controlled U.S. Shareholder does in fact have direct or indirect ownership in Foreign Controlled

---

15 See Code Sec. 7701(b)(1) and Code Sec. 7701(b)(9).

16 See section 951(a)(1) and section 951A(e)(2) which cross-references only section 958(a) for the determination of the amount of an income inclusion. Section 958(a) requires actual direct or indirect ownership. Importantly, neither section 951(a)(1) nor section 951A(e)(2) cross-references section 958(b) when it determines the amount of an income inclusion, and this is critical as section 958(b) is the provision that allows for the expanded constructive ownership principles to be used.

Foreign Corporation #1 and Foreign Controlled Foreign Corporation #2 as depicted in the below revised Diagram #27.

Diagram #27

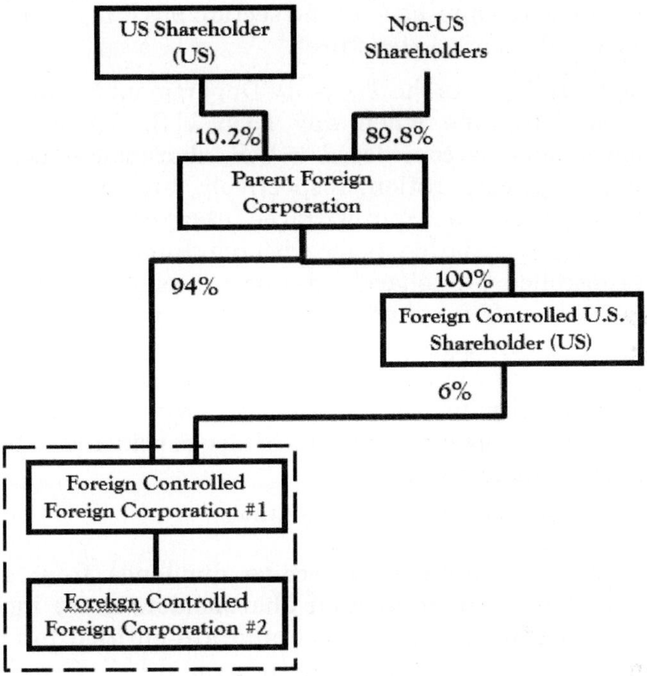

Under these revised facts, the foreign controlled U.S. shareholder in Diagram #27 owns a 6 percent direct interest in Foreign Controlled Foreign Corporation #1 and a 6 percent indirect interest in Foreign Controlled Foreign Corporation #2, so the foreign controlled U.S. shareholder in this fact pattern is required to include 6 percent of the subpart F income and net CFC tested income arising in those foreign controlled foreign corporations in the same manner as if those foreign controlled foreign corporations were controlled foreign corporations. Thus while constructive ownership (including downward attribution) applies to treat the foreign entities as foreign controlled foreign corporations in both of the above illustrations, an income inclusion is required to a foreign controlled U.S. shareholder only when that foreign controlled U.S. shareholder has some actual direct or indirect ownership interest in the foreign controlled foreign corporations. By subjecting the foreign controlled U.S. shareholder to income inclusions based only on their direct or indirect interest in foreign affiliates, the effect of the section 951B regime is to ensure that the U.S. anti-deferral regimes are not avoided through internal "de-control structures" where a controlled U.S. shareholder has some ownership in the foreign affiliates but not more than 50 percent in those entities. Congress originally intended to target those internal "de-control structures" when it repealed section 958(b)(4) in the 2017 Tax Act, but that outright repeal of section 958(b)(4) proved to have broader unintended consequences, and so Congress instead chose to enacted the targeted approach of the section 951B regime to address these internal "de-control structures."

Section 951B grants the Treasury Department broad regulatory authority to determine when any such U.S. person or foreign corporation should be considered a U.S. shareholder or a foreign controlled foreign corporation, respectively, and to prescribe anti-avoidance measures consistent with the intent of this provision. The provision also grants the Treasury with regulatory authority to treat a foreign controlled U.S. shareholder or a foreign controlled foreign corporation as a U.S. shareholder or as a controlled foreign corporation, respectively, for purposes of other tax Code provisions (including any reporting requirement). The Treasury Department is also given authority to provide guidance with respect to foreign controlled foreign corporations that are also considered to be passive foreign investment companies.

5. Individual U.S. Shareholders

For U.S. individuals who receive dividends from a foreign corporation, those U.S. individual shareholders must include the dividend in their worldwide income and are entitled to claim any direct foreign taxes incurred by the individual U.S. shareholder on that foreign dividend. If the foreign corporation were located in a jurisdiction that had an income tax treaty with the United States, then the individual may be entitled to claim a preferential capital gains rate on the receipt of a qualified dividend.[17]

The ability to defer the receipt of foreign dividends and thus the potential incidence of U.S. taxation on the unremitted foreign earnings of a foreign corporation is subject to the constraint of the Subpart F regime and the net CFC tested income regime, but those regimes only apply to controlled foreign corporations. A separate anti-deferral regime applies to any foreign corporation that is considered to be a passive foreign investment company, and that regime is addressed separately in chapter 12.

The first anti-deferral regime to consider is the U.S. Subpart F regime of section 951. When foreign earnings of a controlled foreign corporation are determined to be Subpart F income, the consequence is that the individual U.S. shareholder is required to include immediately in income her pro rata share of the Subpart F income of

---

17 § 1(h)(11)(C)(i).

the controlled foreign corporation. It is as if this income was earned directly by the U.S. shareholder. Thus, the income inclusion is an inclusion of ordinary income and is not treated as a qualified dividend that is eligible for preferential rates.[18] If an individual U.S. shareholder has a Subpart F inclusion from a controlled foreign corporation, then when those earnings are actually distributed the individual U.S. shareholder excludes that distribution from her income. This outcome, mandated by section 959, obviates double taxation. To avoid double taxation to the individual U.S. shareholder with respect to the same foreign earnings, the actual dividend is treated as a distribution of previously taxed earnings and profits ("PTEP") that is excluded from the individual U.S. shareholder's income at the time of actual distribution to prevent double inclusion of the same earnings.

If the earnings of a controlled foreign corporation are not subject to immediate taxation to the individual U.S. shareholder under the Subpart F regime, then a determination must be made as to whether the earnings of the controlled foreign corporation are immediately taxable to the individual U.S. shareholder under the net CFC tested income regime described in section 951A. If so, then the individual U.S. shareholder must include immediately into income her pro rata share of the net CFC tested income inclusion as ordinary income. However, when the earnings of the foreign corporation are actually remitted, then the actual dividend is treated as a distribution of PTEP that is excluded from income. Because the earnings were already subject to taxation under section 951A, these earnings are not taxable at the time of actual remittance in order to avoid double taxation of the U.S. shareholder on the same earnings.

If an individual U.S. shareholder has an immediate inclusion in her income by reason of the Subpart F regime or the net CFC tested income regime or both, the individual U.S. shareholder can make an election under section 962 to have that inclusion treated in the same manner as if that individual were a domestic corporate U.S. shareholder. The benefits of being treated as a domestic corporate U.S. shareholder are discussed in the following paragraph. However, if this election is made, then the later distribution of the income that was the subject of an election under section 962(b) is now taxable to the individual U.S. shareholder but only in an amount in excess of any previously paid taxes on the earlier income inclusion, and the later distribution may be entitled to preferential capital gains rates if the dividend is a qualified dividend.

---

[18] Rodriguez v. Commissioner, 722 F.3d 306 (5th Cir. 2013); Notice 2004–70, 2004–2 Cum. Bull. 724. SIH Partners LLLP v. Commissioner, 923 F.3d 296 (3rd Cir. 2019) (same involving a section 956 inclusion).

6. Domestic Corporate U.S. Shareholder

A domestic corporate U.S. shareholder has a different outcome depending upon whether there is a Subpart F inclusion by reason of section 951 or a net CFC tested income inclusion by reason of section 951 or a combination of the two. In this regard, a domestic corporate U.S. shareholder must include in its income its pro rata share of the Subpart F income plus its associated section 78 gross-up, but then the domestic corporate U.S. shareholder is entitled under section 960 to claim an indirect foreign tax credit for any income taxes paid by the controlled foreign corporation with respect to that Subpart F inclusion. If the earnings of a controlled foreign corporation are determined to be net CFC tested income, then the domestic corporate U.S. shareholder is required to include in its income its pro rata share of the net CFC tested income inclusion plus the associated section 78 gross-up on that net CFC tested income inclusion, but the domestic corporate U.S. shareholder is entitled to a deduction under section 250 with respect to that grossed-up net CFC tested income inclusion and also is entitled to a partial indirect foreign tax credit under section 960. However, once the earnings of the foreign corporation have created an income inclusion to the domestic corporate U.S. shareholder, then those earnings when actually remitted are treated as a distribution of previously taxed income that is excluded from the income of the domestic corporate U.S. shareholder. Because the earnings were already subject to taxation under Subpart F prescribed in section 951 or net CFC tested income prescribed under section 951A, as the case may be, these earnings are not taxable at the time of actual remittance in order to avoid having the domestic corporate U.S. shareholder bear double taxation on the same foreign earnings.

In general, if a foreign corporation is a controlled foreign corporation at any time in the year, then "each United States shareholder which owns stock in such corporation during the CFC tax year shall include in gross income such shareholder's pro rata share of the corporation's subpart F income for the CFC year."[19] Moreover, each United States shareholder which owns stock in such corporation on the last day . . . shall include in gross income the amount determined under section 956 . . . (but only to the extent not excluded from gross income under section 959(a)(2))."[20]

A U.S. shareholder may transfer an ownership interest in a controlled foreign corporation to a non-U.S. shareholder that will not be taxed with respect to an inclusion under the subpart F of section 951 or net CFC tested income under section 951A without itself being

---

[19] § 951(a)(1)(A).

[20] § 951(a)(1)(B).

subject to such an inclusion. Absent any specific limitation in these circumstances, any earnings and profits of the controlled foreign corporation distributed as a dividend to the transferor U.S. shareholder during the controlled foreign corporation's taxable year might be eligible for the section 245A deduction. However, had the transfer not occurred (or had the controlled foreign corporation ceased to be a controlled foreign corporation as a result of the transfer), the earnings and profits may have been subject to tax under the subpart F or the net CFC tested income regimes and, therefore, would not have been eligible for the section 245A deduction.

Mechanically, to prevent the double exclusion of Subpart F income or net CFC tested income inclusions in the context where an extraordinary reduction of interest occurs during the year, the regulations limit the amount of the section 245A deduction allowed to a "controlling section 245A shareholder" with respect to a dividend from a controlled foreign corporation to the portion of the dividend that is paid out of earnings other than the "extraordinary reduction amount."[21] A "controlling section 245A shareholder" of a controlled foreign corporation is a section 245A shareholder of the corporation that, taking into account ownership of the controlled foreign corporation by certain other persons (such as related persons), owns more than 50 percent of the stock of the CFC.[22] The "extraordinary reduction amount" is the portion of the earnings and profits that would have been Subpart F income or net CFC tested income to the transferor domestic corporate U.S. shareholder had there not been a reduction in the stock ownership during the taxable year.[23] Thus, for an extraordinary reduction amount to exist with respect to a controlling section 245A shareholder of a CFC, an "extraordinary reduction" must occur during the controlled foreign corporation's taxable year with respect to the shareholder's ownership of the CFC.[24] Moreover, a reduction is considered *extraordinary* only if either:

(i) the controlling section 245A shareholder transfers more than 10 percent of its stock of the controlled foreign corporation (for example, an extraordinary reduction occurs if the shareholder owns 90 percent of the stock of the controlled foreign corporation and it transfers stock representing more than nine percent of the stock of the CFC) or

---

21 Reg. § 1.245A–5(b)(1) and (e).

22 Reg. § 1.245A–5(i)(2).

23 Reg. § 1.245A–5(e)(1)(ii) and (f)(2).

24 Reg. § 1.245A–5(e).

(ii) there is a greater than ten percent change in the controlling section 245A shareholder's overall ownership of the controlled foreign corporation (for example, if the shareholder owns 90 percent of the stock of the controlled foreign corporation and, as a result of an issuance to a foreign person, the shareholder's ownership of the controlled foreign corporation is reduced such that it no longer owns at least 81 percent of the stock of the CFC).[25]

The effect of denying section 245A's deduction is to cause the domestic corporate U.S. shareholder to include in income these amounts with neither the benefit of the section 245A deduction nor any benefit for a deemed paid foreign tax credit under section 960 nor any benefit of the deduction afforded by section 250 if there had been a net CFC tested income inclusion. So, the outcome to the domestic corporate U.S. shareholder is far worse than the result that would have occurred if the underlying earnings had been subject to taxation to the domestic corporate U.S. shareholder under either the Subpart F regime or the net CFC tested income regime in most foreseeable contexts.

To ameliorate the admittedly harsh treatment contemplated by these regulations, the regulations allow the U.S. domestic corporate U.S. shareholder to elect to close the taxable year of its CFCs immediately prior to any extraordinary reduction event.[26] In that event, the Subpart F inclusion and net CFC tested income inclusion would be made as of the end of the shortened taxable year with the consequence that the domestic corporate U.S. shareholder would then have its full pro rata share of Subpart F income and net CFC tested income inclusion before any extraordinary reduction in interest has occurred. The benefit of that outcome is that the domestic corporate U.S. shareholder would then be entitled to claim the deemed paid credits allowable as part of such an inclusion, and with respect to the net CFC tested income inclusion would be eligible to claim a section 250 deduction. Basis adjustments would also be afforded under section 961(a) for any such inclusions. The regulations frame this option as an "election," but to the mind of this author it appears to be an offer that one cannot refuse in the vast majority of likely situations, so it is likely that U.S. shareholders will need to comply "voluntarily" with the requirements of this election.[27] In addition, pursuant to an exception intended to limit compliance and administrative burdens, for a taxable year in which an

25 Temp. Reg. § 1.245A–5(e)(2)(i)(A).

26 Reg. § 1.245A–5(e)(3)(i)(A).

27 For the requirements of this election, see Reg. § 1.245A–5(e)(3)(i)(C), (D) and (E).

extraordinary reduction occurs, no amount is considered an extraordinary reduction amount if the sum of the CFC's subpart F income and tested income for the taxable year does not exceed the lesser of $50 million or 5 percent of the CFC's total income for the year.[28]

Complicated? Yes, and one needs a clear compass to divine where the issues converge and where they diverge. The key terms of "controlled foreign corporation," "U.S. shareholder," and the definition of the types of income that represent Subpart F income or net CFC tested income are determined without consideration of the identity of the shareholder. However, once Subpart F income or net CFC tested income is found to exist in a controlled foreign corporation ("CFC") environment, then the effects for a U.S. shareholder diverge in important ways depending on whether the U.S. shareholder is an individual or a domestic corporation and also depending on whether the income inclusion is by reason of the Subpart F regime or by reason of the net CFC tested income regime.

B. Subpart F Regime

In the early years of the income tax, foreign corporations were widely used by U.S. persons to avoid U.S. taxation of foreign income, or at least to defer it indefinitely. The separate identity of corporations in the U.S. tax system means that a foreign corporation is not formally a U.S. person, even if owned by U.S. citizens or residents. Consequently, a foreign corporation has no immediate U.S. income tax obligation on foreign source income earned outside the United States.

1. Foreign Base Companies

A foreign "base company" is essentially a center of profit severed from its economic moorings. A foreign corporation, located in a low-tax jurisdiction and owned by U.S. shareholders, became an attractive vehicle to create homeless income and engage in base erosion and profit strategies with other affiliates. A picture can be worth a thousand words, so consider the following Diagram #28:

> **Diagram #28:** In an effort to reduce foreign tax costs of the multinational group and also to avoid the incidence of U.S. taxation on business activities conducted outside the United States, a U.S. multinational enterprise establishes a foreign base company (Foreign Base Co.) in a low-tax jurisdiction (Switzerland in this example). The foreign base company then engages in the following "base erosion" strategies with affiliates operating in high-tax jurisdictions

---

28 Reg. § 1.245A–5(e)(3)(ii).

that are themselves treated as either regarded entities (like Foreign Opco #1) or as disregarded entities (like Foreign Opco #2). Examples of such "base erosion" strategies include the following:

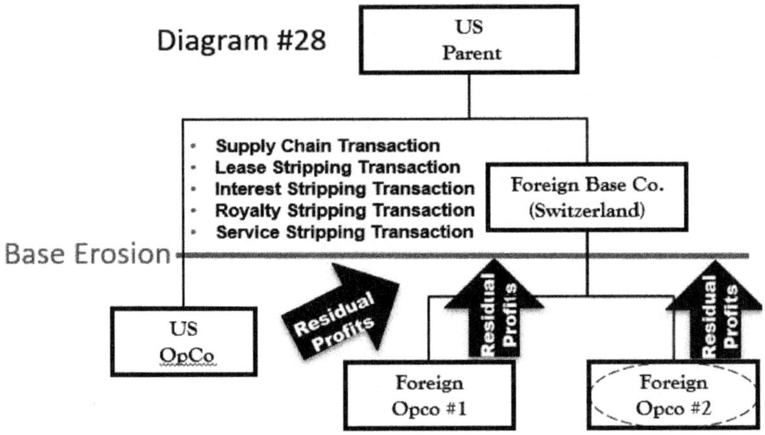

1. Foreign Base Co. leases tangible personal property (machinery and equipment) to foreign operating affiliates located in high-tax jurisdictions and charges rent for its use ("lease stripping transaction").

2. Foreign Base Co. makes related party loans to fund the working capital and capital investment needs of the various affiliates located in high-tax jurisdictions ("interest stripping transaction").

3. Foreign Base Co. obtains ownership of intellectual property and licenses the intellectual property to various foreign operating affiliates located in high-tax jurisdictions for their use of the U.S. developed intellectual property ("royalty stripping transaction").

4. Foreign Base Co., through a contract manufacturing arrangement with operating affiliates, obtains manufactured goods that are resold by Foreign Base Co. to other affiliates and thereby earns a significant profit due to its insertion into this intercompany trading pattern ("supply chain transaction").

5. Foreign Base Co. charges affiliates for management services, accounting and back-office support, and risk

management services and technical services ("service stripping transactions").[29]

Each of the above base erosion techniques allows Foreign Base Co. to extract profits from affiliates[30] located in high-tax jurisdictions and to earn this income in the low-tax jurisdiction of Foreign Base Co. By the early 1960s, foreign base companies were widely used for international production, marketing, and services of all kinds. The U.S. Treasury was not entirely helpless against foreign base companies in the days before Subpart F,[31] but none of the countermeasures available to it made a large dent in the profit shifting opportunities. A further backstop was needed to prevent profit shifting of multinational enterprises to tax haven subsidiaries that escaped U.S. taxation.

2. Subpart F Historical Origins[32]

On April 20, 1961, President Kennedy announced a new major tax reform initiative that included elimination of deferral for "tax haven" subsidiaries and for income earned in the developed countries of Europe.[33] The House Ways and Means Committee held hearings on international tax reform[34], and the Joint Committee on Taxation presented a report detailing the base erosion strategies like those set forth in Diagram #28 that were utilized by "two actual international corporations, which are subsidiaries of large American corporations" that shifted income to tax haven subsidiaries like the foreign base

---

[29] These base erosion techniques have been studied and well-documented. See e.g., JOINT COMM. ON TAXATION, 112TH CONG., PRESENT LAW AND BACKGROUND RELATED TO POSSIBLE INCOME SHIFTING AND TRANSFER PRICING (JCX–37–10) (July 20, 2010); see also U.S. DEP'T OF THE TREASURY, REP. TO THE CONG. ON EARNINGS STRIPPING, TRANSFER PRICING AND U.S. INCOME TAX TREATIES (2007).

[30] Foreign multinational enterprises can engage in each of the above base erosion strategies subject only to the United States transfer pricing rules of section 482, except that interest stripping transactions must also comply with section 163(j)'s earnings stripping rules, section 59A's minimum tax on base erosion payments, and U.S. withholding tax on outbound payment of interest, rentals, and royalties when not eliminated by treaty.

[31] For example, the transfer prices for goods and services between a U.S. enterprise and a foreign affiliate could be attacked under section 482, which in effect forces U.S. taxpayers to recognize income properly attributable to their economic activity in the United States. See chapter 4.

[32] For a more detailed analysis of this historical evolution of the Subpart F regime, see Bret Wells, *Territorial Taxation: Homeless Income is the Achilles Heel*, 12 HOUS. BUS. & TAX L.J. 1 (2012).

[33] See Special Message to the Congress on Taxation, 1961 PUB. PAPERS 290 (Apr. 20, 1961).

[34] See *President's 1961 Tax Recommendations: Hearing Before the H. Comm. on Ways and Means*, 87th Cong. (1961), *reprinted in* BERNARD D. REAMS, JR., U.S. REVENUE ACTS: 1953–72 LEGISLATIVE HISTORIES, LAWS & CONGRESSIONAL DOCUMENTS (William S. Hein & Co., Inc., 17th ed. 1985).

company in Diagram #28.[35] In the course of extended testimony, Secretary of the Treasury Dillon defended the Kennedy administration's Subpart F proposals as a way to deal with the untoward transfer pricing results that arose with tax haven subsidiaries. Secretary Dillon testified that "the reductions in tax that can be achieved through the use of tax haven operations assume that the income attributed to the tax haven companies [sic] are fair and reasonable" and then stated that the problem is that "the incomes are often allocated to tax haven companies which are not economically justified,"[36] thus taking square aim at the income shifting and base erosion opportunities afforded to taxpayers in Diagram #28. Similarly, IRS Commissioner Chapman testified that the IRS believed that section 482 was not effectively protecting the U.S. tax jurisdiction from tax haven subsidiary opportunities,[37] thus arguing that the homeless income mistake made possible in Diagram #28 required a further legislative response. Secretary Dillon alleged that the explosive growth of tax haven subsidiaries was "a very recent and growing phenomenon."[38] The Kennedy administration's Subpart F proposal was motivated by a "general objective of getting at this basic tax haven problem and does not hurt or affect the corporation, which is operating in a country with a tax structure similar to ours."[39] Secretary of Commerce Grudeman reiterated the charge that "the various paper transactions serve as a medium by which large sums [of income] are diverted from the U.S. tax base"

---

[35] See STAFF OF THE JOINT COMMITTEE ON INTERNATIONAL REVENUE TAXATION, TAX EFFECTS OF CONDUCTING FOREIGN BUSINESS THROUGH FOREIGN CORPORATIONS, at 9–18 (JCS–5–61) (1961) (setting forth base erosion opportunities used with two actual U.S. multinational corporations).

[36] See *President's 1961 Tax Recommendations: Hearing Before the H. Comm. on Ways and Means*, 87th Cong. 29 (1961) (statement of Hon. C. Douglas Dillon, Secretary of the Treasury), *reprinted in* BERNARD D. REAMS, JR., U.S. REVENUE ACTS: 1953–72 LEGISLATIVE HISTORIES, LAWS & CONGRESSIONAL DOCUMENTS (William S. Hein & Co., Inc., 17th ed. 1985).

[37] See *President's 1961 Tax Recommendations: Hearing Before the H. Comm. on Ways and Means*, 87th Cong., 3549 (1961) (statement of M. Chapman, IRS Commissioner), *reprinted in* BERNARD D. REAMS, JR., U.S. REVENUE ACTS: 1953–72 LEGISLATIVE HISTORIES, LAWS & CONGRESSIONAL DOCUMENTS (William S. Hein & Co., Inc., 17th ed. 1985); 107 CONG. REC. 6456, 6458 (1961) (Federal Tax System—Message From the President of the United States).

[38] See *President's 1961 Tax Recommendations: Hearing Before the H. Comm. on Ways and Means*, 87th Cong. 349 (1961) (statement of Hon. C. Douglas Dillon, Secretary of the Treasury), *reprinted in* BERNARD D. REAMS, JR., U.S. REVENUE ACTS: 1953–72 LEGISLATIVE HISTORIES, LAWS & CONGRESSIONAL DOCUMENTS (William S. Hein & Co., Inc., 17th ed. 1985).

[39] See *President's 1961 Tax Recommendations: Hearing Before the H. Comm. on Ways and Means*, 87th Cong. 343, 345 (1961) (statement of Hon. C. Douglas Dillon, Secretary of the Treasury *reprinted in* BERNARD D. REAMS, JR., U.S. REVENUE ACTS: 1953–72 LEGISLATIVE HISTORIES, LAWS & CONGRESSIONAL DOCUMENTS (William S. Hein & Co., Inc., 17th ed. 1985).

and into the hands of tax haven subsidiaries.[40] A transfer pricing case (involving DuPont) involved a supply chain transaction that shifted significant export profits out of Dupont's U.S. manufacturing affiliate and into a tax-haven Swiss marketing and distribution company.[41] Thus, a mounting concern was that the U.S. transfer pricing rules were not sufficient to prevent inappropriate income-shifting of profits away from the country where the economic activity occurred, and the proposed Subpart F regime was seen as an important "backstop" to prevent these abuses.

C. Income Subject to Current Taxation Under Subpart F

Current taxation of CFCs under the Subpart F regime extends to what Congress considers to be "tax haven" income (a notion with a somewhat shifting definition over the years) and not (with significant exceptions) to active business operations. What the tax writers understand as tax haven income includes passive income arising in a no-tax or low-tax environment and income artificially shifted to such an environment when it has no indigenous economic connection there. Thus, income subject to current taxation under Subpart F is a mix of passive investment income and income artificially deflected from high-tax to low-tax environments ("base company" income, the quintessential object of Subpart F).[42] There are other categories of income that constitute Subpart F income (namely certain insurance income,[43] international boycott income,[44] illegal or corrupt payments,[45] and income derived from enemy nations as designated by the U.S. State Department),[46] but those topics are not the core topics and are not separately discussed here further. The

---

[40] See *President's 1961 Tax Recommendations: Hearings Before the H. Comm. on Ways and Means,* 87th Cong. 416 (1961) (statement of Secretary Grudeman), *reprinted in* BERNARD D. REAMS, JR., U.S. REVENUE ACTS: 1953–72 LEGISLATIVE HISTORIES, LAWS & CONGRESSIONAL DOCUMENTS (William S. Hein & Co., Inc., 17th ed. 1985).

[41] DuPont attempted to shift approximately half of their profits in 1959 and 1960 to a Swiss tax-haven subsidiary that had little substance. See E.I. Du Pont de Nemours and Co. v. United States, 78–1 U.S.T.C. ¶ 9374 (Ct. Cl. 1978) (finding as a factual matter the prominent role of Mr. Baker's views on the resulting tax planning efforts of DuPont). The taxpayer eventually lost the *DuPont* case twenty years later in 1979. See E.I. Du Pont de Nemours and Co. v. United States, 608 F.2d 445 (Ct. Cl. 1979). But, in the intervening twenty year period, the government was concerned that the transfer pricing rules may not adequately address cases such as the *DuPont* case, and so Congress enacted the Subpart F regime as a "backstop" regime to counteract this type of tax planning that might not have been adequately addressed under section 482.

[42] See § 952(a); § 954(a).

[43] See § 953.

[44] See § 952(b)(3).

[45] See § 952(b)(4).

[46] See § 952(b)(5).

core topics relate to foreign base company income and section 956 inclusions, and those topics are discussed in some detail.

1. Foreign Base Company Income

Among the several items taxed currently under Subpart F, the most important is "foreign base company income," a category itself made up of several elements. A brief traversal of its composition may give you a somewhat clearer picture of the taxation of CFCs.

"Foreign base company income" occupies its own Code section.[47] The term describes several types of income—both passive and active in form. In the original form of Subpart F (1962), foreign base company income included only passive investment income and income from tax haven arrangements between related persons. The common element of this income is that it is relatively easily shifted from a high-tax to a low-tax environment. One way to encapsulate Subpart F is that it imposes current taxation on foreign operations in which relatively liquid or relatively mobile capital is a dominant factor.[48]

Foreign base company income, as defined in section 954(a), is made up of three different components:

1) Foreign personal holding company income,

2) Foreign base company sales income, and

3) Foreign base company services income.

2. Foreign Personal Holding Company Income

The first component of foreign base company income is "foreign personal holding company income" ("FPHCI"), itself defined in section 954(c)(1) as an assemblage of several components. The core element of foreign personal holding company income is the "portion of gross income which consists of. . . dividends, interest, royalties, rents, and annuities."[49] To this are added various gains and losses from transactions in property that produce passive income or are not used in a trade or business,[50] income from various financial transactions,[51] and, most recently, income from "personal service

---

[47] § 954. This is equivalent in statutory real estate to having your own zip code.

[48] Note, however, that the change in Subpart F (1996) actually *removed* a significant class of financial services income—mainly from banking, securities brokerage, and insurance—from its reach.

[49] § 954(c)(1)(A).

[50] These include gains from property producing passive income, gains from commodities transactions not arising in the normal course of business, and many foreign currency gains. See § 954(c)(1)(B)–(D).

[51] These include income "equivalent to interest," income from "notional principal contracts" (commonly known as interest rate and commodities "swaps"), and payments under "repo" agreements. See § 954(c)(*l*)(E)–(G).

contracts" carried out by controlled foreign corporations.[52] The components of foreign personal holding company income mostly have the form of income from passive investments, although several may arise in the course of an active business. Sometimes, however, a connection with a business shifts income from foreign personal holding company income to another category for the purposes of Subpart F.[53]

Active Financial Services Income and Insurance Income Excluded. An important exclusion from foreign personal holding company income, since the 1998 Act,[54] is that income (including interest, dividends, and gains from the sale of property that generates those categories of income) that is generated from active foreign banking and financing businesses is excluded from the definition of foreign personal holding company income in section 954(h). A companion provision provides a similar exemption for qualified insurance income in section 954(i). U.S. banks and other financial intermediaries can now do business outside the United States without current U.S. taxation.[55] The legislative undergirding of this exception is formidable. The effect of the "active financing exception" and the "active insurance exception" is that a foreign finance subsidiary located in a low-tax jurisdiction can engage in lending, leasing and insurance activities with unrelated parties, and the financial services income and insurance income generated in these transactions would not be subject to immediate U.S. taxation under the Subpart F rules. Public interest advocates have argued that the reinstatement of the "active financing exception" of section 954(h) has allowed companies to shift significant profits to tax haven subsidiaries.[56]

---

52 § 954(c)(*l*)(I). This is income from personal services furnished by a controlled foreign corporation if some other person has the right to designate the individual actually performing the services. This provision, which prevents U.S. individuals from deferring tax on income from services performed outside the United States, was moved to Subpart F from the older foreign personal holding company rules, most of which were repealed in 2004.

53 § 954(c)(2).

54 There were complications with the late line-item veto that kept these provisions from definitive effect until 1999.

55 § 954(h).

56 Compare CITIZENS FOR TAX JUSTICE AND THE INSTITUTE ON TAXATION AND ECONOMIC POLICY, CORPORATE TAXPAYERS & CORPORATE TAX DODGERS, 2008–2010, 13 (Nov. 2011):

> It is oxymoronically titled the "active financing exception" (the joke is that financing is generally considered to be a quintessentially *passive* activity). This tax break allows financial companies (GE has a major financial branch) to pay no taxes on foreign (or ostensibly foreign) lending and leasing, apparently while deducting the interest expenses of engaging in such activities from their U.S. taxable income. This is an exception to the general rule that U.S. corporations can defer their U.S. taxes on offshore profits only if they take the form of *active* income rather than passive income.

Rents and Royalties from an Active Business. After the general rule of section 954(c)(1) that rents and royalties are considered foreign personal holding company income, a series of exceptions and exceptions to those exceptions follow. As one exception, foreign personal holding company income does not include rents and royalties derived in an active business, unless received from a related person.[57] A number of rent-producing undertakings—such as the ownership and operation of rental real estate, equipment leasing, and film distribution—can thus be conducted through a CFC without triggering current U.S. taxation as long as there is no obvious income-shifting among related persons.

Dividends, Interest, Rents, and Royalties Between Controlled Foreign Corporations. An exception has long existed for dividends, interest, rents, and royalties paid from one controlled foreign corporation to another controlled foreign corporation that was incorporated in the same foreign country.[58] However, starting in 2006 and extended multiple times thereafter, Congress enacted section 954(c)(6) to give non-Subpart F treatment to related-party interest, rents, royalties, and dividends paid by one controlled foreign corporation to another controlled foreign corporation regardless of where incorporated.[59] The effect of section 954(c)(6) is that the foreign base company in Diagram #28 can engage in lease stripping transactions, interest stripping transactions, and royalty stripping transactions with other controlled foreign corporations without generating Subpart F income. Thus, through the enactment of section 954(c)(6), the Subpart F planning opportunities were expanded beyond the same-country exception that has long existed in section 954(c)(3)(A). However, as an exception to both of these exceptions, the non-Subpart F treatment generally afforded to these related party CFC payments is not available if the related party

---

with Letter to the Editor by Kenneth Kies, *Kies Critiques CTJ Corporate Tax Report*, 2011 TNT 224–13, Doc 2011–24017 (November 21, 2011) (stating that active financing exception to Subpart F is narrowly tailored and consistent with historic compromise contained in the Subpart F rules).

[57] § 954(c)(2)(A).

[58] § 954(c)(3)(A).

[59] See Tax Increase Prevention and Reconciliation Act of 2005, PUB. L. NO. 109–222, § 103(b)(1), 120 Stat. 345, 346 (2006) (enacted section 954(c)(6) and made it applicable for tax years through December 31, 2008). Section 954(c)(6) has been extended to apply for tax years through December 31, 2011. See Tax Extenders and Alternative Minimum Tax Relief Act of 2008, Pub. L. No. 110–343, § 304, 122 Stat. 3765 (2008) (extended section 954(c)(6) to tax years beginning before January 1, 2010); Tax Relief, Unemployment Insurance Reauthorization, and Job Creation Act of 2010, Pub. L. No. 111–312, § 751(a), 124 Stat. 3321, 3321 (2010) (extended section 954(c)(6) through tax years beginning before January 1, 2012). In 2025, after years of extending it on a temporary basis, Congress made the exception found in section 954(c)(6) a permanent provision of the Code. See PUB. L. NO. 119–21, Sec. 70351, 139 Stat. 72, 208 (July 4, 2025).

payment reduced the Subpart F income of the payor[60] or if the domestic corporate U.S. shareholder engaged in an extraordinary reduction of its interest in the year of the related party payment.[61] Consequently, section 954(c)(6) broadly allows interest stripping, royalty stripping, and rental stripping transactions between Foreign Opco #1 and Foreign Base Co. depicted in Diagram #28 to avoid being classified as foreign personal holding company income by reason of section 954(c)(6) unless the deduction arising from the payment reduced the Subpart F income of the payor CFC.

Check-the-Box Planning. A favorable development for tax planning occurred in 1996 when the Treasury Department changed its regulations to provide that the tax classification of foreign entities was a matter of taxpayer election and that a disregarded entity held by one taxpayer would be considered a "branch" for U.S. tax purposes.[62] With the flexibility of the check-the-box regulations, taxpayers were able to have the foreign base company in Diagram #28 to engage in lease stripping transactions, interest stripping transactions, and royalty stripping transactions with lower-tier entities that are treated as "disregarded entities" for U.S. tax purposes by reason of a check-the-box election. The effect of treating the lower-tier foreign operating entity as a disregarded entity (like Foreign Opco #2 in Diagram #28) is that transactions with that entity and its owner are disregarded and not tested under the foreign personal holding company income rules of section 954(c). You will note that the lower-tier foreign entity called Foreign Opco #2 in Diagram #28 in fact is depicted as a hybrid entity that is disregarded for U.S. tax purposes. The Treasury Department in 1999 issued proposed regulations that would attack this use of hybrid entities, but the Treasury Department has set the effective date for any regulatory change to be five years after the date that final regulations were adopted.[63] After more than twenty years, the

---

[60] See § 954(c)(3)(B); § 954(c)(6)(B). For rents and royalties, those amounts are allocated and apportioned based on the rules that exist under Reg. § 1.861–8. Interest, however, is *first* allocated against the passive Subpart F income of the payor to the extent of the passive Subpart F income of the payor and then is prorated to all other income based on the relative gross income of the other categories of income. Reg. § 1.904–5(c)(2)(ii)(C) and (D). This allocation methodology for interest means that related party interest stripping is likely to be to some extent treated as passive if the payor has any net passive income.

[61] See chapter 13 for a discussion of the limitation on the ability to rely on section 954(c)(6) in the context of an extraordinary reduction of the U.S. shareholder's interest in the controlled foreign corporation that receives such payment.

[62] See T.D. 8697, 61 FED. REG. 66,584 (Dec. 18, 1996); Reg. § 301.7701–3(b)(2)(C) (2006).

[63] See T.D. 8767, 63 FED. REG. 14,613 (March 26, 1998); Prop. Reg. 113909–98, 64 FED. REG. 37727 (1999). The earliest possible effective date for the provisions of the hybrid branch regulations is five years from the date that such regulations are finalized. See Prop. Reg. § 1.954–9(c), 64 FED. REG. 37731. These proposed regulations

proposed regulations have still not been finalized, and it is doubtful they ever will be. Consequently, interest stripping, royalty stripping, and rental stripping transactions involving Foreign Opco #2 (which is designated as a disregarded entity in Diagram #28) represent "disregarded transactions" and thus do not create foreign personal holding company income.

High-Tax Exception and High-Tax Kick-Out. If passive income is subject to high taxation, then that income is not considered "passive basket income" but instead is kicked out of the passive basket.[64] Moreover, income that is subject to high taxation (at least 90 percent of the U.S. rate) is excluded from Subpart F.[65] Again, if the income in fact were subject to high taxes, then this is not the income that was of concern. Returning again to Diagram #28, the Subpart F rules were concerned about the deflection of low-tax income to the foreign base company, so when that is not what has happened, the taxpayer can elect not to have an inclusion with respect to high-tax income.

Section 245(e) Hybrid Dividends. A hybrid dividend is a payment of interest or royalties that is deductible by the paying controlled foreign corporation, but the payee controlled foreign corporation treats the payment as a dividend.[66] The inconsistent treatment of the payment between the payor jurisdiction's allowance of a deductible expense, and the payee jurisdiction's dividend treatment creates the potential for homeless income due to the fact that many foreign jurisdictions provide a participation exemption for foreign dividend income. Thus, Congress in 2017 enacted section 245A(e) to require payments that would otherwise meet a foreign personal holding company exception to be treated nonetheless as foreign personal holding company income if the payment is a hybrid dividend. However, as long as a payment is treated consistently as interest, rents, and royalty payments in each of the two relevant foreign jurisdictions (namely the tax jurisdiction of the foreign operating subsidiary and the tax jurisdiction of the foreign base company), then the amounts are not treated as a hybrid dividend even though from a U.S. perspective Foreign Opco #2 in Diagram #28 is a hybrid entity because the U.S. is not the payor or recipient jurisdiction in Diagram #28.[67]

Finally, in applying the foreign personal holding company rules to income earned by a controlled foreign corporation via an

---

have not yet been finalized even though these proposed regulations have been outstanding for over two decades. Id.

64 § 904(d)(2)(B)(iii)(II); Reg. § 1.904–4(c)(1); Reg. § 1.904–4(c)(1).

65 § 954(b)(4).

66 § 245A(e)(4).

67 See Reg. § 1.245A–2(b)(2).

investment in a partnership, the controlled foreign corporation's distributive share of partnership income is determined to be foreign personal holding company income at the partner level by looking at whether the partnership activities would have met any of the above exceptions if the CFC partner had earned the income and engaged in the activities directly, but the partnership's activities and income are considered in isolation at the partner level from all of the other activities of the partner.[68]

Extraordinary Reductions. Chapter 9 set out a discussion of the 100 percent foreign dividends received deduction afforded under section 245A. In that discussion, Reg. § 1.245A–5T restricted the eligibility for dividends that arise as part of an extraordinary reduction"[69] of a taxpayer's interest in the CFC. As a conforming changes, section 954(c)(6) is limited in situations where these transactions occur. In this regard, if a lower-tier CFC makes a dividend payment in the context of an extraordinary reduction, the section 954(c)(6) exception only applies to the extent the dividend exceeds the distributing lower-tier CFC's "tiered extraordinary reduction amount," taking into account certain prior inclusions under section 951(a).[70] The regulations then go through some detail on how to calculate this amount.[71] Finally, a controlling section 245A shareholder of a lower-tier CFC may elect to close the taxable year of the CFC in cases where an extraordinary reduction occurs and the CFC would have a tiered extraordinary reduction amount.[72]

Concluding Thoughts on Foreign Personal Holding Company Income. In light of the above rules, let's consider how the foreign personal holding company income rules and its exceptions impact the base erosion and profit shifting techniques depicted in Diagram #28. To begin with, the foreign personal holding company income rules include in their scope income that is derived from interest, rents, royalties, and gains from property that generate these types of income. However, if Foreign Base Co. were in an active banking or similar financial services entity that could avail itself of the section 954(h) exception or if it were able to meet the active rents and royalties exception, then it would be entitled to an exception from the

---

68 Reg. § 1.954–2(a)(5)(ii).

69 Reg. § 1.245A–5T(e).

70 See Reg. § 1.245A–5T(f)(1).

71 Reg. § 1.245A–5T(f)(2). The amount is multiplied by 50 percent in order to approximate the reduced tax rate that would have arisen by reason of the deduction provided under section 250(a)(1)(B) with respect to section 951A inclusion with respect to the transition tax. For U.S. shareholders who are ineligible for a section 245A deduction, the effect of this formula is to deny the section 954(c)(6) exception and thus prevent deferral of tax with respect to the applicable subpart F income or tested income.

72 See Reg. § 1.245A–5T(e).

general rule. Moreover, as to the interest stripping, rental stripping, and royalty stripping fact patterns, the payments from Foreign Opco #1 would potentially be excluded from foreign personal holding company income by reason of section 954(c)(6) as long as the payments did not reduce the foreign personal holding company income of Foreign Opco #1 and were not treated inconsistently as a hybrid dividend between those two jurisdictions or the payment reduced the net Subpart F income of the payor CFC. The payment from Foreign Opco #2 is a disregarded transaction, so those payments are "nonevents" for U.S. tax purposes, since Foreign Opco #2 is a disregarded entity as long as the payments are treated consistently as interest, rents, and royalties between the relevant *foreign* jurisdictions. Finally, the interest stripping, royalty stripping, or rental stripping from U.S. Opco to Foreign Base Co. would be classified as foreign personal holding company under section 954(c)(1) and would not be eligible for any relevant exception. Those US Opco payments likely would also be U.S. source income for the reasons discussed in chapter 3.

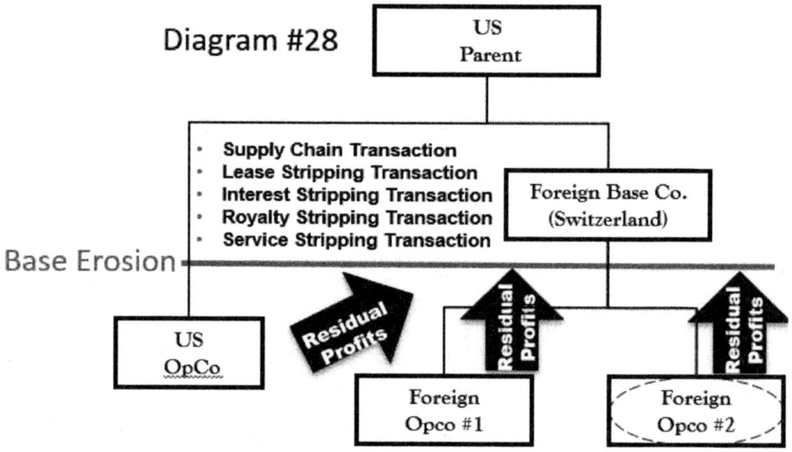

Thus, the foreign personal holding company income rules prevent any related U.S. Opco's payment of interest, rents, or royalty to a controlled foreign corporation from escaping the foreign personal holding company income classification. However, the foreign personal holding company income rules provide exceptions for active foreign banking and active rental and royalty business and also allow related party payments between CFCs of interest, rent, and royalty payments to qualify for exceptions unless those transactions were a hybrid transaction under section 245A(e) or the deduction reduced the payor's Subpart F income. Thus, the foreign personal holding company income rules apply to passive investment portfolio income earned in Foreign Base Co., but earnings stripping conducted entirely among CFCs that operate only in foreign jurisdictions are given significant latitude under the current scope of the foreign personal holding company income rules. This expansive latitude provides the backdrop for why the net CFC tested income regime of section 951A was envisioned as a necessary supplement in the 2017 Act, but let's finish our tour of the Subpart F regime before turning our attention to the companion net CFC tested income regime.

3. Foreign Base Company Sales Income

Foreign base company sales income—perhaps the quintessential form of Subpart F income—is income that results from channeling sales of goods through a low-tax foreign entity that has no significant economic relation to the sales. Broadly, it is income derived from purchases and sales of property between related persons. Persons are "related" within Subpart F if one of them controls the other or if both are under common control.[73]

To be more specific, the following two-part test is a fairly close paraphrase of the Code's definition of foreign base company sales income:

Foreign base company sales income is gain

Test #1

1) derived from the purchase from a related person for resale to any person;

2) derived from the sale to any person on behalf of a related person;

3) derived from the purchase from any person for resale to a related person; or

4) derived from the purchase from any person on behalf of a related person

Test #2

of any personal property manufactured, produced, grown, or extracted outside the country in which a CFC is organized, if the property is sold or purchased for use, consumption, or disposition outside that country.[74]

In order for income to constitute foreign base company sales income, both tests (Test #1 and Test #2) must be satisfied.

Thus, let's return to the supply chain transaction posited in Diagram #7 that was introduced in chapter 3 and is reproduced again here.

---

[73] § 954(d)(3).

[74] § 954(d)(1). Foreign base company sales income includes commissions, fees, and other gains, along with the profits of sale from transactions of this type. Id.

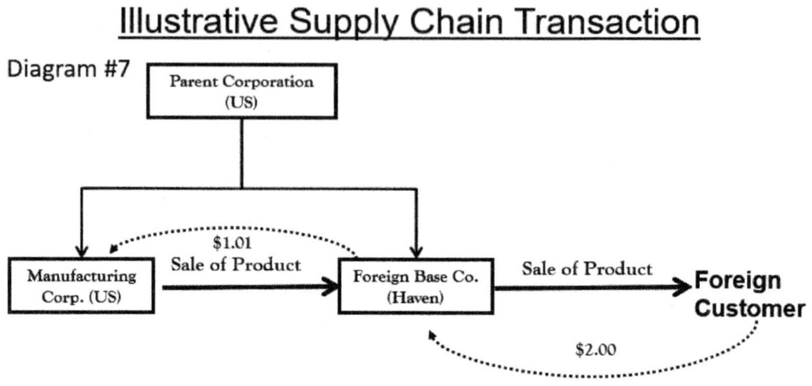

In this Diagram #7, Foreign Base Co. is a distributor of inventory, so its sales of goods do not give rise to interest, rents, royalties, or dividends and thus would not be subject to the foreign personal holding company income rules.[75] However, this is where the foreign base company sale rules then could apply. In this regard, Foreign Base Co. has engaged in a related party purchase of inventory (Test #1 is met) and then resold the inventory that neither originates in its country of incorporation nor is used or consumed in its country of incorporation (thus, Test #2 is met). The foreign customer, you will remember, was located in a European country outside of Haven. Thus, the profits that Foreign Base Co. earns in Diagram #7 are foreign base company sales income and in fact represent the quintessential example for what these rules were designed to address.

Let's take another variation as depicted in Diagram #29.

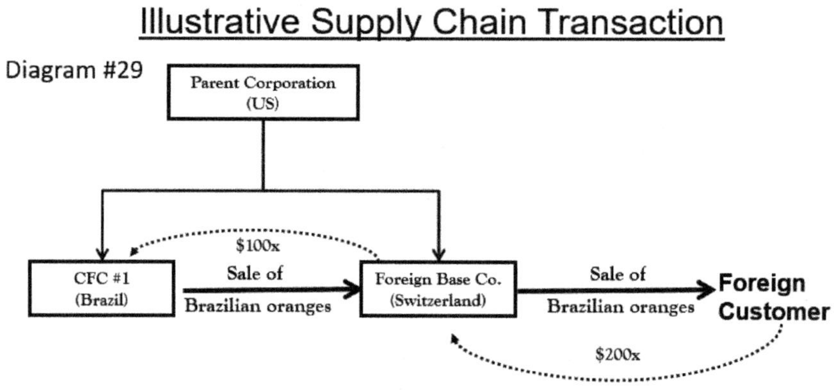

Now, the supplier of the inventory (Brazilian oranges in this example) is a Brazilian CFC that sells its inventory to Foreign Base

75 Reg. § 1.954–2(e).

Co. that then resells the oranges to customers in Switzerland and to customers throughout Europe.

CFC#1 does not have foreign base company income. Yes, CFC#1 has a related party sale (Test #1 is met), but the products were produced or grown in Brazil (thus, Test #2 is *not* met). Because the goods sold by CFC#1 were produced or grown in Brazil (the country of incorporation of CFC#1), then the profit earned by CFC#1 is not foreign base company income. In contrast, Foreign Base Co. has engaged in a related party purchase of inventory goods that were not produced in Switzerland (Test #1 is met), and a *portion* of those goods are sold for use or consumption outside Switzerland. As to the portion that will be sold for use or consumption in Switzerland, the income with respect to those Swiss-destined sales is not foreign base company sales income because Test #2 is not satisfied (the Brazilian oranges are sold for use in Switzerland, the country of incorporation of Foreign Base Co.). However, as to the sale of oranges that will be used or consumed outside of Switzerland (Test #2 is now met), the income earned by Foreign Base Co. on those non-Swiss destined oranges would be foreign base company sales income. The regulations provide presumptions and rules to determine whether goods are presumed to have been sold for use in the country or not.

As a final variation, now assume that CFC#1 acts as a purchasing agent for Foreign Base Co. such that the oranges are purchased directly from the Brazilian growers under the name of Foreign Base Co. In this variation, the commission fee income earned by CFC#1 is paid by a related person for the purchase of property by the related party (Test #1 is met), but CFC#1 earned that commission with respect to the purchase of goods that were grown or produced in its country of incorporation, thus causing Test #2 not to be met. Thus, CFC#1 does not have foreign base company sales income on its commission income. Moreover, Foreign Base Co. now has not purchased from any related party or sold to any related party, so Foreign Base Co. now does not satisfy Test #1 as there is no related party purchase or sale of its inventory. Thus, by removing CFC#1 from the trading pattern's chain of ownership, Foreign Base Co. no longer has foreign base company sales income. Obviously, having a contract concluding agent in Brazil acting on behalf of Foreign Base Co. may create local tax presence issues for Foreign Base Co. in Brazil, so changing the trading pattern may have trade-offs that need to be considered, as the goals of avoiding the foreign base company sales income classification cannot be considered in a vacuum.

Thus, these examples provide a useful framework for understanding the foreign base company sales regime. There must be a related party purchase or sale, or commission income derived from a related party's purchase or sale, and that is one prong of this standard (Test #1 in our analysis). But secondarily, the underlying inventory that is purchased or sold must have been neither (i) produced or manufactured in the country of incorporation of the controlled foreign corporation that is being tested nor (ii) sold for use in the country in which the tested controlled foreign corporation is incorporated (Test #2 in our analysis). The common thread running through the foreign base company sales income regime is that it focuses on purchases and sales between related persons through entities organized in countries with no economic or commercial relation to the production, distribution, or consumption of the property sold. Section 954(d)(1) aims principally at income arising without economic activity in a CFC's country of incorporation.

Agricultural Commodity Exception. If the inventory property that is sold is in fact an agricultural commodity that is not grown in the United States in commercial quantities, then the purchase and sale of such commodities falls outside the foreign base company sales income regime. The connection to the United States for such goods is viewed as remote. The IRS issued proposed regulations in 1976 to implement the exempt agriculture commodity exception.[76] The IRS listed only black pepper, cocoa, coconuts, and tea as agricultural commodities that are not grown in commercial quantities in the United States and then provided a broad facts and circumstances test. In 1978, the Treasury Department issued final regulations and in those final regulations the IRS included bananas, coffee, and crude rubber in the safe harbor as exempt commodities that are not grown in commercial quantities in the United States. It seems a bit of a stretch for the regulations to say that coffee is not grown in the United States in commercial quantities (when did you last have a cup of Kona?), but this expanded safe harbor remains intact. Thus, notwithstanding the above two-part test for determining foreign base company sales income, any purchase or sale of an exempt agricultural commodity in its raw state is not subject to taxation under the foreign base company sales income regime.

Of course, this categorical exemption leads one to ask the following question: when does the processing of an exempt agricultural commodity cause the resulting product to lose its "exempt commodity" status? For example, if coconuts are processed into coconut oil and coconut meal, those are likely separate products and no longer "exempt coconuts" if the raw agricultural commodity has been subjected to a substantial transformation in the manufacturing process even if no non-coconut ingredients were added. Likewise, if Brazilian coffee were first processed into instant coffee packets and Foreign Base Co. only purchased the instant coffee

---

[76] See Notice of Proposed Rulemaking, 41 Fed Reg. 19970 (May 14, 1976).

packets after they were made, then the exempt commodity exception likely no longer applies as to the sale of that derivative coffee product. Thus, if the underlying product that was purchased and sold in Diagram #29 had been Brazilian coffee (an exempt commodity), then neither the Brazilian CFC nor the foreign base company would have had foreign base company sales income because the underlying inventory item would have been an exempt agricultural commodity and thus no testing is required as to that commodity.

Manufacturing Exception and a Substantial Contribution in a Manufacturing Process. The second exception to the foreign base company sales income regime is of more general importance. Section 954(d)(1) deals with the purchase and sale of the same inventory. If the item that is sold is substantially different from the product that was acquired, then the selling party has sold goods that have been manufactured or processed by the controlled foreign corporation and are not treated as foreign base company sales income by reason of the "manufacturing exception."[77]

In Revenue Ruling 75–7,[78] the IRS had ruled that a controlled foreign corporation's use of a contract manufacturer could qualify the controlled foreign corporation for the manufacturing exception of section 954(d)(1) but that use of that controlled foreign corporation would also create a manufacturing branch for the other controlled foreign corporation under section 954(d)(2).[79] Taxpayers relied on the first holding in Revenue Ruling 75–7 to attribute the manufacturing activities of one controlled foreign corporation to another controlled foreign corporation located in a tax haven jurisdiction and then successfully argued against the second holding of Revenue Ruling 75–7 in the courts, thus creating a non-Subpart F result for the profits attributed to the tax haven subsidiary.[80] After several taxpayer victories in the courts, the IRS reversed both of the holdings of Revenue Ruling 75–7 in Revenue Ruling 97–48, holding that the use of a contract manufacturer would not give rise to a manufacturing branch and that the resulting income in the hands of the contract manufacturer did not qualify for the manufacturing exception because the manufacturing activities of the other party

---

[77] The production or processing must be substantial, however. Mere packaging or labeling, or even minor assembly, do not suffice for this purpose, while such activities as transforming wood pulp into paper, steel rods into nuts and bolts, live fish into canned sardines, and so on, *do* constitute sufficient production or processing. The facts of each case are ultimately controlling, but the Regulations provide a safe harbor, acknowledging activity as bona fide manufacturing if production costs (direct labor plus factory costs) account for 20 percent or more of the total cost of goods sold. Reg. § 1.954–3(a)(4)(iii).

[78] Rev. Rul. 75–7, 1975–1 Cum. Bull. 244.

[79] § 954(d).

[80] Ashland Oil Co. v. Commissioner, 95 T.C. 348, 349–50, 360, 362–63 (1990); Vetco, Inc. v. Commissioner, 95 T.C. 579, 590–92 (1990).

would not be attributed to the contract manufacturer.[81] But, in the end, the Treasury Department relented and sanctioned the use of contract manufacturing arrangements as a mechanism to allocate manufacturing activities to a tax haven subsidiary, such as Foreign Base Co., without creating Subpart F income because, in the Treasury Department's view, contract manufacturing arrangements had become "a common way of manufacturing products" and "was deemed to be important to the continued competitiveness of U.S. businesses operating abroad."[82] The checklist of factors that are considered in determining whether Foreign Base Co. provided a "substantial contribution" in the manufacturing process is set forth in Treasury regulations,[83] and those regulations also set forth standards to determine when a process results in a substantial enough transformation so that the resulting product is viewed as having been manufactured.[84]

Thus, let's return to Diagram #29. If Foreign Base Co. purchases the oranges from CFC#1 but then has the Brazilian CFC convert those oranges into frozen concentrate orange juice, the original inventory has been substantially transformed so that the manufacturing exception is implicated. If Foreign Base Co. provided sufficient oversight so that its contribution to that manufacturing process were "substantial," then the sale of its frozen concentrate would be excluded from the foreign base company sale rules by reason of the manufacturing exception.

Branch Rule and the Check-the-Box Regime. One might have expected that the check-the-box regime could provide a way to avoid the foreign base company sales income rules. Said differently, if a separate entity is disregarded for U.S. tax purposes, then perhaps the purchase and sale with that disregarded entity is a nonevent. But, somewhat surprisingly, section 954(d)(2) provides that a branch is to be treated as a separate corporation for purposes of applying the foreign base company sales rules of section 954(d) if the effect of that "branch" is to cause the income earned through that branch to not be taxable with the remainder of the corporation.[85] Thus, supply chain transactions, even if conducted by or with disregarded entities, are separately tested under the foreign base company sale rules. In order to apply this test, Reg. § 1.954–3(b) requires a determination of whether the sales income is separated from the manufacturing

---

[81] Rev. Rul. 97–48, 1997–2 Cum. Bull. 89.

[82] See Notice of Proposed Rulemaking, 73 FED. REG. 10,716 (Feb. 28, 2008). The proposed regulations were eventually finalized in Reg. § 1.954–3(a)(4). See T.D. 9438, 2008–16 I.R.B. 801; T.D. 9563, 76 FED. REG. 78545 (2011).

[83] Reg. § 1.954–3(a)(4)(iv).

[84] Reg. § 1.954–3(a)(4)(ii).

[85] Reg. § 1.954–3(b).

income and then whether the separated sales income is subjected to an actual tax rate that is lower than what would have been the result if it had not been separated away from the manufacturing income (the so-called tax rate disparity test). Thus, under the regulations, section 954(d)(2) is implicated only when the sales income is separated away from the manufacturing activity and that sales income is subjected to a lower tax rate than the hypothetical tax rate that would apply if there had not been such a separation.

The determination of how to apply section 954(d)(2) was addressed in *Whirlpool v. Commissioner*,[86] and that case has become a leading case in terms of interpreting the application of section 954(d)(2). The below Diagram #30 sets forth a simplified corporate structure. In relevant part, a Luxembourg controlled foreign corporation (referred to as "Whirlpool Luxembourg") owned the stock of a Mexican entity (Whirlpool International S. de R.L. de C.V. a.k.a. "WIN").[87] WIN was treated as a disregarded entity for U.S. tax purposes[88] with the consequence that for U.S. tax purposes WIN was a "branch" of Whirlpool Luxembourg. WIN had no employees of its own, but employees were "seconded" to WIN from other undepicted controlled foreign corporations that had operations in Mexico. For its own part, Whirlpool Luxembourg had only one part-time employee that performed minimal administrative functions in Luxembourg. Personnel in Mexico purchased all components in the name of Whirlpool Luxembourg. The manufactured refrigerators and washing machines were then sold on behalf of Whirlpool Luxembourg by personnel located in Mexico to other Whirlpool affiliates. At all times, Whirlpool Luxembourg owned all raw materials, work-in-process, and finished goods inventory. In addition, the sale of the manufactured refrigerators and washing machines was done in the name of Whirlpool Luxembourg. Thus, all income-producing and value-added activities occurred solely from within Mexico. The Whirlpool Luxembourg/WIN maquiladora arrangement, however, was put into place in a tax restructuring exercise that did not involve any movement of actual people or operations into those entities. Through contractual arrangements with other entities, Whirlpool

---

86 Whirlpool v. Commissioner, 154 T.C. 142 (2020), aff'd 19 F.4th 944 (6th Cir. 2021).

87 154 T.C. 142 (2020). Whirlpool's Petition and Motion for Summary Judgment set forth a corporate structure as designating the relevant Luxembourg CFC entity as Whirlpool Overseas Manufacturing S.a.r.l. See Petition, Tax Ct. Docket No. 13986–17, 2017 WL 3392395 (June 23, 2017); Petitioner's Motion for Summary Judgment in Whirlpool v. Commissioner, Tax Ct. Docket No. 13986–17, 2019 WL 4408467 (Feb. 22, 2019). The Tax Court opinion reverses the ownership structure alleged by the taxpayer and believes that a different Luxembourg entity (Whirlpool Luxembourg S.a.r.l.) owned WIN.

88 See Reg. § 301.7701–2(a), Reg. § 301.7701–3(a).

Luxembourg/WIN was entitled to significant profits without any assets or employees of its own.

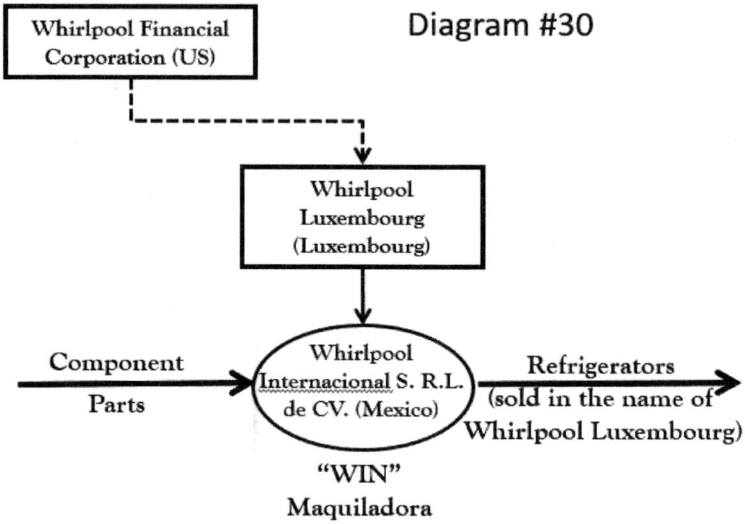

For Mexican tax purposes, Whirlpool Luxembourg's profits were largely exempted from Mexican taxation as the arrangements put into place for the Whirlpool Luxembourg and WIN structure qualified under the concessionary maquiladora regime. Mexico's maquiladora program had been in place for many years, and the Tax Court recognized that the maquiladora regime was "designed to incentivize foreign principals to locate manufacturing operations in Mexico."[89] If the foreign principal (i.e., Whirlpool Luxembourg remainder) and maquila company (i.e., WIN) satisfied specified transfer pricing requirements, one of the benefits was that the foreign principal of the Mexico-resident maquila company was deemed to not have a permanent establishment in Mexico for Mexican tax purposes.[90] Another benefit of the maquiladora regime is that the limited amount of income assigned to the maquila company was allowed to be relatively small in amount, and that small amount of income was subject to Mexican income taxation at a preferential rate of 17 percent (as compared to the normal 28 percent rate).[91] Thus, even though all sales activities and all manufacturing activities occurred solely from within Mexico on behalf of a foreign company (namely Whirlpool Luxembourg), Whirlpool Luxembourg's profits were untaxed in Mexico, and only the small fraction of the overall profits was assigned to the maquila entity and taxed at a

[89] Whirlpool v. Commissioner, 154 T.C. 142, 148 (2020).

[90] Whirlpool v. Commissioner, 154 T.C. 142, 149 (2020).

[91] Whirlpool v. Commissioner, 154 T.C. 142, 149 (2020).

reduced 17 percent rate notwithstanding the fact that everything occurred from within Mexico.

Luxembourg did not tax the profits assigned to Whirlpool Luxembourg either. Luxembourg's tax laws did not seek to tax any extraterritorial active business income earned outside of Luxembourg, and Luxembourg rightly understood that all value-creation occurred outside Luxembourg and in Mexico. For U.S. transfer pricing purposes, no activity occurred in Luxembourg to which any profits rightly could have been allocated to Whirlpool Luxembourg as the substance of the arrangement was that all profits were generated from activities performed solely from within Mexico.[92] However, none of the manufacturing or sales were done by employees of WIN or Whirlpool Luxembourg, and so at the end of the day this controlled foreign corporation that did not directly own any operating assets or employ any operating personnel reported substantial profits. All parties agreed that this arrangement was subject to the strictures of section 954(d)(2), but the parties diverged on the manner in which that statutory provision was to be applied on the facts posited in *Whirlpool*.

In an opinion issued on Cinco de Mayo, the Tax Court found that this arrangement created foreign base company sales income by reason of section 954(d)(2) and its regulations. To begin with, the Tax Court stated that Whirlpool Luxembourg had a branch or similar establishment in Mexico. The business profits earned from Mexico through the maquiladora arrangement had substantially the same tax effect as a separate corporation. The Tax Court then proceeded to apply the branch rule of section 954(d)(2). The Tax Court found that the Whirlpool Luxembourg remainder owned component parts which were used to assemble refrigerators and washing machines, and it also found that the finished goods were then sold in the name of the Whirlpool Luxembourg remainder to other Whirlpool affiliates at a substantial profit. Thus, the Whirlpool Luxembourg remainder obtained profits that arose from sales transactions. The fact that Whirlpool Luxembourg engaged in no sales functions from Luxembourg did not prevent its income from being classified as sales income belonging to the Whirlpool Luxembourg remainder. The Tax Court accepted that only the income attributable to sales activities should be assigned to the Whirlpool Luxembourg remainder. But then, the Tax Court asserted that the sales profits of the Whirlpool Luxembourg remainder included all of the income that was not assigned to WIN and had escaped Mexican taxation. The above handling of the allocation of the profits between the manufacturing

---

[92] This is what the Luxembourg tax authorities had been told by the taxpayer, and the Tax Court also did not disagree with this conclusion. See Whirlpool v. Commissioner, 154 T.C. 142, 150, 158, 161 (2020).

branch (i.e., WIN) and the Whirlpool Luxembourg remainder simply assumes that WIN's allocated profit represented the entirety of the manufacturing income even though for U.S. tax purposes the amount reported by WIN arguably was less than an arm's length manufacturing profit.[93]

The Tax Court then proceeded to address whether this arrangement created a tax rate disparity as required by Reg. § 1.954–3(b)(1)(ii)(b). The Tax Court treated the income not taxed in Mexico as included in the tax base in the Whirlpool Luxembourg remainder and then applied the actual Luxembourg tax paid on that income to determine the actual Luxembourg effective tax rate on that income. Thus, the Tax Court determined that the actual Luxembourg tax rate was zero on all of the profits assigned to the Whirlpool Luxembourg remainder. The Tax Court then proceeded to determine the hypothetical Mexican tax rate that would have applied if the Whirlpool Luxembourg remainder had earned its sales income in Mexico. The Tax Court then posited that the Whirlpool Luxembourg remainder would not have qualified for a concessionary rate in Mexico since Whirlpool Luxembourg did not engage in manufacturing, so the Tax Court then stated that the Mexican hypothetical effective tax rate would have been the statutory rate of 28 percent. Thus, in applying the tax disparity test, the Tax Court used a so-called hypothetical Mexican tax rate of 28 percent notwithstanding the fact that the actual record indicated exactly what rate of Mexican tax would apply assuming all of the relevant sales activities occurred from within Mexico. The Tax Court clearly understood that the actual operations on behalf of Whirlpool Luxembourg, including the sales activities, were all conducted from within Mexico. Yet, when applying the tax rate disparity test, the Tax Court deferred to the foreign law treatment of this Maquiladora arrangement that had provided that these actual sales activities would not be treated as permanent establishment for the Whirlpool Luxembourg remainder for Mexican tax purposes.[94] As to Whirlpool's argument that the same country exception should apply if in fact the Whirlpool Luxembourg remainder is deemed to have sales income, the Tax Court simply stated that Whirlpool Luxembourg was

---

[93] The Tax Court recognized as much when it stated that "[t]he Luxembourg CFC, which had one part-time employee, added no appreciable value to, but earned substantial income from, these sales transactions." See Whirlpool v. Commissioner, 154 T.C. 142, 143 (2020).

[94] Whirlpool v. Commissioner, 154 T.C. 142, 173 (2020). The Tax Court relied on Mexican law that stated that a nonresident company is deemed to not have a permanent establishment in Mexico deriving from the legal or economic relationship with entities carrying on maquila operations. But, a resident corporation was taxed at a 28 percent, and nonresident companies were taxed at a 28 percent rate on any income associated with a permanent establishment. See Whirlpool v. Commissioner, 154 T.C. 142, 148–149 (2020).

incorporated in Luxembourg and thus could not qualify for the same country exception for goods that were manufactured from within Mexico.

As remarkable as the Tax Court decision was, the Sixth Circuit appellate decision is even more so. The Sixth Circuit stated that if the branch rule of section 954(d)(2) applies to a fact pattern, then all of the income of the controlled foreign corporation is foreign base company income without the benefit of any of the exceptions to that treatment that could have existed under section 954(d)(1) notwithstanding that final Treasury regulations provide otherwise.[95] Thus, according to the Sixth Circuit, the manufacturing exception and the same country exception are all inapposite once a transaction is described in section 954(d)(2). The Sixth Circuit stated that section 954(d)(2) consists of two conditions, both of which were satisfied.[96] First, Whirlpool Luxembourg conducted activities in Mexico through a branch located outside of Luxembourg through the activities of WIN as WIN was a disregarded entity. Second, by selling the goods in the name of the Whirlpool Luxembourg remainder, the sales income avoided any taxation in Mexico and in Luxembourg. Thus, the Sixth Circuit concluded that the income was subject to taxation without the need to look into the extensive regulations promulgated under Reg. § 1.954–3(b).

The Sixth Circuit applied section 954(d)(2) as a stand-alone provision that does not need to then re-apply section 954(d)(1) and its various exceptions, if followed by other circuits, would have significant implications. As discussed earlier in this chapter, after the years in issue in *Whirlpool*, the Treasury Department provided a further significant concession by amending its regulations to allow the manufacturing exception to apply to any entity that makes a "substantial contribution" towards the manufacturing process, and so one could imagine a branch arrangement where the head-office remainder did provide a substantial contribution towards the manufacturing process. But, under the Sixth Circuit reasoning, the opportunity for the remainder entity to separately rely on that "substantial contribution" exception would be potentially unavailable under any structure subject to section 954(d)(2) whereas that substantial contribution exception would be available if the entity were tested as a separate CFC under section 954(d)(1). Importantly, the Treasury Department through its 2008 amendments to its final regulation, invited taxpayers to rely on the "substantial contribution" standard across all such structures without distinction. It is an open question whether the Sixth Circuit

95 Whirlpool v. Commissioner, 19 F.4th 944, 953–954 (6th Cir. 2021).

96 Whirlpool v. Commissioner, 19 F.4th 944, 950 (6th Cir. 2021).

would extend its reasoning to find that those arrangements generated foreign base company sales income under section 954(d)(2). In addition, it also remains to be seen what persuasive value the Sixth Circuit's decision will have on controversies decided outside of the Sixth Circuit, both in terms of cases presenting facts similar to those found in *Whirlpool* and also for cases where taxpayers relied on the 2008 amendments to the Treasury regulations in the branch context.

Partnerships and the Foreign Base Company Sales Income Rules. For purposes of applying the foreign base company sale rules to transactions that involve partnerships, a partnership's purchase or sale is considered a related party transaction if controlled by a controlled foreign corporation.[97] In addition, for purposes of determining whether a controlled foreign corporation's distributive share of partnership income is foreign base company sales income, the partnership's transactions are tested under these rules at the partnership level with the partnership treated as a separate entity.[98] Also, for purposes of applying the manufacturing exception, the controlled foreign corporation's distributive share of income is determined to be entitled to that manufacturing exception by looking at whether the partnership activities would have met any of the above exceptions if the partner had earned the income directly and had engaged in the activities directly, but the partnership's activities and income are considered in isolation at the partner level from all of the other activities of the partner for purposes of applying that manufacturing exception.[99]

4. Foreign Base Company Services Income

Similar to foreign base company sales income is foreign base company services income, which includes income (of any kind) derived in connection with the performance of "technical, managerial, engineering, architectural, scientific, skilled, industrial, commercial, or like services" performed for or on behalf of any related person and performed outside the country of organization of a CFC.[100] Thus, two key tests must be met: (i) services performed outside the country of incorporation and (ii) services performed for or on behalf of a related party. This definition includes the type of services that are most easily shifted to a different country, such as

---

[97] § 954(d)(3).

[98] Reg. § 1.954–1(g). This aspect of the regulations was intended to reverse the Eighth Circuit's decision in Brown Group, Inc. v. Commissioner, 77 F.3d 217 (8th Cir. 1996) where the Eighth Circuit held prior to the issuance of these regulations that the activities were tested at the partnership level, not the partner level.

[99] Reg. § 1.954–3(a)(6).

[100] § 954(e)(1).

architecture, engineering, much technical assistance, scientific research, and consulting.

Note, however, that Subpart F does not by itself entirely prevent the use of tax havens to perform services. An engineering firm can create a subsidiary in Bermuda, move personnel there, and carry out actual engineering work beyond the reach of current U.S. taxation.[101] But, if the work is performed by those engineers by going to locations outside of Bermuda, then the services work would be foreign base company services income if performed for or on behalf of a related party.

As to the question of whether or not services are performed for or on behalf of a related party, this requirement can be met even if the services are in form performed for an unrelated party in certain events. In this regard, related party services can arise under any of the following situations: (i) a related person pays the controlled foreign corporation for its services, (ii) a related person is or was obligated to perform the services performed by the controlled foreign corporation, (iii) services are performed by the controlled foreign corporation as a material term of a related party sale, or (iv) a related person contributes "substantial assistance" in the performance of the services provided by a controlled foreign corporation to any other person.[102] However, as to the last category (iv) called the 'substantial assistance" rule, the IRS has stated in Notice 2007–13 that it intends to significantly curtail the scope of the "substantial assistance" rule so that it would only apply if the party providing the substantial assistance is a related *U.S.* person and the cost of that U.S. related party's assistance amounted to 80 percent of the total cost of the controlled foreign corporation's cost of service under its contract.[103] Notice 2007–13 can be relied upon until final regulations are promulgated, and those regulations have not been issued as yet.[104] Note that the above focus is on a U.S. related party providing substantial assistance to a controlled foreign corporation. If the related party that provides substantial assistance is a CFC and it provides this assistance to another related CFC, then the first CFC's assistance will not be considered "substantial assistance" to the other CFC regardless of the amount of its cost, albeit the first CFC that provides the assistance may have foreign base company services income if those service are performed outside of its own country of

---

101 That is because, in this case, the services would be performed in the place of the CFC's incorporation. Note further, though, that if the firm is merely a vehicle for the performance of services by a small number of U.S. individuals, the rules on "personal service contracts" (recently imported into Subpart F from the former foreign personal holding company provisions) may come into play as well. See § 954(c)(1)(I).

102 Reg. § 1.954–4(b)(1).

103 Notice 2007–13, 2007–1 Cum. Bull. 410.

104 See Reg. § 1.954–4(b)(2)(ii) (last amended in 2002).

incorporation.[105] The Treasury Department, as justification for its curtailment of the "substantial assistance" prong of its existing regulations, stated that, "it does not seem appropriate in the current global economy to treat the profits of the [second] controlled foreign corporation contracting to furnish services to the unrelated person as "foreign base company services income" simply because of the assistance provided by another controlled foreign corporation. Thus, the first controlled foreign corporation may have foreign base company services income if its services were provided outside of its country of incorporation, but the second controlled foreign corporation would not be considered to have foreign base company services income merely due to the fact that it received substantial assistance from another foreign related party. In addition, these foreign-to-foreign assistance patterns can be structured to avoid the foreign base company services regime in its entirety by making check-the-box elections on the related entities, as the foreign base company services income regime does not have a branch rule like section 954(d)(2).

Foreign base company services income does not include income from services directly related to the sale of property produced by a CFC and performed before the time of sale, as that income is addressed by the foreign base company sales income regime.[106] Displaying shoes to a potential customer therefore does not produce Subpart F income nor do installation services or essential training to enable the use of property by its buyer. Also, foreign base company services income does not apply to services performed in the sale or purchase of property; instead, that income is treated as income earned as part of the procurement and sale of inventory and tested under the foreign base company sales income regime.[107] In applying these provisions to income earned by a partnership that is owned by controlled foreign corporations, a controlled foreign corporation's distributive share of a partnership's services income will be deemed to be derived from services performed for or on behalf of a related person if the partnership (when separately tested as a separate entity) is a related person with respect to the controlled foreign corporation.[108]

---

[105] Id.

[106] § 954(e)(2).

[107] Services that directly relate to the purchase and sale of inventory are excluded from the foreign base company services income rules. See Reg. § 1.954–4(d)(1). Sales commissions are tested under the foreign base company sales rules. See Reg. § 1.954–3(a)(1)(iii) Ex. (3).

[108] Reg. § 1.954–4(b)(2)(iii).

5. Investment in U.S. Property Inclusions

Section 956 was enacted alongside the Subpart F regime in the 1962 Act to ensure that a controlled foreign corporation's earnings not subject to immediate tax when earned (under the Subpart F regime) would be taxed when repatriated either through a dividend or an effective repatriation. Recognizing that repatriation of foreign earnings was possible through means other than a taxable distribution, Congress enacted section 956 "to prevent the repatriation of income to the United States in a manner which does not subject it to U.S. taxation."[109] Congress determined that the investment by a CFC of its earnings in United States property, including obligations of a U.S. person, "is substantially the equivalent of a dividend."[110] Thus, from the outset of the Subpart F regime, Congress envisioned section 956 as an anti-abuse measure to tax a controlled foreign corporation's investment of its earnings in United States property in the same manner as if it had distributed those earnings to the United States.[111] Without section 956, taxpayers might have circumvented the U.S. system of deferral by effectively repatriating earnings without paying U.S. tax on the substantial equivalent of a taxable dividend. Section 956 was thus designed to ensure symmetry between the tax treatment of repatriations through dividends and effective repatriations.[112]

To accomplish these goals, section 951(a)(1)(B) requires a U.S. shareholder of a controlled foreign corporation to include in gross income the amount determined under section 956 (the "section 956 amount") to the extent not excluded from gross income under section 959(a)(2) (the inclusion, a "section 956 inclusion"). A U.S. shareholder's section 956 amount with respect to a controlled foreign corporation for a taxable year is the lesser of (1) the excess (if any) of such shareholder's pro rata share of the average of the amounts of

---

[109] H.R. REP. NO. 87-1447, 87th CONG. 2d SESS. at 58 (1962).

[110] See S. REP. NO. 87-1881, 87th CONG. 2d SESS. at 88 (1962). See also S. REP. NO. 94–938, 94th CONG. 2d SESS. at 226 (1976) ("[S]ince the investment . . . in the stock or debt obligations of a related U.S. person or its domestic affiliates makes funds available for use by the U.S. shareholders, it constitutes an effective repatriation of earnings which should be taxed.").

[111] See JCS–10–87 at 1081–82 (1987) ("In general, two kinds of transactions are repatriations that end deferral and trigger tax. First, an actual dividend payment ends deferral. . . . Second, in the case of a controlled foreign corporation, an investment in U.S. property, such as a loan to the lender's U.S. parent or the purchase of U.S. real estate, is also a repatriation that ends deferral (Code sec. 956).").

[112] See generally Notice 2014–52, 2014–42 I.R.B. 712 ("In the absence of section 956, a U.S. shareholder of a CFC could access the CFC's funds (untaxed earnings and profits) in a variety of ways other than by the payment of an actual taxable dividend, such that there would be no reason for the U.S. shareholder to incur the dividend tax. Section 956 eliminates this disincentive to pay a dividend by ensuring parity of treatment for different ways that CFC earnings can be made available for use in the United States or for use by the U.S. shareholder.")

United States property held (directly or indirectly) by the controlled foreign corporation as of the close of each quarter of such taxable year, over the amount of earnings and profits described in section 959(c)(1)(A) with respect to such shareholder or (2) such shareholder's pro rata share of the applicable earnings of the CFC.[113] Applicable earnings are defined as the sum of accumulated earnings and profits (not including deficits) described in section 316(a)(1) and current earnings and profits described in section 316(a)(2), reduced by distributions made during the year and earnings and profits described in section 959(c)(1).[114] Under section 956(c), United States property includes tangible property located in the United States, stock of a domestic corporation, an obligation of a United States person, and any right to use in the United States certain intangible property.

Yet, with the enactment of section 245A(a), in the case of any dividend received from a specified 10 percent owned foreign corporation by a domestic corporate U.S. shareholder, there is now a 100 percent foreign dividends received deduction available to a domestic corporate U.S. shareholder for the foreign source portion of such dividend. Thus, if there is no avoidance of a U.S. tax any longer on an actual distribution due to the fact that an actual distribution would be nontaxable to a domestic corporate U.S. shareholder, what anti-abuse policy goal does section 956 play in that context? The Treasury Department determined that, as a result of the enactment of section 245A, the broad application of section 956 to corporate U.S. shareholders would be inconsistent with the enactment of section 245A. Before the 2017 Act, section 956 applied appropriately to domestic corporate U.S. shareholders because both dividends from, and investments in United States property by, controlled foreign corporations were included in income by such domestic corporations. Thus, section 956 provided symmetry between the taxation of actual repatriations and the taxation of effective repatriations, by subjecting effective repatriations to tax in the same manner as actual repatriations. Under existing law, however, earnings of a controlled foreign corporation that are repatriated to a corporate U.S. shareholder as a dividend are effectively exempt from tax under section 245A. As a result, the application of section 956 after the 2017 Act to a corporate U.S. shareholder would result in disparate treatment of actual dividends and amounts "substantially the equivalent of a dividend"—a result directly at odds with the purpose of section 956. Accordingly, the Treasury Department issued regulations that exclude corporate U.S. shareholders from the application of section 956 to the extent necessary to maintain

---

113 § 956(a).

114 § 956(b)(1).

symmetry between the taxation of actual repatriations and the taxation of effective repatriations. To achieve this result, the regulations provide that the amount otherwise determined under section 956 with respect to a U.S. shareholder is reduced to the extent that the domestic corporate U.S. shareholder would have been allowed a 100 percent foreign dividends received deduction under section 245A if the U.S. shareholder had received an actual distribution from the controlled foreign corporation in an amount equal to the amount otherwise determined under section 956.[115] Due to the broad applicability of section 245A, in many cases a corporate U.S. shareholder will not have a section 956 inclusion as a result of the regulations.

Section 956 will continue to apply, however, with respect to U.S. shareholders other than corporate U.S. shareholders, such as individuals, to ensure that, consistent with the purposes of section 956, amounts that are substantially the equivalent of a dividend will be treated similarly to actual dividends. This treatment will apply to individuals regardless of whether they make an election under section 962. Because individuals are not eligible for a foreign dividends received deduction under section 245A, the current application of section 956 to individuals is still necessary to ensure substantial equivalence between an actual repatriation and a deemed repatriation.

D. Foreign Tax Credit for Taxes Paid by Foreign Corporation on Subpart F Income

Mechanically, double taxation is even more difficult to pacify when U.S. corporations engage in foreign operations through separately chartered foreign subsidiaries. If there were no special provision for taxes paid by foreign corporations, in fact, the foreign tax credit would be of no avail in such situations. To illustrate, let's return to Diagram #28 and assume that income earned by Foreign Base Co. was subject to immediate taxation to the U.S. parent corporation under the U.S. Subpart F rules of section 951(a). Foreign Base Co. itself has no claim to the foreign tax credit under section 901 because it is not a U.S. person and in any event pays no U.S. income tax. Foreign Base Co.'s payment of foreign income tax therefore brings no immediate U.S. tax benefit. However, US Parent is subject to taxation immediately on those earnings under section 951(a), so the same earnings are at risk of being subject to international double taxation because section 901 by itself allows US Parent no foreign tax credit for Foreign Base Co.'s foreign income tax

---

115 Reg. § 1.956–1(a)(2).

payments because US Parent did not pay them.[116] US Parent has borne Foreign Base Co.'s foreign taxes only *indirectly* as a reduction of distributable earnings. The income tax paid by US Parent is therefore a second layer of tax.

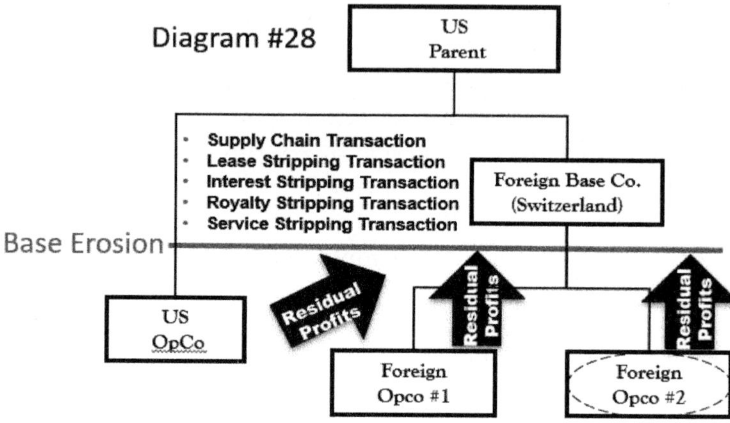

If US Parent had carried out its foreign business as a direct branch operation (i.e., without using a separately chartered foreign entity for its foreign operations) or through a U.S.-chartered subsidiary, there would be no problem. Foreign income tax would be offset (within the limitation, of course) by the foreign tax credit available to a U.S. person paying a foreign tax directly. There would be a single corporate-level tax (at the higher of the U.S. or foreign tax rate). With no further adjustment, therefore, the taxation of separately incorporated foreign subsidiaries of U.S. corporations would be more severe than the taxation of their direct foreign branches or their domestic subsidiaries.

The problem was evident from the start, and so long as there has been a foreign tax credit and foreign earnings earned by a foreign corporation taxable to the domestic corporate U.S. shareholder, there have been provisions extending it to foreign income taxes paid by foreign subsidiaries of U.S. corporations.

Note further that only corporations are ever "deemed" to have paid foreign income taxes.[117] Accordingly, there is no indirect foreign tax credit for individual shareholders of corporations outside the

---

[116] Bear in mind that we are considering here the effect of a tax imposed by Foreign Base Co. on Foreign Base Co.'s earnings, not on its dividend distributions to US Parent. A foreign withholding tax on Foreign Base Co.'s distribution would be a tax paid by US Parent and creditable as such.

[117] Individuals are entitled to elect under section 962 to be treated as a domestic corporate U.S. shareholder, but absent that election no indirect foreign tax credits would be allowed. The implications of such an election are discussed at the end of this chapter.

context of a section 962 election which is discussed more fully below. On first encounter with the *indirect* foreign tax credit system, some students think that it establishes a second form of the foreign tax credit, known as the "indirect" or "deemed paid" credit. This is not so. Let me underscore that there is *only one* foreign tax credit, allowed in section 901. All that section 960 does is to "deem" a U.S. corporation to have paid some part of the foreign income tax actually paid by a foreign subsidiary (hence the term "deemed paid" credit). The foreign tax deemed paid is entitled to credit only within the constraints of the foreign tax credit generally. It is subject to the section 904(a) overall and section 904(d) separate limitation regimes, which is applied by combining foreign taxes deemed paid and actually paid within each separate limitation basket, and so on. A foreign tax deemed paid by a U.S. corporation, in other words, is simply another amount that may give rise to the foreign tax credit.

However, in 2017, a Great Schism was created. Now, foreign dividends of earnings that are not subject to the anti-deferral rules are no longer subject to any U.S. worldwide taxation when distributed to a domestic corporate U.S. shareholder because section 245A provides for a 100 percent foreign dividends received deduction. Thus, in that instance, it is fair and appropriate to deny any *indirect* foreign tax credit relief as section 245A(d) seeks to do. However, when the foreign earnings of a foreign corporation are taxable to the domestic corporate U.S. shareholder under Subpart F without the benefit of a 100 percent foreign dividends received deduction, then an *indirect* foreign tax credit under section 960 is needed in that instance to prevent double international taxation on those same corporate-level earnings.

A fundamental problem, however, with an indirect foreign tax credit is that it can overcompensate the U.S. domestic corporate shareholder if appropriate adjustments are not made. In this regard, in the 1921 system the foreign corporation's payment of foreign taxes created a double tax benefit for the foreign corporate earnings in the form of a simultaneous deduction *and* credit of foreign income taxes paid by foreign subsidiaries. Foreign income taxes paid by the subsidiaries were excluded from the income of their U.S. parents as a simple consequence of the fact that Subpart F applies on the after-tax corporate earnings created by those transactions. From the parent's perspective, this is functionally the same as a deduction of the foreign taxes paid by the subsidiary.[118] If the entire amount of the foreign income taxes paid by the subsidiary were in addition

118 If the full pre-tax earnings of the subsidiary had been included in the parent corporation's income (which would have occurred if a direct branch had been used instead of a foreign subsidiary) and the parent had then deducted the foreign income tax, the result would be the same.

deemed paid upon distributions to the parent and were creditable in full, the parent would have in effect a deduction and a credit for the same foreign taxes.

The IRS attacked this double tax benefit, with partial success, in *American Chicle Co. v. United States*.[119] The IRS contended that the amount of tax deemed paid, and hence the foreign tax credit, should be less than the total foreign income tax paid by a foreign subsidiary because some part of the tax had been paid not with respect to the earnings distributed as dividends but with respect to the very earnings paid over to the foreign government as tax. In other words, only part of the tax paid upon the entire pre-tax income of the subsidiary was attributable to the accumulated profits remaining after the tax itself was paid. It is easier to understand the competing contentions in *American Chicle* with some numbers.

Assume the foreign income tax rate is 25 percent. Tax of 25¢ would be paid to the foreign government on every dollar of the subsidiary's earnings, leaving 75¢ available for distribution. The taxpayer's position was that 25¢ of tax had been paid for each 75¢ of distributable profits and that a 75¢ dividend should therefore bring 25¢ of tax deemed paid with it as the amount of tax paid "with respect to" the earnings. The IRS countered that when 25¢ of tax was paid "upon" a dollar of pre-tax earnings, only three-quarters of the tax (or 18.75¢) was paid "with respect to" after-tax profits, while 6.25¢ of tax was paid upon the 25¢ of earnings that subsequently left the company in the form of taxes paid to a foreign treasury. No matter how much was distributed as a dividend, therefore, some portion of the tax paid (specifically the amount of tax paid on earnings that left the company as tax payments to a foreign government) could not be brought along with a dividend as a tax deemed paid, and would therefore produce no credit.

The government prevailed in *American Chicle*, and foreign "taxes" deemed paid under the 1921 Act were understood to be less than the total tax paid by a foreign subsidiary. The case left the deemed paid system in shambles. The foreign tax credit for taxes paid by foreign subsidiaries was scaled down somewhat, but the effective deduction of the foreign income tax remained intact.[120] In the *American Chicle* regime foreign income taxes paid by foreign subsidiaries afforded their U.S. parents a one-and-a-half tax benefit consisting of a total deduction and a partial credit.

This problem was fixed in 1962 with the addition to the Code of section 78. Now, the amount of any foreign income tax deemed paid

---

[119] 316 U.S. 450 (1942).

[120] Strictly, what we call a "deduction" here was an *exclusion* from income, as explained above.

by a domestic corporation under section 960 in any taxable year is included in the corporation's gross income *as a dividend* in that year. Amounts included in income under section 78 are treated as dividends for all income tax purposes and not entitled to the foreign dividends received deduction benefit. When a U.S. corporation is deemed to have paid a foreign tax because that tax is allocable to a Subpart F inclusion, its taxable income from the Subpart F inclusion is the sum of the actual Subpart F after-tax earnings plus the foreign tax deemed paid. This amount is usually the same as the pre-tax income of the foreign subsidiary from which the dividend was paid. The taxable income of the U.S. parent corporation is in this manner "grossed-up" to the pre-tax income of the subsidiary,[121] and there is in effect no deduction of foreign income taxes from the U.S. tax base. To this extent, direct branch operations and foreign subsidiaries are taxed the same. Credit for the full amount of income tax paid by a foreign subsidiary when deemed paid now produces only a single tax benefit.

E. Controlled Foreign Corporations: Net CFC Tested Income

In the previous section, we looked at the Subpart F regime and saw its mixed success in preventing homeless (or tax haven) income. The scope of the Subpart F regime has changed over time, but these changes have not obscured its core mission. Its current scope does serve as a backstop to prevent U.S. inbound earnings stripping where a controlled foreign corporation engages in earnings stripping transactions to base erode a U.S. affiliate. Several of the earnings stripping transactions are addressed in that context. However, significant exceptions to the Subpart F regime apply in the CFC-to-CFC earnings stripping context. Thus, the Subpart F regime as currently constructed does generally allow broad latitude to the U.S. multinational enterprise to engage in the full range of base erosion strategies between its controlled foreign corporations when those strategies are directed at the foreign-to-foreign context.

This situation could have elicited at least three different responses. One response could have been that Congress simply kept the existing paradigm unchanged. In that alternative, Subpart F would have remained largely focused on preventing the U.S. inbound base erosion and profit shifting strategies of a U.S. multinational enterprise while remaining largely ambivalent about addressing the CFC-to-CFC base erosion strategies that create low-taxed earnings. The argument here would have been that any concerns over base erosion and profit shifting out of a different jurisdiction's tax base is appropriately addressed by that impacted foreign jurisdiction. The

---

121 Section 78 is often known as the "gross-up" provision.

impacted foreign jurisdiction is the one that should solve its own base erosion problem. The United States cannot effectively do so itself as its extraterritorial rules do not extend to all of the multinational enterprises that are involved in that other foreign country, so any unilateral effort to do so by the United States would create a competitive disadvantage for the U.S. multinational enterprise vis-à-vis its other global (non-U.S.) multinational competitors in that other jurisdiction.

Another possible response could have been for Congress to expand the Subpart F regime to more fully address base erosion and profit shifting strategies that create tax haven income in the foreign-to-foreign earnings stripping context. Now that section 245A affords a 100 percent foreign dividends received deduction for untaxed earnings remitted to a domestic corporate U.S. shareholder, the ability to create a lower tax rate on foreign business income in a CFC environment creates an incentive to shift business opportunities to foreign jurisdictions due to the tax benefits of deriving low-taxed income and then claiming a 100 percent foreign dividends received deduction when those earnings are eventually repatriated back to the United States. Even when a foreign jurisdiction has a comparable income tax rate to that of the United States, income of a multinational enterprise could still become low-taxed income if earnings stripping strategies are available to shift profits from where the operations are conducted and into a controlled foreign corporation incorporated in a low-tax jurisdiction. Thus, once Congress decided to enact section 245A's 100 percent foreign dividends received deduction, Congress might have wanted to refocus the Subpart F regime's effort to target foreign-to-foreign base erosion and profit shifting strategies due to the risk of promoting the offshoring of U.S. businesses activities. To that end, Congress might have removed the look-through exception to the foreign personal holding company income rules set forth in section 954(c)(6), expanded the foreign personal holding company rules to apply to interest, rents, and royalties paid from a disregarded entity to the controlled foreign corporation that owns the disregarded entity, removed the active banking and financing exception in section 954(h), and/or curtailed the ability of contract manufacturing arrangements to be used by tax haven subsidiaries to avail themselves of the manufacturing exception to the foreign base company sales income rules.

However, Congress did not pursue any of the above approaches. Congress instead chose a new path to address the tension between its concern over preserving the competitiveness of U.S. multinational enterprises and its competing concern to not provide an incentive for the offshoring of U.S. businesses to low-tax jurisdictions. In this regard, Congress enacted section 951A to provide for a minimum U.S. tax on "excessive" amounts of low-taxed income earned within a controlled foreign corporation environment. When originally enacted in 2017, Section 951A sought to assert taxation over "global intangible low-taxed income." Although one must concede that this term of art allowed for the clever acronym "GILTI,"[122] this term of art in fact was a bit of a misnomer. The GILTI regime did not seek to determine whether the low-taxed income was in fact attributable to an intangible asset. It simply sought to tax excessive profits earned in a CFC environment that were low-taxed income. In the 2025 Act, Congress expanded the scope of section 951A so that it would broadly require inclusions of all net CFC tested income. Thus, Congress is not focused on a particular transaction of interest or a particular activity that should trigger an income inclusion. Under section 951A, Congress is largely agnostic as to why net CFC tested income was generated. Instead, the singular question is whether or not net CFC tested income does arise within CFCs in a particular year for whatever reason. If so, then an income inclusion is generally required. However, if a foreign minimum tax of at least 14 percent were imposed on those earnings, then sufficient foreign tax credits would be available to offset the potential U.S. income inclusion to a domestic corporate U.S. shareholder arising by reason of section 951A, and a high-tax exception may be elected by the taxpayer to avoid an inclusion if sufficient foreign tax were paid on the net CFC tested income.

Because section 951A defines several new terms of art and then fundamentally involves a formulaic application of those concepts, it is helpful to organize one's study of the statute in terms of an illustrative set of facts. In Table #13A, three controlled foreign corporations are set forth. In Column (a) of Lines 1 through 6 of Table #13A, CFC1 is shown to have had a $40 loss and paid no foreign taxes. In Column (b) of Lines 1 through 6 of Table #13A, CFC2 earned $180 of after-tax earnings and paid $10 of foreign tax. Finally, in Column (c) of Lines 1 through 6 of Table #13A, CFC3 had after-tax earnings of $120 and paid $20 of foreign tax. These basic facts are going to be used to work through how the statutory provisions of section 951A interrelate. Other examples are certainly possible, but this Table #13A provides an adequate basis for a student to understand how section 951A is intended to operate.

---

[122] You are guilty if you have GILTI!

Table #13A: Net CFC Tested Income Example

Item		CFC1 (a)	CFC2 (b)	CFC3 (c)	US Parent
1	Tested Income[1]		$180	$120	$300
2	Tested Loss	($40)	$0	$0	−$40
3	Net CFC Tested Income (L1 – L2)				$260
4	Tested Foreign Income Taxes		$10	$20	$30
5	*Foreign effective tax rate on tested income*		*5.3%*	*14.3%*	*9.1%*
6	Section 78 Gross-Up		$8.67	$17.33	$26.00
7	Deemed Paid Credit after 10% haircut (90% * L6)				$23.40
8	Grossed up Net CFC tested income (L3 + L6)				$286.00
9	40% § 250 Deduction (40% * L8)[3]				$114.40
10	Other U.S. allocable & apportionable expenses (§ 904(b)(4))				None
11	Taxable income before credit (L8 – L9 – L10)				$171.60
12	US tax before credit (21% * L13)				$36.04
13	Foreign tax credit (L7)[4]				$23.40
14	US Tax on High Return Amount (L12 – L13)				**$12.64**

[1] Excess of gross income reduced by effectively connected income, Subpart F income, income that would be Subpart F income but for high-tax exception, and foreign oil and gas extraction income, less allocable deductions.

[2] Average of end-of-quarter adjusted bases in tangible depreciable property that generates tested income or loss, determined under alternative depreciation system.

[3] The deduction is reduced to 37.5% for tax years beginning after 12/31/2025.

[4] A separate foreign tax credit limitation applies to the net CFC tested income regime, with no carryforward or carryback of excess credits. No indirect expenses are allocated against this income.

1. Tested Income

Tested income is defined to be the gross income of the related controlled foreign corporations (with certain exclusions) over the deductions (including taxes) properly allocable to that income. Thus, tested income is determined as the after-tax earnings of each related CFC, but the following items of income are excluded from this computation: any income effectively connected to the conduct of a U.S. trade or business, income that is taxable under the Subpart F regime, any income that would be Subpart F income but meets the "high-tax exception" to the foreign base company income rules, dividends received from another affiliate, and any foreign oil and gas extraction income that is subject to a separate regime.[123]

There are two key points worth making here. First, tested income excludes amounts that are subject to U.S. taxation under the Subpart F rules, so the Subpart F rules need to be applied first before the net CFC tested income provisions of section 951A. Moreover, income that is subject to U.S. taxation under another provision has no need for a further minimum tax, hence the existence of exceptions for these items of income. In Line 1 of Table #13A, tested income of $180 and $120 is aggregated, but those two components of "tested income" must have been non-excluded income. Once the CFC tested income is determined, then all of the tested income of all related controlled foreign corporations is included to determine the total CFC tested income. Starting with total CFC tested income is the beginning point for what follows, and only the controlled foreign corporations that have a positive tested income are included at this point.

2. Net CFC Tested Income

In order to arrive at "net CFC tested income," "tested losses" from controlled foreign corporations that have a loss (not income) are then deducted from the CFC tested income that was determined on Line 1. Thus, the calculation is attempting to arrive at a concept of aggregate net CFC income. For this purpose, a controlled foreign corporation has a "tested loss" if it suffered net losses (deductions in excess of gross income), but then any loss that reduced the Subpart F inclusion that would otherwise have been included by the U.S. shareholders are excluded from this net loss. Thus, if a controlled foreign corporation had Subpart F income in excess of its current earnings and profits, the Subpart F inclusion would have been limited to no more than the current earnings and profits.[124] The effect of this exclusion of losses that reduced a potential Subpart F

---

[123] § 954(c)(2).

[124] § 952(c)(1)(A)(i).

inclusion is designed to prevent a double benefit. If a loss in a controlled foreign corporation created an earnings and profits limitation so as to reduce an otherwise includible Subpart F amount, then that loss cannot be used in a duplicate fashion to reduce potential inclusions under section 951A.[125] Thus, Line 2 of Table #13A includes the loss from CFC1 (the amount by which deductions exceeded its gross income), but this amount necessarily must not include any loss that reduced a potential Subpart F inclusion. Once the tested losses are determined, the net CFC tested income can be derived. Based on these posited facts, the amount of "net CFC tested income" is shown on Line 3 as $260 (the difference between tested income of $300 and tested losses of $40). Once net CFC tested income is determined, the amount of net CFC tested income is the reference amount for the income inclusion by reason of section 951A.

3. Section 78 Gross-Up

The section 78 gross-up is now a straightforward application of two ratios. First, the net CFC tested income is prorated between each of controlled foreign corporations that had tested income.[126] In Table #13A, CFC2 had $180 of tested income and CFC3 had $120 of tested income for combined tested income of $300. Thus, $156 of net CFC tested income is allocable to CFC2 (i.e., $260 of net CFC tested income multiplied by $180 of CFC 2's tested income divided by $300 of total tested income of all CFCs equals CFC2's allocable share of net CFC tested income of $156). By the same token, $104 of net CFC tested income is allocated to CFC3 (i.e., $260 of net CFC tested income multiplied by $120 of CFC 3's tested income divided by $300 of total tested income of all CFCs equals CFC3's allocable share of net CFC tested income of $104).

Once the net CFC tested income is allocated to each controlled foreign corporation that had tested income, then the ratio of the net CFC tested income to the total earnings for that particular controlled foreign corporation can be determined. The percentage that the net CFC tested income amount bears to the total current earnings of the controlled foreign corporation provides the percentage to determine the amount of total foreign taxes that are allocable to the net CFC tested income inclusion with respect to each controlled foreign corporation. Thus, for CFC2, $8.67 of its $10 taxes are allocable to

---

[125] In a later year, when the controlled foreign corporation has earnings in excess of its Subpart F income, then the excess income in that later year is recharacterized as Subpart F income. See § 952(c)(2). But, that recharacterized Subpart F income would be excluded from tested income as it would be taxed under Subpart F. See § 951A(c)(2)(A)(i)(II). Thus, because section 951A excludes the recapture of the earnings and profits limit from tested income, the earnings and profits limit is excluded to prevent an asymmetrical result of allowing a deduction and excluding the future income.

[126] § 951A(f)(2).

the net CFC tested income inclusion (i.e., $156 of allocable net CFC tested income to CFC 2 dividend by $180 of CFC 2 earnings multiplied by $10 of CFC 2 foreign taxes equals $8.67 of taxes allocable to the net CFC tested income inclusion). For CFC3, $17.33 of its $20 of foreign taxes are allocable to the net CFC tested income inclusion from CFC3 (i.e., $104 of allocable net CFC tested income to CFC 3 divided by $120 of CFC 3 earnings multiplied by $20 of CFC 3 foreign taxes equals $17.33 of taxes allocable to the net CFC tested income inclusion). Thus, the total foreign taxes related to the net CFC tested income inclusion is $26 in total, so the section 78 gross-up is $26. Thus, the net CFC tested income inclusion of $260 plus the section 78 gross-up of $26 creates a total grossed-up net CFC tested income inclusion of $286.00. Each U.S. shareholder would be required to include its pro rata share of the net CFC tested income inclusion, and if the shareholder were a domestic corporation then it would also include its share of any section 78 gross-up. Except for individuals that make an election under section 962 discussed below, the only shareholders that could potentially claim a deemed paid credit under section 960 is a domestic corporation and thus only a domestic corporation would have a section 78 gross-up absent a section 962 election.

4. Section 250

Section 250 provides a *domestic corporate U.S. shareholder* that receives a net CFC tested income inclusion with a deduction equal to 40 percent of the net CFC tested income inclusion plus the section 78 gross-up on that inclusion. In Table #13A, the U.S. parent corporation owned all of the stock of the controlled foreign corporations and had a net CFC tested income inclusion plus section 78 gross-up of $286 (see Line 8), so the U.S. parent corporation is entitled to a section 250 deduction of $114.40 as shown on Line 9.

5. Foreign Tax Credit and Foreign Tax Credit Limitation

The amount of earnings in CFC2 and CFC3 that are considered net CFC tested income is moved from the basket that it otherwise would have been in (presumably the general basket) and into a separate basket for income that applies solely to income described in section 951A. Thus, the section 951A inclusion of $260 of earnings and profits is placed in the U.S. shareholder's section 951A basket. If the U.S. shareholder is a domestic corporation entitled to section 960 indirect credits, then the section 78 gross-up on the net CFC tested income inclusion ($26 per Line 6) is placed in the domestic corporation's section 951A basket as well. Thus, all of the associated taxes are moved out of the original basket to which it resided and into this section 951A basket as well.

The next issue to address is the amount of the *indirect* foreign tax credits that can be claimed on the net CFC tested income inclusion. After thinking about this for a few moments, I would hope that my students (and the reader of this book) would anticipate that the taxpayer should not be entitled to claim a section 250 deduction to offset 40 percent of the grossed-up net CFC tested income inclusion and simultaneously retain the right to claim the entire amount of foreign tax credits associated with that excluded portion of the net CFC tested income inclusion, as doing so creates a double benefit. When a taxpayer receives a dividend eligible for the 100 percent foreign dividends received deduction, then section 245A(d) denies any foreign tax credit relief in its entirety to avoid a double benefit. Section 245A's 100 percent foreign dividends received deduction avoids the risk of international double income taxation, so no further foreign tax credit relief is justified or allowed in that context. Thus, when a 100 percent foreign dividends received deduction offsets the entire amount of the foreign dividend, it is appropriate to disallow the entire amount of foreign tax credit or else an asymmetrical double benefit would be created.

After thinking of this further, the student might well conclude that the normatively correct result is that 40 percent of the foreign tax credit should be disallowed in the situation where section 250 provides a 40 percent deduction against the grossed-up net CFC tested income inclusion. This line of reasoning provides the rationale for why a partial disallowance of the foreign tax credit is required, and the student would be commended in anticipating that in fact section 960(d) does disallow a portion of the foreign tax credit, but it does not disallow a normatively correct amount. In this regard, section 960(d) provides that the amount of the allowable foreign tax credits is 90 percent of the amount of the indirect credits that are otherwise allocable to the income included under section 951A. Thus, although section 960(d) provides for a partial disallowance of the foreign tax credits, this disallowance preserves a partial double benefit in that 90 percent of the foreign taxes are allowed as a credit, whereas a more justifiable outcome would have been to allow only 60 percent of the credits. Thus, of the $26 of foreign taxes that are allocable to the net CFC tested income inclusion ($8.67 from CFC2 and $17.33 from CFC3 per columns (b) and (c) of Line 6) only 90 percent of that amount (or $23.40 per Line 7) is able to be claimed as an indirect foreign tax credit under section 960.

The section 904(d)(1)(A) foreign tax credit limitation for the net CFC tested income inclusion is equal to the U.S. tax rate of 21 percent multiplied by the income in that separate basket ($171.60 per Line 11). Thus, the foreign tax credit limitation is $36.04 on these facts, and so the U.S. parent corporation is entitled to claim all of the

$23.40 of indirect tax credits that are allowable by reason of section 960(d), as there is sufficient limitation in the section 951A basket to utilize those credits. Because the amount of the foreign tax credits that are allowed to be claimed is less than the U.S. tax liability created by the section 951A inclusion, a residual U.S. tax of $12.64 is created in this example.

It is at this point that the reader can glean the purpose of the section 951A regime. If a CFC paid no foreign tax on its net CFC tested income, the U.S. residual tax on net CFC tested income would be 12.6 percent.[127] If net CFC tested income is subject to a foreign tax of 14 percent or higher, then no residual U.S. tax would apply.[128] If net CFC tested income is subjected to a foreign tax that is below 14%, then those earnings are subjected to a residual U.S. taxation as a top-up tax so that the overall effective rate would range from 12.6 percent to 14 percent. Thus, the import of section 951A is that the U.S. will impose a top-up tax whenever the income in the U.S. shareholder's controlled foreign corporations are subjected to less than a 14 percent foreign tax, but if that 14 percent foreign tax threshold is met then no residual U.S. tax would apply.

Of course, alternative examples could be given where the allocable credits could have been posited to have exceeded the foreign tax credit limitation on the section 951A basket. If those alternative facts had existed, then U.S. parent corporation would be entitled to claim the lesser of the amount of the allowable foreign tax credits or the foreign tax credit limitation in that basket. Those excess credits, because they are placed in a separate section 951A basket, are unable to be used to offset any residual U.S. tax on other items of income. What is more, if there are any excess credits in the section 951A basket, section 904(c) explicitly indicates that no credit carryover is allowed with respect to credits placed in that basket. Thus, unlike other categories of income where a credit carryover for one preceding year and 10 succeeding years is generally allowed, that is not allowed with respect to taxes placed in the section 951A basket.

If the above complexity were not enough, a final complexity should be highlighted with respect to the foreign tax credit limitation for the section 951A basket. The key question is whether any U.S. expenses of the U.S. parent corporation should be allocated and apportioned among all of the separate basket categories of the foreign

---

[127] Net CFC tested income (100%) less 40% deduction under § 250 leaves 60 percent CFC tested income to be taxed at a 21 percent tax rate resulting in a net tax amount of 12.6%.

[128] The 12.6 percent U.S. tax liability before allowance of foreign tax credit can be offset by 90 percent of the allowable foreign tax credits. Ninety percent of foreign income taxes paid of 14 percent would be sufficient to result in a 12.6 percent allowable credit to offset the 12.6% residual U.S. tax amount.

income of the U.S. parent corporation. If U.S. expenses are allocated and apportioned to the income including the section 951A basket income, then the effect of such an allocation would be that the net foreign source income in that separate basket would be reduced to the extent of the U.S. expense allocation and thus would decrease the resulting net foreign source income that exists in that basket to which foreign tax credits can be claimed. Said differently, because the separate limitation is determined based on a 21 percent tax rate on the net foreign source income that is in section 951A basket, any allocation and apportionment of U.S. expenses against that basket of income would create a corresponding reduction in the net foreign source income in that basket and thus would create a reduction in the foreign tax credit limitation, as the foreign tax credit limitation is simply 21 percent of the net foreign source income in the section 951A basket. The allocation and apportionment of expenses represents a significant potential area of controversy. To forestall such controversies, the 2025 Act added section 904(b)(5) to provide that only directly allocable expenses are to be included in the computation of the section 951A foreign tax credit limitation with any indirectly allocable and apportionable expenses that would have been assigned to this category of income under section 861 would instead be assigned to U.S. source income.

F. Previously Taxed Income of Section 959

The provisions of Subpart F in section 951(a) and net CFC tested income in section 951A are anti-deferral regimes that attempt to accelerate the timing of income but are not intended to create double taxation. Thus, if the earnings of a controlled foreign corporation are taxable to the U.S. shareholder under one of those anti-deferral regimes, what should be the result when those earnings are actually distributed? Obviously, they should not be taxed yet again. The U.S. shareholder has already been subject to U.S. taxation on those foreign earnings on a deemed basis and thus should not be taxed again at the time those earnings are actually distributed. Otherwise, double taxation on the same earnings would arise. Congress recognized from the outside the inequity of such a double inclusion and thus provided a remedy from the beginning of the Subpart F regime under section 951 and has extended that remedy to include net CFC tested income under section 951A. Specifically, section 959(a) provides that when earnings of a foreign corporation that are attributable to amounts that are, or have been, included in the gross income of a U.S. shareholder, then those earnings when actually distributed are excluded from the U.S. shareholder's income. Section 959(c) provides ordering rules that allows any distribution to be treated first as a distribution of amounts that were taxed under section 951(a) or under section 951(a).

G. Individual U.S. Shareholders of Controlled Foreign Corporations and Section 962 Elections

An important point of divergence exists with respect to the manner in which a Subpart F inclusion under section 951 and a net CFC tested income inclusion under section 951A applies to a U.S. shareholder that is a U.S. individual. Because section 960 credits are only allowed for domestic corporations and because the deduction equal to 40 percent of the grossed-up net CFC tested income inclusion that is allowed under section 250 is only allowed to domestic corporations, the pro rata share of the Subpart F inclusion or net CFC tested income inclusion would generally be included in the individual shareholder's gross income and taxed at ordinary income rates without either of those nuances.[129] Thus, if one assumes the same facts as in Table #13A except that the U.S. shareholder is now an individual, the facts are now depicted in this modified Table #13B. In this fact pattern, the individual U.S. shareholder would be required to include in her income the pro rata amount of net CFC tested income set forth on Line 3 (i.e., pro rata share of $260) and would be subject to ordinary individual tax rates at a 37 percent maximum rate in turn creating a U.S. tax liability of $44.40 (i.e., 37% of Line 10 of Table #13B). No indirect foreign tax credit is allowed. And, no section 250 deduction on the net CFC tested income inclusion or its section 78 gross-up is allowed either.

Table #13B: Net CFC Tested Income Example

Item		CFC1 (a)	CFC2 (b)	CFC3 (c)	Individual US Shareholder
1	Tested Income		$180	$120	$300
2	Tested Loss	($40)	$0	$0	−$40
3	Net CFC Tested Income				$260

Section 962 was an obscure provision that had very limited attention prior to 2017. With the advent of the adoption of the net CFC tested income anti-deferral regime of section 951A and the availability of a 40 percent deduction against that income under section 250 deduction and a substantial reduction in corporate tax

[129] See Rodriguez v. Commissioner, 722 F.3d 306 (5th Cir. 2013) (section 951 and section 956 inclusions were not qualified dividends and thus were not eligible for preferential individual rate under section 1(h)(11)); SIH Partners LLLP v. Commissioner, 923 F.3d 296 (3rd Cir. 2019) (same involving a section 956 inclusion). Section 951A(f)(1)(A) generally requires net CFC tested income to be treated the same as a Subpart F inclusion, and the Treasury Department has authority to make this explicit for other sections in the Code per section 951A(f)(1)(B).

rates, the previously somewhat obscure provision of section 962 has now been thrust into the limelight.

Section 962 provides, in relevant part, that an individual may elect to include in gross income any Subpart F amount under section 951(a) as if that person were a domestic corporation and as such would be entitled to claim indirect foreign tax credits under section 960 to offset that Subpart F inclusion. However, section 951A(f)(1)(A) makes clear that an inclusion under section 951A should be treated the same as an inclusion under section 951(a) for purposes of applying section 962. Congress enacted section 962 to ensure that individuals' tax burdens with respect to undistributed foreign earnings of their CFCs "will be no heavier than they would have been had they invested in an American corporation doing business abroad."[130] However, the "cost of admission" for the individual shareholder's section 962 election is that the subsequent actual distribution is not eligible to be treated as a distribution of previously taxed income and the shareholder only is able to deduct the prior amount of U.S. taxes paid on the Subpart F or net CFC tested income inclusion, but if the actual dividend (which is now taxable) were from a qualified foreign corporation, the individual U.S. shareholder may be entitled to preferential rates for qualified dividends under section 1(h)(11).

There is one more piece to add to the equation. Although existing Reg. § 1.962–1(b)(1)(i) provides that a deduction of a U.S. shareholder does not reduce the amount included in gross income under section 951(a), the Treasury Department nevertheless concluded that allowing a section 250 deduction to an individual that makes a section 962 election is consistent with the purpose of that provision of ensuring that such individual's tax burden with respect to its CFC's undistributed foreign earnings is no greater than if the individual owned such CFC through a domestic corporation. Accordingly, the Treasury Department provided in proposed regulations that, for purposes of section 962, "taxable income" as used in section 11 of an electing individual is reduced by the portion of the section 250 deduction that would be allowed to a domestic corporation with respect to the individual's net CFC tested income inclusion and the section 78 gross-up attributable to the shareholder's net CFC tested income inclusion.[131] Thus, if an individual U.S. shareholder makes a section 962 election in the facts that accompanied Table #13A, then the results to the individual U.S. shareholder at the time of the net CFC tested income inclusion is set

---

[130] S. Rept. 1881, 1962–3 Cum. Bull. 784, at 798.

[131] See proposed Reg. § 1.962–1(b)(1)(i)(B)(3).

forth in Table #13C, which now is identical to the original Table #13A results that were afforded to the domestic corporation.

Table #13C: Net CFC Tested Income Example with Section 962 Election					
Item		CFC1 (a)	CFC2 (b)	CFC3 (c)	Individual US Shareholder
1	Tested Income		$180	$120	$300
2	Tested Loss	($40)	$0	$0	–$40
3	Net CFC Tested Income				$260
4	Tested Foreign Income Taxes		$10	$20	$30
5	*Foreign effective tax rate on tested income*		*5.3%*	*14.3%*	*9.1%*
6	Section 78 Gross-Up		$8.67	$17.33	$26.00
7	Deemed Paid Credit after 10% haircut (90% * L6)				$23.40
8	Grossed-up Net CFC Tested Income (L3 + L6)				$286.00
9	40% § 250 Deduction (40% * L8)				$114.40
10	Other US allocable expenses (§ 904(b)(5))				None
11	Taxable income before credit (L8 – L9 – L10)				$171.60
12	US tax before credit (21% * L11)				$36.04
13	Foreign tax credit (L7)				$23.40
14	US Tax on Net CFC Tested Income (L12 – L13)				**$12.64**

This equivalency is only maintained at the time of the Subpart F or net CFC tested income inclusion and is removed at the time of the later actual distribution of the earnings. In an important change, section 962(d) provides that the earnings of a foreign corporation attributable to amounts which were included in the gross income and subject to a section 962(a) election shall again be included in the shareholder's gross income when distributed to the extent that such earnings and profits exceed the amount of tax paid on the prior Subpart F or net CFC tested income inclusion. Thus, section 959 is not available at the time of the actual distribution if the individual U.S. shareholder made a section 962 election. If the shareholder had been a domestic corporate U.S. shareholder, then it would have been entitled to rely on section 959 but is denied that outcome if he or she avails of the benefits of a section 962 election.

In Table #13C, the earnings of $260 were subject to a tax of $12.64, so when the $260 of earnings are distributed, then the U.S. shareholder would be subject to taxation on $247.36 (i.e., $260 less $12.64). If the controlled foreign corporation is located in a jurisdiction that has a tax treaty with the United States, then the dividend would be from a "qualified foreign corporation" and thus treated as a qualified dividend subject to a 20 percent maximum qualified dividends rate of $49.47 in the above example (i.e., a 20% qualified dividend rate on $247.36 of taxable dividend upon distribution).

Thus, the section 962 election allows two advantages and has one disadvantage. The first advantage of a section 962 election is that at the time of the Subpart F and/or net CFC tested income inclusion(s) the individual shareholder could claim the benefits of section 960 credits and (as to the net CFC tested income inclusion) also the section 250 deduction. The second advantage of a section 962 election is that at the time of actual distribution the shareholder could then potentially avail herself of the qualified dividend rate, thus effectively side-stepping the adverse result in *Rodriguez v. Commissioner* where an actual Subpart F inclusion was held to not be entitled to the preferential rate for qualified dividends regardless of the tax treaty status of the controlled foreign corporation. However, the disadvantage of a section 962 election is that the actual dividend distribution is taxable again at the time of actual distribution less a deduction for any U.S. taxes paid on the prior inclusion, as section 959 is supplanted.

Let's synthesize this further. If an individual were going to incur a section 951A inclusion and no section 962 election were in effect, then the amount of that inclusion would be included and taxed at the shareholder's normal marginal tax rates up to 37 percent under current law. If, however, a section 962 election were made on the section 951A inclusion from a qualified foreign corporation, then the worst case scenario appears to be that the U.S. individual shareholder would be taxable at 12.6 percent on the net CFC tested income inclusion (assuming no deemed paid credits) and would be taxable on 87.4 percent of an actual distribution at the time of actual distribution but at a 20 percent rate (or 17.48%), so the all-in maximum rate of tax would be 30.08 percent in this situation (i.e., 12.6% plus 17.48%). If the deemed paid credits were available to completely offset the net CFC tested income inclusion plus its section 78 gross-up, then the U.S. individual's only tax would be at the time of the actual distribution and would be entitled to a 20 percent tax rate. If the foreign tax credits only partially offset the inclusion as depicted in Table 13C, then an intermediate tax result would arise as depicted in Table 13C where there is a reduced residual inclusion under section 951A and a partial amount of the dividend that would not be taxable at the time of distribution. Regardless of the scenario, however, the section 962 election provides a significant benefit versus a 37 percent rate that would apply in the scenario where a section 962 election were not made and an inclusion under section 951A is required. However, if the controlled foreign corporation is not located in a jurisdiction that has a tax treaty with the United States, then the foreign dividend is not eligible for preferential rates at the time of the distribution and the taxable dividend distribution would be subjected to a 37 percent individual tax rate at the time of distribution.

What if the inclusion is not a section 951A inclusion but instead is an inclusion under Subpart F? A similar analysis would apply. If the U.S. tax liability from the Subpart F inclusion is sufficiently offset by deemed paid indirect foreign tax credits and the controlled foreign corporation is a qualified foreign corporation, then the U.S. shareholder may well benefit from making a section 962 election to claim the section 960 deemed paid credit relief and then would be entitled to treat the actual distribution as a qualified dividend eligible for preferential rates. That combination may well create a tax cost that is as low as 20 percent assuming the deemed paid indirect foreign tax credits fully offset the U.S. tax liability on the Subpart F inclusion. However, if the foreign corporation is not a qualified foreign corporation (not incorporated in a jurisdiction with a U.S. tax treaty), then the actual distribution would be subject to ordinary income rates to the U.S. shareholder. In that event, the taxation under Subpart F and the non-applicability of section 959 to the actual distribution can cause the cost to be higher to the U.S. individual shareholder in that scenario.

Of course, the obvious planning exercise is for the U.S. individual shareholder to ensure that its controlled foreign corporation is incorporated in a treaty jurisdiction or for the individual U.S. shareholder to transfer the shares of the controlled foreign corporation to a wholly-owned U.S. domestic corporation. In that latter alternative, the U.S. shareholder would always be entitled to treat a dividend from the domestic corporation to the individual shareholder as a qualified dividend eligible for preferential rates as that dividend is received from a domestic corporation, and the domestic corporation would be the entity that would have the Subpart F inclusions or the net CFC tested income inclusions and would be entitled to the benefits of section 250 and section 960 in all events. There would be no added tax cost on distributions from the controlled foreign corporation to the domestic corporation with respect to earnings that were not subject to U.S. taxation under the Subpart F regime or the net CFC tested income regime because the domestic corporation would be entitled to rely on section 959 with respect to any earnings it had already included in income by reason of a prior Subpart F inclusion or net CFC tested income inclusion and would be entitled to a 100 percent foreign dividends received deduction under section 245A on the receipt of any actual foreign dividends that related to CFC earnings that had not been taxed under those regimes.

H. Concluding Thoughts

Before moving on, let's step back and think about the earnings in a controlled foreign corporation environment a bit more. Conceptually, as depicted in Diagram #31, the income in the controlled foreign corporation environment is now comprised of three types of CFC earnings: (1) earnings that are not subjected to an anti-deferral regime due to the high-tax exception or tested income was offset by tested losses, (2) earnings that are classified as Subpart F income, and (3) earnings that are classified as net CFC tested income. From a U.S. perspective, these three types of CFC earnings have markedly different U.S. tax implications. No further residual U.S. taxation will exist on earnings that are not subjected to taxation under subpart F or the net CFC tested income regime if remitted to a domestic corporate U.S. shareholder because domestic corporations obtain a 100 percent foreign dividends received deduction to the extent those earnings are foreign source income. Thus, those earnings potentially could be subject to as low as a zero percent tax rate, since the only relevant tax is the applicable foreign tax, if any. To the extent that foreign taxes are paid on those earnings, there is no U.S. foreign tax credit opportunity for those taxes because all foreign tax credits are disallowed if associated with a dividend that is eligible for the 100 percent foreign dividends received deduction. For individual U.S. shareholders, actual dividends remains subject to U.S. taxation either as qualified dividends or regular dividends.

Diagram #31

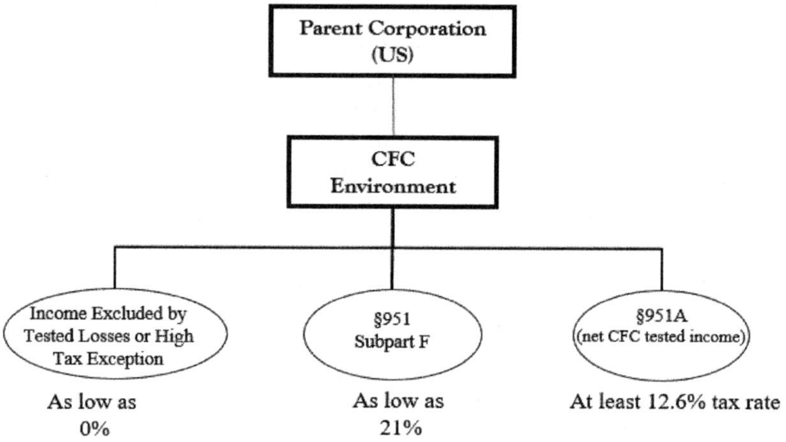

Earnings that are classified as Subpart F income have a dramatically different treatment. Earnings taxable under Subpart F are subject to residual U.S. taxation, but the domestic corporate U.S. shareholder is afforded an indirect foreign tax credit under section 960 for the allocable foreign income taxes paid by the controlled foreign corporation. If the grossed-up Subpart F inclusion had allocable high foreign taxes that exceeded the U.S. tax rate,[132] then the grossed-up Subpart F inclusion generally would be placed in the general basket income and the indirect foreign income tax credits would be placed there as well. Those indirect foreign tax credits could then be used to offset the residual U.S. tax liability of the domestic corporate U.S. shareholder with respect to any of its general basket income that also resides in that domestic corporate U.S. shareholder's general basket. Thus, excess indirect foreign tax credits associated with a Subpart F inclusion provides the domestic corporate U.S. shareholder with an opportunity for cross-crediting at the domestic corporate U.S. shareholder level against other low-taxed general basket foreign source income that may exist at the domestic corporate U.S. shareholder level, and in addition the foreign tax credits placed in the domestic corporate U.S. shareholder's general basket would be eligible to be carried back one year and carried forward to 10 succeeding years if sufficient limitation did not exist in the general basket in that particular year. Thus, the Subpart F regime is helpful in the fact pattern where foreign taxes were

---

132 A student might object and say that the income could be passive income. But, if it were high-taxed passive income, then it would be kicked out of the passive basket and placed in the general basket. See § 904(d)(2)(B)(iii)(II) and (F). Thus, under the assumption that the Subpart F inclusion involves high-taxed income, it would necessarily be placed in the general basket either because it was general basket income initially or because it was high-tax passive income that is subject to the kick-out rule.

assessed on the Subpart F income in an amount that exceeded the U.S. tax rate, since the Subpart F regime provides a mechanism to allow cross-crediting opportunities with respect to the CFC's high taxes both in the current year and other years. However, if the Subpart F income were low-taxed, then a Subpart F inclusion creates a potential residual U.S. tax absent cross-crediting. Thus, in that low-tax scenario, the domestic corporate U.S. shareholder has the opposite incentive and would seek to avoid or minimize low-taxed Subpart F income in the CFC environment. Said differently, it would be better to restructure to avoid low-taxed Subpart F income even if the result were solely that the low-taxed income were then subjected to U.S. taxation under the net CFC tested income regime, as the net CFC tested income regime provides a favorable 40 percent deduction under section 250. As a result, due to the 40 percent deduction allowed by reason of section 250, a net CFC tested income inclusion creates at most a 12.6 percent U.S. residual tax, so if the low-taxed income is going to be taxed it would be better to have it taxed there. With that said, any indirect foreign tax credits attributable to the net CFC tested income inclusion would be placed in the section 951A basket and could only be used to offset net CFC tested income and are ineligible for any carryover. Thus, cross-crediting is minimized, and carryover is eliminated. This is a bad place for excess foreign tax credits to reside, but a better place for low-taxed income to reside at least in comparison to the Subpart F regime. Subpart F creates a potentially higher U.S. tax liability, but it allows for more cross-crediting opportunities if in fact high foreign taxes were paid.

Thus, in situations where a company bears foreign taxes above the U.S. tax rate within a CFC, one would expect that the taxpayer may want to affirmatively plan for ways to have that high-taxed income subjected to Subpart F income treatment to access an indirect foreign tax credit that can provide cross-crediting opportunities against other general basket income at the domestic corporate U.S. shareholder level. If the activity that is creating high foreign tax were conducted in a foreign branch of the domestic corporate U.S. shareholder instead of a CFC, then those taxes would have provided a direct foreign tax credit to the United States shareholder, but the income and its credits would no longer be in the general basket and would instead be in the foreign branch basket. Thus, the ultimate foreign tax credit basket for high-taxed active business income is dependent upon a formal corporate structure decision of whether the active foreign business income is earned in a foreign branch or is instead earned in a CFC. The foreign tax credit basket limitation implications of this corporate structure choice may justify revisiting the decision as to whether the domestic corporate U.S. shareholder conducts its active foreign business activities through a branch or through a CFC.

The point of these insights is to simply state that the different types of CFC earnings, coupled with the application of differing foreign tax credit basket regimes and the inconsistent foreign tax credit carryover rules, create interesting trade-offs. Whether a particular domestic corporate U.S. shareholder desires or disdains a Subpart F inclusion is impacted by whether or not that Subpart F inclusion brings sufficient foreign tax credits to offset the U.S. tax liability on that immediate Subpart F income inclusion and brings excess credits beyond that amount to afford further cross-crediting opportunities. If the income is low-taxed, then the domestic corporate U.S. shareholder may well prefer planning that allows that income to avoid subpart F and is captured by the net CFC tested income regime of section 951A so that the added section 250 deduction could be accessed. Thus, whether or not a taxpayer seeks to avoid or avail of Subpart F's anti-deferral regime is going to be impacted significantly by the foreign tax credit posture of the domestic corporate U.S. shareholder. Now that earnings in a CFC environment have three different outcomes and direct foreign investment has yet a different set of foreign tax credit basket outcomes, the current law creates complex trade-offs and a need for overall foreign tax credit planning that is even more complicated and complex than what existed under the earlier law that pre-dated the 2017 Act.

Chapter 12

PASSIVE FOREIGN INVESTMENT COMPANIES (PFICs)

A further exception to the regime of deferral for foreign corporations is the taxation of Passive Foreign Investment Companies (or PFICs). A PFIC[1] is a foreign corporation that receives predominately passive foreign source income. U.S. persons owning shares of PFICs are generally subject to current U.S. taxation or the equivalent. As with Subpart F, the PFIC tax regime is exceedingly complex in its full detail. This chapter sketches only the big picture and even then omits a number of landmarks.

A. Background and Overview

Until the 1986 Act, current U.S. taxation of foreign corporations was strictly tied to control of the corporation held by U.S. persons. Minority and portfolio interests in foreign corporations owned by U.S. persons were not to any extent subject to look-through taxation. The PFIC regime, introduced in the 1986 Act, considerably enlarged current taxation of foreign passive investments of United States persons through foreign corporations. PFIC taxation applies without regard to the extent of U.S. ownership.

The taxation of PFICs is built on the idea of denying to United States persons (and hence capturing for the U.S. Treasury) the value of deferral of U.S. taxation on *all* passive investments channeled through foreign entities. The rules achieve this end either in the obvious way—current taxation of U.S. investors in PFICs—or in the indirect way of imposing an interest charge on the deferred distributions and gains of those investors. Among the notable features of PFIC taxation is that it does not depend on any threshold of ownership or control by U.S. persons.

The central elements in the taxation of PFICs are 1) the definition of a PFIC and 2) the tax regime imposed on U.S. owners of shares. Noteworthy in the former is that any foreign entity holding passive investments may be a PFIC regardless of the extent of U.S. ownership or control. The unique feature of the latter is an interest charge (equivalent to the value of deferred U.S. taxes) imposed on the realized gains of U.S. shareholders unless the U.S. shareholders make an election that results in current taxation.

---

1 "PFIC" is usually pronounced as a semi-acronym ("pee-fick") rather than a full acronym (which would be "pfick").

B. PFIC Defined

A "passive foreign investment company" (PFIC) is any foreign corporation if "(1) 75 percent or more of the gross income of such corporation for the taxable year is passive income or (2) the average percentage of assets . . . held by such corporation during the taxable year which produce passive income or which are held for the production of passive income is at least 50 percent."[2] A PFIC is thus an entity that receives mainly passive investment income or holds mainly passive investment assets.

Section 1297(b)(1) defines "passive income" as "foreign personal holding company income" as defined in section 954(c) with two qualifications. "Passive income" in Code Sec. 1297(a) does *not* include 1) income derived in the active conduct of a banking or insurance business by a corporation which is predominantly a financial intermediary,[3] 2) interest, dividends, rents, or royalties from a related person paid from income that is not itself passive income,[4] or 3) active financing interest.[5] The definition of a "related person" is the same in this provision as in section 954(d)(3), with the qualifications made necessary by the shift from the context of controlled foreign corporations ("CFCs") to PFICs.

An important definitional question is to what extent the exceptions to the definition of passive income under the exceptions to section 954(c)'s general rule should carry over for purposes of the PFIC provisions definition of the term "passive income." The regulations issued under section 1297(b)(1) incorporate some of the section 954(c) exceptions into the PFIC regime but also provide for areas of divergence. In this regard, the final regulations provide that the following subpart F exceptions to section 954(c) also apply for purposes of applying section 1297(b)(1) of the PFIC regime:

(i) the exceptions contained in Code Sec. 954(c)(1),[6]

(ii) the exception contained in section 954(c)(2)(A) (relating to active rents and royalties),[7]

(iii) the exception in section 954(c)(2)(B) (relating to export financing income),[8]

---

2 § 1297(a).

3 § 1297(b)(2)(A), (B).

4 § 1297(b)(2)(C).

5 § 1297(b)(2)(D).

6 Reg. § 1.1297–1(c)(1)(i)(A).

7 Reg. § 1.1297–1(c)(1)(i)(A).

8 Reg. § 1.1297–1(c)(1)(i)(A).

(iv) the exception in section 954(c)(2)(C) (relating to dealers),[9]

(v) the exception in section 954(c)(4) (relating to sales of certain partnership interests),[10] and

(vi) the exception in section 954(c)(5) (relating to certain commodity hedging transactions).[11]

On the other side of the ledger, the following exceptions that apply to determine passive income under the subpart F regime are not relevant exceptions to be taken into account for purposes of determining passive income for purposes of applying section 1297(b)(1) in the PFIC regime:

(i) the exception in section 954(c)(3) (relating to certain income received from related persons) and section 954(c)(6) (relating to certain amounts received from related controlled foreign corporations),[12]

(ii) the exception in section 954(h) (relating to entities engaged in the active conduct of a banking, financing, or similar business),[13] and

(iii) the exception in section 954(i) (relating to entities engaged in the active conduct of an insurance business) are not taken into account.[14]

The lack of incorporation of the Subpart F exceptions found in section 954(i) and section 954(h) into a comparable exception under section 1297(b)(1) is ameliorated somewhat by the fact that section 1297(b)(2) provides its own analogous albeit narrower set of exceptions for banking and insurance activities for the PFIC context. In addition, the inapplicability of the carve-outs for related party payments in section 954(c)(3) and section 954(c)(6) is not as ominous as one might first expect, as alternative look-through exceptions are available by reason of section 1297(c) for the PFIC context. In this regard, instead of applying the section 954(c)(3) and the section 954(c)(6) exceptions, the PFIC regime provides in section 1297(c) that any related party payments of interest, dividends, rents and royalties are determined as passive income based on the ratio of the payor's passive income to its current earnings and profits.[15] This pro rata approach is likely to be a more favourable outcome than the one

---

9 Reg. § 1.1297–1(c)(1)(i)(A).

10 Reg. § 1.1297–1(c)(1)(i)(C).

11 Reg. § 1.1297–1(c)(1)(i)(C).

12 Reg. § 1.1297–1(c)(1)(i)(B).

13 Prop. Reg. § 1.1297–1(c)(1)(i)(B).

14 Reg. § 1.1297–1(c)(1)(B).

15 § 1297(d)(2)(C); Reg. § 1.1297–1(c)(3).

afforded under the subpart F provisions, as typically related party payments under the subpart F regime are first characterized as passive income to the extent of any passive income in the payor entity.

Assets are passive assets for purposes of determining PFIC status if they produce passive income, or are held by a foreign corporation to that end.[16] Undeveloped land held for investment can therefore confer PFIC status on a foreign corporation if its value is large in relation to any active business assets. Dual use property is property that produces both passive and non-passive income.[17] When dual use property exists, the general rule is that the value of dual-character asset is allocated between a passive asset and a non-passive asset in proportion to the relative amounts of passive income to non-passive income produced by the asset during the taxable year. The definition of a PFIC does not, however, seek to reach pure holding entities that own substantial interests in active businesses through ownership of their shares. This is revealed by the treatment of interest, dividends, rents and royalties from related persons and by section 1297(c), under which a foreign corporation owning 25 percent or more of the stock of another corporation is treated, for the purpose of determining its status as a PFIC, as if it held directly its proportionate share of the assets of the other corporation and received its proportionate share of the other corporation's income.[18] Accordingly, a foreign holding company owning all the shares of an active business corporation and nothing else is not treated as a PFIC. Various "look-through" rules apply to a tested foreign corporation's subsidiaries and related parties for purposes of the PFIC tests. These look-through rules extend to lower-tier subsidiaries owned indirectly by a foreign corporation.[19]

C. Taxation of PFICs

The U.S. persons who own a PFIC are subject to a special (indeed unique) income tax regime. The specifics depend on whether the shareholders of the PFIC have elected to be taxed as shareholders of a "qualified electing fund," or whether the "pure" PFIC tax regime of section 1291 applies.

1. The PFIC Regime of Section 1291

Under section 1291, amounts received by a U.S. person from a PFIC (whether as a distribution or the proceeds of a sale of shares) are first allocated "ratably" to all the separate years of the taxpayer's

---

16 Reg. § 1.1297–1(d)(1).

17 Reg. § 1.1297–1(d)(3)(i).

18 § 1297(b)(2)(C); Reg. § 1.1297–1(c)(3).

19 § 1297(c).

holding period of the PFIC stock.[20] Amounts allocated to earlier years are included in income and subject to U.S. tax *plus* a "deferred tax amount,"[21] which is an increase in tax determined by adding an interest element reflecting and offsetting the prior deferral of U.S. taxation.[22]

Very roughly, the system of section 1291 negates the tax benefit of deferral. If you bear in mind that the economic value of deferral of U.S. taxation is the time value of the deferral itself, you will understand how PFIC taxation, by taking back the time value of deferral through the deferred tax amount, undoes the advantage.

There is an admirably clear summary of the workings of section 1291 in, of all places, the preamble of the Treasury Regulations on PFICs:

> Pursuant to section 1291, a U.S. person that is a shareholder of a section 1291 fund pays tax and an interest charge on receipt of certain distributions and upon disposition of stock of the section 1291 fund. Under this rule, gain from a disposition or the portion of any distribution that is an excess distribution (defined in section 1291(b)) is treated as ordinary income earned ratably over the shareholder's holding period of the stock of the section 1291 fund. The portion allocated to the current year, and to years when the corporation was not a PFIC, are included in the shareholder's gross income for the year of the distribution; the remainder is not included in gross income, but the shareholder must pay a deferred tax amount (defined in section 1291(c)) with respect to that portion. The deferred tax amount is, in general, the amount of tax that would have been owed if the allocated amount had been included in income in the earlier year, plus interest.

2. The QEF Election

As an alternative to this complex and generally severe tax regime, U.S. shareholders of PFICs can elect current U.S. taxation of their share of the earnings of a "qualified electing fund" ("QEF"). An election by a U.S. person brings the allocable earnings of a QEF within a tax regime[23] similar (but not identical) to that of Subpart F, which you may remember from the preceding chapter.

---

[20] § 1291(a)(1)(A).

[21] § 1291(a)(1)(C).

[22] § 1291(c)(2).

[23] See § 1293(c) for the details.

3. The Mark-to-Market Election

The most recent feature of the landscape is the election of section 1296, designed to mitigate the complexities of PFIC taxation for U.S. investors in foreign mutual funds. Small[24] U.S. holders of foreign mutual funds, many of which are PFICs in the hands of U.S. shareholders, would often find it difficult to either comply with the pure PFIC tax regime of section 1291 or to a QEF election.[25]

To ease the plight of such U.S. investors, the "mark-to-market" election of section 1296 allows shareholders of PFICs, if their stock is marketable, to recognize unrealized gain or loss in the shares annually instead of suffering the PFIC tax system.[26] Specifically, a U.S. person owning "marketable stock" in a PFIC may elect to include in income (as ordinary income) the excess of the fair market value of the stock at the close of the taxable year over its adjusted basis or to deduct (as an ordinary loss) the excess of its adjusted basis over the year-end fair market value.[27] The shareholder's basis is adjusted up or down to reflect amounts included or deducted pursuant to this election.[28] PFIC stock that has been marked to market takes a carryover basis (instead of the usual fair market value basis) at the death of its owner.[29]

Needless to say, a taxpayer who has made a mark-to-market election under section 1296 is not subject to the pure PFIC tax regime of section 1291.[30]

It also goes without saying that only "marketable" stock can be marked to market. PFIC stock is "marketable" for this purpose if it is regularly traded on a suitably regulated securities exchange or if it is a foreign open-end or closed-end mutual fund that makes periodic reports of net asset values.[31]

---

24 Note that we mean "small" in the financial sense, not the Lilliputian sense.

25 The difficulty of the latter is getting enough information about the earnings of the fund from its managers, given different requirements of reporting outside the United States.

26 Annual recognition of unrealized gain or loss is known as "marking to market." It is a regime that also applies to many traded commodities contracts. See § 1256.

27 § 1296(a).

28 § 1296(b)(1).

29 § 1296(i).

30 § 1291(d)(1).

31 § 1296(e).

Chapter 13

DISPOSITIONS, LIQUIDATIONS, AND REORGANIZATIONS OF CONTROLLED FOREIGN CORPORATIONS AND INCORPORATIONS OF FOREIGN BRANCHES

This chapter brings together several different forms of restructuring of a foreign investment into one heading. The general rules for the treatment of a taxable disposition of the stock of a foreign corporation are modified by section 961 and section 1248 when the entity being sold is a controlled foreign corporation. The application of those rules is dealt with immediately in the following section. The tax-free incorporations or reorganizations of businesses, as provided in the corporate provisions of Subchapter C, are modified by section 367 in the international setting. The manner in which section 367 applies to branch incorporations, foreign-to-foreign reorganizations, and liquidations will be addressed thereafter.

A. Taxable Dispositions of Controlled Foreign Corporations

1. Section 961

If a U.S. shareholder has been subject to taxation with respect to the undistributed earnings of a controlled foreign corporation either under the Subpart F regime or the net CFC tested income regime, then those earnings, as we have seen in chapter 11, are excluded from gross income when actually distributed to the U.S. shareholder under section 959 in order to avoid double taxation of the U.S. shareholder on the same earnings. Section 959, therefore, understandably allows the previously taxed earnings and profits (or "PTEP") of the U.S. shareholder to be excluded from that shareholder's gross income when those earnings are later distributed.

However, what if the U.S. shareholder sells its interest in the controlled foreign corporation before its previously taxed earnings and profits is actually distributed? Part of the value of the controlled foreign corporation represents the undistributed (but previously taxed) earnings in the controlled foreign corporation, so again it would create an asymmetrical result if the U.S. shareholder did not get credit for already having paid tax on these undistributed but previously taxed earnings. Section 961 provides symmetrical relief for this situation. Under section 961(a), the U.S. shareholder is allowed to increase its basis in the stock of not only the controlled foreign corporation but also each intervening CFC tier as a result of a Subpart F or net CFC tested income inclusion with respect to the earnings of the controlled foreign corporation from which the income inclusion originated. Section 961(b) reduces that basis back down, in the controlled foreign corporation and in each intervening tier, at the time the previously taxed earnings is distributed up the ownership chain and ultimately to the U.S. shareholder. Moreover, if the distribution of PTEP is in excess of the adjusted basis in the stock, then any excess is treated as gain to the taxpayer on the sale or exchange of the foreign stock.[1] However, assuming no intervening return of capital distribution occurred with respect to that controlled foreign corporation before it were sold, the basis adjustments afforded by section 961 serve to ensure that the taxpayer receives an equivalent tax outcome whether the PTEP is distributed or not. Thus, as a general rule, if the controlled foreign corporation has undistributed previously taxed earnings and profits, the U.S. shareholder will have had a section 961(a) increase in its basis for the amount of that undistributed previously taxed income so that it would not be taxed a second time on those earnings if it sold the shares before distributing the previously taxed earnings. Said differently, the U.S. shareholder could certainly distribute the previously taxed earnings and have its stock basis correspondingly reduced. Thus, the gain on the sale of CFC stock is calculated with basis adjustments under section 961. That said, it is important to note that section 961 provides basis adjustments only with respect to previously taxed earnings. If the controlled foreign corporation's earnings are not subject to taxation under an anti-deferral regime, then the value of the corporation will have been increased by the amount of these undistributed and untaxed earnings but the shareholder will not have been taxed on those earnings as yet and will not have had an increase in the basis in the stock of the controlled foreign corporation (or "CFC").

2. Section 1248 and Its Companion Provision of Section 964(e)

So, what is the result with respect to the sale of stock of a controlled foreign corporation with undistributed earnings that have not created an inclusion under either Subpart F or net CFC tested income regime? Certainly, the buyer will have paid a higher purchase price for the company if it has additional undistributed assets that remain in the controlled foreign corporation. Thus, part of the gain in the sale of the controlled foreign corporation represents the

---

[1] Reg. § 1.961–2(c).

earnings that have not been distributed but could have been. What should be the tax result in this situation? The answer to this question is provided by section 1248.

The capital gains preference explains both the existence and the mechanics of section 1248. Section 1248, simplifying a bit for the moment, treats gains from the sale of shares of controlled foreign corporations as dividends, rather than capital gains, to the extent of the undistributed earnings and profits of the controlled foreign corporation that have not been previously taxed to the U.S. shareholder. Before the adoption of Subpart F in 1962, the sale by a United States shareholder of shares of a foreign corporation, like the sale of any other shares, produced capital gains. Liquidations of foreign corporations were similarly taxed. If the earnings of the foreign corporation had been untaxed or lightly taxed outside the United States, the U.S. capital gains tax (at the time much lower than the U.S. tax on ordinary income) would ultimately be the only tax imposed on the foreign earnings after their capture through the sale of shares or effective repatriation through liquidation. The resulting tax regime for low-taxed foreign earnings was less onerous than the domestic regime. For an individual U.S. shareholder, for example, a deferred tax at capital gains rates might be the only tax cost of foreign operations.[2] Within its four corners, Subpart F does not change this result.[3] That is the province of section 1248.

Filling the gap left open by Subpart F is a companion provision, also adopted in 1962, codified as section 1248. In outline, section 1248 imposes taxation as dividends on gains from the liquidation of a controlled foreign corporation or a sale of its shares to the extent those gains are attributable to earnings on which U.S. taxation has been deferred. In effect, section 1248 backstops Subpart F by cutting off the repatriation of foreign earnings at capital gains rates.

Subpart F and section 1248 together form the overall framework of taxation of controlled foreign corporations. Subpart F limits deferral for tax-haven income earned in a CFC environment. Section 1248 reaches their active business income as well. Their deferred foreign earnings must eventually be taxed as dividends. Together Subpart F and section 1248 establish the tax regime imposed on controlled foreign corporations, the central element of which is that

---

2 For *corporate* shareholders of high-taxed controlled foreign corporations, however, capital gains from sales of shares could spell a gratuitous and costly extra layer of U.S. tax. Dividends may allow the domestic corporate shareholder to claim a 100 percent foreign dividends received deduction on its pro rata share of the section 1248 amount that effectively exempts the dividend income from U.S. taxation. See § 1248(j).

3 Nothing in Subpart F itself curtails the possibility of capital gains from the liquidation or sale of controlled foreign corporations.

all overseas earnings of controlled foreign corporations must be treated as actually or constructively distributed either currently (under Subpart F or net CFC tested income) or eventually when a deemed dividend is recast at the time of sale under section 1248.

Section 1248(a) is triggered by the sale or exchange of stock in a foreign corporation by a United States shareholder, including sales in redemption or liquidation treated as exchanges in the Code.[4] If the selling shareholder's ownership of stock of the foreign corporation crossed the threshold of a "United States shareholder" at any time during the five years preceding the sale when the foreign corporation was also a controlled foreign corporation, then part or all of the gain recognized on the sale is included in the income of the seller as a dividend.[5] The amount of the dividend (up to the gain recognized) is the amount of the earnings and profits of the foreign corporation accumulated during the periods in which the seller held the stock while the foreign corporation was a controlled foreign corporation.[6]

Since the enactment of the 2003 Act, the rate of tax on qualified dividends received by individuals has been the same preferential rate as imposed on long-term capital gains. Thus, to the extent that a recast foreign dividend by reason of section 1248 is a qualified dividend, then the recast has no adverse rate effect on an individual U.S. shareholder. A qualified dividend includes foreign dividends paid (or deemed paid by reason of section 1248) by a "qualified foreign corporation." A "qualified foreign corporation" is defined in section 1(h)(11)(C) to include corporations chartered in countries with which the United States has an income tax treaty and foreign corporations traded on U.S. securities markets. Thus, for an individual, section 1248 no longer represents a detriment if the recast foreign dividend is deemed to have been paid by a qualified foreign corporation. If the recast dividend were deemed paid by a foreign corporation that fails to satisfy the requirements of a qualified foreign corporation, then the recast creates a detriment to an individual U.S. shareholder as the recast dividend in that event would be subject to taxation at ordinary rates.

However, the picture is much different for a U.S. shareholder that is a domestic corporation. In this regard, assuming the domestic corporation has held the CFC stock for the requisite holding period, then the recast of what would have been capital gain into a dividend creates the positive benefit of entitling the domestic corporate shareholder to claim a 100 percent foreign dividends received

---

4 The relevant provisions are sections 302 and 331.

5 § 1248(a)(1). You may remember from chapter 11 that a "United States shareholder" is a U.S. person owning directly, indirectly, or by attribution 10 percent or more of the voting power of a foreign corporation. § 951(b).

6 § 1248(a) (flush language).

deduction under section 245A for the portion of the gain that is so recast.[7] Thus, for the domestic corporation that sells the stock of a controlled foreign corporation, the recast from a capital gain to a dividend makes that portion of its gain *nontaxable*. To the extent that the capital gain is greater than the amount of the undistributed earnings, however, then the excess gain remains a capital gain.

The above rules can be illustrated by a combined example that helps to illustrate the principles that are set forth above. In Table #15, a controlled foreign corporation is sold for $200. The original cost basis in the shares of the controlled foreign corporation was $50. Prior Subpart F and net CFC tested income inclusions of $100 occurred, which resulted in a positive basis adjustment of $100 under section 961(a), but $30 of that previously taxed earnings was distributed thus creating a negative basis adjustment of $30 by reason of section 961(b). Thus, the final adjusted basis in the CFC stock at the time of sale is $120 (see Line 5 of Table #15). As a result, a gain of $80 is triggered. Now, Table #15 indicates that the U.S. shareholder's pro rata share of the undistributed untaxed earnings (the so-called section 1248 "applicable earnings") is $35, so the lesser of the gain realized or the section 1248 applicable earnings is $35 in this example. Therefore, $35 of the gain is recast as a deemed dividend to the U.S. shareholder and $45 of the gain remains a capital gain. If the U.S. shareholder were a domestic corporation, then that domestic corporation would be eligible to claim a 100 percent foreign dividends received deduction for the $35 deemed dividend. If the U.S. shareholder were an individual, then that individual U.S. shareholder is taxable on the dividend but would be entitled to claim the preferential capital gains rates if the dividend were deemed paid by a qualified foreign corporation within the meaning of section 1(h)(11)(C).

---

7 See § 1248(j).

Table #14: Section 1248 Example			
Item			
1	Sales Price		$200
2	Original Cost Basis in CFC Stock	$50	
3	Basis Adjustment for Previously Taxed Earnings	$100	
4	Portion of Previously Tax Income Distributed	($30)	
5	Adjusted Basis in CFC Stock (∑ L2 through L4)		$120
6	Gain on Sale of Stock (L1 minus L5)		$80
7	Undistributed & Untaxed Earnings (§ 1248 Amount)		$35
8	Dividend Amount (Lesser of L6 or L7)		$35
9	Excess Capital Gain (Excess of L6 over L8)		$45

What is the result to the U.S. shareholder if an upper-tier controlled foreign corporation sells a lower-tier controlled foreign corporation at a time when the lower-tier controlled foreign corporation had undistributed earnings that had not been taxed under Subpart F or net CFC tested income? One would expect that if there is an answer to this question involving the sale of an indirectly owned CFC that it would be in section 1248, but Congress answered this question in section 964(e) (titled as part of "miscellaneous provisions"). Specifically, section 964(e) provides that the principles of section 1248(a) are to be applied to the selling controlled foreign corporation so that its capital gain is recast as a dividend from the unwanted controlled foreign corporation to the extent of the lesser of the undistributed earnings or the capital gain in the transaction. This recast dividend is treated as Subpart F income to the selling CFC shareholder that is not eligible for an exception to the Subpart F regime.[8] However, if the U.S. shareholder is a domestic corporation, the domestic corporation is able to claim a 100 percent foreign dividends received deduction with respect to its pro rata share of the Subpart F inclusion.[9] This is a unique exception as Subpart F inclusions are not generally eligible for a foreign dividends received deduction except for this specially recast dividend by reason of section 964(e).

If the U.S. shareholder were an individual, then the individual U.S. shareholder's pro rata share of the Subpart F inclusion would

[8] § 964(e)(4)

[9] § 964(e)(4)(A)(iii).

be subject to ordinary income rates. Thus, for an individual U.S. shareholder, this outcome is a trap for the unwary as an actual dividend from the lower-tier CFC to an upper-tier CFC may have been eligible for a Subpart F exception by reason of section 954(c)(6) whereas this recast dividend by reason of section 964(e)(4) creates an immediate Subpart F income inclusion with no section 245A dividends received deduction for an individual U.S. shareholder.

A possible disposition planning idea brought about by *Dover v. Commissioner*[10] is worthy of comment at this juncture. Suppose that the entity classification of the lower-tier CFC entity were changed to that of a disregarded entity immediately before the ownership interest in that entity were sold. Now, the upper-tier controlled foreign corporation is deemed to have sold the underlying trade or business assets of the lower-tier entity, which may not generate foreign base company sales income if these assets were active business assets.[11] Thus, instead of selling stock that would create stock gain subject to the foreign personal holding company income rules or a deemed dividend under section 964(e), the transaction would now represent a disposition that is not subject to those rules but instead treated as a sale of active business assets. The IRS attacked such a transaction in *Dover*, claiming that the upper-tier CFC's transitory "asset ownership" should not entitle it to claim that it sold active business assets, since it did not use those assets in its own business. The Tax Court disagreed, reasoning that the upper-tier CFC inherited the tax history of the lower-tier entity (per section 381) in the deemed liquidation that was tax-free by reason of section 332. Given that those assets had been used in the lower-tier entity's business operations prior to its deemed liquidation by reason of the change of the lower-tier entity's election, the upper-tier CFC was able to claim that these assets were active business assets at the time of the sale. Finally, the Tax Court rejected substance over form arguments to recast the change in the entity's tax classification that had been made shortly before the disposition of the lower-tier entity. This *Dover* planning idea would seem to be an alternative disposition strategy in the right factual situation, but now, with the net CFC tested income regime in place, the income would be tested income and may create an income inclusion under that minimum tax regime.[12]

---

10 122 T.C. 324 (2004).

11 See Reg. § 1.954–2(e); Reg. § 1.954–3(a).

12 The results under section 951A would be somewhat complex. All the income would be included as additional tested income, but the domestic corporate U.S. shareholder (or an individual who elects section 962) would be eligible for a 40 percent section 250 deduction and also 90 percent of any section 960 credits which in certain fact patterns could afford a more favorable outcome overall.

3. Interaction of Section 1248, Section 964(e), and Section 954(c)(6) with Earnings That Would Have Been Taxable Under Subpart F or Net CFC Tested Income

In the case of a deemed dividend by reason of section 1248, its companion provision of section 964(e), or the claim of an exclusion from Subpart F income by reason of section 954(c)(6), the Treasury Department believed that those provisions could create inappropriate results when applied in the same year as an extraordinary reduction of the U.S. shareholder's interest in the pro rata share of earnings that otherwise would have been classified as Subpart F income or net CFC tested income. Thus, through temporary regulations, the Treasury Department has restricted the availability of section 245A's foreign dividends received deduction and section 954(c)(6)'s exclusion so that those provisions do not apply to any "extraordinary reduction amount."[13]

In order to illustrate the concern that motivated these complex rules in the section 245A context, consider the following example. A domestic corporate U.S. shareholder (the transferor) transferred stock in a CFC to another U.S. shareholder (the transferee), and the transferor recast its capital gain from the transfer into a deemed dividend from the CFC by reason of section 1248(a). Now assume that a portion of the CFC earnings that were part of the recast deemed dividend would have created an income inclusion under Subpart F or net CFC tested income to the transferor except for the fact that the transferor only includes its pro rata share of the Subpart F income or net CFC tested income inclusion as of the end of the CFC's taxable year.[14] Obviously, the transferor's ownership was reduced before the end of the year by reason of the disposition of a portion of the CFC stock, and so the transferor's pro rata share of any Subpart F income and/or net CFC tested income was reduced as a result of the transaction to which section 1248(a) applied. Thus, if section 245A applied without limitation to the deemed dividend included by reason of section 1248(a) (or in a lower tier context by reason of section 964(e)),[15] then the CFC earnings could be excluded from the

---

[13] See Reg. § 1.245A–5T(b)(2)(ii).

[14] See § 951(a); § 951A(c)(1).

[15] The rules in these temporary regulations for determining eligibility for the section 245A deduction also apply to deemed dividends arising by reason of section 964(e)(4). Section 964(e)(4) provides that the gain on the sale of a foreign corporation by a CFC is recast as a deemed dividend from the target foreign corporation to the selling CFC that is, in turn, treated as Subpart F income of the selling CFC and included in the gross income of the U.S. shareholders of the selling CFC. Pursuant to section 964(e)(4)(A)(iii), the section 245A deduction is allowed to any U.S. shareholder with respect to such Subpart F income included in gross income in the same manner as if such Subpart F income were a dividend received by the shareholder from the selling CFC. Thus, section 964(e)(4) presents the same concerns as presented by section 1248's application to a domestic corporate U.S. shareholder that sold the stock

transferor's income by reason of the 100 percent foreign dividends received deduction allowable under section 245A. As to the transferee U.S. shareholder that acquired the interest of the transferor, the transferee is a shareholder as of the end of the CFC's taxable year, but the transferee's pro rata share of Subpart F income or net CFC tested income would generally not include any Subpart F income or net CFC tested income that has been actually distributed by the CFC in that year. In this regard, section 951(a)(2)(B),[16] a longstanding provision in the Subpart F regime, prevents double taxation of the same earnings by reducing the transferee U.S. shareholder's pro rata share of Subpart F income of a CFC by the dividends received by another person with respect to the same share of stock.[17] Thus, the combination of section 245A and the exclusion of section 951(a)(2)(B) could be read to create the outcome that the Subpart F income and net CFC tested income inclusion amount is not included by anyone. This possible double exclusion of Subpart F income and net CFC tested income was seen as inappropriate, so the Treasury Department through temporary regulations sought to avoid this result by denying a foreign dividends received deduction for the portion of the deemed dividend that relates to earnings that would otherwise have been taxable under Subpart F or net CFC tested income if there had been no reduction of the transferor's interest in the pro rata share of the CFC's Subpart F income or net CFC tested income inclusion amount.

By the same token section 954(c)(6), in the CFC-to-CFC dividend context, could provide a similar inappropriate double exclusion if section 954(c)(6) applied to exclude a CFC-to-CFC dividend from the Subpart F income of the U.S. shareholder and the U.S. shareholder had an extraordinary reduction of interest in the payor CFC in that

---

of a CFC. Therefore, the temporary regulations treat the portion of the target corporation's earnings that would have generated Subpart F income or a net CFC tested income inclusion to be ineligible for the foreign dividends received deduction in this context as well. See Reg. § 1.245A–5T(g)(2).

16 Section 951A has a companion provision that services the same purpose. See § 951A(c)(2)(A)(iv).

17 Prior to the enactment of section 245A, the broad application of section 951(a)(2)(B) made sense as the first shareholder would have had an income inclusion with no benefit of a foreign dividends received deduction, and so it would have been inequitable to have the second shareholder be taxed on those same earnings under Subpart F. But, with the enactment of section 245A, the dual application of a 100 percent foreign dividends received deduction under section 245A as to the transferor coupled with the exclusion of Subpart F income or net CFC tested income inclusion that accrued from the transferee U.S. shareholder by reason of section 951(a)(2)(B) prior to the ownership, could have the effect of preventing either U.S. shareholder from being taxable on the Subpart F income or net CFC tested income arising in the current year if applied in tandem to earnings that otherwise should have been taxable under Subpart F or net CFC tested income.

same year.[18] In this regard, section 954(c)(6) allows the CFC-to-CFC dividend received by the recipient CFC to be excluded from Subpart F income even though the underlying earnings and profits related to that dividend would have been subject to Subpart F income or a net CFC tested income inclusion. And, the new owner of the payor CFC generally would be able to exclude the Subpart F income and net CFC tested income inclusion that was distributed as a dividend in that year by reason of section 951(a)(2)(B). Again, a double exclusion of the Subpart F income or net CFC tested income is possible but is viewed as inappropriate. Thus, the Treasury Department, through temporary regulations, has sought to curtail the scope of section 954(c)(6) so that it cannot apply where (1) there is an "extraordinary reduction" (addressed in the next paragraph) in the U.S. shareholder's interest in the pro rata share of Subpart F income or net CFC tested income of the payor CFC entity, and (2) the earnings that are remitted as a dividend would have been included as Subpart F income or net CFC tested income "but for" the distribution and the extraordinary reduction of interest that occurred in the same year.[19]

Mechanically, to prevent the double exclusion of Subpart F income or net CFC tested income inclusions in the context where an extraordinary reduction of interest occurs, the regulations limit the amount of the section 245A foreign dividends received deduction that can be claimed by the U.S. shareholder and then separately limits the availability of section 954(c)(6)'s exclusion from Subpart F income so that neither section 245A nor section 954(c)(6) applies to any "extraordinary reduction amount."[20] The "extraordinary reduction amount" is the portion of the earnings and profits that would have been Subpart F income or net CFC tested income to the transferor domestic corporate U.S. shareholder had there not been a reduction in the stock ownership during the taxable year.[21] In the section 245A context, an extraordinary reduction occurs only if a domestic corporate U.S. shareholder reduces by more than 10 percent the amount of such stock that the shareholder owned at the beginning of the CFC's taxable year.[22] In the context of section 954(c)(6), any reduction in a pro rata share of Subpart F income or net CFC tested income inclusion through a reduction in interest of the U.S.

---

[18] Section 951A(c)(2) provides a companion provision that excludes this a dividend received from a related party from tested income.

[19] Reg. § 1.245A–5T(f).

[20] For the application of this extraordinary reduction amount in the context of deemed dividends under section 1248 or section 964(e), see Reg. § 1.245A–5T(b)(1) and (e). For the application of this extraordinary reduction amount in the context of a CFC-to-CFC dividend to which section 954(c)(6) is relevant, see Reg. § 1.245–5T(f).

[21] See Reg. § 1.245A–5T(e)(1)(ii) and (f)(2).

[22] See Reg. § 1.245–5T(e)(2)(i).

shareholder would represent an extraordinary reduction.[23] The effect of denying section 245A's foreign dividends received deduction and denying section 954(c)(6)'s Subpart F exclusion is to cause the domestic corporate U.S. shareholder to include in income these amounts with neither the benefit of a foreign dividends received deduction under section 245A nor the benefit of an exclusion from Subpart F income under section 954(c)(6). What is more, as to the deemed dividend received by the U.S. shareholder that is denied the benefits of section 245A, that foreign dividend income would not entitle the domestic corporate U.S. shareholder to claim any benefit of a deemed paid foreign tax credit under section 960 nor any benefit of the deduction afforded by section 250 if there had been a net CFC tested income inclusion. So, the outcome to the domestic corporate U.S. shareholder is worse than the result that would have occurred if the underlying earnings had been subject to taxation to the domestic corporate U.S. shareholder under either the Subpart F regime or the net CFC tested income regime in most foreseeable contexts.

To ameliorate the admittedly harsh treatment contemplated by these regulations, the regulations allow the U.S. domestic corporate U.S. shareholder to elect to close the taxable year of its CFCs immediately prior to any extraordinary reduction event.[24] In that event, the Subpart F inclusion and net CFC tested income inclusion would be made as of the end of the shortened taxable year with the consequence that the domestic corporate U.S. shareholder would then have its full pro rata share of Subpart F income and net CFC tested income inclusion before any extraordinary reduction in interest has occurred. The benefit of that outcome is that the domestic corporate U.S. shareholder would then be entitled to claim the deemed paid credits allowable as part of such an inclusion, and with respect to the net CTC tested income inclusion would be eligible to claim a section 250 deduction. Basis adjustments would also be afforded under section 961(a) for any such inclusions. The temporary regulations frame this option as an "election," but to the author it appears to be an offer that one cannot refuse in a vast majority of likely situations, so it is likely that U.S. shareholders will need to comply "voluntarily" with the requirements of this election.[25]

As discussed in chapter 11, transactions that create disqualified basis that are addressed in the anti-abuse rule under the regulations that implement section 951A can also create gain arising from extraordinary dispositions that are addressed in the anti-abuse rules

---

[23] See Reg. § 1.245A–5T(f)(2).

[24] See Reg. § 1.245A–5T(e)(3)(i)(A).

[25] For the requirements of this election, see Reg. § 1.245A–5T(e)(3)(i)(C), (D) and (E).

found in the regulations that implement the foreign dividends received deduction under section 245A.[26] As mentioned in chapter 11, absent a coordination mechanism, the simultaneous application of the extraordinary disposition rule of section 245A and the disqualified basis rule of section 951A could lead to punitive double taxation because the earnings and profits to which the extraordinary disposition rules apply and the basis to which the disqualified basis rules apply generally arise from the same amount of gain.

As a result, the government issued regulations to coordinate these two rules to mitigate against the potential for punitive double tax treatment.[27] The regulations coordinate the extraordinary disposition rule and disqualified basis rule through two operative rules. The first rule is a disqualified basis reduction rule, which reduces the amount of basis subject to the disqualified basis rule when the anti-abuse rule dealing with extraordinary dispositions has created U.S. taxation under those rules. The second rule is an extraordinary disposition reduction rule, which reduces the amount of earnings and profits that are subject to the extraordinary disposition rules when the anti-abuse rule that applies to disqualified basis has created U.S. taxation for that same amount previously.[28] The application of the coordination rule seeks to ensure that the simultaneous application of the disqualified basis rule in the regulations under section 951A and the extraordinary disposition rule in the regulations that implement section 245A preserves U.S. taxation over low-taxed income once but does so in a manner so that the simultaneous application of those two rules does not result in punitive double tax results. Thus, implicating immediate taxation by reason of one rule in effect turns off a corresponding risk of taxation under the other rule.

B. Effect of Section 367 on Transactions That Would Otherwise Have Received Nonrecognition Treatment

Subpart F and net CFC tested income, which are summarized in chapter 11, create separate tax regimes for controlled foreign corporations ("CFCs") and their U.S. shareholders. The rules governing passive foreign investment companies (PFICs) similarly create a separate tax regime for PFICs and their U.S. owners. There are, as a result, several distinct corporate income tax environments

---

26 Reg. § 1.245A–5(c).

27 Reg. § 1.245–6(a).

28 See Reg. § 1.245A–7; Reg. § 1.245A–8. These regulations were initially proposed in August 2020. See Notice of Proposed Rulemaking, REG-124737–19, 85 FED. REG. 53,098 (Aug. 27, 2020). The regulations were then finalized in December of that same year with minimal comment. See T.D. 9934, 85 FED. REG. 76,960 (Dec. 1, 2020).

within the U.S. tax system. There is the domestic corporate environment, combining full current taxation of worldwide corporate income with separate taxation of shareholders. There is the CFC environment—a mix of current taxation and deferral, with eventual taxation of foreign earnings upon repatriation as dividends to U.S. individual shareholders and exemption for distributions to domestic corporate U.S. shareholders. There is the PFIC environment, consisting of current taxation of passive investment income or the equivalent, backed up by deferred interest charges. And there is the wholly foreign (or non-CFC) environment, in which full deferral of U.S. taxation is generally possible with eventual taxation of foreign earnings upon repatriation as dividends to U.S. individual shareholders and exemption for distributions to domestic corporate U.S. shareholders.

Income and assets move around and among these tax environments. Foreign corporations receive capital from domestic corporations, distribute dividends back, merge, divide, liquidate, and so on. The U.S. international tax system must therefore follow and coordinate transitions between various tax regimes. In the wholly domestic setting, the Code contains an extensive set of rules—known as Subchapter C to its aficionados—governing the movement of assets into, out of, and within corporate solution. A key element of Subchapter C is the transfer of assets into and within the corporate environment without recognition of gain. Contributions of assets to corporations by their controlling shareholders, most distributions between affiliated corporations (including liquidations), and mergers and divisions are often either partly or wholly free of immediate tax. Assets and shares involved in these nonrecognition transactions generally retain their tax attributes, including basis, intact.

An unstated premise of the corporate nonrecognition rules is that an appropriate amount of gain should be preserved for future taxation. Earnings and profits shifted from one entity to another in a nonrecognition transaction will produce dividends upon ultimate distribution to shareholders. Unrealized appreciation is preserved when the basis of assets is carried over to a new entity and survives there as a tax attribute. If there were no curtailment of the nonrecognition rules in international transactions, however, the movement of assets from a taxable to a nontaxable environment could mean forgiveness rather than deferral of taxation given the different tax regimes applicable to different classes of domestic and foreign corporations. The nonrecognition rules are therefore considerably modified in international corporate transactions. The provision carrying the freight in this area is section 367.

C. Section 367

Section 367 applies differently to different patterns of corporate transactions, which include outbound, inbound, and wholly foreign transfers and exchanges. Section 367 itself contains relatively little detail. It consists largely of a mandate to the Treasury to issue regulations on different types of international corporate reorganizations coupled with some broadly sketched guidelines. The regulations under section 367, in provisions of numbing complexity, severely limit nonrecognition of gain in international corporate transactions according to a somewhat elusive notion of tax avoidance. The regulations work by imposing conditions—known colloquially as "toll charges"—on international reorganizations. Sometimes, the condition is partial or complete immediate recognition of gain; in other cases, it is the preservation of certain tax attributes and prescribed adjustments to others.

Despite the overwhelming clutter and obscurity of the regulations under section 367, the basic idea of section 367 is nearly fathomable. It aims to preserve for U.S. taxation all gains that originally arose within the reach of U.S. taxation. This entails limiting the transfer of unrealized appreciation from the United States to a foreign corporate environment and preventing the earnings of CFCs (to the extent not currently taxed to U.S. shareholders) from slipping into wholly foreign corporate solution or domestic corporate solution without recognition of gain. The regulations under section 367 can be understood only in light of these objectives.

1. Outbound Transfers Under Section 367(a)

Section 367(a)(1) generally requires recognition of gain on transfers of property to a foreign corporation by a U.S. person, overriding in this regard the nonrecognition provisions of Subchapter C. Four notable exceptions remain to the outbound transfer of property from a U.S. person: (i) when the transfer is stock in a foreign corporation, which is dealt with in section 367(a)(2), (ii) when the underlying property is an intangible owned by a U.S. person, in which case section 367(a) is made inapplicable and section 367(d) applies, (iii) when the distribution is of the stock in a foreign corporation to which section 355 would otherwise apply, in which event section 367(e)(1) applies, and (iv) when the distribution is the complete liquidation of a domestic corporation into a foreign corporation, in which event section 367(e)(2) applies.

Transfers of Stock. By far the most complex aspect of section 367(a) is outbound transfers of shares of stock. These are generally taxable under section 367(a)(1), but section 367(a)(2) allows exceptions (pursuant to regulations, naturally) for certain transfers of stock pursuant to a valid tax-free reorganization. The regulations spell out this possibility in considerable detail. In broad outline, the regulations permit nonrecognition treatment in outbound transfers of stock of domestic corporations (such as a stock-for-stock "B" reorganization) if U.S. transferors of stock of a domestic corporation hold no more than 50 percent of the stock of a transferee foreign corporation.[29] There must, in other words, be some dilution of U.S. ownership in a combination of a domestic corporation with a foreign entity.

There are further wrinkles. If U.S. ownership of the stock of the transferee foreign corporation is widely dispersed in small holdings after the transfer, there are no other requirements. U.S. persons who own 5 percent or more of the stock of the foreign corporation, however, must enter into specific gain recognition agreements (a "GRA") with the IRS, whereby upon certain subsequent events within 5 years (such as a disposition by the *foreign* corporation of the transferred domestic stock) gain initially deferred is recognized in full.[30]

Nonrecognition is possible in outbound transfers of a foreign corporation's stock if either the U.S. transferor owns less than 5 percent of the transferee foreign corporation after the transfer or the U.S. transferor enters into a five-year gain recognition agreement with respect to the transferred stock as described above.[31] Therefore, a transferor that ends up with less than 5 percent of the transferee foreign corporation escapes recognition of gain without taking any action, while holders of 5 percent or more of the transferee foreign corporation must either recognize gain immediately or enter into a five-year gain recognition agreement.

2. Outbound Transfer of an Intangible Asset Under Section 367(d)

Section 367(d) seeks to prevent residual profits related to U.S. developed intangible assets from migrating out of the U.S. tax jurisdiction via the outbound tax-free contribution or transfer of intangibles to a related foreign corporation. Seen in its historical context, section 367(d) is best understood as an effort to expand the applicability of the assignment of income doctrine past its historic scope, providing in effect that no transfer of intangible property (whether the fruit, the tree, or the tree with its fruit) will serve to deflect the intangible income away from the U.S. developer. Thus,

---

29 Reg. § 1.367(a)–3(c)(1).

30 Reg. § 1.367(a)–8(e).

31 Reg. § 1.367(a)–3(b)(1).

rightly viewed, section 367(d) is a denial of the possibility of transferring the income generated by U.S. developed intangibles away from the U.S. developer to a related foreign corporation by means of outbound transfers of income-producing intangibles, as was allowed in cases such as *E.I. Dupont de Nemours & Co. v. United States,*[32] *Eli Lily & Co. v. Commissioner,*[33] *G.D. Searle & Co. v. Commissioner,*[34] and *Bausch & Lomb, Inc. v. Commissioner.*[35] Section 367(d) assigns the income derived from the transferred intangible back to the U.S. developer even when ownership of the underlying "tree" (i.e., the income-producing intangible asset) has been transferred to a related foreign corporation. Thus, section 367(d) fits like a glove with section 482. If the owner-developer of an intangible seeks to license the intangible, then section 482 applies in that context. If the owner-developer attempts to transfer its intangible to a related foreign person, then section 367(d) recasts that transaction as if the U.S. developer still owned the intangible and is required to include a superroyalty in income that complies with the arm's length standard. Thus, section 367(d) is a backstop that prevents the owner-developer from being able to assign away its intangible asset to a related foreign corporation and achieve a different outcome than what would occur from the ongoing ownership and licensing of that intangible by the U.S. person.

In 1986, concurrent with the addition of the "commensurate with income" standard to section 482, Congress incorporated this same standard into section 367(d), providing that the amount of the ongoing annual section 367(d) superroyalty payment must be commensurate with the income generated by the transferred intangible.[36] Said differently, this commensurate with income standard was intended to make clear that where taxpayers transfer an enumerated intangible with high profit potential, the ongoing superroyalty cannot be benchmarked with generic industry data. Instead, it must be valued based upon the actual ongoing profit experience of the transferred intangible.[37] This commensurate with income standard accomplishes its objective by deeming the foreign

---

[32] See E.I. Dupont de Nemours & Co. v. United States, 471 F.2d 1211 (Ct. Cl. 1973) (stating that the grant of a non-exclusive license with respect to a patent constituted a "transfer of property" within the meaning of section 351).

[33] Eli Lily & Co., 84 T.C. 996, 1116–27 (1985), *aff'd in part and rev'd in part,* 856 F.2d 855 (7th Cir. 1988) (manufacturing intangibles transferred to Puerto Rican subsidiary).

[34] G.D. Searle & Co. v. Commissioner, 88 T.C. 252 (1987) (manufacturing intangibles transferred to Puerto Rican subsidiary).

[35] Bausch & Lomb, Inc. v. Commissioner, 92 T.C. 525 (1989), *aff'd,* 933 F.2d 1084 (2d Cir. 1991) (manufacturing intangibles transferred to Irish subsidiary).

[36] Tax Reform Act of 1986, PUB. L. NO. 99–514, § 1231(e), 100 Stat. 2085 (1986).

[37] See JOINT COMM. ON TAX'N, 100TH CONG., GENERAL EXPLANATION OF THE TAX REFORM ACT OF 1986, at 1016 (Comm. Print 1987).

transferee corporation as paying a royalty to the U.S. transferor that is determined in amount by the actual income generated from the exploitation of the transferred intangible.[38] Thus, the addition of the commensurate with income standard to section 367(d)(2) in 1986 was an important step towards harmonizing section 367(d)'s superroyalty amount with Congress's underlying goal of codifying the assignment of income doctrine because it made clear that income arising from the contributed intangible would be assigned back to the original U.S. transferor by reason of the fact that the superroyalty must always remain commensurate in amount with the amount of the income actually generated by the transferred intangible. Thus, whereas the government had failed to convince the courts to expand their judicially created assignment of income doctrine to assign the income attributable to transferred income-generating intangible property back to the U.S. developer-transferor,[39] Congress in 1986 statutorily codified this doctrine thus preventing the deflection of intangible returns away from the U.S. developer via the transfer of income-generating intangibles to a foreign corporation.

In 1997, Congress modified section 367(d) again to provide that the superroyalty would be considered foreign source income to the extent that section 482 would have so sourced an actual ongoing royalty if one had been paid between the parties,[40] thus allowing the tax results afforded under section 367(d) to approximate more closely the results attained under section 482.[41]

Notwithstanding the statutory language that requires that the annual payments be taken into account "over the useful life of the property," the final regulations provide that the annual contingent payments could be included by the transferor into income over 20 years but then provide that the amount of the royalty over that limited timeframe must be calculated to ensure that the entire value of the intangible over its entire useful life is included within that shortened 20 year timeframe.[42]

---

[38] See Reg. § 1.367(d)–1T(c)(1) (states super royalty amount is determined consistently with section 482); Reg. § 1.482–6(c)(3)(i)(B) (residual profits allocated to those functions that make a non-routine contribution and only those functions); Reg. § 1.482–4(f)(2)(ii)(C)(4), –4(f)(2)(iii) Ex. (2) (specifies proposition in text and then demonstrates via example that the allocation of residual profits must approximate the actual profit experience to meet the commensurate with income standard).

[39] See, e.g., Eli Lily & Co. v. Commissioner, 84 T.C. 996, 1123 ("Respondent's reallocations conflict with a fundamental principle of Federal income tax law: that income from property is earned by the owner of the property. See Helvering v. Horst, 311 U.S. 112 (1940); Blair v. Commissioner, 300 U.S. 5 (1937)").

[40] Taxpayer Relief Act of 1997, PUB. L. NO. 105–34, 111 Stat. 788.

[41] H.R. CONF. REP. NO. 105–220, 105th CONG. 1st SESS. at 629 (1997).

[42] Reg. § 1.367(d)–1(c)(3). The final regulations provide an example that demonstrates that the entire operating profits for the intangible assets entire useful

In addition, section 367(d)(2)(ii)(II) provides an acceleration rule if there is a direct or indirect disposition of the intangible property. The legislative history makes clear that a direct disposition occurs if there is a disposition of the underlying intangible by the transferee corporation, and an indirect disposition occurs where the transferor corporation disposes of an interest in the transferee corporation,[43] and temporary regulations provide that this occurs if the transferee corporation transfers the intangible asset to an unrelated person.[44] In like manner, the transferor's transfer of the stock of the transferee foreign corporation to an unrelated person represents an indirect disposition that triggers the acceleration rule.[45] The regulations then provide that the transferor's transfer of the stock in the transferee foreign corporation to a related U.S. person is not an indirect disposition that triggers the acceleration rule.[46]

The contours of what constitutes an indirect disposition that triggers the acceleration rule of section 367(d)(2)(A)(ii)(II) outside the contours of the above explicitly contemplated contexts was the issue in *Timberland LLC v. Commissioner*.[47] In a simplified version of the legally relevant facts, Timberland was acquired by a Luxembourg affiliate (referred to as "VF Sarl") for cash in a taxable stock purchase where VF Sarl was ultimately indirectly owned by VF Corporation. After its acquisition, Timberland engaged in an outbound section 368(a)(1)(F) reorganization[48] where it became a Swiss corporation (referred to as TBL GmbH"). All parties agreed that the outbound section 368(a)(1)(F) reorganization of Timberland into TBL GmbH caused the foreign intangible assets owned by Timberland (previously a U.S. corporation) were the subject of an outbound transfer governed by section 367(d) as a result of Timberland becoming a foreign corporation.

---

life are utilized to determine the royalty rate over the 20 year period. See Reg. § 1.367(d)–1(c)(3) Example.

[43] H.R. REP. NO. 98–861, 98th CONG. 2d SESS. at 955 (1984).

[44] Reg. § 1.367(d)–1T(f)(1).

[45] Reg. § 1.367(d)–1T(d)(1).

[46] Reg. § 1.367(d)–1T(e)(1).

[47] Timberland LLC f.k.a. Timberland Company v. Commissioner, 158 T.C. No. 1 (2022).

[48] This reorganization was accomplished by transferring stock in a disregarded entity that owned Timberland to TBL GmbH and immediately thereafter the election for Timberland was changed to treat it as a disregarded entity. Thus, the contribution and change in election was treated as an outbound section 368(a)(1)(F) reorganization. This characterization was undisputed by all parties. In any event, I commend to you the benefits of taking a course on corporate taxation where the topics of tax-free reorganizations and the affirmative use of the step transaction doctrine can be considered in further detail.

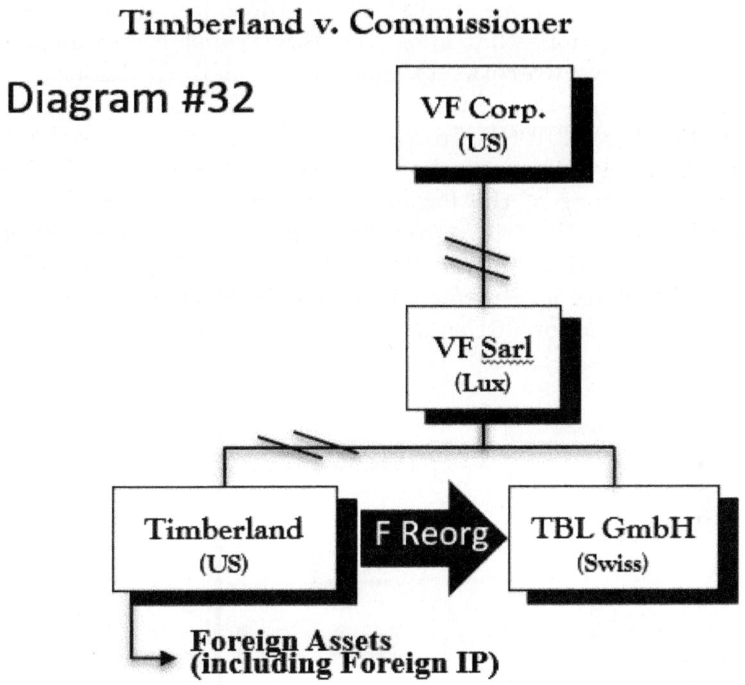

The parties diverged on the timing for the recognition of the income required under section 367(d). The taxpayer took the position that it was entitled to report the deemed royalty on the outbound transfer of the intangibles to TBL GmbH over a twenty year period under the general rule of section 367(d)(2)(ii)(I). The government took the position that the section 368(a)(1)(F) outbound reorganization represented an indirect disposition that triggered the application of the acceleration rule of section 367(d)(2)(ii)(II) and thus required the taxpayer to include the full value of the intangible into income immediately. The Tax Court ruled that the absence of any regulatory exception to the deemed disposition of the stock in Timberland is the taxpayer's problem, not the government's, and so any disposition within the group that did not meet a regulatory exception implicated the acceleration rule of section 367(d)(2)(ii)(II). The Tax Court holding was consistent with the approach taken in a Treasury Department notice that was issued after the year the transaction occurred.[49]

After *Timberland*, a stark contrast exists in terms of the consequences of an internal restructuring. In the below Diagram #33, the far left diagram depicts the basic structure that was forestalled in the *Timberland* decision. In the middle diagram and the far right

[49] See Notice 2012–39, Sec. 4.03, 2012–31 I.R.B. 95.

diagram, the intangible transfers in those diagrams meet the regulatory exceptions that allow the U.S. transferor to include the deemed royalty over a twenty year period under section 367(d)(2)(ii)(I) and thus do not run afoul of the acceleration rule of section 367(d)(2)(A)(ii)(II). In the middle diagram, this is the result notwithstanding the fact that a section 361(a) transfer occurs because the owner of the foreign transferee corporation is a U.S. corporation and thus is a qualified successor under the notice whereas VF Sarl is not.[50] In the far right diagram where a disregarded entity is transferred to a CFC, that transfer avoids any concern under section 361 as it is a section 351 transfer.[51]

Diagram #33

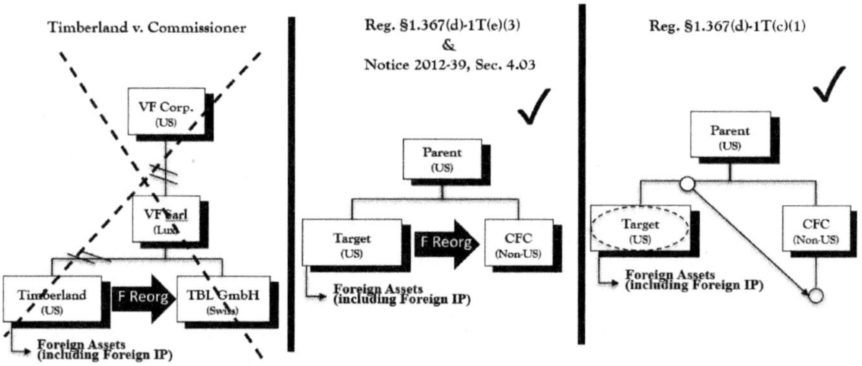

The government's litigating position in *Timberland* is based on a historical policy concern that no longer exists, and yet an important decision about the interpretation of section 367(d)(2)(A)(ii)(II) now exists. If one reviews the above Diagram #33, the acquisition of the U.S. company directly at the CFC level (as attempted in *Timberland*) allowed the multinational corporation to utilize unrepatriated foreign earnings of its CFCs to fund the acquisition of the U.S. company. The acquired U.S. company (Timberland in that case) then engaged in an outbound section 368(a)(1)(F) reorganization where its foreign intangibles were transferred in a transaction that purportedly did not create immediate gain recognition. In its issuance of Notice 2012–39, the government stated that it was "aware that certain taxpayers are engaging in transactions [under section 367(d)] intended to repatriate earnings from foreign

---

[50] See Reg. § 1.367(d)–1T(e)(3); Notice 2012–39, Sec. 4.03, 2012–31 I.R.B. 95. Note that the difference is that the owner of the transferee corporation in the middle diagram is a U.S. corporation (US Parent), so it is a qualified successor. The holder of the transferee corporation in the Timberland fact pattern is VF Sarl, a foreign corporation, which is not a qualified successor.

[51] See Reg. § 1.367(d)–1T(c)(1).

corporations without the appropriate recognition of income,"[52] and then the government asserted in the notice that forthcoming regulations would explicitly require immediate gain recognition on the outbound transfer of intangibles by reason of section 367(d)(2)(A)(ii)(II) to address this concern.[53]

In contrast to the *Timberland* fact pattern, the acquisition structures set forth in the above middle diagram and in the above far right diagram do not present that same repatriation concern, and so those transactions are not treated as deemed disposition events under the regulations or the notice. Thus, the government construes the meaning of an "indirect disposition" that triggers section 367(d)(2)(A)(ii)(II) not simply by whether or not a transfer of the stock interest in the transferee foreign corporation is made to an unrelated party. Instead, the government interprets an indirect disposition expansively to include situations where an opportunity exists to repatriate CFC earnings in a nontaxable manner.

The 2017 Tax Act reverses the justification, but not holding, in *Timberland*. After the enactment of the 2017 Tax Act, section 245A now allows for the tax-free repatriation of unremitted foreign earnings from CFCs through the allowance of a 100 percent foreign dividends received deduction. And, the Treasury Department, through regulations, has asserted that section 956 no longer applies to cause an income inclusion of unrepatriated earnings when a CFC makes an investment in U.S. property and when earnings would otherwise be entitled to section 245A status if distributed.[54] Thus, the policy goals that motivated the government's effort to attack the *Timberland* fact pattern no longer have a connection to today's policy goals but instead harken back to a bygone era. As a result, the likely import of *Timberland* now is that it represents a significant trap for the unwary: a disposition of the interest in the transferee corporation to any member other than a U.S. person creates an indirect disposition that triggers section 367(d)(2)(ii)(II). This outcome creates a stark hazard in terms of how internal restructurings are later accomplished within the wholly-owned multinational corporate context if an annual deemed royalty obligation is ongoing under section 367(d)(2)(ii)(I). If such an ongoing deemed royalty exists or should exist, then a later internal restructuring needs to consider the holding of *Timberland*. This seems like an unfortunate hazard given how the law has evolved after the 2017 Tax Act. Still, the U.S. tax system would not quite be itself if it did not sprinkle a few unexpected hazards in taxpayers' way.

---

[52] Notice 2012–39, Sec. 3, 2012–31 I.R.B. 95.

[53] Notice 2012–39, Sec. 4.03, 2012–31 I.R.B. 95.

[54] Reg. § 1.956–1(a)(2)(i).

3. Cost Sharing Agreements and Section 367(d)

Section 367(d) provides the IRS with authority to require all transfer pricing arrangements, including cost sharing agreements, to comply with the commensurate with income requirements regardless of which entity owns the intangible. However, instead of exercising that authority to harmonize the residual profit allocations afforded under the cost sharing regulations to the residual profit allocations afforded under Reg. § 1.482–6, the IRS has instead limited its policing of cost sharing agreements to contesting (1) the buy-in payment amount for pre-existing intangibles[55] and (2) whether the multinational enterprise had included all of the intangible development costs as part of the cost shares.[56] Furthermore, the existing cost sharing regulations grandfathered even more lenient cost sharing agreements entered before the issuance of the current regulations.[57] Thus, existing Reg. § 1.482–7 provides significant opportunities for a multinational enterprise to side step section 367(d). A qualified cost sharing agreement allows a taxpayer to assign the development rights in an intangible created by other affiliates to a related foreign risk-taker entrepreneur affiliate without the need for the risk-taker entrepreneur affiliate to provide any further significant contribution towards the intangible's creation other than internal funding. Consequently, just as we saw in chapter 4 in the discussion of the transfer pricing rules involving the licensing of an intangible, the IRS provides an exception to section 367(d) with respect to intangibles developed under a qualified cost sharing agreement. If an intangible is created and does not have the benefit of a cost sharing agreement, then the licensing arrangements of the U.S. developer must comply with the commensurate with income standard (by reason of section 482), and any effort to transfer that intangible to a related foreign person would in effect be recharacterized such that the U.S. developer is required to receive an ongoing royalty "as if" it had licensed that intangible to the foreign related party and that deemed superroyalty must be in an amount that complies with the commensurate with income standard. Those results are side-stepped if the foreign affiliate designates the owner-developer upfront in a qualified cost sharing agreement. The stakes

---

[55] See Veritas Software Corp. v. Commissioner, 133 T.C. 297 (2009) (where the IRS unsuccessfully argued that the buy-in payment should have been 1000 percent higher than the one utilized by the taxpayer, and the Tax Court sustained the taxpayer's valuation of the buy-in payment); A.O.D. 2010–005, 2010–49 I.R.B. 803.

[56] See Xilinx, Inc. v. Commissioner, 567 F.3d 482 (9th Cir. 2009) (rejecting IRS position that stock option costs should be included in the cost to be shared among the parties), *withdrawn*, 592 F.3d 1017 (9th Cir. 2010).

[57] See Reg. § 1.482–7(m)(1).

could not be higher with respect to whether or not an intangible is developed under a qualified cost sharing agreement.[58]

4. Outbound Transfers Under Section 367(e)

Section 367(e) applies to situations where a U.S. corporation distributes stock of a subsidiary in a transaction that would otherwise be entitled to nonrecognition treatment under section 355 or when the domestic corporation liquidates into a foreign corporation that would otherwise be entitled to nonrecognition treatment under section 332. Section 367(e) states that these distributions are taxable unless allowed by regulations.

As to section 355 tax-free distributions, the regulations provide that the distributing corporation must recognize gain (but not loss) upon its distribution of stock of a foreign corporation to its shareholders unless the distributee shareholders are qualified U.S. persons.[59] Otherwise, to the extent that the distributee shareholders are not qualified U.S. persons, then to that extent the distributing corporation must recognize gain up to the amount recognized. The regulations set forth a series of rebuttable presumptions as to the status of shareholders[60] and set forth rules to determine whether to presume that a shareholder is not a U.S. person. These rules do not apply if the distributed corporation is a domestic corporation.

As to a liquidation of a domestic corporation into a foreign parent corporation, that transaction is generally subject to immediate gain recognition as well by reason of section 367(e)(2).[61] However, if the distributed assets relate to assets that will remain used in a U.S. trade or business by the foreign parent corporation, then nonrecognition treatment is allowed in that situation as long as the foreign parent corporation uses that property for ten years in a U.S. trade or business and other certification requirements are met.[62]

5. Inbound and Wholly-Foreign Transfers Under Section 367(b)

The regime set forth in regulations under section 367(b) for inbound and wholly-foreign transfers is even more complex, but, in general, section 367(b) prevents untaxed accumulated earnings that arise within a CFC environment (the so-called "section 1248

---

58 For further analysis of section 367(d), see Bret Wells, *Revisiting § 367(d): How Treasury Took the Bite Out of Section 367(d) and What Should Be Done About It*, 16 FLORIDA TAX REV. 519 (2014).

59 Reg. § 1.367(e)–1(b)(1).

60 Reg. § 1.367(e)–1(d).

61 The regulations make clear that section 367(e)(2) applies and not section 367(a) to cover this fact pattern. See Reg. § 1.367(e)–2(a)(2).

62 Reg. § 1.367(e)–2(b)(2).

amount") from leaving that CFC environment, or else the section 1248 amount would be immediately taxable to the United States shareholder. If the earnings and assets of a controlled foreign corporation remain in a controlled foreign corporation in the course of a corporate adjustment—a frequent but not invariable consequence of a wholly-foreign reorganization—current U.S. taxation of the section 1248 amount is generally not imposed under section 367(b). However, certain tax attributes are identified and preserved to prevent erosion of the U.S. tax base later. When assets and earnings move from a controlled foreign corporation to a foreign corporation that is not a controlled foreign corporation, current U.S. taxation generally *is* imposed on the section 1248 amount that leaves the CFC environment. The reason for this is the greater possibility of subsequent escape by those earnings from full U.S. taxation. Finally, when assets move from a controlled foreign corporation to a domestic corporation (often by a liquidation that would normally be tax-free under section 332), a "toll charge" is imposed on foreign earnings (in the form of a constructive dividend) because this is the last occasion to ensure that those earnings are taxed to the U.S. shareholder at a time when the foreign corporation that has those earnings is a controlled foreign corporation.

Taken together, these patterns ensure that all earnings arising in controlled foreign corporations will eventually be subject to U.S. tax as dividends.[63] To this end, toll charges are imposed when earnings slip out of controlled foreign corporate solution or are repatriated, and the earnings are reckoned and preserved for future taxation when adjustments occur within the CFC environment.

After stating these rules and the existing regulatory framework, one is befuddled by the complexity afforded in section 367(b) in light of the changes brought by the 2017 Act. Section 1248(j) indicates that a constructive dividend by reason of section 1248 is eligible for the 100 percent foreign dividends received deduction to a domestic corporate U.S. shareholder under section 245A.[64] Pending further guidance to the contrary, it would seem that the same entitlement to a 100 percent foreign dividends received deduction should be available to a domestic corporate U.S. shareholder for any inclusion of the section 1248 amount under section 367(b). The IRS has issued regulations under section 956 to provide that an investment in U.S. property is no longer a policy concern vis-à-vis a domestic corporation U.S. shareholder when the underlying section 1248 amount would

---

[63] There is the further qualification that, since 2003, some dividends received by individuals are taxed preferentially at lower rates. This has relatively little bearing, however, on the universe of CFCs and corporate reorganizations involving CFCs. Furthermore, the low rate of tax on dividends is slated for extinction in 2011.

[64] § 1248(j).

have been eligible for a 100 percent foreign dividends received deduction under section 245A if actually distributed, so the Treasury Department has ruled that section 956 will have minimal application to the domestic corporate U.S. shareholder in that context.[65] Thus, with the enactment of section 245A, the concern about the escape of the undistributed foreign earnings out of a CFC environment seems to be an irrelevant concern in the context of a U.S. shareholder that is a domestic corporation entitled to an exemption of any taxation as to those earnings, but section 367(b) has not been recalibrated for this new reality. If section 367(b) were to have a continuing policy concern, it would seem to only be in the context of U.S. shareholders who are individuals. Thus, as of the writing of this edition, one would anticipate that section 367(b) is ripe for pruning, as its regulatory provisions seem overgrown in light of the enactment of section 245A and the current policy issues that now are relevant after the 2017 Act.

D. Branch Loss Recapture of Section 91

A U.S. domestic corporation is subject to taxation on its worldwide income under section 61(a), and this is particularly beneficial to the U.S. domestic corporation if that domestic corporation has a foreign branch that has losses. The ability to include foreign branch losses as deductible trade or business expenses can thus reduce the overall U.S. taxable income of the domestic corporation. However, suppose that after several years of incurring losses in its foreign branch, the foreign branch operations are just about to turn the corner and finally become profitable. The domestic corporation can see that the foreign branch is on the verge of "kicking the ball out of the stadium" in terms of future profitability. It is at that moment that the domestic corporation decides to incorporate the foreign branch. By doing so, the domestic corporation hopes to claim that any future earnings from the foreign corporation would be eligible for a 100 percent foreign dividends received deduction under section 245A when actually distributed. The asymmetry is obvious. The domestic corporation had claimed the foreign branch losses as part of an ongoing trade or business that was engaged in for profit, but at the moment the business is just about to become profitable it is transferred to a foreign corporation and out of the domestic corporation. The original assumption about the potential future profitability is thus shown to be inconsistent with what has actually transpired. Envision Charlie Brown running as hard as he can to kick the football being held by Lucy only to find that she pulls the ball away moments before he kicks the football,

---

65 Reg. § 1.956–1(a).

leaving Charlie Brown flat on his back and having missed the football.

Congress eventually grew weary of the "Lucy tax planning strategy" indicated above. Originally contained in section 367 and relocated in 2017 (and somewhat revamped to only apply to domestic corporations), section 91 exists to address this apparent asymmetry. At its core, section 91 provides that upon the incorporation of a foreign branch, the prior branch losses must be recaptured. Thus, if the domestic corporation incurred $5 million of branch losses in prior years, then the incorporation of the foreign branch would require recapture of the $5 million.

The amount of the branch loss recapture can be reduced to the extent branch income was recognized in a year after the branch loss was deducted, and if the branch assets have built-in gain that is recognized and taxable by reason of section 367(a) at the time of the branch's incorporation, then the amount of the branch loss recapture is reduced to the extent of that built-in gain.

Chapter 14

MISCELLANEOUS FOREIGN INCENTIVES REGIMES

A. Income Tax Incentives for Exports (Foreign Derived Eligible Income or "FDEI")

Since the 1930s, the U.S. tax laws have included provisions favoring exports from the United States. In the past 50 years, three successive sets of statutory tax benefits for exports have embroiled the United States in disputes with several foreign countries before two international trade organizations. The first set of major export incentives was introduced in 1971 in the form of "domestic international sales corporations," more commonly known as "DISCs." A DISC is a domestic corporation principally involved in selling U.S.-made goods overseas.[1] DISCs were allowed to defer U.S. income tax on one-half of their export profits until their distribution to shareholders. In 1981, however, the General Agreement on Tariffs and Trade (GATT) issued a ruling that DISCs were an illegal direct export subsidy in violation of the GATT accords. In an attempt to bring the U.S. system's export incentives into compliance, Congress introduced new provisions establishing "foreign sales corporations," known as "FSCs,"[2] in 1984. In 1999, the World Trade Organization, or "WTO" (the successor organization to the GATT), struck down FSCs on much the same ground as the GATT's previous condemnation of DISCs, to wit, that FSCs were an illegal export subsidy in violation of international trade accords.[3] Congress responded, in 2000, with a third set of export incentives, the "extraterritorial income exclusion," known as ETI.[4] The ETI system allowed U.S. importers to exclude part of their export trade earnings from U.S. taxable income. But, the WTO was not assuaged. In 2002, it struck down the ETI system, again as an illegal export subsidy. The vice of the ETI system, in the WTO's view, was that it was of substantially the same effect as the banished FSC system. In the 2004 Act, Congress gave up on earmarked export incentives in the U.S. tax system. Instead, Congress added section 199 in the 2004 Act which in turn provided tax rate reductions and other benefits to U.S.-

---

1 DISCs survive even today, unrecognizably transformed, as a tiny enclave in the Code.

2 "FSC" is usually pronounced as rhyming with "DISC."

3 This is why the first edition of this book had no discussion of export incentives. It was published in 1999, after FSCs were gone but before the ETI system hit the fan.

4 "ETI" is not an acronym and is voiced as "ee tee eye."

based corporations engaged in manufacturing and other production within the United States. That section provided a rate benefit for manufacturing activities, but its connection to exports was somewhat tenuous.

In 2017 Act, Congress repealed section 199 and enacted a replacement regime called section 199A. Because section 199A, similar to section 199, did not condition its incentive on exports but instead on U.S. domestic business activity, those provisions did not provide export subsidies. But, as an additional measure, the 2017 Act provided an additional deduction for "foreign derived intangible income" under section 250(a)(1)(A), a new term created by the 2017 Tax Act. In the 2025 Tax Act, the provision was modified and the term of art changed to "foreign derived eligible income." Through the enactment of section 250(a)(1)(A), Congress returned to providing export subsidies more directly for foreign derived eligible income.

The professed rationale for this export subsidy was to provide greater parity of outcomes in terms of earning foreign income in a domestic corporation versus earning such income within the confines a controlled foreign corporation. After adoption of a 100 percent foreign dividends received deduction and the adoption of a concessionary tax rate on net CFC tested income earned by controlled foreign corporations as a result of section 250(a)(1)(B), Congress was concerned that foreign income earned directly by a domestic corporation would suffer a tax disadvantage versus the result if the foreign income were earned in a CFC environment. Absent a deduction with respect to foreign income derived from overseas activity of a domestic corporation, the lower effective tax rate applicable to net CFC tested income by reason of the deduction provided in section 250(a)(1)(B) creates a potential incentive for domestic corporations to allocate foreign income opportunities to controlled foreign corporations located in low-tax jurisdictions. Therefore, to partially offset the effect of providing a lower U.S. effective tax rate with respect to net CFC tested income inclusions from a controlled foreign corporation, section 250(a)(1)(A) was adopted as a companion provision to provide a lower effective U.S. tax rate with respect to foreign derived eligible income ("FDEI") that is earned directly by the domestic corporation.

Specifically, section 250(a)(1)(A) provides to a domestic corporation a deduction equal to 33.34 percent of the foreign derived eligible income of the domestic corporation. The key term, FDII is defined formulaically as the result of the following equation:

$$\text{FDEI} = \frac{\text{foreign-derived deduction eligible income}}{\text{deduction eligible income}}$$

Deduction eligible income is defined as the domestic corporation's gross income less all allocable deductions but excluding the following seven categories of income: (i) income from Subpart F inclusions, (ii) income from net CFC tested income inclusions, (iii) financial services income, (iv) dividend income from controlled foreign corporations, (v) domestic oil and gas extraction income, (vi) foreign branch income, and (vii) income or gain from the sale of intangible or depreciable property except as provided otherwise in regulations.

Once the total deemed eligible income amount is determined, then the percentage of the deemed eligible income that is *foreign* must be determined. The remaining defined term is the "foreign-derived deduction eligible income." "Foreign-derived deduction eligible income" is the deduction eligible income that is attributable to property sold and services performed for foreign use. The Treasury Department has issued extensive regulations that set out the requirements for a domestic corporation to document that its deduction eligible income was foreign-derived. Once the foreign-derived deduction eligible income is determined, then the ratio of that amount to the total deduction eligible income is used to calculate the percentage of the deemed intangible income that is *foreign*, and this ratio in turn is used to determine the amount of the deemed eligible income that constitutes foreign deemed eligible income or FDEI.

Table #15: Example of U.S. Tax on Foreign-Derived Intangible Income		
Item		
1	Deduction eligible income (tested income)[1]	$200
2	Foreign-derived deduction eligible income[2]	$40
3	Foreign percentage (L2/L1)	20%
4	§ 250(a)(1) Deduction (L1 × L3 × 33.34%)	$13.34
5	Taxable income attributable to deduction eligible income (L1 – L4)	$186.44
6	Tax benefit from foreign-derived eligible income (21% × L7)	**$2.80**

[1] Gross income of U.S. corp. determined without regard to: Subpart F income, net CFC tested income inclusions, dividends from CFCs, domestic oil & gas extraction income, foreign branch income, and certain gains from sale of intangibles and depreciable property excess as provided otherwise in regulations.

[2] Property sold to a foreign person for use, consumption, or disposition outside the U.S. and services provided to a person or with respect to property located outside the U.S. "Sale" includes lease, exchange or other disposition.

The above formulaic exercise is perhaps best understood through an example. In Table #15, the deduction eligible income amount is indicated on Line 1 as $200. To determine that amount, all gross income of the domestic corporation less allocable deductions was considered except for income attributable to the seven categories listed in footnote 1 of Table #15. The foreign-derived deduction eligible income is $40 per Line 2. The ratio of the foreign-derived deduction eligible income ($40 per Line 5) over the total deduction eligible income ($200 per Line 1) provides the ratio for determining the amount of the foreign derived deduction eligible income (20 percent per Line 1). Thus, the deduction under section 250(a)(1)(A) is equal to 33.34 percent of the foreign-derived deduction eligible income (200 x 20% x 33.34% = $13.34). The tax benefit for this $13.34 deduction is $2.80 as indicated in Line 6.

Section 250(a)(1)(A)'s allowance of a tax preference for foreign-derived deduction eligible income remains controversial. In a joint letter sent on December 11, 2017, finance ministers of France, Germany, Italy, Spain, and the United Kingdom claimed that the concessionary rate that applies on foreign-derived intangible income raises concerns of another illegal export subsidy under WTO's Subsidies and Countervailing Measures Agreement. This is ironic in that some of the countries that joined in this letter have adopted their own form of a patent box regime. It remains to be seen whether the WTO will be asked to rule on the legality of section 250.

B. U.S. Citizens Abroad and Section 911 Exclusions

For 50 years, Americans living and working abroad have experienced a somewhat different income tax environment from the rest of us. They have been allowed under section 911 an annual exclusion from income of a substantial amount of foreign source earned income. The exclusion, $20,000 when it was introduced in 1962, has risen to roughly $132,900 for 2026.[5] Several explanations, of which some may even have merit, have been offered for this apparent windfall. Among them are that 1) Americans living abroad do not derive the full benefit of public expenditures financed by taxation in the United States; 2) the cost of living overseas is higher, particularly for U.S.-style amenities; 3) the U.S. foreign tax credit provides no offset for foreign taxes when foreign governments rely heavily (as they often do) on indirect taxes (which can neither be credited nor deducted); 4) tax incentives are necessary to induce Americans to suffer the discomforts of living and working in less developed areas.

Wholly apart from the force of these considerations, the exclusion of section 911 is of little import today, because of changes in its formulation introduced in 2006, confining its power to reduce U.S. income tax substantially to a far narrower range of taxpayers.

Section 911 provides an income tax exclusion and a "housing allowance" for Americans abroad. Under section 911(a), a "qualified individual" may elect to exclude "foreign earned income" from income and exempt the "housing cost amount" from taxation for any taxable year.[6] The rest of section 911 fleshes out such matters as who can claim the exclusion, how much, with respect to what income, and in what years.

1. Qualified Foreign Residents

To qualify for the exclusion, a U.S. citizen must 1) have a "tax home" in a foreign country and 2) *either* be a "bona fide resident" of one or more foreign countries for at least one entire taxable year *or* have spent at least 330 full days in foreign countries during a period of 12 consecutive months.[7] The notion of a "tax home" has already

---

5 Rev. Proc. 2025–32, Sec. 2.39, 2025–45 I.R.B. 695. Taking inflation into account, today's exclusion is considerably smaller in real value than the 1962 original.

6 The dollar amount of the earned income exclusion and the housing cost exemption are specified in sections 911(b) and 911(c).

7 § 911(d)(1). The exclusion is also available to individual alien residents of the United States who have the requisite foreign "tax home" and spend a minimum of 330 days in foreign countries. Note further that international waters (and certain international protectorates such as Antarctica) do not qualify as "foreign countries."

come up in chapter 2, in connection with the definition of a resident alien in section 7701(b). It is much the same in section 911, except that it has a more specifically residential character. The central element of a tax home under section 911(d)(3) is an individual's "abode." As for "bona fide" foreign residence under section 911, it is essentially the same as "residence" for all individuals under the older common-law standard of residence that preceded section 7701(b).[8]

There is a profusion of cases on the nature of an "abode," involving workers on rotating shifts on offshore oil rigs. In *Bujol v. Commissioner*,[9] the taxpayer worked on an offshore oil rig near the United Arab Emirates for continuous periods of 28 days alternating with 28-day periods in Louisiana, where he lived with his family in his own house. The court's conclusion that the taxpayer's "abode" was in the United States forestalled any further consideration of his "tax home," and forced the conclusion that he was not a "bona fide resident" of a foreign country.

In apparent contrast to the oil rig cases, *Jones v. Commissioner*[10] was resolved against the Service. The taxpayer, an airline pilot employed by Japan Airlines, lived in a hotel while in Japan and spent fewer than 165 nights in Japan during the taxable year, a lower percentage than the taxpayers in the oil rig cases. The court found the taxpayer's hotel to be an "abode" nonetheless because it was a dwelling rather than predominantly a place of work. Where *Jones* differs from the oil rig cases, in the court's view, is in the additional cost borne by the taxpayer (from his own pocket) to maintain a place to live in Japan. The court found in the foreign "abode" requirement a particular concern on Congress's part to channel the tax benefits of section 911 to those who "actually incurred increased living expenses while living abroad."[11]

In *Cutting v. Commissioner*,[12] a U.S. citizen was employed by a U.S. airline to primarily transport military personnel and cargo on international routes. The taxpayer's wife resided in Thailand, but his principal place of business (his home base) was in California as that was the location of his gateway travel airport. Moreover, the taxpayer failed to demonstrated that he was a resident in Thailand. He also held a temporary visa that required him to leave Thailand every 30

U.S. citizens serving in the merchant marine therefore are generally not entitled to the exclusion of section 911.

8 See chapter 2 for further discussion.

9 53 T.C.M. 762 (1987), *aff'd without published opinion*, 842 F.2d 328 (5th Cir. 1988).

10 927 F.2d 849 (5th Cir. 1991), *reversing* T.C. Memo. 1989–616.

11 927 F.2d 856.

12 Cutting v. Commissioner, 120 T.C.M. 350 (2020), *aff'd* 2022–1 U.S.T.C. ¶ 50,150 (9th Cir. 2021).

days. On those facts, the Tax Court held that the taxpayer did not have a foreign home, but even if the taxpayer did have a tax home in Thailand the Tax Court alternatively stated that the taxpayer was not a bona fide resident of Thailand and did not meet the physical residence test of section 911(d)(1).

2. Foreign Earned Income

Excludable "foreign earned income" is earned income from sources within a foreign country attributable to services performed by an individual during the period of qualifying overseas presence.[13] It includes wages, salaries, and other amounts received as compensation for personal services actually rendered.[14] Earned income does not include, however, amounts received by a shareholder-employee of a corporation that represent a distribution of corporate earnings.[15] An individual engaged in a trade or business as a sole proprietor may treat the income attributable to personal effort as earned income, but where capital is also a material income producing factor in the business, an individual's earned income cannot exceed 30 percent of her share of the net profits of the business.[16] Significant litigation has resulted in what businesses utilize capital that is an income producing factor that subjects one to the 30 percent limitation.[17]

3. Excluded Amount

The amount of the exclusion under section 911 settled in at $80,000 in 2002. For taxable years beginning in 1997 and earlier, the exclusion amount was $70,000.[18] It increased to $80,000 in increments of $2,000 per year for taxable years beginning in 1998 and later.[19] Since 2006, the exclusion has been indexed for inflation (based on cost of living changes after 2004).[20] In 2026, the exclusion was $132,900. It has been subject since then to the cost-of-living adjustment prescribed in section 1(f)(3).

4. Allowance for Housing Costs

A separate allowance for overseas Americans is the "housing cost amount." A qualifying foreign resident can elect to exclude from income the "housing cost amount" for any taxable year. This

---

13 § 911(b)(1)(A).

14 §§ 911(b)(1)(A), 911(d)(2).

15 §§ 911(b)(1)(A), 911(d)(2); Reg. § 1.911–3(b)(1).

16 § 911(d)(2)(B).

17 See e.g., Rousku v. Commissioner, 56 T.C. 548 (1971) (auto repair business utilized capital as a material income producing factor).

18 § 911(b)(2)(D)(i).

19 Id.

20 § 911(b)(2)(D)(ii).

allowance for housing costs is designed to offset the frequently heavy expense of obtaining American-style housing overseas. Reflecting this cost, the terms of employment for overseas Americans commonly include either free housing or a separate housing allowance. Section 911(c) accommodates either pattern.

The "housing cost amount" is, in fact, the excess of actual housing costs over a basic norm measured by an average middle-class housing cost in the United States.[21] Since 2006, the housing cost allowance has been limited to 16 percent of the basic exclusion. To illustrate, the maximum amount of the housing cost allowance within this limitation for 2026 was $21,264, in contrast to earlier years where the exclusion could easily exceed $60,000.

5. The Mechanics of the Exclusion: "Stacking"

The most important mechanical element in the exclusion is the "stacking" rule of section 911(f), introduced in 2006.

Until the 2006 Act, the exclusion of section 911 worked the same way as any other exclusion or deduction. It reduced taxable income by an amount that otherwise would have been subject to the taxpayer's highest marginal tax rate. Under section 911(f), added in 2006, any exclusion, deduction, or housing cost amount allowed under section 911 comes "off the bottom." That is, it produces a tax reduction as though it had been deducted from income taxable in the lowest rate brackets. To achieve the effect of a deduction from lower rate brackets, section 911(f) determines the income tax imposed after the exclusion as the excess of the tax that would have been imposed absent any exclusion over the tax that would have been imposed on an amount of taxable income equal to the excluded amount. The resulting amount of tax is the same as the tax that would have been imposed on the non-excluded income if it had been stacked on top of the excluded amount in determining the applicable rate. Hence the term "stacking rule" used to describe section 911(f) in tax vernacular.

In the absolute amount of tax paid, taxpayers in the highest rate brackets are most affected by the stacking rule of section 911(f). This is so because the exclusion—formerly from income in a range subject to the highest marginal rate—is now drawn from income that would otherwise be the most lightly taxed.

In relative amount, however, middle to upper-middle income taxpayers experienced the greatest tax increase from the stacking rule. Consider, for example a U.S. expatriate employee earning $165,000 a year. Before 2006, the exclusion would have reduced taxable income to $85,000. Now, our expatriate was taxed in 2019 on

---

21 § 911(c)(2).

$59,100 but at the rates imposed on income between $105,900 and $165,000. A rough back-of-the envelope computation suggests that the amount of U.S. income tax was greater by at least 15 percent than it would have been under the pre-2006 exclusion mechanism.

For lower income taxpayers (i.e., with incomes below $105,900 or so), the new exclusion mechanism generally made only a small difference, particularly for expatriate employees able to exclude the full amount provided in section 911. In an income of $105,900, for example, the top $105,900 and the bottom $105,900 are one and the same. An exclusion of $105,900 reduces taxable income to zero either way. In this instance, the benefit of the exclusion is the same as it was before 2006. For lower income taxpayers able to exclude only part of the full statutory allowance,[22] however, the new rules will have an adverse effect when taxable income is greater than the allowable exclusion. Thus, if the $80,000 income of an overseas American includes only $40,000 of foreign earned income, the stacking rule would now significantly diminish the tax benefit compared to the prior regime.

22 This would be the case, for example, of an employee who spent less than a full year outside the United States.

TABLE OF CASES